# Prizewinning Books for Children

# The LexingtonBooks Special Series
# in
# Libraries and Librarianship
## Richard D. Johnson, General Editor

**International Business Reference Sources**
*Cynthia C. Ryans*

**The Parliament of Great Britain: A Bibliography**
*Robert U. Goehlert* and *Fenton S. Martin*

**Prizewinning Books for Children**
*Jaqueline Shachter Weiss*

**The Feminization of Librarianship in France**
*Mary Niles Maack*

**The Public Library in the 1980s**
*Lawrence J. White*

**Vietnam War Bibliography**
*Christopher L. Sugnet* and *John Hickey*

# Prizewinning Books for Children

**Themes and Stereotypes in
U.S. Prizewinning Prose Fiction
for Children**

**Jaqueline Shachter Weiss**
Temple University

**LexingtonBooks**
D.C. Heath and Company
Lexington, Massachusetts
Toronto

**Library of Congress Cataloging in Publication Data**

Weiss, Jaqueline Shachter.
 Prizewinning books for children.     93048

 Includes bibliographies and index.
 1. Children's stories, American—Themes, motives.
2. Stereotype (Psychology) in literature.   3. Literary
prizes—United States.   4. Subject headings—Children's
literature.   I. Title.
PS374.C45W44 1983       813'.009'9282           82–48624
ISBN 0–669–06352–5

*Copyright © 1983 by Jaqueline Shachter Weiss*

Published simultaneously in Canada

Printed in the United States of America

International Standard Book Number: 0–669–06352–5

Library of Congress Catalog Card Number: 82–48624

*To my devoted husband, George,*
*and children, Sherry, Ross,*
*Scott, and Steve*
*with love and gratitude*

# Contents

# Preface

This book is intended for present and future children's teachers and librarians as well as parents and the general public. Elementary teachers need this book to help pupils think about story themes, and it is especially beneficial for those who pursue individualized reading or bibliotherapy. A renowned children's librarian, who reviewed this book before publication, said:

> Topics and themes are different. We don't have enough books on themes in children's literature. It is the primary theme of each prizewinner that's presented in this [book] though themes are grouped under appropriate headings. If anyone claims a review of primary themes is simplistic, tell them, "It's not simplistic; it's simple and clear." That's what harassed elementary teachers and children's librarians want for quick referral, not extensive literary criticism.

This book emphasizes primary themes of readily obtainable children's literary works that have won U.S. prizes. It is the only known review of children's literature based exclusively on prizewinners, a logical source for those who want to read what has been judged best. Some may question if all past prizewinners are prizeworthy, but it is helpful to see winners in historical perspective, noting changes with the passage of time in that which is valued.

Information concerning 717 U.S. fictional-prose prizewinners comes mainly from the 1979 edition of *Children's Books: Awards & Prizes* compiled and edited by The Children's Book Council.[1] The Lewis Carroll Shelf Award[2] is not cited completely in the 1979 edition, but the writer traced it back to 1958, and all available winners were made a part of the study. While not all-inclusive, the 1979 edition gives around sixty U.S. awards in children's literature. Forty-two of them list the specific book prizewinners used in this study. Award names are in singular form in the study.

Some prizes reflect input from boys and girls who vote on lists prepared by librarians, often with assistance from parents and educators. Other choices are made only by librarians or special-interest groups. Children's choices reflect their values and are an important counterbalance to prizes given solely by adults.[3] Adults may judge books on the basis of values they think children *should* hold, but child-awarded books are more reflective of what *actually* appeals to young people. In some cases, adults and children agree.

Shortly before publication, I included all appropriate books for 1980–1982 that are winners or Honor Books of The John Newbery and

The Randolph Caldecott Medals.[4] I did the same with hardcover fiction and picture-storybook winners in the children's-book category of The American Book Award, which succeeded the National Book Award.[5] I also made the appendix lists more current than some parallel lists in the newly received 1981 edition of *Children's Books: Awards and Prizes.* The appendix contains facts about forty-two awards given to specific children's books. It also has information about three well-known awards given to creators of children's books for their total production.

This book represents a long-term scholarly undertaking. All books listed in *Children's Books: Awards & Prizes,* 1979 edition; the complete list of Lewis Carroll winners; and the latest Newbery, Caldecott, and The American Book Award hardcover winners for children were categorized according to genre. All that were readily available were read to determine primary theme and possible stereotypes (often documented with quotations). For collective short-story prizewinners, the entire book was read to judge if there was an overall theme. Otherwise, the theme of the title story or another representative tale was analyzed. Within chapters, books were grouped under the most appropriate heading for discussion of their themes. Because of the size of the task, these types of prizewinners were excluded: nonfiction (informational books and autobiographies or biographies); alphabet and counting books, considered to be informational; rhyming and wordless picture books as well as poetry and drama; and books published abroad. Although themes are stated definitely, readers are encouraged to be critical and make their own interpretations.

Stereotypes were criticized throughout the book. There is less stereotyping in new prizewinners than in old ones. When reference was made to race, the words Black and White were capitalized.

Picture storybooks for preschool and primary grades were presented according to genre in chapters preceding those dealing with books for middle- and upper-elementary grades. The genres are traditional or folk literature, fantasy (divided into modern fantasy and animal fantasy), historical fiction, and contemporary realistic fiction. Each category makes special contributions and is essential to a balanced study of literature.

In this book, the sources of literature reading levels were librarians and often *Best Books for Children, Preschool through the Middle Grades,* the reference also sometimes used in determining genre.[6] Preschool stories are those that adults read to children who are below grade 1. For books young people read themselves, the term *primary grades* refers to grades 1–2; *middle grades,* to grades 3–4; and *upper grades,* to grade 5 or 6 and beyond. Chapter bibliographies supply specific grade designation in parentheses when each book is listed. Such practical information helps teachers, librarians, and even parents match books to children's reading levels.

Chapter references include names of translators. They also list illustrators, except in instances when authors create their own illustrations.
Publishers of hardcover editions are credited, though many of the prizewinners are so popular they also appear in paperback.

Interesting information about themes was supplied on occasion by
the authors themselves, transcribed from *Profiles in Literature,* video-
taped interviews. Fifty-six outstanding authors and illustrators have par-
ticipated in the series that is distributed by Temple University in
Philadelphia. The regular interviewers are the writer and Carolyn Field
of The Free Library of Philadelphia. These interviews reveal facts about
themes not found in book-jacket blurbs. In some instances, authors'
intended primary themes do not project to the readers, but it is fascinating
to learn what was intended and to reread a prizewinner with the author's
stated purpose in mind.

**Notes**

1. The Children's Book Council (CRC) is at 67 Irving Place, New
York, New York 10003.

2. A committee of librarians, teachers, parents, and writers, sponsored by the University of Wisconsin School of Education, selects from
publisher-nominated books those they consider worthy to sit next to *Alice
in Wonderland.*

3. Each children's-choice award is determined in a unique way. For
example, for the Mark Twain Award, librarians select thirty-five titles
that they submit to three representatives from Missouri organizations,
such as International Reading Association, Parents-Teachers Association,
and the Association of Elementary School Principals. The twenty titles
rated highest by these readers comprise the master list from which children choose the winner. (See appendix descriptions, ''Cited Children's
Book Awards,'' for other children's-choice awards.)

4. The John Newbery Medal and The Randolph Caldecott Medal
are awarded annually to the writer and illustrator, respectively, of U.S.
children's books found by the American Library Association to be most
distinguished. Honor Books are leading medal contenders.

5. In the children's-book category, the National Book Award and
its 1980 successor, The American Book Award, is given to children's books published in the United States in the preceding year, written
by United States citizens, and considered most distinguished by a panel
of judges.

6. John T. Gillespie and Christina B. Gilbert, eds., *Best Books for
Children, Preschool through the Middle Grades* (New York: Bowker,
1981).

# Acknowledgments

I acknowledge the Temple University Research and Study Leaves Committee, who made full-time work on this book possible. I appreciate the help of Temple University vice-presidents of research and development, Edwin Adkins and Eunice Clarke.

I thank local reviewers of my manuscript—from The Free Library of Philadelphia: Carolyn Field, coordinator, Office of Work with Children; her assistant, Kit Breckenridge, head of children's materials selection; and Jeanne Berdine, Northeast Area children's coordinator. Other reviewers to whom I owe a debt of gratitude include Florence Shankman, Temple University professor emeritus; and Muriel Feelings, a critic of chapter 13, "Contemporary Realistic Fiction about U.S. Minorities," and author of two Caldecott Honor Books, *Moja Means One* (1972) and *Jambo Means Hello* (1975).

I also thank Faith Matthews, dedicated former graduate student and friend, and many equally dedicated children's librarians. From The Free Library of Philadelphia, I thank those in the Central Library: librarian Ellen Whitney, head of the Children's Department, DianeJude McDowell, and Margaret Plotkin; and library assistants Julie Baga, Gloria Cosby, and Edith McCray. I also express appreciation to those in the Northeast Regional Library: librarians Mary Ellen Den, head of the Children's Department, and Irene Reed; library technician Lorraine Brill; and library assistants Ruth Cohn and Karen Siderick. From the Norristown Public Library, I thank Marian Peck, head of Children's Services, and Celeste Cygal, library assistant.

My family helped make this book possible. Aside from my immediate family, who faithfully assisted me and to whom this book is dedicated, I thank Jewell Brownstein and Walter and Cheryl Harrell. I thank the following family members for their general supportiveness: Sylvia and Marcos Corona, Cyrel and Al Cohen, Ruth and Joseph Sikora, Helen Weiss, Eve and Murray Jankow, Julius Brownstein, Miriam and Martin Nelson, Lucie and Philip Nelson, and Phyllis and Stuart Kaufman.

I also express appreciation to my students; my editor, Margaret Zusky; and countless friends, such as Ida and Morris Schiff, Lil and Max Millman, Rose and Abe Mamlin, Fran and Bob Kleiner, Lucy Cruz, and Rose and Max Rosenfeld, all of whom have helped me endure.

# Part I
# For All Children

# 1

# Themes in Children's Literature and Teaching Children about Them

*I read books that have won prizes the same way I go to Academy Award movies. I can't stand books or movies that show all Orientals alike. When I read, I think about a book's main idea. I'm learning to separate big notions from small details. I even think about main ideas in social studies. Best of all, knowing a main idea helps me remember a story better.*
—Hoang, aged twelve

Hoang is wise beyond his years. His main-idea search is actually probing for theme. Intuitively, when he senses a conventional, formulaic treatment of characters, he expresses opposition to stereotypes without using that terminology. His interest in awarded volumes can be satisfied by this book, believed to be the first to deal exclusively with prizewinners for children. Since more has been written on stereotypes than on themes, the book mentions stereotypes only when they occur but focuses solidly on the primary theme of each of 717 prizewinners.

## Meaning of Theme

A theme is important because it expresses the main idea of a book, a short story, or a poem or shows significance behind action. Poet John Ciardi, who calls many of his verses for children "sheer nonsense," adds that even nonsense is discarded if it has no unifying theme.[1]

Currently, there are over forty thousand children's books in print, and it is no small job to evaluate them. The criteria by which those in literary circles evaluate these books generally include examination of theme, plot, writing style, characterization, setting, format, and sometimes, point of view. The least-understood criterion is theme, which requires pondering large, underlying ideas: the forest. The most popular criterion is plot, which involves noting details: individual trees.

Bernice E. Cullinan says:

> A plot tells the action, but a theme reveals the significance of the action; a theme tells the reader what an experience means. A theme is not merely the discourse or topic with which the author deals but is his message or comment on that topic as his story evolves. . . . Seem-

ingly, our psychological makeup demands a theme, a necessity for making sense of events, hence the structural equation: *no theme, no story.*[2]

Arthur N. Applebee in *The Child's Concept of Story, Ages 2–17* says that a story may operate at more than one level of meaning. Immature readers tell about a story as a patterning of events. Mature readers, however, generalize about a work, seeing a theme, message, or point of view. He contrasts generalization with analysis in the following way:

> Generalization, . . . while often beginning in analysis, puts its emphasis on the work as the statement of a point of view. The reader may agree with the author or offer an alternative, but the response differs from analysis in that it is now consciously concerned with understanding the world through the work, rather than with understanding the function or structure of the work itself.[3]

Themes are the unifying threads that are so woven into a tale they bind it together and provide a sense of completeness. They may be illustrated beyond the world of literature. In music, for example, themes are the first tentative statements of melody that appear and reappear and eventually possess the listener with their power. The main melody of a musical composition is akin to the main theme of a literary work.

Concept books, often for young children, always have a theme, and often the concept and theme are the same. Counting books, as an example, develop the concept of numbers and alphabet books, the concept of letters. In *Count and See,*[4] Tana Hoban uses her photographs of common objects—five garbage cans, for instance—to develop a concept of the number five. In *Look Again!,*[5] her photographs establish the concept and theme: effect of viewpoint on appearance. Her camera captures a turtle, for example, showing dorsal and ventral surfaces. Through ingenious peepholes, a viewer sees an item in part and then resees it, causing the person to *Look Again!* Though the picture book is wordless, prereaders understand the theme, that something can look different from its front, back, or side.

Themes should not be confused with issues, such as divorce or sibling rivalry. An issue is likely to be the subject, not the theme, of a book, but at times the theme and the subject or topic overlap.

Philosopher Monroe C. Beardsley explains:

> It may not always be possible to draw a sharp line between theme and subject. . . . We refer to a subject by a concrete noun or nominative construction: a war, a love affair, the Aztecs, the taming of a shrew. More puzzling is the general idea or underlying concept (the theme),

a general statement that the literature may contain, some observation, or reflection about life or art or human beings or reality.[6]

Beardsley refers to a theme as the ideological content of a literary work, discovered through interpretation. A theme, in his opinion, is a general concept which the reader abstracts from literature and relates to life. A subtle theme may come from a story's deep structure. A theme may focus on a conflict that is not fully resolved even though the plot conflict may be. This is exemplified in a book by James Lincoln Collier and Christopher Collier, *My Brother Sam Is Dead*,[7] whose theme questions justification of a war that divides families and punishes innocent victims.

Beardsley says that a theme cannot be called true or false, but a thesis can. By definition a thesis is "a claim put forward: statement, proposition . . . that a person . . . advances and maintains or offers to maintain by argument."[8]

The issue, subject or topic, symbol (sometimes present), theme, and thesis can be distinguished in several examples. A disabled boy is the issue and subject of Marguerite deAngeli's historical fiction for upper-elementary grades, *The Door in the Wall*.[9] The lad's crutches symbolize his disability. The primary theme is ingenuity in opening doors to independence. The thesis is that ingenuity and independence are admirable goals.

Pioneer life and relations with Native Americans are the issue and subject of Alice Dalgleish's historical fiction for middle-elementary grades, *The Courage of Sarah Noble*.[10] An eight-year-old girl's cloak symbolizes her need for mustering courage as she cooks for her father in the wilderness while he builds a house for his family. The theme is the lonely girl's courage. The thesis is that perseverance is possible with courage.

Migratory workers are the issue and subject of Doris Gates's *Blue Willow*,[11] realistic fiction for upper-elementary grades. A ten-year-old daughter of migratory workers cherishes a blue willow plate, symbol of a dimly remembered past home. She displays the plate when her father finally gets a good job and the family settles down. The theme is a need for permanence, and the thesis is that permanence brings stability.

Book illustrations may help emphasize a theme. For example, true love seems to be the theme of Hans Christian Andersen's *The Steadfast Tin Soldier*,[12] illustrated by Marcia Brown. The picture-book romance between a tin soldier and a toy dancer ends when the two are thrown into a fire. Brown's final picture depicts the theme, for in the hearth are remnants of a tin soldier, melted into the shape of a heart, that lies next to a charred dancer's spangle.

A book's setting can also reinforce its theme. Eleanor Cameron's fantasy, *The Court of the Stone Children,*[13] has the following theme: rendering justice by removing barriers of time periods. Modern-day Nina visits a San Francisco French Art Museum where she alone can see Dominique, a young noblewoman from Napoleon's era. Nina proves that Dominique's father was falsely accused of murder, for in a dream, she sees a museum statue point to a painting showing his innocence. The setting helps merge past and present, for the museum has old furnishings from the French girl's home. Hanging in the museum is a Chagall painting, *Time Is a River without Banks,* the book's symbol.

## Explicit and Implicit Themes

A theme is particularly joyous to discover when it is implicit, or implied. The opposite of an implicit theme is one that is explicit, or stated. (The Greek word, *thema,* means something set down.) A book's title is often the best explicit expression or clue to its primary theme. Kristin Hunter's short stories for upper-elementary grades, *Guests in the Promised Land,*[14] seem to have the theme of being Black in a White world, for the stories highlight discrimination. The title is the precise theme of Janice May Udry's simple picture book, *A Tree Is Nice,*[15] a theme that even young children can understand. The book's few words tell about the pleasure of sitting in a tree's shade, swinging from its branches, or picking its fruit.

A book may have both explicit and implicit themes. Moreover, there are subjective responses to literature, so what is explicit to one reader may be implicit to another. Readers interact with stories in determining theme. They need guidance to help them distinguish between explicit and implicit themes, but they are entitled to their own interpretations.

Whether it is explicit or implicit, a theme may at times be named by an abstract noun or phrase: nonconformity, vanity, the price of mischief, or the futility of war. Two winners of The John Newbery Medal, for example, have the same abstract theme: the power of love. It is explicit in the 1963 winner, Madeleine L'Engle's *A Wrinkle in Time,*[16] and implicit in the 1966 winner, Elizabeth Borton de Treviño's *I, Juan de Pareja.*[17]

In the climax of the fantasy, *A Wrinkle in Time,* the heroine discovers how she can save her brother from the evil, mechanical IT, ruler of imaginary Camazotz. She announces, ''Love. That was what she had that IT did not have.''[18] The power of her love rescues the boy from IT's spell.

The theme is stated in *A Wrinkle in Time,* but it is implied in *I, Juan de Pareja.* Treviño's primary theme is frequently interpreted as the desire for freedom to paint by Juan de Pareja, enslaved to artist Velásquez. No slave in seventeenth-century Spain was allowed to paint, so Pareja was a secret artist until his master freed him. Treviño intended a different primary theme, however, and it is the power of love. She says:

> The theme is the same in every book I've ever written. I personally think that is why we're here on this earth. We're here to learn to love. The relationship between Juan and Velásquez can only be described by that word, love. Of course, it began as a friendship, a friendship between two men of different races.[19]

Treviño's statement about her primary theme casts a soft light on *I, Juan de Pareja*. The main records from both artists are their paintings, and Velásquez's moving portrait of Pareja could support Treviño's view of their relationship.

Like Treviño, Katherine Paterson favors implicit themes which she sometimes repeats. The main idea of her Newbery Honor Book, *The Great Gilly Hopkins*,[20] is: "Life is tough, but there's nothing better than doing well at a tough job."[21] She thinks this book has the same theme "in American dress" as her earlier Japanese historical fiction, *The Sign of the Chrysanthemum:* "Becoming what you are through fire."[22]

Young children may sense an implicit theme without articulating it, and a clever picture book with an implicit theme may be as popular as one whose theme is stated. Maurice Sendak's *Where the Wild Things Are* is an example of an appealing picture-book fantasy with an implicit theme: remembered childhood emotions.[23] Sendak shows Max, a boy who defies his mother and becomes angry when she sends him to bed without supper. He fantasizes he rules a kingdom of wild monsters until he returns home to find supper waiting. The author-illustrator, whose work is based on his own boyhood memories, says his book infers, "It's all right to be a child. It's all right to defy your parents. It's all right to get angry. It's all right to be alive and enjoy yourself!"[24]

## Primary and Secondary Themes

A primary theme is essential in every fine literary work, and it may be related to secondary or less important themes. A book with an explicit primary theme may have implicit secondary themes. Jean Craighead George's Alaskan story, *Julie of the Wolves*,[25] has an explicit title that emphasizes the primary theme, Julie's relationship to wolves. Julie's becoming an independent person is an illustration of a secondary implicit theme. Relationship to animals (wolves) and becoming an independent person are universal experiences often embodied in themes.

In *A Wrinkle in Time,* Madeleine L'Engle contrasts her explicit primary theme, the power of love, with greed of power seekers. An implicit secondary theme is individualization as opposed to regimentation. Both notions fascinate her and recur in her works.

A title may relate to a secondary theme, as does Elizabeth George Speare's *The Witch of Blackbird Pond.*[26] The title refers to Puritan abuse of a Quaker in seventeenth-century New England. Being a misfit is the explicit primary theme, for a high-spirited girl from Barbados was out of place in Puritan New England. She states, "I don't seem to fit in."[27] This book exemplifies that themes may be negative and may raise profound questions without presupposing answers. Speare identifies still another explicit secondary theme in her popular historical fiction: the colonists' preparation for revolution.[28]

Because of space limitation, this book emphasizes only primary themes. However, an example is provided of a fable that has not one but several explicit primary themes and at least six implicit secondary themes. A fable is an excellent model because its stated moral is an undisputed theme. The Aesop fable, "The Grasshopper and the Ant," is treated in a new, poetic way by John Ciardi in his *John J. Plenty and Fiddler Dan.*[29] Among the implicit secondary themes in Ciardi's story are:

1. Industry. As he prepares for winter, John J. Plenty, the hardworking ant, can't stop to play.
2. Love. The ant's sister falls in love the moment she sees the grasshopper violinist, Fiddler Dan, and she marries him.
3. Entertainment. Though Fiddler Dan doesn't work, his music entertains his bride and the world of nature.
4. Hoarding. The ant wants his sister and brother-in-law to stay away from his stored winter food.
5. Self-denial. The miserly ant goes hungry while he saves his good mosquito steaks, remembering how hard they are to obtain.
6. Frailty. The ant is so weak from fasting, he collapses.

Ciardi's moral or explicit primary themes are: While saving is optional, eating is essential, and no matter what you do, music makes it easier for you. This moral or primary theme may be summarized as the importance of food for soul (music) and body. Poet Ciardi says:

> *John J. Plenty and Fiddler Dan* is my effort in favor of the musicians' union. The fable always has it that the busy person comes out ahead, but I think musicians should be paid. I think they should have their share of successes, and in this telling of it, John J. Plenty, the ant, spends all of his time gathering and then almost starves to death, because he's afraid to eat what he's gathered. He comes out in the spring

and thinks, "Ha, Fiddler Dan is gone by now," but somehow from somewhere, the music starts over.

I don't know what keeps musicians alive. My daughter is a musician, and my son wants to be. I guess their father keeps them alive.[30]

Ciardi says he is particularly proud of the last line in his moral praising the enduring quality of music. A moral, unless it is inferred, is expected at the end of a fable, but moralizing is appropriate only in fables. A story written to convey a theme can lapse into preaching, the function of sermons, or instructing (didacticism), the function of text-books. Neither preaching nor instructing is welcome in general literature, so teachers and librarians should avoid both temptations in discussing story themes.

Bernice E. Cullinan says:

In children's literature, theme is generally simpler than in adult literature; it embodies significance of experiences that children can understand. Furthermore, there is usually only one theme, whereas in adult literature, there may be several.[31]

Actually, beyond the simplest picture books, most literary selections offer multiple or multileveled themes, and one's degree of mental maturity plus experiential background determines which themes one identifies. Though themes are stated definitely in this book, they may be refuted, so the book fulfills a purpose of motivating critical thinking, which is important to adults and children alike.

**Encouraging Children to Think about Themes**

Ideas about developing the notion of theme with children have been field-tested. After boys and girls read a selection, they answer the question, "What's the main idea?" or "What's the meaning behind the words?" Such questions stimulate thinking, even if children are only aware of a theme but are unable to express it.

In trial discussions of main idea, elementary pupils had problems distinguishing theme from plot. It helped them to begin with fables that have stated morals or themes. Pupils gained confidence as they moved to picture storybooks, then short stories and longer books, each with a title stating its primary theme. Children reread the longer books to discover secondary themes and exchanged ideas with peers. Finally, classes read books with implicit themes and especially enjoyed picture storybooks, like *Madeline,*[32] written and illustrated by Ludwig Bemelmans, and folk tales, like Charles Perrault's *Cinderella, or the Little Glass Slipper*.[33] Class analysis of primary and secondary implicit themes helped bolster readers when they progressed to challenging short stories and books.

Results after a short period show that pupils are beginning to understand the notion of theme. Paula in second grade read *Sam, Bangs, and Moonshine* by author-illustrator Evaline Ness.[34] This picture storybook concerns motherless Samantha (everyone calls her Sam), who fantasizes or moonshines until she endangers a friend. Paula believes the main idea is: "Danger from lies."

In third grade, Jonathan read the picture storybook, *Crow Boy*, by author-illustrator, Taro Yashima.[35] It is the tale of a poor, isolated Japanese pupil who hears crows for six years on his long trips to school. His only friend, his last teacher, lets him imitate the birds in a talent show. Jonathan feels the main idea is: "How a child can change with help."

Lucy in fourth grade read E.B. White's *Charlotte's Web*.[36] The fantasy is about a spider who befriends a pig, preventing his slaughter, and he, in turn, saves her egg sac. Lucy views the main idea as: "Friends helping each other."

David in fifth grade read Lloyd Alexander's *The High King*.[37] In this story, set in imaginary Prydain, the hero defeats the Lord of the Land of Death, and David says its theme is: "The battle between good and evil."

All the children seemed excited to be discussing the meaning of a story and felt it required more thinking than plot reviews. They believed their early understanding of themes would help create a positive lifetime attitude toward literature. What they requested was ample adult guidance.

Obviously, if teachers and librarians cannot comprehend themes themselves, they cannot guide pupils. They must be enlightened first and can then help children grasp the full significance of a story, probing beyond surface to core.

### Selected Games and Activities to Popularize Themes with Children

Games and activities may develop the notion of theme with some children. Only a few activity examples are offered in the following section. They often cite specific grades, themes, or prizewinners, but some may be extended to other grades, themes, and books. Though the word *theme* appears at times in this description, *main idea* is the term to use with children. Themes are stated precisely in the next section, but there should

be leeway for individual interpretation. The activities stimulate reading
for main idea, *encouraging thinking, not memorizing fixed themes.* Classes
exchange games, and enthusiastic pupils often design their own.


*Activities for All Ages*

1. A public library and a first-grade classroom feature the theme friendship on the bulletin board surrounded by appropriate titles and
   pictures.
2. Creative dramatization of themes of carefully chosen books takes
   place in many grades. Second graders wear headdresses in enacting
   *Who's in Rabbit's House? A Masai Tale* recorded by Verna Aardema, and afterward peers discuss its main idea: Being wise helps
   more at times than being big. From a dramatization of Watty Piper's
   *The Little Engine that Could,* first graders extract a related notion:
   important work by something small.

   Third graders appreciate the theme, a daughter's love for her mother,
from a skit of Becky Rehyer's *My Mother Is the Most Beautiful Woman
in the World.* Fourth graders portray deceptive cleverness, using Nonny
Hogrogian's *The Contest.* Fifth-grade pupils convey ingenuity with James
Thurber's *Many Moons,* and sixth graders, heroic capabilities with Dell
McCormick's *Paul Bunyan Swings His Axe.*
   A teacher writes:

> I have a fourth-grade class of small-town and semi-rural pupils whose
> top I.Q. is 110–115. I give them a reading list of easily-dramatized
> prizewinners. After they read the same books, we divide into groups,
> each picking a book to enact. The group determines the main idea,
> records it on a card, rehearses in a corner of the room or hall, and does
> a short, informal skit for others who try to guess the theme. They
> improvise props, using chairs, for example, for the ship in Uri Shule-
> vitz's *The Fool of the World and the Flying Ship.* I'm amazed at group
> independence, the learning that results, and above all, the enthusiasm!

3. Puppet dramatizations of book themes are popular. Puppets can be
   made from paper bags; socks; papier mâché; tongue depressors;
   wooden spoons; cookies cut in characters' shapes; paper plates, cones,
   or tubes; yarn; felt; raffia; or fabric. They are often simple hand,
   ring, or two-finger puppets or ones painted on a fist. Cardboard
   figurines with metal attached to their stands move when guided under
   a cardboard puppet stage by a pupil-held magnet. In shadow plays,
   silhouette puppets are manipulated behind a screen. A strong light
   behind them casts their shadows on the screen.

*Activities for Grades K to 3*

4. After hearing Arnold Lobel's *Frog and Toad Are Friends* or *Frog and Toad Together,* kindergarteners graphically portray the friendship theme by using a crayon on a simple maze to link a picture of Frog crying in one page corner to Toad waiting for him with open arms in the opposite corner. The teacher asks why Frog and Toad want to be together. (Older children try more complex mazes, such as one symbolizing the love theme, linking Agba and King of the Wind, the stallion in Marguerite Henry's book by that name.)
5. First graders arrange in proper sequence three pictures from Harve Zemach's *Duffy and the Devil: A Cornish Tale Retold,* and they do the same with three from Ruth Sawyer's *Journey Cake, Ho!* Then they decide which story is about a chase and which is about trouble from lying.
6. Reading Leo Lionni's *Swimmy* occurs before a teacher asks third graders how its central idea (cooperation) enters into any team project. She organizes circle dancing and then asks for a parallel between what pupils and fish alike achieve.
7. A second-grade class reads Marcia Brown's *Stone Soup.* Then each pupil brings a vegetable to school, helps make soup, eats it, and discusses sharing food as part of the story's main idea. (The book shows soldiers resourcefully overcoming villagers' reluctance to share their food.)
8. Third graders read Taro Yashima's *Crow Boy* before playing a circle game to comprehend how the protagonist changed from inferior-feeling Chibi to accepted Crow Boy. When children receive a ball or bean bag, they have to compliment its thrower. Though praise is required, pupils feel more valued, just as Crow Boy did when his teacher, Mr. Isobe, appreciated him.
9. A third-grade class decodes the theme of Ellen Raskin's *Spectacles,* a book showing a girl's need for eyeglasses. Once letters, arranged in diminishing size, as on a Snellen eye chart, are unscrambled, they reveal the theme: importance of good vision.

*Activities for Grades 4 to 6*

10. Children solve a crossword puzzle or cryptogram of a book's theme.
11. After reading Thomas Rockwell's *How to Eat Fried Worms,* fourth graders play Hang Worm modeled after Hang Man. The teacher

draws part of a worm for each incorrect response to book questions. Correct respondents guess letters placed in thirteen blanks for the theme: determination. Pupils then discuss their own interpretation of the book's theme.

12. A fourth-grade class makes a card deck based on E.B. White's *Charlotte's Web,* replacing a joker's picture on a card with that of Charlotte the spider. The person stuck with the spider card after playing ''Go Fish'' has to find the book's theme (friendship) on a seek-and-find sheet. This is a sheet with letters written horizontally, vertically, and diagonally embedded among which, in this case, is the word *friendship.*

13. Fourth graders play a concentration game. When children correctly answer questions about Madeleine L'Engle's *A Wrinkle in Time,* they are allowed to seek a pair of cards, the hidden backs of which have matching names from the book. As they remove pairs, they reveal underneath parts of a rebus (a riddle made of pictures that suggest word sounds). The rebus message is the theme: Love (a heart picture) rules (a measuring ruler picture).

14. Several teams of fifth graders take turns dramatizing book themes with charades.

15. Fifth graders play a Dike Walk board game motivated by Meindert DeJong's Dutch story, *The Wheel on the School,* first making a cardboard windmill with arms attached by a paper fastener. After spinning windmill arms to determine how many spaces to advance on the board, players answer book questions on their space. The first at the dike unscrambles letters to form determination, the book's theme.

16. After reading the same prizewinners, every member of a fifth-grade class contributes a visual interpretation of the theme of one book. Each art-exhibit entry is numbered, including posters, murals, dioramas, paper sculptings, clay models, collages, linoleum block prints, and mobiles. Classmates act as viewers and keep a list of entry numbers and book titles they associate with each. Later, viewers learn titles that actually inspired creations.

17. Fifth graders read Virginia Hamilton's *The House of Dies Drear,* a book about an historic underground railroad station. Each pupil who correctly answers questions about the book can try to rearrange letters of a theme word in slots on a poster showing an overhead view of a railroad. The six words are on separate railroad ties and, when unscrambled, read: keeping an historic underground railroad station.

18. Sixth graders have a treasure hunt based on Kin Platt's *Sinbad and*

*Me,* a book about breaking a code to find treasure. Code numbers that stand for the theme are hidden around the room and clues to find them are written on paper scorched around the edges for an aged effect. Once found, the code has to be deciphered to form the theme: facing personal challenges.

19. A sixth-grade class makes book mosaics: designs or pictures in which each book read within a given period is recorded, perhaps on separate flower petals. The unique feature is that petals of books with similar themes are colored the same. In a box on the mosaic is a legend clarifying themes and color scheme.

20. A sixth-grade teacher caps each pupil with a headband on which a theme is written, but no child sees his or her own theme. Themes are anything from friendship or courage to survival or good conquers evil. To ascertain their themes, players question each other, but respondents can only reply, "Yes" or "No."

21. In a literary newspaper, sixth graders report events in prizewinners, artfully citing the theme of each in CAPITAL LETTERS. A weather report tells of green fall-out in the Kingdom of Didd and "THE KING'S NEED TO ADMIT ERROR WHEN DISTURBING NATURE" (Dr. Seuss' *Bartholome and the Oobleck*). A Times Square concert announcement mentions Chester Cricket's honoring "New York FRIENDS before returning to Connecticut" (George Selden's *The Cricket in Times Square*). A real-estate advertisement requires "LOVING FAMILY to rent or purchase forest cottage" (Laura Ingalls Wilder's *The Little House in the Big Woods*). Dear Abby replies to Cinderella, assuring her, "VIRTUE WILL BE REWARDED" (Marcia Brown's version of *Cinderella, or the Little Glass Slipper*).

22. After a sixth-grade class reads the same books, they play records relating to their primary themes, and children try to match record to book title. For example, they play "The Impossible Dream" for Scott O'Dell's *Sing Down the Moon,* a story of courage when doomed Navahos seek justice. They play "Love Makes the World Go Round" for Hans Christian Andersen's tale of two toys' romance, *The Steadfast Tin Soldier*. For Paula Fox's *The Slave Dancer,* they offer "Born Free"; for Marcia Brown's version of *Cinderella, or the Little Glass*

22. *Slipper,* "Someday My Prince Will Come"; and for July Blume's *Are You There, God? It's Me, Margaret,* "Circle Game," a song that emphasizes maturing.

These classroom activities highlight the fun of finding themes. The most popular primary themes among reviewed prizewinners are cited next.

## Most Popular Themes and Topics under Which Themes Are Grouped

Some of the 717 prizewinners in the sample have popular themes. As shown in an appendix chart, the top ten themes or topics under which themes are grouped in rank order are as follows: (1) friendship, (2) family relationships, (3) love, (4) survival, (5) determination and courage, (6) maturing, (6) nature, (8) adventure, (9) search for identity, (10) good overcoming evil, and (10) virtue rewarded. The two ties reflect identical frequency.

Some themes are associated with a particular genre. Unique to modern fantasy, for example, is fusion of past, present, or future. War's effect is important in historical fiction as is search for identity, reflective of the fiction concerning pioneers raised by Native Americans. Love, largely between animals and owners, is frequently the theme of realistic animal stories. In contemporary realistic fiction, there are also certain characteristic themes. In fiction that involves families, friends, and problems, accepting responsibility often dominates. In literature set in other lands, learning new ways is appropriate. In stories that concern U.S. minorities, Black in a White world and integrated education both fit.

An overview of frequent themes has been offered. The section that follows gives another kind of overview, for it cites books that are especially popular.

## Findings about Multiple Prizewinners and Some Newbery/Caldecott Medalists

Some choice books for theme games may be those with clear main ideas drawn from the appendix list, "Winners of Three or More Awards." Compiling this list of multiple prizewinners occurred after theme analysis of 717 books. The list gives equal weight to all forty-two studied awards, including those in which boys and girls have input. (Fourteen children's-choice awards are asterisked in the appendix listing of all studied awards.)

Pupils may benefit from reading and analyzing themes of books awarded prizes by children and adults alike. The children's-choice awards among multiple prizewinners were especially examined, and results were interesting. The list proves children prefer to read about animals, both in fantasy and in realistic stories. Children gave three of their awards to each of the following animal fantasies: Beverly Cleary's *The Mouse and the Motorcycle*, Robert C. O'Brien's *Mrs. Frisby and the Rats of NIMH*, and E.B. White's *The Trumpet of the Swan*, reserving one of their awards for George Selden's *The Cricket in Times Square* and one for William Steig's *Dominic*.

Realistic animal stories include historical and contemporary ones. Children gave four awards to Sterling North's historical *Rascal: A Memoir of a Better Era*. Among contemporary realistic stories, they gave four awards to Fred Gipson's *Old Yeller*, three to Sheila Burnford's *The Incredible Journey*, and one to a story that reaches beyond animal-human relationships, Jean Craighead George's *My Side of the Mountain*.

Besides animal stories, children prefer humorous contemporary fiction. They gave six awards to Thomas Rockwell's *How to Eat Fried Worms*, four each to Judy Blume's *Tales of a Fourth Grade Nothing* and Beverly Cleary's *Ramona the Pest*, and one to Beverly Cleary's *Ramona and Her Father*.

Among contemporary fiction on the list are two books about American minorities, each receiving a children's-choice award: Alice Childress's *A Hero Ain't Nothin' but a Sandwich* and Miska Miles's *Annie and the Old One*. In the same genre, again with one children's-choice award apiece, is a book about interracial friendship, Zilpha Keatley Snyder's *The Egypt Game*, and a book set in India, Aimée Sommerfelt's *The Road to Agra*.

One children's-choice award among multiple winners went to a folk tale, Taro Yashima's *Seashore Story*, and one to a collection of fantasies in folktale style, Jane Yolen's *The Girl Who Cried Flowers and Other Tales*.

In historical fiction, beyond previously cited *Rascal: A Memoir of a Better Era*, children gave three awards to Scott O'Dell's *Island of the Blue Dolphins*, two to William H. Armstrong's *Sounder*, and one each to Robert Burch's *Queenie Peavy*, Meindert DeJong's *The House of Sixty Fathers*, Sid Fleischman's *By the Great Horn Spoon!*, Mildred D. Taylor's *Roll of Thunder, Hear My Cry*, and Theodore Taylor's *The Cay*.

It is important to note child-awarded historical fiction because there are librarian-awarded prizewinners in this genre that children do not read unless librarians promote them. Many old winners and Honor Books of The John Newbery Medal, begun in 1922, are historical fiction children seldom read today, no matter how fine the writing. While the same may be true of some new prizewinners, the most hopeful sign is child-awarded historical fiction.

A surprise is that one very popular book, E.B. White's *Charlotte's Web*, recipient of three awards on the multiple list, has not received a major children's-choice award, though E.B. White's less-known *The Trumpet of the Swan* received five. *Charlotte's Web* was also deprived of The John Newbery Medal in 1953 when it was named an Honor Book, second to Ann Nolan Clark's *Secret of the Andes*. There is no better proof of the importance of Honor Books! Equally strange is the fact that Eleanor Estes's *The Moffats* received no Newbery recognition in 1942 when Walter D. Edmonds's *The Matchlock Gun* won The John Newbery Medal, but her less-known *Ginger Pye* won The John Newbery Medal in 1952.

What seems like another mistake with two Newbery Honor Books has a logical explanation. In 1929, Wanda Gág's *Millions of Cats* was a Newbery (not Caldecott) Honor Book, as was her *The ABC Bunny* in 1934. Her books may have inspired a separate illustration award, The Randolph Caldecott Medal, begun in 1938.

It was not until 1981 that the Association for Library Services of the American Library Association named separate selection committees for Newbery and Caldecott Medals, but in 1982, there were unusual results. A picture book of poetry, Nancy Willard's *A Visit to William Blake's Inn* won The John Newbery Medal and was simultaneously a Caldecott Honor Book.

Newbery and Caldecott winners and Honor Books are among those in the list of multiple prizewinners. Unfortunately, no picture storybooks in the appendix list were given children's-choice awards. This is because young children are just beginning to be consulted, as with the Little Archer Award sponsored by the Department of Library Science at the University of Wisconsin, Oshkosh campus.

Among multiple prizewinners, child-awarded books may particularly appeal to children. Adults should promote those with clear primary themes when encouraging boys and girls to think about themes.

## Summary

A literary work must have a theme, its unifying thread, which may be explicit (stated) or implicit (implied). Generally, the title is a clue to an explicit theme. Concept books for young children always have a theme, and often the concept and theme are the same. It is an exciting challenge to discover not only a primary theme, but also secondary or less-important themes. Illustrations, particularly in picture storybooks, may help portray a theme.

In this book, the most popular themes and topics under which themes are grouped are tabulated. The top four in rank order are friendship, family relationships, love, and survival.

If teachers and librarians have time to ask a child only one comprehension question about a completed book, it might well be, "What's the main idea?" or "What's the meaning behind the story?" Using the words *main idea,* adults can assist children to understand what a theme is, particularly with the support of field-tested games and activities. Twenty-two are offered, easier ones for children in grades K to 3 and then challenging ones for those in grades 4 to 6. When encouraging boys and girls to think about themes, adults may select a book with a clear primary theme from an appendix list of multiple prizewinners. The list includes children's-choice awards that should be popular with both boys and girls.

Often with supportive quotations, this book offers an interpretation of the primary theme of each of 717 prizewinners. Others may present their own documented interpretations. In this way, readers may spend less time on minutia, giving priority instead to exciting critical thinking, particularly about a main theme at the heart of a story.


**Notes**

1. Jaqueline Shachter Weiss, executive producer, "John Ciardi," *Profiles in Literature* (Philadelphia: Temple University, 1976).

2. Bernice E. Cullinan, *Literature for Children, Its Discipline and Content* (Dubuque, Iowa: Brown, 1971), p. 36.

3. Arthur N. Applebee, *The Child's Concept of Story, Ages 2–17* (Chicago: The University of Chicago Press, 1978), p. 110.

4. In 1972, *Count and See* was a *New York Times* Choice of Best Illustrated Children's Book of the Year.

5. In 1971, *Look Again!* was a *New York Times* Choice of Best Illustrated Children's Book of the Year.

6. Monroe C. Beardsley, *Aesthetics, Problems in the Philosophy of Criticism* (New York: Harcourt, 1958), p. 403.

7. In 1975, *My Brother Sam Is Dead* was a Newbery Honor Book and a finalist for the National Book Award in the children's-book category.

8. Philip Babcock Gove, ed., *Webster's Third New International Dictionary of the English Language Unabridged* (Springfield, Mass.: Merriam, 1971), p. 2374.

9. In 1950, *The Door in the Wall* won The John Newbery Medal.

10. In 1955, *The Courage of Sarah Noble* was a Newbery Honor Book.

11. In 1940, *Blue Willow* won the Commonwealth Club of California Award, and in 1941, it was a Newbery Honor Book.

12. In 1954, *The Steadfast Tin Soldier* was a Caldecott Honor Book.

13. In 1974, *The Court of the Stone Children* won the National Book Award in the children's-book category.

14. In 1973, *Guests in the Promised Land* won the Christopher Award in the children's-book category for ages twelve and up. In 1974, it was a finalist for the National Book Award in the children's-book category.

15. In 1957, *A Tree Is Nice,* illustrated by Marc Simont, won The Randolph Caldecott Medal.

16. In 1963, *A Wrinkle in Time* won The John Newbery Medal and in 1965, the Sequoyah Children's Book Award.

17. In 1966, *I, Juan de Pareja* won The John Newbery Medal.

18. Madeleine L'Engle, *A Wrinkle in Time* (New York: Farrar, 1962), p. 207.

19. "Elizabeth Borton de Treviño," *Profiles in Literature* (Philadelphia: Temple University, 1977).

20. In 1978, *The Great Gilly Hopkins* won the Christopher Award in the children's-book category for ages nine to twelve. In 1979, it won the National Book Award and was a Newbery Honor Book.

21. "Katherine Paterson," *Profiles in Literature* (Philadelphia: Temple University, 1979).

22. Ibid.

23. In 1963, *Where the Wild Things Are* was a *New York Times* Choice of Best Illustrated Children's Book of the Year. In 1964, it won The Randolph Caldecott Medal, and in 1966, it was put on the International Board on Books for Young People Honor List.

24. "Maurice Sendak," *Profiles in Literature* (Philadelphia: Temple University, 1977).

25. In 1973, *Julie of the Wolves* won The John Newbery Medal and was a finalist for the National Book Award.

26. In 1959, *The Witch of Blackbird Pond* won The John Newbery Medal and in 1960, it was put on the International Board on Books for Young People Honor List.

27. Elizabeth George Speare, *The Witch of Blackbird Pond* (Boston: Houghton Mifflin, 1958), p. 127.

28. "Elizabeth George Speare," *Profiles in Literature* (Philadelphia: Temple University, 1974).

29. In 1963, *John J. Plenty and Fiddler Dan,* illustrated by Madeleine Gekiere, was a *New York Times* Choice of Best Illustrated Children's Book of the Year.

30. "John Ciardi," *Profiles in Literature* (Philadelphia: Temple University, 1976).

31. Bernice E. Cullinan, *Literature for Children, Its Discipline and Content* (Dubuque, Iowa: Brown, 1971), p. 36.

32. In 1940, *Madeline* was a Caldecott Honor Book.

33. In 1955, *Cinderella, or the Little Glass Slipper,* illustrated by Marcia Brown, won The Randolph Caldecott Medal.

34. In 1967, *Sam, Bangs, and Moonshine* won The Randolph Caldecott Medal.

35. In 1955, *Crow Boy* won the award of the Child Study Children's

Book Committee at Bank Street College, and in 1956, it was a Caldecott Honor Book.

36. In 1953, *Charlotte's Web* was a Newbery Honor Book. In 1959, it won the Lewis Carroll Shelf Award, and in 1970, the George G. Stone Center for Children's Books Recognition of Merit Award.

37. In 1969, *The High King* won The John Newbery Medal and was a National Book Award finalist in the children's-book category.

## References

*(Estimated Reading Grade Level in Parentheses)*

Aardema, Verna, ed. *Who's in Rabbit's House? A Masai Tale*. Illustrated by Leo and Diane Dillon. New York: Dial, 1977 (K–3).

Alexander, Lloyd. *The High King*. New York: Holt, 1968 (5–8).

Andersen, Hans Christian. *The Steadfast Tin Soldier*. Illustrated by Marcia Brown. New York: Scribner, 1953 (K–4).

Armstrong, William H. *Sounder*. Illustrated by James Barkley. New York: Harper, 1969 (6–9).

Bemelmans, Ludwig. *Madeline*. New York: Viking, 1939 (K–3).

Blume, Judy. *Are You There, God? It's Me, Margaret*. Scarsdale, N.Y.: Bradbury, 1970 (4–6).

———. *Tales of a Fourth Grade Nothing*. Illustrated by Roy Doty. New York: Dutton, 1972 (3–4).

Brown, Marcia. *Stone Soup*. New York: Scribner, 1947 (1–4).

Burch, Robert. *Queenie Peavy*. Illustrated by Jerry Lazare. New York: Viking, 1966 (4–7).

Burnford, Sheila. *The Incredible Journey*. Illustrated by Carl Burger. Boston: Little, Brown, 1961 (6–9).

Cameron, Eleanor. *The Court of the Stone Children*. New York: Dutton, 1973 (5–7).

Childress, Alice. *A Hero Ain't Nothin' but a Sandwich*. New York: Coward, 1973 (6–9).

Ciardi, John. *John J. Plenty and Fiddler Dan*. Illustrated by Madeleine Gekiere. Philadelphia: Lippincott, 1963 (3–6).

Clark, Ann Nolan. *Secret of the Andes*. Illustrated by Jean Charlot. New York: Viking, 1952 (4–8).

Cleary, Beverly. *The Mouse and the Motorcycle*. Illustrated by Louis Darling. New York: Morrow, 1965 (3–5).

———. *Ramona and Her Father*. Illustrated by Alan Tiegreen. New York: Morrow, 1977 (3–5).

————. *Ramona the Pest*. Illustrated by Louis Darling. New York: Morrow, 1968 (3–5).

Collier, James Lincoln and Christopher. *My Brother Sam Is Dead*. New York: Four Winds, 1974 (6–9).

Dalgleish, Alice. *The Courage of Sarah Noble*. Illustrated by Leonard Weisgard. New York: Scribner, 1954 (3–5).

deAngeli, Marguerite. *The Door in the Wall*. New York: Doubleday, 1949 (5–7).

DeJong, Meindert. *The House of Sixty Fathers*. Illustrated by Maurice Sendak. New York: Harper 1956 (6–9).

————. *The Wheel on the School*. Illustrated by Maurice Sendak. New York: Harper, 1954 (4–7).

Edmonds, Walter D. *The Matchlock Gun*. Illustrated by Paul Lantz. New York: Dodd, 1941 (5–7).

Estes, Eleanor. *Ginger Pye*. New York: Harcourt, 1951 (4–6).

————. *The Hundred Dresses*. Illustrated by Louis Slobodkin. New York: Harcourt, 1944 (3–5).

————. *The Middle Moffat*. Illustrated by Louis Slobodkin. New York: Harcourt, 1942 (4–6).

————. *The Moffats*. Illustrated by Louis Slobodkin. New York: Harcourt, 1941 (4–6).

————. *Rufus M*. Illustrated by Louis Slobodkin. New York: Harcourt, 1943 (4–6).

Fleischman, Sid. *By the Great Horn Spoon!* Illustrated by Eric Von Schmidt. Boston: Little, Brown, 1963 (4–6).

Fox, Paula. *The Slave Dancer*. Illustrated by Eros Keith. Scarsdale, N.Y.: Bradbury, 1973 (6–9).

Gág, Wanda. *The ABC Bunny*. New York: Coward, 1933 (PS–1).

————. *Millions of Cats*. New York: Coward, 1928 (PS–1).

Gates, Doris. *Blue Willow*. Illustrated by Paul Lantz. New York: Viking, 1940 (4–6).

George, Jean Craighead. *Julie of the Wolves*. Illustrated by John Schoenherr. New York: Harper, 1972 (5–8).

————. *My Side of the Mountain*. New York: Dutton, 1959 (5–7).

Gibson, Fred. *Old Yeller*. Illustrated by Carl Burger. New York: Harper, 1956 (6–9).

Hamilton, Virginia. *The House of Dies Drear*. Illustrated by Eros Keith. New York: Macmillan, 1968 (5–8).

Henry, Marguerite. *King of the Wind*. Illustrated by Wesley Dennis. Chicago: Rand McNally, 1948 (5–8).

Hoban, Tana. *Count and See*. New York: Macmillan, 1972 (PS–2).

————. *Look Again!* New York: Macmillan, 1971 (PS–2).

Hogrogian, Nonny. *The Contest*. New York: Greenwillow, 1976 (3–5).

Hunter, Kristin. *Guests in the Promised Land*. New York: Scribner, 1977 (6–9).

Lionni, Leo. *Swimmy*. New York: Pantheon, 1963 (PS–1).

Lobel, Arnold. *Frog and Toad Are Friends*. New York: Harper, 1970 (K–2).

————. *Frog and Toad Together*. New York: Harper, 1972 (K–2).

McCormick, Dell J. *Paul Bunyan Swings His Axe*. Caldwell, Id.: Caxton, 1936 (4–6).

Miles, Miska. *Annie and the Old One*. Illustrated by Peter Parnall. Boston: Little, Brown, 1971 (2–5).

Ness, Evaline. *Sam, Bangs, and Moonshine*. New York: Holt, 1966 (K–2).

North, Sterling. *Rascal: A Memoir of a Better Era*. Illustrated by John Schoenherr. New York: Dutton, 1963 (6–8).

O'Brien, Robert C. *Mrs. Frisby and the Rats of NIMH*. Illustrated by Zena Bernstein. New York: Atheneum, 1971 (5–7).

O'Dell, Scott. *Island of the Blue Dolphins*. Boston: Houghton, 1960 (5–8).

————. *Sing Down the Moon*. Boston: Houghton, 1970 (5–8).

Paterson, Katherine. *The Great Gilly Hopkins*. New York: Crowell, 1978 (4–6).

————. *The Sign of the Chrysanthemum*. Illustrated by Peter Landa. New York: Crowell (5–7).

Perrault, Charles. *Cinderella, or the Little Glass Slipper*. Illustrated by Marcia Brown. New York: Scribner (2–4).

Piper, Watty. *The Little Engine that Could*. Illustrated by George and Doris Hauman. New York: Platt and Munk, 1930 (PS–3).

Platt, Kin. *Sinbad and Me*. Philadelphia: Chilton, 1966 (6–9).

Raskin, Ellen. *Spectacles*. New York: Atheneum, 1968 (K–3).

Reyher, Becky. *My Mother Is the Most Beautiful Woman in the World*. Illustrated by Ruth Gannett. New York: Lothrop, 1945 (2–5).

Rockwell, Thomas. *How to Eat Fried Worms*. Illustrated by Emily McCully. New York: Watts, 1973 (4–6).

Sawyer, Ruth. *Journey Cake, Ho!* Illustrated by Robert McCloskey. New York: Viking, 1953 (K–3).

Selden, George. *The Cricket in Times Square*. Illustrated by Garth Williams. New York: Farrar, 1960 (3–6).

Sendak, Maurice. *Where the Wild Things Are*. New York: Harper, 1963 (K–3).

Seuss, Dr. *Bartholomew and the Oobleck*. New York: Vanguard, 1949 (K–3).

Snyder, Zilpha Keatley. *The Egypt Game*. Illustrated by Alton Raible. New York: Atheneum, 1967 (5–7).

Sommerfelt, Aimée. *The Road to Agra*. Illustrated by Ulf Aas. New York: Criterion, 1961 (4–6).

Speare, Elizabeth George. *The Witch of Blackbird Pond*. Boston: Houghton, 1958 (6–9).

Taylor, Mildred D. *Roll of Thunder, Hear My Cry*. Illustrated by Jerry Pinkney. New York: Dial, 1976 (6–8).

Taylor, Theodore. *The Cay*. New York: Doubleday, 1969 (5–8).

Thurber, James. *Many Moons*. Illustrated by Louis Slobodkin. New York: Harcourt, 1944 (4–5).

Treviño, Elizabeth Borton de. *I, Juan de Pareja*. New York: Farrar, 1965 (6–9).

Udry, Janice May. *A Tree Is Nice*. Illustrated by Marc Simont. New York: Harper, 1956 (PS).

White, E.B. *Charlotte's Web*. Illustrated by Garth Williams. New York: Harper, 1952 (2–5).

———. *The Trumpet of the Swan*. Illustrated by Edward Frascino. New York: Harper, 1970 (3–6).

Wilder, Laura Ingalls. *The Little House in the Big Woods*. Illustrated by Garth Williams, New York: Harper, 1932 (4–7).

Willard, Nancy. *A Visit to William Blake's Inn*. New York: Harcourt, 1981 (3 and up).

Yashima, Taro. *Crow Boy*. New York: Viking, 1955 (K–3).

———. *Seashore Story*. New York: Viking, 1967 (K–2).

Yolen, Jane. *The Girl Who Cried Flowers and Other Tales*. Illustrated by David Palladini. New York: Crowell, 1974 (5–6).

Zemach, Harve. *Duffy and the Devil: A Cornish Tale Retold*. Illustrated by Margot Zemach. New York: Farrar, 1973 (1–3).

*Professional References*

Applebee, Arthur N. *The Child's Concept of Story, Ages 2–17*. Chicago: University of Chicago Press, 1978.

Beardsley, Monroe C. *Aesthetics, Problems in the Philosophy of Criticism*. New York: Harcourt, 1958.

Cullinan, Bernice E. *Literature for Children, Its Discipline and Content*. Dubuque, Iowa: Brown, 1971.

Huck, Charlotte S. *Children's Literature in the Elementary School*, 3rd ed. New York: Holt, 1979.

Lukens, Rebecca J. *A Critical Handbook of Children's Literature*, 2nd ed. Glenview, Ill.: Scott, Foresman, 1981.

Rees, David. *The Marble in the Water*. Boston: Horn Book, 1980.

Sebesta, Sam Leaton, and Iverson, William J. *Literature for Thursday's Child*. Chicago: Science Research Associates, 1975.

Sutherland, Zena, and Arbuthnot, May Hill. *Children and Books,* 5th ed. Glenview, Ill.: Scott, Foresman, 1977.

Townsend, John Rowe. *Written for Children*. Philadelphia: Lippincott, 1974.

Whitehead, Robert. *Children's Literature: Strategies of Teaching*. Englewood Cliffs, N.J.: Prentice-Hall, 1968.

*Audiovisuals*

Weiss, Jaqueline Shachter. *Profiles in Literature,* No. 1–47, 1969–present, 3023 De Kalb Boulevard, Norristown, Penn. 19401. Phone 215 (AC) 279-1330.

# 2 Prose Classics

*When I was young, I liked* The Tale of Peter Rabbit, *especially because my name's Peter, but now I keep* Charlotte's Web *under my pillow.*
                                                                —Peter, aged nine

## Perspective

Peter's early favorite, published in 1902, is a classic, and *Charlotte's Web,* published in 1952, is considered a modern classic. Classics are distinguished literary works that have "weathered at least one generation."[1] A generation is about thirty years, so modern classics presented here in the 1980s end with books published in the 1950s. Mary Elisabeth Edes believes book sales indicate if a modern book is a classic because many families buy treasured volumes:

> The sale of just how many books does it take to make a classic? Well, to be utterly crass about it, the answer seems to be at least 100,000 copies and more, likely, 175,000.[2]

First choice in Edes's poll of librarians, reviewers, and sellers of children's books is *Charlotte's Web,* enjoyed in paperback alone by over 3 million readers. Modern classics in this chapter are chosen from Edes's list and "Modern Classics" issued by The Free Library of Philadelphia.[3]

Classics should be read by choice, never by duress. Some are appreciated if shared aloud when children are old enough to understand them. Reading should not be confined to classics, and such material should not be revered as flawless.

This chapter criticizes stereotypes in the classics. In a day when there are many divorces and remarriages, young children are being exposed to picture storybooks that continually show evil stepmothers. They are sexist stereotypes, for rarely are cruel stepfathers depicted. Similarly, boys and girls read more often about wicked witches than evil wizards. Even the wizard in *The Wizard of Oz* proves to be a jolly bungler. Tales with stereotyped characters are not taboo. They should still be shared critically, reminding children that classics reflect cultural values of the era when they were created.

This chapter discusses only U.S. prizewinning prose classics. The Lewis Carroll Shelf Award is the main prize given to older titles believed "worthy to sit on the shelf with *Alice in Wonderland.*" Modern classics are among winners and Honor Books of The John Newbery Medal mainly and, to a lesser extent, of The Randolph Caldecott Medal. Illustration awards have been given to picture-storybook editions of *Fables of Aesop, Beauty and the Beast,* and classical folk tales recorded by Charles Perrault, the Grimm brothers, and Hans Christian Andersen. Other chapters discuss less-known old traditional literature.

## Themes of Prizewinning Prose Classics Grouped under These Topics

*Friendship*

**Primary through Upper Grades.** Faithful friendship, emphasized in humorous illustrations by Garth Williams, is the explicit primary theme of E.B. White's *Charlotte's Web* (1952).[4] Wilbur, a pig, grieves for a friend until he meets Charlotte, a spider. She, helped by Templeton, a self-centered rat, saves the pig's life. In her web she spins compliments about him that the public notices. She says:

> You have been my friend . . . That in itself is a tremendous thing. I wove my webs for you because I liked you. . . . By helping you, perhaps I was trying to lift up my life a trifle.[5]

After Charlotte dies on the fair grounds, Wilbur brings her egg sac back to the barn and befriends her babies. (Death is among many secondary themes in this fantasy.)

Master writer E.B. White speaks of this story as one of friendship and salvation on a farm.[6] He says it originated one day in his barn when he saw a spider cleverly weaving while he was thinking of ways to save a doomed pig's life.

An Englishman with a light pen, A.A. Milne, the former assistant editor of *Punch,* uses White's same theme, friendship, in *Winnie-the-Pooh* (1926) and *The House at Pooh Corner* (1928). These two episodic domestic fantasies are now in a single edition, *The World of Pooh,*[7] illustrated by *Punch* cartoonist Ernest H. Shepard. Milne gently humanizes stuffed-toy animals, Winnie-the-Pooh (a teddy bear), Piglet, Tigger (a tiger), Kanga, Roo (mother and baby kangaroos), Rabbit, Eeyore (a donkey whose name comes from the sound he makes), and others. It was Mrs. Milne who suggested writing about their son, Christopher Robin, in an imaginary world with his nursery animals animated.

Moved by friendship, Pooh and Piglet, in one of many adventures, construct a house to shield Eeyore from the cold. The problem is they use sticks from the home gloomy Eeyore previously built. Eeyore laments that his friends have no brains, and Christopher Robin charitably jokes, "Silly old bear." The characters' childish pretending contributes to humor.

**Upper Grades.** In 1929, Kenneth Grahame, English author of *The Wind in the Willows* (1908),[8] enjoyed Milne's adaptation of his book as a play, "Toad of Toad Hall." Friendship is the theme of *The Wind in the Willows,* an allegory and fantasy that personifies animals. Water Rat is an extrovert; Mole, an introvert; Badger, a philosophical recluse; and Toad, a playboy. At each other's dwellings, they share food and fireside armchairs. When Mole gets homesick, Rat accompanies him home. Mole, in turn, helps Rat overcome depression by encouraging him to become a writer:

> . . . scribbling and sucking the top of his pencil. It is true that he sucked a good deal more than he scribbled; but it was a joy to the Mole to know that the cure had at least begun.[9]

Rat, Mole, and Badger, reliable in times of danger, help Toad oust tenants from Toad Hall. When Toad takes all the credit, his companions chide him for boasting, kindly calling him Toady. Toad likes motor cars, which Grahame satirizes, favoring the natural Wild Wood, where wind sings in the willows.

*The Wind in the Willows,* Grahame's only book especially for children, was inspired by his son, Alastair or "Mouse." On his fourth birthday, Mouse requested a story about a mole, a giraffe, and a rat. Grahame forgot the giraffe, so interested was he in Mole and Rat, but he added Badger, and Mouse's caricature, Toad. He continued the tale as a three-year bedtime story and recorded the end in letters to vacationing Mouse.

Grahame was delighted with the illustrations of Ernest H. Shepard, whom he told, "I love these little people. Be kind to them."[10] The fine writing and illustrations moved President Theodore Roosevelt to promote American publication of *The Wind in the Willows.*

*Loyalty*

**Middle and Upper Grades.** Loyalty is the theme of *Lassie Come-Home* (1940),[11] written when Eric Knight was in Pennsylvania. Author of an adult bestseller, *This Above All,* Knight was born in Yorkshire, England, where most of *Lassie* takes place. Lassie is Joe Carraclough's faithful collie, but in hard times, the boy's poor family sells her to a Scottish duke. Loyalty forces her to travel home hundreds of miles from Scotland to Yorkshire.

**Upper Grades.** Loyalty of friends is the theme of *The Adventures of Huckleberry Finn* (1884) by Mark Twain (pseudonym for Samuel L. Clemens).[12] This account of a Mississippi River voyage is nineteenth-century historical fiction. The author specifies on the title page: "Time: Forty to fifty years ago."[13] Reared haphazardly in the South, adolescent narrator Huckleberry Finn finds that helping a runaway slave bothers his conscience, but it would bother him more to betray such a good friend as Jim. Finn reflects:

> I couldn't seem to strike no places to harden me against him, but only the other kind. I'd see him standing my watch on top of his'n, 'stead of calling me, so I could go on sleeping; . . . and at last I struck the time I saved him by telling the men we had smallpox aboard, and he was so grateful, and said I was the best friend old Jim ever had in the world, and the *only* one he's got now.[14]

Finn decides he will "go to hell" rather than return Jim to his owner. The boy feels loyalty to the man, not opposition to slavery. Jim announces he will work in a free state where he will buy his wife's liberty and buy or steal his two children. Finn is incensed that Jim might steal his children.

Jim shows great loyalty to Finn and Tom Sawyer. When Finn tricks him, Jim tells of his deep friendship: "My heart wuz mos' broke bekase you wuz los', en I didn't k'yer no mo' what become er me en de raf'."[15] Later, when Finn is rumored dead, Jim waits for him, and once united with the hungry boy, feeds him. Jim stops hiding, sacrificing cherished liberty, to help treat wounded Tom Sawyer. He does not realize his own captivity has been prolonged by playful Sawyer. This boy wants the adventure of freeing Jim, though he knows Jim's owner has already freed him. Light treatment of liberty is incongruous.

Color consciousness pervades the humorous satire. With self-denigration, Jim interprets Finn's drunken father to be misled by a Black angel, and Finn says of Jim, "I knowed he was white inside."[15] Jim is shown to be very superstitious, often childlike. The characters, speaking in vernacular, use an objectionable term for Black, and Finn says he sweats "like an Injun."[16] These weaknesses, reflective of some nineteenth-century thought, have caused occasional efforts to censor Twain, but critical reading, not censorship, should be encouraged.

Finn is based on Samuel Clemens's childhood friend, Tom Blankenship, the town drunk's son. His older brother, Ben Blankenship, who came upon a runaway slave in the swamps, refused to disclose him, even though he denied himself a reward and violated the law.

## Adventure

**Upper Grades.** The theme, adventures of a mischievous boy, characterizes *The Adventures of Tom Sawyer*[17] (1876), an earlier work by Mark Twain. In his preface, Twain indicates the work is historical fiction, taking place thirty or forty years prior to 1876. It is a period when Tom's boyhood adventures include humorous whitewashing of a fence and finding cures for warts, but more important, witnessing a murder, testifying about it, and locating buried treasure. In the beginning, Tom is a prank-prone boy in a conformist small town, but by the end, he begins to mature.

The story's villain is Injun Joe. Unfortunately, the character's name insults Native Americans and so do references to him as "half-breed."[18] Injun Joe offends another minority when he reports being treated cruelly, "horsewhipped in front of the jail, like a nigger! with all the town looking on!"[19] A robber accomplice is a "deaf and dumb Spaniard,"[20] negative casting of a third minority.

The author knew Injun Joe, a drunkard, in his hometown, Hannibal, Missouri, called St. Petersberg in the book. Tom's tattling half-brother, Sid, a "model boy," is based on the author's younger brother, Henry, and Aunt Polly, Tom's guardian, stems from his joking, red-haired mother. Twain created the book on a new invention, the typewriter. This melodrama is known, not for theme or plot, but for humorous style and local color.

Adventures of a different sort are in *Mary Poppins* (1934),[21] which has a magical-nursemaid theme. This is the first of five fantasies about Mary Poppins by P.L. Travers, a former Australian living in New York. Mary Poppins is Nanny to four English children, Jane, Michael, John, and Barbara Banks. Among her magical acts, she commands a compass to take her and the children in any direction. As directions change, the author presents stereotyped views of Eskimos, Africans, a Chinese Mandarin, and Native Americans. Of the Africans she says:

> Beneath the palm trees sat a man and a woman, both quite black all over and with very few clothes on. . . . On the knee of the negro [sic] lady sat a tiny black pickaninny with nothing on at all. It smiled at the children as the Mother spoke.
>
> "Ah bin 'specting you a long time, Mar' Poppins," she said, smiling.

"You bring dem chillun dere into ma li'l house for a slice of watermelon right now. My, but dem's very white babies. You wan' use a
li'l bit black boot polish on dem."[22]

A 1972 paperback edition changes the woman's words but does not
alter stereotyped illustrations by Mary Shepard or the following child's
nightmare:

> There were four gigantic figures bearing down toward him—the Es-
> kimo with a spear, the Negro Lady with her husband's huge club, the
> Mandarin with a great curved sword, and the Red Indian with a
> tomahawk.[23]

The latest edition still has these expressions, "Come away from those
dreadful street arabs [sic]!"[24] and "You will *not* behave like a Red
Indian, Michael."[25]
In a 1974 interview, Travers says:

> Remember, *Mary Poppins* was written a long time ago when racism
> was not as important. . . . When the next edition, which was the
> paperback, came out, I altered one or two things which had nothing to
> do with "picaninny" talk at all . . . I grew up in a rarefied atmosphere.
> I loved *Little Black Sambo* as a child. . . . I only came across racism
> since I came to the United States.[26]

## Courage

**Middle Grades.** Courage is the theme of Alice Dalgliesh's true story of
1707, *The Courage of Sarah Noble* (1954).[27] Eight-year-old Sarah Noble
accompanies her father into the Connecticut wilderness while he builds
a house. The girl holds her cloak tightly around her, a symbol of mustering courage. She discards the cloak after local Native Americans befriend her, and she is reunited with the rest of her family.

**Upper Grades.** Another historical work with courage as its theme is
Esther Forbes's *Johnny Tremain* (1943).[28] In Boston in 1773, Johnny
Tremain, a fourteen-year-old silversmith's apprentice, maims his right
hand. Forced to abandon his trade, he bravely becomes a rider for the
Committee of Public Safety. During the Battle of Lexington in 1775, he
has the courage to permit a surgeon, unassisted, to operate on his hand.
The operation helps him achieve his goal of using a musket in the fight
for liberty.

*Materialism*

**Preschool through Middle Grades.** Emphasis on materialism pervades Charles Perrault's *Puss in Boots* (1697).[29] Clever provider is the theme of this talking-beast folk tale published in French as part of *Contes de ma Mere l'Oye (Tales of Mother Goose)*. Charles Perrault is probably the recorder, though it was believed beneath his dignity as a member of the French Academy to issue a children's book, so he signed his son's name, Pierre Perrault-Darmancour.

In *Puss in Boots,* the miller's youngest son is disappointed to inherit only a cat. However, Puss in red boots mounts a campaign that results in his master's marrying the king's daughter. Marcia Brown's illustrations project the picture-storybook theme, a saucy cat as a clever provider, one who turns an ogre into a mouse by appealing to his pride.

**Middle and Upper Grades.** Destructive materialism is the primary theme of a fantasy with details about miniature people, *The Borrowers* (1952).[30] The English author, Mary Norton, is a former actress and playwright, but Joe and Beth Krush are American illustrators. The Clock family consists of Homily, Pod, and their daughter, Arrietty, who live below the floorboards under the kitchen clock. Homily drives her husband, Pod, to ''borrow'' items from the house, like an emerald watch to time her cooking. Pod sometimes escapes her demands by using the house as his ''club.'' Mainly to satisfy her, he takes chances, is exposed to people, and is forced to emigrate with his family.

*Finding a Home and Permanence*

**Preschool through Middle Grades.** The theme of *Make Way for Ducklings* (1941) by author-illustrator Robert McCloskey is ducks finding a home.[31] In Boston, a pair of mallards nest along the Charles River. When they move to the Public Gardens, Mrs. Mallard leads her brood of seven. Police stop traffic to make way for ducklings.

During an interview, Robert McCloskey says the theme of his picture storybook is universal. He shows newspaper photographs and a Copenhagen, Denmark handkerchief of ducks obstructing traffic. To do his illustrations, he bought mallards, sketched them in his apartment, and fed them red wine to keep them still. They awakened at sunrise and started quacking, ruining the sleep of an illustrator, Marc Simont, who shared the New York apartment. McCloskey thinks his poultry models look a little like their creator when he has a crewcut.[32]

**Middle and Upper Grades.** A need for permanence is the theme of Doris Gates's realistic fiction, *Blue Willow* (1940).[33] Ten-year-old Janey Larkin, an adopted daughter of migratory workers, cherishes a blue willow plate, symbol of a dimly remembered home and a deceased mother. She displays the plate when her father takes the job formerly held by an irresponsible foreman, and the family moves into a permanent California home. The theme is explicit because the book ends as the girl asks, "How long can we stay?" and her father's employer replies, "As long as you want to."[34] She celebrates with a Latino friend, Lupe Romero, with whom she enjoys the kind of nonpatronizing relationship that is rare in children's books of the 1940s.

*Give or Take with Animals*

**Preschool through Middle Grades.** In a picture storybook, *Caps for Sale* (1947) by author-illustrator Esphyr Slobodkina, animals take caps, then give them back.[35] A peddler gets monkeys in a tree to return his caps that they are wearing. He is not successful when he talks to them, but when he throws his own cap on the ground, they imitate him, and he resumes peddling. Success through imitation is the book's theme.

**Middle and Upper Grades.** A doctor serves animals in a series of books by English author-illustrator Hugh Lofting. A naturalist communicating with animals and curing them is the theme of twelve fantasies, including *The Story of Doctor Dolittle* (1920) and *The Voyages of Doctor Dolittle* (1922).[36] The series is based on illustrated letters Lofting wrote his children in America while he was an Irish Guards officer hospitalized during World War I. Concerned about battle-wounded beasts, he wrote his books about a physician who prefers to be a veterinarian.

Lofting shows color consciousness in *The Story of Doctor Dolittle* when monkeys in Africa praise Dolittle as "the Good White Man."[37] Stereotyped in *Voyages* is "a whole band of Red Indians watching us with great curiosity from among the trees . . . and shaking their spears threateningly at us."[38] They make Dolittle their king before he escapes and returns with his animal menagerie to England.

**Middle and Upper Grades.** Mr. Popper is a house painter, not a doctor, but he makes his home a penguin haven in *Mr. Popper's Penguins* (1939).[39] Accomodation is the theme of Richard and Florence Atwater's humorous book, illustrated by Robert Lawson. Mr. Popper, who lets his refrigerator be a penguin home, thinks inconvenience is unimportant as he makes twelve penguins comfortable. He pays expenses by having the spirited animals perform in theaters. Most of the book shows Mrs. Popper as a stereotyped housewife who sweeps, cooks, and mends while her husband reads. However, in the end, she plays the piano for the performing penguins and decides on the money for their contract. The authors were teachers, but Richard Atwater was suffering from a lengthy illness when he wrote this book.

Compassionate help is the theme of a story Beatrix Potter wrote and illustrated for twelve-year-olds, *The Tailor of Gloucester* (1903),[40] a tale with mice as heroes. Potter sent her original manuscript as a picture-letter to Freda Moore, daughter of her former governess. The English author heard of assistants who secretly helped a tailor in Gloucester, England, but she chose mice as subjects. In her tale, mice sew a mayor's waistcoat when a tailor, who left pieces cut, is too ill to stitch them.

Another fantasy by an author-illustrator is Robert Lawson's humorous *Rabbit Hill* (1944),[41] whose theme is sharing with animals or "live and let live." In Connecticut's Pine Wood are humanized animals, Georgie Rabbit, his Uncle Analdas, Phewie the Skunk, and others. They are happy that new folks in the big house are benefactors. Readers may question the folks' credibility when they put food for animals beside a Saint Francis of Assissi pool labeled "There is enough for all."[42] This is a fine example of an explicit theme. The theme is emphasized in illustrations, like the one on page 78 with the new folks' sign, "Please drive carefully on account of small animals."

Large animals, horses, are the subject of Marguerite Henry's true story, *Misty of Chincoteague* (1947),[43] illustrated by Wesley Dennis. A relationship with horses is the theme of this realistic animal story. Siblings Paul and Maureen Beebe bring captured wild mare Phantom and foal Misty to a horse ranch on Chincoteague Island, Virginia. The children tame Misty and win a race on Phantom before granting her freedom to join her wild sire. This story is flawed only by Paul's sexist statements to his sister, such as "Quit acting like a girl."[44]

*Animal Fantasy*

**Middle and Upper Grades.** Beast myths is the theme of separate fantasies in *Just So Stories* (1902) written by English author Rudyard Kipling and illustrated by him.[45] These are *pourquoi* explanations telling why man has dominion over animals and why animals have physical peculiarities. In "How the Leopard Got His Spots," Kipling has one of his stereotyped characters, the Ethiopian, who just became Black, mark the Leopard with "spots off five fat black finger tips (there was plenty of black left on his new skin still)."[46]

Before he recorded the stories, Kipling told them to a friend and to his daughter, whom he calls "Best Beloved" in the tales. The title comes from his insisting they were factual: "Just so."

*Revenge*

**Preschool through Middle Grades.** Pride avenged is the theme of Jacob and Wilhelm Grimm's recording of *King Grisly-Beard* (1823),[47] first published in English in Edgar Taylor's translation, *German Popular Stories,* Volume I, illustrated by George Cruikshank. The tale is about a proud princess who insults so many suitors, her father forces her to marry a beggar. After she earns her bread as a kitchen maid, her beggar husband reveals he is really King Grisly-Beard. Maurice Sendak's humorous illustrations show the husband curing his wife of haughty pride.

**Upper Grades.** Revenge is the theme of "The Juniper Tree" (1826), first published in English in Volume II of Taylor's *German Popular Stories. The Juniper Tree and Other Tales from Grimm* consists of two books with a total of twenty-seven folk tales, each with a distinct theme.[48] "The Juniper Tree" is singled out because it is emphasized in the title. In this folk tale, a stepmother decapitates her stepson, but makes her daughter feel guilty. The stepmother butchers the boy, cooks him in a stew, and serves him to her husband, who unwittingly devours him. After his half sister puts his bones under the juniper tree, the boy is resurrected as a bird. When the bird kills the cruel stepmother, the boy emerges whole to live happily with his father and half sister.

Few folk tales show evil stepfathers. "The Juniper Tree" contributes to sexism by depicting a stereotyped, super-wicked stepmother. Though *Best Books for Children* suggests this story, illustrated by Maurice Sendak, for readers in grades 4 to 8, the tale is grim enough to be reserved for adults.

*Love*

**Preschool through Middle Grades.** True love is the theme of Hans Christian Andersen's *The Steadfast Tin Soldier,*[49] first published in New York in 1846. The love affair is between a tin soldier and a toy dancer, each balanced on a single leg. In the end, the tin soldier is thrown into a fire and dies, joined by the toy dancer. Marcia Brown's final picture depicts the theme, for in the hearth are remnants of a tin soldier melted into the shape of a heart, and next to it, a charred dancer's spangle.

**Middle Grades.** Another Andersen work, *Thumbelina* (1846),[50] has a matchmaking theme. Thumbelina, a thumb-sized girl who sleeps in a walnut shell, avoids marriage, first to a toad and then to a mole, before she is united with a thumb-sized flower king. *Thumbelina,* issued in English in 1846, was printed in Denmark in 1835, the first year the great Danish storyteller published stories for children.

**Middle and Upper Grades.** *The Light Princess* (1867),[51] written by Scottish author George MacDonald and illustrated by Maurice Sendak, has a primary theme of love overcoming lightness. A princess is deprived of her gravity by an aunt who is angry at not being invited to her christening. The princess is not only light in body, she also acts foolishly light-minded. She acquires gravity and conquers frivolity by falling in love and maturing.

The theme of *Beauty and the Beast* (1756) is the power of love.[52] Mariana Mayer adapted the story from a longer one by Madame Leprince de Beaumont, and Mercer Mayer illustrated it. In the French fairy tale, Beauty loves her father so much, she saves his life by living at the Beast's palace. Beauty's unselfish love for the Beast breaks his evil enchantment, and he becomes a handsome young prince before they marry. The girl's love for her father is a forerunner of her love for her husband.

A different kind of affection from that of sweethearts is the devotion a horseboy feels for a horse, the theme of Marguerite Henry's *King of the Wind* (1948).[53] Mute Agba, slave of a Sultan of Morocco's groom, tends an Arabian colt born in the Sultan's stables. He nurses it with camel's milk when its mother dies. He accompanies the stallion after it is gifted to the King of France and when it is sent to England, where it sires the legendary Godolphin Arabians. To the horseboy, the stallion is King of the Wind.

*Humor*

**Middle and Upper Grades.** Humor and nostalgia provide the theme of *Homer Price* (1943),[54] six episodes written and illustrated by Robert McCloskey. Midwestern life is shown in the small town of Centerburg, formerly known as Edible Fungus. In tall-tale tradition, Uncle Ulysses's doughnut machine won't stop making doughnuts, and pet skunk Aroma helps Homer Price capture robbers. Homer and a friend represent stereotypes only when they are tomahawk-bearing Native Americans in a pageant.

McCloskey still receives mail about drawing five robbers in bed on page 25 when his text mentions only four. He explains that, before being drafted in World War II, at his publisher's request, he added this illustration, but did it quickly. He says the Japanese in their edition redid that one illustration while keeping his others.[55]

**Middle and Upper Grades.** Humor is the theme of *Uncle Remus, His Songs and His Sayings* (1880), written by Georgia journalist Joel Chandler Harris and illustrated comically by Arthur Frost.[56] The first of five books, it contains thirty-four talking-beast tales of African origin. Many show Brer Rabbit humorously outwitting other animals.

Uncle Remus, a slave storyteller, makes fun of fellow Blacks, intended humor that is actually insulting. The book is drawn from the column Harris began in 1878 in the *Atlanta Constitution,* a column intended for White readers. A White audience is emphasized by having Uncle Remus tell the stories to his White master's seven-year-old son. Feeling superior to Blacks was a nineteenth-century diversion of some Confederate-minded Whites, and the Uncle Remus stories cater to that attitude.

For example, in a *pourquoi* folk tale, "Why the Negro Is Black," Uncle Remus explains why Blacks have white palms and soles.[57] He says originally everyone was Black, but bathers in a certain pond were washed off "nice en w'ite."[58] He claims everyone wanted to be White, but those who came when the water was low are mulattos, and those who found only enough water to wet the bottom of their hands and feet are Blacks. He includes the "Injun" and "Chinee" among mulattos, but they kept their heads in water long enough to "onkink der ha'r."[59]

Uncle Remus offends his people, saying they're "too lazy to work" and discourages their education:[60] "Put a spellin'-book in a nigger's han's, en right den en dar' you loozes a plow-hand."[61] In "A Story of the [Civil] War," Uncle Remus shoots the arm off a Union soldier to prevent injury to a Confederate soldier, his master's son, Mars Jeems. Uncle Remus shows his primary loyalty to his master, though he knows the Union soldier is fighting for slaves' freedom.

The book's weakness lies in having Uncle Remus as ideological spokesman, and the dialect is difficult for children to read. Universal humor is found only in the African animal folk tales Harris faithfully records.

*Negative Emotions*

**Preschool and Primary Grades.** Destructive vanity is the theme of *Millions of Cats* (1928),[62] an accumulative picture storybook by Wanda Gág, a Bohemian artist from Minnesota. In this animal fantasy, a lonely, aged couple request the prettiest cat from millions at their doorstep, and competing cats claw each other to death. The only survivor, a scraggly kitten, explains that, being homely, he did not compete and was safe. He becomes the household pet.

**Primary and Middle Grades.** Destructive envy is the theme of *Snow-White and the Seven Dwarfs* (1823),[63] told by Jacob and Wilhelm Grimm and published in English in *German Popular Stories,* Volume I. Two English editions have won prizes for illustrations. One is in color by Nancy Ekholm Burkert and translated by Randall Jarrell. The other is in black and white by Wanda Gág, who freely translated the work herself. Gág shows midgets, not dwarfs.

A vain queen, envious of the beauty of her stepdaughter, Snow-White, banishes the seven-year-old girl from the palace. The child finds a forest home with seven dwarfs. Here is another stereotyped evil stepmother, one who makes four attempts on her stepdaughter's life. The queen pays dearly for her envy. She has to wear red-hot slippers and dance to her death. Violence, as in this ending, is found in other faithfully recorded Grimm folktales.

One of the first folktales collected by the Grimm brothers, *The Fisherman and His Wife* (1823),[64] has the theme of a wife's discontentment. A fisherman tries unsuccessfully to satisfy his wife after he finds a wish-granting fish. They first get a pretty cottage, but she wants more, so they progressively occupy a mansion, a castle, a palace, and a cathedral, winding up finally in their original hut. With such a meek husband, the wife's shrewish tendencies flower.

The *Emperor's New Clothes,*[65] believed to be a folktale recorded by Hans Christian Andersen, has pretense and insecurity as its theme.[66] It was first published in New York in 1846. Two swindlers convince a vain emperor to pay them while they pretend to weave cloth and sew his imperial outfit. They intimidate observers by announcing that anyone who cannot see the clothes is unfit for office or stupid. An honest child looks at the parading emperor, supposedly in the new clothes, and says that the emperor is naked. Students enjoy this tale that unmasks deceit and insecurity.

*Maturity*

**Middle and Upper Grades.** Maturing is the theme of Carol Ryrie Brink's *Caddie Woodlawn*[67] (1935). This nineteenth-century historical fiction is based on the life of the author's grandmother, Caddie Woodhouse. In a Wisconsin pioneer family, eleven-year-old Caddie Woodlawn enjoys outdoor life until her mother starts to make her "ladylike." The theme is apparent in these words:

> When she awoke she knew that she need not be afraid of growing up. It was not just sewing and weaving and wearing stays. It was something more thrilling that that. It was a responsibility.[68]

Sexist conversion of Caddie the tomboy into a lady is less offensive than the book's anti-Native American expressions. Though local Native Americans are friendly with the heroine and her father, the author frequently refers to characters as "savage." When the heroine buys red handkerchiefs for children who have one Native American parent, the author states: "The red was like music to their half-savage eyes."[69] The attitude toward intermarriage is summarized thus: "Father marry an Indian? . . . He never would!"[70] Much ado is made over Indian John's scalp belt without explaining that Whites started the practice of scalping victims.[71]

Another work of historical fiction, *The Door in the Wall* (1949) by author-illustrator Marguerite deAngeli, tells about a lonely ten-year-old boy, Robin, in thirteenth-century England who is crippled when his parents are away.[72] The book's primary theme is ingenuity in opening doors to independence. The author says her main theme is: "There's always a way out."[73] Friars and friends teach Robin to whittle, read, write, swim, play a harp, walk with crutches, ride a horse, and above all, have patience. Robin is more self-sufficient after each experience. This is shown in deAngeli's illustrations whose backgrounds were sketched in England. The boy earns knighthood when he helps save his lord's besieged castle. The book's title is a clue to its theme, for Robin hears, "If we do what we are able, a door always opens to something else."[74]

Robin's name comes from his prototype, Harmon Robinson, deAngeli's New Jersey neighbor, who was crippled. A gifted cabinetmaker, Robinson played the viola in a quartet with the author's husband. DeAngeli's book seems timely, although it was written long before today's emphasis on special education.

## Positive Experiences

**Middle and Upper Grades.** Frances Hodgson Burnett, who was born in England and emigrated to the United States, wrote *The Secret Garden* (1910) with recovery of health as its theme.[75] In an English manor, there is simultaneous blossoming of a neglected garden and revitalizing of two ten-year-old cousins, Mary Lennox and Colin Craven. Mary is an orphan from India, and Colin is a spoiled heir who feels he is going to die soon. They thrive in fresh air as they, aided by Yorkshire friends, cooperate to cultivate a secret garden.

**Upper Grades.** Redemption is the primary theme of *The Water-Babies: A Fairy Tale for a Land Baby* (1863),[76] written by an English clergyman, Reverend Charles Kingsley, for his young son. Tom, a dirty, ten-year-old chimney sweep, drowns and fairies turn him into a four-inch water baby. (Water babies are neglected children befriended by such fairies as Bedonebyasyoudid and Doasyouwouldbedoneby.) Tom completes a quest to find his old apprentice master and help him repent of his wickedness. The water baby is working out his own salvation, and the strongest symbolism is that of being washed free from sin. The Kathleen Lines 1961 edited version of this parable is better than the original text, whose latter part is tedious.

*Negative Experiences*

**Preschool through Middle Grades.** *Rumplestiltskin* (1823) has trouble from deceit as its theme.[77] The tale, recorded by Jacob and Wilhelm Grimm, was first published in English in *German Popular Stories,* Volume I. A miller lies when he says his daughter can spin gold from straw, and a king, "very fond of money," tests her. A little man performs the miracle for her, but she has to promise him her first child after she becomes queen. The promise is nullified when she identifies him as Rumplestiltskin. She possesses power over him by naming him.

**Middle and Upper Grades.** Prejudice and cowardice are among the negative experiences in Eleanor Estes's *The Hundred Dresses* (1944),[78] illustrated by Louis Slobodkin. Fourth-grade pupils taunt Wanda Petronski about her name and her fantasies. The motherless, poverty-stricken girl always wears the same faded blue dress, which the illustrator shows with just a splash of color on the frontispiece. In a move for peer acceptance, Wanda says she has one hundred dresses at home. Rich, popular Peggy teases her, and insecure Maddie, who wears hand-me-down dresses herself, offers no opposition. When Wanda's drawings of one hundred dresses win the class art prize after she has moved away, Maddie is especially sorry.

Many readers infer Estes's theme to be isolation of an outcast, but the author herself says it is "no second chance."[79] From the author's point of view, the protagonist is not Wanda, creator of the hundred dresses, but Maddie, who wants to stop teasing Wanda, yet is afraid.

Maddie, illustrated on page 63 in gray tones and forlorn mood, is determined "she was never going to stand by and say nothing again."[80] Maddie's thematic brooding is described as, "She felt sad because she knew she would never see the little tight-lipped Polish girl again and couldn't ever really make things right between them."[81]

Being unattainable, a negative experience, is the theme of "The Fox and the Grapes," from Alexander Calder's version of *Fables of Aesop*.[82] Calder's selection is made from fables told by Sir Roger L'Estrange in his 1692 London publication, *Fables of Aesop and Other Eminent Mythologists with Morals and Reflexions* [sic]. L'Estrange was English censor or Surveyor of the Imprimery (Printing Presses) from 1663–1688.

Each of more than two-hundred entries in *Fables of Aesop* has its own theme, but "A Fox and Grapes" is best known. A hungry fox tries unsuccessfully to reach ripe grapes high on a trellis. When he finds they are unattainable, he rationalizes they must be green and sour, source of the universal expression, "sour grapes." The moral or theme concerns acting indifferent when disappointed.

L'Estrange recorded over five hundred fables of Aesop. He also wrote Aesop's biography, though no one is certain such a man existed. L'Estrange says the name of the slave, Aesop, means Ethiopian, which he spells Aethiop. He states that Aesop served Greek masters in Asia Minor in 560 B.C. when Croesus was Lydia's king.[83] However, some of the fables were known centuries earlier in Greece and, before that, in India and Egypt. William Caxton first printed them in English in 1484. Though he did not record fables, Aesop supposedly told them to entertain his master's guests, using animal characters to avoid offending people.

*Self-Knowledge*

**Primary and Middle Grades.** Learning to distinguish what is natural from what is artificial is a form of self-knowledge. Real versus imitation is the theme of Hans Christian Andersen's fable, *The Nightingale*,[84] published in New York in 1846. After enjoying a nightingale's song, a Chinese emperor ignores the bird and listens to a mechanical nightingale. The artificial one wears out. It is the real one who helps restore the emperor's health and promises to tell him what he learns from people as he flies across the land. Now the emperor appreciates the real bird. Nancy Burkert illustrates with brush and colored ink Eva Le Gallienne's translation of Andersen's *The Nightingale*.

**Middle and Upper Grades.** Self-knowledge, expressed by a desire to return home, is the primary theme of L. Frank Baum's fantasy, *The*

*Wizard of Oz* (1899).[85] Dorothy, an orphan, is blown with her spaniel in a Kansas cyclone to the Land of Oz. She travels with Scarecrow, Tin Woodman, and Lion to see the Wizard of Oz. But it is Glinda, the Good Witch, not the Wizard, who returns her to Kansas relatives. She learns that home, and what is more important, self-reliance and self-knowledge, were always available. In "The Wiz," a musical adaptation of the book, Glinda the Good Witch says, "When you know who you are, you are always home." Dorothy's traveling companions find they get courage, intelligence, and compassion by acting as if they have these attributes. Positive thinking is magical.

An analyst of the deep structure of *The Wizard of Oz* finds the book to be an Industrial Revolution allegory. He says:

> The Scarecrow stands for agriculture (the "hick" seeking brains), the Tin Man is technology (looking for a heart so to love everyone and not to hurt any living thing), and the Cowardly Lion prefigures Nature's animal world, mastered easily once controlled ("slapped down").[86]

*The Wizard of Oz* implies at the end that home is where all is in place and appropriate. In his introduction to the book, Baum announced his departure from the stereotyped genie. The midwestern journalist created one of the first fairy tales involving America. He wrote fourteen Oz books, taking the Oz name from an O to Z filing cabinet drawer.

### Virtue Rewarded

**Primary and Middle Grades.** Virtue rewarded is the theme of the universal fairy tale, *Cinderella* (1697),[87] recorded by Charles Perrault in France. The subtitle of Marcia Brown's self-illustrated translation is *The Little Glass Slipper*, but Perrault did not stipulate a glass slipper for the heroine. He recorded it as made of *vair*, a rare, costly fur, restricted by law in early times to highest royalty. Through a printer's error in France, *vair* was spelt *verre*, which means glass. Cinderella was to have worn royal fur on her delicate feet, not glass slippers.[88]

A virtuous, passive maiden, servant of a cruel stepmother and stepsisters, earns the nickname, Cinderseat or Cinderella, because she often sits in ashes. Her fairy godmother dresses her in finery, including glass slippers, and sends her to a royal ball. There a wealthy prince falls in love with her and eventually marries her. In Marcia Brown's ending, Cinderella lets her stepsisters live in the palace, but there are hundreds of versions, and endings vary.

Negative association with the word *stepmother* derives largely from

Cinderella's wicked stepmother. Other stereotyped notions are that female passivity is admirable and that marrying a wealthy person guarantees happiness.

**Middle and Upper Grades.** A modern Cinderella story about a virtuous child, *A Little Princess* (1892) has the theme that true nobility is internal.[89] Frances Hodgson Burnett's melodrama is about an Englishman's compassionate daughter, Sara Crewe, born in India, who is a pupil in a Parisian boarding school from the age of seven until thirteen. The school mistress, Miss Minchin, treats the wealthy girl like a little princess until the child's father dies, leaving her penniless. Then the mistress moves her to a rat-infested attic, reducing her to a raggedy errand girl. But the girl's character remains noble. In hard times, she is as unselfish as a princess. When her wealth is restored, the girl rebuffs evil Miss Minchin.

Frank Stockton's *The Griffin and the Minor Canon* (1894) has virtue rewarded as its theme.[90] (Stockton is famous for "The Lady or the Tiger?") Though Stockton describes the Griffin with a serpent's tail, illustrator Maurice Sendak in a 1963 edition shows him, as in Greek mythology, with an eagle's head, wings, and forelegs but a lion's body, hind legs, and tail. When a Griffin comes to see his likeness over a church door, terrified people leave town, including high-church officers, because they know it is almost time for the creature's semiannual meal. The kind Minor Canon remains. He is a young, unappreciated priest who conducts services and helps the poor, sick, or wayward. He complies when people ask him to go into the wilds, thinking the Griffin will follow. To their surprise, the Griffin stays and does the Canon's work. Then the Griffin brings the Canon back, threatening vengeance unless people honor the Canon. The virtuous Canon finally receives these rewards:

> The Minor Canon was appointed to the highest office of the church, and before he died, he became a bishop . . . In the course of time, they [the people] learned to honor and reverence their former Minor Canon without the fear of being punished . . . [91]

Virtue overcoming evil is the theme of the allegory, *The Lion, the Witch, and the Wardrobe: A Story for Children* (1950)[92] by English author, C.S. Lewis. A Cambridge literature professor fascinated by medieval allegory, Lewis has the lion in his story represent Christ. In this first book of seven about imaginary Narnia, four English children, Peter, Susan, Edmund, and Lucy, in a professor's home during World War II, go through his wardrobe to enter Narnia. There a noble lion, Aslan, dies to save the life of Edmund, his betrayer. The lion is resurrected and frees Narnia from a White Witch's evil spell.

*Inner Spirit*

**Middle and Upper Grades.** Valuing inner spirit, not appearance is the theme of *Dwarf Long-Nose* (*circa* 1827),[93] the best-known story of Wilhelm Hauff, the Hans Christian Andersen of early nineteenth-century Germany. On an errand for his mother, a vegetable vender, handsome twelve-year-old Jacob insults an evil fairy. She changes him into a squirrel and, at the end of seven years, releases him as an ugly dwarf with hunched back and foot-long nose. These words convey hope that still lingers:

> The evil hag may have transformed his body, but she couldn't have stunted his spirit, of that he was sure . . . He believed he had grown wiser and more sensible.[94]

When his family rejects him, Jacob remembers culinary skills learned under the fairy and becomes a Duke's chef. He buys a goose, only to learn she is enchanted Mimi, a magician's daughter. Mimi helps him prepare an unusual guest dish, complete with Sneezewithease herb. The herb transforms him into a handsome youth, and when Jacob takes Mimi to her father, he changes her into a girl. The bitter experience teaches Jacob to value inner spirit more than physical appearance.

*Destiny*

**Middle and Upper Grades.** Inescapable destiny is the theme of *Undine* (1817),[95] Friedrick Fouque de la Motte's fairy tale originally written in German and retold by Gertrude C. Schwebell. The story, reminiscent of classical tragedies, focuses on eighteen-year-old Undine, a water nymph who is the foster child of a fisherman and his wife. She acquires a soul when she marries a human being, Huldbrand, a knight, though he worries about her magical powers. Destiny links him with Undine and another woman, Bertalda, a spoiled, immature beauty. When Undine magically withdraws a gift for Bertalda from the Danube River, her husband is angry about her use of magic. He asks her to stay with water witches, so the river absorbs her. The knight weeps, but soon marries Bertalda who inadvertently admits Undine into their home. Undine gives Huldbrand a death kiss, his destined penalty for remarriage. She then becomes a gushing spring encircling his grave.

*Family Relationships*

**Preschool and Primary Grades.** A mother's love for a mischievous child is the theme of *The Tale of Peter Rabbit* (1902) by English author-

illustrator, Beatrix Potter.[96] With succinct text, this diminutive (5½" ×
4"), watercolored picture storybook personifies a rabbit family. Mischievous Peter disobeys his mother when he goes to Mr. McGregor's garden
to eat. He narrowly escapes, but is too sick for the dinner enjoyed by
his obedient sisters, Flopsy, Mopsy, and Cotton-tail. His loving mother
gently puts him to bed and gives him camomile tea. In a snug home, the
recalcitrant son is not lectured but cured.

Potter's book is based on a picture letter she sent Noël Moore, the
ill, five-year-old son of a former governess and brother of the girl who
received *The Tailor of Gloucester*. When publishers rejected her manuscript, Potter prepared inked drawings and paid for the first edition. In
1902, Warne issued the second edition in London for one shilling, now
worth about nine cents. Warne distributed the English edition in New
York without copyrighting it, so the book is in U.S. public domain.[97]

**Middle and Upper Grades.** Family solidarity is the theme of Eleanor
Estes's humorous historical fiction, *The Moffats* (1941),[98] *The Middle
Moffat* (1942), and *Rufus M.*(1943),[99] all illustrated by Louis Slobodkin.
*The Moffats* introduces four siblings, fifteen, twelve, ten, and five-and-
a-half-years old, of Cranbury (actually West Haven), Connecticut. They
live with their widowed mother, a seamstress, whom they admire even
for the way she peels apples. The threat of sale of their rented home
haunts the family in the first book. The episodic stories are told mainly
from the point of view of the two youngest children. *The Middle Moffat*
is about the youngest daughter, Janey, now eleven years old, and her
efforts to see the Oldest Inhabitant through to his hundredth birthday.
*Rufus M.*, set during World War I, concerns the youngest son, now seven
years old.

Financial plight pulls the family together. In *The Moffats,* when
Mama thinks a child lost the coal money, she does not scold, but says,
"Well, if it's gone, it's gone. We'll manage somehow."[100] Material
poverty contrasts with genuine affection.

Eleanor Estes, whose first book was *The Moffats,* says her own
mother inspired all her fictional mothers. She relates that Rufus's appli-
cation for a library card in *Rufus M.* is based on her experiences as a
former librarian. ("M." in the title was as far as Rufus could get in the
space for his name on his library card.) It was Eleanor Estes who interested Slobodkin, an architectural sculptor, in becoming an illustrator,
beginning with *The Moffats.*[101]

Family solidarity is the theme of the nine *Little House* books by
Laura Ingalls Wilder. Garth Williams traveled to the areas described

before illustrating these books. Though the events reported are factual, the books are not considered as autobiography, but as historical fiction, narrated in third person as stories. The series begins with *Little House in the Big Woods* (1932) in the year 1871 when Laura is not quite five years old. The pioneering Ingalls family is traced westward to Kansas in *Little House on the Prairie* (1935), to Minnesota in *On the Banks of Plum Creek* (1937), and to Dakota Territory in *By the Shores of Silver Lake* (1939). In *Farmer Boy* (1933), Laura Ingalls Wilder tells about the boyhood of her future husband, Almanzo Wilder, and in *Little Town on the Prairie* (1941), she meets him. At eighteen, she marries him in *These Happy Golden Years* (1943) and has a daughter in *The First Four Years* (1971, published posthumously).

One of Wilder's best books is *The Long Winter* (1940),[102] which effectively contrasts the warmth of the six in the Ingalls household with the whirling snow outside. *Little Town on the Prairie* depicts sacrifices the family makes to send Laura's blind sister, Mary, to college. Always Pa's fiddle and Ma's meals, including specially prepared biscuits, help create family solidarity.

A forerunner of realistic fiction that avoids the nineteenth-century authoritarian stereotype of family life is Louisa May Alcott's *Little Women* (1868).[103] Individualization within a loving family is its theme. This first great family story begins with distinct characterizations of four March sisters: Meg, a sixteen-year-old plump nursery governess; Jo, a fifteen-year-old thin, sharp-tongued bookworm and amateur playwright (modeled after the author); Beth, a thirteen-year-old shy pianist whose death saddens each generation of readers; and Amy, the youngest, an artist who laments her flat nose. During half of the book, the father, a Civil War chaplain, is absent, but the unselfish mother holds the family together.

In 1868, Alcott, who preferred to write for boys, wrote the girls' story, *Little Women,* at her editor's suggestion. Though she found it rather dull, it brought income. She was supporting her family, so a year later, she wrote the second part, *Good Wives,* about the maturing sisters. Both parts are now bound together as *Little Women.*

Laurie in Alcott's book is patterned after a friend met in Europe. Aunt March is based on a regal aunt, John Hancock's widow. The classic pays tribute to Alcott's mother, who wrote inspirationally in her daughters' diaries, just as "Marmee" does in *Little Women.* The father is underdeveloped, perhaps because the author did not fully understand her own father, Bronson Alcott. A brilliant idealist and educator, he was a poor provider for his family. However, she includes his ideas on education in her writing.

*Relationship to Society*

**Middle and Upper Grades.** Being ostracized is the theme of the Mowgli fantasies included among the seven wild animal tales in *The Jungle Book* (1893).[104] English author Rudyard Kipling was born in India, which provides the book's setting. Kipling remembered being ostracized himself when he came to England as a swarthy seven-year-old pupil with a Hindi accent. He describes Mowgli as "a naked brown baby" raised by jungle wolves. The youth introduces "the red flower" of fire to the animals and kills the dreaded tiger, Shere Khan. However, he suffers rejection: "Man Pack and Wolf Pack have cast me out. Now I will hunt alone in the jungle."[105] When Mowgli is seventeen, he returns to his village, motivated by need for a mate.

**Upper Grades.** Being a nonconforming misfit is the primary theme of Elizabeth George Speare's book of historical fiction, *The Witch of Blackbird Pond* (1958).[106] Sixteen-year-old Kit Tyler, a free-spirited girl from Barbados, is a misfit in Puritan New England. She says, "It's very different here. I don't seem to fit in."[107] Her friend, Nat Eaton, agrees and compares her to an exotic Jamaican bird that is out of place in Connecticut. Other themes the author identifies are Puritan abuse of a Quaker in seventeenth-century New England and the colonists' preparation for war.[108] Secondary themes include Puritan labeling of some independent-thinking women as witches in order to silence them.

Kit Tyler is not a stereotype and neither is a dragon who wants to live peacefully with his neighbors, the theme of *The Reluctant Dragon* (1899).[109] This book was written with tongue-in-cheek humor by English author, Kenneth Grahame, and illustrated by Ernest H. Shepard. In knighthood days, a boy makes friends on the downs with a dragon who enjoys writing poetry, trusts his English neighbors, and wants to settle peacefully with them. They, however, have preconceived ideas and distrust the dragon without investigating his character. To appease villagers, the boy arranges for St. George to have a mock battle. The villagers, not anxious for the dragon's death, are mollified when the animal submits. The dragon is happy because, far from being hurt in the fight, he "won popularity and a sure footing in society."[110] St. George warns villagers against future prejudice.

In describing the mock battle, Grahame includes a stereotyped comment about the dragon who "began to leap from one side to the other with huge ungainly bounds, whooping like a Red Indian."[111] *Best Books for Children* recommends this book for pupils in grades 2 to 4. While they can understand the short story, pupils in grades 4 to 6 will appreciate better the tongue-in-cheek humor and will not be overwhelmed by lengthy sentences with such challenging vocabulary as "pestilential scourge," "affable gentry," or "antediluvian anecdotes."

A new perspective of society is the theme of *Alice's Adventures in Wonderland* (1865). English author Lewis Carroll called it a fairy tale. The satire's major target is Victorian society with its overemphasis on certainty and dictates of behavior. In Wonderland, politeness is overthrown. At the Mad Hatter's tea party, for example, dirty dishes are everywhere and characters are rude. The Queen of Hearts's croquet party is a high society parody from the viewpoint of ten-year-old Alice. The language is nonsense but has the essence of truth.

The story begins as Alice sees a rabbit and falls asleep. The rest is her dream after following White Rabbit down his hole. Protected by Cheshire Cat, she is a calm, rational girl in an irrational world. A court scene is the height of illogic. Causality is reversed when the Queen of Hearts asks for a penalty first and a verdict afterward, so Alice calls the court a pack of cards. Just as the child sees through adults' false customs, she awakens to reality.

Lewis Carroll is the pseudonym mathematician Charles Lutwidge Dodgson used when writing his children's stories. It was derived by (1) Latinizing Charles Lutwidge as Carolus Ludovicus, (2) reversing them, and (3) Anglicizing Ludovicus as Lewis and Carolus as Carroll.

The book is based on a story Dodgson told ten-year-old Alice Liddell and her two sisters on July 4, 1862. He recorded it and convinced Sir John Tenniel, *Punch* cartoonist, to do inked illustrations. Though Dodgson's photographs show Alice Liddell with dark hair, Tenniel made her a blonde.

It is interesting to note that Dodgson had migraine headaches preceded by periods in which he saw things in distorted sizes and shapes. These illusions must have influenced his writing. Neurologists today identify the distortion before onset of migraine with the term, *Alice in Wonderland* syndrome.

There is jollity in *Alice*'s parodies and homonyms. Humor and profundity in this book and its sequel, *Through the Looking-Glass,* are understood best by older children. However, both classics may be appreciated at more than one level.

## Summary

This chapter focuses on themes of sixty-five books that are among the prizewinning children's classics. These are distinguished literary works that have weathered at least one generation, ending with books published in the 1950s. Themes of classics are grouped under twenty-two headings.

Sexual and racial stereotypes are also identified. Almost half of the books are for a range of middle- and upper-elementary grades. The balance divide just about equally into those for upper grades alone and those for preschool or primary through middle grades.

Prizewinning children's classics are split approximately three ways: (1) led by Lewis Carroll Shelf Award winners, (2) then Newbery Medalists or Honor Books (modern classics), and (3) either recipients of illustration or children's-choice awards. A few modern classics have received prizes based on votes by children. Lewis Carroll Awards were also given to two recordings, "Tom Sawyer" and "More Just So Stories."

**Notes**

1. Alice M. Jordan, *Children's Classics* (Boston: Horn Book, 1947), p. 4.

2. Mary Elisabeth Edes, "Children's Books of 1930–1960 That Have Become Modern Classics," *Readings about Children's Literature,* ed. Evelyn Robinson (New York: McKay, 1966), p. 168.

3. Office of Work with Children, *Modern Classics* (Philadelphia: The Free Library of Philadelphia, 1977).

4. In 1953, *Charlotte's Web* was a Newbery Honor Book. In 1959, it won the Lewis Carroll Shelf Award, and in 1970, the George G. Stone Center for Children's Books Recognition of Merit Award.

5. E.B. White, *Charlotte's Web* (New York: Harper, 1952), p. 164.

6. Lee Bennett Hopkins, *More Books by More People* (New York: Citation, 1974), p. 378.

7. In 1958, *The World of Pooh* won the Lewis Carroll Shelf Award.

8. In 1958, *The Wind in the Willows* won the Lewis Carroll Shelf Award.

9. Kenneth Grahame, *The Wind in the Willows* (New York: Scribner, [1908] 1954), p. 188.

10. Ibid., p. 4 of preface.

11. In 1943, *Lassie Come-Home* won the Pacific Northwest Library Association Young Reader's Choice Award.

12. In 1962, *The Adventures of Huckleberry Finn* won the Lewis Carroll Shelf Award.

13. Mark Twain, *The Adventures of Huckleberry Finn* (New York: Harper, [1884] 1931). The time period is not specified in all editions.

14. Ibid., p. 296.

15. Ibid., p. 381.

16. Ibid., p. 20.

17. In 1967, the recording, ''Tom Sawyer,'' Caedmon Records R 1088, by Samuel Clemens, read by Boris Karloff, won the Lewis Carroll Shelf Award. The book is entitled *The Adventures of Tom Sawyer*.

18. Mark Twain, *The Adventures of Tom Sawyer* (New York: Macmillan, 1966), pp. 87, 91.

19. Ibid., p. 238.

20. Ibid., p. 213.

21. In 1965, *Mary Poppins* won the Nene Award.

22. P.L. Travers, *Mary Poppins* (New York: Harcourt, 1934), p. 60.

23. Ibid., p. 65.

24. Ibid., p. 35.

25. Ibid., p. 135.

26. Albert V. Schwartz, ''Mary Poppins Revised: An Interview with P.L. Travers,'' *Interracial Books for Children*, V, 3 (1974), pp. 1, 3.

27. In 1955, *The Courage of Sarah Noble* was a Newbery Honor Book.

28. In 1944, *Johnny Tremain* won The John Newbery Medal.

29. In 1953, *Puss in Boots*, illustrated by Marcia Brown, won The Randolph Caldecott Medal.

30. In 1960, *The Borrowers* won the Lewis Carroll Shelf Award.

31. In 1942, *Make Way for Ducklings* won The Randolph Caldecott Medal.

32. ''Robert McCloskey,'' *Profiles in Literature* (Philadelphia: Temple University, 1977).

33. In 1940, *Blue Willow* was a Newbery Honor Book and won the Commonwealth Club of California Award.

34. Doris Gates, *Blue Willow* (New York: Scholastic, 1940), p. 153.

35. In 1947, *Caps for Sale* won the Lewis Carroll Shelf Award.

36. In 1923, *The Voyages of Doctor Dolittle* won The John Newbery Medal, and in 1958, *The Story of Doctor Dolittle* won the Lewis Carroll Shelf Award.

37. Hugh Lofting, *The Story of Doctor Dolittle*, part of *Doctor Dolittle, a Treasury* (Philadelphia: Lippincott, 1967), p. 17.

38. Hugh Lofting, *The Voyages of Doctor Dolittle*, part of *Doctor Dolittle, a Treasury* (Philadelphia: Lippincott, 1967), p. 146.

39. In 1939, *Mr. Popper's Penguins* was a Newbery Honor Book. In 1941, it won the Pacific Northwest Library Association Young Reader's Choice Award and in 1958, the Lewis Carroll Shelf Award.

40. In 1962, *The Tailor of Gloucester* won the Lewis Carroll Shelf Award.

41. In 1945, *Rabbit Hill* won The John Newbery Medal.

42. Robert Lawson, *Rabbit Hill* (New York: Viking, 1944), p. 123.

43. In 1948, *Misty of Chincoteague* was a Newbery Honor Book.

44. Marguerite Henry, *Misty of Chincoteague* (Chicago: Rand, McNally, 1947), p. 36. See also p. 34, "That's because you're a girl," and p. 132, "Just girls' fribble."

45. In 1967, the recording, "More Just So Stories," Caedmon Records R 1205, by Rudyard Kipling, read by Ed Begley, won the Lewis Carroll Shelf Award. The book is entitled *Just So Stories*.

46. Rudyard Kipling, *Just So Stories* (New York: Doubleday, 1902), p. 57.

47. In 1973, *King Grisly-Beard,* was a *New York Times* Choice of Best Illustrated Children's Book of the Year.

48. In 1973, *The Juniper Tree and Other Tales from Grimm,* was a *New York Times* Choice of Best Illustrated Children's Book of the Year.

49. In 1954, *The Steadfast Tin Soldier,* illustrated by Marcia Brown, was a Caldecott Honor Book.

50. In 1962, *Thumbelina* won the Lewis Carroll Shelf Award.

51. In 1969, *The Light Princess* was a *New York Times* Choice of Best Illustrated Children's Book of the Year.

52. In 1979, *Beauty and the Beast,* illustrated by Mercer Mayer, was selected for the American Institute of Graphic Arts Book Show.

53. In 1949, *King of the Wind* won The John Newbery Medal.

54. In 1947, *Homer Price* won the Pacific Northwest Library Association Young Reader's Choice Award.

55. "Robert McCloskey," *Profiles in Literature* (Philadelphia: Temple University, 1977).

56. In 1963, *Uncle Remus, His Songs and His Sayings* won the Lewis Carroll Shelf Award.

57. *Pourquoi* refers to folktales that explain appearances or customs.

58. Joel Chandler Harris, *Uncle Remus, His Songs and His Sayings* (New York: Appleton [1880], 1921), p. 167.

59. Ibid., p. 168.

60. Ibid., p. 206.

61. Ibid., p. 261.

62. In 1929, *Millions of Cats* was a Newbery Honor Book.

63. Two distinct editions of *Snow-White and the Seven Dwarfs* were Caldecott Honor Books, Wanda Gág's in 1939 and Nancy Ekholm Burkert's in 1973.

64. In 1957, *The Fisherman and His Wife,* illustrated by Madeleine Gekiere, was a *New York Times* Choice of Best Illustrated Children's Book of the Year.

65. In 1973, *The Emperor's New Clothes,* illustrated by Monika Laimgruber, was a *New York Times* Choice of Best Illustrated Children's Book of the Year.

66. On the last page in their Random House 1971 edition of *The Emperor's New Clothes,* Jack and Irene Delano reveal that this is a traditional folktale that Andersen recorded but did not create. The Delano illustrations show a Puerto Rican setting.

67. In 1936, *Caddie Woodlawn* won The John Newbery Medal.

68. Carol Ryrie Brink, *Caddie Woodlawn* (New York: Macmillan, 1973–1935), p. 246.

69. Ibid., p. 163.

70. Ibid., p. 158.

71. Masha Kabakow Rudman, *Children's Literature, An Issues Approach* (Lexington, Mass.: Heath, 1976), pp. 261–262.

72. In 1950, *The Door in the Wall* won The John Newbery Medal.

73. "Marguerite deAngeli," *Profiles in Literature* (Philadelphia: Temple University, 1976).

74. Marguerite deAngeli, *The Door in the Wall* (New York: Doubleday, 1949), p. 71.

75. In 1959, *The Secret Garden* won the Lewis Carroll Shelf Award.

76. In 1963, *The Water-Babies* won the Lewis Carroll Shelf Award.

77. In 1955, *Rumpelstiltskin,* illustrated by Jan B. Balet, was a *New York Times* Choice of Best Illustrated Children's Book of the Year.

78. In 1945, *The Hundred Dresses* was a Newbery Honor Book.

79. "Eleanor Estes," *Profiles in Literature* (Philadelphia: Temple University, 1975).

80. Eleanor Estes, *The Hundred Dresses* (New York: Harcourt, 1944), p. 63.

81. Ibid., p.76

82. In 1967, *Fables of Aesop,* illustrated by Alexander Calder, was a *New York Times* Choice of Best Illustrated Children's Book of the Year. Calder is famous for his mobiles and sculpture.

83. Sir Roger L'Estrange, *A History of the Life of Aesop* (Philadelphia: Southwark Office, 1798).

84. In 1965, *The Nightingale* won the Lewis Carroll Shelf Award.

85. In 1968, *The Wizard of Oz* won the Lewis Carroll Shelf Award.

86. Raymond J. Cormier, "Star Wars: The Rebirth of Oz?," *Temple University Alumni Review,* XXXI, 3 (1980), p. 17.

87. In 1955, *Cinderella, or the Little Glass Slipper,* illustrated by Marcia Brown, won The Randolph Caldecott Medal.

88. d'Alte A. Welch, *Bibliography of American Children's Books Printed Prior to 1821* (Worcester, Mass.: American Antiquarian Society and Barre Publishers, 1972), p. 325.

89. In 1964, *A Little Princess* won the Lewis Carroll Shelf Award.

90. In 1963, *The Griffin and the Minor Canon* won the Lewis Carroll Shelf Award.

91. Frank Stockton, *The Griffin and the Minor Canon* (New York: Holt, 1963), p. 54.

92. In 1965, *The Lion, the Witch, and the Wardrobe: A Story for Children* won the Lewis Carroll Shelf Award.

93. In 1963, *Dwarf Long-Nose* won the Lewis Carroll Shelf Award.

94. Wilhelm Hauff, *Dwarf Long-Nose* (New York: Random, 1960), p. 28.

95. In 1971, *Undine* won the Lewis Carroll Shelf Award.

96. In 1958, *The Tale of Peter Rabbit* won the Lewis Carroll Shelf Award.

97. Jane Quinby, *Beatrix Potter: A Bibliographical Check List* (New York: Quinby, 1954), p. 18.

98. In 1941, *The Moffats* won the Lewis Carroll Shelf Award.

99. The following books were Newbery Honor Books: *The Middle Moffat* in 1943 and *Rufus M.* in 1944.

100. Eleanor Estes, *The Moffats* (New York: Harcourt, 1941), p. 205.

101. "Eleanor Estes," *Profiles in Literature* (Philadelphia: Temple University, 1975).

102. The following were Newbery Honor Books: *On the Banks of Plum Creek* (1938), *By the Shores of Silver Lake* (1940), *The Long Winter* (1941), *Little Town on the Prairie* (1942), and *These Happy Golden Years* (1944).

103. In 1969, *Little Women* won the Lewis Carroll Shelf Award.

104. In 1960, *The Jungle Book* won the Lewis Carroll Shelf Award.

105. Rudyard Kipling, *The Jungle Book* (New York: Doubleday [1893], 1964), p. 95.

106. In 1959, *The Witch of Blackbird Pond* won The John Newbery Medal, and, in 1960, it was put on the International Board on Books for Young People Honor List.

107. Elizabeth George Speare, *The Witch of Blackbird Pond* (Boston: Houghton, 1958), p. 127.

108. "Elizabeth George Speare," *Profiles in Literature* (Philadelphia: Temple University, 1974).

109. In 1963, *The Reluctant Dragon* won the Lewis Carroll Shelf Award.

110. Kenneth Grahame, *The Reluctant Dragon* (New York: Holiday House [1899], 1938), p. 51.

111. Ibid., p. 43.

112. Since the Lewis Carroll Shelf Award is given to books "worthy

to sit on a shelf with *Alice in Wonderland,*" it is logical to include *Alice in Wonderland* among prizewinners.

## References of Prizewinning Prose Classics Listed Chronologically

*(Estimated Reading Grade Level in Parentheses)*

L'Estrange, Sir Roger. *Fables of Aesop and Other Eminent Mythologists with Morals and Reflexions.* London: R. Sare et al., 1692.

———. *Fables of Aesop.* 1692. Illustrated by Alexander Calder. New York: Dover, 1966 (4–6).

Perrault, Charles. "Cinderella, Puss in Boots." *Conte de ma Mere l'Oye* (Tales of Mother Goose). Paris: Claude Barbin, 1697; *Histories or Tales of Past Times.* London: J. Pote; R. Montague, 1729.

———. *Cinderella, or the Little Glass Slipper.* 1697. Translated and illustrated by Marcia Brown. New York: Scribner, 1954 (2–4).

———. *Puss in Boots.* 1697. Translated and illustrated by Marcia Brown. New York: Scribner, 1952 (K–3).

Madame Leprince de Beaumont. *Beauty and the Beast.* 1756. Adapted by Mariana Mayer. Illustrated by Mercer Mayer. New York: Four Winds, 1979 (4–6).

Fouque de la Motte, Friedrick. *Undine.* 1817. Retold by Gertrude C. Schwebell. Illustrated by Eros Keith. New York: Simon and Schuster, 1957 (4–6).

Grimm, Jacob and Wilhelm. "The Fisherman and His Wife," "King Grisly-Beard," "Rumpelstiltskin," "Snow-White and the Seven Dwarfs." *Kinder- and Hausmärchen* (Nursery and Household Tales). *German Popular Stories,* Vol. I. Translated by Edgar Taylor. London: C. Baldwyn, 1823.

———. *The Fisherman and His Wife.* 1823. Translated by Edgar Taylor. Illustrated by Madeleine Gekiere. New York: Pantheon, 1957 (1–3).

———. *King Grisly-Beard.* 1823. Translated by Edgar Taylor. Illustrated by Maurice Sendak. New York: Farrar, 1973 (K–3).

———. *Rumplestiltskin.* 1823. Translated by Edgar Taylor. Illustrated by Jan B. Balet. Chicago: Rand McNally, 1955 (K–3).

———. *Snow-White and the Seven Dwarfs.* 1823. Translated by Randall Jarrell. Illustrated by Nancy Ekholm Burkert. New York: Farrar, 1972 (1–4).

———. *Snow-White and the Seven Dwarfs.* 1823. Translated and illustrated by Wanda Gág. New York: Coward, 1938 (1–4).

————. "The Juniper Tree." *Kinder- und Hausmärchen* (Nursery and Household Tales). *German Popular Stories,* Vol. II. Translated by Edgar Taylor. London: James Robins, 1826.

————. *The Juniper Tree and Other Tales from Grimm.* 1826. Vol. I and II. Translated by Lore Segal and four tales Randall Jarrell. Illustrated by Maurice Sendak. New York: Farrar, 1973 (4–8 and adult).

Hauff, Wilhelm. *Dwarf Long-Nose.* 1827. Translated by Doris Orgel. Illustrated by Maurice Sendak. New York: Random House, 1960 (3–5).

Andersen, Hans Christian. "Emperor's New Clothes," "The Nightingale," "The Steadfast Tin Soldier," "Thumbelina." *Wonderful Stories for Children.* Translated by Mary Howitt. New York: Wiley and Putnam, 1846.

————. *The Emperor's New Clothes.* 1846. Illustrated by Monika Laimgruber. Reading, Mass.: Addison-Wesley, 1973 (2–4).

————. *The Nightingale.* 1846. Illustrated by Nancy Ekkolm Burkert. New York: Harper, 1965 (1–4).

————. *The Steadfast Tin Soldier.* 1846. Translated by M.R. James. Illustrated by Marcia Brown. New York: Scribner, 1953 (K–4).

————. *Thumbelina.* 1846. Translated by R.P. Keigwin. Illustrated by Adrienne Adams. New York: Scribner, 1961 (3–4).

Kingsley, Charles. *The Water-Babies: A Fairy Tale for a Land Baby.* 1863. Illustrated by Heath Robinson. Boston: Houghton, 1915 (5–9).

Carroll, Lewis, pseudonym. (Charles L. Dodgson.) *Alice's Adventures in Wonderland,* 1865. Reprint. Illustrated by John Tenniel. New York: Dutton, 1965 (5–7).

MacDonald, George. *The Light Princess.* 1867. Illustrated by Maurice Sendak. New York: Farrar, 1977 (3–6).

Alcott, Louisa May. *Little Women.* 1868–1869. Illustrated by Betty Fraser. New York: Macmillan, 1962 (4–7).

Twain, Mark, pseudonym. (Samuel L. Clemens.) *The Adventures of Tom Sawyer.* 1876. Illustrated by John Falter. New York: Macmillan, 1966 (5–8). Recording Caedmon R 1088, "Tom Sawyer," read by Boris Karloff.

Harris, Joel Chandler. *Uncle Remus, His Songs and His Sayings.* 1880. Reprint. Illustrated by A.B. Frost. New York: Appleton, 1921 (3–5).

Twain, Mark, pseudonym. (Samuel L. Clemens.) *The Adventures of Huckleberry Finn.* 1884. Illustrated by John Falter. New York: Harper, 1965 (6–8).

Burnett, Frances Hodgson. *A Little Princess.* 1892. Illustrated by Tasha Tudor. Philadelphia: Lippincott, 1963 (4–6).

Kipling, Rudyard. *The Jungle Book*. 1893. Illustrated by Philip Hays. New York: Doubleday, 1964 (4–7).

Stockton, Frank R. *The Griffin and the Minor Canon*. 1894. Illustrated by Maurice Sendak. New York: Holt, 1963 (3–5).

Baum, L. Frank. *The Wizard of Oz*. 1899. Reprint. Illustrated by W.W. Denslow. New York: Macmillan, 1962 (3–6).

Grahame, Kenneth. *The Reluctant Dragon*. 1899. Illustrated by Ernest H. Shepard. New York: Holiday House, 1953 (4–6).

Kipling, Rudyard. *Just So Stories*. New York: Doubleday, 1902 (4–6). Recording Caedmon R 1205, ''More Just So Stories,'' read by Ed Begley.

Potter, Beatrix. *The Tale of Peter Rabbit*. London: Warne, 1902 (K–2).

Potter, Beatrix. *The Tailor of Gloucester*. 1903. Reprint. London: Warne, 1968 (4–6).

Grahame, Kenneth. *The Wind in the Willows*. 1908. Reprint. Illustrated by Ernest H. Shepard. New York: Scribner, 1954 (5 and up).

Burnett, Frances Hodgson. *The Secret Garden*. 1910. Illustrated by Tasha Tudor. Philadelphia: Lippincott, 1962 (4–6).

Lofting, Hugh. *The Story of Doctor Dolittle*. Philadelphia: Lippincott, 1920 (3–6).

———. *The Voyages of Doctor Dolittle*. Philadelphia: Lippincott, 1922 (3–6).

Milne, A.A. *Winnie-the-Pooh*. 1926. Reprint. Illustrated by Ernest H. Shepard. New York: Dutton, 1974 (2–5).

Gág, Wanda. *Millions of Cats*. 1928. Reprint. New York: Coward, 1977 (PS–1).

Milne, A.A., *The House at Pooh Corner*. Illustrated by Ernest H. Shepard. New York: Dutton, 1928 (K–5).

Travers, P.L. *Mary Poppins*. 1934. Reprint. Illustrated by Mary Shepard. New York: Harcourt, 1981 (5–7).

Brink, Carol Ryrie. *Caddie Woodlawn*. 1935. Illustrated by Trina Schart Hyman. New York: Macmillan, 1973 (4–6).

Atwater, Richard and Florence. *Mr. Popper's Penguins*. Boston: Little, Brown, 1938 (3 and up).

Wilder, Laura Ingalls. *On the Banks of Plum Creek*. 1938. Reprint. Illustrated by Garth Williams. New York: Harper, 1953 (4–7).

Gates, Doris. *Blue Willow*. Illustrated by Paul Lantz. New York: Viking, 1940 (4–6).

Knight, Eric. *Lassie Come-Home*. 1940. Illustrated by Don Bolognese. New York: Holt, 1971 (4–7).

Wilder, Laura Ingalls. *By the Shores of Silver Lake*. 1940. Reprint. Illustrated by Garth Williams. New York: Harper, 1953 (4–7).

Estes, Eleanor. *The Moffats*. 1941. Reprint. Illustrated by Louis Slobodkin. New York: Harcourt, 1969 (4–6).

McCloskey, Robert. *Make Way for Ducklings*. New York: Viking, 1941 (PS–3).

Wilder, Laura Ingalls. *The Long Winter*. 1941. Reprint. Illustrated by Garth Williams. New York: Harper, 1953 (4–7).

Estes, Eleanor. *The Middle Moffat*. 1942. Reprint. Illustrated by Louis Slobodkin. New York: Harcourt, 1970 (4–6).

Wilder, Laura Ingalls. *Little House on the Prairie*. 1942. Reprint. Illustrated by Garth Williams. New York: Harper, 1953 (4–7).

Estes, Eleanor. *Rufus M*. Illustrated by Louis Slobodkin. New York: Harcourt, 1943 (4–6).

Forbes, Esther. *Johnny Tremain*. Illustrated by Lynd Ward. Boston: Houghton, 1943 (6–9).

McCloskey, Robert. *Homer Price*. 1943. Reprint. New York: Viking, 1971 (3–6).

Estes, Eleanor. *The Hundred Dresses*. Illustrated by Louis Slobodkin. New York: Harcourt, 1944 (3–5).

Lawson, Robert. *Rabbit Hill*. New York: Viking, 1944 (4–7).

Wilder, Laura Ingalls. *These Happy Golden Years*. 1944. Reprint. Illustrated by Garth Williams. New York: Harper, 1953 (4–7).

Henry, Marguerite. *Misty of Chincoteague*. Illustrated by Wesley Dennis. Chicago: Rand, McNally, 1947 (4–6).

Slobodkina, Esphyr. *Caps for Sale*. Reading, Mass.: Scott, 1947 (K–3).

Henry, Marguerite. *King of the Wind*. Illustrated by Wesley Dennis. Chicago: Rand, McNally, 1948 (4–6).

deAngeli, Marguerite. *The Door in the Wall*. New York: Doubleday, 1949 (5–7).

Lewis, C.S. *The Lion, the Witch and the Wardrobe*. Illustrated by Pauline Baynes. New York: Macmillan, 1950 (4–7).

Norton, Mary. *The Borrowers*. Illustrated by Joe and Beth Krush. New York: Harcourt, 1952 (4–6).

White, E.B. *Charlotte's Web*. Illustrated by Garth Williams. New York: Harper, 1952 (2–5).

Dalgliesh, Alice. *The Courage of Sarah Noble*. Illustrated by Leonard Weisgard. New York: Scribner, 1954 (3–4).

Speare, Elizabeth George. *The Witch of Blackbird Pond*. Boston: Houghton, 1958 (6–9).

# Part II
# For Preschool and
# Primary Grades

# 3 Traditional or Folk Literature in Picture Storybooks

*I want to hear over and over* Once a Mouse *and see how the mouse changes. But funnier pictures are in* Journey Cake, Ho!. *I get tickled to see a pancake rolling down a road.* —Maggie, aged six

## Perspective

Maggie abbreviated the title of her first book, for it is Marcia Brown's *Once a Mouse . . . A Fable Cut in Wood.* Fables and Bible tales that teach a lesson consistent with religious ethics were among the earliest literature Puritans in this country shared with children. The stated or implied moral, most apparent in a short fable, is equivalent to its theme.

Maggie's second choice, *Journey Cake, Ho!,* is Ruth Sawyer's adaptation of an English folk tale, *Johnny-Cake.* The tale is cumulative because Johnny chases a rolling journey cake, and other animals join him, one by one. The climax or resolution is quick.

Maggie is a prereader who champions two picture storybooks. In a true picture book, the dominant pictures convey the theme or concept, as in an alphabet or counting book, and there is little or no text. A picture storybook, however, derives a primary theme from equally important pictures and text combined. After Maggie and others like her hear such a story once, they may reread it from the pictures alone. In illustrated books, the story conveys the theme, sometimes aided by pictures, but the enriching pictures are not necessary for understanding the story.

In an interview, editor Ann Durell, author Lloyd Alexander, and author-illustrator Evaline Ness discuss the challenge of the picture storybook which Alexander feels is almost a poetic form. Ness says, "I like the limitation of knowing I only typewrite two pages double spaced, and it has to be finished."[1] Durell comments:

> Picture storybooks are the hardest books to write. . . . As an editor, I can tell you one of the greatest faults with most would-be picture storybook writers is that they write too much. What the artist really likes is a manuscript that leaves a lot to the artist, that doesn't spell everything out.[2]

The author may be obscure about setting and time period, letting those be determined by the illustrator, but the text must convey the theme. That is why discussion in this book centers mainly on text. It is essential to appreciate that illustrators contribute to theme portrayal using a variety of artistic media and techniques that often need to be identified on book jackets. Illustrations may also contribute to stereotyping sexes, minorities, the aged, the disabled, or other groups.

Both of Maggie's cited picture storybooks, tattered from use, are part of folk or traditional literature. These are stories that spring from the culture and are passed in the oral tradition from one generation to another. Folktales include myths (stories about gods and creation) and legends (tales of prehistoric heroes' deeds). They also include fables, romantic so-called fairy tales, and folk songs. They may feature farm families, royalty, giants, or animals talking and acting like people. The characters, sometimes aided by magic, have universal, timeless human traits.

Folk literature, sometimes erroneously termed *fairy tales,* may spur imagination. Before the late Louis I. Kahn received the American Institute of Architects' National Gold Medal, he said he relished *The Arabian Nights,* tales that reveal the nature of man. His enthusiasm was shared by Leopold Stokowski, who acquired a sense of power through reading about the incredible in fairy tales. When Kahn was in Venice, he discussed with students the idea of preserving the city from industry's destructiveness. Among other things, he suggested building smoke and chemical eaters, a figment of his imagination, but one that could inspire technology. He concluded, "The wish in a fairy tale is the beginning of all science."[3]

Children like folk literature that is short and ends happily. They identify with the youngest of three characters who generally fulfills tasks to receive rewards. A primary theme in folk literature is usually clear and appeals to children's sense of justice. They see how those who are poor but kind, courageous, or hardworking achieve goals, such as comfort, longevity, a loving spouse, and freedom from fear of a giant or of hunger. Most of these old tales extol virtue, but they are not free of gore. After all, they were originally told by adults to the whole community at a time when survival depended on brute strength.

Some folk stories are *pourquoi* tales that are literary explanations for animal behavior or appearance and human customs.

### Themes of Prizewinning Folk Literature in Picture Storybooks Grouped under These Topics

Pourquoi *Tales*

**Preschool and Primary Grades.**  Arlene Mosel retells a Chinese folk tale, *Tikki Tikki Tembo.*[4] Explaining why Chinese children have short names is its theme. A Chinese mother names her older son Tikki, Tikki, Tembo-no sa rembochari bari ruchi-pipperi pembo, which means the most wonderful thing in the world. She names her younger son Chang, which means little or nothing. When Chang falls in the well, his brother gets help at once, naming him quickly. When Tikki is a similar victim, he almost drowns, because Chang is slow pronouncing his long name. Illustrator Blair Lent uses yellow, blue, green, and grey watercolors and shows Tikki in dire circumstances at the bottom of the well with water covering his nose.

**Preschool through Middle Grades.** A cumulative *pourquoi* story from the animal's point of view is *Why Mosquitoes Buzz in Peoples' Ears: A West African Tale, retold by Verna Aardema.*[5] Mosquito tells a lie to Iguana, who avoids hearing more by putting sticks in his ears. This upsets Python who scares Rabbit who alarms Crow who causes Monkey to break a tree branch from which Owlet falls and dies. Grief-stricken Mother Owl refuses to call the sun to rise, so darkness prevails until the council of animals decides to punish Mosquito. She escapes, but her guilty conscience drives her to buzz people. Then she is slapped, so the book's primary theme is long-awaited justice. Illustrators Leo and Diane Dillon show the long nights of postponed justice with a black background that shifts to white when Mother Owl awakens the sun. Moreover, the last picture shows Mosquito receiving just punishment. The Dillons's bold, stylized compositions, painted in soft watercolors and pastels, are inspired by African fabric designs.

Ashanti designs influence Gerald McDermott, author-illustrator of another African folktale, *Anansi the Spider.*[6] Explaining why the moon is in the sky is the book's primary theme. When Anansi finds a globe of light in the forest, he wants to give it to one of his six sons who saved his life, but the six rescued him together. He asks for help from Nyame, God of All Things, and Nyame puts the moon in the sky for all to see, a theme depicted in McDermott's final vivid picture. Anansi has a black-spider's body with a stylized African face.

**Primary and Middle Grades.** Ananse's name is spelled differently, and he looks different, like an old man, in *A Story, a Story,*[7] an African folktale retold by author-illustrator Gail E. Haley. The title reflects the theme: explaining why and how stories reached earth, for originally Nyame, the Sky God, kept them with him in a golden box. Ananse fulfills tasks, earns the golden box of spider stories, and brings them to earth. When "he opened the box all the stories scattered to the corners of the world, including this one."[8] Haley illustrates with forceful wood-cuts arranged artistically in fourteen full-color two-page spreads. Her text gains authenticity with repetitions, like "so small, so small, so small,"[9] an African form of emphasis.

*Animal Importance in the Bible*

**Primary and Middle Grades.** The Bible, one of the oldest collections of traditional literature, is the source of the text of *Animals of the Bible*,[10] edited and illustrated by Dorothy P. Lathrop. The book's theme, the important role of animals in the Bible, is extracted from Old and New Testament tales, among which are a creation myth and stories of Noah's Ark and the peaceable kingdom. Winner of the first Caldecott Medal, Lathrop used black-and-white illustrations of Bible scenes, highlighting animals.

*Contentment*

**Preschool and Primary Grades.** From Scotland comes the folktale, *Always Room for One More*,[11] recorded by Sorche Nic Leodhas and illustrated by Nonny Hogrogian. Contentment from sharing is the theme of this story about Lachie MacLachlan, his wife, and ten children who live in a two-room house. When a traveler knocks at his door, Lachie says:

> We will be sharing whatever we've got. . . . There's room galore. Och, come awa' in! There's room for one more, always room for one more![12]

The house becomes so full the walls collapse, so travelers build Lachie a bigger house. The book ends with the song, "Always Room for One More," and the feeling of being crowded but contented is conveyed in Nonny Hogrogian's pen and ink drawings with grey wash and pastels.

    Cramped living conditions are also featured in the next story. Margot Zemach recorded and illustrated *It Could Always Be Worse: A Yiddish Folk Tale*,[13] whose theme is finding contentment. This colorfully illustrated European story is about a poor Jewish man who complains that his mother, wife, and six children live with him in a small hut. He follows his Rabbi's advice to bring his farm animals inside, experiencing sweet contentment when he removes the creatures. He states, "With just my family in the hut, it's so quiet, so roomy, so peaceful."[14]

**Preschool through Middle Grades.** Celestino Piatti is the Swiss recorder and illustrator of a Dutch legend, *The Happy Owls*,[15] translated into English from German. Its theme is disclosing a source of contentment to an inflexible, argumentative audience. When self-centered barnyard fowl question why a pair of owls are happy, the two reply, "When spring comes we are happy to see everything come to life after the long winter sleep.''[16] They speak similarly about other seasons, but the chickens, ducks, peacock, and geese do not understand and continue preening, stuffing themselves, and quarreling. This is the first picture storybook done by Piatti, a prizewinning poster artist, who uses dark outlines around full-color figures.

**Primary and Middle Grades.** Finding contentment is the theme of a Russian folktale, *No Room, an Old Story Retold,*[17] recorded by Rose Dobbs and illustrated humorously by Fritz Eichenberg. An old peasant lives with his wife in a small hut and complains that there is no room when his daughter writes, requesting permission to visit with her husband and baby. A wise man advises the peasant to invite his daughter and bring his farm animals into the hut. When he moves the animals out, he sees how much space there is and understands the wise man's words, ''Peace is not a commodity to be bought and sold; nor is it to be had for the wishing. Each man must find it for himself.''[18]

Contentment when true identity prevails is the theme of *Usha the Mouse Maiden,*[19] one of eighty-four *niti* or moral tales in India's Panchatantra (meaning five books) that is several thousand years old. It is retold and illustrated in full color by Mehlli Gobhai, a Bombay-born writer and painter who authentically paints Usha with a single gold earring. A thousand years ago near the Ganges River, an Indian magician, Yajnavalkya, changes a mouse into a baby girl, and he and his wife raise her like their daughter. When it is time for her to marry, her father seeks the mightiest husband. Usha rejects sun, clouds, wind, even a mountain, and meets a mouse who is mightiest because he nibbles at a mountain. Falling in love with the mouse, the maiden goes into the forest with him after having this wish granted, ''Dear Father, please change me into a mouse. I will be truly happy only if I can marry him and no other.''[20]

While the other books have only one story, *The Knee-High Man and Other Tales* is a collection of Afro-American folk tales retold by Julius Lester and colorfully illustrated by Ralph Pinto.[21] The book contains six animal tales, each with a distinct theme. These tales told among slaves often reveal their relationship to their masters. Two are wise-beast/foolish-beast tales, two are *pourquoi* tales, and two are moralistic tales, including ''The Knee-High Man.'' The theme of this title story is the need for contentment. A short, knee-high man wants to become as tall as Mr. Horse and Mr. Bull, so he asks Mr. Owl for advice. Mr. Owl says he does not need height for protection, because he has no enemy, and he can climb a tree to see a distance. Mr. Owl concludes:

> I'm smaller than you, and you don't see me worrying about being big. Mr. Knee-High Man, you wanted something that you didn't need.[22]

*A Chase and a Search*

**Preschool and Primary Grades.** Ruth Sawyer's folktale adaptation, *Journey Cake, Ho!*,[23] has humorous blue and maroon illustrations by Robert McCloskey. After a fox steals their livestock, an old couple with enough food for themselves alone send their farm boy, Johnny, to search for a better home. The woman makes Johnny a journey cake to eat on the trip, but it falls out of his sack and rolls away. In this cumulative tale, Johnny chases the cake, joined separately by a cow, ducks, sheep, a pig, chickens, and a donkey. The journey cake goes around the mountain, back to the couple's home, where Johnny and the animals stay permanently. The book's theme is a successful chase. The illustrator shows joy in the chase, for Johnny is a nonchalant rural boy, and the elusive journey cake seems to have a smiling face.

**Primary Grades.** An endless search with a theme of hope is featured in the Russian Christmas folk tale, *Baboushka and the Three Kings*,[24] recorded by Ruth Robbins and illustrated by Nicholas Sidjakov. Three kings ask old Baboushka to join their search for the Christ child and offer Him gifts, but she asks them to wait until morning. They go without her and the next day, she brings gifts for Him, looking in vain. Every year at Christmas, she searches with new hope, leaving her gifts for children instead. The illustrator gives the holiday story an appropriate stained-glass effect using red, blue, green, and yellow watercolors with black-pen outlines for block figures, including that of the searching, hopeful Baboushka.

*Resourcefulness*

**Preschool through Middle Grades.** Resourcefulness, a trait more important than size, is the theme of *Who's in Rabbit's House? A Masai Tale*,[25] retold by Verna Aardema. It appears as "The Long One" in her collection, *Tales for a Third Ear from Equatorial Africa*. When the Long One enters Rabbit's house, Frog offers to eject him, but Rabbit's refusal is: "You are so small."[26] Larger creatures, such as Jackal, Leopard, Elephant, and Rhinoceros are not able to get the Long One out, because Rabbit will not let them destroy his house. Now Rabbit lets Frog, resourcefully pretending to be Cobra, threaten, "Come out or I'll squeeze under the door and spit poison into your eyes."[27] That is when a long green caterpillar emerges.

Leo and Diane Dillon illustrated *Who's in Rabbit's House? A Masai Tale* in a novel way, as a play by Masai villagers wearing animal masks that change expression. They traced their originial drawing, applied pastels to the background, and painted the foreground in tempera. Their four-color work shows authentic Masai terrain, housing, sparkling jewelry, hairstyles, and costumes. They depict Frog as the small but clever hero of this humorous folktale.

**Primary and Middle Grades.** Another humorous folktale is from France. Marcia Brown records and illustrates *Stone Soup* with the theme of resourcefully overcoming reluctance to share.[28] When three tired, hungry French soldiers ask peasants for food, they hear excuses. The wily soldiers offer to make stone soup, and then the curious villagers contribute a big pot, water, and firewood for the clean stones. They even add, one by one, carrots, cabbage, beef, and milk, because they want to make the stone soup richer. The villagers and soldiers feast together. Marcia Brown's orange and brown illustrations are earthy, like the rogues who overcome the villagers' reluctance to share.

Author-illustrator Marcia Brown turns to England for a second folktale, *Dick Whittington and His Cat*.[29] Its theme is resourcefulness that leads from rags to riches. Orphaned, homeless Dick Whittington lives on villagers' potato parings but humbly works at any job he can get. For one penny he buys a cat and lets her go on a voyage, killing mice and rats aboard ship. The merchant captain pays Whittington for his cat with jewels, so the lad dresses like a gentleman. He marries the wealthy merchant-captain's daughter, Miss Alice Fitzwarren, and becomes Lord Mayor of London. Marcia Brown's amber and black linoleum cut prints trace Whittington from the time he is a pauper receiving parings at the door of a thatch hut to the day when he resourcefully bargains with the merchant and finally, to his wealthy period when, as mayor, he entertains King Henry.

Resourcefulness is also James Still's theme in *Jack and the Wonder Beans*,[30] illustrated by Margot Tomes. This Appalachian variant of the English *Jack and the Beanstalk* has mountaineer dialect, for Jack and his mother are poor as "Job's turkey." When Jack sells their only cow for magic beans, the disgusted mother throws the beans outside, and a beanstalk grows that Jack climbs to a giant's dwelling. He returns home with a hen that lays brown eggs, and he chops down the beanstalk in time to end the descending giant's life. James Still summarizes Jack's cleverness when he declares, "As the saying goes, to get ahead of Jack you would have to have long ears and a bushy tail."[31] The illustrations, appropriately done in rustic blue, grey, and brown tones, magnify Jack's resourcefulness because he is so small in comparison with the giant and his "high tall woman."


## Luck

**Primary and Middle Grades.** Chih-Yi's *The Good-Luck Horse*,[32] has fine-colored illustrations by twelve-year-old Plato Chan. This old Chinese legend tells how a lad, Wah-Toong, makes a paper horse that blows in front of a magician. The man changes it into a real horse, names it Good-Luck, and gives it to the boy. The horse gets into so much trouble, it leaves China, and in a neighboring land, marries the No-Good Mare. The horse pair return to the boy. When the child gets thrown from the mare on a mountain, the Good-Luck Horse saves his life. The stallion and boy end a war between China and the mare's homeland. A horse bringing good luck is the story's theme, for everyone finally agrees the animal is well named.


## Cooperation

**Preschool and Primary Grades.** Félicité Lefèvre's recording of *The Cock, the Mouse, and the Little Red Hen* is illustrated by Tony Sarg.[33] Learning cooperation is the theme of this English folktale about a little red hen who industriously does all the housework while a cock and mouse sleep by the fire. Catching them off guard, a fox seizes the three and puts them in his sack. The little red hen, armed with her sewing bag, cuts a hole in the sack, and the three escape. Once they return home, the cock and mouse share work with the hen. The illustrator shows in color and black and white how the three characters learn to cooperate.

Sharing work takes a slightly different twist with a role-reversal theme in "Changing Places," a German folktale adapted by Bernard Garfinkel and illustrated by Tomi Ungerer. It is among the six stories in *A Storybook*,[34] Ungerer's collection that contains four folktales with no common theme. In "Changing Places," a farmer envies his wife's easy work cleaning the house, caring for the baby, and feeding the animals. She objects and switches places the next day. Ungerer's illustrations show her first as an efficient, smiling housewife, then going to work cheerfully in the fields. He also captures the overwhelmed husband trying to manage the house with the baby soiled and the cow on the thatch roof. A final picture shows the frustrated man putting himself in a pot to stew.

Cooperation is obvious in Sorche Nic Leodhas's *All in the Morning*

*Early,*[35] with Evaline Ness's olive, ocher, black, and turquoise illustrations. This Scottish accumulative tale, told by three or more generations, has a task-completion theme, for Sandy, a Perthshire boy, fulfills his mother's request to take a sack of corn to the mill, "and the miller ground it into meal—all in the morning early."[36] The story is primarily in prose, but recurring, accumulative poetry describes the crowd of villagers and animals who accompany the boy en route and disappear at the mill.

Cooperation for survival is the theme of the Grimm brothers' *The Bremen Town Musicians,*[37] retold with full-color illustrations by author-illustrator Ilse Plume. The tale begins with a donkey, later joined by a dog, cat, and rooster, all old, all escaping before masters get rid of them. They decide to go to Bremen to be street musicians. At night, they see a cozy cottage occupied by robbers. They scare the thieves away by standing on each other's backs and crashing through the window with loud "music." Then the quartette enjoys their retirement home together.

*Excessiveness*

**Preschool and Primary Grades.** Elphinstone Dayrell retells a Nigerian folktale, *Why the Sun and the Moon Live in the Sky,*[38] whose theme is excessive hospitality. According to the story, Sun often visits Water, but not the reverse, because Sun's house is not big enough for Water and his people. Sun and his wife, Moon, build a larger house. When Water and water-dwelling creatures visit, Water asks Sun if he wants more water people to enter. "And the sun and the moon both answered, 'Yes,' not knowing any better."[39] To accommodate so many guests, Sun and Moon first have to sit on their house's thatch roof and later, are forced into the sky where they remain. Blair Lent's stylized illustrations portray Sun in a brown-with-ocher color scheme and Water and his followers in blue with green.

Excessive pasta causes problems in *Strega Nona* by author-illustrator Tomie de Paola.[40] His humorous illustrations done in pastel emphasize the theme that disobedience leads to disaster. This Italian folktale is about Strega Nona, meaning Grandma Witch, who cooks pasta after an incantation over a magic pot, an act that amazes her hired hand, Big Anthony. She warns him, "The one thing you must never do . . . is touch the pasta pot."[41] However, when she leaves town, he uses the pot to cook pasta for the village. Since he does not know "three blows of a kiss" to end the process, the pasta overflows into the streets. Luckily, Strega Nona returns in time to end the cooking, but she punishes Big Anthony by making him eat the excessive pasta.

*Frivolity*

**Preschool through Middle Grades.** The danger of frivolity is Arlene
Mosel's theme when she retells a Japanese folktale, *The Funny Little
Woman,*[42] illustrated by Blair Lent. A woman chases one of her rice
dumplings underground and, because she laughs at the wrong time, gets
caught by a wicked *oni,* an impish, grotesque underground god, who
forces her to cook for all the *oni.* After months of captivity, she tries to
escape by rowing across a river in a boat. The *oni* drink all the river
water, so she is stuck in mud, but they make a mistake. When they laugh
at her, the water flows from their mouths back into the river, and the
woman rows to freedom. She keeps an *oni* magic paddle which multiplies
one rice grain, so she becomes the richest woman in Japan. The final
full-color picture shows her merchandising a quantity of rice dumplings,
getting the last laugh.

*Greed*

**Preschool and Primary Grades.** Ruth Hürlimann retells and illustrates
*The Cat and Mouse Who Shared a House,*[43] a German folktale with the
theme of greed destroying friendship. In a joint dwelling, a mouse does
the housework. A cat secures food, such as a big pot of butter hidden
in the church for their winter meals. The cat makes excuses to sneak to
the church and eat the winter butter, saying he left to name his godchil-
dren Top-off and Half-gone. When winter comes, the mouse understands
the reason for the unusual names and accuses the cat. Then the cat's
greed is apparent for:

> . . . the mouse had All-gone on the tip of her tongue, and out it came.
> No sooner had she said it, than the cat pounced on her and ate her
> up.[44]

Hürlimann's stylized full-color illustrations show the cat's greed.

**Primary and Middle Grades.** Ancient India is the source of *Once a
Mouse . . . A Fable Cut in Wood,*[45] retold and illustrated by Marcia
Brown with a theme of forgetting origin through greed and arrogance.
A hermit protects a mouse from predators, changing him first into a cat,
then a dog, and finally a tiger. The hermit tells the proud tiger, "Without
me, you would be a wretched little mouse, that is, if you were still alive.
There is no need to give yourself such airs."[46] The hermit avoids the
tiger's effort to kill him by changing the beast into a mouse once more.

Marcia Brown's woodcuts contribute to the theme by cleverly showing the tiger with the shadow of a dog, his former self. She gradually adds red to her forest-green and mustard-yellow drawings as in a crescendo that warns about impending danger, but she omits this color in her final picture after the crisis.

*Deceit*

**Primary and Middle Grades.** Evaline Ness retells and illustrates *Tom Tit Tot,*[47] based on Joseph Jacob's English version of the German tale, *Rumplestiltskin,* with the theme, trouble from deception. Knowing a king can hear her song, a mother deceptively claims her daughter daily spins five skeins. The greedy king marries the girl on condition that she spin that amount for one month or be decapitated. A little man, Tom Tit Tot, does the spinning for her, but if she cannot guess his name, she promises to belong to him. The king overhears the little man's name in time to save his wife. Ness's blue, gold, black, and brown illustrations capture the girl's dilemma.

Trouble from deception is again the theme of a humorous Cornish variant of *Rumplestiltskin, Duffy and the Devil,*[48] told by Harve Zemach and illustrated by his wife, Margot Zemach. Nineteenth-century residents of Cornwall, England—mummers—went door to door at Christmastime performing this folktale as a play. It is about young Duffy, fired for being lazy, who lies that she is a fine knitter and spinner, so Squire Lovel of Trove hires her to help his housekeeper, Jone. When Jone asks Duffy to spin and knit, the incapable girl shouts that the devil can do the task, and so he does. He wants to claim her at the end of three years, but she saves herself by naming him Tarroway. Told with verve, the story has soft-toned, humorous illustrations.

*Selfishness*

**Preschool and Primary Grades.** *Seashore Story,*[49] a Japanese legend recorded and illustrated by Taro Yashima, is built around a theme of selfishness. A Japanese fisherman, Urashima, travels on a turtle's back to a beautiful palace under the sea where he stays so long he forgets his loved ones. Carrying a box from the sea people, he returns home, but cannot recognize anyone. After he learns that his house and family are gone, he goes up a hill and opens his box; when only white smoke escapes, he becomes an old man. The smoke is the fisherman's punish-

ment for selfishly forgetting his loved ones. The pastel illustrations muted
with white produce a dreamy effect.

*Bravery*

**Primary and Middle Grades.** Stephen Gammell's sensitive black-and-
white illustrations depict the bravery theme that is apparent in Olaf Baker's *Where the Buffaloes Begin*.[50] First published in 1915 in *St. Nicholas
Magazine,* this story is about ten-year-old Little Wolf, who has no fear.
He hears Nawa, the wise man, tell a legend of buffaloes who rise from
a lake, and he makes the arduous journey south to that lake. He sees the
buffaloes rise at the same time he identifies an enemy, the Assiniboins,
traveling toward his people. Little Wolf, riding to warn his home camp
about the Assiniboins, is surrounded though untrampled by the stamped-
ing herd. He successfully directs the herd to gallop over the enemy.
Little Wolf's bravery becomes part of the buffalo legend.

*Determination*

**Preschool through Middle Grades.** Nonny Hogrogian focuses on the
theme of determination as she retells and illustrates an Armenian accumulative folktale, *One Fine Day*.[51] An old woman cuts off the tail of a
thirsty fox who drinks her pail of milk. She promises to sew it on if the
fox replaces her milk, so he asks the cow for milk, but must give her
grass in exchange. With determination, the fox trades items in return for
the milk, and the woman sews on his tail. Hogrogian shows the persevering fox in bright, full-color oil paintings.

Determination is the primary theme of three Native American stories:
*Arrow to the Sun: A Pueblo Indian Tale,*[52] *The Angry Moon,*[53] and *The
Legend of Scarface: A Blackfeet Indian Tale*.[54] Gerald McDermott adapts
and illustrates the Pueblo myth about a boy who brings the spirit of the
Lord of the Sun, his father, back to his people after he is changed into
an arrow. With determination, he proves himself worthy to have such a
great father by fulfilling dangerous tasks. A filmmaker, McDermott shows
a moviemaker's eye for color, contrasting predominantly yellow and
orange with black and brown in stylized full-color illustrations.

An Alaskan tale, *The Angry Moon,* recorded by William Sleator and
illustrated by Blair Lent, shows the determination of a Tlinget boy, Lupan, to rescue a girl, Lapowinsa. When she criticizes the Moon, that
celestial body spirits her away. Lupan tries to defend her by shooting
arrows toward the sky. Surprisingly, the arrows form a ladder which

Lupan climbs. After he brings her down the ladder to Earth, the arrows fall to the ground, the end of an adventure long remembered in the village. Highlighting the book are Lent's spectacular full-color drawings.

**Primary and Middle Grades.** Robert San Souci's recording of *The Legend of Scarface: A Blackfeet Indian Tale* is enhanced by full-color realistic illustrations done by his brother, Daniel. Scarface, named for the birthmark on his cheek, and the chief's daughter, Singing Rains, fall in love, but she previously made a vow to Father Sun not to marry. With determination, Scarface travels to Father Sun to ask him to release her from the vow. After Scarface saves the life of Morning Star, Father Sun's son, his wish is granted, and as an added bonus, the scar on his face vanishes. The illustrations show the hazardous, successful journey of this determined brave.

The final book with a theme of determination is Arthur Ransome's recording, *The Fool of the World and the Flying Ship,*[55] a Russian folktale illustrated by Uri Shulevitz. When the czar announces he will marry his daughter to a man who builds him a flying ship, the fool's older brothers leave to compete. The fool wants to follow, but his parents consider him a simpleton, so he announces, "I am going. I am going. I am going."[56] He takes stale bread and water which, when shared with an old man, become fine food. The man builds him a flying ship, and he flies to the palace, offering transportation en route to seven strangers, all extraordinary. Thanks to the strangers, the fool performs difficult tasks assigned by the czar and marries the princess. With great perseverence, he wins respect. The illustrations in brilliant color faithfully show Russian background.

## Summary

This chapter analyzes the primary theme of thirty-six samples of prize-winning folk literature in picture-storybook form. Themes are discussed under fourteen topics, the most popular being contentment, resourcefulness, determination, cooperation, and *pourquoi* or literary explanations for animal and human traits or appearance. Young nonreaders appreciate hearing the tales, so grade indicates listening-comprehension level as well as independent-reading level. An equal number of books in this sample are intended for those in preschool and primary grades, preschool through middle grades, and primary and middle grades.

Most of the picture storybooks have received illustration awards. Over half are Caldecott Medal winners or Honor Books. In this sample, Marcia Brown retells and illustrates three prizewinners and Gerald

McDermott, two. Nonny Hogrogian, Evaline Ness, and Margot Zemach
are illustrators of two separate prizewinners and author of one of them.
Illustrators of multiple prizewinners include Blair Lent with four to his
credit and Leo and Diane Dillon with two.

The chapter presents folktales from nineteen cultural groups. Their
origins are as follows: six African or Afro-American and English, Cornish, or Anglo-American; three German, Native American, and Russian;
and two Chinese, Japanese, Scottish, and Jewish, including one Yiddish
and one Hebrew. There are two tales from India, and one from every
other source.

**Notes**

1. "Lloyd Alexander, Evaline Ness, and Ann Durell," *Profiles in
Literature* (Philadelphia: Temple University, 1972).

2. Ibid.

3. Hans Knight, "Architect Kahn Is Avid Reader of Fairy Tales,"
*The Evening Bulletin* (June 24, 1971), p. 3B.

4. In 1968, *Tikki Tikki Tembo* won the *Boston Globe-Horn Book*
Award for illustration.

5. In 1976, *Why Mosquitoes Buzz in People's Ears: A West African
Tale, retold by Verna Aardema* won The Randolph Caldecott Medal.

6. In 1973, *Anansi the Spider* was a Caldecott Honor Book.

7. In 1971, *A Story, a Story* won The Randolph Caldecott Medal.

8. Gail E. Haley, *A Story, a Story* (New York: Atheneum, 1970),
no page.

9. Ibid., no page.

10. In 1938, *Animals of the Bible* won The Randolph Caldecott
Medal.

11. In 1966, *Always Room for One More* won The Randolph Caldecott Medal.

12. Sorche Nic Leodhas, *Always Room for One More* (New York:
Holt, 1965), pp. 1–2.

13. In 1977, *It Could Always Be Worse: A Yiddish Folk Tale* was a
*New York Times* Choice of Best Illustrated Children's Book of the Year,
and in 1978, it was a Caldecott Honor Book.

14. Margot Zemach, *It Could Always Be Worse: A Yiddish Folk Tale*
(New York: Farrar, 1976), no page.

15. In 1964, *The Happy Owls* was a *New York Times* Choice of Best
Illustrated Children's Book of the Year.

16. Celestino Piatti, *The Happy Owls* (New York: Atheneum, 1964),
p. 14.

17. In 1968, *No Room, an Old Story Retold* won the Lewis Carroll Shelf Award.

18. Rose Dobbs, *No Room, an Old Story Retold* (New York: McKay, 1944), no page.

19. In 1969, *Usha the Mouse Maiden* won the Lewis Carroll Shelf Award.

20. Mehlli Gobhai, *Usha the Mouse Maiden* (New York: Hawthorn, 1969), p. 23.

21. In 1972, *The Knee-High Man and Other Tales* won the Lewis Carroll Shelf Award.

22. Julius Lester, *The Knee-High Man and Other Tales* (New York: Dial, 1972), p. 28.

23. In 1954, *Journey-Cake, Ho!* was a Caldecott Honor Book.

24. In 1960, *Baboushka and the Three Kings* was a *New York Times* Choice of Best Illustrated Children's Book of the Year, and in 1961, it won The Randolph Caldecott Medal.

25. In 1978, *Who's in Rabbit's House? A Masai Tale* won the Lewis Carroll Shelf Award.

26. Verna Aardema, *Who's in Rabbit's House? A Masai Tale* (New York: Dial, 1977), no page.

27. Ibid., no page.

28. In 1948, *Stone Soup* was a Caldecott Honor Book.

29. In 1951, *Dick Whittington and His Cat* was a Caldecott Honor Book.

30. In 1977, *Jack and the Wonder Beans* was a *New York Times* Choice of Best Illustrated Children's Book of the Year.

31. James Still, *Jack and the Wonder Beans* (New York: Putnam, 1977), no page.

32. In 1944, *The Good-Luck Horse* was a Caldecott Honor Book.

33. In 1947, *The Cock, the Mouse, and the Little Red Hen* won the Lewis Carroll Shelf Award.

34. In 1974, *A Storybook* was a *New York Times* Choice of Best Illustrated Children's Book of the Year.

35. In 1964, *All in the Morning Early* was a Caldecott Honor Book.

36. Sorche Nic Leodhas, *All in the Morning Early* (New York: Holt, 1963), no page.

37. In 1981, *The Bremen Town Musicians* was a Caldecott Honor Book.

38. In 1969, *Why the Sun and the Moon Live in the Sky* was a Caldecott Honor Book.

39. Elphinstone Dayrell, *Why the Sun and the Moon Live in the Sky* (Boston: Houghton, 1968), p. 23.

40. In 1976, *Strega Nona* was a Caldecott Honor Book.

41. Tomie de Paola, *Strega Nona* (Englewood Cliffs, N.J.: Prentice-Hall, 1975), no page.

42. In 1973, *The Funny Little Woman* won The Randolph Caldecott Medal.

43. In 1976, *The Cat and Mouse Who Shared a House* (translated by Anthea Bell) won the Mildred L. Batchelder Award.

44. Ruth Hürlimann, *The Cat and Mouse Who Shared a House* (New York: Walck, 1973), p. 21.

45. In 1961, *Once a Mouse . . . A Fable Cut in Wood* was a *New York Times* Choice of Best Illustrated Children's Book of the Year, and in 1962, it won The Randolph Caldecott Medal.

46. Marcia Brown, *Once a Mouse . . . A Fable Cut in Wood* (New York: Scribner, 1961), p. 23.

47. In 1966, *Tom Tit Tot* was a Caldecott Honor Book.

48. In 1973, *Duffy and the Devil* won the Lewis Carroll Shelf Award, and in 1974, The Randolph Caldecott Medal.

49. In 1967, *Seashore Story* was a *New York Times* Choice of Best Illustrated Children's Book of the Year. In 1968, it was a Caldecott Honor Book and won the Southern California Council on Literature for Children and Young People Award.

50. In 1982, *Where the Buffaloes Begin* was a Caldecott Honor Book.

51. In 1972, *One Fine Day* won The Randolph Caldecott Medal.

52. In 1975, *Arrow to the Sun: A Pueblo Indian Tale* won The Randolph Caldecott Medal.

53. In 1971, *The Angry Moon* was a Caldecott Honor Book.

54. In 1978, *The Legend of Scarface: A Blackfeet Indian Tale* was a *New York Times* Best Illustrated Children's Book of the Year.

55. In 1969, *The Fool of the World and the Flying Ship* won The Randolph Caldecott Award.

56. Arthur Ransome, *The Fool of the World and the Flying Ship* (New York: Farrar, 1968), p. 46.

## References of Prizewinning Folk Literature in Picture Storybooks Arranged according to Place of Origin

*(Estimated Reading or Listening Grade Level in Parentheses)*

*Africa*

Aardema, Verna, ed. *Who's in Rabbit's House? A Masai Tale.* Illustrated by Leo and Diane Dillon. New York: Dial, 1977 (K–3).

———. *Why Mosquitoes Buzz in Peoples' Ears: A West African Tale,* retold by Verna Aardema. Illustrated by Leo and Diane Dillon. New York: Dial, 1975 (K–3).

Dayrell, Elphinstone. *Why the Sun and the Moon Live in the Sky.* Illustrated by Blair Lent. Boston: Houghton, 1968 (K–2).

Haley, Gail E. *A Story, a Story.* New York: Atheneum, 1970 (1–4).

McDermott, Gerald. *Anansi the Spider.* New York: Holt, 1972 (K–3).

## Africa and America

Lester, Julius. *The Knee-High Man and Other Tales.* Illustrated by Ralph Pinto. New York: Dial, 1972 (1–3).

## Armenia

Hogrogian, Nonny. *One Fine Day.* New York: Macmillan, 1971 (K–3).

## China

Chih-Yi. *The Good-Luck Horse.* Illustrated by Plato Chan. New York: Whittlesey, 1943 (2–4).

Mosel, Arlene. *Tikki Tikki Tembo.* Illustrated by Blair Lent. New York: Holt, 1968 (K–2).

## England

Brown, Marcia. *Dick Whittington and His Cat.* New York: Scribner, 1950 (1–4).

Lefèvre, Félicité. *The Cock, the Mouse, and the Little Red Hen.* Illustrated by Tony Sarg. Philadelphia: Macrae, Smith, 1947 (K–3).

Ness, Evaline. *Tom Tit Tot.* New York: Scribner, 1965 (1–3).

## Cornwall, England

Zemach, Harve. *Duffy and the Devil.* Illustrated by Margot Zemach. New York: Farrar, 1973 (1–3).

*France*

Brown, Marcia. *Stone Soup*. New York: Scribner, 1947 (1–4).


*Germany*

Hürlimann, Ruth. *The Cat and Mouse Who Shared a House*. Translated
   by Anthea Bell. New York: Walck, 1973 (K–2).
Plume, Ilse. *The Bremen Town Musicians*. New York: Doubleday, 1980
   (K–3).
Ungerer, Tomi, ed. *A Storybook*. New York: Watts, 1974 (1–4).


*India*

Brown, Marcia. *Once a Mouse . . . A Fable Cut in Wood*. New York:
   Scribner, 1961 (1–3).
Gobhai, Mehlli. *Usha the Mouse Maiden*. New York: Hawthorn, 1969
   (1–3).


*Israel*

Lathrop, Dorothy P., ed. *Animals of the Bible*. Philadelphia: Lippincott,
   1937 (1–3).


*Italy*

de Paola, Tomie. *Strega Nona*. Englewood Cliffs, N.J.: Prentice-Hall,
   1975 (K–3).


*Japan*

Mosel, Arlene. *The Funny Little Woman*. Illustrated by Blair Lent. New
   York: Dutton, 1972 (PS–4).
Yashima, Taro. *The Seashore Story*. New York: Viking, 1967 (K–2).


*Netherlands*

Piatti, Celestino. *The Happy Owls*. New York: Atheneum, 1964 (K–3).

*Poland (Possibly Yiddish)*

Zemach, Margot. *It Could Always Be Worse*. New York: Farrar, 1976 (1–3).

*Russia*

Dobbs, Rose. *No Room, an Old Story Retold*. Illustrated by Fritz Eichenberg. New York: McKay, 1944 (2–4).

Ransome, Arthur. *The Fool of the World and the Flying Ship*. Illustrated by Uri Shulevitz. New York: Farrar, 1968 (1–4).

Robbins, Ruth. *Baboushka and the Three Kings*. Illustrated by Nicolas Sidjakov. San Francisco: Parnassus, 1960 (1–2).

*Scotland*

Leodhas, Sorche Nic. *All in the Morning Early*. Illustrated by Evaline Ness. New York: Holt, 1963 (K–3).

Leodhas, Sorche Nic. *Always Room for One More*. Illustrated by Nonny Hogrogian. New York: Holt, 1965 (K–3).

*United States*

**Alaska:**

Sleator, William. *The Angry Moon*. Illustrated by Blair Lent. Boston: Little, Brown, 1970 (K–9).

**Arizona and New Mexico:**

McDermott, Gerald. *Arrow to the Sun: A Pueblo Indian Tale*. New York: Viking, 1974 (1–3).

**Montana:**

Baker, Olaf. *Where the Buffaloes Begin*. New York: Warne, 1981 (2–4).

San Souci, Robert. *The Legend of Scarface: A Blackfeet Indian Tale*. Illustrated by Daniel San Souci. New York: Viking, 1978 (2–4).

*United States (Appalachia) and England*

Sawyer, Ruth. *Journey Cake, Ho!* Illustrated by Robert McCloskey. New York: Viking, 1953 (PS–3).

Still, James. *Jack and the Wonder Beans*. Illustrated by Margot Tomes. New York: Putnam, 1977 (1–3).

# 4 Modern Fantasy in Picture Storybooks

*Eva, my sister, is seven. She says* The Maggie B. *is her best book and next to that comes* The Girl Who Loved the Wind. *I like a wind story, too:* Little Pieces of the West Wind. *But I'm different from Eva. Give me a book about monsters! I like it when the monsters in* Where the Wild Things Are *show their terrible teeth.*                    —Yuri, aged five

## Perspective

In *The Maggie B.*, author-illustrator Irene Haas shows through full-color paintings and brush drawings how her character, Margaret Barnstable, fulfills dreams of becoming a sailor on her own boat. The wind talks in Jane Yolen's *The Girl Who Loved the Wind,* and Princess Danina rides the wind, using her cape like a magic carpet. After illustrator Ed Young decided on a Persian setting for the princess, he created watercolor illustrations that incorporate tissue-paper collage. (From the French verb *coller,* meaning to paste, collage involves integrating in art such pasted items as figured wallpaper or fabric.)

Yuri's books include Christian Garrison's *Little Pieces of the West Wind,* a cumulative tale in which the wind is personified. Diane Goode's full-color pastel illustrations for Garrison's book are done on parchment with brush and China ink. Yuri also cites *Where the Wild Things Are* by author-illustrator Maurice Sendak. His tale of a dreamed visit to a land of monsters is drawn with tempera paints and black felt pen.

Yuri's and Eva's selections are fanciful picture storybooks, the subject of this chapter. Another chapter deals with animal fantasy in picture storybooks, an important aspect of modern fantasy discussed separately because of the large number of pertinent prizewinners. As in all picture storybooks, many art styles are used in fanciful works, varying from realistic to stylized or abstract approaches to cartoons or caricatures. Illustrators have distinctive styles though they may change their method to suit particular stories, at times preferring to use photography. In addition to photography, illustrators' preferred media may include acrylics, oils, pastels, charcoal, sponge prints, woodcuts, linoleum cuts, lithographs, or scratchboards (scratching on a crayoned surface overlaid with

India ink). They may have to do a separate overlay for each color, a cheaper process than printing in full color.

Picture storybooks of high-quality fantasy nourish imagination and are never out of date. Effective fantasy is made believable by numerous devices, including moving gradually from reality into fantasy, using sensory imagery to describe a new world, or offering fake documentation with coined vocabularly and spurious references.

This chapter analyzes prizewinning fanciful picture storybooks that mention a dragon or Loch Ness Monster. Actual animals, though personified, are characters in animal fantasy picture storybooks discussed in another chapter.

## Themes of Prizewinning Modern Fantasy in Picture Storybooks Grouped under These Topics

*Personification*

**Preschool through Middle Grades.** Proving himself is the theme that pervades the story of a personified tugboat, *Little Toot*,[1] by author-illustrator Hardie Gramatky. Big ships consider Little Toot, the smallest tugboat in the harbor, to be a nuisance because he is lazy and blows silly smoke balls. He makes his father, Big Toot, proud when he rescues an ocean liner jammed between rocks in a storm. Gramatky's illustrations in red, blue, black, yellow, and green help stress the theme, for one shows Little Toot blowing S.O.S. signals with smoke balls. He is personified with a human face and in this kind of description, "Little Toot was a hero! . . . Well, after that, Little Toot became quite a different (industrious) fellow."[2]

**Primary and Middle Grades.** Author-illustrator Virginia Lee Burton personifies her subject in *The Little House,* a prizewinner with a renaissance theme.[3] Her watercolor illustrations initially show a smiling house "watching the sun rise in the morning, the moon at night, and the change of the seasons."[4] Then the city encroaches on the countryside, and the Little House dwells in the shadows of skyscrapers and elevated train tracks. It is the great-great-granddaughter of the original owner who moves the Little House into the country again and cares for her. The final illustration shows a smile replacing previous frowns as the Little House feels reborn.

*Wind*

**Preschool and Primary Grades.** A single element, wind, is personified in two distinct ways. The first book, Christian Garrison's *Little Pieces* *of the West Wind*,[5] illustrated humorously by Diane Good, has the theme of reward for fulfilling promises. In the beginning, the blustery West Wind agrees to look for a man's lost socks, but the distrustful man takes a piece of the wind as security. This sets off a chain of events because a woodchopper with the socks will give them back only when the wind promises to find his gloves, and the wind leaves a piece of himself until his return. The cycle continues as a gypsy, sheep, and bird extract promises, taking so many pieces of the wind that he is reduced to a breeze. A little girl playing with the bird's missing feather trusts the wind to cool her every afternoon, so she does not take the final piece of him. Now he grows in strength in this accumulative tale as he fulfills each promise and receives his missing pieces. The last illustration of the West Wind cooling the girl underscores the theme.

**Primary and Middle Grades.** Jane Yolen's *The Girl Who Loved the Wind,* illustrated by Ed Young, has the theme of a sheltered girl seeking life's challenges.[6] A wealthy merchant surrounds his only child, Princess Danina, with perfection, but the wind takes her away to experience the real world, preparing her by announcing, ''I am not always kind. Nothing is always.''[7] The book cover reinforces the theme, for it shows the girl riding the wind to the real world. The artist, Ed Young, talented in book design, offers illustrations in watercolor that are reminiscent of Persian miniatures.

*Accomplishments Despite Small Size*

**Preschool through Middle Grades.** A personified train is the hero of Watty Piper's *The Little Engine that Could*,[8] illustrated by George and Doris Hauman. The book's theme is accomplishment despite small size. A little train loaded with Christmas toys and holiday food exerts great effort to travel to the other side of the mountain, saying, ''I think I can. I think I can. I think I can. I think I can.''[9] When he is successful, he expresses, ''I thought I could. I thought I could. I thought I could. I thought I could.''[10] The full-color, nursery-type illustrations are relatively stereotyped.

Another book with the theme, accomplishment despite small size, is Jane Yolen's *The Emperor and the Kite*.[11] An emperor neglects his youngest, tiny daughter, Djeow Seow (the smallest one). He forces her to eat and fly her kite alone. When evil men lock him in a tower and leave him to die, Djeow Seow rescues him. She flies her kite to her father's window, and he slides down its long rope. When they return to his kingdom, she helps rule, sitting beside him on the throne, and she reigns when he dies. The book's illustrator, Ed Young, born in Shanghai, depicts the book's Chinese setting with authenticity.

## Night

**Preschool and Primary Grades.** Gail Radley's *The Night Stella Hid the Stars*,[12] illustrated by John Wallner, has the theme: being needed. As the star lady, Stella dusts the stars each day and puts them in the sky each night to shine. One evening, wanting to enjoy daytime, she hides the stars in her closet. People in the universe become upset, so the following night when she puts out the stars, "people began to shout for joy, and the happy sound grew so loud that Stella looked down and smiled."[13] In this way, Stella realizes she is needed.

Unlike Stella, Hildilid, in Cheli Durán Ryan's *Hildilid's Night*,[14] hates the night. Stubbornness is the book's theme, for Hildilid futilely tries to sweep the night away, put it in a sack, sing it away, and even spit at it. It is daybreak when Hildilid gives up, but she is so tired, she falls asleep and misses a beautiful day. Arnold Lobel presents black-and-white pen-and-ink illustrations, creatively using yellow overlays for the sun in only the last three. He supports the theme by showing the stubborn woman yawning and going to sleep when her hut is bathed in sunlight.

## Nature

**Preschool and Primary Grades.** The hope of summer is the theme of Astrid Lindgren's *The Tomten*,[15] illustrated by Harold Wiberg. This story, adapted from Viktor Rydberg's poem, tells about the Tomten, a friendly troll who roams at night speaking to sleeping animals in a language only they understand. He expresses the hope that when summer comes, they can be grazing in the fields.

An island is a natural phenomenon, and the concept of an island is the theme of Golden MacDonald's *The Little Island*.[16] The theme is clarified in Leonard Weisgard's illustrations which show flora and fauna on a small island. Told from the island's perspective, the story describes the effect of seasonal change there. When a kitten visits with picnickers, he brags about being part of the big world. The island, who claims the same distinction, invites the kitten to ask fish how the island is part of the land. "And the fish told the kitten how all land is one land under the sea. The cat's eyes were shining with the secret of it."[17]

**Preschool through Middle Grades.** Author-illustrator Dr. Seuss offers the theme of admitting error when disturbing nature in his *Bartholomew and the Oobleck*.[18] Bored King Derwin commissions his wizards to invent something new, oobleck, a sticky green substance descending from the sky. Dr. Seuss does black-and-white illustrations with oobleck accentuated in green as it drips through ceilings, rolls down chimneys, and even destroys birds' nests. A boy, Bartholomew, stops the mess by having the king admit his error in changing nature.

*Mischief and Magic*

**Preschool through Middle Grades.** *The Devil Did It* by author-illustrator Susan Jeshke is about a young girl, Nana, who alone sees the devil, a symbol of mischief, which is the book's theme.[19] Humorous illustrations emphasize this theme. Nana's mother says, "The devil did it!" when asked the source of hair knots. Naturally Nana similarly shifts the blame when she rips the bathroom curtain. However, mystery surrounds who put her father's clothes in the refrigerator and who dangles a turkey from a chandelier. If the devil did it, he leaves when Nana ceases to fear him.

**Primary through Upper Grades.** Chris Van Allsburg, whose sculpture and drawings have been exhibited at New York's Museum of Modern Art, offers as his first picture storybook *The Garden of Abdul Gasazi*.[20] Magic, the book's theme, is largely communicated in his black-and-white illustrations done with carbon pencil on Strathmore paper. The story is about young Alan Mitz who lets Miss Hester's dog, Fritz, lead him on a walk. The dog enters a forbidden area, a garden where he gets lost among the topiary trees and shrubs that are animal-shaped. Alan asks the garden's owner, Abdul Gasazi, for the dog. The evil magician says he temporarily changed it into a duck which Alan tries to carry home. The duck flies away with Alan's hat. When the anxious boy reports to Miss Hester, she shows him Fritz is safe at home. Only after the boy's departure does the dog reveal Alan's hat.

*Excessiveness*

**Preschool through Middle Grades.** Excessiveness is the theme of Judi Barrett's *Cloudy with a Chance of Meatballs*.[21] In a town appropriately named Chewandswallow, everything is wonderful at first. Meals rain from the sky (for example, frankfurters already in rolls). When food becomes excessive, giant meatballs damage stores and school is canceled. People are forced to abandon the town, sail elsewhere on bread rafts, and shop at supermarkets. Ron Barrett's illustrations add to the humor.

Equally humorous is *The Sweet Touch* by author-illustrator Lorna Balian.[22] The book's theme is excessive sweetness that becomes undesirable. A young genie, Oliver, grants little Peggy's wish that everything she touches will turn to candy. While her dog watches, she and Oliver eat too much before she has the wish removed. Then Oliver's winged mother takes home her winged son. Color is used ingeniously because the illustrations begin and end in black and white, but when Peggy has her magic touch, the candy she creates is in bright colors.

*Etiquette*

**Primary and Middle Grades.** A comical approach to manners is the theme of Sesyle Joslin's *What Do You Say, Dear?*,[23] illustrated by Maurice Sendak. The book has suggestions for proper eitquette in ridiculous situations. Here is an example of the text, which is accompanied by a humorous illustration:

> You are picking dandelions and columbines outside the castle. Suddenly, a fierce dragon appears and blows red smoke at you, but just then a brave knight gallops up and cuts off the dragon's head. What do you say, dear?
>
> Thank you very much.[24]

The only weakness in *What Do You Say, Dear?* is the stereotyped role of the same little boy and girl who are in every situation. The boy is the brave knight, and the girl is the scared damsel in distress.

*Indifference*

**Primary through Upper Grades.** Edward Gorey's black-and-white illustrations for Florence Parry Heide's *The Shrinking of Treehorn* confirm the theme of indifference to others.[25] Treehorn, a boy who is about seven years old, is actually shrinking, but no one sympathizes. When his shrinking affects people, they react selfishly. After he becomes so small he must stand on a chair to reach his piggy bank, his mother exclaims, "You know how I hate to have you climb up on the chair, dear."[26] When Treehorn shrinks so much, he has to jump off his bed, he notices a game he began a few days ago. It's "The Big Game for Kids to Grow On," and instead of moving backwards as he did previously, he moves forward until he grows to be his regular size. He puts the game away, but notices at the end of the story that he is turning green. Neglected Treehorn decides, "If I don't say anything, they won't notice."[27]

## Christmas

**Preschool.** Christmas sharing is the theme of *Morris's Disappearing Bag: A Christmas Story* by author-illustrator Rosemary Wells.[28] Morris is the youngest member of a family of personified rabbits. His siblings won't let him play with their Christmas toys until he shares something with them. It is a bag that makes him disappear. This small book has watercolor illustrations of rabbits dressed and acting like people. Rosemary Wells cleverly draws Morris's partial body showing him crawling into and emerging from the disappearing bag.

**Preschool and Primary Grades.** Marie Hall Ets illustrates *Nine Days to Christmas, a Story of Mexico,*[29] using pink, orange, brown, yellow, purple, and black tones on a gray background. She wrote the story with Aurora Labastida, telling about Ceci, a kindergartener from a comfortable Mexico City home. She is to have her first *posada,* a Christmas party in different houses, one on each of the nine nights before the holiday. She goes with her mother to market to buy a *piñata,* a container of candy and gifts that blindfolded children break open at a party. *Piñatas* talk to her, asking her to buy them, but she selects a silent gold star. When guests break the star *piñata* at her party, Ceci is sad until a star in the sky says, "Don't cry, Ceci . . . I'm a *real* star now!"[30] A young child's Mexican Christmas celebration is the book's theme.

## Virtue Rewarded

**Preschool and Primary Grades.** William Lipkind's *The Magic Feather Duster,*[31] illustrated by Nicolas Mordvinoff, has virtue rewarded as its primary theme. When four brothers request their old neighbor's magic feather duster, she promises it to the one who brings her the right apple. The three oldest brothers try, refuse a frog who asks for their apples, and change respectively into a rabbit, mouse, and bear. The youngest brother gives his apple to the frog, who transforms magically into the old neighbor. Before she vanishes, she lets him have her feather duster, house, and cats. With the magic feather duster he restores his brothers. Mordvinoff's humorous illustrations help develop the theme.

**Preschool through Middle Grades.** Another book with virtue rewarded as its theme is Jay Williams's *Everyone Knows What a Dragon Looks Like* illustrated by Mercer Mayer.[32] Han, the poor, friendly gate sweeper for the city of Wu, takes a messenger to the Mandarin's palace. The visitor warns that Wild Horsemen will attack, so advisors agree to pray to the Great Cloud Dragon for help. The next day, a fat, bald man comes to the city gate, and Han takes him to the palace, where everyone treats him discourteously. When Wild Horsemen approach, Han tells the stranger, "I don't think we have much time. If you are hungry and thirsty, please come to my house."[33] The man replies, "I don't think much of the people of Wu, but for your sake I will save the city."[34] The man transforms himself into a dragon and destroys the army of the Wild Horsemen. Then people call Han "The Honorable Defender of the City." The theme and Chinese setting are emphasized in full-color, bordered paintings with fine details and in pen-and-ink sketches on some facing pages.

Kindness reciprocated is the specific kind of virtue-rewarded theme in a dragon story with an ingenious ending, *How Droofus the Dragon Lost His Head* by author-illustrator Bill Peet.[35] After a sensitive four-year-old dragon, Droofus, strays from the horrible beasts in his family, a king sees him. He wants to mount Droofus' head as a trophy on his castle wall and offers a hundred golden quadrooples for his capture. A young farm boy, aware of the reward, finds Droofus beside a lost lamb, Flossie, and acknowledges, "If he wouldn't hurt my lamb then he must be a good dragon."[36] The boy refuses to sacrifice Droofus for prize money, and Droofus reciprocates his kindness by moving boulders, plowing fields, weeding, sowing seeds, cutting firewood, and scarecrowing for the farm boy's family. When the king discovers the dragon's hideaway, the boy refuses to sell Droofus, so the dragon occasionally loans himself to the king, provided the boy gets thirty quadrooples each time. When on loan, Droofus projects his neck through an opening, displaying his head on the wall. He once "loses his head" by laughing hysterically during village festivities, but by now he is safe. The illustrations alone effectively tell the story.

*Good and Evil*

**Preschool and Primary Grades.** Changing from being evil to being good is the theme of *The Three Robbers* by author-illustrator Tomi Ungerer.[37] There were three terrifying robbers in large black capes and tall black hats. Dark, mysterious watercolor illustrations underscore the men's threatening natures. The men try to rob a carriage with only one passenger, five-year-old Tiffany, and take her to their hideout. After she asks what they intend to do with their wealth, they buy a castle where they house unhappy children. When the children mature, they, ''in memory of their kind foster fathers built three tall high roofed towers. One for each of the three robbers.''[38]

**Primary and Middle Grades.** Mitchell Miller's pencil sketches illustrate Jack Sendak's *The Magic Tears,*[39] whose theme is distinguishing good from evil. A magician, Marvo, saves the life of a young boy, Yanos, and asks in return that Yanos kill a magic wolf, Senta. Yanos must also collect tears from a magic girl, Chiardi, who lives in the forest. She tells the boy that Marvo is the evil one, and though confused, he agrees with her. ''He hoped that he would always know the difference between good and bad.''[40] In the end, Yanos causes Marvo to melt by kissing him on the nose.

*Ingenuity*

**Primary and Middle Grades.** In black and white with red and amber highlights, Robert E. Barry offers humorous illustrations that support the bravery-through-ingenuity theme of his book, *Faint George.*[41] Motivated to be a bold knight, Faint George makes himself the shiniest armor and builds the finest castle but cannot slay a dragon. Instead, he tricks one to come inside his castle, and the dragon becomes a base for a mobile home. A stylized illustration shows the castle on the dragon's back and Faint George riding the creature. The knight feels brave at last, not from slaying the dragon, but through ingenuity.

*Friendship*

**Preschool and Primary Grades.** Friendship between a boy and a reptile is the theme of *The Mysterious Tadpole* by author-illustrator Steven Kellogg.[42] On his fifth birthday, Louis receives from his uncle in Scotland a so-called tadpole that the boy names Alphonse. The friendly green creature with pink spots soon outgrows a jar, then a sink and a bathtub. During the summer, Louis takes Alphonse to the junior-high pool to keep him from being sent to the zoo. Louis visits him daily, bringing cheeseburgers that he earns by delivering newspapers. A librarian, Miss Seeves, guides Alphonse to buried treasure in the ocean. This discovery yields enough money to purchase a parking lot and convert it into a pool where city children swim with Alphonse. The disconcerting note in the happy ending is that, on his sixth birthday, Louis receives from the same Scottish uncle an egg that hatches into an unusual bird, initiating what may become a new cycle of events. Full-color illustrations humorously depict the book's theme, friendship with a Loch Ness Monster.

**Preschool through Middle Grades.** David L. Harrison's *The Book of Giant Stories,* illustrated by Philippe Fix, has three stories with a theme of friendship and honesty in the world of giants.[43] In "The Little Boy's Secret," three giants free a young lad who is honest enough to share his secret: He is getting measles. "The Giant Who Was Afraid of Butterflies" is about a giant bewitched into seeing everything doubly enlarged. A friendly lad corrects his vision with glasses before the giant gets the spell removed. "The Giant Who Threw Tantrums" shows how a lad teaches a giant to whistle, ending his tantrums and earning his praise: "You're a good friend."[44] Each illustration by the Parisian illustrator, Philippe Fix, is a small, full-color masterpiece. The boy's head is shown so small it equals a giant's eye.

**Primary and Middle Grades.** The power of friendship is the theme of *The Amazing Bone,*[45] a book about personified animals by author-illustrator William Steig. A young pig, Pearl, discovers a talking bone, puts it in her purse, and chats with it in a friendly way. When robbers attack, the bone frightens them away. A fox captures them and plans to eat Pearl, but the bone puts a spell on the fox that causes him to shrink. Free at last, Pearl takes the bone home to be her lifetime friend. Steig's humorous illustrations in watercolor show the power of friendship in a world where animals dress like people.

*Love*

**Primary and Middle Grades.** Another book by author-illustrator William Steig, *Caleb and Kate,*[46] has true love as its theme. After a husband and wife have a lovers' quarrel, Caleb takes a walk in a forest where the witch, Yedida, turns him into a dog. The dog becomes Kate's pet, but when he tries to protect her from burglars, his paw is slashed. The cut breaks the spell, and he becomes a man again, one who loves his wife dearly. An illustration that accentuates the theme shows Kate crying for her missing husband.

*Dreams and Wishes*

**Preschool and Primary Grades.** Ruth Krauss's *I Want to Paint My Bathroom Blue,*[47] illustrated by Maurice Sendak, is built around a theme of dreams. A young boy speaks of forbidden things he dreams about doing, such as: "I want to paint my bathroom blue—my papa won't let me paint it blue."[48] He adds, "I'll make a house the kind I dream about, not the kind I see," one with a horse in the bedroom or painted like a rainbow. Sendak's illustrations extend the theme.

Equally fanciful are the illustrations of Andre François in John Symonds's *The Magic Currant Bun*,[49] which is built around a theme of wishes leading to adventure. When Pierre hears a currant bun in a bakery begging to be rescued, he grabs it. People think he is a thief and chase him, but he escapes with the help of the currant bun, who grants him wishes as he eats the currants. After a policeman captures Pierre, the boy uses his last wish to make the short policeman nine feet tall, and the officer is grateful. At last, Pierre returns home where he dreams of buns without currants. His fanciful adventures are illustrated humorously in black and white with green highlights.

Irene Haas provides full-color paintings and black-and-white illustrations for her book, *The Maggie B.*,[50] which has the theme of wish fulfillment. Young Margaret Barnstable realizes her wish to be joined by her younger brother, James, and sail for a day on a boat named for her. The illustrations help depict the theme, for they show Margaret in charge of her boat, *The Maggie B.* In one view, she is an artist on the upper deck surrounded by a goat, rooster, and chickens in a garden.

Maggie fantasizes being aboard ship, and Shirley is at the shore fantasizing in *Come Away from the Water, Shirley* by English author-illustrator John Burningham.[51] Two different points of view are expressed in text and full-color illustrations. The right-hand wordless pages show in watercolor and colored-pencil illustrations exciting experiences of the child and a dog. From Shirley's point of view, the primary theme is daydreamed adventures resulting in her becoming a pirate queen. On the left-hand side in colored-pencil illustrations are Shirley's parents in beach chairs. The father is silent, but a realistic point of view is expressed by a stereotyped nagging mother. She issues endless warnings, like "Of course it's too cold for swimming, Shirley," and "Don't stroke that dog, Shirley, you don't know where he's been."[52]

**Preschool through Middle Grades.** Author-illustrator Maurice Sendak says the common theme in his books may be grossly simplified thus: "It's all right to be a child. It's all right to defy your parents. It's all right to get angry. It's all right to be alive and enjoy yourself!"[53] He shows the gamut of these emotions before, during, and after a dream sequence in *Where the Wild Things Are*.[54] The night a young boy, Max, wears his wolf suit, his mother calls him a Wild Thing. After defying her, he has to go to his room without supper. He dreams that his room is a jungle where the Wild Things are, and he tames these monsters before becoming their king. Then he returns to his room where his loving mother has left a hot supper for him. Sendak uses tempera paints and black felt pen for his illustrations, increasing the size of his monsters for emphasis during their rumpus.

Sendak considers *In the Night Kitchen* to be a companion volume to *Where the Wild Things Are*,[55] but he changes Max's name in the second book to Mickey. In humorous cartoon-like illustrations, he shows Mickey dreaming about shedding his clothes to visit the night kitchen where there are three cake bakers who look like Oliver Hardy. When they need milk, he gets it by traveling on a homemade bread-dough airplane to the Milky Way (a huge milk bottle). After his dreamed adventure, Mickey returns to his room and resumes sleeping.

Sendak created *In the Night Kitchen,* which shows a subway train made of bread, as an homage to New York City. He completed it before moving to Connecticut. It has drawn criticism from some librarians because of Mickey's nudity. The total work, inspired by a Sunshine Bakers' advertisement, "We bake while you sleep," embodies "nine hundred condensed fantasies."[56]

## Imagination

**Primary through Upper Grades.** According to Maurice Sendak, his book, *Outside Over There* is part of a trilogy that includes *Where the Wild Things Are* and *In the Night Kitchen*.[57] The latest book, set in the eighteenth century, appeals to more sophisticated children than its predecessors. In two beautiful pastel illustrations, Sendak includes his dog, Agamemnon. Near the end in a view beside a stream, he shows a pianist, apparently Mozart. In an interview, Sendak, who plays music while he creates, says, "For this particular book, I listened only to Mozart."[58] Sendak tells about young Ida who tends her baby sister while her father is at sea and her lonely mother is in the arbor. Inside, when Ida turns her back to play her wonder horn, faceless goblins kidnap her sister, taking her to an imaginary place: outside over there. Ida follows, plays her wonder horn, and makes goblin babies dance in such frenzy, they dissolve in a stream. After rescuing her sister, Ida brings her home where her mother reads Papa's letter urging Ida to watch baby and Mama in his absence. An imaginary rescue is the book's theme.

The power of convincing imagination is the theme of *Jumanji*,[59] written by Chris Van Allsburg and illustrated by him in black and white with Conte dust used with Conte pencil. The surreal story describes how, alone for an afternoon, Judy and Peter are bored until they discover in the park a mystical jungle board game, Jumanji. A child's note taped on the box warns, "Free game, fun for some but not for all. P.S. Read instructions carefully."[60] The directions state the game, once started, is over only when a player reaches Golden City and says, "Jumanji." Unusual is the fact that adventures cited on the board actually come to life. Judy and Peter experience a lion, python, monsoon, volcano, and two monkeys, along with tsetse flies and rhinoceros stampedes before Judy reaches the Golden City, yelling "Jumanji!" The house instantly becomes as it was before the onslaught, and the children quickly return the game to the park. They are asleep when their parents and guests come home, but adults believe Peter's report of the afternoon is a dream. A guest, Mrs. Budwing, complains that her sons, Daniel and Walter, never read game instructions. Meanwhile, a view from the window shows Daniel and Walter leaving the park carrying a box.

## Summary

This chapter discusses the primary theme of thirty-seven examples of prizewinning fanciful picture storybooks. Animal fantasy is treated in another chapter. Themes are presented under seventeen topics, the most popular being dreams and wishes. Most of the books are appropriate for preschool and primary grades or preschool through middle grades. Only one book is intended for preschool alone and only one for primary through upper grades.

In this sample, several prizewinners have been created by the same author or illustrator. Maurice Sendak is illustrator of five fanciful prizewinners, three of which he has also written. William Steig and Chris Van Allsburg are author-illustrators of two, and Jane Yolen has written two, both of which are illustrated by Ed Young.

## Notes

1. In 1969, *Little Toot* won the Lewis Carroll Shelf Award.
2. Hardie Gramatky, *Little Toot* (New York: Putnam, 1939), no page.
3. In 1943, *The Little House* won The Randolph Caldecott Medal.
4. Virginia Lee Burton, *The Little House* (Boston: Houghton, 1942), p. 1.
5. In 1976, *Little Pieces of the West Wind* won the Southern California Council on Literature for Children and Young People Award for illustrations.

6. In 1973, *The Girl Who Loved the Wind* won the Lewis Carroll Shelf Award and the Children's Book Showcase.

7. Jane Yolen, *The Girl Who Loved the Wind* (New York: Crowell, 1972), no page.

8. In 1958, *The Little Engine that Could* won the Lewis Carroll Shelf Award.

9. Watty Piper, *The Little Engine that Could* (New York: Platt and Munk, 1930), no page.

10. Ibid, no page.

11. In 1968, *The Emperor and the Kite* was a Caldecott Honor Book.

12. In 1979, *The Night Stella Hid the Stars* won the American Institute of Graphic Arts Book Show Award.

13. Ibid.

14. In 1972, *Hildilid's Night* was a Caldecott Honor Book and a finalist for the National Book Award in the children's-book category.

15. In 1969, *The Tomten* won the Lewis Carroll Shelf Award.

16. In 1947, *The Little Island* won The Randolph Caldecott Medal.

17. Golden MacDonald, *The Little Island* (New York: Doubleday, 1946), no page.

18. In 1950, *Bartholomew and the Oobleck* was a Caldecott Honor Book.

19. In 1976, *The Devil Did It* won the Friends of American Writers Award.

20. In 1979, *The Garden of Abdul Gasazi* was a *New York Times* Best Illustrated Children's Book of the Year. In 1980, it was a Caldecott Honor Book and won the *Boston Globe-Horn Book* Award for illustration and the Irma Simonton Black Award.

21. In 1978, *Cloudy with a Chance of Meatballs* was a *New York Times* Choice of Best Illustrated Children's Book of the Year, and in 1979, it was in the American Institute of Graphic Arts Book Show.

22. In 1978, *The Sweet Touch* won the Colorado Children's Book Award and the Georgia Children's Picture Storybook Award.

23. In 1958, *What Do You Say, Dear?* was a *New York Times* Choice of Best Illustrated Children's Book of the Year, and in 1959, it was a Caldecott Honor Book.

24. Sesyle Joslin, *What Do You Say, Dear?* (Reading, Mass.: Scott, 1958), p. 5.

25. In 1971, *The Shrinking of Treehorn* was a *New York Times* Choice of Best Illustrated Children's Book of the Year.

26. Florence Parry Heide, *The Shrinking of Treehorn* (New York: Holiday House, 1971), no page.

27. Ibid., no page.

28. In 1976, *Morris's Disappearing Bag: A Christmas Story* won the Irma Simonton Black Award.

29. In 1960, *Nine Days to Christmas, a Story of Mexico* won The Randolph Caldecott Medal.

30. Marie Hall Ets and Aurora Labastida, *Nine Day to Christmas, a Story of Mexico* (New York: Viking, 1959), p. 46.

31. In 1958, *The Magic Feather Duster* was a *New York Times* Choice of Best Illustrated Children's Book of the Year.

32. In 1977, *Everyone Knows What a Dragon Looks Like* won the Irma Simonton Black Award and was a *New York Times* Choice of Best Illustrated Children's Book of the Year.

33. Jay Williams, *Everyone Knows What a Dragon Looks Like* (New York: Four Winds, 1976), p. 14.

34. Ibid., p. 20.

35. In 1976, *How Droofus the Dragon Lost His Head* won the Colorado Children's Book Award and the Young Reader Medal.

36. Bill Peet, *How Droofus the Dragon Lost His Head* (Boston: Houghton, 1971), p. 19.

37. In 1962, *The Three Robbers* was a *New York Times* Choice of Best Illustrated Children's Book of the Year.

38. Tomi Ungerer, *The Three Robbers* (New York: Atheneum, 1962), p. 35.

39. In 1971, *The Magic Tears* was a *New York Times* Choice of Best Illustrated Children's Book of the Year.

40. Jack Sendak, *The Magic Tears* (New York: Harper, 1971), p. 49.

41. In 1957, *Faint George* was a *New York Times* Choice of Best Illustrated Children's Book of the Year.

42. In 1978, *The Mysterious Tadpole* won the Irma Simonton Black Award.

43. In 1972, *The Book of Giant Stories* won the Christopher Award in the children's-book category.

44. David L. Harrison, *The Book of Giant Stories* (New York: American Heritage, 1972), p. 42.

45. In 1977, *The Amazing Bone* was a Caldecott Honor Book.

46. In 1978, *Caleb and Kate* won the National Book Award in the children's book category.

47. In 1956, *I Want to Paint My Bathroom Blue* was a *New York Times* Choice of Best Illustrated Children's Book of the Year.

48. Ruth Krauss, *I Want to Paint My Bathroom Blue* (New York: Harper, 1956), p. 1.

49. In 1952, *The Magic Currant Bun* was a *New York Times* Choice of Best Illustrated Children's Book of the Year.

50. In 1976, *The Maggie B.* won the Irma Simonton Black Award.

51. In 1977, *Come Away from the Water, Shirley* was a *New York Times* Choice of Best Illustrated Children's Book of the Year.

52. John Burningham, *Come Away from the Water, Shirley* (New York: Crowell, 1977), no page.

53. "Maurice Sendak," *Profiles in Literature* (Philadelphia: Temple University, 1977).

54. In 1963, *Where the Wild Things Are* was a *New York Times* Choice of Best Illustrated Children's Book of the Year. In 1964, it won The Randolph Caldecott Medal, and in 1966, it was put on the International Board on Books for Young People Honor List.

55. In 1970, *In the Night Kitchen* was a *New York Times* Choice of Best Illustrated Children's Book of the Year, and in 1971, it was a Caldecott Honor Book.

56. "Maurice Sendak," *Profiles in Literature* (Philadelphia: Temple University, 1977).

57. In 1982, *Outside Over There* was a Caldecott Honor Book and won The American Book Award for picture books.

58. "Maurice Sendak," *Profiles in Literature* (Philadelphia: Temple University, 1977).

59. In 1982, *Jumanji* won The Randolph Caldecott Medal.

60. Chris Van Allsburg, *Jumanji* (Boston: Houghton, 1981), no page.

**References of Prizewinning Modern Fantasy
in Picture Storybooks**

*(Estimated Reading or Listening Grade Level in
Parentheses)*

Balian, Lorna. *The Sweet Touch*. Nashville: Abingdon, 1976 (K–3).

Barrett, Judi. *Cloudy with a Chance of Meatballs*. Illustrated by Ron Barrett. New York: Atheneum, 1979 (PS–3).

Barry, Robert E. *Faint George*. Boston: Houghton, 1957 (1–3).

Burningham, John. *Come Away from the Water, Shirley*. New York: Crowell, 1977 (K–2).

Burton, Virginia Lee. *The Little House*. Boston: Houghton, 1942 (1–3).

Ets, Marie Hall, and Labastida, Aurora. *Nine Days to Christmas, a Story of Mexico*. Illustrated by Marie Hall Ets. New York: Viking, 1959 (K–2).

Garrison, Christian. *Little Pieces of the West Wind*. Illustrated by Diane Goode. New York: Bradbury, 1975 (PS–1).

Gramatky, Hardie. *Little Toot*. New York: Putnam, 1939 (K–3).

Haas, Irene. *The Maggie B*. New York: Atheneum, 1978 (K–2).

Harrison, David L. *The Book of Giant Stories*. Illustrated by Philippe Fix. New York: American Heritage, 1972 (K–3).

Heide, Florence Parry. *The Shrinking of Treehorn*. New York: Holiday House, 1971 (2–6).

Jeshke, Susan. *The Devil Did It*. New York: Holt, 1975 (K–3).

Joslin, Sesyle. *What Do You Say, Dear?* Illustrated by Maurice Sendak. Reading, Mass.: Scott, 1958 (1–3).

Kellogg, Steve. *The Mysterious Tadpole*. New York: Dial, 1977 (PS–2).

Krauss, Ruth. *I Want to Paint My Bathroom Blue*. Illustrated by Maurice Sendak. New York: Harper, 1956 (PS–1).

Lindgren, Astrid. *The Tomten*. Illustrated by Harold Wiberg. New York: Coward, 1967 (PS–2).

Lipkind, William. *The Magic Feather Duster*. Illustrated by Nicolas Mordvinoff. New York: Harcourt, 1958 (K–2).

MacDonald, Golden. *The Little Island*. Illustrated by Leonard Weisgard. New York: Doubleday, 1946 (PS–2).

Peet, Bill. *How Droofus the Dragon Lost His Head*. Boston: Houghton, 1971 (K–3).

Piper, Watty. *The Little Engine that Could*. Illustrated by George and Doris Hauman. New York: Platt and Munk, 1930 (PS–3).

Radley, Gail. *The Night Stella Hid the Stars*. Illustrated by John Wallner. New York: Crown, 1978 (K–2).

Ryan, Cheli Durán. *Hildilid's Night*. Illustrated by Arnold Lobel. New York: Macmillan, 1971 (K–2).

Sendak, Jack. *The Magic Tears*. Illustrated by Mitchell Miller. New York: Harper, 1971 (1–3).

Sendak, Maurice. *In the Night Kitchen*. New York: Harper, 1970 (K–3).

———. *Outside Over There*. New York: Harper, 1981 (2–5).

———. *Where the Wild Things Are*. New York: Harper, 1963 (K–3).

Seuss, Dr. *Bartholomew and the Oobleck*. New York: Random, 1947 (K–3).

Steig, William. *The Amazing Bone*. New York: Farrar, 1976 (1–3).

———. *Caleb and Kate*. New York: Farrar, 1977 (1–3).

Symonds, John. *The Magic Currant Bun*. Illustrated by Andre François. Philadelphia: Lippincott, 1952 (K–2).

Ungerer, Tomi. *The Three Robbers*. New York: Atheneum, 1962 (PS–1).

Van Allsburg, Chris. *The Garden of Abdul Gasazi*. Boston: Houghton, 1979 (2–5).

———. *Jumanji*. Boston: Houghton, 1981 (2–5).

Wells, Rosemary. *Morris's Disappearing Bag*. New York: Dial, 1975 (PS–K).

Williams, Jay. *Everyone Knows What a Dragon Looks Like*. Illustrated by Mercer Mayer. New York: Four Winds, 1976 (K–3).

Yolen, Jane. *The Emperor and the Kite*. Illustrated by Ed Young. New York: World, 1967 (K–3).

———. *The Girl Who Loved the Wind*. Illustrated by Ed Young. New York: Crowell, 1972 (1–3).

# 5 Animal Fantasy in Picture Storybooks

*I like* Chanticleer and the Fox, *a story about animals that act like people. I also like* The Girl Who Loved Wild Horses, *about a girl who turns into a horse. These two books are about different times and are drawn differently, but both have great pictures. Another good book is very easy. It's* Inch by Inch, *about an inchworm that's used to measure things. The man who drew it must like jokes.* —Stella, aged seven

## Perspective

Stella's first-choice book, *Chanticleer and the Fox,* is adapted by author-illustrator Barbara Cooney from ''The Nun's Priest's Tale'' in Geoffrey Chaucer's *Canterbury Tales.* Cooney had a live rooster and chickens in her studio as models for Chanticleer and his harem. She also studied rare illuminated manuscripts, bringing their brilliantly colored portrayal of medieval life into some of her illustrations.

While *Chanticleer and the Fox* shows animals personified, the second book Stella mentions, *The Girl Who Loved Wild Horses* by author-illustrator Paul Goble, moves in the opposite direction. Here a Native American identifies so much with horses, she herself becomes a mare. Goble's illustrations are full-color paintings in dark, bold tones. He knows much about Native Americans, for he is artist-in-residence at the Gallery of Indian and Western Arts at Mount Rushmore National Memorial in the Black Hills of South Dakota.

Stella's third picture storybook, *Inch by Inch,* has less text than the two previous ones. With watercolors, author-illustrator Leo Lionni depicts ingenuity as a theme, showing an inchworm in a collage setting that includes tissue-paper foliage.

Stella's three titles are animal-fantasy picture storybooks, popular prizewinners. The animals that predominate in such tales are often personified, talk, or reflect human values, like wanting to reciprocate kindness or be heroic. The primary theme of each prizewinner will be discussed after books are organized in topical groups.

**Themes of Prizewinning Animal Fantasy
in Picture Storybooks Grouped under These Topics**

*Nature*

**Preschool and Primary Grades.** Ruth Krauss's *The Happy Day,*[1] illustrated by Marc Simont, expresses the joy of seasonal change as its theme. The black-and-white illustrations first show animals hibernating and then awakening to play in the snow. The forest creatures celebrate in the following way when they see the first signs of spring:

> The field mice, ground hogs, bears, squirrels, and snails . . . sniff, run, stop, laugh, dance. . . . They cry, "Oh! A flower is growing in the snow."[2]

**Preschool through Middle Grades.** Alice and Martin Provensen are the authors and illustrators of *The Animal Fair*[3], a collection of short stories and poems with themes centering on animals. For example, the theme of "A Winter Story" is protecting a pet deer, and for "The Carpenters," it is personified animals uniting against a suspected enemy. There are full-color illustrations of wild and tame animals as well as birds and fish.

Animal survival during a snowy winter is the theme of Berta and Elmer Hader's *The Big Snow,*[4] which they illustrate in black and white and in watercolor. The Haders tell how the sight of geese heading south alerts animals to prepare for winter, and a rainbow around the moon warns them of snow. Deer and rabbits grow thicker coats, and raccoons, skunks, and groundhogs get ready to hibernate. When the big snow covers the animals' stored feed, an aged couple leaves food in their yard for the forest creatures until spring.

Another book by Berta and Elmer Hader, *The Mighty Hunter,*[5] has the theme of learning reverence for life. The Haders present some black-and-white and some watercolor illustrations as well as end papers with a blue-and-white pictograph of their story. They tell about Little Brave Heart, who one day chooses to hunt rather than go to school. He aims his bow and arrow at a wood rat, prairie dog, rabbit, wildcat, antelope, wolf, and buffalo. Each one asks him to defer shooting until he has larger prey. The buffalo leads the boy to a grizzly who growls, "Hunting for fun! . . . I only hunt when I am hungry. And I am hungry right now!"[6] To escape the bear, Little Brave Heart runs to school.

**Primary and Middle Grades.** Arnold Lobel's colorful, humorous illustrations are in his *Fables,*[7] a collection of twenty fables with animals as an overall theme. Each tale concerns a different animal and has its own

theme. For example, learning from parents is the theme and moral of
"The Bad Kangaroo." This fable is about a kangaroo pupil in school
who throws spitballs, ignites firecrackers, and spreads glue on door-
knobs. When the principal sees the same behavior from the kangaroo's
parents in their home, he concludes, "A child's conduct will reflect the
ways of his parents."[8]

**Primary and Middle Grades.** Explaining why birds have feathers is the
theme of a *pourquoi* fantasy, *Feather Mountain*,[9] by author-illustrator
Elizabeth Olds. Formerly naked and taunted by other animals for being
bare, birds stop singing and resume only when, directed by the Great
Spirit, they receive feathers from trees on Feather Mountain. Colorful
illustrations and inked line drawings show birds ashamed to leave their
nests because they are naked, candidates getting measured for plumage,
and turkey buzzard distributing glue to adhere feathers. There is a two-
page spread of a variety of identified birds.

*Maturing*

**Preschool.** A. Birnbaum illustrates his book, *Green Eyes*,[10] in watercolors. The first year of life, the book's theme, is revealed by the narrator, a white cat named Green Eyes. He cites his experiences on a farm
throughout the seasons.

**Preschool and Primary Grades.** Growing, but still loved, is the theme
of Ruth Bornstein's *Little Gorilla*.[11] When Little Gorilla is small, everyone loves him. Then one day, something happens: Little Gorilla begins
to grow and grow. Despite his huge size, everyone still loves him. This
notion is conveyed in humorous red, green, and brown illustrations with
few details.

Jean Charlot's rose, green, and white lithographs are featured in
Miriam Schlein's *When Will the World Be Mine? The Story of a Snowshoe
Rabbit*.[12] This story with a growing-up theme tells how Little Rabbit's
extended paws serve as snowshoes. He has protective coloring, a white
coat in winter and a brown one in summer. Mother Rabbit teaches her
child to strip tree bark, hide in a thicket, and drink from a stream. She
asks, "Now do you see how easy it is for all of the world that you need
to be yours?"[13] When he comprehends, he is ready for his own nest.

*Changing*

**Preschool through Middle Grades.** The title, *Nothing at All* by author-
illustrator Wanda Gág, suggests the theme of changing from invisibility

(nothing at all) to visibility in order to be nurtured.[14] A boy and girl adopt two out of three brother dogs, but the third one is left behind because no one can see him. He says, "I never minded looking like nothing-at-all . . . but now I long to look like other dogs so I will be adopted and fed like my two brothers."[15] He meets Jackdaw who has a Book of Magic with a chapter on "Nothingness and Somethingness." Jackdaw gradually changes empty space into a dog known as Roundy when adopted by the boy and girl. The last colored illustration is a lithograph showing three dogs, Pointy, Curly, and Roundy, identified by ear shapes, standing before appropriate dog houses with pointed, curled, or rounded roofs.

The theme, change is not always desirable, pervades *Sylvester and the Magic Pebble* by author-illustrator William Steig.[16] A donkey, Sylvester, excited because he finds a magic wishing pebble, wishes himself to change into a stone to escape a lion. He regrets the granted wish, because he is petrified. The following spring, the donkey's parents, who miss him, happen to picnic on the stone that is Sylvester. They find the magic pebble, put it on the stone, and instantly, Sylvester's wish to become himself again is granted. The family is joyously reunited with no need for further wishes since they "had all that they wanted."[17] The final watercolor illustration shows their happiness. A source of controversy when the book was published in 1969 is Steig's portrayal of police as pigs.

*Young and Old*

**Preschool and Primary Grades.** Photographs by Ylla, the world's foremost animal photographer, support the theme of dream fulfillment in Arthur Gregor's *The Little Elephant*.[18] After Japu, a little elephant, dreams of attending the king's parade and learns to walk independently, his parents take him to the procession. Upon the king's invitation, Japu becomes the first baby elephant to lead a parade.

At the opposite end of the age spectrum is Limpy in *Mister Penny's Race Horse* by Marie Hall Ets.[19] The book's theme, the value of an aged creature, is revealed when a farmer, Mister Penny, rejects his horse, Limpy, while entering other animals and produce in a fair. He explains, "Limpy is too old and knobby. The judges would laugh at him."[20] His other animals want to win to get a ride on the ferris wheel. They are so anxious, they free themselves, harm produce, including their owner's prize pumpkin, and are disqualified. It is Limpy, linked to a race cart and tethered next to the horse races, who enters the track and entertains the crowd. "That afternoon so many people came to see Limpy run on the racetrack that they could not get seats in the grandstands.''[21] The reward is a free ferris-wheel ride for Mister Penny's animals and for him, fifty dollars. Black-and-white lithographs reinforce the theme, for they show old Limpy, complete with bandages, capable of a great feat.

*Pretense and Imagination*

**Preschool and Primary Grades.** Lucy Bates's *Little Rabbit's Loose Tooth* depicts pretense as a theme, supported by Diane Degroat's full-color illustrations.[22] When Little Rabbit's loose tooth falls into her ice cream, she puts the tooth under her pillow and before retiring, cautions her mother, ''Just in case there isn't a tooth fairy, . . . after I'm asleep, could you sneak a peek under my pillow and look in the envelope? And if there isn't a present, could you leave one?''[23]

Like Little Rabbit, Little Fox enjoys pretending in Ann Tompert's *Little Fox Goes to the End of the World*,[24] illustrated by John Wallner. The book's theme is an imaginary escape that brings satisfaction with reality. A young female fox, bored with playing near her den, fantasizes adventures to her mother. The child pretends she will travel to the end of the world, taming angry bears with honey, sailing down a river full of hungry crocodiles, and even crossing a desert and snowy mountain. In the end, she tells her mother, ''And I shall miss you, so I'll let out the North Wind and head straight for home.''[25] The spectacled mother, who is dressed in socks and stereotyped in an apron, promises to have her child's favorite dinner waiting. The theme is emphasized in black-penciled illustrations with pencil-colored overlays printed in four hues.

*Self-Awareness*

**Preschool and Primary Grades.** Nancy Moore's *The Unhappy Hippopotamus* is illustrated simply in black, gray, white, and pink by Edward Leight.[26] Self-awareness, the book's theme, becomes apparent after Harriet decides she no longer wants to be a hippopotamus, moves into a house, and forgets how to smile. Mouse, a friend, tries to help, but it is Owl who wisely diagnoses, ''I know what's the matter with you! You've got to be YOU! You can't be somebody else!''[27] Harriet understands him when she goes to the riverbank, sheds her clothes, feels the soft mud between her toes, and wades into the water. Then she smiles and smiles.

Self-awareness is also the theme of Louise Fatio's *Hector Penguin*,[28] illustrated by Roger Duvoisin. When Hector Penguin is lost in a forest,

animals ridicule him because they have never before seen a penguin. He
starts to doubt his own worth until a learned crow announces:

> I am a well educated fellow who travels to learn about the world. I
> visited zoos and that is why I can tell you who this charming stranger
> is. He is a bird. He is a penguin. . . .[29]

After Hector proves his swimming prowess in a race with fish and ducks,
he is proud to be a penguin and makes friends near his new home, the
forest pond.

**Preschool through Middle Grades.** Adrienne Adams is author-illustrator
of *The Easter Egg Artists* which features the Abbotts, a rabbit family.[30]
The parents paint the town's Easter eggs, but in the beginning, their son
Orson does not help. The book, which shows Orson's discovery of his
talents, is created with a theme of self-awareness. After Orson helps
paint Easter egg decorations on the family's car and vacation house, an
aviator gets him to decorate the top and bottom of his plane. He even
decorates a bridge and flagpole and originates comical Easter eggs. The
precise watercolor illustrations depicting Orson's new talents are essential
for theme appreciation.

In *Pitschi* by author-illustrator Hans Fischer, the theme of self-awareness is expressed, for Pitschi is at first dissatisfied that he is a kitten.[31]
After traveling around the farm, he realizes he does not want to be a
rooster, goat, duck, or rabbit. When he is sick and his owner, Lisette,
cares for him, he appreciates being a kitten. Pitschi is sympathetically
drawn in illustrations with blue, red, green, yellow, and brown highlights.

*Mischief Maker*

**Preschool and Primary Grades.** A mischief maker in a hospital is the
theme of *Curious George Goes to the Hospital* by authors and illustrators
Margret and H.A. Rey.[32] When a monkey, Curious George, swallows a
jigsaw-puzzle piece, he goes to a hospital for an operation. While he is
recovering in the children's ward, he races on a go-cart down a hospital
ramp, upsetting lunch carts and landing in a visiting mayor's arms. Authorities forgive him because his antics make a sad patient laugh. George
is personified in cartoon style but does not talk.

*Curious George Gets a Medal* is another book in the series illustrated
in watercolor and written by H.A. Rey alone.[33] The book's theme is
purposeful activity at last from a mischief maker. When George receives
a letter, he tries to respond, spilling ink. In an effort to clean the ink,

he floods the house. He needs a pump and gets into more trouble when he tries to borrow one from a farmer. He escapes on a truck that takes him to a museum. The museum director, Professor Wiseman, wants to punish him for ruining a museum display, but learns that the letter to George invites him to participate in an outer-space experiment. George accepts, successfully bails from a space ship in flight, and receives a gold medal in recognition.

*Learning to Give*

**Preschool and Primary Grades.** Eve Titus's *Anatole* takes place in a village near Paris, France.[34] Illustrator Paul Galdone at times aptly adds to his black-line drawings purple and the colors of the French flag, blue, white, and red. Anatole is a beret-wearing, bicycling mouse who takes cheese from the cheese factory for his wife, Ducette, and their six mice children. Anatole tells Ducette how upset he is to learn people despise mice, and she laments, "If only we could give people something in return—But alas, that is impossible!"[35] Anatole, a mouse of honor, proves that giving is not impossible. Therefore, learning how to give is the book's theme. Anatole's contribution is to write notes on the cheeses in M'sieur Duval's factory, suggesting improvements. The factory recognizes his skill as cheese taster and allows this mouse *magnifique* to take whatever cheese he needs.

**Preschool through Middle Grades.** Learning to give is the primary theme of *Exactly Alike* by author-illustrator Evaline Ness,[36] who dresses her characters in nineteenth-century attire, using red, blue, olive, and brown as her color scheme. Elizabeth cannot distinguish between quadruplets in red middy suits who are her young identical brothers, Benny, Bertie, Buzzie, and Biff. Her small toy, William, a talking horse, counsels her to observe carefully, then give and take. She says her brothers may play with her most precious toys if they supply her with their names, but they refuse. When she gives them her toys without expecting anything, they give her their playthings and supply their names which she associates with characteristics, like Benny Freckle Nose, Bertie Fox Ears, Buzzie Blue Eye, and Biff Dimple. She self-critically concludes:

> She had treated it like "give and get." She realized now that "give" meant giving, without asking for something in return as she had done.[37]

*Ingenuity*

**Preschool and Primary Grades.** Eve Titus's *Anatole and the Cat*,[38] a sequel to *Anatole*, reflects its French setting in the flag on the book's cover. Paul Galdone's illustrations are in black and white with blue and red added on some pages. The book's ingenuity theme becomes apparent when the mouse, Anatole, copes with a cat who threatens his factory position as vice president in charge of cheese tasting. He decides, "If a man may build a mouse-trap, then a mouse may build a cat-trap!"[39] Anatole puts a cord with a bell on it around the neck of the sleeping cat. The bell cautions Anatole when the cat approaches. Before belling the cat, frightened Anatole puts the wrong suggestions on cheese, accidently inventing a new type of cheese.

*A Holiday for Mister Muster* by author-illustrator Arnold Lobel is created on an ingenuity theme.[40] A loving zoo keeper, Mister Muster, takes zoo animals for a seashore ride to breathe salt air. When it is departure time, the animals refuse to leave amusement-park rides, so Mister Muster cleverly wears a disguise and gets animals on board by making his bus seem like an amusement ride. Lobel's yellow-and-black illustrations show how they "all wanted to try the most exciting ride in the whole amusement park and quickly climbed on the bus."[41] Arriving at the zoo, the upset animals think they left Mister Muster behind, but are delighted when the driver removes his disguise.

Ingenuity is also the theme of *Inch by Inch,*[42] written and illustrated with collage by Leo Lionni. An inchworm measures a toucan's beak and the legs of a heron. When a nightingale wants his song measured, the inchworm at first replies, "I measure things not songs."[43] If his demand is not fulfilled, the bird threatens to eat the worm, so the inchworm asks for the song to begin. The nightingale closes his eyes to concentrate on singing, and the inchworm cleverly measures until he inches out of sight. The illustrations of the backward-moving worm help convey the theme.

**Preschool through Middle Grades.** The illustrations also help convey the ingenuity theme of *The Church Mice Adrift* by author-illustrator Graham Oakley.[44] The full-color pictures, often arranged in two columns on a page, have so many comical details, the reader may need a magnifying glass to appreciate posted signs. Forced out of their town-hall home, rats displace mice in the church vestry. With ingenuity, Sampson the cat helps mice repossess their church home. Sampson laments:

> "What I do for those mice," he sighed as he strolled out to think up a plan, but deep down he knew it was really his own reputation he had to do something for.[45]

Sampson's successful plan lures rats from the church with free food that mice scavenge. The mice convert a dollhouse into Riverside Restaurant. The plan is to get all mice away from the restaurant before setting it afloat with only rats aboard, but two mice, Arthur and Humphrey, fail to escape. Sampson rescues them, and the church mice return to the vestry.

*Origin*

**Primary and Middle Grades.** Humorous lithographs by William Pène du Bois illustrate his book, *Lion*.[46] The origin of the lion is the theme of this fanciful *pourquoi* tale which explains that long ago, heavenly artists designed each beast and sent a pair to Planet Earth. In the sky, 104 artistic angels, with ermine brushes dipped in gold paint, work in the drawing room of the Animal Factory, determining the sight and sound of each animal. It is the boss, Artist Foreman, who thinks of a new word, lion. With the help of his colleagues, he draws the present King of Beasts, finally deciding the lion should roar, not say, ''Peep peep!'' In his black-and-white illustrations, du Bois colors animals to accentuate them. He has bright, inviting end paper with a lion's heraldic crest.

*Sharing*

**Preschool and Primary Grades.** Will Lipkind's *Finders Keepers*[47] illustrated by Nicolas Mordvinoff, has sharing as its theme. When two dogs, Nap and Winkle, fight over the same bone, they bury it and seek a third party who can judge their dispute. A haymaker, goat, and barber are indifferent, but a mean dog gets them to dig up the bone, and he tries to take it. After Nap and Winkle chase their enemy away, the story concludes:

> Nap took one end of the bone and Winkle took the other end of the bone and they both chewed away at it together, without another word.[48]

**Primary Grades.** Papa Mouse tells seven bedtime stories, one to each of his mouse sons in *Mouse Tales* by author-illustrator Arnold Lobel.[49] There is no common theme in this beginning reader, though all tales concern mice. One of the longest stories, ''The Very Tall Mouse and the Very Short Mouse,'' has sharing as its theme. Because of the difference in their heights, two mice see the same item differently. The tall mouse looks at a house and appreciates its roof while the short mouse inspects its cellar. However, when the tall mouse looks out a window at a rainbow, he feels he must share its beauty and lifts the short mouse. This short story's theme is enhanced by small illustrations in purple, amber, and pink tones, one of which shows tall and short mice sharing the rainbow.

**Preschool through Middle Grades.** Laurent de Brunhoff writes the series about Babar the elephant in French and illustrates it in cartoon style in bright watercolors. Sharing is the theme of one book, *Babar's Fair*.[50] At King Babar's suggestion, on the anniversary of the founding of the elephant city, Celesteville, different animals hold a fair. They display fine items from their countries for a month and share their cultures.

*Cooperation*

**Preschool and Primary Grades.** *Swimmy* by author-illustrator Leo Lionni depicts the theme of cooperation in both text and illustrations.[51] The underwater scenes combine watercolor, linoleum block prints, and collage with lace paper doilies. Lionni tells about a small black fish who is alone in the sea after a large fish devours his kin. When he meets a school of red fish hiding in a cave, he convinces them for self-protection "to swim all together like the biggest fish in the sea!"[52] The final illustration shows Swimmy acting like an eye of black hue with red fish surrounding him in the shape of a fish that is large enough to scare contenders.

**Primary and Middle Grades.** Nancy Sherman's *Gwendolyn and the Weathercock*,[53] with page-by-page illustrations by Edward Sorel, has cooperation as its theme. Gwendolyn, a hen, organizes Farmer Brown's animals, and they help him survive attacks by a wicked man, Nimbus Flood.

*Virtue Rewarded*

**Preschool through Middle Grades.** Kindness returned by kindness is the virtue-rewarded theme of *The Happy Hunter* written by Roger Duvoisin and illustrated by him in pen and ink highlighted by earth-tone watercolors.[54] Mr. Bobbin, who lives alone in the woods, buys a hunting outfit, gun, and cartridges. Every autumn, he goes hunting, but as he starts to pull the trigger, he hums, sings, whistles, sneezes, coughs, or blows his nose. Af first, animals hide, but later realize Mr. Bobbin is near and continue their activities. Though he never fires his gun, he says at night, "Well that was another beautiful hunting day. I had a lovely walk through the forest."[55] After Mr. Bobbin is too old to hunt, he sits on his porch, and his animal friends reward the kind man by visiting him.

Virtue rewarded is also the theme of *Mouse Café*,[56] written by Patricia Coombs and illustrated by her in black, white, brown, and pink. Lollymops, a diligent, forgiving mouse, is unjustly expelled from her mother's house by her sisters and becomes a waitress for Ella, owner of Mouse Café. Other mouse waitresses resent the newcomer, thinking;

> Lollymops was dumb because she was happy and smiled as she wrote down orders and poured coffee and set the tables and propped up the menus.[57]

When Ella assigns Lollymops to wait on wealthy Mr. Hodges, other waitresses trip her, and she spills soup on him. The forgiving man loves her, so he proposes, and the next day, they marry.

**Primary and Middle Grades.** *Andy and the Lion*,[58] a modern version of Aesop's *Androcles and the Lion,* is written by James Daugherty and illustrated by him with humor and vigor in ocher and brown tones. This is historical animal fantasy set *circa* 1900, as judged from the illustrations of women in high-buttoned shoes and long dresses and men with handlebar, waxed moustaches. Its virtue-rewarded theme is stated on the title page as ''a tale of kindness remembered or the power of gratitude.''[59] In the town of Andersonville, Andy is so influenced by the library's copy of *Androcles and the Lion* that he imagines meeting his own lion and extracting a thorn from its paw. He also imagines later going to a circus where the escaping lion recognizes Andy in the audience and, remembering his kindness, dances with him. Andy won't allow the crowd to hurt the lion. He is honored for his bravery with a parade and a medal from the mayor. The next day, Andy leads the lion while finishing his book en route to the library, and the reader infers the lion will disappear with the return of the book.

*Heroism*

**Preschool and Primary Grades.** David McPhail, author-illustrator of *Captain Toad and the Motorbike* portrays a theme of heroism in his text and expressive pictures done in pencil and soft color washes.[60] Captain Toad, a former Navy hero and renowned jumper, lives in quiet retirement in Basher's Hollow. Upset because cross-country motorbike racers will come through their village, the residents dig a ditch to trap racers. Captain Toad prevents the catastrophe. When he sees the lead motorbike heading for the ditch, he substitutes himself for the rider, jumps over the ditch on his bike, and wins the silver cup. Other racers are frightened away, so villagers celebrate the captain's heroism with a sign:

> Here lives Captain Toad
> Who won the race
> And saved this place.[61]

Heroism that wins friends is the theme of *Lyle, Lyle, Crocodile* by author-illustrator Bernard Waber.[62] Mr. and Mrs. Primm and their son, Joshua, live in a Manhattan apartment with a pet personified crocodile, Lyle. Two neighbors, Mr. Grumps and his cat, Loretta, do not appreciate Lyle even when the reptile flashes a friendly toothsome smile. These neighbors have Lyle sent to the zoo where he meets his former stage partner, Signor Valenti. Before the partners leave to perform in Australia, Lyle visits the Primms. He notices smoke from Mr. Grumps's house and rescues the sleeping occupants. Mr. Grumps admits:

> Lyle is the bravest, kindest, most wonderful crocodile in the whole, wide world. I would consider it a privilege and a pleasure to have him as our neighbor once more.[63]

Lyle's heroism and good nature are shown in humorous black-and-white illustrations enriched with yellow and red on some pages, but always with the green crocodile outstanding.

**Preschool through Middle Grades.** Heroism, the theme of Reiner Zimnik's *Little Owl*,[64] is conveyed in Hanne Axmann's colorful red, yellow, blue, green, and purple illustrations. No one knows that little owl lives in the horse's leg of a park statue of General Josef Castulus Wassowitsch. At night, the lonely owl observes a house where the park keeper lives with his wife, his son Klaus, and tenants, including Clotilda the washerwoman. Klaus talks to little owl, but others, like Clotilda, are afraid of him. One snowy night when little owl sees the house roof on fire, he hoots to awaken the park keeper. Scorching his feathers, he circles near Clotilda's apartment until she is the last one rescued. When the fire is extinguished, the park keeper says, "It was little owl who saved us."[65] Ever since, his hoots no longer scare Clotilda.

*Seeking Peace*

**Preschool and Primary Grades.** Learning to live in peace is the theme of *Mr. T.W. Anthony Woo* written by Marie Hall Ets and illustrated by her with black-and-white lithographs.[66] While Michael the cobbler works, a little mouse, Mr. T.W. Anthony Woo, sits placidly on his shoulder. Michael's two other animals, Rodrigo the dog and Meola the cat, at first resent the mouse. They champion him, however, when he does their bidding and scares away Michael's sister, Miss Dora, and her precious parrot, Pollyandrew, who had come to stay. Mr. T.W. Anthony Woo is responsible for Michael and his three animals living in harmony, for the dog and cat appreciate the mouse so much, they "all lived together in peace."[67]

*Bear Party* by author-illustrator William Pène du Bois features real teddy bears who live in trees in Austrialia's Koala Park.[68] The bears become angry and stop speaking to each other, so the book's peacemaking theme is one of improving relationships. Following the wise old bear's advice, the group gives a costume party. The illustrations in colorful oil pastels and ink show the elaborate costumes of the personified bears. When they remove their costumes and masks at sundown, they do not recognize each other and start to growl again, though they enjoyed themselves during the party. For the sake of peace, they once more don their costumes at night and the following day, wear remnants, relating to each other as a Nurse Bear or Clown Bear.

**Primary and Middle Grades.** Another book, *The Forbidden Forest*,[69] by author-illustrator William Pène du Bois has a theme of stopping a war. The prologue specifically states, "This is the story of the three heroes who stopped the Great World War."[70] The three heroes are Lady Adelaide, a kangaroo boxing champion humorously drawn in woman's clothing, Spider Max, her promoter, and Buckingham, a bulldog. The night the Great War was to start, the Australian kangaroo is in Germany on a boxing tour with her promoter. In a restaurant she rescues a bulldog abused by a German officer, and he becomes her companion, Buckingham. The menu is on the back of a sign telling people to stay out of Forbidden Forest, so the two animals go there, chasing the cruel German officer. She uses a slingshot to fire a grape in his eye, he misfires in the direction of his own army, and the shell, called "The Lady Adelaide Magic Whizzbang," causes so much destruction, the war ends. Spider Max fulfills the task of getting the two animals to Australia where they are known as "The Stoppers of the Great War." The full-color precise illustrations show dramatically the peacemaking role of the trio.

*Getting a Second Chance*

**Preschool and Primary Grades.** Author-illustrator Françoise conveys the theme of getting a second chance in the text of *Chouchou* and in its simple, bright watercolor illustrations.[71] Children visit and feed Chouchou, a French photographer's donkey. When he accidently bites a boy's finger, gendarmes jail the donkey. Children explain to the Police Captain, "It's the little boy's fault. Instead of giving sugar on a flat hand he held it between his thumb and first finger."[72] After they feed Chouchou for a week without mishap, gendarmes free him, giving him a second chance. Because boys and girls then get their pictures taken with the donkey, the photographer can afford a wedding, a joyous event for Chouchou and his young friends.

**Preschool through Middle Grades.** Getting a second chance to improve is also the theme of *Five Little Monkeys* written by Juliet Kepes and illustrated by her in simplified style.[73] Eight illustrations are in color, and the balance are in black and white. Five mischievous monkeys, Buzzo, Binki, Bulu, Bibi, and Bali, have played so many pranks that other animals trap them in a pit filled with bananas. When the monkeys want to leave, they realize, "We better call for help. . . . But who will help us after all those tricks we've played?"[74] The other animals gathered around the pit help the monkeys because they "think they have learned their lesson."[75] The monkeys are so thankful, they never harm another animal again. In fact, the monkeys give a second chance to Terrible, the animal-eating Tiger, who finally learns responsibility.

*Danger from Trusting Flattery*

**Primary and Middle Grades.** An adaptation of "The Nun's Priest's Tale" from Chaucer's *Canterbury Tales, Chanticleer and the Fox* is recorded and illustrated with authenticity by Barbara Cooney.[76] To her excellent line drawings she adds blue, brown, yellow, red, and green tones and offers inviting red-and-blue end paper. The tale concerns a widow who lives in a cottage with two young daughters. Among her livestock are the vain rooster, Chanticleer, and his favorite hen, Partlet. One night, a fox enters the hen yard and compliments the rooster, Chanticleer, on the way he sings with closed eyes. When the rooster shuts his eyes to crow, the fox grabs him, and takes him into a grove. Since the widow and her daughters follow them, Chanticleer advises the fox to tell them to turn back, and when the fox complies, Chanticleer escapes into a tree. As the widow recovers Chanticleer, she tells him, "That is the result of trusting in flattery."[77] The widow's advice is the moral or theme of Chaucer's fable.

*Learning*

**Preschool and Primary Grades.** *Turtle Tales* is written by Frank Asch and illustrated by him with black outlining of colored subjects.[78] A young turtle profits from an apple's falling on his head. Becoming wise is the book's theme, for the apple hurts so much, the turtle learns to keep his head inside his shell. When a fox attacks, he is glad his head is in the shell. One illustration is completely black to impart how the shell appears inside. The book ends when the central figure has become a wise old turtle.

**Primary and Middle Grades.** Learning is the theme of *Andy Says Bonjour,*[79] written by Pat Diska and illustrated by Chris Jenkyns with black, red, and gray detailed pictures. An English-speaking boy, Andy, who just arrived in Paris, learns French words from Minou, his French-speaking cat and tour guide. After Andy lives in Paris a long time, he learns to speak French well.

*Family Relationships*

**Preschool and Primary Grades.** Else Holmelund Minarik's *Father Bear Comes Home* is part of the Little Bear series of beginning readers that have short, easy sentences, controlled vocabulary, much repetition, and large type, but still are literary.[80] The theme of *Father Bear Comes Home,* family unity, is conveyed in the tender illustrations of Maurice Sendak. He chose the Victorian period for the series, preferring the nostalgia of old-fashioned oil-wick lamps and long skirts that accentuate female laps. He uses pen and ink and in this book, adds pale-blue and rose tints. Minarik tells how Father Bear, back from a fishing trip, hugs Little Bear and even helps rid him of hiccups.

Family unity is also the theme of Else Holmelund Minarik's *Little Bear's Visit,*[81] illustrated by Maurice Sendak in ink with pale-green and buff watercolor highlights. When Little Bear visits his grandparents, he enjoys listening to their stories and tells them, " 'I like it here.' . . . He hugged them."[82] The final illustration expresses the theme, for Grandmother, Grandfather, Mother, and Father Bear all look tenderly at sleeping Little Bear.

**Preschool through Middle Grades.** *Fly High, Fly Low* is written by Don Freeman and illustrated by him with colored pencils in blue, rose, and yellow tones.[83] A desire for family unity is the theme of this San Francisco story about two pigeons, Sid and Midge, who build a nest in the

bottom of the letter ''B'' atop the Bay Hotel. Sid is away, but Midge is
sitting on two eggs in the nest when sign men remove the letter ''B''
and its clinging inhabitant. Sid hunts for Midge through fog and rain at
the waterfront and even at the top of the Golden Gate Bridge. It is his
friend, Mr. Hi Lee, who takes him to a bakery with a new letter ''B''
on its sign. Sid flies to the nest before both eggs hatch, so family unity
occurs just in time. After a while, the two little ones occupy the upper
loop of the ''B'' while Sid and Midge are cozy below.

*Relationship with One Parent*

**Preschool and Primary Grades.** Mitchell Preston's *Where Did My Mother
Go?,*[84] with detailed illustrations in full color by Chris Conover, has as
its theme a son's concern for his mother. When little cat realilzes his
mother is not at home, he gets on his tricycle and looks for her at such
locations as a supermarket, laundromat, and library. She actually has
been at those places doing things for her son, but he finds her when he
returns home. Because he worries, she never leaves in the future without
telling him where she is going.

   Miriam Young's *Miss Suzy's Birthday,*[85] illustrated by Arnold Lobel,
has the empty-nest syndrome as its primary theme. Miss Suzy Squirrel
worries that her four adopted squirrel children, when fully grown, will
go off on their own,[86] but she learns one of them, little Steve, is not as
old as she thinks. He tells her about her surprise birthday party. ''Steve
was too little to keep a secret, Miss Suzy realized. And the others weren't
much bigger. They would be with her for a long, long time.''[87]

**Preschool through Middle Grades.** *Emmet Otter's Jug-Band Christmas,*[88] written by Russell Hoban and illustrated by Lillian Hoban, has
warmth between mother and son as its theme. Emmet and his mother,
Alice, have been poor otters since Emmet's father died. Ma does laundry
and Emmet, odd jobs, but Emmet wants to buy Ma a piano for Christmas,
and she wants to get him a guitar. They hope to purchase items by
winning a talent show and receiving a fifty-dollar cash prize. Both secretly enter, Ma as a singer and Emmet with his newly formed jug band.
Ma gets money for a dress to wear at the contest by selling Emmet's
odd-jobs tools. Ma cannot do laundry because Emmet put a hole in her
wash tub for his band's wash-tub instrument. Worse still, they lose the
contest. Their songs on the way home, appreciated by patrons who over-
hear them at Riverside Rest Restaurant, motivate the owner, Doc Bull-
frog, to hire Ma and Emmet's Frogtown Hollow Boys as musicians. The

mother and son, secure in their relationship, now have financial security as well.

**Primary and Middle Grades.** *Little Though I Be* by author-illustrator Joseph Low has the theme of help from animal friends that wins a father's praise.[89] A father favors his tall sons, Ted and Tad, rather than Tim, his short son. Tim finds solace in animal friends, the horse, goose, mouse, and crow, who help him impress his father. The father's attitude changes from "What a useless baggage you are, Tim! Little you do for what you get. . . ."[90] to "Now then, me fine buckos, didn't I always tell you and all others this lad carried a great weight of brain above his shoulders?"[91]

*Treachery Punished*

**Primary and Middle Grades.** *Mice Twice* is another book written and illustrated in watercolor by Joseph Low.[92] Treachery punished is the theme of this book about a clever mouse who tricks a hungry cat. The mouse accepts the cat's invitation for dinner if he can invite a friend, and the cat is willing because he thinks two mice will come or mice twice. Actually, the mouse appears with a dog. After several other invitations, the cat has to leave home, but the mouse is safe.

*Love*

**Preschool and Primary Grades.** Else Holmelund Minarik's *A Kiss for Little Bear* is illustrated by Maurice Sendak in pen and ink with pale-green and buff watercolor added.[93] The theme, shared love, becomes clear when Little Bear asks Hen to deliver one of his drawings to Grandmother. The Grandmother, whose attire is complete with Victorian headdress, is so happy with the picture, she requests that Hen give Little Bear a kiss. The kiss is relayed by Hen to Frog, to Cat, to boy Skunk, and then to pretty girl Skunk. However, the girl Skunk returns the kiss to the boy Skunk. When Hen sees this, she brings the kiss to Little Bear herself. Little Bear gets another kiss from the bride when he is best man at the two skunks' wedding.

**Preschool through Middle Grades.** The theme of author-illustrator Paul Gobel's *The Girl Who Loved Wild Horses* is mirrored in its title.[94] In a Native American village, one girl has a special way with horses, for they follow her everywhere. During a storm, she and the horses she attends are lost. A handsome stallion, leader of wild horses, finds the girl with her animals and invites them to live with him. She accepts, but a year later, hunters from her village take her home to her parents. When she becomes ill and doctors cannot help, her parents ask what will make her well. She replies:

> I love to run with the wild horses. They are my relatives. If you let me go back to them I shall be happy forevermore.[95]

After her parents release her, she returns year after year with a colt for them. Eventually, she disappears, but hunters who see a beautiful mare galloping beside the stallion believe she is one of the wild horses.

*Friendship*

**Preschool and Primary Grades.** With precise watercolor illustrations and clever text, William Pène du Bois created *Bear Circus*,[96] a book with true friendship as its theme. In Australia, kangaroos help move koala teddy bears whose gum-tree leaves have been eaten by grasshoppers. Aboard a circus plane that crashed near their new home, the bears find costumes that fit them. For seven years, the bears rehearse with the equipment on the plane before inviting the kangaroos to be guests at a bear circus. During the performance, grasshoppers once more invade, and the kangaroos again put the teddy bears in their pouches, finding them another home. The bears apologize because they cannot have another circus to show their gratitude, but the kangaroos explain that "true friends never owe each other anything."[97]

In *Bear Circus*, two different kinds of animals are friends, but in *Mr. Gumpy's Outing* by author-illustrator John Burningham,[98] the theme is animal/human friendship. Burningham alternates pencil sketches with green, brown, blue, and amber stylized watercolor illustrations as he shows Mr. Gumpy taking two children and a group of animals for a boat ride. The boat capsizes because the guests are unruly. Friendship is shown when everyone helps each other to land, joins Mr. Gumpy for tea, and responds to his last words, "Come for a ride another day."[99] Sunny-yellow end papers contribute to the book's predominant mood of joy.

Friendship is also the theme of *Alexander and the Wind-Up Mouse* by author-illustrator Leo Lionni.[100] Alexander, a mouse, is sad because everyone is afraid of him, and he wishes to be loved, like Willie, a toy wind-up mouse. Alexander wants to ask the magic Lizzard to change him into a toy mouse, but he learns Willie, now broken, will be discarded. Impulsively, Alexander asks the magic Lizzard to transform Willie into a real mouse. Thereafter the two companions share a hole together.

A cat is the subject of *Jenny's Birthday Book* by author-illustrator Ester Averill,[101] who alternates inked illustrations with those done in bold tempera paint. Friendship shown by those who give a birthday party is the theme of this book which tells about animals who prepare a memorable park birthday picnic for Jenny, a little black cat. That night Jenny prays, "Please, may all cats everywhere have happy birthdays when their birthday comes."[102]

Another talking cat, called Red because of the color of his fur, is in *The Two Reds*,[103] written by Will Lipkind and illustrated by Nicolas Mordvinoff. The other Red is a redheaded boy whose real name is Joey. The book's theme is development of friendship because in the beginning, the two did not relate. The cat coveted Joey's goldfish, a source of initial friction. The two Reds narrowly escape trouble and sit on a stoop together while people chasing them run past. The cat agrees when Red the boy questions him, " 'Paws off my fish and friends? ' . . . Now the two Reds are together all the time."[104]

Arnold Lobel is author-illustrator of two companion beginning readers that are literary and have friendship as their theme. These amusing books are *Frog and Toad Are Friends*[105] and *Frog and Toad Together,*[106] both with five stories apiece and illustrated in black, brown, and green watercolors. Frog and Toad have a unique friendship they cannot share with anyone else. In the first book when Frog is sick, Toad is beside his bed to cheer him. After Frog learns his companion is sad waiting for mail he never receives, Frog writes him:

Dear Toad, I am glad
that you are my best friend.
Your best friend, Frog.[107]

Dependent friendship permeates the second book, *Frog and Toad Together*. When Frog and Toad try to prove their bravery by climbing mountains or encountering snakes and hawks, the outcome is always the same: They run away quickly. The two return home, content with the security and dependence they feel with one another. Their mood is captured in these words: "They stayed there for a long time, just feeling very brave together."[108] On other occasions, Frog shares garden seeds with Toad, Toad gives his chum home-baked cookies, and both help each other find the willpower to stop eating them.

In an interview, Arnold Lobel states that there is a Frog and Toad Fan Club. He says toads, not frogs, eat in captivity, so they are better pets. He adds he got the idea for his two books in Vermont when his own children brought frogs and toads into the house. He explains:

The reason I picked these two characters is that they're so close, yet so different. . . . The books are Harper "I Can Read" beginning readers. They're all limited to black and two colors. I tend to like the books with fewer colors better than the full-color books by me and by other artists.

I don't use controlled vocabulary, but I have an "I Can Read" mind. In *Frog and Toad Together,* I use the word "avalanche," a good word for a child to know. . . .

I have no plans for any more Frog and Toad books, but stories with the same kind of feeling because I like their gentleness and simplicity.[109]

An interviewer questions Lobel how he felt when *Frog and Toad Together* was named a Newbery Honor Book, since few books for young readers are given this award. He replies:

I consider myself an illustrator who also writes. Now I am suddenly a Writer with a capital "W." I hope it doesn't make me self-conscious and constricted. I think that would be very dangerous for me because up till now, I've only used my writing as a support for my pictures.[110]

**Preschool through Middle Grades.** Friendship between a little girl and a rabbit is the theme of Charlotte Zolotow's *Mr. Rabbit and the Lovely Present.*[111] Illustrator Maurice Sendak uses watercolors in jewel tones to help depict the theme. With her mother's birthday imminent, a serious little girl asks sophisticated Mr. Rabbit for gift ideas. He helps her choose a basket with different kinds of fruit.

A lion is the center of interest in a series by author-illustrator Roger Duvoisin that includes *The Happy Lion*[112] and *The Happy Lion in Africa.*[113] Both concern friendship between a lion and a French boy. Duvoisin alternates black-and-white illustrations with those done in amber, red, and black. A popular, sophisticated lion in a French zoo strolls from his open cage but finds people who liked him at the zoo are now frightened. He walks back to the zoo in the company of the keeper's son, François. François visits him every afternoon, and the lion "swished his tail for joy, for François remained always his dearest friend."[114]

In *The Happy Lion in Africa,* the lion escapes a kidnapper by boarding a ship that happens to land in Africa. There animals run from or after him, but he feels at home only when he finds the camp of Monsieur Lentille, a friend who is an animal photographer. The people celebrate after Lentille returns the lion by plane to his French hometown. The final illustration shows the lion in the zoo happily reunited with his true friend, Françoise.

Another series book, *The Story of Babar,*[115] was originally written in French by Jean de Brunhoff and humorously illustrated by him in bright green, red, yellow, gray, and pink watercolors. (His son, Laurent de Brunhoff, has continued the Babar series.) As a young elephant, Babar flees to a town when a hunter kills his mother in the forest. An old lady adopts Babar, giving him clothes and comforts, but he "is not quite happy, for he misses playing in the great forest with his little cousins and his friends, the monkeys."[116] The story ends when Babar returns to his forest friends and marries his cousin, Celeste. His old chums are so delighted he is back, they choose Babar and his bride as king and queen.

Babar's bulk is matched by that of two hippopotami named in the title, *George and Martha*,[117] whose friendship gives the book its theme. James Marshall creates five short stories and illustrates them humorously with bright red, yellow, and green watercolors. When George pours Martha's hated split pea soup into his loafers, she assures him she is not hurt by declaring:

> Friends should always tell each other the truth. As a matter of fact, I don't like split pea soup very much myself. I only like to make it.[118]

When George breaks his favorite front tooth and visits her with a new gold tooth, Martha tells him how wonderful he looks.

> "That's what friends are for," he said. "They always look on the bright side and they always know how to cheer you up."
>
> "But they also tell you the truth," said Martha with a smile.[119]

Unusual friends as rescuers is the theme of *Amos & Boris* written by William Steig and illustrated by him in blue, yellow, and orange watercolors.[120] This modern version of "The Lion and the Rat" fable tells how Amos the mouse falls overboard while on a sea adventure. His rescuer, Boris the whale, takes Amos ashore, but when the mouse promises to help Boris, the whale silently laughs. However, after Hurricane Yetta, Amos finds Boris washed ashore, and with the help of two elephants, returns Boris to the sea. As both part for the last time, Boris expresses:

> I wish we could be friends forever. . . . We *will* be friends forever, but we can't be together. You must live on land and I must live at sea. I'll never forget you, though.[121]

**Primary Grades.** Author-illustrator Marie Hall Ets makes imaginary friends the theme of *In the Forest*.[122] During a forest walk, a little boy fantasizes that he plays games and picnics with a lion, two baby elephants, two big brown bears, a kangaroo family, an old gray stork, two little monkeys, and a shy rabbit. After eating peanuts, jam, ice cream and cake, the animals play hide-and-seek with the little boy as It. When he opens his eyes, the animals are gone, but his father, who has been looking for him, wants to know with whom he has been talking. The little boy answers, "To my friends the animals. Can't you see them?"[123]

**Primary and Middle Grades.** Mainly black-and-white, detailed illustrations by Joseph Schindelman help convey the theme of friendship in Leon A. Harris's *The Great Picture Robbery*.[124] From a small French village, Maurice the mouse comes to Paris and lives at the Louvre where a museum worker, Madame Marina, feeds him and plays with him. He reciprocates her friendship by telling her when two men steal the Mona Lisa. He also points to the hiding place of the robbers and the painting. Since she calls the police, she will receive the legion of honor medal, but she tells Maurice he should get it. The mouse, an unselfish friend, replies, "I am proud to have done something for you at last. . . . If anyone deserves a medal, Madame, it's you."[125]

*Individualized Contribution*

**Preschool and Primary Grades.** A field mouse stars in *Frederick,*[126] written by Leo Lionni and illustrated by him in watercolor and collage. Frederick is unusual, for while his family gathers nuts, corn, wheat, and straw for the coming winter, he collects sunrays, colors, and words. In this adaptation of "The Grasshopper and the Ant" fable, the theme, individualized contribution, is apparent. In winter, food supplies dwindle, and mice ask Frederick to offer something. They close their eyes and listen.

> And as Frederick spoke of the sun, the four little mice began to feel warmer. . . . They saw the colors as clearly as if they had been painted in their minds.[127]

Next, Frederick recites a poem to alleviate winter's bitterness. Visual imagery reinforces the theme, for one illustration uses yellow splashes to symbolize the sun's warmth, and another has bright dots representing the colors Frederick describes. Even the inner binding, which repeats the word Frederick, reflects the theme, for words are Frederick's contribution.

**Summary**

This chapter examines themes of seventy-three examples of prizewinning animal-fantasy picture storybooks grouped under twenty-four topics.

Friendship is the theme of about one-fifth of the books in the sample. Ingenuity and self-awareness are among the next-most-popular themes. A handful of books concern nature and relationship to a parent.

More than half of the prizewinners are intended for children in the range from preschool through primary grades and about a third for those in the broader range from preschool through middle-elementary grades. Most of the balance are for those in the range from primary through middle grades with only two designated for primary grades alone.

Mice are the most popular subjects in this sample, for they are heroes of eleven prizewinning animal-fantasy picture storybooks. They are also the most popular subjects of animal fantasy for older elementary pupils, as noted in chapter 8. This is significant because they are among the smallest animal subjects. Beyond mice, there are six picture storybooks in this sample dealing with cats and kittens, five concerning bears, four revolving around lions or rabbits, and three apiece focusing on birds, elephants, horses, or monkeys.

Prolific author-illustrators of animal-fantasy picture storybooks in this sample are creators of the following number of prizewinners: Arnold Lobel, five; William Pène du Bois and Leo Lionni, four apiece; Marie Hall Ets, three; and Joseph Low, H.A. Roy, and William Steig, two apiece. In addition, illustrators alone of several animal-fantasy picture storybook prizewinners in this sample have created the following number of books: Maurice Sendak, four (three by Else Holmelund Minarik and one by Charlotte Zolotow); Roger Duvoisin, three by Louise Fatio; and Paul Galdone, two by Eve Titus.

## Notes

1. In 1950, *The Happy Day* was a Caldecott Honor Book.
2. Ruth Krauss, *The Happy Day* (New York: Harper, 1949), no page.
3. In 1952, *The Animal Fair* was a *New York Times* Choice of Best Illustrated Children's Book of the Year.
4. In 1949, *The Big Snow* won The Randolph Caldecott Medal.
5. In 1944, *The Mighty Hunter* was a Caldecott Honor Book.
6. Berta and Elmer Hader, *The Mighty Hunter* (New York: Macmillan, 1943), no page.
7. In 1981, *Fables* won The Randolph Caldecott Medal.
8. Arnold Lobel, *Fables* (New York: Harper, 1980), p. 28.
9. In 1952, *Feather Mountain* was a Caldecott Honor Book.
10. In 1954, *Green Eyes* was a Caldecott Honor Book.
11. In 1977, *Little Gorilla* won the Southern California Council on Literature for Children and Young People Award.

12. In 1954, *When Will the World Be Mine? The Story of a Snowshoe Rabbit* was a Caldecott Honor Book.

13. Miriam Schlein, *When Will the World Be Mine? The Story of a Snowshoe Rabbit* (Reading, Mass.: Scott, 1953), no page.

14. In 1942, *Nothing at All* was a Caldecott Honor Book.

15. Wanda Gág, *Nothing at All* (New York: Coward, 1941), no page.

16. In 1970, *Sylvester and the Magic Pebble* won The Randolph Caldecott Medal and was a finalist for the National Book Award in the children's-book category. In 1978, it won the Lewis Carroll Shelf Award.

17. William Steig, *Sylvester and the Magic Pebble* (New York: Simon & Shuster, 1969), no page.

18. In 1956, *The Little Elephant* was a *New York Times* Choice of Best Illustrated Children's Book of the Year.

19. In 1957, *Mister Penny's Race Horse* was a Caldecott Honor Book.

20. Marie Hall Ets, *Mister Penny's Race Horse* (New York: Viking, 1956), p. 6.

21. Ibid., p. 60.

22. In 1975, *Little Rabbit's Loose Tooth* was a *New York Times* Choice of Best Illustrated Children's Book of the Year.

23. Lucy Bates, *Little Rabbit's Loose Tooth* (New York: Crown, 1975), no page.

24. In 1976, *Little Fox Goes to the End of the World* was in the American Institute of Graphic Arts Book Show, and in 1977, it won the Friends of American Writers Award.

25. Ann Tompert, *Little Fox Goes to the End of the World* (New York: Crown, 1976), no page.

26. In 1957, *The Unhappy Hippopotamus* was a *New York Times* Choice of Best Illustrated Children's Book of the Year.

27. Nancy Moore, *The Unhappy Hippopotamus* (New York: Vanguard, 1957), no page.

28. In 1973, *Hector Penguin* was a *New York Times* Choice of Best Illustrated Children's Book of the Year, and in 1974, it was in the American Institute of Graphic Arts Book Show.

29. Louise Fatio, *Hector Penguin* (New York: McGraw, 1973), no page.

30. In 1977, *The Easter Egg Artists* won the Irma Simonton Black Award.

31. In 1953, *Pitschi* was a *New York Times* Choice of Best Illustrated Children's Book of the Year.

32. In 1966, *Curious George Goes to the Hospital* received a special citation from the Child Study Children's Book Committee at Bank Street College.

33. In 1957, *Curious George Gets a Medal* was a *New York Times* Choice of Best Illustrated Children's Book of the Year.

34. In 1957, *Anatole* was a Caldecott Honor Book.

35. Eve Titus, *Anatole* (New York: McGraw, 1956), p. 16.

36. In 1964, *Exactly Alike* was a *New York Times* Choice of Best Illustrated Children's Book of the Year.

37. Evaline Ness, *Exactly Alike* (New York: Scribner, 1964), no page.

38. In 1958, *Anatole and the Cat* was a Caldecott Honor Book.

39. Eve Titus, *Anatole and the Cat* (New York: McGraw, 1957), p. 23.

40. In 1963, *A Holiday for Mister Muster* was a *New York Times* Choice of Best Illustrated Children's Book of the Year.

41. Arnold Lobel, *A Holiday for Mister Muster* (New York: Harper, 1963), no page.

42. In 1961, *Inch by Inch* was a Caldecott Honor Book.

43. Leo Lionni, *Inch by Inch* (New York: Astor-Honor, 1960), no page.

44. In 1977, *The Church Mice Adrift* was a *New York Times* Choice of Best Illustrated Children's Book of the Year.

45. Graham Oakley, *The Church Mice Adrift* (New York: Atheneum, 1976), no page.

46. In 1957, *Lion* was a Caldecott Honor Book.

47. In 1952, *Finders Keepers* won The Randolph Caldecott Medal.

48. Will Lipkind, *Finders Keepers* (New York: Harcourt, 1951), no page.

49. In 1973, *Mouse Tales* won the Irma Simonton Black Award.

50. In 1956, *Babar's Fair* was a *New York Times* Choice of Best Illustrated Children's Book of the Year.

51. In 1963, *Swimmy* was a *New York Times* Choice of Best Illustrated Children's Book of the Year, and in 1964, it was a Caldecott Honor Book.

52. Leo Lionni, *Swimmy* (New York: Pantheon, 1962), no page.

53. In 1963, *Gwendolyn and the Weathercock* was a *New York Times* Choice of Best Illustrated Children's Book of the Year.

54. In 1961, *The Happy Hunter* was a *New York Times* Choice of Best Illustrated Children's Book of the Year.

55. Roger Duvoisin, *The Happy Hunter* (New York: Lothrop, 1961), p. 23.

56. In 1972, *Mouse Café* was a *New York Times* Choice of Best Illustrated Children's Book of the Year.

57. Patricia Coombs, *Mouse Café* (New York: Lothrop, 1972), no page.

58. In 1939, *Andy and the Lion* was a Caldecott Honor Book.

59. James Daugherty, *Andy and the Lion* (New York: Viking, 1938), no page.

60. In 1979, *Captain Toad and the Motorbike* won the American Institute of Graphic Arts Book Show Award.

61. David McPhail, *Captain Toad and the Motorbike* (New York: Atheneum, 1978), no page.

62. In 1979, *Lyle, Lyle, Crocodile* won the Lewis Carroll Shelf Award.

63. Bernard Waber, *Lyle, Lyle, Crocodile* (Boston: Houghton, 1965), p. 45.

64. In 1962, *Little Owl* was a *New York Times* Choice of Best Illustrated Children's Book of the Year.

65. Reiner Zimnik, *Little Owl* (New York: Atheneum, 1962), p. 26.

66. In 1952, *Mr. T.W. Anthony Woo* was a Caldecott Honor Book.

67. Marie Hall Ets, *Mr. T.W. Anthony Woo* (New York: Viking, 1951), p. 54.

68. In 1971, *Bear Party* was a *New York Times* Choice of Best Illustrated Children's Book of the Year.

69. In 1978, *The Forbidden Forest* was a *New York Times* Choice of Best Illustrated Children's Book of the Year.

70. William Pène du Bois, *The Forbidden Forest* (New York: Harper, 1978), no page.

71. In 1958, *Chouchou* was a *New York Times* Choice of Best Illustrated Children's Book of the Year.

72. Françoise, *Chouchou* (New York: Scribner, 1958), no page.

73. In 1952, *Five Little Monkeys* was a *New York Times* Choice of Best Illustrated Children's Book of the Year, and in 1953, it was a Caldecott Honor Book.

74. Juliet Kepes, *Five Little Monkeys* (Boston: Houghton, 1952), p. 20.

75. Ibid., p. 23.

76. In 1959, *Chanticleer and the Fox* won The Randolph Caldecott Medal.

77. Barbara Cooney, *Chanticleer and the Fox* (New York: Crowell, 1948), no page.

78. In 1979, *Turtle Tale* won an American Institute of Graphic Arts Book Show Award.

79. In 1954, *Andy Says Bonjour* was a Caldecott Honor Book.

80. In 1959, *Father Bear Comes Home* was a *New York Times* Choice of Best Illustrated Children's Book of the Year.

81. In 1962, *Little Bear's Visit* was a Caldecott Honor Book.

82. Else Holmelund Minarik, *Little Bear's Visit* (New York: Harper, 1961), p. 17.

83. In 1958, *Fly High, Fly Low* was a Caldecott Honor Book.

84. In 1979, *Where Did My Mother Go?* won the American Institute of Graphic Arts Book Show Award.

85. In 1974, *Miss Suzy's Birthday* was a *New York Times* Best Illustrated Children's Book of the Year.

86. Miriam Young, *Miss Suzy's Birthday* (New York: Parent's Magazine, 1974), no page.

87. Ibid., no page.

88. In 1971, *Emmet Otter's Jug-Band Christmas* won the Christopher Award for ages four to eight, and in 1972, it won the Lewis Carroll Shelf Award.

89. In 1976, *Little Though I Be* was a *New York Times* Choice of Best Illustrated Children's Book of the Year.

90. Joseph Low, *Little Though I Be* (New York: McGraw, 1976), p. 5.

91. Ibid., p. 33.

92. In 1981, *Mice Twice* was a Caldecott Honor Book.

93. In 1968, *A Kiss for Little Bear* was a *New York Times* Choice of Best Illustrated Children's Book of the Year.

94. In 1979, *The Girl Who Loved Wild Horses* won The Randolph Caldecott Medal.

95. Paul Goble, *The Girl Who Loved Wild Horses* (Scarsdale, N.Y.: Bradbury, 1978), no page.

96. In 1971, *Bear Circus* was a *New York Times* Choice of Best Illustrated Children's Book of the Year.

97. William Pène du Bois, *Bear Circus* (New York: Viking, 1971), p. 48.

98. In 1971, *Mr. Gumpy's Outing* was a *New York Times* Choice of Best Illustrated Children's Book of the Year, and in 1972, it won the *Boston Globe-Horn Book* Award for illustrations.

99. John Burningham, *Mr. Gumpy's Outing* (New York: Holt, 1970), no page.

100. In 1969, *Alexander and the Wind-Up Mouse* won the Christopher Award for ages four to eight. In 1970, it was a Caldecott Honor Book and won the Brooklyn Art Books for Children Citation.

101. In 1954, *Jenny's Birthday Book* was a *New York Times* Best Illustrated Children's Book of the Year.

102. Ester Averill, *Jenny's Birthday Book* (New York: Harper, 1954), no page.

103. In 1951, *The Two Reds* was a Caldecott Honor Book.

104. William Lipkind and Nicolas Mordvinoff, *The Two Reds* (New York: Harcourt, 1950), pp. 44–45.

105. In 1971, *Frog and Toad Are Friends* won The Randolph Caldecott Medal and the National Book Award.

106. In 1973, *Frog and Toad Together* was a Newbery Honor Book and was in the Children's Book Showcase.

107. Arnold Lobel, *Frog and Toad Are Friends* (New York: Harper, 1970), p. 62.

108. Arnold Lobel, *Frog and Toad Together* (New York: Harper, 1971), p. 51.

109. "Arnold Lobel," *Profiles in Literature* (Philadelphia: Temple University, 1973).

110. Ibid.

111. In 1963, *Mr. Rabbit and the Lovely Present* was a Caldecott Honor Book.

112. In 1954, *The Happy Lion* was a *New York Times* Choice of Best Illustrated Children's Book of the Year.

113. Louise Fatio, *The Happy Lion* (New York: McGraw, 1954), no page.

114. In 1955, *The Happy Lion in Africa* was a *New York Times* Choice of Best Illustrated Children's Book of the Year.

115. In 1959, *The Story of Babar* won the Lewis Carroll Shelf Award.

116. Jean de Brunhoff, *The Story of Babar* (New York: Random, 1933), p. 24.

117. In 1972, *George and Martha* was the *New York Times* Choice of Best Illustrated Children's Book of the Year.

118. James Marshall, *George and Martha* (Boston: Houghton, 1972), p. 12.

119. Ibid., p. 46.

120. In 1971, *Amos & Boris* was a *New York Times* Best Illustrated Children's Book of the Year. In 1972, it was a National Book Award finalist in the children's-book category, and it was in the Children's Book Showcase.

121. William Steig, *Amos & Boris* (New York: Farrar, 1971), no page.

122. In 1945, *In the Forest* was a Caldecott Honor Book.

123. Marie Hall Ets, *In the Forest* (New York: Viking, 1944), no page.

124. In 1963, *The Great Picture Robbery* was a *New York Times* Choice of Best Illustrated Children's Book of the Year.

125. Leon A. Harris, *The Great Picture Robbery* (New York: Atheneum, 1963), no page.

126. In 1967, *Frederick* was a *New York Times* Choice of Best

Illustrated Children's Book of the Year, and in 1968, it was a Caldecott Honor Book.

127. Leo Lionni, *Frederick* (New York: Pantheon, 1967), no page.

## References of Prizewinning Animal Fantasy in Picture Storybooks

*(Estimated Reading or Listening Grade Level in Parentheses)*

### Assorted Animals

Burningham, John. *Mr. Gumpy's Outing*. New York: Holt, 1970 (PS–2).
Duvoisin, Roger. *The Happy Hunter*. New York: Lothrop, 1961 (K–3).
Ets, Marie Hall. *In the Forest*. New York: Viking, 1944 (1–2).
Hader, Berta and Elmer. *The Big Snow*. New York: Macmillan, 1948 (K–3).
―――. *The Mighty Hunter*. New York: Macmillan, 1943 (K–3).
Krauss, Ruth. *The Happy Day*. Illustrated by Marc Simont. New York: Harper, 1949 (PS–1).
Lobel, Arnold. *Fables*. New York: Harper, 1980 (2–4).
―――. *A Holiday for Mister Muster*. New York: Harper, 1963 (PS–1).
Low, Joseph. *Little Though I Be*. New York: McGraw, 1976 (1–3).
Provensen, Alice and Martin. *The Animal Fair*. New York: Simon & Schuster, 1952 (PS–3).

### Bears

du Bois, William Pène. *Bear Circus*. New York: Viking, 1971 (PS–2).
―――. *Bear Party*. New York: Viking, 1971 (PS–2).
Minarik, Else Holmelund. *Father Bear Comes Home*. Illustrated by Maurice Sendak. New York: Harper, 1959 (K–2).
―――. *A Kiss for Little Bear*. Illustrated by Maurice Sendak. New York: Harper, 1968 (K–2).
―――. *Little Bear's Visit*. Illustrated by Maurice Sendak. New York: Harper, 1961 (K–2).

### Birds

Freeman, Don. *Fly High, Fly Low*. New York: Viking, 1952 (K–3).
Olds, Elizabeth. *Feather Mountain*. Boston: Houghton, 1951 (2–4).

Zimnik, Reiner. *Little Owl*. Illustrated by Hanne Axmann. New York: Atheneum, 1962 (K–3).


## Cats and Kittens

Averill, Ester. *Jenny's Birthday Book*. New York: Harper, 1954 (K–2).
Birnbaum, A. *Green Eyes*. Irvington, New York: Capitol, 1953 (PS–K).
Diska, Pat. *Andy Says Bonjour*. Illustrated by Chris Jenkyns. New York: Vanguard, 1954 (1–3).
Fischer, Hans. *Pitschi*. New York: Harcourt, 1953 (K–3).
Lipkind, William. *The Two Reds*. Illustrated by Nicolas Mordvinoff. New York: Harcourt, 1959 (1–2).
Preston, Mitchell. *Where Did My Mother Go?* Illustrated by Chris Conover. New York: Four Winds, 1978 (PS–1).
(See Mice, Low, Joseph. *Mice Twice*.)
(See Mice, Oakley, Graham. *The Church Mice Adrift*.)


## Crocodile

Waber, Bernard. *Lyle, Lyle, Crocodile*. Boston: Houghton, 1965 (K–2).


## Dogs

Gág, Wanda. *Nothing at All*. New York: Coward, 1941 (PS–3).
Lipkind, Will. *Finders Keepers*. Illustrated by Nicolas Mordvinoff. New York: Harcourt, 1951 (K–2).


## Donkeys

Françoise. *Chouchou*. New York: Scribner, 1958 (K–2).
Steig, William. *Sylvester and the Magic Pebble*. New York: Simon & Schuster, 1969 (K–3).


## Elephants

Brunhoff, Jean de. *The Story of Babar*. Translated by Merle Haas. New York: Random House, 1933 (PS–3).
Brunhoff, Laurent de. *Babar's Fair*. Translated by Merle Haas. New York: Random House, 1956 (PS–3).

Gregor, Arthur. *The Little Elephant*. Illustrated by Ylla. New York: Harper, 1956 (K–2).

*Fish*

Lionni, Leo. *Swimmy*. New York: Pantheon, 1962 (K–2).

*Fowl (Hens and Rooster)*

Sherman, Nancy. *Gwendolyn and the Weathercock*. Illustrated by Edward Sorel. New York: Golden, 1963 (1–3).
Cooney, Barbara. *Chanticleer and the Fox*. New York: Crowell, 1958 (1–4).

*Frog*

Lobel, Arnold. *Frog and Toad Are Friends*. New York: Harper, 1970 (K–2).
———. *Frog and Toad Together*. New York: Harper, 1971 (K–2).

*Foxes*

Tompert, Ann. *Little Fox Goes to the End of the World*. Illustrated by John Wallner. New York: Crown, 1976 (K–2).
(See Fowl, Cooney, Barbara. *Chanticleer and the Fox*.)

*Gorilla*

Bornstein, Ruth. *Little Gorilla*. New York: Seabury, 1976 (PS–1).

*Hippopotami*

Marshall, James. *George and Martha*. Boston: Houghton, 1972 (K–3).
Moore, Nancy. *The Unhappy Hippopotamus*. New York: Vanguard, 1957 (PS–2).

*Horses*

Ets, Marie Hall. *Mister Penny's Race Horse*. New York: Viking, 1956
   (PS–2).
Goble, Paul. *The Girl Who Loved Wild Horses*. New York: Bradbury,
   1978 (K–3).
Ness, Evaline. *Exactly Alike*. New York: Scribner, 1964 (K–3).


*Inchworm*

Lionni, Leo. *Inch by Inch*. New York: Astor-Honor, 1960 (K–2).


*Kangaroos*

du Bois, William Pène. *The Forbidden Forest*. New York: Harper, 1978
   (2–4).
(See Bears, du Bois, William Pène. *Bear Circus*.)


*Lions*

Daugherty, James. *Andy and the Lion*. New York: Viking, 1938 (1–4).
du Bois, William Pène. *Lion*. New York: Viking, 1955 (1–3).
Fatio, Louise. *The Happy Lion*. Illustrated by Roger Duvoisin. New
   York: McGraw, 1954 (K–3).
———. *The Happy Lion in Africa*. Illustrated by Roger Duvoisin. New
   York: McGraw, 1955 (K–3).


*Monkeys*

Kepes, Juliet. *Five Little Monkeys*. Boston: Houghton, 1952 (K–3).
Rey, H.A. *Curious George Gets a Medal*. Boston: Houghton, 1957
   (PS–2).
Rey, H.A. and Margret. *Curious George Goes to the Hospital*. Boston:
   Houghton, 1966 (PS–2).


*Mice*

Coombs, Patricia. *Mouse Café*. New York: Lothrop, 1972 (K–3).
Ets, Marie Hall. *Mr. T.W. Anthony Woo*. New York: Viking, 1951
   (PS–2).

Harris, Leon A. *The Great Picture Robbery*. Illustrated by Joseph Schindelman. New York: Atheneum, 1963 (1–3).

Lionni, Leo. *Alexander and the Wind-Up Mouse*. New York: Random, 1969 (PS–2).

———. *Frederick*. New York: Pantheon, 1967 (K–2).

Lobel, Arnold. *Mouse Tales*. New York: Harper, 1972 (1–2).

Low, Joseph. *Mice Twice*. New York: Atheneum, 1980 (1–3).

Oakley, Graham. *The Church Mice Adrift*. New York: Atheneum, 1976 (K–3).

Steig, William. *Amos & Boris*. New York: Farrar, 1971 (K–3).

Titus, Eve. *Anatole*. Illustrated by Paul Galdone. New York: McGraw, 1956 (K–2).

———. *Anatole and the Cat*. Illustrated by Paul Galdone. New York: McGraw, 1957 (K–2).

## Otters

Hoban, Russell. *Emmet Otter's Jug-Band Christmas*. Illustrated by Lillian Hoban. New York: *Parents' Magazine,* 1971 (K–3).

## Penguin

Fatio, Louise. *Hector Penguin*. Illustrated by Roger Duvoisin. New York: McGraw, 1973 (K–2).

## Rabbits

Adams, Adrienne. *The Easter Egg Artists*. New York: Scribner, 1976 (PS–3).

Bate, Lucy. *Little Rabbit's Loose Tooth*. Illustrated by Diane de Groat. New York: Crown, 1975 (PS–2).

Schlein, Miriam. *When Will the World Be Mine? The Story of a Snowshoe Rabbit*. Illustrated by Jean Charlot. Reading, Mass.: Scott, 1953 (K–2).

Zolotow, Charlotte. *Mr. Rabbit and the Lovely Present*. Illustrated by Maurice Sendak. New York: Harper, 1962 (PS–3).

## Squirrels

Young, Miriam. *Miss Suzy's Birthday*. Illustrated by Arnold Lobel. New York: *Parents' Magazine,* 1974 (PS–2).

*Toads*

McPhail, David. *Captain Toad and the Motorbike*. New York: Atheneum, 1978 (PS–2).
(See Frog, Lobel, Arnold. *Frog and Toad Are Friends* and *Frog and Toad Together*.)


*Turtle*

Asch, Frank. *Turtle Tale*. New York: Dial, 1978 (PS–2).


*Whale*

(See Mice, Steig, William. *Amos and Boris*.)

# 6 Realistic Fiction in Picture Storybooks

*Grandma and Grandpa tell me about the old country. Maybe that's why I pick four books on other lands. One is* Hanukah Money, *but I don't know where it takes place. The other three are* Crow Boy *about Japan,* Henry Fisherman *about the Virgin Islands, and* Harlequin and the Gift of Many Colors *about Italy, the old country. Grandma and Grandpa tell so many Italian stories, one day I'll write my own book.*

—Gino, aged seven

## Perspective

Gino's preferences are realistic fictional picture storybooks. His first two choices, *Hanukah Money* and *Crow Boy,* are historical fiction, the category of only nine picture storybook prizewinners in the sample. Obviously, this type of book, which requires a concept of past time, often is for older readers.

The setting of *Hanukah Money* that eludes Gino is a Jewish *shtetl* or village in eastern Europe around the turn of the century. This child's story was told originally by the great Yiddish writer, Sholem Aleichem, a pseudonym for Solomon J. Rabinowitz, who lived from 1859 until 1916. Uri Shulevitz is the primary translator and adaptor as well as the sole illustrator. His humorous, faintly tinted line drawings accentuate the theme of holiday memories, including receiving money as gifts.

Gino cites another work of historical fiction, *Crow Boy.* The author, Taro Yashima, born in 1908 on the island of Kyushi, Japan, tells a story based on his own village school days and includes colored-pencil illustrations. This is one of the few picture storybooks that shows character development. The book's theme is change nurtured by a compassionate teacher. Even the butterfly and flower on end papers underscore the theme, the protagonist's metamorphosis from an outsider to an appreciated person.

The last two books Gino likes are contemporary. Marcia Brown is author-illustrator of *Henry Fisherman, a Story of the Virgin Islands.* Her theme, recognition of growing up, is reflected in coral, navy blue, and white illustrations on every other page. Pictures on remaining pages are even brighter—done in coral, brown, turquoise, yellow, dark green, and blue—fitting for sunny Caribbean isles.

Gino's final book, *Harlequin and the Gift of Many Colors,* reveals Remy Charlip's talent as illustrator and coauthor with Burton Supree. The story takes place in Bergamo, Italy, a town that celebrates Carnival season by enacting a medieval masked comedy featuring a character called Harlequin. Both Charlip and Supree visited Bergamo twice to portray the setting accurately. Some of the town's children as well as its balconies and narrow cobblestone streets appear in Charlip's pastel illustrations.

Gino's favorites are set in other lands, but most realistic picture storybooks take place in the United States. Tales that occur in the post-World War II period and earlier are considered historical fiction, and those set later are known as contemporary fiction. Themes of prizewinners that are historical fiction are discussed first, followed by those that are contemporary fiction.

### Themes of Prizewinning Historical Fiction in Picture Storybooks Grouped under These Topics

*Money and Treasure*

**Primary and Middle Grades.** The theme of Sholem Aleichem's *Hanukah Money,*[1] illustrated by Uri Shulevitz, is Hanukah memories of young boys wanting to receive coins they cannot yet calculate. In this story set around the turn of the century, a small boy, the narrator, tells how he and his younger brother, Motl, observe the holiday in an eastern European Jewish village that is poor materially. The notion of the extended family prevails, for aunts and uncles play a major role, such as granting Hanukah *gelt* or money. Father and Uncle Bennie give more readily than Uncle Aaron-Moishe who asks, "What do children do with money? Spend it? Waste it? Hah?"[2] Even he responds when Aunt Pessl coaxes. Moreover, the boys follow this fixed pattern upon receipt of gifts:

> We take it and walk away, slowly at first, like well-mannered boys,
> then faster and faster. We jump, we jig, and when we reach our room,
> do three somersaults, and end up hopping on one leg and singing . . .[3]

The unfortunate part of the ritual is as follows: "We count and we count and we can't add up our money."[4] The boys cope by going to bed and dreaming of their Hanukah money.

Another story with an Old World flavor is *The Treasure,*[5] a full-color book by author-illustrator Uri Shulevitz. The story is about old, poverty-stricken Isaac who travels to the capital city because he dreams three nights of a treasure under the bridge. When he tells the bridge guard captain his dream, the captain says if he believed one of his own dreams, he would go to the old man's city and look under the stove of a man named Isaac. Isaac returns and finds a treasure. The book's theme is discovering treasure by following dreamed instructions. The guard captain's wig helps date the setting to about the eighteenth century.

*Friendship*

**Primary and Middle Grades.** Brinton Turkle writes and illustrates in full color several stories about plucky, redheaded Obadiah Starbuck, the youngest boy in a colonial Quaker family on Nantucket Island. In *Thy Friend, Obadiah,*[6] the theme is a sea gull's friendship with a boy, for a sea gull follows Obadiah, even when he and his family go to Friends Meeting. After the boy removes a large rusty fishhook dangling from the bird's beak, the gull perches near Obadiah's window at night. The lad announces to his mother, "That sea gull is my friend. . . . Since I helped him, I'm *his* friend, too."[7]

*Value of Honesty*

**Primary and Middle Grades.** Brinton Turkle continues the saga of young Obadiah Starbuck, showing in *The Adventures of Obadiah* how he fancies experiences with a wolf and a lion.[8] Its theme is an imaginative child's low credibility when adventure actually occurs. At sheep-sheering, Obadiah strays from his older brother, rides a ram, and is thrown into a sideshow area where he dances, sees a fire eater, and gets his fortune told. No one believes him until a neighbor, Levi Bunker, returns the boy's missing Quaker hat. Then Obadiah tells the story many times "the way it really happened."[9]

*Virtue Rewarded*

**Primary and Middle Grades.** Sixteenth-century Norway is the setting for *Sven's Bridge,*[10] Anita Lobel's first children's book which she illustrates elaborately in blue, yellow, green, and black. Kind Sven, keeper of a bridge, serves hot chocolate to those who use the bridge in winter. When a selfish king, impatient to get home for dinner, shoots the drawbridge apart, separated villagers find it difficult to visit each other. Sven builds a boat to ferry people and once saves the drowning king. Virtue rewarded is the book's theme, for on the old site, the grateful king builds a new, tall bridge, with dependable Sven as caretaker.

Virtue rewarded is also the theme of Joseph Longstreth's *Little Big-Feather*,[11] illustrated by Helen Brown Borton in blue, beige, yellow, and green tones. Since a Native American boy wants a feather as big as his, Chief Great-Eagle tells him:

> No one can have what he wants just because he wants it. When your deeds prove that you deserve it, then you can wear the biggest feather in the land.[12]

While elders are at a powwow and fire threatens the village, the boy drums a warning that brings help in time. The chief honors the drummer with a feast where he announces, ''This young brave shall now be known as Big-Feather.''[13]

A story with virtue rewarded as its theme is set *circa* 1900 and illustrated in homespun brown and blue. The book is *Down Down the Mountain*,[14] which takes place in the Blue Ridge Mountains where author-illustrator Ellis Credle has lived. Credle tells about little Hetty and her brother Hank who raise turnips and travel down the mountain toward town to sell them. They want to buy high-topped shoes for winter. On their trip, they distribute so many turnips to requesting adults, they arrive in town with only one that they enter in the county fair. It wins them a five-dollar gold piece with which they buy squeaky shoes and family gifts.

## Self-Sufficiency

**Primary and Middle Grades.** Donald Hall's *Ox-Cart Man*,[15] a cyclic story of an early nineteenth-century New England family, has early American farm self-sufficiency as its theme. Barbara Cooney's bright illustrations, which support the theme, resemble the early American technique of painting on wood. The story is about a family who brings its ox cart to Portsmouth Market, vending handspun clothing and farm-grown vegetables. They sell everything and begin anew to prepare for the following year.

## Change

**Primary and Middle Grades.** The period roughly from 1916 until the 1920s in Kyushi, Japan is described in *Crow Boy*,[16] a story based on recollections of childhood by author-illustrator Taro Yashima. Among those to whom the book is dedicated is "Takeo Isonaga who appears in this story as a teacher named Isobe."[17] The story begins with a tiny boy, nicknamed Chibi, hiding under the rural schoolhouse on the first day of school. Yashima draws lonely Chibi, whom peers consider stupid, set apart from others in the classroom. Even when it rains he trudges to school in a raincoat of dried zebra grass. After five years, isolated Chibi changes. Change nurtured by a compassionate teacher is the book's theme. The understanding new teacher, Mr. Isobe, "often spent time talking with Chibi when no one was around,"[18] and he displayed Chibi's drawings. In the talent show at the end of sixth grade, Chibi imitates crow voices. The teacher honors him as the only pupil with perfect attendance, citing how far Chibi walked to school every day for six years. Now called Crow Boy instead of Chibi, the lad no longer feels like an outsider. He stands erect at graduation, very different from his first-grade bearing. The book has minimal text, its theme implanted largely through colored-pencil illustrations.

Among the historical-fiction picture-storybook prizewinners are tales from this country and abroad, some set as early as the sixteenth century. Next themes of realistic picture storybooks that take place afer recovery from World War II are analyzed.

## Themes of Prizewinning Contemporary Fiction in Picture Storybooks Grouped under These Topics

*Concepts*

**Preschool.** Marie Hall Ets's *Just Me* presents her text in brown type and her illustrations in black-and-white lithographs.[19] She tells about a little boy who, after imitating the way various animals move, hears his Dad call and runs to him. He says, "And *now* I ran like nobody else at all! JUST ME."[20] The theme is the same as the concept the book develops for young children: that they are unique in the world of nature.

**Preschool and Primary Grades.** Janice May Udry's first book for children conveys its underlying concept and theme in its title, *A Tree Is Nice,*[21] a book whose slender, vertical shape suggests a tree. Marc Simont's illustrations, half in full color, accentuate the author's simple statements about delights to be had in or under a tree, such as picking apples, raking leaves, or swinging. There may be subtle sexual stereotyping in Simont's illustrations of tree climbers, seven boys and only one clearly defined girl, while a girl on the ground boosts a boy up a limb.

Margaret Wise Brown's *A Child's Good Night Book* conveys the theme and concept that animals as well as children sleep.[22] She says, "The little fish in the darkened sea sleep with their eyes wide open. Sleepy fish."[23] There is minimal, large-type text. Featured are Jean Charlot's colored-pencil illustrations of sleeping birds, fish, animals, and children.

**Preschool through Middle Grades.** The concept of a storm is the theme of Charlotte Zolotow's *The Storm Book*,[24] illustrated in watercolor and line drawings by Margaret Bloy Graham. A little boy observes an electrical storm in the country from the period of stillness before it starts to the rainbow afterward. His mother explains that lightning is the source of lamplight, and thunder comes from "rain clouds breaking against each other."[25] Her answers help remove his fears and those of other children.

The importance of good vision is the theme and concept projected in *Spectacles* by author-illustrator Ellen Raskin.[26] Young Iris Vogel sees her baby-sitter as a chestnut mare, her aunt as a fire-breathing dragon, and her friend, Chester, as a fat kangaroo until she gets corrective spectacles. Humorous illustrations show the way Iris sees people without glasses and the way they really look.

**Primary and Middle Grades.** Helen Coutant's *First Snow* is illustrated by the author's husband, Vo-Dinh.[27] The book's concept and theme is accepting death as a part of life. This Buddhist belief is communicated by a Vietnamese grandmother who believes she will die when it first snows in New England, and she prepares her granddaughter, Liên, for what actually transpires.

*Inviting Pleasant Dreams*

**Preschool and Primary Grades.** Susan Jeffers's fanciful, colored illustrations enhance Jean Marzollo's *Close Your Eyes*.[28] This book, inspired by a lullaby, shows how a father tries to dispel his son's fear of the night with the theme of inviting pleasant dreams. The story is about a non-stereotyped father who brings his young son from outside, gives him a bath, and dresses him in pajamas. While the father is not looking, the child hides under the bed. The father urges the boy to close his eyes and overcome fears by having nice thoughts, so he might dream about them. The boy finally falls asleep.

*Discovery*

**Primary and Middle Grades.** Lavinia R. Davis's *Roger and the Fox* is illustrated in blue, brown, black, and white by Hildegard Woodward.[29] The story tells about seven-year-old Roger, a city boy who moves with his family to a farm and readily sees squirrels, rabbits, mice, turtles and chipmunks. He learns to ski because he is determined to see the Red Fox by himself in its habitat. The book's theme is discovery, for Roger is rewarded by seeing not one, but two foxes before they disappear in the snow.

The joy of discovery is also the theme of *Time of Wonder* by author-illustrator Robert McCloskey.[30] He shows his daughter Sal and her younger sister Jane exploring a Maine seacoast island. With soft gray and yellow watercolor he paints a foggy morning so quiet one can hear "the sound of growing ferns."[31] On another day, the quiet yields to a thunderous hurricane, and the artist, his wife, and daughters face it together. Afterward, the girls walk on tops of giant fallen trees and find shell heaps where trees were uprooted. Some discoveries await them, for the book ends encouraging a time to wonder about such questions as "Where do hummingbirds go in a hurricane?"[32]

In an interview, McCloskey shows his drawing of Sal in her flute-playing days with Jane at the piano. He says:

> My daughters went on strike when they found that other children didn't have to pose for their father. I had to take advantage of every time that they were quiet to make drawings of them.[33]

He explains that, in the dozen years transpiring since that sketch, both daughters have built their own homes in Maine. While Jane is a former boat builder, Sal and her husband are attorneys.

*Nature*

**Preschool and Primary Grades.** Janice May Udry's *The Moon Jumpers* is enhanced by Maurice Sendak's illustrations in jewel tones on seven double-page spreads.[34] Enjoying moonlight is the book's theme. Four children, turned into night nymphs by moonlight, dance, turn somersaults, and try to touch the moon by jumping. They call themselves The Moon Jumpers, but their pleasure ends at bedtime.

**Primary and Middle Grades.** Leonard Wesigard uses a yellow, dark brown, gray, and rust palette for Alvin Tresselt's *Rain Drop Splash*,[35] whose theme is ever-larger bodies of water from prolonged rain. Tresselt tells about rain so heavy it increases a puddle into a pond which then becomes a brook. The brook tumbles into a lake that flows into a river that merges with the sea. Finally, the rain stops.

Gene Zion's *Really Spring* is colorfully illustrated by Margaret Bloy Graham.[36] Its theme—impatience for spring—is expressed as city dwellers paint artificial flowers to evoke spring. They ask, ''Why wait for spring to change everything to grass and flowers? Let's change it ourselves right now!''[37] Rain washes their art away, but from the rain grow lush plants that Graham illustrates in green, blue, and yellow tones.


*Winter Preparations and Survival*

**Preschool and Primary Grades.** The blue-and-white illustrations of author-illustrator Robert McCloskey in *Blueberries for Sal* add to the homespun effect of this story whose theme is mothers preparing for winter.[38] The main characters are McCloskey's wife and his daughter Sal when she was a toddler. Little Sal's mother takes her to Blueberry Hill to gather blueberries for winter. On the hill's other side, Little Bear's mother brings him to eat berries to keep him fat over winter. The young ones become attached to the wrong mothers. Before returning them peacefully, McCloskey captures as much fear on Mother Bear's face as on that of Sal's mother. Properly reunited, the bears descend one side of the hill eating berries, storing their winter food in their stomachs. Down the other side go Little Sal and her mother, gathering four pails of berries for winter. The book helps children realize that animals and human beings alike prepare for winter.

In an interview, McCloskey tells the origin of *Blueberries for Sal:*

> The story occurred to me one afternoon when we were all out as a family in the blueberries. Peggy [my wife] was picking industriously and Sal was picking and eating and kuplink, kuplank, kuplunking a few berries in her little pail. I was sitting there with my sketchbook in a dreamy fashion when the story occurred to me. I added the bear.

> The model for the old-fashioned kitchen stove on the end paper of *Blueberries for Sal* came from the house of Peggy's mother, Ruth Sawyer [a famous storyteller and author]. I thought her stove would make a more interesting drawing than the white gas stove we were using.[39]

McCloskey doesn't show winter, but Roger Duvoisin does in his red, yellow, and black illustrations for Alvin Tresselt's *White Snow, Bright Snow*.[40] The book's theme is winter occurrences and seasonal changes viewed differently by adults and children. When it snows, the postman wears rubbers, and the policeman buttons his coat.

> But the children laughed and danced, trying to catch the lacy snow-flakes on their tongues. They dreamed of snow houses and snowmen as they slept in their beds.[41]

Fun on a snowy day is the theme of *The Snowy Day* by author-illustrator Ezra Jack Keats.[42] Marbleized end paper decorated with snow-flakes appropriately introduces this story of Peter, a little Black boy in a red snowsuit, who enjoys tracking in the snow, lying down to fashion angels, and building a snowman. He puts a snowball in his pocket when he goes into his warm home to nap, but finds it gone when he awakens.

Keats illustrates *The Snowy Day* in full color, using collage exten-sively for the fabric of Peter's pajamas and his mother's dress, the wall-paper, tree, and much of the background paper. He marbleizes the paper by first dropping diluted oil paints into a shallow pan of water, stirring them, and gently pressing the paper atop the surface to form a print.

The salient points Keats makes in an interview are as follows:

> I deal with universal themes. The things I've experienced in my own childhood in Brooklyn, both good and bad, come into play. . . .

> *The Snowy Day* was the first book that was really my own. It was also the first full-color picture book where the hero is Black, and he doesn't appear through the courtesy of other people. He's there because he ought to be. . . .

> Where does Peter come from? Long before I ever thought of doing children's books, I found photos of him in a magazine. The boy's expressive face, his clothes, his gestures captivated me. For years he was on my studio wall or tucked in a drawer. When *The Snowy Day* was finished, I inquired of the magazine how long ago these pictures were printed. To my astonishment, I found I had known this little boy for twenty-two years. . . .

> In addition to being inspired by a clipping, when I did *The Snowy Day*, I did use a model. I wanted to be sure when I did Peter that he looked like a Black boy, not like a White kid colored black, so I made many studies of his face. . . .

> Peter's become like a real person to me. After the third book on Peter, I noticed he's growing, and I wasn't even aware of it. He grew so big, I introduced Archie to have a younger boy in the series.[43]

Keats comments on abstract elements in *The Snowy Day:*

> The figure of Peter you see walking through the snow is almost an

abstract shape. Peter and the background are both simplified. The hills
of snow are pure shapes, no shadows. When I started *The Snowy Day,*
I didn't have that much experience in collage. I wanted to keep it
simple, but I've been able to put more detail and paint more as the
stories became more complex.[44]

Keats's ability to relate to children is apparent in the interview. When
a third-grade pupil asks how long it takes him to write a story and draw
its pictures, Keats encourages a guess, and the response, ''Two days?''
invites chuckles.

**Preschool through Middle Grades.** Bernice Freschet's *Bear Mouse* is
illustrated in black, white, and amber by Donald Carrick.[45] This is a
factual account presented in story form of a small mouse who is so
shaggy, she looks like a bear when she stands. The book's theme is
survival, for it is winter, and a mother mouse in a snow tunnel must
provide nourishment for her four babies. Her enemies, a large snow owl
and hungry bobcat, wait nearby, but despite their threatening presence,
she manages to bring her babies food from a squirrel's nest.

*Birds*

**Preschool through Middle Grades.** In rose-tinted and multicolored illustrations, author-illustrator Leo Politi presents *Song of the Swallows,*[46]
a modern story set in California's San Juan, Capistrano where there is
an old Spanish mission. The book's theme is friends sharing an interest
in swallows. Young Juan hears old Julian, the mission caretaker, explain
how the swallows winter in an unknown place, but always return to
Capistrano on Saint Joseph's Day. Juan helps Julian prepare the mission
gardens as a nesting place for the swallows, and the boy even plants a
garden at his own home. The two ring the mission bell together to signal
the return of the swallows. Juan is delighted when two birds choose to
nest at his home.

Seasonal migrations is the theme of a story from another part of the
world, *Wheel on the Chimney,*[47] by Margaret Wise Brown and Tibor
Gergely. Gergely is the illustrator of this full-color, life-cycle story about
storks who nest in the spring in Hungary. A Hungarian farmer ties a
wheel to his chimney as a nesting site, believing a nesting stork brings
good luck. The storks fly to Hungary from Africa with some secret
knowledge of seasons expressed as follows:

How did they [storks] know in that far away land that spring had come in the lands of the North? This is still a secret of the storks—North or South.[48]

When Hungarian air grows colder, these white storks fly with black storks from wild northern forests to their winter abode. It is the land of the Nile where they meet their cousins, crimson flamingos.

*Patience Rewarded*

**Preschool and Primary Grades.** Taro Yashima uses colored pencils to illustrate his story, *Umbrella*,[49] which is about his daughter Momo when she was three years old. She receives rubber boots and an umbrella for her birthday, but cannot use them until a rainy day.

> Momo asked her mother, who used to take her to the nearby nursery school, "Why the rain doesn't fall?" The answer was always the same: "Wait, wait; it will come."[50]

A rainy day does come, and Momo's patience is rewarded, the book's theme.

Patience rewarded is also the theme of Alvin Tresselt's *Hide and Seek Fog*,[51] illustrated by Roger Duvoisin with gouache (tempera paint with white color added). Tresselt tells about a New England seaside resort community plagued for days during vacation season with a fog that tests everyone. "The fathers scowled and complained about spending their vacations in the middle of a cloud."[52] Finally, the fog lifts, the "damp cotton-wool" thins out, and patience is rewarded. The theme is depicted in illustrations that are hazy during the fog and sharper once it clears.

*Fish*

**Primary and Middle Grades.** Text and small black-and-white illustrations arc simple in M.B. Goffstein's *Fish for Supper*.[53] The theme of this diminutive book is a routine centered on fishing. Goffstein tells how Grandmother arises at five in the morning, goes fishing, brings her catch home, and fries fish for supper. She retires early, so she can repeat her routine the next day.

A boy who fries fish as often as Goffstein's Grandmother is Si in Marcia Brown's *Skipper John's Cook*.[54] Brown illustrates her book in red, black, blue, and ocher tones. Her story is about Skipper John who wants a new cook because his previous chefs antagonized the crew by serving only beans. Si, a plucky boy, not only makes beans, but also fries fish for every meal. The theme is a chef needing to vary meals, for when the ship lands, Skipper John seeks another cook.


*Growth*

**Primary and Middle Grades.** Berta and Elmer Hader are author-illustrators of *Cock-a-Doodle Doo, the Story of a Little Red Rooster,*[55] enhanced with delicate watercolor and black-and-white illustrations. Growing up is the theme of this story of a baby chick, Little Red, who is a misfit because he hatches with ducklings. When he hears a rooster crow from a neighboring farm, he follows the call, though he travels through a dangerous meadow to reach the farm. Once in the safety of the farm's chicken house, he finally feels at home. In time he becomes a rooster.

**Primary and Middle Grades.** Conrad Buff does brown-and-white gentle illustrations and three beautiful two-page colored spreads which help depict the growth theme of *Dash and Dart.*[56] This book by Mary and Conrad Buff is written in prose that clearly approximates poetry. It traces the childhood of two fawns, Dash, and his sister, Dart, from a period after their birth until they become independent. They learn to eat acorns, willow twigs, grasses, and leaves. "And they eat and eat and eat and they grow and grow and grow."[57] His reflection in the lake shows Dash two tiny knobs that will become antlers. "Some day Dash will be a great buck. . . . When he grows up."[58]

The subject of development shifts from animals to human beings. Robert McCloskey's blue-and-white detailed illustrations emphasize the growth theme of *One Morning in Maine,*[59] a story of his own family in a Maine island summer home. The tale focuses on the fact that his older daughter, Sal, has her first loose tooth. She announces this to a loon among other island animals, adding, "And today I have started to be a big girl."[60] She loses her tooth while digging for clams with her father. He reminds her, "You are growing into a big girl, and big girls don't cry about a little thing like that."[61] Even though she has no tooth to put under her pillow, Sal gets her wish for a chocolate ice cream cone. Feeling mature, she orders vanilla for her younger sister, Jane, "so the drips won't spot, . . . because she's still almost a baby."[62]

In an interview, McCloskey says that *One Morning in Maine* is his first book with illustrations of himself. He adds:

I keep a mirror in my studio at all times. I use it not only when I'm drawing myself, but when I'm drawing a hand, a foot, or an action. I'm often my own model.[63]

Older than McCloskey's daughters in *One Morning in Maine* is the protagonist in *Henry Fisherman, a Story of the Virgin Islands* by author-illustrator Marcia Brown.[64] When Henry, who lives in the Virgin Islands, wants to fish in the deep sea, his father says, "Oh, you'll have to do plenty growing, Mon."[65] Illustrations show him fulfilling many tasks, like carrying water pails on his head, washing clothes, and marketing, before his father needs a helper and takes him fishing. From then on, he goes to sea daily, his mother declaring him "a fisherman now for true."[66] Recognition of growing up is the book's theme.


*Imagination*

**Preschool.** On a tan background, Maurice Sendak does humorous illustrations in blue, black, and white for Ruth Krauss's *A Very Special House*.[67] The book's theme, imagination, becomes apparent when the boy explains, "I know a house . . . it's not a house you'd see . . . it's just a house for me Me ME."[68] In this house, one could write on the walls, jump on the bed, spill drinks, and have all kinds of pets. Instead of saying, "Stop!" everyone would yell, "More!" He admits the house exists "root in the moodle of my head head head."[69]

**Primary and Middle Grades.** Phyllis McGinley's *The Most Wonderful Doll in the World* has Helen Stone's illustrations, some in black and white and some in full color.[70] The illustrations in this small book show how young, dissatisfied Dulcy improves her dolls with wishful thinking. They clarify the theme of an imaginative child who finally begins to distinguish between fantasy and reality. When Dulcy loses her doll, Angela, she imagines her wonderful assets. Upon recovering her, however, she notes:

> I found her. And she doesn't have a lot of clothes or talk or sing or skate or wave, or anything all that wonderful. I must have just made it all up out of my head.[71]

Danger in fantasizing is the theme of Evaline Ness's *Sam, Bangs and Moonshine*.[72] She uses collage with line and wash to illustrate her story in somber green, black, and olive, fitting for its sensitive contents. She tells about a fisherman's young daughter, Samantha, nicknamed Sam, a lonely, motherless child. Bangs is her cat, and moonshine is her term for her wild imagination. Her father warns, "Moonshine spells trouble,"[73] but she tells trusting young Thomas to look for her baby kangaroo at Blue Rock. Both he and Bangs go there during high tide and almost die. Ness illustrates Sam's remorseful face. The girl gives her pet gerbil, Moonshine, to rescued Thomas and thereafter, no longer moonshines. This is one of the few picture storybooks that show character development.

*Impression*

**Preschool.** Eugene Ionesco's *Story Number 1*,[74] with watercolor illustrations by Etienne Delessert, is built on a theme of incorrect impressions. Josette, who is thirty-three months old, listens to her father's story about a girl, Jacqueline. The girl's mother is Mrs. Jacqueline, the father is Mr. Jacqueline, and all other story characters are named Jacqueline. Later, when the maid takes Josette shopping, the child meets a peer named Jacqueline. Josette says, "I know. Your papa is named Jacqueline, your mama is named Jacqueline, . . ."[75] When other shoppers stare, the maid explains the child's source of information.

*Resolving Problems*

**Preschool through Middle Grades.** Clare Turlay Newberry offers red-captioned, gentle illustrations in rose, black, and red tones in her book, *April's Kitten*.[76] Her father says six-year-old April lives in a one-cat apartment, but Sheba, their cat, has three kittens. April gives away two and will reluctantly relinquish Brenda, a favorite kitten, if she must choose between Brenda and the mother cat. Resolving a problem, the book's theme, is apparent when April's parents decide to move to a bigger, two-cat apartment.

**Primary and Middle Grades.** Benjamin Elkin's *Gillespie and the Guards* is humorously illustrated in brown, black, and white by James Daugherty.[77] The contemporary story's theme is problem solving by ingenuity. A king is so proud of three guards' superior vision, he promises a gold and diamond medal to anyone who can trick them. A little boy, Gillespie, enters the contest and daily brings a wagonload of worthless materials, like leaves, sand, and trash, past the guards. Gillespie wins the medal because the guards only consider the contents, and he brings from the palace storeroom to his home "dozens and dozens and dozens of little red wagons!"[78]

Resolving a problem is also the theme of Munro Leaf's *Wee Gillis*,[79] illustrated by Robert Lawson in pen and ink with cross-hatching and humorous detail. The green-and-white end papers set the mood for a story about Scotland. The relatives of Wee Gillis, a young boy, want him to become either a Lowlander, like his mother's folks who raise cows, or a Highlander, like his father's family who stalk stags. He takes turns living in both areas and expands his lungs by calling cows or holding his breath to be quiet near stags. He now can breathe like a bagpiper, and that is what he chooses to be, living in a house "half-way up the side of a medium-sized hill."[80]

*Deciding What Is Best*

**Primary and Middle Grades.** Kurt Wiese's *Fish in the Air* is illustrated by him in purple, blue, yellow, black, green, and brown.[81] Wiese, who has been to China on business, draws a Chinese setting with authenticity. His book has a theme of big not always being best. In China, a boy named Little Fish has a lantern and shoes that look like fish. At his request, his father, Big Fish, buys him a huge fish-shaped kite. When wind carries the kite high in the air, Little Fish ascends with it and falls into a fisherman's net only after a hawk bites the kite. The retrieved boy now tells his father, "Honorable Fish, I want you to buy me the smallest fish kite there is."[82]

Margot Zemach's humorous illustrations in watercolor help depict the theme of Yuri Suhl's *Simon Boom Gives a Wedding*.[83] His theme suggests judging what is best for each occasion. For his only daughter's wedding, he wants to serve the best food. He plans to buy fish, but the fisherman indirectly sends him to a sugar merchant by claiming, "Our fish are sweet as sugar."[84] He thinks sugar must be best, but gets redirected so many times, he winds up serving only cool spring water. When his wife protests, Boom shouts:

> Only water! . . . But what *kind* of water? I served them water that is sweeter than sugar, dearer than honey, purer than oil, and better then all three of them. I served them the Best. The very Best![85]

*Establishing a Creative Tradition*

**Primary and Middle Grades.** Illustrations are essential in Katherine Milhous's *The Egg Tree*,[86] whose theme is establishing a creative tradition. She illustrates every other page in orange, brown, and rose. Her color scheme for the remaining pages is pink, yellow, green, gray, blue, black, and white. Writing about a Pennsylvania Dutch family, she appropriately borders some pages with their traditional designs. Her story begins when Katy, in her first Easter egg hunt at Grandmom's, explores the attic and finds six ornate eggshells in an old hatbox. Grandmom hangs the eggs on a little tree in the house. She teaches children how to decorate eggs, and each year, people visit her red farmhouse to see an ever-expanding egg tree.

*Contentment*

**Primary Grades.** Arnold Lobel illustrates Anne Rose's *As Right as Right Can Be*,[87] a story whose theme is finding contentment. After Ron Ronson buys new shoelaces, he decides to buy a new outfit to go with the laces. Since his wife, Rona, buys new clothes to match his, their house seems too drab. In keeping with their new clothes, they borrow money for a large new house and new furniture, but creditors take everything back. After the Ronsons carry their old furnishings into their old house, their crumbling old things match nicely. When Ron Ronson expresses that everything's all right, Rona happily replies, "As right as right can be."[88]

**Primary and Middle Grades.** Contentment with a realized goal is the theme of *Ben's Trumpet* by author-illustrator Rachel Isadora.[89] With minimal text and jazzy, black-and-white illustrations, Isadora tells about Ben, a young Black boy, who pretends to play a trumpet until a Zig Zag Jazz Club musician starts to teach him on a real instrument.

Hope Newell's *The Little Old Woman Who Used Her Head and Other Stories* has black-and-white illustrations by Margaret Ruse.[90] The book's theme is a nonsensical thinker finding contentment. When a little old woman has to solve a difficult problem, she ties a wet towel around her head and sits with closed eyes and forefinger against her nose. For instance, when she needs a new blanket, she buys geese for a feather quilt, makes coats to keep the geese warm after she plucks their feathers, and lets them sleep in her house while she sleeps in the barn. Pleased with her illogical solutions, the little old woman concludes:

> I have used my head so much this year that I will give it a rest. . . .
> It will be very pleasant to sit by my fire and think how contented and
> happy we are, all because I used my head.[91]

Somewhat more predictable is the protagonist in *Jonah the Fisherman* by French author-illustrator Reiner Zimnik.[92] The book's theme, contentment upon returning to one's homeland, is reinforced in pen-and-ink illustrations. The story is about Jonah who fishes on the banks of the Seine and learns how to catch only big fish, one as big as a hog. Jealous fishermen have him arrested and exiled. He travels in Europe and America telling sea captains how to catch big fish, they reward him, and he becomes wealthy. Though king of fishermen, he is unhappy. Homesick, he returns to Paris to catch only little fish, giving his money to students and market women. Other Parisians make him content when they welcome "our Jonah."

*Responsibility*

**Preschool and Primary Grades.** Leonard Weisgard's illustrations amplify the explicit theme, feeling responsible, in Golden MacDonald's *Little Lost Lamb*.[93] A shepherd lad cannot sleep at night because he worries about a lost black lamb who needs him. He leaves his bed to search, worrying that a mountain lion's roar may mean his lamb is hurt. "The shepherd was more afraid for his black sheep than he was afraid for himself."[94] When the lad finds the lamb unharmed, he gratefully carries it. Weisgard's first eleven illustrations of the shepherd during the day show bright, sunlit colors. Commencing on page 31 with the words, "And then the sun began to go down," his next eight illustrations depict night in soft black, white, and brown tones.

Curiosity that leads to being responsible is the theme of Marguerite deAngeli's *Yonie Wondernose*,[95] illustrated by her in black and white and in watercolor. The story is about an Amish boy, Yonie, nicknamed Yonie Wondernose because of his curiosity. One night, when his parents are away and others in the house are asleep, lightning sets the barn on fire. Yonie is so responsible, he leads the animals to safety. His father, who returns in time to help extinguish the fire, praises Yonie by saying, "This time it pays to be a Wondernose!"[96] His father rewards Yonie with a pig, a calf, and the privilege of helping with fall planting.

Like Marguerite deAngeli, Edward Ardizzone is both author and illustrator of his books. An English master of watercolor and pen-and-ink sketches, Ardizzone at times projects cartoon-style conversation in his illustrations for *Tim's Last Voyage*.[97] His full-color seascapes show the ocean's threat and highlight the theme of being responsible and brave. Tim, a young boy who lives on the coast at Goodwin Sands, joins the Arabella's crew with his friend, Ginger, for an intended three-day voyage. When the ship is caught in a gale, engines are flooded and stop, so the trip is prolonged. Scared Ginger acts as a foil or contrasting character highlighting Tim's bravery. Tim helps a carpenter, Joey Adze, stitch a sail to steady the ship.

> When Tim's fingers became too sore to go on stitching he would wedge himself into a corner and read *Moby Dick* to Joey. This made them both feel happier.[98]

After the captain admits they are lost, Tim sees Goodwin Sands and guides them home. Abandoning the sinking vessel, the boy is responsible enough to take the ship's cat on a lifeboat. Not until he is an adult does he go to sea again, but he becomes a captain then.

*War*

**Primary and Middle Grades.** Louise Fitzhugh's illustrations for her book with Sandra Scoppettone, *Bang Bang You're Dead,*[99] help depict the theme of the difference between play war and real war. Four boys, James, Bert, Timothy, and Stanley, play "Bang bang you're dead," but another group claims their same hill and announces, "You'll have to take it away from us . . . three o'clock tomorrow . . ."[100] When the Great War begins, there are screams, yells, clubbing, blood, and painful bruises, all depicted graphically in the illustrations. Fortunately, the gangs decide to share the hill, return the following day for play war, and become friends. This book is considered controversial though it speaks against violence.

*Bored or Challenged by Neighborhood*

**Preschool through Middle Grades.** Failure to appreciate a neighborhood is the theme of Ellen Raskin's *Nothing Ever Happens on My Block.*[101] Raskin's humorous illustrations prove her main character, Chester Filbert, is wrong when he complains that nothing ever happens in the block of 5264 West 177 Street. Chester is oblivious to his surroundings, however, and in the end announces, "When I grow up, I want to move."[102]

Another viewpoint is found in Martha Whitmore Hickman's *I'm Moving,*[103] realistically illustrated by Leigh Grant. The book's theme is anxiety assuaged by love. Young William is disturbed to leave his old neighborhood, but adjusts to his new setting, concluding, "I still have my same mommy and daddy and turtle and me."[104]

*Family Relationships*

**Preschool through Middle Grades.** Clare Turlay Newberry's *Barkis*,[105] with her gentle brown, black, and beige illustrations, has sharing as its theme. On his ninth birthday, James gets Barkis, a cocker spaniel puppy with curly ears. James's ten-and-a-half-year-old sister, Nell Jean, owns a cat, Edward, but still covets the puppy. After Barkis falls in a cold creek and Nell Jean saves him, she bargains with her brother thus:

> "Barkis can be partly mine, but *mostly* yours, and Edward can be partly yours, but *mostly* mine. Okay?"
>
> "Okay!" cried James.[106]

A sadder book, small in size, is Charolotte Zolotow's *My Grandson Lew*,[107] which has colored-pencil illustrations by William Pène du Bois. The book's theme, shared memories, is conveyed when young Lew discovers his Grandfather is dead and tells his mother warm recollections of him. After Lew confides that he misses the tall, bearded man, his mother replies:

> So do I. . . . But now we will remember him together and neither of us will be so lonely as we would be if we had to remember him alone.[108]

**Primary and Middle Grades.** The birth of a child can be traumatic for the older sibling, as Eloise Greenfield shows in *She Come Bringing Me that Little Baby Girl*,[109] a vernacular tale of a warm Black family. John Steptoe's bold illustrations help depict the theme of conquering jealousy over a new baby. Five-year-old Kevin asks his mother for a brother, but she brings home a girl too little for football. Guests forget him when seeing the baby. Then Mother embraces him, asking for his help. He notes when friends come to his home:

> They just stood there looking at my sister like they had never seen a baby that pretty before. I was watching them though. I had to be sure they didn't squeeze her too hard or anything.[110]

In an interview, Steptoe answers a question about outlining the illustrated figures in Greenfield's book. He states, "The things that people usually think are lines are dark backgrounds around foregrounds."[111] He says he and Eloise Greenfield are Black creators of children's books who, in other stories, are concerned with unique Black experiences.

*Chinese Culture*

**Preschool through Middle Grades.** Appreciating Chinese culture is the theme of *Moy Moy* by author-illustrator Leo Politi.[112] The story is told from the viewpoint of Lily, the only daughter and youngest of four children. Her nickname, Moy Moy, means little sister in Chinese. Her parents, who come from China, perpetuate their culture by living in Los Angeles's Chinatown and sending their school-age sons to afternoon Chinese classes. Moy Moy is free to enjoy Chinese shops and Chinese New Year preparations, aspects of the theme portrayed in Politi's bright illustrations.

**Primary and Middle Grades.** *Mei Li,*[113] by author-illustrator Thomas Handforth, features black-and-white detailed illustrations by a master craftsman whose etchings and lithographs hang in New York's Metropolitan Museum of Art. Handforth's Chinese characters on the back of his book jacket mean Mei Li's Chinese New Year. Search for a role within and beyond the family is the theme of this story that occurs during the Chinese New Year in a walled city near the Great Wall of North China. In the morning, Mei Li's family prepares a feast for the Kitchen God who visits at midnight to tell them what to do during the coming year. Escaping kitchen chores, the young girl joins her older brother, San Yu, at a fair where a fortune teller says Mei Li will rule a kingdom. Later, when the tired girl gratefully returns home, her mother welcomes "the princess who rules our hearts."[114] Mei Li questions where her kingdom is, and the Kitchen God answers, "This house is your kingdom and palace."[115]

*Chicano Culture*

**Preschool through Middle Grades.** Giving and receiving during a Chicano Christmas celebration is the theme of Leo Politi's *Pedro, the Angel of Olvera Street.*[116] Politi has lived on Olvera Street, Los Angeles's small Chicano street where venders sell curios to tourists. His illustrations, many in full color, show the setting, accenting red-tile roofs, booths, and nighttime Christmas *posadas* or processionals where participants walk with lit candles, reenacting the quest of Mary and Joseph for lodging. The small book shows how young Pedro, a singing angel with red wings, makes a contribution as procession leader. Afterward, though blindfolded, he breaks a *piñata,* a decorated container filled with candy and gifts, and rushes to get a gift.

Pedro came out of the rush . . . smiling and in his hands he held a small music box. It was this music box he had wished for most.[117]

Other illustrations in watercolor of Olvera Street enhance Leo Politi's *Juanita*,[118] a larger book whose theme is love of family and pet. Dressmaker María and basket weaver Antonio are Olvera Street venders at a booth called Juanita in honor of their four-year-old daughter. For her birthday, Antonio gives Juanita a dove. The loving child dressed in pink takes her white dove in the parade for the Blessing of the Animals, and she sleeps with it on Easter eve.

*Laughter*

**Primary through Middle Grades.** Georges Schreiber's illustrations in watercolor for his *Bambino the Clown*[119] help convey the theme of a desire to make others laugh. The story is about a clown from Italy who is small and called Bambino because that is the Italian word for child. Bambino makes children laugh. "In fact, he lived to make everyone laugh."[120] When he finds little Peter crying over a lost hat, Bambino gives him one with a feather. After a fine circus show with Flapper, a sea lion, Bambino tells Peter:

Now you know how to be a clown. You must remember just one thing. To laugh and make everybody laugh . . . even when you lose your hat.[121]

*Friendship*

**Preschool.** Marie Hall Ets's illustrations in yellow, white, black, and green on a beige background reflect her theme, need for playmates, stated in her title, *Play with Me*.[122] A preschool girl invites a grasshopper, frog, turtle, chipmunk, blue jay, rabbit, and snake to play with her. At first, they leave, but they later sit beside her, joined by a fawn who licks her cheek. She exudes happiness for "All of them—ALL OF THEM—were playing with me."[123]

**Preschool and Primary Grades.** Clare Turlay Newberry's soft black-and-white illustrations for her book, *T-Bone, the Baby Sitter*,[124] help her brief text convey a friendship theme. She tells about T-Bone, a large black-and-white cat who pushes the Pinny's baby in her swing and watches over her as she sleeps. One day, in a mischievous mood, T-Bone plays with Mrs. Pinny's stockings and tears her best hat. The furious mother sends T-Bone elsewhere, but when the baby cries without him, she takes him back. Baby, upon seeing her friend again, says her first word, "Kitty."

A boy's friendship with a professor is the theme of Lavinia R. Davis's *The Wild Birthday Cake,*[125] illustrated by Hildegard Woodward in blue, green, yellow, and black tones suitable for an outdoor setting. Davis tells about seven-year-old Johnny who celebrates the birthday of his favorite friend, the Professor, with a card on birch bark. He also gives the man a lame wild duck, a female mallard he captures on his hike and puts in the Professor's pond. The boy calls her Birthday Cake because he catches her with cake crumbs, and she later gets some of the Professor's birthday cake.

A cat is the subject of Ezra Jack Keats's *Hi, Cat!,*[126] illustrated by him in bright acrylics and collage with shreds of newspaper, other printed matter, and marbleized background paper. The book's theme is a cat's friendship incurred with an innocent "hi." The story begins when Archie says, "Hi, Cat!" to a black cat with white paws and white throat. After ruining Archie's sidewalk show for friends, the cat follows the boy home. Archie tells his mother, "I think that cat just kinda liked me!"[127]

**Preschool through Middle Grades.** *Goggles,*[128] another book by author-illustrator Ezra Jack Keats, has cooperative friendship as its theme. Keats relates that, after finding motorcycle goggles, Peter and his young chum, Archie, have to protect themselves from covetous bullies. In a fight, the goggles fall, and Peter's dachshund, Willie, retrieves them, returning them to the boy.

Another Black boy is featured in *Stevie,*[129] a book created in full color by Black author-illustrator John Steptoe when he was only seventeen. Steptoe gives credit for *Stevie* to Ursula Nordstrom, an editor "with a terrific sense of timing."[130] Concern for a young chum, though often a tag-along pest, is the book's theme. Robert, the narrator, resents Stevie, the child with whom his mother baby-sits, until the child leaves. Then the narrator misses the small boy.

A relationship between two animals—a big black cat, Oliver, and a white rabbit, Marshmallow—is portrayed in Clare Turlay Newberry's *Marshmallow.*[131] Newberry's black, white, and rose illustrations project the adoptive-friendship theme. At first, Oliver wanted to bounce on the rabbit, but Marshmallow kissed him on the nose. Oliver "adopted the little bunny and brought him up as his own kitten."[132]

One kitten and seventeen cats share a coastal house with an old lady in Margaret Wise Brown's small book, *When the Wind Blew.*[133] Geoffrey Hayes's humorous, diminutive illustrations in watercolor support the

theme, companionship with animals. Hayes's illustrations are more appealing than those by another artist which appeared in the 1937 edition
of the book. Brown tells about a day when the cold wind blows, and the
old lady has a bad toothache. She goes to bed, and the little grey kitten
she especially likes puts its warm body next to her painful cheek, like a
fur-covered hot water bottle. In the end:

> The cabin grew warmer, and the little blue, grey kitten purred on by
> the old lady's cheek until she forgot that she had ever had a toothache,
> and it almost seemed as though the old lady were purring, too . . .[134]

A more unusual comrade, a pelican, is in *Come Again, Pelican* by
author-illustrator Don Freeman.[135] Helpful friendship, the book's theme,
is projected in colorful illustrations showing how the pelican teaches Ty
to fish and to recover his lost boot. In this story, Ty shows his appreciation by giving his friend a fish.

Human friends are featured in *The Beast of Monsieur Racine*,[136] a
full-color, humorous farce by author-illustrator Tomi Ungerer. Companionship outweighing greed is the theme of this story set in France. Ungerer tells about a retired tax collector and gardener, Monsieur Racine,
whose motto concerning his prizewinning pears is "No selling, no sharing." However, he befriends a strange beast who eats his pears, and
only after he takes the beast before the Academy of Sciences in Paris
does he discover a hoax. After the creature begins to giggle on stage, a
boy and girl pop from under blankets. Monsieur Racine's sense of humor
prevails, and he returns home to raise "a new crop of pears, which he
happily shared with his two young friends."[137]

**Primary and Middle Grades.** Evaline Ness uses experimental techniques
and a blue, olive, orange, and black color scheme in her book, *A Double
Discovery*,[138] whose theme is friendship based on sharing. This story set
in Japan centers on three characters: Norio, a lonely, bespectacled farm
boy; Saru, a monkey with double vision; and Hoki, a wild pony. Wanting
a ride, the boy chases the pony among the monkeys until he loses his
glasses. Saru the monkey finds them, wears them, and sees well enough
to swing from tree to tree. The boy gets his glasses back but discovers
if he shares them with the monkey, Saru coaxes the pony to take him
riding. A second discovery is the three are becoming friends.

Evaline Ness's inventive techniques and some of her favorite colors—
olive, ocher, orange, and black—again appear in the illustrations for
Rebecca Caudill's *A Pocketful of Cricket*.[139] Friendship with a cricket is
the theme of this story about six-year-old Jay who delights in his rural
setting. Whatever appeals to Jay goes in his pocket, including a cricket.

Though the cricket chirps in school, the boy will not part with it. The sensitive teacher asks, "Jay, . . . is this cricket your friend?"[140] When he nods his head, the teacher lets him display the cricket in "Show and Tell" and share information that delights classmates.

Ness's bright colors seem ideal for the sunny countryside, but Remy Charlip favors full-color pastel illustrations for the book he coauthors with Burton Supree, *Harlequin and the Gift of Many Colors*.[141] The book takes place in Bergamo, Italy before Lent, a time when people relinquish a favorite item. Giving plays a role in this story, whose theme is friends' generosity. Harlequin, a poor lad, cannot afford a carnival costume, so each of his friends donates a piece of cloth, and his mother, a seamstress, sews them together in a bright, patchwork suit. His peers are delighted when he joins them for carnival, "And Harlequin was the happiest of them all on this happy night, for he was clothed in the love of his friends."[142]

Friendship, the theme of Lynd Ward's *The Biggest Bear*,[143] is emphasized in his brown-and-white illustrations that create both pathos and humor. The story is about young Johnny Orchard who befriends a lovable bear cub in the woods and brings it home as a pet. In time, the bear eats so much, he becomes gigantic. When the boy tries to get rid of the pet by rowing him to an island, the bear returns. Mr. Orchard orders his son to shoot the bear, so he takes it into the woods, but both fall into a trap set by zoo personnel. Johnny approves when the zoo contact asks to keep the bear, promising:

> He will have a fine place to live, and all he wants to eat. . . . And you can come and see him whenever you want to.[144]

In an interview, Lynd Ward, a master lithographer and wood engraver, discusses his medium in *The Biggest Bear:*

> *The Biggest Bear* is done in opaque watercolor. Instead of being transparent as ordinary water color is, when you lay down a layer with opaque watercolor, it hides what's underneath it. This quality makes it invaluable . . . because it is possible to change things as I go along.[145]

Upon request, Lynd Ward analyzes an illustration on page 60 of *The Biggest Bear* which shows small Johnny rowing the huge bear to an island. He says:

> You have the main element and other things that go on in a picture. Each of them contribute to the whole, such as the pattern of the wings of the gulls leading back to the circular motion that starts with the

upraised bow of the boat with the island towards which they're going seen in the far distance.

The inspiration for the immense bear being rowed on a lake was really a huge woman who liked to fish near our Canadian summer home.[146]

Ward displays a copy of his Caldecott winner which the publisher covered for him in bearskin. The artist jokes about brushing off any dandruff before having it photographed.

## Summary

This chapter analyzes the primary theme of seventy-seven sample realistic-picture-storybook prizewinners. Nine books are historical fiction, all of which are appropriate for those in primary and middle grades. Stories that require understanding the concept of past time generally are not intended for a preschool audience. Themes of historical fiction are examined under six topics, the most popular being virtue rewarded.

Themes of sixty-nine sample contemporary realistic-picture-storybook prizewinners are examined under twenty-two topics. Though there is only one book with a friendship theme in the chapter's historical fiction, there are thirteen books with this most-popular theme in the chapter's contemporary fiction. The one historical story and nine of those that are contemporary involve friendship between human beings and animals. Other popular topics are: concepts, growth, winter preparations and survival, imagination, resolving problems, contentment, nature, responsibility, and family relationships.

Four contemporary realistic-picture-storybook prizewinners are intended only for a preschool audience. Slightly more books are appropriate for primary and middle grades than for preschool through middle grades, and a lesser number are for preschool and primary grades only. This is fairly good distribution of prizewinners.

Brinton Turkle created two historical-picture-storybook prizewinners in the sample and Taro Yashima one that is historical and one that is contemporary. Prolific author-illustrators of contemporary realistic picture storybooks are creators of the following number of prizewinners: Clare Turlay Newberry and Leo Politi, four apiece; Ezra Jack Keats and Robert McCloskey, three apiece; Evaline Ness, one as illustrator and two as author-illustrator; and Marcia Brown, Marie Hall Ets, and Ellen Raskin, two apiece.

Authors alone of several books in this chapter's contemporary sample have created the following number of prizewinners: Margaret Wise Brown, three; Janice May Udry and Charlotte Zolotow, two apiece; Lavinia R.

Davis, two with Hildegard Woodward as illustrator; and Alvin Tresselt, two with Roger Duvoisin as illustrator. Illustrators alone of two prize-winners in this chapter's contemporary sample are Margaret Bloy Graham, Maurice Sandak, and Leonard Weisgard.

## Notes

1. In 1974, *Hanukah Money* was a *New York Times* Choice of Best Illustrated Children's Book of the Year, and in 1979, it was in the American Institute of Graphic Arts Book Show.

2. Sholem Aleichem, *Hanukah Money* (New York: Morrow, 1978), p. 24.

3. Ibid., p. 13.

4. Ibid., p. 27.

5. In 1979, *The Treasure* was a *New York Times* Best Illustrated Children's Book of the Year. In 1980, it was a Caldecott Honor Book, and it was in the American Institute of Graphic Arts Book Show.

6. In 1970, *Thy Friend, Obadiah* was a Caldecott Honor Book.

7. Brinton Turkle, *Thy Friend, Obadiah* (New York: Viking, 1969), no page.

8. In 1972, *The Adventures of Obadiah* won the Christopher Award in the children's-book category for ages four to eight.

9. Brinton Turkle, *The Adventures of Obadiah* (New York: Viking, 1972), no page.

10. In 1966, *Sven's Bridge* was a *New York Times* Choice of Best Illustrated Children's Book of the Year.

11. In 1956, *Little Big-Feather* was a *New York Times* Choice of Best Illustrated Children's Book of the Year.

12. Joseph Longstreth, *Little Big-Feather* (New York: Abelard, 1956), no page.

13. Ibid., no page.

14. In 1971, *Down Down the Mountain* won the Lewis Carroll Shelf Award.

15. In 1979, *Ox-Cart Man* was a *New York Times* Best Illustrated Children's Book of the Year, and in 1980, it won The Randolph Caldecott Medal.

16. In 1955, *Crow Boy* won the Child Study Children's Book Committee at Bank Street College Award, and in 1956, was a Caldecott Honor Book.

17. Taro Yashima, *Crow Boy* (New York: Viking, 1955), no page.

18. Ibid., p. 23.

19. In 1966, *Just Me* was a Caldecott Honor Book.

20. Marie Hall Ets, *Just Me* (New York: Viking, 1965), no page.

21. In 1957, *A Tree Is Nice* won The Randolph Caldecott Medal.

22. In 1944, *A Child's Good Night Book* was a Caldecott Honor Book.

23. Margaret Wise Brown, *A Child's Good Night Book* (Reading, Mass.: Scott, 1943), no page.

24. In 1953, *The Storm Book* was a Caldecott Honor Book.

25. Charlotte Zolotow, *The Storm Book* (New York: Harper, 1952), no page.

26. In 1968, *Spectacles* was a *New York Times* Choice of Best Illustrated Children's Book of the Year.

27. In 1974, *The First Snow* received the Christopher Award in the children's-book category for ages eight to twelve.

28. In 1974, *Close Your Eyes* was in the American Institute of Graphic Arts Book Show.

29. In 1948, *Roger and the Fox* was a Caldecott Honor Book.

30. In 1958, *Time of Wonder* won The Randolph Caldecott Medal and the Ohioana Book Award.

31. Robert McCloskey, *Time of Wonder* (New York: Viking, 1957), p. 14.

32. Ibid., p. 62.

33. "Robert McCloskey," *Profiles in Literature* (Philadelphia: Temple University, 1977).

34. In 1960, *The Moon Jumpers* was a Caldecott Honor Book.

35. In 1947, *Rain Drop Splash* was a Caldecott Honor Book.

36. In 1956, *Really Spring* was a *New York Times* Choice of Best Illustrated Children's Book of the Year.

37. Gene Zion, *Really Spring* (New York: Harper, 1956), p. 3.

38. In 1949, *Blueberries for Sal* was a Caldecott Honor Book and won the Ohioana Book Award.

39. "Robert McCloskey," *Profiles in Literature* (Philadelphia: Temple University, 1977).

40. In 1948, *White Snow, Bright Snow* won The Randolph Caldecott Medal.

41. Alvin Tresselt, *White Snow, Bright Snow* (New York: Lothrop, 1947), p. 13.

42. In 1963, *The Snowy Day* won The Randolph Caldecott Medal.

43. "Ezra Jack Keats," *Profiles in Literature* (Philadelphia: Temple University, 1970).

44. Ibid.

45. In 1974, *Bear Mouse* won the Irma Simonton Black Award.

46. In 1950, *Song of the Swallows* won The Randolph Caldecott Medal.

47. In 1955, *Wheel on the Chimney* was a Caldecott Honor Book.

48. Margaret Wise Brown and Tibor Gergely, *Wheel on the Chimney* (Philadelphia: Lippincott, 1954), no page.

49. In 1959, *Umbrella* was a Caldecott Honor Book.

50. Taro Yashima, *Umbrella* (New York: Viking, 1958), p. 6.

51. In 1965, *Hide and Seek Fog* was a *New York Times* Choice of Best Illustrated Children's Book of the Year, and in 1966, it was a Caldecott Honor Book.

52. Alvin Tresselt, *Hide and Seek Fog* (New York: Lothrop, 1965), no page.

53. In 1977, *Fish for Supper* was a Caldecott Honor Book.

54. In 1952, *Skipper John's Cook* was a Caldecott Honor Book.

55. In 1940, *Cock-a-Doodle Doo, the Story of a Little Red Rooster* was a Caldecott Honor Book.

56. In 1943, *Dash and Dart* was a Caldecott Honor Book.

57. Mary and Conrad Buff, *Dash and Dart* (New York: Viking, 1942), p. 46.

58. Ibid., p. 75.

59. In 1953, *One Morning in Maine* was a Caldecott Honor Book.

60. Robert McCloskey, *One Morning in Maine* (New York: Viking, 1952), p. 19.

61. Ibid., p. 37.

62. Ibid., p. 60.

63. "Robert McCloskey," *Profiles in Literature* (Philadelphia: Temple University, 1977).

64. In 1950, *Henry Fisherman, a Story of the Virgin Islands,* was a Caldecott Honor Book.

65. Marcia Brown, *Henry Fisherman, a Story of the Virgin Islands* (New York: Scribner, 1949), no page.

66. Ibid., no page.

67. In 1954, *A Very Special House* was a Caldecott Honor Book.

68. Ruth Krauss, *A Very Special House* (New York: Harper, 1953), no page.

69. Ibid., no page.

70. In 1951, *The Most Wonderful Doll in the World* was a Caldecott Honor Book.

71. Phyllis McGinley, *The Most Wonderful Doll in the World* (Philadelphia: Lippincott, 1950), p. 53.

72. In 1967, *Sam, Bangs and Moonshine* won The Randolph Caldecott Medal.

73. Evaline Ness, *Sam, Bangs and Moonshine* (New York: Holt, 1966), no page.

74. In 1968, *Story Number 1* was a *New York Times* Choice of Best Illustrated Children's Book of the Year.

75. Eugene Ionesco, *Story Number 1* (New York: Harlin, 1968), no page.

76. In 1941, *April's Kittens* was a Caldecott Honor Book.

77. In 1957, *Gillespie and the Guards* was a Caldecott Honor Book.

78. Benjamin Elkin, *Gillespie and the Guards* (New York: Viking, 1956), p. 52.

79. In 1939, *Wee Gillis* was a Caldecott Honor Book.

80. Munro Leaf, *Wee Gillis* (New York: Viking, 1938), no page.

81. In 1949, *Fish in the Air* was a Caldecott Honor Book.

82. Kurt Wiese, *Fish in the Air* (New York: Viking, 1948), no page.

83. In 1972, *Simon Boom Gives a Wedding* was a *New York Times* Choice of Best Illustrated Children's Book of the Year, and in 1973, it was in the Children's Book Showcase.

84. Yuri Suhl, *Simon Boom Gives a Wedding* (New York: Four Winds, 1972), no page.

85. Ibid., no page.

86. In 1951, *The Egg Tree* won The Randolph Caldecott Medal.

87. In 1976, *As Right as Right Can Be* was a *New York Times* Choice of Best Illustrated Children's Book of the Year.

88. Anne Rose, *As Right as Right Can Be* (New York: Dial, 1976), no page.

89. Rachel Isadora, *Ben's Trumpet* (New York: Greenwillow, 1979), no page.

90. In 1935, *The Little Old Woman Who Used Her Head* won the Lewis Carroll Shelf Award.

91. Hope Newell, *The Little Old Woman Who Used Her Head* (New York: Nelson, 1935), p. 62.

92. In 1956, *Jonah the Fisherman* was a *New York Times* Choice of Best Illustrated Children's Book of the Year.

93. In 1946, *Little Lost Lamb* was a Caldecott Honor Book.

94. Golden MacDonald, *Little Lost Lamb* (New York: Doubleday, 1945), p. 39.

95. In 1945, *Yonie Wondernose* was a Caldecott Honor Book.

96. Marguerite deAngeli, *Yonie Wondernose* (New York: Doubleday, 1944), p. 35.

97. In 1973, *Tim's Last Voyage* was a *New York Times* Choice of Best Illustrated Childen's Book of the Year.

98. Edward Ardizzone, *Tim's Last Voyage* (New York: Walck, 1972), no page.

99. In 1969, *Bang Bang You're Dead* was a *New York Times* Choice of Best Illustrated Children's Book of the Year.

100. Louise Fitzhugh and Sandra Scoppettone, *Bang Bang You're Dead* (New York: Harper, 1969), p. 19.

101. In 1966, *Nothing Ever Happens on My Block* was a *New York Times* Choice of Best Illustrated Childen's Book of the Year.

102. Ellen Raskin, *Nothing Ever Happens on My Block* (New York: Atheneum, 1968), no page.

103. In 1976, *I'm Moving* won the Friends of American Writers Award in the younger-children's-book category.

104. Martha Whitmore Hickman, *I'm Moving* (Nashville: Abingdon, 1974), no page.

105. In 1939, *Barkis* was a Caldecott Honor Book.

106. Clare Turlay Newberry, *Barkis* (New York: Harper, 1938), p. 30.

107. In 1974, *My Grandson Lew* won the Christopher Award in the children's-book category for ages four to eight.

108. Charlotte Zolotow, *My Grandson Lew* (New York: Harper, 1974), p. 30.

109. In 1975, *She Come Bringing Me that Little Baby Girl* won the Irma Simonton Black Award.

110. Eloise Greenfield, *She Come Bringing Me that Little Baby Girl* (Philadelphia: Lippincott, 1974), no page.

111. "John Steptoe," *Profiles in Literature* (Philadelphia: Temple University, 1975).

112. In 1961, *Moy Moy* won the Southern California Council on Literature for Children and Young People Award.

113. In 1939, *Mei Li* won The Randolph Caldecott Medal.

114. Thomas Handforth, *Mei Li* (New York: Doubleday, 1938), no page.

115. Ibid., no page.

116. In 1947, *Pedro, the Angel of Olvera Street* was a Caldecott Honor Book.

117. Leo Politi, *Pedro, the Angel of Olvera Street* (New York: Scribner, 1946), no page.

118. In 1949, *Juanita* was a Caldecott Honor Book.

119. In 1948, *Bambino the Clown* was a Caldecott Honor Book.

120. Georges Schreiber, *Bambino the Clown* (New York: Viking, 1947), p. 12.

121. Ibid., p. 30.

122. In 1956, *Play with Me* was a Caldecott Honor Book, and it was put on the International Board on Books for Young People Honor List.

123. Marie Hall Ets, *Play with Me* (New York: Viking, 1955), p. 31.

124. In 1951, *T-Bone the Baby Sitter* was a Caldecott Honor Book.

125. In 1950, *The Wild Birthday Cake* was a Caldecott Honor Book.

126. In 1970, *Hi, Cat!* won the *Boston Globe-Horn Book* Award.

127. Ezra Jack Keats, *Hi, Cat!* (New York: Macmillan, 1970), no page.

128. In 1970, *Goggles* was a Caldecott Honor Book.

129. In 1978, *Stevie* won the Lewis Carroll Shelf Award.

130. "John Steptoe," *Profiles in Literature* (Philadelphia: Temple University, 1975).

131. In 1943, *Marshmallow* was a Caldecott Honor Book.

132. Clare Turlay Newberry, *Marshmallow* (New York: Harper, 1942), no page.

133. In 1977, *When the Wind Blew* was a *New York Times* Choice of Best Illustrated Children's Book of the Year.

134. Margaret Wise Brown, *When the Wind Blew* (New York: Harper, 1973), p. 30.

135. In 1962, *Come Again, Pelican* won the Southern California Council on Literature for Children and Young People Award for illustration.

136. In 1971, *The Beast of Monsieur Racine* was a *New York Times* Choice of Best Illustrated Children's Book of the Year.

137. Tomi Ungerer, *The Beast of Monsieur Racine* (New York: Farrar, 1971), no page.

138. In 1965, *A Double Discovery* was a *New York Times* Choice of Best Illustrated Children's Book of the Year.

139. In 1965, *A Pocketful of Cricket* was a Caldecott Honor Book.

140. Rebecca Caudill, *A Pocketful of Cricket* (New York: Holt, 1981), no page.

141. In 1974, *Harlequin and the Gift of Many Colors* won the Irma Simonton Black Award.

142. Remy Charlip and Burton Supree, *Harlequin and the Gift of Many Colors* (New York: Parents Magazine Press, 1973), no page.

143. In 1953, *The Biggest Bear* won The Randolph Caldecott Medal.

144. Lynd Ward, *The Biggest Bear* (Boston: Houghton, 1952), p. 82.

145. "Lynd Ward and May McNeer," *Profiles in Literature* (Philadelphia: Temple University, 1974).

146. Ibid.

## References of Prizewinning Realistic Literature in Picture Storybooks

*(Estimated Reading or Listening Grade Level in Parentheses)*

*Historical Fiction*

Aleichem, Sholem. *Hanukah Money*. Translated by Uri Shulevitz and Elizabeth Shub. Illustrated by Uri Shulevitz. New York: Morrow, 1978 (1–3).

Credle, Ellis. *Down Down the Mountain*. New York: Nelson, 1934 (1–3).

Hall, Donald. *Ox-Cart Man*. Illustrated by Barbara Cooney. New York: Viking, 1979 (1–3).

Lobel, Anita. *Sven's Bridge*. New York: Harper, 1965 (2–4).

Longstreth, Joseph. *Little Big-Feather*. Illustrated by Helen Brown Borten. New York: Abelard, 1956 (1–3).

Shulevitz, Uri. *The Treasure*. New York: Farrar, 1979 (1–3).

Turkle, Brinton. *The Adventures of Obadiah*. New York: Viking, 1972 (1–3).

Wynants, Miche. *The Giraffe of King Charles X*. New York: McGraw, 1961 (1–3).

Yashima, Taro. *Crow Boy*. New York: Viking, 1955 (1–4).

*Contemporary Fiction: Animal Stories*

**Assorted Animals:**

Brown, Margaret Wise. *A Child's Good Night Book*. Illustrated by Jean Charlot. Reading, Mass.: Scott, 1943 (PS–1).

Ets, Marie Hall. *Just Me*. New York: Viking, 1965 (PS–K).

———. *Play with Me*. New York: Viking, 1955 (PS–K).

**Bears:**

McCloskey, Robert. *Blueberries for Sal*. New York: Viking, 1948 (PS–2).

Ward, Lynd. *The Biggest Bear*. Boston: Houghton, 1952 (1–3).

**Birds:**

Brown, Margaret Wise. *Wheel on the Chimney*. Illustrated by Tibor Gergely. Philadelphia: Lippincott, 1954 (1–3).

Freeman, Don. *Come Again, Pelican*. New York: Viking, 1961 (K–3).

Politi, Leo. *Song of the Swallows*. New York: Scribner, 1945 (K–3).

## Cats:
Brown, Margaret Wise. *When the Wind Blew*. Illustrated by Geoffrey Hayes. New York: Harper, 1937 (K–4).

Keats, Ezra Jack. *Hi, Cat!* New York: Macmillan, 1970 (K–2).

Ness, Evaline. *Sam, Bangs and Moonshine*. New York: Holt, 1966 (1–4).

Newberry, Clare Turlay. *April's Kittens*. New York: Harper, 1940 (K–3).

————. *T-Bone, the Baby Sitter*. New York: Harper, 1950 (K–2).

## Cricket:
Caudill, Rebecca. *A Pocketful of Cricket*. Illustrated by Evaline Ness. New York: Holt, 1960 (1–3).

## Deer:
Buff, Mary and Conrad. *Dash and Dart*. Illustrated by Conrad Buff. New York: Viking, 1942 (1–3).

## Duck:
Davis, Lavinia R. *The Wild Birthday Cake*. Illustrated by Hildegard Woodward. New York: Doubleday, 1949 (K–2).

## Dog and Cat:
Newberry, Clare Turlay. *Barkis*. New York: Harper, 1938 (K–3).

## Fish:
Goffstein, M.B. *Fish for Supper*. New York: Dial, 1936 (1–3).

## Fox:
Davis, Lavinia R. *Roger and the Fox*. Illustrated by Hildegard Woodward. New York: Doubleday, 1947 (1–3).

## Lamb:
MacDonald, Golden. *Little Lost Lamb*. Illustrated by Leonard Weisgard. New York: Doubleday, 1945 (PS–1).

## Mice:
Freschet, Bernice. *Bear Mouse*. Illustrated by Donald Carrick. New York: Scribner, 1950 (K–3).

**Monkey and Pony:**
Ness, Evaline. *A Double Discovery*. New York: Scribner, 1965 (2–4).

**Rabbit and Cat:**
Newberry, Clare Turlay. *Marshmallow*. New York: Harper, 1942 (K–3).

**Rooster:**
Hader, Berta and Elmer. *Cock-a-Doodle Doo, the Story of a Lit'le Red Rooster*. New York: Macmillan, 1939 (K–3).

*Stories in Other Lands*

**China:**
Handforth, Thomas. *Mei Li*. New York: Doubleday, 1932 (1–3).
Wiese, Kurt. *Fish in the Air*. New York: Viking, 1942 (1–3).

**England:**
Ardizzone, Edward. *Tim's Last Voyage*. New York: Walck, 1972 (1–4).

**France:**
Ungerer, Tomi. *The Beast of Monsieur Racine*. New York: Farrar, 1971 (K–3).
Zimnik, Reiner. *Jonah the Fisherman*. Translated by Richard and Clara Winston. New York: Pantheon, 1956 (1–4).

**Italy:**
Charlip, Remy, and Supree, Burton. *Harlequin and the Gift of Many Colors*. Illustrated by Remy Charlip. New York: Parents Magazine, 1973 (1–3).

**Scotland:**
Leaf, Munro. *Wee Gillis*. Illustrated by Robert Lawson. New York: Viking, 1938 (1–4).

**Virgin Islands:**
Brown, Marcia. *Henry Fisherman, a Story of the Virgin Islands*. New York: Scribner, 1949 (1–3).

*Stories about U.S. Minorities*

**American Blacks:**
Greenfield, Eloise. *She Come Bringing Me that Little Baby Girl*. Illustrated by John Steptoe. New York: Lippincott, 1974 (1–3).

Isadora, Rachel. *Ben's Trumpet*. New York: Greenwillow, 1979 (1–3).
Keats, Ezra Jack. *Goggles*. New York: Macmillan, 1969 (K–3).
————. *The Snowy Day*. New York: Viking, 1962 (PS–1).
Steptoe, John. *Stevie*. New York: Harper, 1969 (PS–3).

**Amish:**
deAngeli, Marguerite. *Yonie Wondernose*. New York: Doubleday, 1944
    (2–4).

**Chicanos:**
Politi, Leo. *Juanita*. New York: Scribner, 1940 (1–3).
————. *Pedro, the Angel of Olvera Street*. New York: Scribner, 1946
    (1–3).

**Chinese Americans:**
Politi, Leo. *Moy Moy*. New York: Scribner, 1960 (K–3).
Yashima, Taro. *Umbrella*. New York: Viking, 1958 (PS–1).

**Italian:**
Schreiber, Georges. *Bambino the Clown*. New York: Viking, 1947
    (2–3).

**Jewish:**
Suhl, Yuri. *Simon Boom Gives a Wedding*. Illustrated by Margot Ze-
    mach. New York: Four Winds, 1972 (K–3).

**Pennsylvania Dutch:**
Milhous, Katherine. *The Egg Tree*. New York: Scribner, 1950 (1–4).

**Vietnamese Americans:**
Coutant, Helen. *First Snow*. Illustrated by Vo-Dinh. New York: Knopf,
    1974 (1–3).


*General Stories*


Brown, Marcia. *Skipper John's Cook*. New York: Scribner, 1951 (1–3).
Elkin, Benjamin. *Gillespie and the Guards*. Illustrated by James Daugh-
    erty. New York: Viking, 1956 (1–3).
Hickman, Martha Whitmore. *I'm Moving*. Illustrated by Leigh Grant.
    Nashville: Abingdon, 1974 (K–3).
Ionesco, Eugene. *Story Number 1*. Illustrated by Etienne Delessert. New
    York: Harlin, 1968 (PS–K).

Krauss, Ruth. *A Very Special House*. Illustrated by Maurice Sendak. New York: Harper, 1953 (PS–K).

Marzollo, Jean. *Close Your Eyes*. Illustrated by Susan Jeffers. New York: Dial, 1978 (K–2).

McCloskey, Robert. *One Morning in Maine*. New York: Viking, 1952 (1–3).

———. *Time of Wonder*. New York: Viking, 1957 (1–4).

McGinley, Phyllis. *The Most Wonderful Doll in the World*. Illustrated by Helen Stone. Philadelphia: Lippincott, 1950 (1–4).

Newell, Hope. *The Little Old Woman Who Used Her Head*. Illustrated by Margaret Ruse. New York: Nelson, 1973 (1–4).

Raskin, Ellen. *Nothing Ever Happens on My Block*. New York: Atheneum, 1968 (K–3).

———. *Spectacles*. New York: Atheneum, 1968 (K–3).

Rose, Anne. *As Right as Right Can Be*. Illustrated by Arnold Lobel. New York: Dial, 1976 (1–3).

Scoppettone, Sandra, and Fitzhugh, Louise. *Bang Bang You're Dead*. Illustrated by Louise Fitzhugh. New York: Harper, 1969 (1–4).

Tresselt, Alvin. *Hide and Seek Fog*. Illustrated by Roger Duvoisin. New York: Lothrop, 1965 (PS–2).

———. *Rain Drop Splash*. Illustrated by Leonard Weisgard. New York: Lothrop, 1946 (K–3).

———. *White Snow, Bright Snow*. Illustrated by Roger Duvoisin. New York: Lothrop, 1947 (PS–2).

Udry, Janice May. *A Tree Is Nice*. Illustrated by Marc Simont. New York: Harper, 1956 (PS–2).

———. *The Moon Jumpers*. Illustrated by Maurice Sendak. New York: Harper, 1959 (K–2).

Zion, Gene. *Really Spring*. Illustrated by Margaret Bloy Graham. New York: Harper, 1956 (1–3).

Zolotow, Charlotte. *My Gandson Lew*. Illustrated by William Pène Du Bois. New York: Harper, 1974 (K–3).

———. *The Storm Book*. Illustrated by Margaret Bloy Graham. New York: Harper, 1952 (K–3).

**Part III
For Middle- and Upper-
Elementary Grades**

# 7

## Traditional or Folk Literature

*I go for folktales, like* Zlateh the Goat and Other Stories. *I can't help giggling when I read about foolish people in Zlateh's Chelm village or in* Pecos Bill, *about superheroes. Tall tales chase away my blues!*
—Olga, aged ten

### Perspective

Hyperbolic tall tales are the only distinctly American folktales. *Pecos Bill,* which deals with a monumental cowboy, is compiled by Dr. James Cloyd Bowman. A surprising number of scholars, like Dr. Bowman, are folklorists. As early as 1806 in Germany, linguists Jacob and Wilhelm Grimm, who later began a German dictionary, recorded old folk literature, some of which is found in the classics chapter. In 1948 and 1955, Harold Courlander, famous for Black folktale collections, won Guggenheim Fellowships for studies of African and Afro-American cultures. Isaac Bashevis Singer, who tells Yiddish stories about Eastern European life in *Zlateh the Goat and Other Stories,* is a 1978 Nobel Prizewinner for literature.

Both *Pecos Bill* and *Zlateh the Goat and Other Stories* contain folktales. As the name implies, these stories stem from folk culture, not individual authors. Originally transmitted in oral tradition to adults and young people alike, the tales now are often recorded and are considered part of children's literature.

Folk or traditional literature, which dates to antiquity, includes Bible tales, myths, legends, fables, and folk songs. Myths are prescientific efforts to explain creation and the universe. Legends are accounts of heroes who lived before recorded history. Fables are short stories that teach a lesson.

Magic is often featured in folktales, especially in so-called fairy tales which present some royal characters. The Puerto Rican folklorist, Pura Belpré, finds publishers more willing to accept tales about kings and queens than translations about Brazilian jungle animals. She complains, ''They're used to just one type of storytelling.''[1]

Folktales generally end happily showing the success of those who are poor but kind over those who are evil, including royalty. Triumph of good over evil and virtue rewarded are among popular themes.

Love is another popular theme, exemplified in *Tristan and Iseult,* an ancient Celtic legend told around the peat fire of Irish or Welsh chieftains. First recorded around 1150, it later became one of Richard Wagner's famous operas.

Since every ethnic group has its own folktales, cultural values are often conveyed in themes. For instance, judging inner spirit not external details is the theme of an old Chinese story originally written in 350 B.C., *The Superlative Horse.* Cooperation is the theme of both a Russian tale, *Seven Simeons,* and a Spanish story, *Padre Porko: The Gentlemanly Pig.* Social values may represent those of an entire continent, as shown in *The Legend of Africania,* an allegory about African plunder, with a need for individualism as its theme. By studying folktale themes, readers may contrast unique and universal culture values.

### Themes of Prizewinning Traditional or Folk Literature Grouped under These Topics

*Capabilities and Limitations*

**Middle and Upper Grades.** The theme of Glen Rounds's tall tale, *Ol' Paul, the Mighty Logger,*[2] is heroic capabilities. The book contains ten tales about Paul Bunyan, legendary father of logging, each depicting the giant's strength and ingenuity. Born in Maine of French-Canadian parents, Bunyan is so restless as a three-year-old, he rolls around and ruins four square miles of timber. Aided by Babe the Blue Ox, Bunyan digs the Mississippi and clears Iowa and Kansas. He uses "a big sledge hammer and pounds the hills out flat as flapjacks."[3]

Heroic capabilities is also the theme of Dell McCormick's *Paul Bunyan Swings His Axe,*[4] seventeen tall tales set in mid-nineteenth century. Bunyan, who drags his axe by the handle while traveling west from North Dakota, accidently digs the Grand Canyon. The power of his voice alone knocks down three men. A friend, Hot Biscuit Slim, and his cooks skate on a hot ten-acre griddle in order to make pancakes for thousands of hungry men.

Heroic capabilities is the theme of another tall tale, James Cloyd Bowman's *Pecos Bill.*[5] One of eighteen children, Pecos Bill is not missed by his parents when he rolls out of their covered wagon in Texas. He is raised by coyotes, communicating in animal talk, until found as a man by his brother, Chuck. They go to I.X.L. (I Excell) Ranch where Pecos becomes a leader. He ropes and rides a cyclone from Texas to the West

Coast. On the day he is to wed Slue-foot Sue, she insists on riding his horse, Widow Maker, and is bucked high.

> She had to duck her head to let the moon go by . . . . Sue fell back to earth with the speed of a meteor. She struck exactly in the middle of the spring-steel bustle and rebounded like a rocket . . . . At last, at the end of the sixth day, Pecos succeeded in lassoing Sue.[6]

After her adventure, Sue no longer wants to be a cowgirl and reverts to a stereotyped prim and proper lady.

Tall tales emphasize capabilities, but human limitations in the struggle for Jewish survival is the theme of *The Golem: A Jewish Legend* by author-illustrator Beverly Brodsky McDermott.[7] Warned by God that Prague Jews will be harmed, Rabbi Yehuda Lev ben Bezalel makes the Golem, a live, speechless clay man, to protect his people. On Passover eve, mobs enter the ghetto to avenge alleged use of Christian blood in matzos. The angry Golem grows into a giant who not only destroys the enemy but everything in his path. Lamenting, "God in heaven, what imperfect thing have I created?,"[8] Rabbi Lev destroys the Golem.

*Cleverness*

**Middle and Upper Grades.** Deceptive cleverness is the theme of an Armenian folktale, *The Contest*,[9] by author-illustrator Nonny Hogrogian. Cunning Ehleezah, betrothed to robber-by-night Hrahad and robber-by-day Hmayag, is proud each man is unaware of the other. The robbers happen to meet while eating identical lunches packed by Ehleezah. They suggest a contest to determine the cleverest thief, who should win Ehleezah. After doing daring feats, they both become convinced Ehleezah does not deserve them. She merely finds a new beau.

Resourceful cleverness is the theme of many of the sixteen ancient Chinese short stories found in Arthur Bowie Chrisman's *Shen of the Sea*.[10] Some trace the origin of kites, china dishes, gunpowder, different tea names, even printing. The latter is explained in "Ah Mee's Invention," which tells about a mischievous boy, Ah Mee, whose father tells him not to get into jars of jam. He literally interprets the warning, being too big for the little jars anyway, and pours jam on his father's carved wall plaques, using them as plates. His father is so angry, he flings the plaques at the wall, and they leave an impression, creating the idea for printing. It is only one step further to carve words on wooden blocks, spread the blocks with black jam, and press the blocks on paper to print stories.

From China'a neighbor, Japan, comes *The Wave,*[11] Margaret Hodges's adaptation of a folktale found in Lafcadio Hearn's *Gleanings in Buddha Fields.* The book has Blair Lent's handsome illustrations. The tale's theme, unselfish wisdom or cleverness, is demonstrated by quick actions of an elderly rice farmer, Ojiisan. From his mountain home, he sees an approaching tidal wave threatening four hundred inhabitants who live in a fishing village below. There is no time to descend the mountain to sound a warning, so he attracts villagers to climb the mountain by setting his rice fields afire. He sacrifices "his precious rice, all of his work for the past year, all of his food for the year to come,"[12] to save the villagers. Now a poor man, Ojiisan opens his home to the homeless. When they reconstruct the village, the inhabitants build a temple to honor their wise, unselfish savior.

The Jewish village of Chelm in the Ukraine is the setting for the eight stories translated from Yiddish in Isaac Bashevis Singer's *When Shlemiel Went to Warsaw and Other Stories.*[13] Cleverness and foolishness in Chelm is the book's overall theme emphasized in Margot Zemach's humorous line illustrations. Most of the stories are folktales, and each has its own theme. A sample story, "Shrewd Todie and Lyzer the Miser," has the theme of cleverness outwitting greed. It is about poverty-stricken Todie who needs to support his wife, Shaindel, and seven children. For his daughter's potential engagement, he borrows a silver tablespoon from rich Lyzer the miser. He returns it with a silver teaspoon, explaining that the tablespoon gave birth to a teaspoon. He repeats this two more times before borrowing a tablespoon and silver candlesticks. He sells the candlesticks, giving his family needed money, but he returns the tablespoon, apologizing that it didn't give birth, and the candlesticks died. When Lyzer complains, the rabbi dismisses his case, explaining, "If you accept nonsense when it brings you profit, you must also accept nonsense when it brings you loss."[14]

## Outwitted

**Middle and Upper Grades.** In contrast with Todie, the main character in Peggy Appiah's *Ananse the Spider* pays a price for being clever but selfish.[15] Being outwitted is the theme of most of the thirteen African stories about the adventures of Ananse (the Ashanti word for spider that may refer to man or spider. The more common English spelling is Anansi.) His greedy, amusing plots generally backfire.

Anansi is also the only character repeated in several of the eighteen folktales, *The Cow-Tail Switch and Other West African Stories,*[16] recorded by Harold Courlander and George Herzog. Being outwitted is the theme of two Gold Coast Anansi tales, "Hungry Spider and the Turtle" and "Anansi's Fishing Expedition." In the first story, greedy Spider offers visiting Turtle a meal, but eats the food himself, claiming that Turtle is not clean enough to be a dinner guest. Turtle gets even when he hosts hungry Spider. Turtle serves dinner at the bottom of a lake, and light Spider floats on the water, unable to eat.

In the second story, "Anansi's Fishing Expedition," lazy Anansi is outwitted when he invites another man, Anene, on a fishing trip, hoping to make his friend do all the work. Anene offers to make and set fish traps if Anansi just expresses the groans of fatigue, but Anansi reverses procedures. Even when it comes to claiming the fish in the traps, Anene gets the most. Anansi lets him take today's catch, thinking tomorrow's will be larger, but greedy Anansi waits too long.

*Cooperation*

**Middle and Upper Grades.** Cooperation is the theme of the Russian folktale, *Seven Simeons,*[17] retold by author-illustrator Boris Artzybasheff. Handsome young King Douda wants to marry Princess Helena of the Boozan Islands, but she lives ten sailing years away. Seven peasant brothers, each called Simeon, use their magical powers cooperatively to bring Helena to Douda. The first Simeon builds a tower to the sky, the second climbs it to see Helena, the third builds a ship, the fourth sails it to her island, the fifth shoots magical Helena so she flies like a bird, the sixth recovers her, and the seventh takes her aboard ship. They bring Helena to Douda as his bride and ask for no reward beyond returning to their cooperatively planted wheat fields.

Cooperation is also the theme of Alf Evers's *The Three Kings of Saba,*[18] a story believed to extend information about the New Testament's Magi. Balthasar, Melchior, and Jaspar are brothers who each want selfishly to rule the region of Saba alone. (Saba is the Arabic name for Sheba.) A child prophet teaches them to cooperate and offer their subjects more by joint reign.

Solving problems through cooperation is again a theme of folktales, this time from Spain, *Padre Porko: The Gentlemanly Pig,*[19] recorded by Robert Davis. Padre Porko, a benevolent pig who speaks all languages, spends his life helping human and animal friends. In "Pablo's Goose and the Evil Eye," he demonstrates his thesis, "We animals can do anything, if we will work together."[20] The Evil Eye or wicked magic is believed to cause the king's gluttonous goose to stop eating. Padre Porko solves the problem by sending for the stork to withdraw a wooden piece blocking the goose's esophagus. In "The Outlaw," forest animals want to kill an obnoxious bear who challenges Padre Porko as animal chief. Instead, the kind pig leads the bear to trap himself in a no-exit beehive (a cage) before shipment to a zoo that will pamper him.

In *Padro Porko,* the pig asks crows for errand service. His question, "Will one of you black boys do me a favor?"[21] is considered racially stereotyped today.

## Good Overcoming Evil

**Middle and Upper Grades.** Good wins over evil is the most popular theme in Sorche Nic Leodhas's collection of ten Scottish dialect tales, *Thistle and Thyme: Tales and Legends from Scotland.*[22] In "St. Cuddy and the Gray Geese," St. Cuddy punishes a selfish old woman. The legend, "The Drowned Bells of the Abbey," tells about pirates who suffer because they rob an abbey of its bells. "The Beekeeper and the Bewitched Hare" features a beekeeper who overcomes an evil witch. "Michael Scott and the Demon" shows how a man outwits an annoying demon. In "The Bride Who Outtalked the Water Kelpie," a newlywed couple overcomes the water kelpie's spell on the bride. "The Changeling and the Fond Young Mother" concerns a fairy who substitutes her ugly crying baby for a pretty baby whose mother brags excessively. Helped by a wise old woman, the mother gets her baby back and stops boasting. "The Lass Who Went Out at the Cry of Dawn" is an account of a young kind girl who rescues her older sister from an evil wizard. The lass kills the wizard and lifts a spell from the sisters' future husbands. Happy endings are consistent with the theme, good wins over evil.

Good triumphs over evil is the theme of most of the South American folktales in Charles J. Finger's collection, *Tales from Silver Lands.*[23] In "The Magic Dog," for example, Maconahola, whom the Princess loves, suffers when an evil witch, Tlapa, casts a spell that makes most people dislike him. He helps a hungry dog who magically gives him fields of growing corn and a furnished house. He hides to study the dog and finds the animal is really the Princess covered with a dog skin. When he throws the skin into the fire, it disappears and so does the kingdom's wicked spell. Maconahola slays the witch and becomes ruler with the Princess.

## Determination

**Upper Grades.** Jamake Highwater draws upon tales from his Blackfeet and Cherokee heritage, adding Anpao, a fictitious hero, in *Anpao: An American Indian Odyssey.*[24] *Anpao* is based on tales passed down through generations of Great Plains and Southwest people. Highwater explains the world's genesis through Anpao whose name means Dawn. His theme, determination, is apparent as the warrior goes on a dangerous quest to ask the Sun to remove his facial scar and permit him to marry a lovely maiden, Ko-ko-mik-e-is. While en route, he learns the Sun is his father. He is determined to fulfill his task though he breaks a leg and almost dies from poison. To those who would deter him, he says:

> I cannot stay with you. . . . I must continue my search for the Sun. It is what I have been dreaming about and if I give up that dream I will become a sullen old fellow.[25]

Reaching the Sun's lodge, Anpao meets his brother, Morning Star, and saves him from monster birds. The Sun repays Anpao by eliminating his facial scar and granting his marriage request. Anpao returns to the village to wed Ko-ko-mik-e-is.

Determination is also the theme of Kate Seredy's *The White Stag*,[26] based on a legend of the founding of Hungary. The story traces the Huns' arrival in their chosen land after a long migration from Asu (Asia) to Ereb (Europe). Hunor is in charge of the Huns and Magyar, of the Magyars, but Attila is the only leader actually to reach Hungary. After twenty years of wars, Attila the Conqueror leads his cold, hungry people westward. When the correct path is snow-covered, a white stag guides them to the Promised Land.

At first driven to avenge a father's murder, Fionn, a Gaelic warrior, changes and becomes determined to have a meaningful life, the theme of Ella Young's *The Tangle-Coated Horse and Other Tales*.[27] This single story, with many tales from Gaelic sagas interwoven, tells how gods and goddesses give Fionn truth, power, and knowledge. Their enchanting powers are both beneficial and detrimental in his attempts to defend the land now known as Ireland. Gods and goddesses show him beauty beyond belief, but at the same time, he is a subject of the Goddess of Death. Before his death, he temporarily transforms into a salmon who embodies wisdom. Even the Tangle-Coated Horse, a supernatural character, cannot prevent Fionn's death.

*Individualism*

**Middle and Upper Grades.** Need for individualism is the theme of Dorothy Robinson's story based on African oral tradition, *The Legend of Africania*.[28] Rewarded for his pride in Africa, Prince Uhuru is allowed to marry Africania, daughter of the Sun King and Earth Queen. The couple love each other and their continent, but ruthless Takata drugs the Prince for many years, strips Africa of its beauty, and makes Africania his prisoner. When she asks for freedom, Takata tells her she is too different, so she changes her ways to his. Each time she changes, more vines grow around her hut until they entirely cover the dwelling, enclosing her. When her awakened husband finally finds her, she is imprisoned, not by chains, but by vines. She reverts to her old individualism, the vines wither, and she is reunited with Uhuru. Takata has imprisoned others, and the couple free them by encouraging them to be their own true selves. This allegory about African plunder suggests that individualism and pride in being unique can disarm opponents.

## Inner Spirit

**Middle and Upper Grades.** An ancient Chinese story recorded by Jean Merrill, *The Superlative Horse,* has a theme of judging inner spirit, not external details.[29] Duke Mu has the finest stables in China, thanks mainly to his Chief Groom, Po Lo, who is about to retire. The trusted old groom suggests as his successor an uneducated peasant boy, Han Kan, who has no breeding and is physically unimpressive. However, Han Kan proves he has the ability to judge a horse's inner spirit, for "The excellence of a horse does not reside in its color or sex or breed or build. Excellence is a matter of the heart and spirit of a horse."[30] Han Kan selects for the stables a superlative horse that defeats the Duke's favorite in a major chariot race. This proves the boy worthy to become Chief Groom. The theme emphasizes inner spirit as the basis for judging both boy and horse.

## Keeping a Secret

**Middle and Upper Grades.** The need to keep a secret is the theme of "The Boar Who Was a Man," one of the Italian folktales retold by Mary Gould Davis in *The Truce of the Wolf and Other Stories of Old Italy.*[31] In old Italy, a kind, beautiful maiden marries a boar and learns on her wedding night that he is a handsome man under a witch's spell. As long as she keeps his secret, he is a man from sunset to sunrise, but a boar the rest of the time. For many years, the two are content with this arrangement until she tells the secret. Then she sees her husband as a man for the last time, and a witch changes her into a frog.

## Patience

**Middle and Upper Grades.** "Don't Be in as Great a Hurry as Your Father" is an Algerian story with patience as its theme. It is found in

William Kaufman's *UNICEF Book of Children's Legends*.[32] A carpenter postpones making a cradle for his friend's expected child until the child is grown and seeks a cradle for his own baby. When prodded, the carpenter scolds:

> Patience, my son. You shall have your cradle soon. But please, I beg
> you, don't be in as great a hurry as your father.[33]

## *Survival*

**Middle and Upper Grades.** Survival is the theme of "Zlateh the Goat," one of seven Yiddish folktales about late nineteenth-century Jewish life in Poland, found in Isaac Bashevis Singer's *Zlateh the Goat and Other Stories*.[34] A rare realistic folktale, "Zlateh the Goat" tells how Reuven the furrier suffers financially during an unseasonably warm winter, so he has to sell his goat, Zlateh, to Feyvel the butcher. Reuven's twelve-year-old son, Aaron, begins the sad trip to town with Zlateh. When caught in a three-day snowstorm, the two take refuge in a haystack. Their survival depends on each giving warmth to the other. While Zlateh eats the hay, Aaron sucks the goat's milk. After the storm ends, they return home, and no one ever again mentions selling Zlateh.

## *Love*

**Middle and Upper Grades.** *Jonah and the Great Fish*,[35] an Old Testament tale retold by Clyde Robert Bulla, has God's love as its theme. At first, Jonah does not understand that the Lord loves everyone. He refuses God's command to preach against wickedness in Nineveh, Assyria, because the Assyrians are enemies of his people, the Israelites. He flees and tries to hide aboard ship. When a storm arises, the sailors believe it is Jonah's fault, so they throw him overboard. God spares his life by having a great fish swallow him whole, then cast him safely on land. Now Jonah preaches to his Nineveh enemies, and the sinners repent, but he cannot understand why God loves sinners instead of destroying them. After God creates a plant that Jonah likes, He kills it. When Jonah protests, God explains that thousands of people in Nineveh should be cherished more than one plant.

The themes of the remaining stories concern human love. A daughter's love for her mother is shown in Becky Rehyer's adaptation of a Russian folktale, *My Mother Is the Most Beautiful Woman in the World*.[36] Varya, a six-year-old Ukrainian girl, is tired after helping harvest wheat with her mother and father, Marfa and Ivan. She falls asleep and awakens to find both parents missing. When strangers ask their names, the scared child replies only that her mother is the most beautiful woman in the world. The village leader, Kolya, has pretty village women appear before Varya, but the girl shakes her head until someone not summoned comes puffing breathlessly from the crowd. It is chubby, plain-looking Marfa, and Varya cries with joy, "See, I told you, this is my mother, the most beautiful woman in the world."[37] Kolya then cites the Russian proverb, "We do not love people because they are beautiful, but they seem beautiful to us because we love them."[38]

**Upper Grades.** Romantic love is the theme of Rosemary Sutcliff's version of an ancient Celtic legend, *Tristan and Iseult*.[39] Tristan, whose name prophetically means sadness, is loved like a son by Cornwall's King Marc. Tristan promises to bring the King a wife, Princess Iseult of the Swallow's Hair, a woman with hair so dark red it is almost purple. Her father wishes her to marry the man who rids Ireland of a dragon. Since Tristan kills the beast, he may marry her, but though he and she are in love, he keeps his promise to King Marc.

Iseult marries King Marc and continues to be Tristan's lover, first secretly and then as a runaway. After King Marc leaves his glove at the couple's hiding place, Tristan returns Iseult to Marc, promising to protect her even if he leaves.

Tristan goes to Brittany where he marries Iseult of the White Hands, hoping for partial happiness. Before Tristan settles with his wife, he visits the first Iseult, and both lovers promise to aid each other when needed.

It is wounded Tristan who sends for the first Iseult, requesting a white sail if she is on the returning ship and a black sail if she refuses. Learning her lover is dying, Iseult hastens to him with healing herbs. As the ship approaches, Tristan's wife sees the white sail, but jealously tells Tristan it is black, a lie that kills him. Tristan's wife confesses to the first Iseult that her husband "loved you more than ever he loved me."[40] Iseult of the Swallow's Hair dies across Tristan's body, and King Marc buries them side by side. Over Tristan he plants a hazel tree and over Iseult, a honeysuckle, greenery that "intertwined so that they could never be separated any more."[41]

### Summary

This chapter discusses themes of twenty-six examples of prizewinning folktales. The themes are analyzed under twelve topics, such as capabilities and limitations, cleverness, love, and cooperation. Almost all these books are intended for readers in middle- through upper-elementary grades, though four are only for upper-grade pupils.

Ranked according to frequency in this sample, the largest number of prizewinning folktales are from Europe, followed by North America, Africa, Asia, and finally, South America. Since only a handful are realistic, it is fantasy that predominates. Fantasy, as in tall tales, often contributes to humor.

**Notes**

1. "Pura Belpré," *Profiles in Literature* (Philadelphia: Temple University, 1971).

2. In 1958, *Ol' Paul, the Mighty Logger* won the Lewis Carroll Shelf Award.

Some investigators believe Paul Bunyan tales to be "fakelore," not folklore, conceived in the early 1900s as a promotional effort by the lumber industry in Wisconsin and Michigan.

3. Glen Rounds, *Ol' Paul, the Mighty Logger* (New York: Holiday House, 1949), p. 110.

4. In 1940, *Paul Bunyan Swings His Axe* won the Pacific Northwest Library Association Young Reader's Choice Award.

5. In 1938, *Pecos Bill* was a Newbery Honor Book.

6. James Cloyd Bowman, *Pecos Bill* (Chicago: Whitman, 1972), pp. 251–256.

7. In 1977, *The Golem: A Jewish Legend* was a Caldecott Honor Book.

8. Beverly Brodsky McDermott, *The Golem: A Jewish Legend* (Philadelphia: Lippincott, 1976), no page.

9. In 1977, *The Contest* won The Randolph Caldecott Medal.

10. In 1926, *Shen of the Sea* won The John Newbery Medal.

11. In 1964, *The Wave* was a *New York Times* Choice of Best Illustrated Children's Book of the Year, and in 1965, it was a Caldecott Honor Book.

12. Margaret Hodges, *The Wave* (Boston: Houghton, 1964), p. 22.

13. In 1969, *When Shlemiel Went to Warsaw and Other Stories* was a Newbery Honor Book.

14. Isaac Bashevis Singer, *When Shlemiel Went to Warsaw and Other Stories* (New York: Farrar, 1968), p. 12.

15. In 1966, *Ananse the Spider,* illustrated by Peggy Wilson, was a *New York Times* Choice of Best Illlustrated Children's Book of the Year.

16. In 1948, *The Cow-Tail Switch and Other West African Stories* was a Newbery Honor Book.

17. In 1938, *Seven Simeons* was a Caldecott Honor Book.

18. In 1955, *The Three Kings of Saba,* illustrated by Helen Sewell, was a *New York Times* Choice of Best Illustrated Children's Book of the Year.

19. In 1962, *Padre Porko: The Gentlemanly Pig* won the Lewis Carroll Shelf Award.

20. Robert Davis, *Padre Porko: The Gentlemanly Pig* (New York: Holiday House, 1948), p. 23.

21. Ibid., p. 161.

22. In 1963, *Thistle and Thyme: Tales and Legends from Scotland* was a Newbery Honor Book.

23. In 1925, *Tales from Silver Lands* won The John Newbery Medal.

24. In 1978, *Anpao: An American Indian Odyssey* was a Newbery Honor Book.

25. Jamake Highwater, *Anpao: An American Indian Odyssey* (Philadelphia: Lippincott, 1977), p. 101.

26. In 1938, *The White Stag* won The John Newbery Medal.

27. In 1930, *The Tangle-Coated Horse and Other Tales* was a Newbery Honor Book.

28. In 1975, *The Legend of Africania* won the Coretta Scott King Award.

29. In 1963, *The Superlative Horse* won the Lewis Carroll Shelf Award.

30. Jean Merrill, *The Superlative Horse* (Reading, Mass.: Scott, 1961), p. 60.

31. In 1932, *The Truce of the Wolf and Other Stories of Old Italy* was a Newbery Honor Book.

32. In 1970, *UNICEF Book of Children's Legends* won the Christopher Award in the children's-book category for all ages.

33. William Kaufman, *UNICEF Book of Children's Legends* (Harrisburg, Penn.: Stockpole Books, 1970), p. 14.

34. In 1966, *Zlateh the Goat and Other Stories,* illustrated by Maurice Sendak, was a *New York Times* Choice of Best Illustrated Children's Book of the Year.

35. In 1970, *Jonah and the Great Fish* won the Commonwealth Club of California Award.

36. In 1946, *My Mother Is the Most Beautiful Woman in the World,* illustrated by Ruth Gannett, was a Caldecott Honor Book.

37. Becky Reyher, *My Mother Is the Most Beautiful Woman in the World* (New York: Lothrop, 1945), no page.

38. Ibid., no page.

39. In 1972, *Tristan and Iseult* won the *Boston Globe-Horn Book Award*.

40. Rosemary Sutcliff, *Tristan and Iseult* (New York: Dutton, 1971), p. 149.

41. Ibid., p. 150.


## References of Prizewinning Folk Literature Arranged according to Place of Origin

*(Estimated Reading Grade Level in Parentheses)*

*Africa*

Appiah, Peggy. *Anase the Spider*. Illustrated by Peggy Wilson. New York: Pantheon, 1966 (4–7).

Courlander, Harold, and Herzog, George. *The Cow-Tail Switch and Other West African Stories*. Illustrated by Madye Lee Chastain. New York: Holt, 1947 (4–6).

Robinson, Dorothy. *The Legend of Africania*. Illustrated by Herbert Temple. Chicago: Johnson, 1974 (4–6).

*Armenia*

Hogrogian, Nonny. *The Contest*. New York: Morrow, 1976 (3–5).

*China*

Chrisman, Arthur Bowie. *Shen of the Sea*. Illustrated by Else Hasselnis. New York: Dutton, 1966 (4–6).

Merrill, Jean. *The Superlative Horse*. Illustrated by Ronni Solbert. Reading, Mass.: Scott, 1961 (4–6).

*Czechoslovakia*

McDermott, Beverly Brodsky. *The Golem: A Jewish Legend*. Philadelphia: Lippincott, 1976 (4–6).

*Hungary*

Seredy, Kate. *The White Stag*. New York: Viking, 1937 (5–9).

*Ireland or Wales*

Sutcliff, Rosemary. *Tristan and Iseult*. New York: Dutton, 1971 (5–adult).
Young, Ella. *The Tangle-Coated Horse and Other Tales*. Illustrated by Vera Beck. New York: McKay, 1929 (5–7).

*Israel*

Bulla, Clyde Robert. *Jonah and the Great Fish*. Illustrated by Helga Aichinger. New York: Crowell, 1970 (2–5).

*Italy*

Davis, Mary Gould. *The Truce of the Wolf and Other Stories of Old Italy*. Illustrated by Jay Van Everen. New York: Harcourt, 1931 (2–5).

*Japan*

Hodges, Margaret. *The Wave*. Illustrated by Blair Lent. Boston: Houghton, 1964 (2–5).

*Poland*

Singer, Isaac Bashevis. *When Shlemiel Went to Warsaw and Other Stories*. Translated by Isaac Bashevis Singer and Elizabeth Shub. Illustrated by Margot Zemach. New York: Farrar, 1968 (4–7).
———. *Zlateh the Goat and Other Stories*. Translated by Isaac Bashevis Singer and Elizabeth Shub. Illustrated by Maurice Sendak. New York: Harper, 1966 (4–6).

*Russia*

Artzybasheff, Boris. *Seven Simeons*. New York: Viking, 1937 (4–6).
Reyher, Becky. *My Mother Is the Most Beautiful Woman in the World*. Illustrated by Ruth Gannett. New York: Lothrop, 1945 (2–5).

*Scotland*

Nic Leodhas, Sorche. *Thistle and Thyme: Tales and Legends from Scotland*. Illustrated by Evaline Ness. New York: Holt, 1962 (4–7).

*South America*

Finger, Charles J. *Tales from Silver Lands*. Illustrated by Paul Honoré. New York: Doubleday, 1924 (4–6).

*Spain*

Davis, Robert. *Padre Porko: The Gentlemanly Pig*. Illustrated by Fritz Eichenberg. New York: Holiday House, 1948 (4–6).

*United States*

**Great Plains:**
Highwater, Jamake. *Anpao: An American Indian Odyssey*. Illustrated by Fritz Scholder. Philadelphia: Lippincott, 1977 (5–8).

**Idaho, Washington, and North Woods:**
McCormick, Dell J. *Paul Bunyan Swings His Axe*. Caldwell, Id.: Caxton, 1972 (4–6).

**Maine and North Woods:**
Rounds, Glen. *Ol' Paul, the Mighty Logger*. New York: Holiday House, 1976 (3–6).

**Texas and Southwest:**
Bowman, James Cloyd. *Pecos Bill*. Illustrated by Laura Bannon. Chicago: Whitman, 1972 (4–6).

*Yemen*

Evers, Alf. *The Three Kings of Saba*. Illustrated by Helen Sewell. Philadelphia: Lippincott, 1955 (3–6).

*Multiple or Nonspecified Places*

Kaufman, William T. *UNICEF Book of Children's Legends*. Harrisburg, Penn.: Stockpole, 1970 (3–6).

# 8 Modern Fantasy

*I get an eerie feeling when I read* The Black Cauldron *and* Tom's Midnight Garden, *but I'll never give up these treasures.*

—Angelo, aged eleven

## Perspective and Standards

*Tom's Midnight Garden* is by Ann Philippa Pearce, a writer of modern fantasy, who lives in England. Children appreciate modern fantasy more in England than in the United States. An American fantasy writer is Lloyd Alexander, author of *The Black Cauldron.* Alexander compares fantasy to realism in the following way:

> There are different kinds and levels of experience—the everyday experiences of the real world, and the inner experiences of the imagination. Both provide the raw materials of literature. Realism, in a way, is fantasy pretending to be true; and fantasy is truth pretending to be a dream. I try, through imagination, to express attitudes and feelings about real people, real human relationships. In that sense, all my work is based on personal experience.[1]

Alexander notes that the author of fantasy studies his craft and "what appears gossamer is, underneath, solid as prestressed concrete."[2] He explains the importance of internal consistency to a writer of fantasy:

> Once committed to his imaginary kingdom, the writer is not a monarch but a subject. Characters must appear plausible in their own setting, and the writer must go along with the inner logic. Happenings should have logical implications. Details should be tested for consistency. . . . Are there enchantments? How powerful? If an enchanter can perform such-and-such, can he not also do so-and-so?[3]

If there is consistency, a work of fantasy is more believable. Modern fantasy includes individually authored fairy tales while those that spring from the culture are part of traditional literature. Though fantasy may involve strange kingdoms, miracles, time magic, personification of toys, and odd transformations of characters, it still must be believable to be of literary quality.

This chapter includes a section on science fiction. Though modern fantasy encompasses animal fantasy, a separate chapter is devoted to animal fantasy because of the volume of books. The chapter on animal fantasy features works involving live animals, but they have the power of speech and often other human traits as well. The present chapter discusses toy animals, like a velveteen rabbit, or nonexistant animals, such as a dragon. A mermaid and a witch are among other imaginary characters in modern fantasy.

A universal truth often underlies a fantasy, and that truth is its primary theme. While the fantasy may occur in a magical kingdom in any age, the tale is meaningful because the theme applies to the known, current world.

## Themes of Prizewinning Modern Fantasy Grouped under These Topics

*Good Overcoming Evil*

**Middle and Upper Grades.** Good overcoming evil is the primary theme or universal truth underlying *The Wolves of Willoughby Chase,*[4] a melodramatic spoof by English author, Joan Aiken. This is fantasy because it takes place in nineteenth-century England under King James III who actually ruled in the fifteenth century. The Victorian story unfolds in a country mansion, Willoughby Chase, with wild wolves outside and human wolves inside. When Bonnie Willoughby's parents are on an extended vacation, cruel Miss Slighcarp becomes governess for courageous Bonnie and her timid cousin, Sylvia. Miss Slighcarp, a human *wolf-pack leader* preoccupied with taking over the estate, dismisses servants and turns the place into a den of deceit. A second *wolf,* Mr. Grimshaw, helps Miss Slighcarp plan to sink Sir Willoughby's ship with him and his wife aboard and then forge his will. Miss Slighcarp calls Bonnie, " 'Insolent, ungovernable child!' . . . With iron strength, she thrust Bonnie into a closet . . . and turned the key on her.' "[5] Realizing the children are against her, the governess sends them to an orphanage run by Mrs. Brisket, a third *wolf.* After the girls escape, police return with them to Willoughby Chase and jail the villains. Bonnie's righteous parents, saved from the shipwreck, have a home reunion with loved ones.

Another tale set in Europe, specifically in rural Poland, is Isaac Bashevis Singer's *The Fearsome Inn,*[6] translated from Yiddish. Nonny Hogrogian's watercolor illustrations extend the good-overcoming-evil theme, showing how evil the witch Dohoshova is. She and her half-devil husband, Lapitut, are keepers of a fearsome inn. They hold three spellbound maidens as servants, and they bewitch three male travelers, Vel-

vel, Herschel, and Leibel. Leibel is a student of cabala, mystical interpretation of Scriptures. He draws a magic chalk circle around the witch and her husband which traps them until he lets them leave the area. Then the good maidens and men marry. One of the three pairs remains at the inn to make it a haven for lost travelers.

Good overcoming evil is also the theme of Sid Fleischman's humorous tall tale, *McBroom Tells the Truth*.[7] After leaving a Connecticut farm, Josh McBroom, his wife, and their eleven redheaded children stop in Iowa, looking for fertile land. Old Heck Jones, a scoundrel, takes McBroom's meager ten dollars in exchange for a deed to eighty acres of farmland. What McBroom actually receives is a one-acre pond, but dishonest Jones argues:

> There are a full eighty acres—one piled on the other, like griddle cakes.
> I didn't say your farm was all on surface. It's eighty acres thick,
> McBroom, read the deed.[8]

Hot and disgusted, McBroom's family goes for a swim in the pond, but when they jump into the water, it evaporates. McBroom feels the rich topsoil, drops a bean seed on it, and harvests a crop in an hour. After the farm yields four crops daily, Jones tries several times to repossess the land. Unsuccessful, he retaliates by planting weeds on McBroom's property, but the farmer destroys them. On his final attempt to threaten McBroom, Jones visits while eating watermelon and spitting seeds on the ground. Watermelons erupt and catapult Jones into oblivion!

**Upper Grades.** More serious is Lloyd Alexander's *The Black Cauldron*,[9] whose theme is good overcoming evil as part of destiny. Alexander's five books set in imaginary Prydain are created with a series theme of good overcoming evil. The second book in the cycle is *The Black Cauldron*. Welsh names abound in the chronicles which center around Taran, an assistant Pig Keeper who matures under stress. Taran wants to find and destroy the cauldron which changes men killed in battle into silent, deathless warriors, the hated Cauldron-Born. With three enchantresses he exchanges a magical brooch for the cauldron, but they warn him:

> A living person must climb into it. When he does, the Crochan will
> shatter. . . . The poor duckling who climbs in will never climb out
> again alive. The Crochan only cost you a brooch, but it will cost a life
> to destroy it.[10]

Though the heavy iron cauldron seems grimly alive, Taran moves it to his camp with the help of Prince Ellidyr who claims the prize as his own in an ego contest. "There is a destiny laid on everything,"[11] and

Ellidyr fulfills his destiny when he sacrifices his life to destroy the cauldron, a source of cruelty. Taran, a survivor, is destined to continue leading positively in triumph over negative forces.

The masterful conclusion of Taran's rise to fame is Lloyd Alexander's *The High King,*[12] whose theme echoes anew good overcoming evil. Taran leads the Sons of Don against the Death-Lord whose "domain is as much a treasure-house as a stronghold of evil,"[13] a rocky waste stifling all living things. From the Death-Lord he regains the sword, Drnwyn, and is ordained High King. Taran dedicates his life to rebuilding his land and combating the evil that threatens "so long as men still hate and slay each other."[14]

Lloyd Alexander's *Westmark,*[15] named for an imaginary kingdom, again has the theme of good overcoming evil. Alexander tells about an idealistic youth, Theo, a printer's devil who accidently kills a gruff soldier on assignment from the wicked chief minister, Cabbarus. Theo flees, becoming part of a road show with a charlatan, Las Bambas, his dwarf assistant, Musket, and later, a vagrant girl, Mickel. After many adventures, the group arrives at the palace to find the king grieving over the loss of his daughter. Mickel reveals she is his missing daughter whom Cabbarus tried to kill. Exposed, Cabbarus escapes and is banished from the kingdom. An honest physician, Dr. Torrens, whom Cabbarus also tried to kill, replaces him as chief minister. As the story ends, Theo and Mickel show interest in sharing their future.

Another series of five modern fantasies with the good-overcoming-evil theme, is the creation of Susan Cooper, an Englishwoman living in Boston. She equates good with Light and evil with Dark, as seen in the second book of the cycle, *The Dark Is Rising.*[16] This is reflected in her statement, "They [powers of the Dark] love to twist good emotion to accomplish ill."[17] In the prizewinner, which takes place in England, Will Stanton, aged eleven, learns he is the last of the Old Ones, immortals destined to prevent the dark from rising. He hears:

> The powers of the Dark can do many things; but they cannot destroy. They cannot kill those of the Light. Not unless they gain a final dominion over the whole earth. And it is the task of the Old Ones—your task and ours—to prevent that.[18]

Will lives at home and prepares for Christmas celebration in church. On the holiday, the Old Ones support each other in church while outside, the Dark is destructive, freezing half the country. Finally, the neutral Walker finds strength to join the Light, symbol of love and trust, and for the present, overcomes the Dark.

The fourth book of Susan Cooper's series, *The Grey King,*[19] has the theme of good overcoming evil through a fulfilled quest. Will Stanton, convalescing from hepatitis, leaves England to be with relatives in Wales. After meeting Bran, a Raven Boy, Will recalls his mission to save the world from the evil Grey King. "He remembered the verses that had been put into his head as guide for the bleak, long quest he was destined now to follow."[20] Will and Bran fulfill the verses' request that they seize a golden harp whose notes offer safety to those under its protection, but they must also awaken the Sleepers in this life-or-death war for humanitarianism. Ultimately, Bran's revealed birth and ancestry help destroy the many manifestations of the Dark's Grey King. "As Will plays the final notes on the harp, the prophetic verse is fulfilled, ending his quest, for six horsemen came riding, the Sleepers were awakened."[21]

Another English author, Alan Garner, is responsible for *The Weirdstone of Brisingamen*.[22] The weirdstone is a magical firefrost stone capable of stopping the wicked forces of Nastrond, allowing for fulfillment of the theme, good overcoming evil. The raindrop-shaped crystal on a charm bracelet belongs to nine-year-old Susan. When she and her ten-year-old brother, Colin, meet a wizard, Cadelin Silverbrow, in the English countryside, they learn why the stone's safety is imperative for the pure of heart. Evil goblins, birds, and human beings, such as Selina Place, want to destroy the stone's magic and try to take it from the children as they and dwarfs race to deliver it to the wizard. Finally, despite the pain of death, they give the wizard the stone that can control evil. At once, darkness passes, and survivors of Nastrond's wrath blink in sunlight.

*Maturing*

**Upper Grades.** Lloyd Alexander's *The First Two Lives of Lukas-Kasha*,[23] a story of fifteenth-century Persia, has the theme of personal growth through adventures. At first, Lukas, the vagabond of Zara-Petra village, "took only one holiday and made it last all year. He loved to laugh, to sing, to dance on his hands. . . ."[24] While helping Battisto the magician, he changes into King Kasha of Abadan. In his early reign, he is still childish, but as he becomes more responsible, he tries to prevent war. When he makes enemies and flees for his life, evil King Shugdad rules until his return. A monarch once more, Kasha has matured and writes decrees "not only to set right all Shugdad had done but also to better the laws he himself had made while he first was King."[25] The story ends with Kasha realizing he has been dreaming, because his face is in the magician's bowl just a few moments. He is back in Zara-Petra, but villagers do not realize his personal growth, so he leaves, hoping to rule only himself.[26]

Referring to *The First Two Lives of Lukas-Kasha,* the author says:

> I would almost call this a theological novel. Lukas-Kasha goes through changes of attitude that almost approach changes in attitude toward a deity. Is the deity benevolent or malevolent? Does he have any reason for what he is doing?[27]

In this case, the author not only provides answers but raises questions as well.

*Deviltry or Trickery*

**Middle and Upper Grades.** Natalie Babbitt's ten short stories in *The Devil's Storybook* support a theme of either the Devil outwits creatures or they outwit him.[28] In several tales, he is outwitted. In "Nuts," for example, he wants a woman to crack all his walnuts, searching for a pearl in one, but she discovers the jewel quickly, leaving the Devil to do his own work. "The Very Pretty Lady" tells how the Devil punishes a beautiful woman who spurns him. He makes her ugly, and she finds an equally ugly husband who loves her. The Devil tries to make a good man evil in "A Palindrome" by stealing an artist's painting items, but the victim becomes a sculptor. After the Devil gets a speaking goat into Hell in "The Power of Speech," he regrets it because the goat does nothing but complain.

Some tales in *The Devil's Storybook* show a clever Devil. In "The Harps of Heaven," the Devil orders bickering brothers to steal a harp from Heaven, but when they return with a damaged one, he punishes them by requiring them to take piano lessons. Angela of "Perfection" does everything right, losing her temper only when the Devil marries her to a perfect husband.

Akin to deviltry is the trickery that brings frustration and joy, the theme of Scott Corbett's *The Home Run Trick.*[29] Kerby Maxwell and Fenton Claypool of the Panthers baseball team have a stereotyped attitude toward a girls' team, the Taylorville Toms. They want to lose their game with the Wildcats because the victor will play the girls, so the two boys develop a powerful chemical that turns the Wildcats into superior athletes. During the game, the Panthers suffer from the strain of trying to lose, and the Wildcats, soon aware of the scheme, also make purposeful mistakes. "Both sides tried every trick they could think of to make the other side score."[30] At the same time, the chemical vapor increased the

skills of both teams. The judge arrives when the teams seem so professional, he rules both too good to play the Taylorville Toms. The book
appeals to boys, but under humorous guise, helps implant negative attitudes toward female athletes.

## Revenge

**Middle and Upper Grades.** Consequences of revenge is the theme of a
story in eighteenth-century London, *Mister Corbett's Ghost,*[31] by an English author, Leon Garfield. Benjamin Partridge, who is ten or eleven
years old, hates Mr. Corbett, his boss in an apothecary shop. On New
Year's Eve, the boy wants to rush to a family party, but he fulfills his
boss's request to deliver medicine to an old man. When the boy discovers
the elderly man has special powers, he contracts for the man to receive
a reasonable fee if he kills Mr. Corbett. Benjamin shudders as he leaves
the old man and sees Mr. Corbett running on the road before his death.
Then comes the fatal report: "Mister Corbett was dead. His body dropped
down on the road. And over it stood Benjamin Partridge revenged."[32]
Since the boy cannot remove the corpse, the man with special powers
changes the corpse into a ghost. Benjamin is afraid he will be caught for
murder and declares, "I've had my fill of revenge."[33] When he leads
the ghost into the apothecary shop, the man with special powers is waiting, and at the boy's request, makes Mr. Corbett alive. Benjamin is so
relieved, he develops compassion for Mr. Corbett.

Justice is delayed forty years in Mary Jo Stephens's *Witch of the
Cumberlands,*[34] whose theme is revenge aided by witchcraft. In the Kentucky Cumberland mining area lives Miss Birdie, a woman who communicates with the dead. Over forty years earlier, her father had a coal
mine. When the union came, her father hired a man, Broughton, to be
his bodyguard and spy, taking his advice as gospel. Donald Campbell,
the union organizer, and Miss Birdie fell in love. After the contract was
settled, 150 men, including Campbell, were killed in an explosion. Miss
Birdie is sure of the culprit, but needs proof. Three foretold events help
her. First, Susan, Betsy, and Robin McGregor move into the area with
Miss Birdie as their loving housekeeper, and the children help unravel
the mystery. Second, old Broughton returns, and third, a spirit of the
dead tells Miss Birdie to go to the rock house. "She had waited forty
years for the foretelling to be fulfilled. And now, it seemed, the time
had come."[35] Betsy helps by stumbling onto the rock house, a mountain
cave. It has been the graveyard of Campbell and other destroyed miners
since Broughton, angry at the union contract, caused an explosion. Once
the cave is discovered, Miss Birdie sees Broughton's body there, killed

in a recent rock slide, so she "got her revenge,"[36] as foretold, before she too expires.

## War

**Upper Grades.** One of the rare satires children enjoy is Jean Merrill's *The Pushcart War,*[37] whose theme is probing war's cause and effect. The author's purpose for writing and her theme are identical, for in her introduction, she states that world peace will not be realized until people understand war's cause and effect. Writing as if in 1986, the author describes the Daffodil Massacre on March 15, 1976 when Mack of Mammoth Moving Company runs his truck into Morris the Florist's pushcart. This small incident leads to a New York City war between 509 peddlers and 20,000 truckers hired by three large trucking firms known as The Three. At first, drivers crush pushcarts like matchboxes, but peddlers flatten truckers' tires with pea- and tack-shooters. As trucks become stranded, people sympathize with pushcarts and demonstrate in a Peace March. Finally, truckers surrender and the Courtesy Act is established which "makes it a criminal offense for a larger vehicle to take advantage of a smaller vehicle in any way."[38]

## Obedience

**Middle and Upper Grades.** A need to follow instructions in safeguarding Jewish survival is the theme of Sulamith Ish-Kishor's *The Master of Miracle: A New Novel of the Golem,*[39] a legend-based story set in sixteenth-century Prague. Count Batislav accuses the Jewish people of kidnapping his daughter, Maria-Agnes, to use her blood during Passover. This is an excuse for a *pogrom* or mass slaughter of ghetto Jews. Instructed by God, the High Rabbi creates a manlike clay being, the Golem, to help the Jewish people survive. The tale's fifteen-year-old narrator, Gideon ben Israyel, an orphan, guides the Golem. The two find the missing Maria-Agnes hidden in the Count's castle, so the Count has no excuse to attack the ghetto. Gideon is supposed to destroy the clay man now that he has done his job, but Gideon gives way to the Golem's pleading eyes. Then the High Rabbi ends the Golem's imitation life and punishes Gideon by making him live in isolation with the Golem's charred remains.

## Destiny

**Middle and Upper Grades.** Sulamith Oppenheim's *The Selchie's Seed,*[40] a tale about Scotch islanders over two centuries ago, has the theme of destiny fulfilled. Selchies are seal folk who, by shedding their skin, live as humans on land. All members of Clan MacCodrum, like Ursula Sinclair, have within themselves the selchie's seed. When Ursula's daughter, Marian, turns fifteen, she hears bells from a white whale as only a selchie can. Ursula tells Marian the whale can magically assume any form and take whatever it wishes. Marian is destined to live with the whale. Her father tries to prevent fate by destroying his wife's marriage trunk containing selchie skins, but he learns, "There are no charms against one's own destiny."[41] The whale gives Marian a belt, and when she wears it, she becomes half-human, half-seal. Marian's destiny is fulfilled as a mermaid who sometimes removes her cincture, living ashore a few days before returning to the sea.

*Immortality*

**Middle and Upper Grades.** The problems of everlasting life provide the theme of Natalie Babbitt's *Tuck Everlasting*,[42] a story that takes place during the 1800s. For eighty-seven years, the Tuck family has not aged because they accidently drank from a magical Treegap spring. Jesse Tuck, who is apparently seventeen though born 104 years ago, is drinking at the spring when ten-year-old Winnie Foster discovers its power. Jesse, his brother, Miles, and mother, Mae, kidnap Winnie to silence her. Mae takes the girl to her husband, Angus, who stresses, "You can't have living without dying."[43] He asks, "Can you imagine? All the little ones little forever, all the old ones old forever."[44] Because they are changeless, the Tucks are hermits who move rather than answer questions from the curious. Their secret is safe with Winnie, though not with a man who overhears it, so Mae kills him. Sentenced to hang, Mae escapes, and Winnie substitutes for her in jail before being released. When Winnie is seventeen, she refuses to marry Jesse and drink the water that gives immortality. She lives normally, and sixty years later, the Tucks find her dead whereas they remain unchanged.

*Fusion of Past, Present, or Future*

**Middle and Upper Grades.** Philippa A. Pearce's *Tom's Midnight Garden* has the haunting theme of fused past memory and present time.[45] Separated from his twin, Peter, who has measles, lonely eight-year-old Tom Long is placed in quarantine with his aunt and uncle in Castleford, England. Their flat in a converted house is below that of the owner, old Mrs. Bartholomew. His adventures begin when the grandfather's clock, in-

scribed "Time no longer,"[46] strikes the thirteenth hour. Then Tom explores, finding behind the back door a dream garden that once existed.
In the garden, Tom befriends young Hatty, the only one in her late-
Victorian family who sees him. On nightly visits, he finds time moves
quickly, for seasons change rapidly, and Hatty soon becomes a maiden.
He finally learns Hatty is actually Mrs. Bartholomew as a girl, and the
setting is her remembered childhood garden. She confesses, "When you're
my age, Tom, you live in the Past a great deal. You remember it; you
dream of it."[47]

> He understood so much now: why the weather in the garden had always
> been perfect; why Time in the garden had sometimes gone backwards.
> It had all depended upon what old Mrs. Bartholomew had chosen to
> remember in her dreams.[48]

This masterpiece truly unites present and past in a timeless world.
    L.M. Boston is another English author who skillfully fuses the past
with the present in *The Children of Green Knowe*.[49] Green Knowe, the
author's actual residence, is the basis for the Oldknow English mansion
in the fantasy. Here young motherless Tolly begins to live with his great-
grandmother. Over the drawing-room fireplace hangs a picture of three
children, Toby, Linnet, and Alexander, who lived at Green Knowe, but
died in the Great Plague of 1665. Tolly's great-grandmother tells about
them so convincingly, he seems to see and hear them. The book's theme
is a fantasized family fulfilling a child's needs, for Tolly thinks:

> He wished he had a family like other people—brothers and sisters,
> even if his father were away. His mother was dead. He had a stepmother
> but he hardly knew her and was miserably shy of her.[50]

Since great-grandmother Oldknow talks as if Toby, Linnet, and Alexander are still at Green Knowe, they become the brothers and sisters
Tolly never had.

> He must have known of course that the children could not have lived
> so many centuries without growing old, but he never thought about it.
> To him, they were so real, so near, they were his own family that he
> needed more than anything on earth.[51]

The book concludes as Tolly and his great-grandmother, whom he loves
like a mother, celebrate Christmas with the fantasy family.
    Tolly profits from his ties with the past, and so does young Colin
Hyatt in Jay Williams's *The Hawkstone*.[52] The book's theme is relics
from the past helping solve present problems. In an ancient cave, Colin

finds an eighteenth-century Native American carved hawkstone which helps him relive past episodes involving his ancestors. It also prevents loss of the Hyatt home in Millbridge, Connecticut after a giant tax increase. The hawkstone leads Colin to a hidden black box filled with eighteenth-century gold pieces, enough to pay the family's debts. The box is on a neighbor's land, and Colin trades the right to dig on neighboring land for a valuable knife he wins in an archery contest. He thinks the hawkstone gives him new skills with bow and arrow. The mysterious hawkstone, effective only for Colin, creates past scenes in his mind. He leaves this symbol in the cave to help resolve future problems, for he realizes:

> I know, now, about the stone. It comes when it is needed. It brings with it those who have loved the land and fought for it and saved it in the past. And they will help you if you call on them as I did.[53]

Magical visits to the past, ending with maturity is Julia L. Sauer's theme in *Fog Magic*.[54] This tender story traces Greta Addington in a Nova Scotia fishing village for about two years, ending with her twelfth birthday. Greta is the one person in her generation of Addingtons for whom the seasonal fog seems magical. On a foggy day, Greta discovers secret Blue Cove, a village of a hundred years ago, and a friend, Retha Morrill. On sunny days, this same area consists of empty cellar holes of past houses. Visiting Blue Cove for the final time on her twelfth birthday, she gets a kitten from Retha's mother as a symbol for "the voyage into your teens."[55] When her father shows her his twelfth-birthday gift, a knife received in Blue Cove, she realizes she is crossing the threshold from childhood to adolescence.

Past and present also fuse in "She Cries No More," one of three short stories in Norton Juster's *Alberic the Wise and Other Journeys*.[56] Domenico Gnoli is the illustrator of this book about strange journeys. The theme of "She Cries No More" is an indifferent boy learning to fight for freedom through trips into the past. Claude, who does not care about anything except museums, either enters or is engulfed in a Renaissance painting of sad Princess Elena Grifonetto. Elena's tears form a pool in front of her painting because she grieves over loss of her kingdom to tyrants. He wants to help her, "for now there was something for which he knew he cared."[57] Elena's tears disappear after Claudio successfully leads her fifteenth-century supporters into their walled city. He cannot stay to celebrate since he returns to the present when the 6 P.M. museum bell rings. He later questions if he had been dreaming about "The Young Lady in a Make-Believe Landscape."

Present and future sometimes fuse in Mary Rodgers's *A Billion for*

*Boris,*[58] whose primary theme is gains and losses from knowledge of the future. In New York City, fourteen-year-old Annabel Andrews and her mechanical younger brother, Apeface or Ben, get involved with their fifteen-year-old neighbor, Boris, in a billion-dollar scheme. When Ben repairs Boris's old television set, it forecasts the future by showing the next day's programs. Knowledge of the future prevents Annabel from getting botulism and helps Boris win some bets. However, he is in debt after he bets on the Kentucky Derby based on partial information, having turned off the set before a thought-to-be-winner, Ticker Tape, is disqualified. Boris, who calls his eccentric mother, Sascha, irresponsible, actually is indebted to her for paying his bills, thanks to a movie script she wrote and sold. The television capers are over, for Mrs. Andrews gives the futuristic set away, unaware of its predictive qualities. This sequel to Rodgers's book, *Freaky Friday,* ends after Annabel confesses:

> To know about hijackings and trouble, fires and murders and know people are going to suffer from things you can't prevent—that's not fun. It's very depressing. I don't want that responsibility.[59]

**Upper Grades.** *Earthfasts* by English author, William Mayne,[60] has a theme of past and present fused. Young David and Keith happen upon Nellie Jack John, a lad who rises from the earth beating a drum and clutching a white-flamed candle. Though he went under a castle in 1742 to seek King Arthur's treasure, the drummer emerges in a modern world, a lonely misfit without his parents or girlfriend, Kath. After staying two days, the drummer disappears, leaving his strangely cold candle behind. His disturbance of time results in bizarre events. Ancient stones, called earthfasts, appear in a ploughed field, boars haunt towns they have not molested for two centuries, and in what seems to be lightning, David vanishes. Nellie Jack John's past world absorbs David. Keith concludes:

> I know that when Nellie Jack John took up this candle and brought it out from its place, he disturbed the time that slept and the King [Arthur] that slept with it, and he awoke what was asleep before. . . .[61]

Keith knows the only way to separate past and present is to return the candle, so he joins his two friends in the past. There King Arthur tries to kill Keith but destroys the candle instead. When that happens, Keith and David are restored to the present, and time is again in balance.

Another English author, Jane Louise Curry, offers a story set in England, *Poor Tom's Ghost,*[62] with the theme of past and present intertwined. Tony and Jo Nicholas, each with a child from a previous marriage, Roger and Pippa, inherit a house built in 1603. It is haunted by the ghost of Tom Garland, an actor from Shakespeare's day. Tony, also an actor, suddenly develops an authentic Shakespearian accent in "Hamlet" and becomes a new sleepwalker, searching with the ghost for the ghost's wife, Katherine. "By some strange shift past and present there had run together, overlapped even, so that Tony had walked in both at once."[63] It is thirteen-year-old Roger, however, who rids the house of its ghost by going into the past for five days and assuring Tom of his wife's love.

Putting a ghost to rest is Richard Peck's theme in *The Ghost Belonged to Me*,[64] a story set in Bluff City of the Mississippi River Valley during the early 1900s. A neighbor, Blossom Culp, tells thirteen-year-old Alexander Armsworth that, like her, he has the gift to see ghosts. This is confirmed when he discovers a ghost of his own age, Inez Dumaine, in his barn. She warns about an impending streetcar accident, and he becomes a hero by saving passengers. At their next meeting, Inez asks him to look for her grave beyond the barn and rebury her with her people. She complains, "I had thought to be saved, but my rescuer was my robber. I am even denied a decent grave."[65] Uncle Miles Armsworth sympathizes, because she died in a ship explosion when her father's friend was saving her from war in Europe by bringing her to America. The friend sold jewels found on her and with the money, built the Armsworth house, burying her under the porch. Alexander, his uncle, and Blossom Culp place her remains in a New Orleans cemetery, putting her soul to rest.

Dominique (Domi), also French, is a young noblewoman from Napoleon's era who communicates with modern-day Nina in a San Francisco French Art Museum. This happens in Eleanor Cameron's *The Court of the Stone Children*,[66] whose theme is rendering justice by removing barriers of time periods. Only Nina can see Domi. The Museum is furnished with items from the French girl's home, so the theme is reinforced as furnishings from the past and Domi's journal become part of the present. Domi wants Nina to help clear her father, a count, of murder charges. The mystery is resolved, for in a dream, Nina sees a statue in the Museum's Court of the Stone Children point to a painting proving the count's innocence. The absence of time barriers between Nina and Domi facilitates discussion of clues and this feeling of co-existence: "We are both living beings, each in her own way, only we can't touch one another, that's all."[67] The timeless theme is symbolized by a museum painting that intrigues Nina and her present-day friend, Gil. It is Chagall's "Time Is a River without Banks."

Author Eleanor Cameron originally planned to make the Chagall title the name of her book, because a year before publication, she said in an interview, "In the book I've just written, *Time Is a River without Banks,* . . . I have some stone children in a courtyard and upon them rests the book.''[68] Through fantasy she said she discovered her own unique writing style. She defined style as ''the sound of self. You have to have a self in order to sound like self.''[69]

*Ingenuity*

**Middle and Upper Grades.** Outwitting lazy animals with ingenuity is the theme of Ruth Stiles Gannett's humorous *My Father's Dragon.*[70] Young Elmo Elevator tells what his father, Elmer Elevator, did as a boy on Wild Island near Tangerina to free a baby dragon. The creature was tied to a stake on rope long enough for him to ferry animals and their loads across the river. To rescue the dragon, Elmer distracted tigers with chewing gum, a rhinoceros with toothbrush and paste, lions with comb, brush, and ribbons, a gorilla with a magnifying glass, and crocodiles with lollipops. Elmer showed ingenuity tying lollipops on tips of crocodiles' tails and lining the beasts single file, so each licked the candy in front. This was a crocodile bridge Elmer used to cross the river and reach the dragon. At once, he used his jackknife to cut the rope that tied the dragon. The other animals tried to follow aboard the moody crocodiles who left them stranded in the water. Meanwhile, ingenious Elmer was flying away atop his dragon.

Ingenuity is the theme of another fantasy, James Thurber's *Many Moons,*[71] illustrated by Louis Slobodkin. Sick Princess Leonore can recover from eating too many tarts only if her wish for the moon is granted. The King consults the Lord Chamberlain, the Royal Wizard, and the Royal Mathematician, but only the Court Jester is ingenious enough to solve the problem. He gets an idea from talking to the Princess who says the moon is a small, golden globe she obscures by holding up her thumb. The Court Jester gives her precisely a small, golden globe on a chain to wear around her neck, and she is pleased to get the moon as she sees it.

Willy Wonka shows ingenuity in a sequel to *Charlie and the Chocolate Factory* called *Charlie and the Great Glass Elevator* written by English author, Roald Dahl.[72] The theme of this second book is creative solutions to mistakes. Charlie Bucket, who is about eleven years old, his parents, and his two sets of grandparents are with Willy Wonka in a glass elevator when, through error, it is the only part of the chocolate factory launched into outer space. Willie, the factory's inventive founder, seizes the chance to tow out of orbit an endangered space capsule from Houston containing a deluxe hotel. The capsule is threatened by snakelike Knids that swallow victims. Willy also creatively solves another mistake. Earlier he invented a rejuvenation pill that causes users to be too young, for several grandparents are babies and one is minus two years old. He restores them to their correct age through another pill, Vita-Wonk.

Stereotyping of the aged occurs in *Charlie and the Great Glass Elevator*. Only Grandpa Joe is shown to be active. The other three, who are in their seventies or eighties, usually refuse to leave their beds though they are apparently healthy. Young readers of this book may incorrectly generalize about the elderly.

*Determination*

**Middle and Upper Grades.** A sequel to *Sailing to Cythera and Other Anatole Stories, The Island of the Grass King* by Nancy Willard, has unselfish determination as its theme,[73] for Anatole insists upon finding fennel to relieve his asthmatic grandmother. After he wishes on a rainbow for fennel, a winged horse, Pegasus, takes him and his cat, Plumpet, to the Island of the Grass King where the jailed king has a fennel crown. The only way to unlock the king and queen is with evil Mother Weather-sky's key, but there are hazards which he overcomes. An islander who helps Anatole says:

> If you were traveling for yourself, I might turn your mind another way. But when people want a thing for somebody else, they'll never give up till they've found it.[74]

Indeed, Anatole, not once deterred, gets the golden key. When he frees the monarchs, others under the spell are automatically released. They gladly give Anatole fennel which he presents to his grandmother.

**Upper Grades.** Determination to uproot heathenism is the theme of Marie Elizabeth Pope's *The Perilous Gard*,[75] a story of sixteenth-century England. Queen Mary blames Kate Sutton for a letter her sister, Alicia Sutton, wrote complaining about living conditions for the court's maids of honor. Queen Mary banishes Kate to the Perilous Gard, a remote castle belonging to Sir Geoffrey. Here heathen Fairy Folk are secretly holding Sir Geoffrey's daughter, Cecily, as a tiend or sacrifice for All Hallow's Eve. When Cecily's Uncle Christopher learns about her captivity, he offers to substitute for his niece. Kate, determined to uproot the cult, risks her life confronting him in front of the Fairy Folk, and he opposes the cultists. At last, Sir Geoffrey frees Christopher and Cecily, stopping all heathen practice.

*Wish or Dream Fulfillment*

**Middle and Upper Grades.** Marjorie Kinnan Rawlings's *The Secret River,*[76] set in Florida, has the theme of wish fulfillment in time of need. Calpurnia's father is a fishmonger without fish, so to help financially, she is guided by wise Mother Albirtha to "follow her nose" to a secret river filled with fish. Accompanied by her dog, Buggy-horse, she finds the river and, with pink crepe-paper roses as bait, catches catfish that are profitable for her father. When there is no need, she seeks the same river, but Mother Albirtha says:

> Child, you caught catfish when catfish were needed. Hard times have turned to soft times. So you will not find that river again. . . . The secret river is in your mind. You can go there any time you want to. Close your eyes and you will see it.[77]

Sure enough, Calpurnia imagines or dreams about the secret river to which she can escape in time of need.

As unusual as Calpurnia is Mona Lisa Figg-Newton, a high-school student featured in Ellen Raskin's self-illustrated *Figgs and Phantoms,*[78] whose theme is dream fulfillment. Mona's family of midgets, contortionists, and dancers, often the subject of gossip in the town of Pineapple, invent Capri, an island where dreams can be realized. When her beloved Uncle Florence Italy Figg dies and goes to the Figg family heaven, Capri, Mona visits him. She cannot stay because Capri is different for each Figg, and this Capri is not based on her dreams. One day, she will envision her own Capri, for "We live, as we dream—alone."[79] In her Uncle's Capri, Mona finds him happily married to Phoebe with a child named Mona. In Pineapple once more, Mona is content about her uncle and anticipates future dreams fulfilled in a personal Capri.

*Adventure*

**Middle and Upper Grades.** The theme of Lloyd Alexander's *The Marvelous Misadventures of Sebastian*[80] is finding a life goal after championing underdogs in nearly disastrous adventures. Sebastian is a Baron's unjustly dismissed fourth fiddler in eighteenth-century imaginary Hamelin-Loring. He fights to protect his first underdog, Presto, a tortured cat who becomes his traveling companion. In the fight, his fiddle, the only source of income, is smashed. After meeting Princess Isabel, who is fleeing marriage orders of a repressive Regent, Sebastian takes her into a theatrical group. Here he finds a cursed violin that killed its former master. He is not sure if he plays the violin or it plays him. However, its music saves Sebastian and the Princess while defeating his imprisoner, the Regent. Instead of marrying Isabel, Sebastian ends his adventure by deciding to devote his life to music. He summarizes: "But one thing the fiddle taught me: before, music was my living; now, it's my life."[81]

American author Lloyd Alexander introduces a magical violin and English writer Ian Fleming a fantastic car in his *Chitty Chitty Bang Bang*,[82] whose theme is a magical car protecting adventurers. This detective story parody is the only children's book by the late Ian Fleming, famous for James Bond mysteries. Commander Crackpot Potts, his wife, Mimsie, and their eight-year-old twins, Jeremy and Jemima, buy an old Paragon Panther racer, Chitty Chitty Bang Bang, to explore England and France. Its license, GEN II (genii), is apt for the racer transforms into a boat or plane. After Chitty takes the family into a cave and avoids a trap, they realize, "There really is something almost magical about this car."[83] In the cave the family ignites explosives belonging to a crook, Joe the Monster. When Joe avenges by kidnapping the children, Chitty enables their rescue and the crook's arrest. The family concludes, "You never get real adventures without a lot of risk somewhere."[84]

A young boy who is willing to take risks is imaginative Anatole in Nancy Willard's *Sailing to Cythera and Other Anatole Stories*.[85] This book has three short stories, each with the theme of a child's imagination leading to magical adventures. The title story, "Sailing to Cythera," tells how Anatole journeys via a wallpaper scene to Cythera Island where he confronts Blimlim, a dangerous monster. It has a lizard's body, an eagle's head, and an albatross's wings. When Anatole learns Blimlim is lonely, he and the monster return to his home through the wallpaper with Blimlim content to live under the boy's bed.

In 1887, Mathilda has an unusual one-day adventure described in *The Slightly Irregular Fire Engine: Or The Hithering Thithering Djinn* by author-illustrator Donald Barthelme.[86] His black-and-white collage illustrations on different-colored backdrops are made entirely from nineteenth-century engravings. Escapade is the theme, for Mathilda goes outside to hoop and finds a mysterious Chinese house has grown in her backyard overnight. Inside she sees two fierce-looking Chinese guards, a knitting pirate, a rainmaker, a cat seller on a camel, an elephant, a gigantic popcorn-making machine, and djinn, or supernatural Moslem creatures. She has fried lobster for lunch in the Gray Room that houses treasures. Jugglers, clowns, and fencers entertain until her nurse calls her. The next day, though the Chinese house is gone, she has a requested souvenir, a fire engine. Mathilda lets her parents use the engine that is not red, but bright green.

**Upper Grades.** The adventure of floating at night, the theme of Randall Jarrell's *Fly by Night*,[87] is conveyed through young David who is a normal, obliging child by day. "But at night . . . he wakes up sometimes . . . and after a minute he feels himself float up from the bed. He is flying."[88] He floats nude in his neighborhood, sometimes talking to animals that never answer. When he awakens, he forgets his nocturnal experiences. On page 26 of *Fly by Night,* illustrator Maurice Sendak shows himself as a baby in his mother's arms while David is floating overhead.

An ordinary library becomes the point of departure for fantasy in Edward Eager's *Seven-Day Magic*,[89] whose theme is wishing adventures but with limitation. Susan, John, and neighbors Barnaby, Fredericka, and Abbie return from the library with a magical book that allows the children to take turns wishing themselves included in a favorite story, and it becomes a reality. At first, everyone is overjoyed to adventure with wizards and slay dragons. When they experiment with a baby, keeping his mind infantile and making his body adult, they realize wishes should be limited. John and Barnaby rip the book somewhat in a quarrel. However, the children return it safely after a seven-day loan, and they use their final wish to bring it to the library on wings and magic carpets. As they put it on a shelf, they see the title, *Seven-Day Magic,* emerge and wonder what adventures await the next reader.

*Kindness*

**Upper Grades.** Unselfish kindness is the theme of Jane Yolen's title short story in a collection of five tales, *The Girl Who Cried Flowers and Other Tales*,[90] illustrated by David Palladini. "The Girl Who Cried Flowers" tells about an ancient Greek woman, Olivia, who never sheds tears, only a cascade of flowers that she gives away. The greedy deliberately try to make her sad to collect blossoms. "Still she did not complain for above all things Olivia loved making other people happy. . . ."[91] When Olivia marries Panos, he forbids her to be sad in the service of others, a command that causes her death. As he grieves, a drop of his blood falls, and from it springs a blossoming olive tree. Kind Olivia, even in death, creates greenery for her beloved husband. When Panos dies, the tree yields bitter fruit.

*Insight*

**Middle and Upper Grades.** Mary Rodgers's humorous *Freaky Friday* has the theme of insight gained from role reversal.[92] Since thirteen-year-old Annabel Andrews is impatient with her mother's strictness and Ellen Andrews cannot understand her daughter's demands, the mother offers a day of role reversal as a solution. On a Friday, Annabel's mind is placed in her mother's body and vice versa, leading both to perceive each other's feelings and see themselves as others see them. Annabel becomes frustrated doing laundry, conferencing with teachers, disciplining her children, and coping with her husband's clients as unexpected dinner guests. At day's end, she declares, "Listen, I quit! . . . You wanted to teach me a terrific lesson? OK, I've learned a terrific lesson."[93] Her mother is also frustrated from being treated as an insensitive child. The story ends when the two assume original bodies, but with new insight about self and each other.

*Preferring Myth*

**Middle and Upper Grades.** *Kneeknock Rise* by author-illustrator Natalie Babbitt has the theme of unwillingness to relinquish a myth.[94] In Instep, villagers believe when it rains, Megrimum, a suspected god, wails from the misty top of a low mountain, Kneeknock Rise. One rainy day, pre-adolescent Egan explores the mountain with Annabelle, a dog belonging to a recently disappeared relative, Ott. At the summit, Egan finds Ott, a poet who finds solace there. Ott says wailing sounds come from water boiling like a mineral spring through a narrow hole in this former volcano. Rain increases pressure, and the hot water rises as steam. Then Ott warns:

> For me it's always been important to find out the why of things. . . . As for those people down below, they've had their Megrimum for years and years. And I don't know as I want to spoil it all for them. There's always the possibility that they're happier believing. . . .[95]

Ott's words prove prophetic, because when Egan descends and tells villagers the truth, they refuse to accept his explanation.

*Personification*

**Primary through Middle Grades.** Love bringing a toy to life is the theme of Margery Williams's *The Velveteen Rabbit: Or How Toys Became*

*Real.*[96] In the nursery, the velveteen rabbit listens as the Skin Horse explains:

> When a child loves you for a long, long time, not just to play with, but REALLY loves you, then you become real. . . . Generally by the time you are Real, most of your hair has been loved off, and your eyes drop out and you get loose in the joints and very shabby. But these things don't matter at all, because once you are Real you can't be ugly, except to people who don't understand.[97]

The rabbit values the horse's words when, as the young boy's favorite bedtime companion, he hears his master declare, "He isn't a toy. He's real!"[98] After the boy gets scarlet fever and his rabbit has to be burned, the nursery magic fairy turns him into a live, soft, brown bunny for all to love.

**Middle and Upper Grades.** Adventures that prove the value of companionship is the theme of Rachel Field's *Hitty, Her First Hundred Years,*[99] a first-person account of a doll, Hitty, who tells about her life. She begins with being carved from mountain ash, being passed among owners as a good-luck symbol, surviving the high seas, fires, and theft, and ending in an antique shop. She is depicted almost as a lifelike child with desperate craving to be with loving boys and girls.

Unfortunately, *Hitty,* copyrighted in 1957, has derogatory references to Native Americans. An example is this quotation: "Until then the only dancing I had seen was sailor's hornpipe and those performed by savages."[100]

Less urbane is the country doll, Miss Hickory, found in Carolyn Sherwin Bailey's nature-theme book, *Miss Hickory.*[101] Made of an applewood-twig body and a hickory-nut head, the hardheaded doll survives winter in the New Hampshire woods with Crow, Bull Frog, Ground Hog, and Squirrel. The latter animal is forgetful enough to eat Miss Hickory's head. She contributes her body to nature when she is grafted on an apple tree, helping it bloom and bear fruit.

Personified dolls and toy soldiers are subjects of prizewinning fantasies. In Edward Eager's *Knight's Castle,*[102] eleven-year-old Roger has an heirloom tin soldier, the Old One, who leads four children into the past. The book's theme is imagining knighthood as relief from crisis. When his father needs surgery, Roger and his eight-year-old sister, Ann, accompany their parents to Baltimore, visiting their cousins, eleven-year-old Jack and nine-year-old Eliza. Roger carries his toy soldiers and on the train, talks to a soldier he calls the Old One. When his aunt gives him a knight's castle, he involves his peers in three knighthood experiences with Ivanhoe and Robin Hood. In the final one, Roger proves worthy to be granted a special wish. His father recovers, so his wish is realized.

**Upper Grades.** Twelve nineteenth-century wooden soldiers, toys of Branwell Brontë described in *The History of the Young Men,* are subjects of *The Return of the Twelves* by English author, Pauline Clarke.[103] The theme is a quest to return to a former life in an ancestral home. Set in England during the early 1900s, the story features eight-year-old Max Morley who discovers the Brontë soldiers under the floorboards of his attic. If he plays his great-grandfather's Ashanti drum, they come to life. When in jeopardy, they freeze into mere wood. Anyone who discovers the toys can receive a $5,000 reward, so Max enlists his brother's and sister's help in protecting them. After an American professor comes to take them to a museum, the soldiers leave through the attic window, bound for Haworth, their original home. Max finds them, but instead of offending their dignity by carrying them to Haworth, he lets them march there under their patriarch, Butter Crashley. As the book ends, the twelve arrive at Haworth museum, destined to be wooden by day and alive by night. "It was obvious that Haworth was their place."[104]

*Family Relationships*

**Upper Grades.** Randall Jarrell's poetic *The Animal Family* has the theme of man's need for a family, even if it means accepting different creatures.[105] A lonely hunter on a deserted island becomes fascinated with a mermaid, and she adapts to living with him, though she eats only the raw fish she catches. "The hunter and the mermaid were so different from each other that it seemed to them, finally, that they were exactly alike, and they lived together and were happy."[106] After a mother bear's death, her cub becomes part of the hunter's family, eating at his table though retaining a habit of hibernating. Soon the hunter adopts another forest creature, a lynx, who looks down from the rafters. "The bear was fond of the hunter and mermaid but the lynx adored them."[107] It is the lynx who finds the last family member, an orphan boy in a drifting canoe. In time, the boy thinks:

> He knew that the hunter was his father and the mermaid his mother.
> . . . The two of them were different from him, different from each
> other, but aren't a boy's father and mother always different from him,
> different from each other?[108]

Illustrator Maurice Sendak helps convey the theme of *The Animal*

*Family*. Sendak accentuates differences within the family by preceding each chapter on a family member with a picture of the former habitat: the hunter's home, the mermaid's sea, the cub's cave, the lynx's cliffs, and the boy's canoe. With such distinct origins, characters accept each other admirably.

Integrating an unusual stepsister into a family can be a challenge. Complex family relationships with an occultist is the theme of Zilpha Keatley Snyder's *The Headless Cupid*.[109] Eleven-year-old David, his middle sister, Janie, and four-year-old twins, Blair and Ester, had begun to accept their new stepmother, Molly, when Molly's twelve-year-old daughter, Amanda, becomes a family member. Amanda's belief in the supernatural is fed by Mr. Golanski, an electrician who mentions the presence of a poltergeist or noisy ghost in the house. From then on, plants break, paintings fall, rocks are thrown, furniture is moved, and night noises are heard. Though others suspect a poltergeist, Amanda admits she is the cause. The house has a headless wooden cupid, but Amanda is not the one who suddenly returns its head. It is four-year-old Blair who finds the head in his toy chest and says a girl ghost told him where to look. By now, however, Amanda is less interested in the supernatural, beginning to forgive her mother for divorcing her father, and adjusting to rural California. She explains:

> I was getting even with everybody for everything. Part of the time I thought it was to get them to move out of this house because I didn't want to live way out here in the country and have to go to some hick school with a lot of squares who'd probably hate a person like me.[110]

Amanda no longer needs her pose of superiority as she begins to love her new family.

Nancy Bond's *A String in the Harp* has a theme of a grieving family's learning to communicate again.[111] Mourning for his recently deceased wife, David Morgan leaves Amherst, Massachusetts and becomes a teacher for a year at the University of Wales. His fifteen-year-old daughter, Jen, attends high school in Amherst, but visits her father, twelve-year-old brother, Peter, and ten-year-old sister, Becky, in Borth, Wales. She finds "ever since their mother had been killed last December, their family had seemed to come apart."[112] Her father grieves by focusing on his work. Her brother, with his hard exterior, grieves by yelling at his father. Only her sister Becky is interested in Wales, but this is due to a friend, Gwilyn Davies, not to her family. At first, Peter continues to be withdrawn after he finds a magical silver tuning key to the harp of a Welsh bard, Taliesin, a key that transports him to Taliesin in the sixth century. Then the family draws together as they share visions of the past and protect the key.

"The distance between them dwindled and they could talk."[113] Through a vision, Peter is led to Taliesin's grave and leaves the key there so the bard's spirit can rest. Peter becomes a responsible family member, a string in the Morgan harp that is now in tune.


*Individuality and Freedom*

**Middle and Upper Grades.** Peggy Clifford's *The Gnu and the Guru Go Behind the Beyond,* illustrated by Eric Von Schmidt, has the theme of eschewing conformity in favor of individuality and freedom.[114] The Gnu, an impatient, hairy member of the antelope family, and the Guru, a patient, short, fat man, travel on a mysterious cloud to Behind the Beyond, a land where order and symmetry rule over imagination. The first thing the couple notice is that all trees are boring symmetrical squares. The gatekeeper explains:

> "They weren't always that way. Some were bushy. Some were tall and thin as straws. Some were fat. We thought they were exceedingly messy. So we decided to make all the trees square and all the flowers geometrically satisfying. It makes for a tidier and more functional landscape, doesn't it?"[115]

The heavens are no more interesting, for the sky is painted and rain comes at precise intervals. Furniture is also painted on walls. The critical Gnu and Guru are imprisoned but escape and ride the gatekeeper's cloud to freedom.

> They were free. It seemed such a simple act, opening and closing a gate, but it overjoyed them beyond reason. "We're free!" they called.[116]

Once home, the Gnu and Guru marvel at weeds, wild flowers, shaggy trees, road ruts, and streaky skies.

Similar to the conformity in Behind the Beyond is that in the Land Between the Mountains, described in Carol Kendall's *The Gammage Cup.*[117] The story takes place in the year Gammage 880 among the conventional, isolated Minnipins living in villages along the Watercress River. They obey the edicts of their revered first family, the Periods, who have abbreviated names, like Ltd. and Ave. Five Minnipins rebel as follows: (1) Muggles wears an orange sash when brown or green clothes are required; (2) Curley's door is red instead of green; (3) Gummy writes jingles that Periods hate; (4) Mingy dislikes Period public ex-

penditures; and (5) Walter the Earl questions Period authority. Muggles
tries to explain at a town meeting:

> " . . . it's no matter what color we paint our doors or what kind of
> clothes we wear, we're . . . well, we're those colors inside us. Instead
> of being green inside, you see, like other folk."[118]

Muggles is ineffective; the five are exiled and settle together upriver.
They discover the Mushrooms or Hairless Ones invading and force enemy retreat by alerting reluctant Minnipins. Welcomed home as heroes,
the outlaws discover: "Colored streams of scarlet, orange, . . . from
every house. And the doors! There wasn't a green door on the square."[119]
As a result, Slipper-on-the-Water wins the coveted Gammage Cup for
the most beautiful village in hard-won recognition of individuality.


*Learning and Wisdom*

**Middle and Upper Grades.** Norton Juster's humor derives from a play
on words in *The Phantom Tollbooth,*[120] which has the value of learning
as its theme. Young Milo, disillusioned with school, experiments with
a surprising packaged tollbooth and travels into The Lands Beyond, an
adventure that teaches him he'd "never amount to anything without an
education."[121] After passing through Doldrums where thinking is pro-
hibited, he learns the value of words in Dictionopolis ruled by King Azaz
the Unabridged. His next stop is in Point of View where he appreciates
how different beholders interpret the same thing, like a bucket of water
that appears to be a vast ocean from an ant's point of view, "from an
elephant's just a cool drink, and to a fish, of course, it's home."[122] In
Digitopolis, Mathemagician serves subtraction stew to increase diners'
hunger. At a funny royal banquet, guests eat their words. Milo returns
princesses Rhyme and Reason to the Kingdom of Wisdom before returning home, convinced "whenever you learn something new, the whole
world becomes that much richer."[123]

**Upper Grades.** Seeking wisdom and a better life is the theme of Mary
Q. Steele's *Journey Outside.*[124] Raised among Raft People, young Dilar
escapes from subterranean river tunnels where his grandfather travels in
circles looking for "a better place than where we were before."[125] Dilar
finds a green world of daylight and searches here for answers to questions. "For he had questions and questions and questions and it would
take wise men to answer them."[126] He learns nothing from the fun-loving
People against the Tigers or from the hermit, Wingo, who cares for small

creatures, only to see them become hawk or tiger prey. In the desert, Dilar meets "Not People," who need no one. Finally, he finds an old goatherder, Vigan, who recites Raft People history and comments:

> "Wisdom is like water: there comes a point where it runs into the ground and if you want it you must dig it out yourself."[127]

Vigan tells Dilar how to join his people since the boy wants them to take the same journey he took. In this allegory, everyone except wise Vigan seems to be circling in the dark as much as Dilar's grandfather. Vigan urges the boy to listen to others, separating wisdom from stupidity and drawing his own conclusions.

*Love*

**Upper Grades.** Mozart's German opera, "Die Zauberflöte," is retold in English in Stephen Spender's *The Magic Flute*,[128] illustrated by Beni Montresor. Its theme, earned love, is revealed in the trials of Prince Tamino who is sent by the Queen of the Night to rescue her daughter, Princess Pamina, from the castle of the priest Sarastro. The Prince, who falls in love with the Princess when he sees her portrait, arms himself on his quest with a magic flute. After the Prince and Princess meet, they know their love is genuine. Sarastro tests the couple's affection by making them overcome obstacles, and in the end, they find him "standing on the steps, his arms outstretched to welcome those whose love had overcome great trials."[129] A magic flute helps the Prince and Princess, and silver bells help a comic bird catcher, Papageno, win his intended, Papagena. The opera is allegorical, for the Prince and Princess represent Masonic ideals, not ordinary people, while Sarastro stands for forces of light and the evil Queen of the Night, forces of darkness.

The power of love is the theme of James Thurber's *The White Deer*.[130] King Clode has three sons, Thag and Gallow, who are selfish hunters, and Jorn, who is a poet-musician. The sons stalk a white deer who changes into a lovely maiden when cornered. She assigns them tasks which they fulfill, though she is in danger of becoming a deer again if her love is spurned three times. The older brothers don't want a wife who is half deer, but Jorn, who truly loves the maiden, says, "What you have been, you are not; and what you are, you will forever be. I place this trophy in the hands of love."[131] Jorn adores the mysterious twenty-one-year-old maiden identified by Prince Tel as his sister, Princess Rosanore of Northland.

## Themes of Prizewinning Science Fiction Grouped under These Topics

While modern fantasy departs from reality and often revolves around magic, science fiction is concerned with science or pseudo-science. It may be futuristic, picture life on another planet, or inspire change. Sylvia Louise Engdahl, an author of prizewinning science fiction, explains:

> . . . science fiction differs from fantasy not in subject matter but in aim, and its unique aim is to suggest real hypotheses about mankind's future or about the nature of the universe.[132]

Themes in science fiction often parallel those in fantasy.

### Survival

**Upper Grades.** The theme of Robert C. O'Brien's *Z for Zachariah* is struggling to survive after nuclear war.[133] The unusual title derives from the fact that when Ann Burden learned the alphabet from *The Bible Letter Book,* she found, "The first page said A is for Adam. The last of all was Z is for Zachariah."[134] Believing she is the last person left in the world, Ann is now sixteen and has just withstood a nuclear war. Surrounded by radioactive barrenness, she is fortunate to be in a Pennsylvania valley that escaped the path of the bombing, allowing her to cultivate food and obtain water. She says "I had all summer to . . . get over being afraid, and to think about how I was going to live through the winter."[135] Her loneliness is interrupted by another survivor, John R. Loomis, a New York chemist, who appears wearing a radiation-proof safe suit. He becomes ill after swimming in a radioactive creek, but Ann nurses him back to health. The ungrateful man insanely attempts to kill her, so Ann steals the safe suit and leaves the valley, hoping to survive elsewhere.

### Ingenuity

**Middle and Upper Grades.** Ingenuity is shown in *Danny Dunn and the Homework Machine* by Jay Williams and Raymond Abrashkin.[136] Part of the Danny Dunn series, this book portrays the consequences of inventiveness. Danny Dunn and his mother, a housekeeper, live with a physicist, Professor Bullfinch, who has just invented a computer named Miniac. Danny and two friends, Joe Pearson and Irene Miller, spend three days programming Miniac to do their homework. Irene stays with the group though Joe offers this stereotyped criticism of her: ''Dames! Nothing but trouble.''[137] The trouble comes, however, from Eddie Philips who tells the teacher, Miss Arnold, what is taking place. Danny concludes:

> Somehow it always seemed that when he jumped into something without thinking of the consequences—as for instance when he had jumped into the idea of using the computer for homework—then all sorts of unforeseen . . . things resulted.[138]

One result is the teacher assigns the trio more difficult work than the rest of the class. When Miniac is needed elsewhere, the three once more do their own homework.


*Adventure*

**Middle and Upper Grades.** Another book by Jay Williams and Raymond Abrashkin, *Danny Dunn on the Ocean Floor*,[139] has the theme of creating and solving problems in an oceanic adventure. Danny Dunn and his mother, a housekeeper, live with Professor Bullfinch. Bullfinch and a friend, Dr. Grimes, build a plastic submarine, *Sea Urchin*, reluctantly taking Danny and his friends, Irene Miller and Joe Pearson, on its maiden voyage near Mexico. Danny, anxious to record fish sounds, brings his tape recorder. He causes trouble by blowing a fuse, trapping a shark that damages equipment, and knocking the captain unconscious, resulting in the submarine's being stranded on the ocean floor. On the positive side, the group discovers in an ocean bed the Image of the Sun, an Aztec relic, and a special antibiotic. Danny's recordings attract fish that guide the submarine's safe return.

Fantasies portray adventuring on the ocean floor and in the stratosphere, the site of Ellen MacGregor's *Miss Pickerell Goes to Mars*.[140] Its theme is contributions from an enterprising woman on an unexpected space adventure. Miss Pickerell becomes the first woman on Mars after accidently boarding a rocket ship parked in her pasture. Chief Engineer Haggerty is left on Earth after the unexpected launch. Nervous at first, Miss Pickerell eventually enjoys the expedition. In stereotyped fashion, she is a spaceship cook who wears an apron even when sleeping. Told to stay aboard while the men explore, her spunky reply is: ''If you think for one minute, Captain Crandall, that I'm going to come all the way to Mars without getting out to see what it's like, you are very much mistaken.''[141] After all, it is she who determines how to land on Mars, and it is she who saves the life of Wilbur, a crew member who almost exhausts his oxygen supply. Laden with Mars specimens for her rock

collection, Miss Pickerell returns to Earth to learn Mr. Haggerty has
been caring for her cow and now wants to be a veterinarian.

**Upper Grades.** Robert A. Heinlein's science fiction, *Have Space Suit—
Will Travel,*[142] has the theme of teamwork facilitating adventurous interspacial rescue. A high school student, Clifford (Kip) Russell, happens
to be wearing a space suit won in a contest when he meets a ten-year-
old genius, Peewee. A spaceship lands, and Peewee becomes a prisoner
aboard it along with a loving police space marsupial, the Mother Thing.
Kip boards the ship to rescue the captives and to travel in space, finally
meeting those in command, cruel worm-faced monsters. After the monsters' defeat and the captives' release, Kip and Peewee have to defend
themselves in an interspacial court. Fortunately, they are allowed to
return to Earth under the Mother Thing's interspacial supervision. Kip
concludes that teamwork made rescue possible with him supplying en-
ergy, the Mother Thing offering warmth and nursing wounds, and Peewee
providing information on survival in space. Knowledge from the flight
helps Kip get a four-year college scholarship.

*Service*

**Middle and Upper Grades.** William Maxwell's *The Heavenly Tenants,*[143]
illustrated by Ilonka Karasz, tells what happens when a stargazer, his
wife, and four children leave their Wisconsin farm to visit Virginia relatives. They expected their hired hand August to tend the house, farm,
and animals in their absence, but sick August does not help. In Virginia,
Mr. Marvell cannot see a single zodiac sign in the sky, yet while he is
gone, his farm is bathed in such a bright light each night, neighbors
come to see it. The Marvells, return to find a fire in the stove, clocks
ticking, and sparks flying off many objects. "None of them realized the
whole secret—that while they were away the zodiac people with their
animals had come down from the sky and taken care of the farm."[144]
The theme proves to be zodiac people's service to an earthly friend.

*Maturing*

**Upper Grades.** The theme of Ursula K. Le Guin's *A Wizard of Earthsea*
is reaching manhood by accepting responsibility.[145] Duny, a boy raised
in a world of many islands, is later called Sparrowhawk and then Ged,
his true name known only to trusted friends. He has inborn magical
powers, and learning when to demonstrate this talent leads to early man-

hood. He changes from an immature adolescent studying at the School for Wizards into a wise wizard or mage. At first, he is so impatient, he doesn't listen to advice, "Wait. Manhood is patience."[146] He engages in a forbidden sorcerer's duel and summons from the dead a haunting, life-threatening shadow which he hunts. When he calls the shadow by his own name in recognition of his responsibility for this evil, he halts its power. He frees the world of the dark and allows himself to become a man in this first book of a trilogy. His friend, Vetch, says:

> Ged had neither lost nor won but, naming the shadow of his death with his own name had made himself whole: a man: who, knowing his whole, true self, cannot be used or possessed by any other power other than by himself, and whose life therefore is lived for life's sake and never in the service of ruin, or pain, or hatred, or the dark.[147]

*Self-Identity*

**Upper Grades.** Losing and gaining self-identity is the theme of Ursula K. Le Guin's *The Tombs of Atuan,*[148] sequel to *A Wizard of Earthsea.* Tenar-Arha, destined to become High Priestess when she is fifteen years old, is later allowed self-choice. When Tenar was six, she was taken from home to serve the Nameless Powers of the Earth at the Place of the Tombs in the deserts of Atuan. She was stripped of her identity and assumed the name of Arha or the Eaten One. Bored with perpetual darkness and death, she felt lost, for she couldn't remember her real name or family. In the tombs forbidden to men, she gives food and water to a lost wizard, Ged or Sparrowhawk, and he in return gives her a chance to cease being a slave and regain her identity. He tells her, "You must be Arha, or you must be Tenar. You cannot be both."[149] The two leave with the broken ring, an ancient treasure, joining them, and she faces the problems of assuming a new identity as she copes with the weight of liberty.

*Immortality*

**Upper Grades.** Completing a trilogy, *The Farthest Shore* by Ursula K. Le Guin has a theme of immortality, a struggle between life and death.[150] The story unfolds as young Arren, Prince of Enlad, and respected Ged, the Archmage of Roke, journey to the farthest shore of Earthsea to discover why wizardry has diminished. (Wizardry and wisdom seem indistinguishable.) They learn that a great but corrupted mage, Cob, has threatened the world's equilibrium by opening the door to immortality, catering to those who fear death. Ged argues, "To refuse death is to refuse life."[151] He and Arren finally reach the land of death where evil Cob is master of immortality, and the two witness nameless, loveless eternal life. Ged tells Cob, "You exist: without name, without form. You sold the green earth and the sun and stars to save yourself. But you have no self."[152] Ged restores the balance between life and death before returning with prospective King Arren.

*Insight*

**Upper Grades.** Insight into another way of life is the theme of Alexander Key's *The Forgotten Door*.[153] While watching the stars, Little Jon falls through the "forgotten door" to planet Earth with no memory of the past or knowledge of English. Gifted with ability to read others' minds, he senses hatred and thinks:

> The language was strange, but the hate-driven thoughts behind it were clear enough. For a moment he stood incredulous, . . . Surely the man approaching was a being like himself. But why the intent to kill another creature [deer]?[154]

On Little Jon's planet, man and animal are in harmony, and hating, killing, stealing, and lying do not exist. Accused of thefts because he is different, the boy is protected by the Bean family. Mr. Bean tells him:

> It gave me a glimpse of what a peaceful and wonderful place your world must be—and how strange and terrible ours must look to you. Jon, the awful part is what people here would do to you if they could. They'd use you. They'd pay no attention to the good you could give; they'd use your mind to help fight their secret battles.[155]

The Beans, after prodding the boy's memory, discover the entrance door to Earth is amidst volcanic rock where Earth's magnetism is strong. When Little Jon hears his people calling, he returns. The Beans, unpopular because of help given the boy, go with him since their values are similar to those of Little Jon's kin.

*Destiny*

**Upper Grades.** Sylvia Louise Engdahl's futuristic science fiction, *Enchantress from the Stars*,[156] has human destiny as its theme. On the planet

Andrecia are three levels of civilization: (1) Primitive Andrecians who want to reward a slayer of their enemy's dragon; (2) Imperials whose dragon is an earth-moving machine. It destroys Andrecian forests and people, whom they consider subhuman, to make room for Imperial colonists; and (3) a team of the most advanced human beings, Federalists from the Federation of Planets who use mental telepathy to try to save Andrecians from Imperials. Elana, the book's narrator, is on the Federalist team with her father. He teaches respect of Andrecian destiny when he questions, "What right did the Empire have to take their future away from them just because they were not civilized now?"[157] He adds: "At best their civilization would become poor copies of ours, instead of keeping their uniqueness."[158] An Andrecian woodcutter's son, Georyn, learns skills from the Federalist team to prevent his planet's overthrow. He looks upon mind-reading Elana as an Enchantress from the Stars, and they grow to love each other. Elana not only differentiates among Andrecians but also among Imperials when she gets help from a sympathetic Imperial doctor, Jarel, in defeating the invasion. The book ends with Elana and Georyn painfully parting, for Elana must rejoin her civilization. Both rejoice that Andrecians can now control their destiny.

## Truth

**Upper Grades.** Another futuristic work by Sylvia Louise Engdahl, *This Star Shall Abide*,[159] has a quest-for-truth theme. "I want to know the truth. The truth is the most important thing there is,"[160] says adolescent Noren, a lowly Villager in a planet with three castes. Villagers are farmers, shopkeepers, and traders; Technicians operate machines, like aircars and soil quickeners; and Scholars, who alone reside within City walls, possess all knowledge and power until a future time when, according to the Divine Prophecy, the Mother Star will appear in the sky. Challenging the Prophecy that keeps truth from Villagers, heretic Noren faces punishment by Scholars. To his surprise, punishment consists of learning truth, fulfilling Noren's quest, for Scholars prepare to overthrow the caste system by enlightening heretics, even welcoming some as new Scholars. Stefred the High Scholar tells Noren, "There is something higher and more significant than we are. You, I think, would call it Truth."[161]

## Freedom

**Upper Grades.** *The White Mountains* by English author John Christopher has the theme of escape to freedom.[162] This first book of a futuristic trilogy is set in the twenty-first century when mechanized Tripods from another planet make human beings subservient by "Capping" them, inserting a steel plate in fourteen-year-olds' skulls. Thirteen-year-old Will Parker, his cousin, Henry, and friend, Beanpole, determined to avoid being Capped, receive escape directions from Ozymandias, considered insane because he is an un-Capped Vagrant. They head for a White Mountains haven in what ancients called Switzerland. When Will becomes ill, a comtesse's daughter, Eloise, helps him recover, but he realizes she is Capped. "More and more Will had come to see the Capped as lacking what seemed the essence of humanity, the vital spark of defiance against the rulers of the world."[163] After Will leaves Eloise, a Tripod seizes and releases him, but implants in his skin a metal device so Tripods can follow him. Fortunately, the boys find weapons and use them before escaping to the White Mountains. There are no luxuries in the haven, though Will argues:

> "For it is not quite true to say that we have no luxuries. We have two: freedom and hope. We live among men whose minds are their own, who do not accept the dominion of the Tripods, and who, having endured in patience for long enough, are even now preparing to carry the war to the enemy."[164]

*Love*

**Upper Grades.** Among the best-known science-fictional prizewinners with a power-of-love theme is Madeleine L'Engle's *A Wrinkle in Time*.[165] Twelve-year-old Meg Murray, her brilliant five-year-old brother, Charles Wallace Murry, and fourteen-year-old friend, Calvin O'Keefe, search for Mr. Murry, a government physicist who disappeared a year earlier. The children learn he is a prisoner on an evil planet, Camazotz. Three supernatural women, Mrs. Whatsit, Mrs. Who, and Mrs. Which, guide them to the planet by fifth-dimensional space travel, a tesseract, that reduces distance by creating a wrinkle in time. In Camazotz, an oversized brain, IT, controls and regiments people, even capturing Charles Wallace. (Regimentation versus individualization is one of the book's secondary themes.) Meg frees her father who takes her and Calvin to another planet, but it is Meg alone who goes back for her brother. She saves him, repeating, "I love you. I love you. I love you."[166] He runs into her arms, and they join Mr. Murry and Calvin in tesseracting safely to Earth.

In an interview, Madeleine L'Engle reveals:

> I don't know how many times *A Wrinkle in Time* was rejected for two

reasons mostly: (1) quite a few publishers didn't know if it was for children or grownups and (2) it dealt too overtly with the problem of evil. It showed children that there was evil in the world. Well, there is evil in the world, and we've got to fight it. If you protect children entirely from the fact that there is death, there is evil, there are people who hate and who would like to hurt them, they have no weapons and are going to grow up incapable of loving. You cannot love truly, maturely in an unreal world. Now we've gone to the other end of the pendulum, because we have realism without love.[167]

Elaborating on a favorite theme, love, L'Engle says when you love, you are vulnerable. She offers this example:

During the Second World War, there was a young English war bride. Her husband was in the R.A.F., and they had three little babies. When he came home on leave, she got all of their food coupons together and went off, leaving him with the kids to buy the greatest meal you could possibly buy in wartime London which wasn't going to be very great, but still it would be a party. She was standing in line a long time, and when she got home, a random bomb had dropped. The house was gone and so were her husband and children. She spent the rest of the war working with other homeless people. She was very brave and much admired. Then somebody else fell in love with her and wanted to marry her. She knew that as long as she didn't love again, as long as she didn't marry or have children again, she was safe. She couldn't be hurt. . . . She made the choice for life, married, and had children.

When we love, it can be the most glorious thing in the world, but it can also be the most terrible, and this is a risk we have got to take, I think. Otherwise, we die.[168]

L'Engle's overall view of themes is as follows:

Every writer, every artist, and every musician has a theme. What we do is go over it again and again. You can always recognize a concerto by Rachmaninoff or a fugue by Bach, because they had their own thing to say. I think you're right about what my thing is [stress on love versus evil and on individualization, not regimentation].[169]

## Summary

This chapter discusses fifty-eight examples of prizewinning modern fantasy with their primary themes grouped under twenty-one topics and fourteen examples of prizewinning science fiction with their primary themes grouped under twelve topics. Many books are written about fusion of past, present, or future; adventure; good overcoming evil; and personification. About half of the books are intended for middle- and upper-elementary grades and the other half, for upper grades alone with only one book destined for primary and middle grades. In science fiction, books for upper grades predominate.

English-born writers authored eleven of the reviewed modern fantasy prizewinners, which is not surprising considering that fantasy is the preferred genre of many English children. Among the presented modern fantasy prizewinners, Lloyd Alexander has written five; Natalie Babbitt, three; and Susan Cooper, Edward Eager, Randall Jarrell, Norton Juster, Mary Rodgers, James Thurber, and Nancy Willard, two each. Ursula K. Le Guin has written three of the presented prizewinners in science fiction; Sylvia Louise Engdahl, two; and Jay Williams with Raymond Abrashkin, two (though Jay Williams alone also wrote a reviewed modern-fantasy prizewinner).

## Notes

1. Holt Library Services Department, *Lloyd Alexander* (New York: Holt, 1973), no page.

2. Lloyd Alexander, "The Flat-Heeled Muse" in *Children and Literature, Views and Reviews* by Virginia Haviland (Glenview, Ill.: Scott Foresman, 1973), p. 242.

3. Ibid., p. 243.

4. In 1965, *The Wolves of Willoughby Chase* won the Lewis Carroll Shelf Award.

5. Joan Aiken, *The Wolves of Willoughby Chase* (New York: Doubleday, 1962), p. 66.

6. In 1968, *The Fearsome Inn* was a Newbery Honor Book.

7. In 1969, *McBroom Tells the Truth* won the Lewis Carroll Shelf Award.

8. Sid Fleischman, *McBroom Tells the Truth* (New York: Norton, 1966), p. 17.

9. In 1966, *The Black Cauldron* was a Newbery Honor Book.

10. Lloyd Alexander, *The Black Cauldron* (New York: Holt, 1965), p. 165.

11. Ibid., p. 138.

12. In 1969, *The High King* won The John Newbery Medal and was a finalist for the National Book Award in the children's-book category.

13. Lloyd Alexander, *The High King* (New York: Holt, 1968), p. 54.

14. Ibid., p. 282.

15. In 1982, *Westmark* won The American Book Award for fiction.

16. In 1973, *The Dark Is Rising* won the *Boston Globe-Horn Book* Award, and in 1974, it was a Newbery Honor Book.

17. Susan Cooper, *The Dark Is Rising* (New York: Atheneum, 1974), p. 44.

18. Ibid., p. 40.

19. In 1976, *The Grey King* won The John Newbery Medal.

20. Susan Cooper, *The Grey King* (New York: Atheneum, 1975), p. 31.

21. Ibid., p. 197.

22. In 1970, *The Weirdstone of Brisingamen* won the Lewis Carroll Shelf Award.

23. In 1979, *The First Two Lives of Lukas-Kasha* was a finalist for the National Book Award in the children's-book category.

24. Lloyd Alexander, *The First Two Lives of Lukas-Kasha* (New York: Dutton, 1978), p. 3.

25. Ibid., p. 205.

26. Ibid., p. 213.

27. Lloyd Alexander discussed his themes with the writer on June 8, 1982.

28. In 1975, *The Devil's Storybook* was a finalist for the National Book Award in the children's-book category.

29. In 1976, *The Home Run Trick* won the Mark Twain Award.

30. Scott Corbett, *The Home Run Trick* (Boston: Little, Brown, 1973), p. 87.

31. In 1968, *Mister Corbett's Ghost,* illustrated by Alan E. Cober, was a *New York Times* Choice of Best Illustrated Children's Book of the Year.

32. Leon Garfield, *Mister Corbett's Ghost* (New York: Pantheon, 1968), p. 33.

33. Ibid., p. 75.

34. In 1976, *Witch of the Cumberlands* won the Ohioana Book Award.

35. Mary Jo Stephens, *Witch of the Cumberlands* (Boston: Houghton, 1974), p. 2.

36. Ibid., p. 241.

37. In 1965, *The Pushcart War* won the Lewis Carroll Shelf Award.

38. Jean Merrill, *The Pushcart War* (Reading, Mass.: Scott, 1964), p. 218.

39. In 1971, *The Master of Miracle: A New Novel of the Golem* won the National Jewish Book Award.

40. In 1976, *The Selchie's Seed* won the Southern California Council on Literature for Children and Young People Award.

41. Sulamith Oppenheim, *The Selchie's Seed* (New York: Bradbury, 1975), p. 57.

42. In 1975, *Tuck Everlasting* won the Christopher Award in the children's-book category for ages nine to twelve, and in 1978, it was put on the International Board on Books for Young People Honor List.

43. Natalie Babbitt, *Tuck Everlasting* (New York: Farrar, 1975), p. 64.

44. Ibid., p. 64.

45. In 1961, *Tom's Midnight Garden* won the Lewis Carroll Shelf Award.

46. Philippa A. Pearce, *Tom's Midnight Garden* (Philadelphia: Lippincott, 1958), p. 162.

47. Ibid., p. 224.

48. Ibid., pp. 224–225.

49. In 1969, *The Children of Green Knowe* won the Lewis Carroll Shelf Award.

50. L.M. Boston, *The Children of Green Knowe* (New York: Harcourt, 1955), p. 23.

51. Ibid., p. 75.

52. In 1972, *The Hawkstone* won the Lewis Carroll Shelf Award.

53. Jay Williams, *The Hawkstone* (New York: Walck, 1971), p. 98.

54. In 1944, *Fog Magic* was a Newbery Honor Book.

55. Julia L. Sauer, *Fog Magic* (New York: Viking, 1943), p. 103.

56. In 1965, *Alberic the Wise and Other Journeys* was a *New York Times* Choice of Best Illustrated Children's Book of the Year.

57. Norton Juster, *Alberic the Wise and Other Journeys* (New York: Pantheon, 1965), p. 38.

58. In 1974, *A Billion for Boris* won the Christopher Award in the children's-book category for ages twelve up.

59. Mary Rodgers, *A Billion for Boris* (New York: Harper, 1974), p. 186.

60. In 1968, *Earthfasts* won the Lewis Carroll Shelf Award.

61. William Mayne, *Earthfasts* (New York: Dutton, 1967), p. 140.

62. In 1978, *Poor Tom's Ghost* won the Ohioana Book Award.

63. Jane Louise Curry, *Poor Tom's Ghost* (New York: Atheneum, 1977), p. 110.

64. In 1976, *The Ghost Belonged to Me* won the Friends of American Writers Award.

65. Richard Peck, *The Ghost Belonged to Me* (New York: Viking, 1975), p. 110.

66. In 1974, *The Court of the Stone Children* won the National Book Award in the children's-book category.

67. Eleanor Cameron, *The Court of the Stone Children* (New York: Dutton, 1973), p. 113.

68. "Eleanor Cameron," *Profiles in Literature* (Philadelphia: Temple University, 1972).

69. Ibid.

70. In 1949, *My Father's Dragon* was a Newbery Honor Book and in 1968, it won the Lewis Carroll Shelf Award.

71. In 1944, *Many Moons* won The Randolph Caldecott Medal.

72. In 1978, *Charlie and the Great Glass Elevator* won the Nene Award.

73. In 1979, *The Island of the Grass King* won the Lewis Carroll Shelf Award.

74. Nancy Willard, *The Island of the Grass King* (New York: Harcourt, 1979), p. 32.

75. In 1975, *The Perilous Gard* was a Newbery Honor Book and was in the Children's Book Showcase.

76. In 1956, *The Secret River* was a Newbery Honor Book.

77. Marjorie Kinnan Rawlings, *The Secret River* (New York: Scribner, 1955), p. 49.

78. In 1975, *Figgs and Phantoms* was a Newbery Honor Book and was in the Children's Book Showcase.

79. Ellen Raskin, *Figgs and Phantoms* (New York: Dutton, 1974), p. 194.

80. In 1971, *The Marvelous Misadventures of Sebastian* won the National Book Award in the children's-book category.

81. Lloyd Alexander, *The Marvelous Misadventures of Sebastian* (New York: Dutton, 1970), p. 201.

82. In 1967, *Chitty Chitty Bang Bang* won the Pacific Northwest Library Association Young Reader's Choice Award.

83. Ian Fleming, *Chitty Chitty Bang Bang* (New York: Random, 1964), p. 57.

84. Ibid., p. 62.

85. In 1977, *Sailing to Cythera and Other Anatole Stories* won the Lewis Carroll Shelf Award.

86. In 1972, *The Slightly Irregular Fire Engine: Or The Hithering Thithering Djinn* won the National Book Award in the children's-book category.

87. In 1976, *Fly by Night* was a *New York Times* Choice of Best Illustrated Children's Book of the Year.

88. Randall Jarrell, *Fly by Night* (New York: Farrar, 1976), p. 5.

89. In 1963 *Seven-Day Magic* won the Ohioana Book Award.

90. In 1974, *The Girl Who Cried Flowers and Other Tales* won the Golden Kite Award and was a *New York Times* Choice of Best Illustrated Children's Book. In 1975, it was a finalist for the National Book Award in the children's-book category.

91. Jane Yolen, *The Girl Who Cried Flowers and Other Tales* (New York: Crowell, 1974), p. 2.

92. In 1972, *Freaky Friday* won the Christopher Award in the teenage category, and in 1978, it won the Georgia Children's Book Award.

93. Mary Rodgers, *Freaky Friday* (New York: Harper, 1972), p. 112.

94. In 1971, *Kneeknock Rise* was a Newbery Honor Book.

95. Natalie Babbitt, *Kneeknock Rise* (New York: Farrar, 1970), p. 88.

96. In 1971, *The Velveteen Rabbit: Or How Toys Became Real* won the Lewis Carroll Shelf Award.

97. Margery Williams, *The Velveteen Rabbit: Or How Toys Became Real* (New York: Avon, 1975), pp. 16–17.

98. Ibid., p. 24.

99. In 1930, *Hitty, Her First Hundred Years* won The John Newbery Medal.

100. Rachel Field, *Hitty, Her First Hundred Years* (New York: Macmillan, 1929), p. 139.

101. In 1947, *Miss Hickory* won The John Newbery Medal.

102. In 1957, *Knight's Castle* won the Ohioana Book Award.

103. In 1965, *The Return of the Twelves* won the Lewis Carroll Shelf Award.

104. Pauline Clarke, *The Return of the Twelves* (New York: Coward, 1963), p. 217.

105. In 1965, *The Animal Family* was a *New York Times* Best Illustrated Children's Book of the Year. In 1966, it was a Newbery Honor Book.

106. Randall Jarrell, *The Animal Family* (New York: Random, 1965), p. 54.

107. Ibid., p. 119.

108. Ibid., pp. 156–157.

109. In 1971, *The Headless Cupid* won the Christopher Award in the teenage category. In 1972, it was a Newbery Honor Book and in 1974, it was put on the International Board on Books for Young People Honor List.

110. Zilpha Keatley Snyder, *The Headless Cupid* (New York: Atheneum, 1972), p. 171.

111. In 1977, *A String in the Harp* was a Newbery Honor Book and won the International Reading Association Children's Book Award.

112. Nancy Bond, *A String in the Harp* (New York: Atheneum, 1976), p. 3.

113. Ibid., p. 304.

114. In 1970, *The Gnu and the Guru Go Behind the Beyond* was a *New York Times* Choice of Best Illustrated Children's Book of the Year.

115. Peggy Clifford, *The Gnu and the Guru Go Behind the Beyond* (Boston: Houghton, 1970), p. 34.

116. Ibid., p. 90.

117. In 1960, *The Gammage Cup* was a Newbery Honor Book and won the Ohioana Book Award.

118. Carol Kendall, *The Gammage Cup* (New York: Harcourt, 1959), pp. 91–92.

119. Ibid., p. 215.

120. In 1971, *The Phantom Tollbooth* won the George G. Stone Center for Children's Books Recognition of Merit Award.

121. Norton Juster, *The Phantom Tollbooth* (New York: Random, 1961), p. 52.

122. Ibid., p. 108.

123. Ibid., p. 234.

124. In 1970, *Journey Outside* was a Newbery Honor Book.

125. Mary Q. Steele, *Journey Outside* (New York: Viking, 1969), p. 15.

126. Ibid., p. 53.

127. Ibid., p. 123.

128. In 1966, *The Magic Flute* was a *New York Times* Choice of Best Illustrated Children's Book of the Year.

129. Stephen Spender, *The Magic Flute* (New York: Putnam, 1966), no page.

130. In 1946, *The White Deer* won the Ohioana Book Award.

131. James Thurber, *The White Deer* (New York: Harcourt, 1945), p. 101.

132. Sylvia Louise Engdahl, "The Changing Role of Science Fiction in Children's Literature," *The Horn Book Magazine* 47 (October 1971), p. 450.

133. In 1976, *Z for Zachariah* won the Edgar Allen Poe Award.

134. Robert C. O'Brien, *Z for Zachariah* (New York: Atheneum, 1975) p. 75.

135. Ibid., p. 13.

136. In 1961, *Danny Dunn and the Homework Machine* won the Pacific Northwest Library Association Young Reader's Choice Award.

137. Jay Williams and Raymond Abrashkin, *Danny Dunn and the Homework Machine* (New York: McGraw-Hill, 1958), p. 75.

138. Ibid., p. 188.

139. In 1963, *Danny Dunn on the Ocean Floor* won the Pacific Northwest Library Association Young Reader's Choice Award.

140. In 1956, *Miss Pickerell Goes to Mars* won a Pacific Northwest Library Association Young Reader's Choice Award.

141. Ellen MacGregor, *Miss Pickerell Goes to Mars* (New York: McGraw, 1951), p. 103.

142. In 1961, *Have Space Suit—Will Travel* won the Sequoyah Children's Book Award.

143. In 1947, *The Heavenly Tenants* was a Newbery Honor Book.

144. William Maxwell, *The Heavenly Tenants* (New York: Harper, 1946), p. 57.

145. In 1969, *A Wizard of Earthsea* won the *Boston Globe-Horn Book* Award.

146. Ursula K. Le Guin, *A Wizard of Earthsea* (Berkeley, Calif.: Parnassus Press, 1968), p. 28.

147. Ibid., p. 203.

148. In 1972, *The Tombs of Atuan* was a Newbery Honor Book and was a finalist for the National Book Award.

149. Ursula K. Le Guin, *The Tombs of Atuan* (New York: Atheneum, 1971), p. 126.

150. In 1973, *The Farthest Shore* won the National Book Award in the children's-book category.

151. Ursula K. Le Guin, *The Farthest Shore* (New York: Atheneum, 1974), p. 137.

152. Ibid., p. 204.

153. In 1965, *The Forgotten Door* won the North Carolina Division, American Association of University Women's Award in Juvenile Literature.

154. Alexander Key, *The Forgotten Door* (Eau Claire, Wisc.: Hale, 1965), pp. 15–16.

155. Ibid., p. 108.

156. In 1971, *Enchantress from the Stars* was a Newbery Honor Book.

157. Sylvia Louise Engdahl, *Enchantress from the Stars* (New York: Atheneum, 1970), p. 59.

158. Ibid., p. 135.

159. In 1972, *This Star Shall Abide* won the Christopher Award in the young-adult category.

160. Sylvia Louise Engdahl, *This Star Shall Abide* (New York: Atheneum, 1972), p. 11.

161. Ibid., p. 246.

162. In 1977, *The White Mountains* won the George C. Stone Center for Children's Books Recognition of Merit Award.

163. John Christopher, *The White Mountains* (New York: Macmillan, 1967), p. 110.

164. Ibid., p. 184.

165. In 1963, *A Wrinkle in Time* won The John Newbery Medal and in 1965, the Sequoyah Children's Book Award.

166. Madeleine L'Engle, *A Wrinkle in Time* (New York: Dell, 1962), p. 187.

167. "Madeleine L'Engle," *Profiles in Literature* (Philadelphia: Temple University, 1970).

168. "Madeleine L'Engle," *Profiles in Literature* (Philadelphia: Temple University, 1970).

169. Ibid.

**References of Prizewinning Modern Fantasy**

*(Estimated Reading Grade Level in Parentheses)*

Aiken, Joan. *The Wolves of Willoughby Chase*. Illustrated by Pat Marriott. New York: Dell, 1963 (4–6).
Alexander, Lloyd. *The Black Cauldron*. New York: Holt, 1965 (5–8).
———. *The First Two Lives of Lukas-Kasha*. New York: Dutton, 1978 (5–8).
———. *The High King*. New York: Holt, 1968 (5–8).
———. *The Marvelous Misadventures of Sebastian*. New York: Dutton, 1970 (4–7).
———. *Westmark*. New York: Dutton, 1981 (5–7).
Babbitt, Natalie. *The Devil's Storybook*. New York: Farrar, 1974 (4–6).
———. *Kneeknock Rise*. New York: Farrar, 1970 (4–7).
———. *Tuck Everlasting*. New York: Farrar, 1975 (4–6).
Bailey, Carolyn Sherwin. *Miss Hickory*. Illustrated by Ruth Gannett. New York: Viking, 1967 (4–6).
Barthelme, Donald. *The Slightly Irregular Fire Engine: Or The Hithering Thithering Djinn*. New York: Farrar, 1971 (3–5).
Bond, Nancy. *A String in the Harp*. New York: Atheneum, 1976 (4–6).
Boston, L.M. *The Children of Green Knowe*. Illustrated by Peter Boston. New York: Harcourt, 1955 (4–7).
Cameron, Eleanor. *The Court of the Stone Children*. New York: Dutton, 1973 (5–7).
Clarke, Pauline. *The Return of the Twelves*. Illustrated by Bernarda Bryson. New York: Coward, 1963 (5–7).
Clifford, Peggy. *The Gnu and the Guru Go Behind the Beyond*. Illustrated by Eric Von Schmidt. Boston: Houghton, 1970 (3–5).
Cooper, Susan. *The Dark Is Rising*. Illustrated by Allan E. Cober. New York: Atheneum, 1974 (5–7).
———. *The Grey King*. Illustrated by Michael Heslop. New York: Atheneum, 1975 (5–7).
Corbett, Scott. *The Home Run Trick*. Illustrated by Paul Galdone. Boston: Little, Brown, 1973 (3–5).
Curry, Jane Louise. *Poor Tom's Ghost*. New York: Atheneum, 1977 (5–7).
Dahl, Roald. *Charlie and the Great Glass Elevator*. Illustrated by Joseph Schindelman. New York: Knopf, 1972 (4–6).
Eager, Edward. *Knight's Castle*. Illustrated by N.M. Bodecker. New York: Harcourt, 1956 (4–6).
———. *Seven-Day Magic*. Illustrated by N.M. Bodecker. New York: Harcourt, 1962 (5–6).

Field, Rachel. *Hitty, Her First Hundred Years*. Illustrated by Dorothy P. Lathrop. New York: Macmillan, 1957 (4–6).

Fleischman, Sid. *McBroom Tells the Truth*. Illustrated by Kurt Werth. New York: Norton, 1966 (3–5).

Fleming, Ian. *Chitty Chitty Bang Bang*. Illustrated by John Burningham. New York: Random House, 1964 (4–6).

Gannett, Ruth Stiles. *My Father's Dragon*. Illustrated by Ruth Chrisman. New York: Random House, 1948 (4–6).

Garfield, Leon. *Mister Corbett's Ghost*. Illustrated by Allan E. Cober. New York: Pantheon, 1968 (5–8).

Garner, Alan. *The Weirdstone of Brisingamen*. New York: Watts, 1960 (5–7).

Ish-Kishor, Sulamith. *The Master of Miracle: A New Novel of the Golem*. Illustrated by Arnold Lobel. New York: Harper, 1971 (4–7).

Jarrell, Randall. *The Animal Family*. Illustrated by Maurice Sendak. New York: Random House, 1965 (5–7).

———. *Fly by Night*. Illustrated by Maurice Sendak. New York: Farrar, 1976 (5–7).

Juster, Norton. *Alberic the Wise and Other Journeys*. Illustrated by Domenico Gnoli. New York: Pantheon, 1965 (3–6).

———. *The Phantom Tollbooth*. Illustrated by Jules Feiffer. New York: Random House, 1961 (4–6).

Kendall, Carol. *The Gammage Cup*. Illustrated by Erik Blegvad. New York: Harcourt, 1959 (4–7).

Mayne, William. *Earthfasts*. New York: Dutton, 1967 (6–9).

Merrill, Jean. *The Pushcart War*. Illustrated by Ronni Solbert. Reading, Mass.: Scott, 1964 (5–7).

Oppenheim, Shulamith. *The Selchie's Seed*. Illustrated by Diane Goode. Scarsdale, N.Y.: Bradbury, 1975 (4–6).

Pearce, A. Philippa. *Tom's Midnight Garden*. Illustrated by Susan Einzig. Philadelphia: Lippincott, 1958 (4–7).

Peck, Richard. *The Ghost Belonged to Me*. New York: Viking, 1975 (6–8).

Pope, Elizabeth Marie. *The Perilous Gard*. Boston: Hall, 1974 (6–9).

Raskin, Ellen. *Figgs and Phantoms*. New York: Dutton, 1974 (4–6).

Rawlings, Marjorie Kinnan. *The Secret River*. Illustrated by Leonard Weisgard. New York: Scribner, 1955 (3–5).

Rodgers, Mary. *A Billion for Boris*. New York: Harper, 1974 (4–6).

———. *Freaky Friday*. New York: Harper, 1972 (4–7).

Sauer, Julia L. *Fog Magic*. New York: Macmillan, 1943 (4–6).

Singer, Isaac Bashevis. *The Fearsome Inn*. Translated by Isaac Bashevis Singer and Elizabeth Shub. Illustrated by Nonny Hogrogian. New York: Scribner, 1967 (4–7).

Snyder, Zilpha Keatley. *The Headless Cupid*. Illustrated by Alton Raible. New York: Atheneum, 1972 (5–7).

Spender, Stephen. *The Magic Flute*. Illustrated by Beni Montresor. New York: Putnam, 1966 (4–6).

Steele, Mary Q. *Journey Outside*. Illustrated by Rocco Negri. New York: Viking, 1969 (5–8).

Stephens, Mary Jo. *Witch of the Cumberlands*. Illustrated by Arvis Stewart. Boston: Houghton, 1974 (4–7).

Thurber, James. *Many Moons*. Illustrated by Louis Slobodkin. New York: Harcourt, 1944 (4–5).

———. *The White Deer*. Illustrated by James Thurber and Don Freeman. New York: Harcourt, 1945 (6–7).

Willard, Nancy. *The Island of the Grass King*. Illustrated by David McPhail. New York: Harcourt, 1979 (4–6).

———. *Sailing to Cythera and Other Anatole Stories*. Illustrated by David McPhail. New York: Harcourt, 1974 (4–6).

Williams, Jay. *The Hawkstone*. New York: Walck, 1971 (4–6).

Williams, Margery. *The Velveteen Rabbit: Or How Toys Became Real*. Illustrated by William Nicholson. New York: Doubleday, 1958 (2–4).

Yolen, Jane. *The Girl Who Cried Flowers and Other Tales*. Illustrated by David Palladini. New York: Crowell, 1974 (5–6).

**References of Prizewinning Science Fiction**

*(Estimated Reading Grade Level in Parentheses)*

Christopher, John. *The White Mountains*. New York: Macmillan, 1967 (6–9).

Engdahl, Sylvia Louise. *Enchantress from the Stars*. Illustrated by Rodney Shackell. New York: Atheneum, 1970 (6–9).

———. *This Star Shall Abide*. Illustrated by Richard Cuffari. New York: Atheneum, 1972 (6–9).

Heinlein, Robert. *Have Space Suit—Will Travel*. New York: Scribner, 1958 (5–7).

Key, Alexander. *The Forgotten Door*. Eau Claire, Wisc.: Hale, 1965 (5–7).

Le Guin, Ursula K. *The Farthest Shore*. Illustrated by Gail Garraty. New York: Atheneum, 1974 (6–9).

———. *The Tombs of Atuan*. Illustrated by Gail Garraty. New York: Atheneum, 1971 (6–9).

————. *A Wizard of Earthsea*. Illustrated by Ruth Robbins. Berkeley, Calif.: Parnassus, 1968 (6–9).

L'Engle, Madeleine. *A Wrinkle in Time*. New York: Dell, 1962 (6–9).

MacGregor, Ellen. *Miss Pickerell Goes to Mars*. Illustrated by Paul Galdone. New York: McGraw, 1951 (4–6).

Maxwell, William. *The Heavenly Tenants*. Illustrated by Ilonka Karasz. New York: Harper, 1946 (4–6).

O'Brien, Robert C. *Z for Zachariah*. New York: Atheneum, 1975 (5–9).

Williams, Jay, and Abrashkin, Raymond. *Danny Dunn and the Homework Machine*. Illustrated by Ezra Jack Keats. New York: McGraw, 1958 (3–5).

————. *Danny Dunn on the Ocean Floor*. Illustrated by Brinton Turkle. New York: McGraw, 1960 (4–6).

# 9 Animal Fantasy

The Mouse and the Motorcycle *is made for me. That's 'cause I have a pet mouse, Ichabod. Papa named him Ichabod. I like books that show tiny animals doing funny things. A mouse riding a motorcycle is funny. I pretend Ichabod's driving one. A cricket singing fancy songs in New York City is funny, too. I'm reading about that in* The Cricket in Times Square.

—Hans, aged eight

## Perspective

Many children besides Hans favor animal fantasy by Beverly Cleary or George Selden. This chapter discusses books featuring animals either in the present or past time periods in the United States or abroad. Fantasy stems from the fact that these animals speak and are given other human characteristics.

The first chapter on classics and modern classics includes such revered animal fantasies as *The Wind in the Willows, Winnie-the-Pooh, Rabbit Hill,* and *Charlotte's Web.* Animal fantasy has timeless appeal; it is also a safe vehicle for criticizing society. In *Jonathan Livingston Seagull,* for instance, the elders with closed minds are gulls, and in *Watership Down,* the fascist general is a rabbit, but readers easily note human parallels. Animal fantasies extol old-fashioned ideals such as rewarding the virtuous. As an example, the theme of *The Blue Cat of Castle Town* emphasizes the blue cat's quest: encouraging artisans' pride in creating beauty, not profits. His ideas might seem didactic in realistic fiction but are powerfully presented in animal fantasy.

## Themes of Prizewinning Animal Fantasy Grouped under These Topics

*Animals with Human Traits*

**Middle and Upper Grades.** The overall theme of Margaret Green's collection of twenty-three international tales, *The Big Book of Animal Stories,*[1] is animals with human traits. Egotism is the dominant human foible

229

in a Native American creation myth, "How the Coyote Made Man," for "every one of the animals wanted to make a man exactly like himself."[2] Egotism also ruins Half-Chick in the Spanish tale, "Little Half-Chick," because he begins to think he is as remarkable as his mother believes. He says, "If I am distinguished, I am distinguished. The sooner the world knows it, the better."[3] Being greedy, ungrateful, proud, and power hungry are human traits assigned to other animals.

Vanity is another human trait, and the folly of vanity is the theme of "The Rooster Who Could Not See Enough of Himself," one of Paula Fox's six original fables in *The Little Swineherd and Other Tales*.[4] A rooster who sees himself in a mirror for the first time rebukes hens for not telling him how handsome he is.

> "All these years," he said, "and not a word from any of you! I suppose you were afraid you would lose me if I found out about myself—that I might leave and go where I would be appreciated. Selfish! That's what you all are!"[5]

The rooster wants all the animals in the countryside to appreciate his appearance, so the sheep help him climb to the barn roof. When he wants to descend, no one assists. He finally flies down and heads straight for the mirror, only to discover his beautiful comb and wattles are white. This has a humbling effect, and the Old Hen flings the mirror into the pond, so the rooster isn't further demoralized.

### Virtue Rewarded

**Middle and Upper Grades.** Virtue rewarded is the theme of Julia Cunningham's *Dear Rat*,[6] which takes place in Paris, France. Andrew, the narrator from Humpton, Wyoming, explains, "I'm a rat. I'm tough and I'm tender . . . But the truth is I'm honest."[7] Aided by a bird, Richet, and Princess Angelique (Angie), Andrew recovers emeralds a mobster rat, Groge, stole from a statue. In keeping with his honest nature, he returns the jewels to the Chartres cathedral and, as a reward, marries Angie.

A similar theme, good triumphs over evil, pervades William Steig's philosophical book, *Dominic*.[8] An adventurous, enthusiastic dog, Dominic, helps defend new friends—a mouse, a turtle, a boar, and an invalid pig—from the evil Doomsday Gang. After the sick pig dies and leaves Dominic an inheritance, the Gang threatens, and Dominic outwits them. The theme is explicit when the dog reasons, "One could not be happy among the good ones unless one fought the bad ones."[9] In the end, Dominic shares his wealth with his friends and finds a mate.

Kindness and courage rewarded is the theme of Elizabeth Coatsworth's *The Cat Who Went to Heaven*.[10] In Japan, an artist is so poor, he is sorry his housekeeper spends their few pennies on a cat, Good Fortune, but he is kind to the animal and grows to love her. When a priest asks him for a temple painting of Buddha's death, the artist puts Good Fortune at the end of the line of animals approaching the dying Buddha. He knows a cat once rebelled against Buddha and did not receive his blessing, but does not feel all cats should be punished and courageously thinks for himself. Because the cat is included, the priest refuses the picture until a miracle occurs. The cat dies and suddenly appears in the painting at the head of the line under Buddha's hand outstretched in blessing. Kind Good Fortune, the artist's companion, earns a place in heaven. The compassionate artist, who lets his housekeeper buy dress material with his first money, becomes a rich, honored man as a reward.

It is interesting to note that Lynd Ward's black-and-white lithographs for the 1930 edition of *The Cat Who Went to Heaven* seem more Asian than his precise illustrations for the 1958 edition. The publisher redesigned the book with new illustrations, considering the earlier version outdated and hoping to attract new readers.[11]

*Quest*

**Middle and Upper Grades.** A noncomformist's quest for acceptance in two worlds is the theme of Randall Jarrell's *The Bat-Poet*.[12] Although most bats sleep during the day, one little brown bat enjoys sunlight, but cannot convince bat friends to share his new world. Wanting to be accepted by them, he coaxes his peers to try daytime activities. When fellow bats refuse to change their habits, he begins to write poetry and seeks acceptance with daylight creatures, especially a chipmunk who loves his poems. At last, he writes a poem about bats, acknowledging, "It's wonderful to fly all night. And when you sleep all day with the others it feels wonderful."[13] Realizing it's good to be a bat, he joins those in the barn for a winter daytime nap.

Stranger than a bat poet is a blue cat born "once in a blue moon." He is in Catherine Cate Coblentz's *The Blue Cat of Castle Town*.[14] The blue cat is a nonconformist, and the book's theme is a quest to encourage beauty and creativity. The story begins in the 1830s in the village of Castle Town, Vermont where a blue kitten is destined to learn the river's song of enchantment. The song suggests:

With your life fashion beauty, riches will pass and power. Beauty remains. All that is worth doing, do well. Sing your own song. Sing well.[15]

Villagers forget the song when they are under the spell of Arunah Hyde, a man interested only in riches and power. Reteaching the river's song becomes the blue cat's mission, for he "is like a knight, a small knight sent forth on a quest, armed only with a song."[16] By purring the song again and again, the blue cat teaches lonely Zeruah Guernsey that she doesn't have to be beautiful to weave a beautiful carpet. The cat sings to other craftsmen, and their values change.

**Upper Grades.** Fulfilling a quest to unite two groups is the theme of Sheila Moon's *Knee-Deep in Thunder*.[18] The opposing groups are greedy Beasts and peaceful They. A unique band tries "to find a way to bring Beasts and They together without one completely destroying the other."[17] The band consists of narrator Maris, a thirteen-year-old girl, Scuro, her dog, Jetsam, a young boy, and beetles, a caterpillar, an ant, a bird, a mouse, a gopher, even a spider. In contrast with these small creatures, the Beasts are enormous. The band courageously lures the Beasts into They territory and traps them in pits, so Beasts can later be conditioned to lead peaceful lives. The ant dies in the struggle, but as the story ends, They commend the band for completing their mission by uniting the kingdom.

Though *Knee-Deep in Thunder* shows the activities of a small band, Richard Bach's *Jonathan Livingston Seagull* focuses on a unique individual.[19] A nonconformist's quest for freedom, perfection, and love is the theme of this book. Jonathan is no ordinary bird, for unlike most gulls, he experiments with flight techniques and speed. Others ask him, "Why is it so hard to be like the rest of the flock?"[20] Then elders banish him to a solitary life because they misinterpret his nonconformity as irresponsibility. In exile, he flies beyond the limits of his immediate world into a heaven-like atmosphere where he attains a new level of perfection. He returns to earth to help outcasts, like young Fletcher. He leads them back to the flock, insisting upon their freedom from ritual or superstition. Fletcher, called a devil by the mob, doesn't see how he can love such gulls until Jonathan explains:

> You have to practice and see the real gull, the good in every one of them, and to help them see it in themselves. That's what I mean by love.[21]

Jonathan, a nonconformist who loves brotherhood, achieves self-made goals.

*Survival*

**Middle and Upper Grades.** Survival with a change of life-style is the theme of William Steig's *Abel's Island*,[22] which takes place from 1907 to 1908. Abel, a rich, frivolous town mouse, enjoys a picnic with his wife, Amanda, tries to retrieve her scarf, and is swept away in a storm. He spends a year marooned on a deserted island. Though formerly supported by his parents, he now learns to be resourceful. "He sat there, vaguely smug, convinced that he had the strength, the courage, and the intelligence to survive."[23] After futilely attempting to leave, he builds a house, hunts for food, and defends himself against animal attackers. Abel finally finds a way to swim from the island and return to his family in Mossville.

**Upper Grades.** Migration for survival with self-sufficiency is the theme of Robert C. O'Brien's *Mrs. Frisby and the Rats of NIMH*.[24] Mrs. Frisby, a widowed field mouse with four children, worries because her youngest son, Timothy, ill with pneumonia, cannot be moved for three weeks. Mr. Fitzgibbon will be plowing in five days, and the Frisby house will be destroyed. The crow and owl suggest that the widow ask for advice from the rats living under the rosebush, so that is how Mrs. Frisby meets rat leader Nicodemus. He explains that her deceased husband had been part of their special rat community. The rats are special because they were made literate and intelligent by experiments at NIMH. (While the book doesn't specify, the initials undoubtedly refer to National Institute of Mental Health.) The rats escaped from the laboratory and built their own technologically advanced community. However, the leader, Nicodemus, is conscience-stricken because the rats are stealing food and electrical power from people. He develops the Plan to escape from their present setting threatened by bulldozers, migrate to Thorn Valley, and survive with self-sufficiency. He wants to "live without stealing, of course. That's the whole idea. That's the Plan."[25] The rats move Mrs. Frisby's home, and she tells them information she overheard that makes their escape possible with few casualties. Now they can survive according to the Plan.

Migration for survival is also the theme of *Watership Down* by English author Richard Adams.[26] When Fiver, a rabbit who has visions, foresees the doom of the warren, a rabbit burrowing area, the chief rabbit won't listen. Then Fiver, his brother, Hazel, and some other male rabbits begin a hazardous journey across English downs, searching for a place where they can survive and build a better society. Fiver leads the band away from snares to settle at Watership Down. The male rabbits need females for mating and help some escape from a warren named Efrafa controlled by fascist General Woundwart. The general retaliates but is defeated. Finally, rabbits from both Watership and Efrafa build another warren where they survive peacefully.

### Courage and Determination

**Middle and Upper Grades.** Acquiring courage is the theme of Mary Stolz's *Belling the Tiger*.[27] Portman, a kitchen mouse bully, arbitrarily assigns two gentle cellar mice, Asa and Rambo, to attach a collar with a warning bell to the cat despot, Siri. Fearful of Siri, the two are more afraid of Portman, so they buy a collar with a bell at a dockside shop. Then a waterfront cat chases them to a ship that takes them to a strange land. When they disembark, they hesitantly put the collar on the tail of a tiger, questioning each other, "Are you afraid?"[28] The tiger, who proves friendly, shows Asa and Rambo an elephant terrified of mice. The tiger explains, "It's nothing to be ashamed of . . . a fear or two. Most of us have them."[29] Fortified by such advice, Asa and Rambo have the courage to face dictatorial Portman when their ship returns.

Determination is the theme of E.B. White's *The Trumpet of the Swan*,[30] the story of Louis, a trumpeter swan who cannot communicate verbally. Using chalk and slate, Louis learns to read and write when he goes to school with an eleven-year-old boy, Sam Beaver. However, Louis still cannot attract Serena, a swan he loves, so his father steals a trumpet for his son from a music store. With Sam's help, Louis learns to play the trumpet, becoming a camp bugler and later, an entertainer in the Philadelphia zoo. In the zoo, he wins Serena with his music and realizes, "This was the moment of triumph for a young swan who had a speech defect and had conquered it."[31] Determined to show integrity, Louis and his bride, Serena, give his earnings to his father to pay the store for the stolen trumpet.

### Excessive Size

**Middle and Upper Grades.** Excessive size is the theme of Glen Rounds's *Mr. Yowder and the Giant Bull Snake*.[32] A sign painter who speaks snake language, Xenon Zebulon Yowder, befriends Knute, a bull snake. After he instructs the snake in body-building exercises, Knute becomes immense. Mr. Yowder saddles the snake and rides him to herd buffalo. Knute is so big he causes a stampede when the U.S. President visits the plains, but no one is hurt and afterward, man and snake part company.

*Love*

**Middle and Upper Grades.** Love of a pet dinosaur is the theme of Oliver Butterworth's *The Enormous Egg*.[33] In Freedom, New Hampshire, twelve-year-old Nate Twitchell finds his hen laid an enormous egg. When the egg hatches, a triceratops emerges, and Nate lovingly nurses the infant reptile he calls Uncle Beazley. Nate resists huge sales offers for his pet. Accommodating to the animal's need for a warmer winter climate, he moves it to Washington, D.C. and places it in the zoo. A senator, who objects to the cost of feeding the animal, introduces legislation for it to be killed. Dr. Ziemer, a paleontologist, realizes the triceratops's scientific value and wages a television campaign to save the dinosaur. When Nate appears on television, he says:

> I took care of that dinosaur, and I fed him, and I watched him grow big and strong, and I sure would hate to have him killed. He is no beaut, but I love him a lot . . . Please tell your Senators and Representatives to vote against the Dinosaur Bill. But you better do it fast or there won't be anything to save.[34]

The campaign results in the bill's defeat and contributions to the zoo for the dinosaur's upkeep.

Nate loves one pet, but Bocamp in Brinton Turkle's *The Fiddler of High Lonesome* is fond of many animals.[35] Love of all life is the theme of this book written in mountain dialect. After his parents' death, fiddle-playing Lysander Bocamp travels to his only kin, the rough, crude Fogel clan. When the Fogels learn their guest is opposed to killing critters, they let him stay only because they enjoy his music. One night, the Fogels hide behind a sassafras tree and watch animals magically dance to Bocamp's fiddle. The Fogels kill the animals. In despair, Bocamp leaves, knowing he cannot accept these people as his kin. The ending argues against shooting animals, the author's purpose for writing the story.[36]

*Wish Fulfillment*

**Upper Grades.** Jane Langton's *The Fledgling*,[37] whose theme is wish fulfillment, concerns eight-year-old Georgie and a fledgling goose. The animal comes to her window one night and teaches her to fly, fulfilling her deep desire. They fly above Walden Pond, the story's setting. ''Georgie exulted. At last she was free as air. With the Goose Prince she could fly everywhere, all over the world.''[38] However, a neighbor considers the bird a menace and kills him on his second shooting attempt. The girl becomes too heavy to fly, but she has memories and a gift from the goose, a rubber ball that shows continents and oceans as they look from the sky.


## Running Away

**Middle and Upper Grades.** Beverly Cleary's *Runaway Ralph* has running away as its theme.[39] Ralph is the only mouse in the Sierra Nevada foothills who owns a motorcycle. Tired of being bossed by his mother and Uncle Lester, Ralph decides to run away from his hotel home, Mountain View Inn. After almost being killed by highway traffic, he arrives at a children's camp, Happy Acres, where he has to escape from a dog, cat, gopher, and numerous children—problems not encountered at the hotel. The mouse's freedom ends when a camper, Garf, captures and cages Ralph, leaving him in constant fear of a villainous cat. Garf is also running away. He doesn't leave camp, but he never associates with other children. Finally, Ralph bargains with Garf for his release, admitting, "I'm a hotel mouse,"[41] and Garf takes him home.


## Friendship

**Middle and Upper Grades.** *Runaway Ralph* is the sequel to Beverly Cleary's *The Mouse and the Motorcycle*,[40] written to specifications. Beverly Cleary says:

> I wrote *The Mouse and the Motorcycle* for my son. When he was in the fourth grade, he was disgusted with school and reading. I asked him what he wanted to read about and he said, "Motorcycles." I asked my daughter what she'd like to read about, and she said, "A nice little animal." I put the two together.[42]

Friendship is the theme of *The Mouse and the Motorcycle*. Keith Gridley, who is spending a week with his parents in an old California hotel, Mountain View Inn, finds Ralph, a young mouse, in a wastebasket, and the two share a five-day friendship. Keith loans his toy motorcycle to Ralph at night, and the mouse shows reciprocal friendship, watching over Keith when he is ill:

> Ralph watched anxiously, but this time he was not selfishly concerned about room service. He was concerned about Keith, the boy who had saved him from a terrible fate in the wastebasket and who had trusted him with his motorcycle, the boy who had forgiven him when he had

lost that motorcycle and who had brought food, not only for Ralph, but for his whole family.[43]

Ralph, in turn, risks his life to find an aspirin for his friend. The mouse sneaks into hotel rooms, searches suitcases and dresser drawers, and triumphantly brings one to Keith. Before departing, the boy rewards Ralph by giving him the toy motorcycle.

Friendship is also the theme of a trilogy by George Selden: *The Cricket in Times Square*,[44] *Tucker's Countryside*,[45] and *Harry Cat's Pet Puppy*.[46] In the first book, Chester, a Connecticut cricket, is brought in a picnic basket to a subway station in New York's Times Square. He becomes the pet of Harlo Bellini whose parents struggle to run a subway newsstand. Chester makes his home at the newsstand with two new animal friends, fast-talking Tucker Mouse and sympathetic Harry the Cat. Chester is "touched that a mouse he had known only a few minutes would share his food with him."[47] Beyond liverwurst sandwiches, the three share concern about the Bellinis's financial problems, and Chester tries to help. He performs operatic and concert music at the newsstand, increasing newspaper sales. After the three animals have an anniversary party to celebrate their friendship, Chester decides to return to Connecticut. The trio acknowledges that even a special relationship cannot replace a longing for home. Certain that their friendship will endure, Tucker and Harry remember the love Chester conveys in his farewell chirp.

In *Tucker's Countryside,* George Selden continues the adventures of Chester Cricket, Harry Cat, and Tucker Mouse. The friendship theme extends to chums averting an environmental crisis. Chester, who lives in Old Meadow, Connecticut, sends John Robin to New York City to summon his two friends to help save his home countryside from bulldozers. Though traveling such a distance is a new experience, they come at once, greeted by "exclaiming and laughing the way old friends do when they haven't seen each other for months and months."[48] Chester puzzles how to prevent the town from ruining the meadow with apartments because the animals "want to keep the meadow the way it is."[49] With the help of a girl, Ellen, Tucker solves the problem. He finds a sign marked "Hadley" which he changes to "Hedley," surname of the town's founder. He puts the sign at an abandoned homestead located in the meadow, and citizens demand that so-called historic Hedley's Meadow be preserved. Animals honor their friend by calling the area Tucker's Countryside.

Tucker Mouse and Harry Cat are featured again in George Selden's *Harry Cat's Pet Puppy,* whose specific theme is friends helping a stranger find a home. Harry and Tucker are back at their Times Square subway station. Harry brings a stray mutt, Huppy, to their cramped drainpipe home. "It may seem very strange that a cat should do this, but with his nails withdrawn he reached out and petted and stroked the dog's head."[50] Harry explains that Huppy needs a permanent home:

> Harry explained as gently as he could while Huppy's head hung down to his chest, that a cat and mouse could live in a drainpipe, but a growing dog couldn't. It wasn't that Tucker and he didn't want him there or love him very much.[51]

Harry and Tucker, helped by a Siamese cat, Miss Catherine, place Huppy with Mr. Smedley, the music teacher. The puppy adjusts so well, he declines an invitation for a drainpipe visit. Tucker feels hurt, but Harry reminds him that Huppy finally has a home.

Mice, like Tucker, are Marvin the Magnificent and Fats the Fuse who star with Raymond the Rat in Jean Van Leeuween's *The Great Christmas Kidnapping Caper*.[52] Here the theme is friends solving a mystery. Before Christmas, the mice settle in Macy's toy-department dollhouse, where a new friend, the store's Santa, every night leaves them a crumb in a Snicker's wrapper. When Santa disappears, the mice learn that Gimbel's Santa kidnapped him in an effort to hurt Macy's business. The mice write the press a Concerned Citizens letter, explaining where Santa is. Marvin, seeking fame, is upset because the letter is anonymous and brings no reward or glory, but he gets both on Christmas Eve. Santa returns then, receives a medal from the mayor, and leaves the medal to the mice.

Another mouse, O'Crispin, is featured in Roger W. Drury's *The Champion of Merrimack County*.[53] Development of cooperative friendship is the theme of this book about a champion mouse who at first is unwelcome and later, cheered by Mr. Berryfield, owner of the house invaded by the mouse. O'Crispin uses Berryfield's new bathtub as a track to practice for the state championship. The mouse executes a daring leap, slips on soap in the tub, hurts his tail, and damages the precious tub. Janet, Berryfield's daughter, her mother, and many friends try to mend the hurt mouse and tiny bicycle as well as fix the scratch on the tub before Berryfield sees it. The father, who sets mousetraps and opposes pets, receives this advice from his daughter:

> Being a pet isn't something you do, or whether you wear a collar, or anything like that. It's how people feel about you; if they feed you; if they care when you get hurt; if they don't want you to be caught in a trap.[54]

After Berryfield sees O'Crispin ride his bicycle, his attitude changes, and he proclaims, "Pet, my eye! This is a champion, that's what! Why didn't anybody tell me? What luck for us that he came to live in our house!"[55] Berryfield feels especially proud when O'Crispin wins the trophy for champion bicycle rider of Merrimack County.

**Upper Grades.** Protective friendship and unity, despite differences, is the theme of Agnes Smith's *An Edge of the Forest*.[56] A black leopardess rescues a black lamb from a mad dog, killer of the lamb's mother. In the Children's Grove, "the black leopardess and the black lamb began their friendship."[57] The lamb, symbol of innocence, adapts to life in the forest. Wild creatures befriend the lamb when the leopardess enlists aid from natural prey. The leopardess spares a doe who gives the lamb milk, and both leopardess and doe learn to relate, compelled by love for the lamb. The shepherd's son sees the lamb and wants her. The lamb meets him at the edge of the forest after saying farewell to animal friends. He is astonished to see the lamb followed by beasts who are usually enemies.

**Summary**

Twenty-six books that are among prizewinning animal fantasies are examined in this chapter, and their themes are analyzed under ten headings. The most popular theme is friendship. This chapter discusses more books for middle-elementary grades than most of the chapters dealing with intermediate-grade material. To appeal to this audience, all of the books are illustrated except two, *Watership Down* and *The Fledgling*. *Watership Down* and *Jonathan Livingston Seagull* are often placed in library adult collections. The majority of the books can be appreciated if they are read aloud with enthusiasm. Otherwise, their satire may be understood only by mature readers.

Those who have written more than one prizewinner in this genre are Beverly Cleary, George Selden, and William Steig, all of whom are creators of at least one book about a rodent. Favorite animal-fantasy subjects are mice and rats, heroes in one-third of the prizewinners discussed in this chapter. Mice are also preferred subjects in animal-fantasy picture storybooks, as shown in chapter 4.

**Notes**

1. In 1961, *The Big Book of Animal Stories,* illustrated by Janusz Grabianski, was a *New York Times* Choice of Best Illustrated Children's Book of the Year.

2. Margaret Green, *The Big Book of Animal Stories* (New York: Watts, 1961), p. 103.

3. Ibid., p. 228.

4. In 1979, *The Little Swineherd and Other Tales* was a finalist for the National Book Award in the children's-book category and, illustrated by Leonard Luben, it was in the American Institute of Graphic Arts Book Show.

5. Paula Fox, *The Little Swineherd and Other Tales* (New York: Dutton, 1978), p. 52.

6. In 1960, *Dear Rat,* illustrated by Walter Lorraine, was a *New York Times* Choice of Best Illustrated Children's Book of the Year.

7. Julia Cunningham, *Dear Rat* (Boston: Houghton, 1961), p. 1.

8. In 1972, *Dominic* won the Christopher Award in the children's-book category for all ages. In 1973, it was a finalist for the National Book Awards in the children's-book category. In 1975, it won the William Allen White Children's Book Award.

9. William Steig, *Dominic* (New York: Farrar, 1972), p. 132.

10. In 1931, *The Cat Who Went to Heaven* won The John Newbery Medal.

11. Children's book editor Phyllis Larkin expressed Macmillan's point of view although she had nothing to do with reissuing the book.

12. In 1964, *The Bat-Poet,* illustrated by Maurice Sendak, was a *New York Times* Choice of Best Illustrated Children's Book of the Year, and it won the North Carolina Division, American Association of University Women's Award in Juvenile Literature.

Randall Jarrell, author of *The Bat-Poet,* was Chancellor of the American Academy of Poets and poetry consultant for the Library of Congress. Living with bats on the porch of his forest house and a chipmunk in the yard, he considered himself to be the Bat-Poet.

13. Randall Jarrell, *The Bat-Poet* (New York: Macmillan, 1963), p. 41.

14. In 1950, *The Blue Cat of Castle Town* was a Newbery Honor Book, and in 1958, it won the Lewis Carroll Shelf Award.

15. Catherine Cate Coblentz, *The Blue Cat of Castle Town* (New York: Longmans, 1949), p. 16.

16. Ibid., p. 4.

17. In 1967, *Knee-Deep in Thunder,* illustrated by Peter Parnall, was a *New York Times* Choice of Best Illustrated Children's Book of the Year.

18. Sheila Moon, *Knee-Deep in Thunder* (New York: Atheneum, 1967), p. 167.

19. In 1974, *Jonathan Livingston Seagull* won the Nene Award.

20. Richard Bach, *Jonathan Livingston Seagull* (New York: Macmillan, 1970), p. 13.

21. Richard Bach, *Jonathan Livingston Seagull* (New York: Macmillan, 1970), p. 91.

22. In 1977, *Abel's Island* won the Lewis Carroll Shelf Award and in 1978, it was a Newbery Honor Book.

23. William Steig, *Abel's Island* (New York: Farrar, 1976), p. 16.

24. In 1972, *Mrs. Frisby and the Rats of NIMH* won The John Newbery Medal, the Lewis Carroll Shelf Award, and it was a finalist for the National Book Award in the children's-book category. In 1973, it won the Mark Twain Award. In 1974, it won the Pacific Northwest Library Association Young Reader's Choice Award and the William Allen White Children's Book Award.

25. Robert C. O'Brien, *Mrs. Frisby and the Rats of NIMH* (New York: Atheneum, 1971), p. 157.

26. In 1977, *Watership Down* won the Young Reader Medal for grades 9 to 12.

27. In 1962, *Belling the Tiger* was a Newbery Honor Book.

28. Mary Stolz, *Belling the Tiger* (New York: Harper, 1961), p. 36.

29. Ibid., p. 52.

30. In 1971, *The Trumpet of the Swan* was a finalist for the National Book Award in the children's-book category. In 1972, it was put on the International Board of Books for Young People Honor List. In 1973, it won the Sequoyah Children's Book Award and the William Allen White Children's Book Award. In 1975, it won the Young Hoosier Award.

31. E.B. White, *The Trumpet of the Swan* (New York: Harper & Row, 1970), p. 163.

32. In 1978, *Mr. Yowder and the Giant Bull Snake* won the Lewis Carroll Shelf Award.

33. In 1970, *The Enormous Egg* won the Lewis Carroll Shelf Award.

34. Oliver Butterworth, *The Enormous Egg* (Boston: Little, Brown, 1956), p. 173.

35. In 1968, *The Fiddler of High Lonesome* was a Caldecott Honor Book.

36. Anne Commire, ed., *Something About the Author,* II (Detroit: Gale Research, 1971), p. 20.

37. In 1981, *The Fledgling* was a Newbery Honor Book.

38. Jane Langton, *The Fledgling* (New York: Harper, 1980), p. 94–95.

39. In 1972, *Runaway Ralph* won the Nene Award.

40. Beverly Cleary, *Runaway Ralph* (New York: Morrow, 1970), p. 153.

41. In 1968, *The Mouse and the Motorcycle* won the Pacific Northwest Library Association Young Reader's Choice Award and the William Allen White Children's Book Award. In 1969, it won the Nene Award.

42. "Beverly Cleary," *Profiles in Literature* (Philadelphia: Temple University, 1979).

43. Beverly Cleary, *The Mouse and the Motorcycle* (New York: Morrow, 1965), p. 114.

44. In 1961, *The Cricket in Times Square* was a Newbery Honor Book. In 1963, it won the Lewis Carroll Shelf Award and in 1979, the Massachusetts Children's Book Award.

45. In 1969, *Tucker's Countryside* won the Christopher Award in the children's-book category for ages 8 to 12.

46. In 1977, *Harry Cat's Pet Puppy* won the William Allen White Children's Book Award.

47. George Selden, *The Cricket in Times Square* (New York: Dell, 1960), p. 22.

48. George Selden, *Tucker's Countryside* (New York: Farrar, 1969), p. 24.

49. Ibid., p. 44.

50. George Selden, *Harry Cat's Pet Puppy* (New York: Farrar, 1974), p. 15.

51. Ibid., p. 55.

52. In 1976, *The Great Christmas Kidnapping Caper* won the Ethical Culture School Book Award and in 1978, the William Allen White Children's Book Award.

53. In 1976, *The Champion of Merrimack County* won the Christopher Award in the children's-book category for ages nine to twelve and in 1977, the Ethical Culture School Book Award.

54. Roger W. Drury, *The Champion of Merrimack County* (Boston: Little, Brown, 1976), p. 125.

55. Ibid., p. 196.

56. In 1966, *An Edge of the Forest* won the Lewis Carroll Shelf Award.

57. Agnes Smith, *An Edge of the Forest* (New York: Viking, 1959), p. 16.

## References of Prizewinners Arranged according to Type of Animal in Animal Fantasy

*(Estimated Reading Grade Level in Parentheses)*

*Three or More Different Kinds of Animals as Major Characters*

Fox, Paula. *The Little Swineherd and Other Tales*. Illustrated by Leonard Luben. New York: Dutton. 1978 (4–6).

Green, Margaret. *The Big Book of Animal Stories*. Illustrated by Janusz Grabianski. New York: Watts, 1961 (2–5).

Moon, Sheila. *Knee-Deep in Thunder*. Illustrated by Peter Parnall. New York: Atheneum, 1967 (6–8).

Selden, George. *The Cricket in Times Square*. Illustrated by Garth Williams. New York: Dell, 1960 (3–6).

———. *Harry Cat's Pet Puppy*. Illustrated by Garth Williams. New York: Farrar, 1974 (3–6).

———. *Tucker's Countryside*. Illustrated by Garth Williams. New York: Farrar, 1971 (3–6).

Smith, Agnes. *An Edge of the Forest*. Illustrated by Roberta Moynihan. New York: Viking, 1959 (5–8).

Steig, William. *Dominic*. New York: Farrar, 1972 (4–6).

Turkle, Brinton. *The Fiddler of High Lonesome*. New York: Viking, 1968 (4–6).

## Bats

Jarrell, Randall. *The Bat-Poet*. Illustrated by Maurice Sendak. New York: Macmillan, 1963 (4–6).

## Birds

Bach, Richard. *Jonathan Livingston Seagull*. New York: Macmillan, 1970 (7 and up).

Langton, Jane. *The Fledgling*. New York: Harper, 1980 (5–7).

White, E.B. *The Trumpet of the Swan*. Illustrated by Edward Franscine. New York: Harper, 1970 (3–6).

## Cats

Coatsworth, Elizabeth. *The Cat Who Went to Heaven*. Illustrated by Lynd Ward. New York: MacMillan, 1930 (4–6).

Coblentz, Catherine Cate. *The Blue Cat of Castle Town*. Illustrated by Janice Holland. New York: Longmans, 1949 (3–5).

## Mice and Rats

Cleary, Beverly. *The Mouse and the Motorcycle*. Illustrated by Louis Darling. New York: Morrow, 1965 (3–5).

———. *Runaway Ralph*. Illustrated by Louis Darling. New York: Morrow, 1970 (3–5).

Cunningham, Julia. *Dear Rat*. Illustrated by Walter Lorraine. Boston: Houghton, 1961 (4–6).

Drury, Roger W. *The Champion of Merrimack County*. Illustrated by Fritz Wagner. Boston: Little, Brown, 1976 (4–7).

O'Brien, Robert. *Mrs. Frisby and the Rats of NIMH*. Illustrated by Zena Bernstein. New York: Atheneum, 1978 (5–7).

Steig, William. *Abel's Island*. New York: Farrar, 1976 (4–6).

Stolz, Mary. *Belling the Tiger*. Illustrated by Beni Montresor. New York: Harper, 1961 (3–5).

Van Leeuwen, Jean. *The Great Christmas Kidnapping Caper*. Illustrated by Steven Kellogg. New York: Dial, 1975 (3–5).

*Rabbits*

Adams, Richard. *Watership Down*. New York: Macmillan, 1972 (9–12).

*Reptiles*

Butterworth, Oliver. *The Enormous Egg*. Illustrated by Louis Darling. Boston: Little, Brown, 1956 (3–6).

Rounds, Glen. *Mr. Yowder and the Giant Bull Snake*. New York: Holiday House, 1978 (3–6).

# 10 Historical Fiction

*If I were stuck on a deserted isle, the two books I'd want with me are Scott O'Dell's* Island of the Blue Dolphins *and Bette Greene's* Summer of My German Soldier. *O'Dell gives me tips on how to survive there, but mainly I'd want the books for company.*

—Zipporah, aged eleven

## Perspective and Standards

Both O'Dell's book, which takes place from 1835 until 1853, and Greene's World War II story are historical fiction. This category includes believable stories set in the past. High standards require a good story that is historically accurate and authentic. In this textbook, tales set no later than post-World War II are considered historical fiction, and more recent tales, modern realistic fiction.

Historical research should be included only to enrich a story. Elizabeth Janet Gray (Vining), whose *Adam of the Road* won The John Newbery Medal, emphasizes this point:

> It's absolutely essential to subordinate research to the story. You have to do your research, live with it, assimilate it, and then write your story about life in the past as if it happened to you. I think if I can claim any particular gift, it is imagining myself back in another age and feeling very much as if I really lived there. . . .

> The most difficult thing in writing about the past is to get the climate of thought of the past. It's easy enough to pick up costumes, customs, and events, but people thought differently, entirely differently, in the past period from the way they think now. It's the hardest thing to pick up the thought, express it in your book, and make modern people accept it.[1]

Historical perspective helps readers when previous and current attitudes conflict. Some authentic dialogue from the past may reflect bias, particularly toward women and minorities, but there is no excuse for stereotyped characters.

Too often Native Americans, for example, are shown as so-called savages. (*Native Americans* is preferred to *Indians,* which may be confused with residents of India.) Native Americans are often depicted collecting White scalps, although in fact the scalping practice seems to have originated with Spanish or English colonizers who paid a bounty for Native American scalps.[2]

Historical fiction requires attention to detail. For instance, it is not authentic to mention garment pockets in a novel about seventeenth-century American life or carriage springs in one about the early nineteenth century when leather thongs were used.

The most effective work of historical fiction have universal, timeless primary themes. Such themes will be highlighted in this chapter.

## Themes of Prizewinning Historical Fiction Grouped under These Topics

### Resistance

**Middle and Upper Grades.** Resistance to Black oppression is the theme of Mildred D. Taylor's *Song of the Trees,*[3] and keeping trees is symbolic of that resistance. Taylor tells a story based on fact of attempted racial exploitation of the Black Logan family in Mississippi. In 1932 during the Depression, jobs are so hard to find that David Logan, father of eight-year-old Cassie, has to work in Louisiana. (The author's father is the model for David Logan.) Knowing he is away and Logan's family needs money, Mr. Andersen, a White logger, forces Cassie's grandmother, Big Ma, to sell cherished trees around her home. Alerted, David returns and spends the night setting dynamite in the groves. Threatening to ignite the dynamite, he forces loggers to leave and cancels his fearful mother's agreement. The trees are so important to David he will not even allow those already cut to be removed.

**Upper Grades.** Mildred D. Taylor's sequel to *Song of the Trees* is a full-length novel, *Roll of Thunder, Hear My Cry,*[4] whose theme is again resistance to oppression, as symbolized by keeping the land. The setting is still Mississippi, but the time is one year later, 1933. Nine-year-old Cassie Logan learns why owning land permits the Logans luxuries of pride and courage. This causes resentment in their rich White neighbor, Harlan Granger, and envy in their Black sharecropper neighbors. Cassie overhears her parents plan to help sharecroppers discontinue buying in a store backed by Granger. She worries because her father might use his land as collateral for the purchases, so she asks, "We gonna lose our land?" and he replies, "If you remember nothing else in your whole life, Cassie girl, remember this: We ain't never gonna lose this land."[5] Two sharecroppers withdraw from cooperative purchases when Granger threatens to get them on a chain gang, and the son of one, T.J., is almost lynched. To sidetrack night riders, David Logan sets part of his land on fire. Cassie's final words are: "I cried for T.J. For T.J. and the land,"[6] so the land remains constantly in characters' minds, an obvious binding theme.

*Nature*

**Middle and Upper Grades.** Margot Benary-Isbert's *Blue Mystery* shows Germany in the 1800s and features the theme of appreciation of nature.[7] The life of ten-year-old Annegret and her family revolves around animals and flowers. Her father experiments with new plants, such as "Blue Mystery," a rare gloxinia, now missing. On a peninsula called Crusoe's Island, Annegret helps develop a wildlife preserve that "promised aid and protection to all living creatures."[8]

**Upper Grades.** Man's triumph over nature is the theme of William O. Steele's *Winter Danger*,[9] which takes place in the wilderness of Tennessee in the 1780s. When eleven-year-old Caje Amis, his father, and their neighbors survive a severe winter, they feel triumphant and strengthened in their relationship to each other.

Encounter with Native Americans is of minor importance in *Winter Danger,* but descriptions and illustrations are stereotyped. Here are two references: "There was an Indian coming toward him, a tomahawk in the red man's hand and a cruel scalping knife at his belt,"[10] and "Mostly Jared got along with the savages pretty good. The Chickamaugas hated all white men."[11]

*Maturing*

**Middle and Upper Grades.** Nancy Barnes's *The Wonderful Year,*[12] set in Colorado during the early 1900s, concerns growing up. Twelve-year-old Ellen has adolescent fears about being accepted in a new church and school when her family moves from Kansas to a Colorado ranch. The pigtailed girl faces popularity problems and recognizes how inflexible she is: "Everything was changing and she hated change. Why can't everything stay the same forever? She had never felt so forlorn, so lost."[13] Fortunately, understanding parents help her endure growing-up trials.

Ellen's contemporary is a boy in wooden shoes, Siebren from Weiram, Netherlands, featured in Meindert DeJong's *Journey from Peppermint Street.*[14] A boy beginning to mature and know himself is the theme of this story of Siebren who baby-sits his brother Knillis. Siebren lets the toddler climb rusty railroad ties and feels guilty when Knillis gets rust into head bruises. Relief comes when Grandpa takes Siebren on his first journey from his Peppermint Street home. On the walking trip, the boy befriends a dog, Wayfayer, and leaves it where his father will see a note to bring it home. They come to a former monastery tiny Aunt Hinka occupies with her huge deaf-mute husband. The aunt identifies with Siebren, saying:

> Well, you are wonderful too. . . . Oh, yes you are. See, it *has* to be, because we are so alone. I live in a marsh with a deaf-and-dumb husband, you sit endless hours with a baby brother who can't talk, so both of us have to make up things within ourselves—for ourselves.[15]

Armed with this advice, Siebren, a tornado survivor, returns home to his dog and a brother who now says, "Sieb."

**Upper Grades.** Maturing after surviving hardships is the theme of Eric Scott's *Down the Rivers, Westward Ho!,*[16] based on Colonel John Donelson's diary of 1779 until 1780. Thirteen-year-old Isam helps voyagers on his boat, the *Jonathan,* endure smallpox and whirlpooling rapids on a trip from Fort Henry, West Virginia to Big Salt Lick, Tennessee. Isam feels "neither nature nor man nor beast could stay his way, that he . . . had come to Big Salt Lick well on his way to manhood, a manhood that was more than well earned."[17]

A century later is the period of Joan W. Blos's *A Gathering of Days,*[18] subtitled *A New England Girl's Journal, 1830–32.* Maturing is the theme of the diary entries that tell about Catherine Hall from the time she is thirteen until she is fifteen on a farm near Meredith, New Hampshire. In 1831, her father, Charles Hall, a widower, marries a Boston widow, Ann Higham. She has an adolescent son, Daniel, who helps with farm chores, and she is a fine stepmother. Catherine and her best friend, Cassie Shipman, give a quilt and food items to Curtis, an escaped slave who writes gratefully from Canada. Cassie dies from fever before Catherine leaves town to help Aunt Lucy with a baby. Catherine continues to study with her former teacher, Edward Holt, Lucy's husband.

A French mountain village, St. Chamant, is the setting for Cyrus Fisher's *The Avion My Uncle Flew.*[19] Here thirteen-year-old John Littlehorn narrates an account whose theme is maturing through independent experience. Babied when he fractured his leg, the American boy is left with his French uncle when his parents go to England for post-World War II duty. John acquires French and tries to walk again, despite pain, following his doctor's advice:

From now on it depends on you whether you'll be able to run as well
as you used to run. I can't help you. Your father, he can't help you.
Your mother can't help you. If anything . . . they'll hinder you from
getting well, Johnny.[20]

John does learn to walk, and before returning reluctantly to the United
States, he even learns to fly the glider his uncle made.


*Family Relationships*


**Middle and Upper Grades.** Sydney Taylor's *All-of-a-kind Family,*[21] which
takes place in New York City's East Side at the turn of the century, has
family solidarity as its primary theme. The title derives from the fact
that this close-knit Jewish family of seven only has daughters, five to be
exact. At the end, a son is born. Though they have little money, family
members celebrate holidays, cherish friends, and above all, are loyal to
each other.

**Upper Grades.** Searching for father is Anne D. Kyle's theme in her
story about fifteenth-century Italy, *The Apprentice of Florence,*[22] She
tells how sixteen-year-old Neno travels from his farm to Florence, seeking his father who once worked for Messer Bardo, a silk merchant. He
learns his father may have sailed to the Indies. When he returns to the
farm, his stepmother explains that her husband owes her money for the
farm, and she will claim the farm if she remarries. Neno returns to
Florence, becoming the silk merchant's apprentice to earn money toward
his father's debt. He finds his father didn't die on a voyage, but at an
inn near Visreggio. Pleased to know his father's fate, Neno settles on
the farm with his stepmother who does not remarry.

Sadie Weilerstein's *Ten and a Kid* revolves around the theme of
family life, depicting a traditional nineteenth-century Jewish family in
Lithuania.[23] The family consists of Avrom Itsik, his wife, Gittel, their
eight children, and their goat, Gadya. Twenty-one stories follow the
Jewish calendar year, focusing on the family's traditional celebration of
holidays and Sabbath.

Autobiographical experiences in the village of Massarosa, Italy in
1905 are the basis for author-illustrator Angelo Valenti's *Nino.*[24] Its theme,
close family ties, is apparent as all activities on Grandfather's farm and
all celebrations are observed as a family. Nino is a young artist, en-
courged by his mother, Allinda, who gives him paints for Christmas. In
the end, Nino's father sends money for his wife and son to join him in
America. There is no painful parting from Grandfather, however, because he sells his farm and accompanies them.

Family solidarity is also the theme of a 1903 story in San Francisco's Chinatown, *Dragonwings,*[25] by Laurence Yep. Eight-year-old Moon Shadow is in China until his father, Windrider, who works in America, sends for him. Even when they are an ocean apart, they think of themselves as a loving Chinese household and ask, "What kind of lives do we live without families?"[26] They refer to the United States as the "Golden Mountain," supposedly a land of riches. At the end, Moon Shadow realizes it is not money but people and family that make the new country golden.

Search for family members is the theme of Sid Fleischman's humorous *Chancy and the Grand Rascal,*[27] which begins in Ohio during the post-Civil War period. Orphaned Chancy Dundee travels to Kansas to look for his younger siblings, aided by his foxy Uncle Will Buckthorn, the grand rascal. Near Paducah he finds his older sister, eleven-year-old Indiana, and in Sun Dance, his younger sister Miranda and brother Jamie. The family settles in Sun Dance when Uncle Will, famous for his tall talk, captures outlaws and becomes mayor.

Search for a family is also the theme of Meindert DeJong's *The House of Sixty Fathers,*[28] which features another young Chinese boy, Tien Pao. During World War II, the lad, separated from his family, begins the journey back to them through Japanese-held territory. He takes refuge in an American base where sixty soldiers seem like kind fathers. The boy is sensitive to the soldiers' international language of caring that transcends linguistic barriers.

*Love*

**Upper Grades.** The theme of gaining a father's love is seen in Berniece Rabe's *The Girl Who Had No Name.*[29] In Missouri during the Great Depression year of 1936, motherless twelve-year-old Girlie is shunted from one sister to another, both of whom resent her. Girlie's only wish is to live with her father and earn his love. She convinces him when she says:

> Papa, you need me. I need you too, Papa. I don't got no more sisters
> to take me in. Please, Papa. Even if I ain't your daughter (the father
> felt there may have been another man), let me come live with you.
> Couldn't you sort of adopt me? Don't you like me? Am I that bad a
> person?[30]

Girlie does succeed in winning her father's love after she moves home. His resistance to her was due to guilt feelings. He thought if he were Girlie's dad, he helped kill his wife, because she died at Girlie's birth.

Girlie is more fortunate than twelve-year-old David who has never experienced love, for he has lived most of his life in an eastern European concentration camp. Anne Holm's *North to Freedom,*[31] which takes place in eastern Europe and Denmark during World War II, tells how David escapes from the camp. The book's theme is the difficulty an unloved person has in giving love. David's mistrust of people limits him, but he finally learns to relate to others. He achieves individual freedom even before he experiences freedom to love that comes from a reunion with his mother in Denmark.

Another World War II story, Bette Greene's partly autobiographical *Summer of My German Soldier,*[32] takes place in Jenkinsville, Arkansas. The story is about a Jewish family, mainly twelve-year-old Patty Bergen, a unique girl who searches for love, the book's theme. A Black housekeeper, Ruth, is surrogate mother to Patty, whose parents favor their pretty younger daughter, Sharon. The mother says, "Patricia doesn't care how she looks while Sharon is just like me."[33] Patty thinks of her grandparents' place in Memphis as home. "It was as though I had just left home and was now going to where I lived."[34]

Patty is impressed with cultured twenty-two-year-old Anton Reiker, an antifascist German prisoner of war whom she meets at her father's store. When he escapes from the prison camp, the lonely girl lets him stay in her garage hideout. He observes her father beating her, a frequent practice. Anton tries to help her, but Patty prevents it, and only Ruth sees him. The housekeeper relates:

> That man come a-rushing out from the safety of his hiding 'cause he couldn't stand your pain and anguish no better'n me. That man listens to the love in his heart. Like the Bible tells us, when a man will lay down his life for a friend, well, then there ain't no greater love in this here world than that.[35]

Anton says after the beating, he overhears the cruel father confess, "Nobody loves me. In my whole life nobody has ever loved me."[36] Patty realizes she does not even *like* him or her mother when she tries to run away with Reiker. The prisoner insists upon departing alone, but gives her an heirloom ring, confiding, "I want you to always remember that you are a person of value, and you have a friend who loved you enough to give you his most valued possession."[37] Patty makes the mistake of revealing the ring. She is shunned as a Jewish girl who helped a Nazi and is committed to the Arkansas Reformatory at Bolton. Ruth, fired for helping Patty, is the only one who visits her, declaring, "You got love to give, Honey Babe, ain't nothing better'n that."[38]

*Being Accepted*

**Middle and Upper Grades.** Improving and being accepted is the theme
of Caroline Dale Snedeker's *Downright Dencey,*[39] an account of Nantucket, Massachusetts, in the 1800s. Young Dencey Coffyn and her
Quaker family help Sammie Jetsam, a previously abused orphan waif.
At first, her family scorns the ill-bred boy, and she joins in stoning him.
When he sees her remorse, he says, "Ef ye teach me to read, I will
forgive ye."[40] During reading lessons, friendship develops, but the Cof-
fyns punish Dencey for associating with him. The family's opinion
changes when Sammie rescues Dencey in a blizzard. Stricken with lung
fever as a result, Sammie is nursed at the Coffyn home. There he realizes
he is "hungry for the things beyond bread—the relationship of life,
father, mother, the belonging to anybody."[41] Sammie is transformed
from a rejected to a totally accepted boy.

Acceptance of a Native American girl is the theme of Lois Lenski's
*Bayou Suzette,*[42] a picture of Bayou life in Louisiana in 1892. Ten-year-
old Suzette Durand finds a young, motherless Native American girl,
Marteel, and takes her to her overcrowded home where she is greeted
by these prejudiced statements:

> She one of them good-for-nothing half-breed Indians from the back
> country. She one leetle animal, like all her tribe. . . .[43]
>
> Dirty no-count Injun. I don't know w'at you t'inkin' 'bout, to bring a
> dirty savage in your nice clean bed. . . .[44]
>
> Don't you know Injuns can't never be trusted? Don't you know they
> take everyt'ing they see? . . .[45]

Such attitudes seem insurmountable, but Marteel overcomes bias by
saving Suzette from an alligator and Papa Jules from drowning. Then
Maman confesses, "She en't not'ing to me but she's got herself wrapped
around my heart and me, I can't turn her loose."[46] Papa Jules "took
Marteel in his arms and kissed her. They wanted Marteel to know that
she had found not only a name, not only worthy ancestors, but a home
as well."[47]

Unfortunately, Marteel does not take pride in her Native American
ancestors, for she says, "Marteel not Injun no more. Marteel white girl
now."[48] She identifies with the Bayou family and is welcomed by them.

**Upper Grades.** Sulamith Ish-Kishor's sixteenth-century Czechoslova-
kian tale, *A Boy of Old Prague* has the theme of bigotry due to ignorance
and one boy's acceptance of a religious group after his enlightenment.[49]
Tomás, an illiterate peasant boy in a feudal society, believes Jews are

Harper, lone survivor of a Comanche massacre, is sustained on the prairie
by Sequoyah, a Cherokee. He says:

> My Cherokee name is Sequoyah. My white name is George Gist. I
> lived on the edge of two worlds. . . . To you I am Indian. To them
> I am white. Where two worlds meet they make a lonely place.[55]

Like Sequoyah, Calvin Harper is at the edge of two worlds, anxious to
return to his people, yet obligated to Sequoyah. Neither man's conflict
is resolved.

Mary Jane Carr's *Young Mac of Fort Vancouver*[56] describes a search
for identity in the nineteenth century by Young Mac or Donald Mac-
Dermott, son of a Canadian fur trader and a Cree woman. The fatherless
thirteen-year-old boy, living in the Northwest's Fort Vancouver, is given
a year to choose between White or Native American life. When he elects
to stay with his father's people, he goes to Edinburg to become a physician. Then, at age twenty-three, he visits his paternal grandfather in
Quebec and is reunited with a childhood friend, Mia. The author makes
a point of adding that Mia no longer looks Native American as though
that is complimentary. Young Mac says, "Mia, . . . I have been studying you, looking for a trace of Indian in you, but I can't find any."[57]

Eloise Jarvis McGraw's *Moccasin Trail* takes place around mid-
nineteenth century in Missouri and Oregon territory before they become
states.[58] Rebelling against a whip-lashing father, eleven-year-old Jim
Keath runs away from his Missouri farm with an uncle to trap beaver.
They are separated when a grizzly wounds the boy. Friendly Crow Native
Americans rescue the lad and raise him on the Absaroka plains, giving
him the name, Talks Alone. He leaves them to trap again but finds beaver
scarce. When Big Bull brings him a letter from the Keaths, he goes to
Oregon territory, rejoining his two brothers, Jonnie and young Dan'l,
and his sister, Sally, now orphaned. He arrives in time to help his siblings
through Columbia Gorge and, as the only family member of sufficient
age, claims land in the Willamette Valley. Since Sally cannot accept his
braids and feather, he eliminates them, finding identity, the book's theme.
Eleven-year-old Dan'l worships Jim, so among other stereotyped comments, Jim instructs, "I mean you mustn't ever want to be a Injun any
more! By gor, it ruint me but it ain't gonna git to you."[59] Only mildly
counterbalancing is Jim's statement to his older brother, Jonnie, when
the two relate:

> Once again they "knew each other's heart." He smiled, realizing the
> phrase had come to his mind in Crow. No matter. It was good that
> way.[60]

Rachel Fields's *Calico Bush* has a similar search-for-identity theme.[61] In 1743, during the French and Indian War, thirteen-year-old Marguerite Ledeux is forced to leave France, bound in servitude to a family in Maine. At first, she suffers this ridicule: "You-you're next thing to an Injun, you're French."[62] As she begins to love the American family she serves, she thinks less about France and rejects an opportunity to return. In France, she was called Marguerite, but in America, Maggie, and the change in name symbolizes a change in identity.

Search for identity is the theme of Elizabeth Janet Gray's *Meggy MacIntosh*,[63] another story about an immigrant whose loyalty shifts from mother country to adopted land. Orphaned fifteen-year-old Meggy MacIntosh leaves Scotland and comes to Carolina colony during the American Revolution. She does not know whether to support England or the colonies, but is influenced in the New World by fellow highlander Flora MacDonald and, in time, stands with American patriots, identifying herself as an American. She says:

> I've found myself here too. I was nothing in Edinburgh, but a miserable little poor relation. Now I am needed and useful and happy. I could never go back.[64]

A third story that involves changing homelands is Alice Dalgleish's partially autobiographical *The Silver Pencil*.[65] A writer's accepting new citizenship is the identity theme of this book, believed to be "the first picture in print" of an English girl becoming American. When Janet Laidlaw is young, her father gives her a silver pencil, encouraging her to be a writer. Janet spends her childhood in Trinidad before going to King George V's England, then Scotland, and eventually, America where she attends college and teaches. She becomes a U.S. citizen because she "had grown to feel this was her country, her home."[66]

During the 1940s in Maryland's Chesapeake Bay area, a fisherman's elder twin daughter gropes for self-worth in Katherine Paterson's *Jacob Have I Loved*.[67] Finding identity is the theme of this book narrated by the elder Bradshaw fraternal twin, Sarah Louise, who thinks of herself as Esau and of her younger, successful sister, Caroline, as Jacob. Caroline is always a center of attention, as a child because she is sickly, and as an adolescent, because of her vocal talent. Louise fishes crab floats and culls oysters—hard manual labor—so Caroline can have music lessons. Caroline even robs her sister of a dignified name, calling her Wheeze. Though Louise first befriends Captain Hiram Wallace, he gives Caroline his inheritance so she can go to Juilliard, but leaves nothing for Louise. The neglected twin's chum is a chubby neighbor, Call, who changes into a slender, handsome navy recruit before marrying golden

Caroline. Jealous Louise feels she is stricken by the Bible's ''Jacob have I loved, but Esau have I hated.''[68] Without encouragement, Louise becomes a scholarship student at the University of Maryland and then attends the University of Kentucky's School of Midwifery. Afterward, she goes to a small Appalachian community, Truitt, where she meets and marries Joseph Wojtkiewicz, a kind widower with three daughters. They have a son, and she continues as a midwife, feeling she has found her identity at last.

### Adjustment and Resistance to Change

**Middle and Upper Grades.** A city girl's adjustment to country life is the theme of *The Good Master* by Hungarian author-illustrator Kate Seredy.[69] Prior to World War I, Kate, a young girl from Budapest, visits relatives in rural Hungary. A headstrong imp, she responds to the firmness and love of her uncle, the good master, and begins to adore the countryside. Later, her father sees her and comments:

> I sent a spoiled, cranky, pale little girl to you. I find a husky, happy, busy little farmer. She will never fit into city life again.[70]

A sequel to *The Good Master* is Kate Seredy's *The Singing Tree*.[71] Until World War I, Kate and her cousin Jancsi are carefree at the Hungarian ranch of the good master, Uncle Márton Nagy. They are forced to adjust to change when the good master and other men enter the service. For two years, with help from his mother and Kate, Jancsi is in charge while relatives and prisoners take refuge at the ranch. A desire for peace is the book's theme, symbolized by an apple tree full of singing birds that boosts the spirits of Uncle Márton on the battlefield. When the war ends, the good master adds a fourth word to a monument: '' 'Liberty, equality, fraternity.' . . . Only a fourth one, just born, will ring clearer. *Peace.* . . . Please God. Just peace.''[72]

A small Georgia town in the 1930s is the setting for Robert Burch's *Skinny*,[73] whose theme is resistance to change. Skinny, an eleven-year-old orphan, does not want to leave Miss Bessie's hotel, though he understands this is a temporary home until he can go to a church orphanage. He previously stayed with a tenant farmer who never sent him to school, so he cannot read or write, but he greets hotel visitors professionally. Miss Bessie says if she were not single, she would adopt Skinny, and she adds, ''I intentionally care so much for you that I'll give you up for your own good.''[74] When he receives word of the orphanage opening, hotel-cook Peachy tells him, ''I wishes you would take on a more hopeful outlook, child. You can be happy anywhere if you make up your mind to it.''[75] Skinny feels he leaves a real family at the hotel but has no choice and is treated fairly in his new home.

**Upper Grades.** Colonists' adjustment to American life is Patricia Clapp's theme in *Constance,*[76] which takes place in Plymouth, New England in 1620–1626. Narrator Constance Hopkins relates impressions from the time she is a fourteen-year-old girl until she is an eighteen-year-old married woman. Sickness and death are the biggest hardships. Those who make the adjustment from England enjoy freedom and space, finally feeling that Plymouth is home.

Jacqueline Jackson's *The Taste of Spruce Gum,*[77] which takes place in Vermont in 1903, has a theme of slow adjustment to change. The year before, eleven-year-old Libby Fletcher's father died, and she is upset about Mama's marrying Papa's brother, Uncle Charles. After the wedding, Libby, who is reluctant to share her mother, criticizes their new lumber-camp home. The girl begins to appreciate her stepfather at Christmas when he presents a gift he carved for her. Total acceptance comes when he has an accident, and she rushes to the hospital to call him Papa.

Resistance to change is the theme of A. Linevski's *An Old Tale Carved Out of Stone,*[78] a story about neolithic Siberia four thousand years ago. The author, a noted Soviet archaeologist, speaks with authority since he is familiar with Siberian stone carvings. Seventeen-year-old Liok, his tribe's shaman or medicine man, meets with resistance when he tries new rituals. "Tradition had been broken, and the hunters feared that the hunt would go badly.''[79] Liok rules with cunning ingenuity, but his deviations from tradition cause insecurity in the tribe, and he eventually flees.

*Adventure*

**Middle and Upper Grades.** Sid Fleischman's humorous *By the Great Horn Spoon!* has adventuring during the 1849 Gold Rush as its theme.[80] Orphaned twelve-year-old Jack Flagg leaves the Boston home he shares with his sisters and Aunt Arabella to seek his fortune with Praiseworthy, the aunt's butler. As ship stowaways, the two have one hair-raising experience after another. They find gold but lose it in San Francisco Bay. After they return to Boston, Aunt Arabella and Praiseworthy plan marriage, opening the door to more adventures.

Another humorous book by Sid Fleischman with the theme of adventure is *Humbug Mountain.*[81] It takes place in the latter nineteenth century, probably in the 1870s or 1880s, mainly on the Nebraska-Dakota border. Son of an itinerant newspaperman, thirteen-year-old Wiley Flint, his ten-year-old sister, Glorietta, and their parents settle in a grounded riverboat at the foot of Humbug Mountain. Their adventures include securing the arrest of two prairie killers, Shagnasty John and the Fool Killer, and saving two tons of gold dust.

The theme of youthful adventures pervades Ruth Sawyer's *Roller Skates*,[82] a factually based story set in New York City in the 1890s. While her parents travel in Europe for a year, ten-year-old lively Lucinda lives with Miss Peters, a teacher, and has numerous adventures on her roller skates. She encourages Tony, a fruit-vendor's son, to join her on skates, and she makes friends with whomever she meets. Life is so exciting she wishes she could stay ten forever.

**Upper Grades.** Agnes Danforth Hewes's *Spice and the Devil's Cave* has the theme of nationalistic adventures,[83] as it fictionally describes Vasco da Gama's 1497 voyage around the Cape of Good Hope. The explorer's purpose is to claim the Indian spice trade for Portugal. He gets support for his plans to go around the southern end of Africa from a quiet Arabic adolescent, Nejmi, called only the Girl. She had once lived at the Cape of Good Hope, identified as the Devil's Cave because of its swirling winds and waters. She imparts her knowledge of the area to Magellan and actually sails with da Gama. Dominant feelings of nationalism are expressed by one of the young sailors, Nicolo Conti, who says, "When Portugal reaches the Indies by sea she's going to take trade supremacy from Venice."[84] An example of stereotyped thinking is reflected in these words of a banker and cartographer, Abel Zakuto, " . . . I know that those half-naked savages and those rude gewgaws [trinkets] that Columbus brought back don't tally with . . . the costly trade that men who've been in the Orient tell about . . ."[85]

Four hundred years later, 1848, is the year discussed in Bruce Clements's mildly humorous *I Tell a Lie Every So Often*,[86] a book with the theme of adventure resulting from a lie. The narrator, fourteen-year-old Henry, lies when he claims that lost, redhaired cousin Hanna is living with Native Americans. To investigate his claim, he and his older brother, Clayton, take a five-hundred-mile trip. Clayton, a would-be preacher, is so biased he repeatedly calls Native Americans *savages* and carries a loaded rifle because he wants "to find some very evil Indians and shoot them to death."[87] When Clayton accidentally shoots his brother, the Santec Native Americans treat Henry's wounds. In the end, the brothers return home without Hanna, so their adventures are fruitless.

*Mysticism*

**Upper Grades.** Mysticism is the theme of Adrienne Richard's tale about California in the 1920s, *Wings*.[88] Though the plot revolves around a young girl, Pip de Puyster, her interest in flying, her relationship with separated parents, and her preoccupation with death, a mystical feeling prevails. It stems from such supporting characters as an Indian mystic and an astrologer who influence Pip and her mother.

## Determination

**Middle and Upper Grades.** Determination is the theme of Meindert DeJong's *The Wheel on the School*,[89] a story of the Netherlands during the first quarter of this century. Despite stormy island weather, six young pupils try to attract storks back to the roofs of their village, Shora. A persistent teacher tells his class, "When we wonder, we can make things begin to happen."[90] Things do happen after the children have a wheel placed on the school's roof, and two storks use it as a nesting place.

**Upper Grades.** Determination to fulfill a father's dream is the theme of James Ramsey Ullman's *Banner in the Sky*,[91] which takes place in Kurtal (actually Zermatt), Switzerland in 1865. Swiss guide Josef Matt died trying to climb the greatest Swiss mountain, now a challenge to his sixteen-year-old son Rudi. Rudi is the first to climb the Citadel, a fictional name for the Matterhorn. A red shirt on a flagpole, a banner in the sky, symbolizes his success. Self-motivated Rudi becomes the most famous Alpine guide.

Determination to fulfill a dream is the theme of another book, *The Golden Goblet*,[92] Eloise Jarvis McGraw's tale of ancient Egypt. Ranofer, a fatherless young Egyptian boy, is forced to work for his cruel half brother, a stonecutter, though he wants to become apprenticed to a famous goldsmith. When Ranofer discovers stolen tomb jewels and a missing golden goblet, the Queen asks him to choose a reward. He asks for a donkey to become independent of his brother, explaining:

> I could be a pupil of Zau the goldsmith and then I would become a master goldsmith and grow rich and famous and someday perhaps make necklaces for Your Majesty.[93]

The book ends with Ranofer's triumph.

Elizabeth Foreman Lewis's *Young Fu of the Upper Yangtze* has the theme of determination for self-improvement and elders' approval.[94] In Chungking, China during the 1920s, young Fu is a fatherless thirteen-year-old boy who comes with his mother from the country to work as a coppersmith's apprentice. The ambitious youth learns to read and write while helping in the shop. His mother considers him a man, and his approving master says he will adopt him.

Eleanor M. Jewett's view of medieval England, *The Hidden Treasure*

*of Glaston,*[95] has perseverance as its theme. Although his father wanted
him to become a knight, twelve-year-old crippled Hugh learns to enjoy
being a scribe in a monastery. From documents, Hugh and a friend,
Dickon, piece together clues about the Holy Grail. When Hugh glimpses
the Holy Grail, his leg is no longer lame. He can be a knight now, but
he chooses to be a scribe, documenting his experience with the Holy
Grail.

Self-determination is the theme of Walter D. Edmond's *Bert Breen's
Barn,*[96] which takes place in the state of New York in 1889. Fourteen-
year-old Tom Dolan, deserted by his father, is disgusted because his
grandfather requires his mother to wear a ragged dress and sell berries
door to door. The conscientious lad gets a feed-mill job and arranges to
buy Bert Breen's barn, demolishing it and reassembling it on his own
property. He feels if he has a respectable barn, his life will change, and
it does. When he finds hidden treasure in the barn, he ends his family's
poverty, and with hard work, expands his farm.

### Female Educational Goals

**Upper Grades.** A girl's dream for an education and better life is the
theme of Chaya Burstein's *Rifka Grows Up,*[97] a tale set in a Russian
Jewish *shtetl* or village in 1905. Twelve-year-old Rifka, maturing amidst
cries of "Kill the Jews!," hopes revolutionaries will help stop discrimination so she can continue her studies. The book ends optimistically as
Rifka plans to join her brother in America to fulfull her educational goals.

Another female who yearns to be more than a peasant is Hertha
Seuberlich's *Annuzza, a Girl of Romania.*[98] Longing for a place in life
is the theme of this early twentieth-century book which shows how Annuzza convinces her father to let her take the city's high-school entrance
exams. As a fifteen-year-old high school student, she realizes she belongs
on the farm after all, and she accepts a nursery-school job that will permit
her to live at home.

Betty Underwood's *The Tamarack Tree* has determination for an
education as its primary theme.[99] Despite prejudice against women in the
1800s in Canterbury, Connecticut, Bernadette, a fourteen-year-old White
orphan, and her Black friend, Miriam, insists upon bettering themselves
through schooling. Bernadette turns away from those who say female
brains are feeble and says, "I'm going to be a schoolteacher, have my
own school, because I want to be free and take care of myself."[100]

### Overcoming a Disability

**Primary and Middle Grades.** Jane Yolen's *The Seeing Stick* has overcoming a disability as its theme.[101] In ancient Peking, Princess Hwei

Ming, blind and dependent, learns to see with her hands from an old blind man who carves pictures on his seeing stick. The picture book begins with black-and-white illustrations, but once the Princess copes with her problem, the theme is emphasized with colored pictures. The Princess copes by seeing with mind and heart in addition to fingers and extending this knowledge to other blind children.

**Upper Grades.** Overcoming a disability by finding a purpose in life is Rosemary Sutcliff's theme in *The Witch's Brat*,[102] set in eleventh-century England. Lovel, a fatherless eleven-year-old boy with a lame leg, is stoned by villagers for being a misshappen witch's brat, and he escapes to a monastery where he does errands. His life has meaning when he finds he can heal others, and he helps Rahere build a hospital founded on compassion. He fulfills his grandmother's prophecy, "You will be one of the menders of this world; not the makers, nor yet the breakers."[103]

*Positive Replacing Negative*

**Primary and Middle Grades.** Governing peacefully after previously being cruel is the theme of Ashod Davar's *The Wheel of King Asoka*.[104] The story takes place two thousand years ago when Asoka the Great ruled India. At first, he frightened his subjects. He changed, ruling with love, after he saw his dead and wounded on the battlefield. The title comes from his slogan, "Justice, peace, and love must go on forever in this world like a wheel."[105]

**Middle and Upper Grades.** Florida during the early 1900s is the setting for Lois Lenski's *Strawberry Girl*,[106] whose theme is feuding neighbors resolving conflicts. The feud begins over jealousy and gains momentum after destruction of farm animals and property. Though one father threatens to set fire to the house next door, he changes through religious conversion and eventually adopts a love-your-neighbor attitude.

Robert Burch's *Queenie Peavy* is another story that takes place in the South,[107] this time in a small Georgia town during the Depression of the early 1930s. Queenie is an embittered, lonely thirteen-year-old girl whose mother works long hours in a factory and whose father is in prison. A defiant girl, she throws stones when children taunt her, "Queenie's daddy's in the chain gang."[108] The adolescent feels iron loyalty to her father until he comes home on parole. Then he calls her String Bean,

denies her mother's claim she's getting pretty, and tells her to mind her
own business when she rebukes him for violating parole by carrying a
pistol. After her father becomes a prisoner again, Queenie's attitude in
school improves because she worries she may be sent to a reformatory.
She realizes she has shown foolish loyalty to her father,

> . . . loyalty to him and resentment against almost everyone else. Yet
> she had known all the time, and refused to face up to it, that he had
> brought on his own troubles.[109]

*Queenie's Peavy's* theme is a retaliating girl learning responsibility after
true appraisal of her father. This 1966 book helps end the perfect-parent
image in children's literature.

**Upper Grades.** Elizabeth George Speare's *The Bronze Bow*,[110] set in
Biblical Palestine, has the theme of revenge replaced by love. Since the
Romans killed his parents, Daniel Bar Jamin, a Jewish lad, dedicates
himself to driving them from the Holy Land. Rosh, a revengeful leader,
no longer influences Daniel after the boy meets Jesus and hears how
crippling hate can be. Daniel now accepts that only love can bend the
bronze bow, symbol of his kingdom's struggle against the Romans.

Speare emphasizes the theme of *The Bronze Bow* in an interview,
and she tells why she wrote the book:

> I was teaching Sunday school, and it all seemed so amorphous to my
> students and to me, too. The whole period was just a big blank. . . .
> There was at that time a radio show, "The Greatest Story Ever Told,"
> in which Jesus sometimes spoke. When He did, they used a special
> sound effect for His voice. It was a hollow, portentous, solemn voice,
> inhuman. I wanted to make Jesus a human being and the people who
> followed Him human beings. I started out with that purpose.[111]

Turgen craves love in Nicholas Kalashnikoff's *The Defender*,[112] which
takes place in nineteenth-century Siberia. Warmth substituted for loneliness is the book's theme. Turgen, a lonely mountain shepherd, is shunned
by villagers who look upon his gentleness with his rams as a sign he is
linked with the devil. His solitude ends after Marfa and her two children
befriend him. When Turgen marries Marfa, the village accepts him as
the defender, for he shares food with her family, heals an injured lamb,
and helps those in need.

Turgen's gentleness is in contrast with the conniving boys in John
D. Fitzgerald's *The Great Brain Reforms*[113] and Suzanne Newton's *What
Are You Up To, William Thomas?*[114] Fitzgerald's theme is reformation of
a schemer. His book takes place in Adenville, Utah, in 1898. At home

for summer vacation from the Catholic Academy for Boys, Tom Fitzgerald, alias The Great Brain, swindles buddies with a hypnotism hoax,
outwits three confidence men, and establishes a business as a river rafts-
man. When he endangers the lives of two friends to make thirty cents,
his brother John, the narrator, organizes a mock trial of Adenville children vs. The Great Brain. Tom receives a guilty verdict and a suspended
sentence, provided that he reform. He says:

> When this trial started, I thought it was a big joke and that my great
> brain would make you all look like fools. Instead, for the first time in
> my life, I see myself as others see me.[115]

Craftiness characterizes Tom and fifteen-year-old Will Thomas in
Suzanne Newton's *What Are You Up To, William Thomas?* A developing
sense of fair play is the theme of Newton's book, set in Riverton, North
Carolina in 1923. Will is sure Paul Nesbitt will win the high school's
Douglass History Medal because Paul gets most awards. Paul's father
owns the cotton gin where Will's father works, and Will holds deep-
seated resentment toward Paul. Will, serving under Lilly Fentrice on the
commencement committee, replaces the impressive Douglass Medal with
his brother's tiny Sunday school attendance pin, hoping to embarrass
Paul. His conscience bothers him before the prank backfires and *he*
receives the medal. Perceptive Lilly had put the correct medal in the
box, so Will enjoys his moment of glory.

### Good Overcoming Evil

**Upper Grades.** Julia Cunningham's *The Treasure Is the Rose,*[116], set in
France in 1100, concerns good overcoming evil. The story is about a
young widowed countess, Ariane, who survives with scant food made
by a devoted servant, Moag, in her decrepit Château de Mon Coeur.
Ariane and Moag become hostages of three desperate wayfarers, Yarrow
and his followers, Toadflex and Ragwort. A neighbor, arrogant Baron
de Rincon, offers Ariane protection if he can have her property but she
refuses. She remembers that, on his deathbed, her husband left her the
message, "The treasure is the rose,"[117] and Yarrow seeks that rumored
fortune. He looks near the damask roses in the garden, finding a treasure
in jewels. Instead of leaving with the valuables, Yarrow and his followers
elect to stay to help Ariane. She alone has the power to overcome the
evil ways of the three former robbers volunteering to work constructively
with her.
   The tale of Ariane is set in the Middle Ages, and so is Howard Pyle's

*Otto of the Silver Hand.*[118] Its theme is good triumphs over evil. From the beginning, twelve-year-old Otto Conrad experiences good as well as evil, for he spends part of his life in a monastery and part with his father, a robber baron. He also learns that his dad, so kind to him, has killed others. Enemies slay his father and in revenge, cut off Otto's hand, replacing it with a silver hand. Living now with the German Emperor, Otto matures and realizes loving, not warring, enables him to stand above others. He concludes, "Better a hand of silver than a hand of iron."[119]

### One Dream Fulfilled and Others Aborted

**Middle and Upper Grades.** Author-illustrator Holling Clancy Holling has created *Paddle-to-the-Sea,*[120] a story that takes place in Canada before World War II. Its theme is dream fulfillment. An unnamed Native American boy wants to travel to see the world, but he cannot leave his family. Instead, he whittles a paddling figure to take the voyage for him and a canoe on which he carves "Please put me back in water. I am Paddle-to-the-Sea."[121] The trip is completed from the Great Lakes to the Atlantic Ocean and back, though the toy canoe experiences ice, storms, and fire. The boy, who identifies vicariously with the paddler, indirectly fulfills his dream.

**Upper Grades.** Contrasting with the positive mood of *Paddle-to-the-Sea* is Yoshiko Uchida's *Samurai of Gold Hill,*[122] whose theme is an unrealized dream. Twelve-year-old Koichi and his father leave war-torn Japan in 1869 and go to Gold Hill, California to develop a tea and silk farm. The two face prejudice, drought, money shortage, and their own bias against farming, because in prewar Japan, family members were Samurai warriors. The dream of father and son begins to fade when they acknowledge failure of their farm.

Ending an experience is the negative primary theme of Eleanor Cameron's *To the Green Mountains,*[123] set in a small town, South Angela, Ohio, during World War I. Elizabeth Rule raises her thirteen-year-old daughter, Kath, in a hotel she manages. The mother evaluates:

> I have experiences, and I've always known when each one has come to an end. For me, they're like plants. They grow and come to flower, and die. And this one, here at the hotel, has died.[124]

The experience ends after the tragic death of a Black friend, Tessie Grant. The story is told from the point of view of Kath who shows amazing understanding of adult problems. She influences her mother to ask for a divorce and to move to grandmother's home in the green mountains of Vermont.

In an interview, author Eleanor Cameron reveals autobiographical aspects of *To the Green Mountains:*

> The next book, which I think is going to be called *A Love of Green Mountains,* will be about Black people and White people, but going back to when I was a child . . . . I absolutely adored my mother. She was my property, because we hadn't seen my father for a long time. Incidentally, my mother and father were divorced. . . . There are many things that are interesting for me to get into that I haven't thought about before, but I know the book will open them up. It's going to be more adult than anything I've yet done, more adult in many ways.[125]

*Occupational Choice*

**Upper Grades.** Independent choice of occupation is the theme of Monica Shannon's *Dobry,*[126] which takes place in the past in Bulgaria. Dobry, a young Bulgarian peasant, breaks the family tradition by becoming a sculptor instead of a farmer, but first he has to convince his mother. After he sculpts a snow nativity scene, she is so moved, she says, "God made him an artist and who am I to set my heart against it?"[127]

Similarly Elizabeth Janet Gray's story of thirteenth-century England, *Adam of the Road,*[128] has the underlying theme of discovering one's talent and choosing an occupation. Twelve-year-old Adam and his minstrel father, Roger, are going to the Fair of St. Giles when someone steals Adam's dog, Nick. While hunting for his dog, Adam is separated from his father, but meets strangers who try to convince the boy that their trade is best. Aware of alternatives, Adam chooses to be a minstrel and is happy when he is reunited with Roger and Nick.

In an interview, Elizabeth Janet Gray clarifies the theme of *Adam of the Road:*

> Each one of us has a talent which is ours to develop and use, and if we don't use it, it rusts. This is borne out in Adam. . . . He's a very appealing, attractive youngster. Many people help him along the way, and in helping him, they all want to make him something that he isn't. The parish priest wants to make him a parish priest. Someone else wants to make him a farmer. In the course of the story, he learns he is really a minstrel, and this is what he's supposed to do in his life.[129]

Mari Sandoz's *The Horsecatcher,* apparently set in the early nineteenth century, tells about Big Elk,[130] son of a Cheyenne chief, who refuses to be a full-time warrior and prefers, instead, the occupation of horsecatcher, although he does fulfill tribal obligations. Individuality, this book's theme, is not appreciated by fellow Cheyenne who think Big Elk's preference for horses really reflects his fear of fighting. The brave's difficulties in explaining his point of view are registered below:

> Elk could not tell them how much he regretted killing the horse raider, and that his two moons' time spent under the bare sky without robe or lodge had strengthened his belief that all things of the earth and sky were a part of him.[131]

A weakness in *The Horsecatcher* is frequent mention of violence. A mild example is this description of Cheyenne women wounding themselves in mourning over their slain men: "Young Elk's mother and all his women relatives gashed themselves. . . , arms and legs cut to bleeding. . . ."[132]

The end of the nineteenth century is the time described in *The Great Wheel* written by Robert Lawson and illustrated by him with black-and-white lithographs.[133] This work of fiction begins in Ireland where Aunt Honora, reading tea leaves, tells twelve-year-old Cornelius Terence (Conn) Kilroy, "Your fortune lies to the west. . . . One day you'll ride the greatest wheel in all the world."[134] The prediction comes true, for Conn goes to New York City and at age eighteen, makes an occupational choice. He quits a city-sewer-and-pavement job to help construct a Ferris wheel for the 1893 Chicago World's Columbian Exposition. Conn helps Mr. Ferris engineer the wheel, and he supervises riding it. Being enterprising is the book's theme, for Conn accepts the challenge of a novel job. The story concludes when he marries Trudy, a friend met aboard the ship from Ireland, and a wedding gift is Car Number One from the Ferris wheel, a future playhouse for their first child. There is evidence of stereotyped thinking by several minor characters, such as Conn's mother, who jokes that Irish emigrants to the United States are "likely skelped by the heathen red Indian savages."[135]

### Slavery

**Upper Grades.** Misadventures connected with the slave trade is the theme of Charles Boardman Hawes's *The Great Quest*.[136] This is a narration of voyages in the 1820s by twenty-year-old Josiah Woods from Topham, Massachusetts to Cuba and then to Guinea, Africa. Uncle Seth, with whom Josia lives, buys a ship, *The Adventure,* and the lad joins its crew under Captain Cornelius Gleazen, a greedy man who has a fortune hidden in Guinea. When Gleazen loses the fortune, he forces Blacks from Guinea on board as part of slave trading, causing fights between the crew and the Guineans and destroying the ship's morale, especially Josiah's. As the voyage ends in Topham, Josiah feels the only good part is bringing home a bride from an African mission. The book is replete with stereotyped references to Blacks as "heathen savages,"[137] "black yelling devil,"[138] and "black sons of hell,"[139] perhaps indicative of the 1920 publication year, for *The Great Quest* was the first Newbery Honor Book.

Paula Fox's story of the slave trade in the 1840s, *The Slave Dancer*,[140] has a theme of inhumanity so grave the whole known world at times seems meaningless. The narrator is a Creole musician, thirteen-year-old Jessie Bollier, kidnapped in New Orleans and put aboard a slave ship to exercise captives while playing his fife. He sees that Blacks are regarded as less than animals, chained, beaten, shot, tortured, and thrown overboard, like waste.

In *The Slave Dancer*, the author fails to give a name to most of the slaves, a way of depriving them of individual character. She identifies just one slave, Ras. When there is a shipwreck, Jessie and Ras are sole survivors. After they come ashore, an escaped slave helps Ras to freedom via the Underground Railroad. Jessie, a musician, returns home, but can no longer listen to music because of remembered pain. The author writes this novel at a child's level of understanding.

A Creole lad narrates *The Slave Dancer*, but Julius Lester's *Long Journey Home: Stories from Black History* offers views from a Black perspective.[141] This is a collection of six stories, based on historical fact, whose theme is slaves or exslaves struggling for freedom in a White world. The title refers to forty or fifty slaves in Georgia who could no longer stand degradation and drown themselves as they walk in the ocean toward Africa, a long journey home. One exslave comments after emancipation, "We free, but free don't mean that much if you ain't got a piece of dust in the world to plant a seed in."[142]

*Freedom from Fascism*

**Upper Grades.** Acceptance of freedom or fascism is the theme of Alki Zei's book about Greece in 1936, *Wildcat under Glass*.[143] A stuffed wildcat symbolizes the struggle, for it has a blue eye representing democracy and a black eye representing dictatorship. It is described in these terms:

When it saw out of its blue eye, it was tame like a cat. It walked among

men and helped them, and played with the children and with the small
animals of the forest. But when its black eye was open, it destroyed
the work of man, and the little animals ran and hid in their burrows
when they heard him pass.[144]

In *Wildcat under Glass,* two young sisters, Myrto and Melissa, are
torn by Greece's turmoil. They protect their feedom-fighting cousin but
attend a fascist school. They witness book burnings and imprisonment
of government opponents. Their father supports dictatorship to keep his
job, though he believes in democracy. Amidst split loyalties, Greeks
must decide between freedom and fascism.

Another book by Alki Zei, *Petro's War,*[145] has fighting for freedom
as its theme. It is again set in Greece, but in the 1940s when ten-year-
old Petros and his family see Jewish persecution and executions during
World War II. The Resistance fights back as Petros and his friends post
signs declaring their hunger. When his friends are shot, Petros realizes
the grim reality of the slogan, ''Freedom or death.'' The war ends and
Petros, now fourteen, hopes for human dignity again.

### Revenge

**Upper Grades.** Author-illustrator Marguerite deAngeli tells a story of
Scotland during the tenth century, *Black Fox of Lorne,*[146] with revenge
as its theme. Twin brothers, Brus and Jan, want to avenge their father's
death, but are satisfied when the king kills their parent's murderer,
Gavin, the Black Fox of Lorne. The boys' search for their long-lost
mother ends happily, as they learn she is the Queen's servant, anxious
to make a home for them.

Vengeance is the theme of Yuri Suhl's *Uncle Misha's Partisans,*[147]
set in the Ukraine in the 1940s. Twelve-year-old Motele, member of a
famous anti-Nazi Jewish band, seeks revenge for the death of his parents
and sister, killed because they were Jewish. When he first fired against
fascists, another partisan recalls saying, ''This is for my wife . . . and
for my daughter . . . and my son . . . and my sister . . . and my
father.''[148] Motele, a violinist, gets revenge when he performs at the
German Officers' House, plants a bomb there, and escapes before it
explodes.

### Fear and Courage

**Middle and Upper Grades.** Fear of Native Americans is the theme of
Walter D. Edmonds's *The Matchlock Gun,*[149] which takes place in 1757

when New York was still a British colony. At that time, the French were said to have led Native Americans from Canada against Dutch settlers. In this true story, Teunis Van Alstyne leaves his family for guard duty, but first shows his ten-year-old son, Edward, how to fire a matchlock gun. When Native Americans raid, Edward fires, killing three men, though not before Gertrude, his mother, sustains tomahawk wounds. Edwards drags Gertrude, who is unconscious, from the steps of the burning cabin and waits with his six-year-old sister, Trudy, until his father returns to the fearful group.

The text and pictures of *The Matchlock Gun* stereotype Native Americans as wild-eyed *savages* from no identified nation. Gertrude looks upon five braves as animals "trotting, stooped over, first one and then another coming up, like dogs sifting up to the scent of food."[150] Violence is overplayed, for a child kills three persons. No reason is given for the attack that caused terror. This story also downgrades Blacks, called negro without a capital letter.[151]

Courage, not fear, is the theme of Claire Huchet Bishop's World War II story, *Twenty and Ten*.[152] In German-occupied France, twenty French fifth-grade pupils led by nuns hide ten Jewish children from the Nazis. The twenty share their limited food and are courageous under fascist interrogation, remaining silent about the refugees' cave hiding place.

**Upper Grades.** Ann Weil's *Red Sails to Capri*,[153] which takes place in 1826 on the island of Capri, Italy, has the theme of abolishing fears of the unknown through knowledge. The tale is about Michele whose parents, Signor and Signora Pagano, are struggling operators of one of the island's two inns. When Michele is on a red-sailed boat with an inn guest, Jacques, and a friend, Pietro, they notice a cove which they bypass because of superstitions that it is unlucky. However, a visiting Danish student argues:

> Now there is a cove and we want to find the truth about it. How will we find the truth? Through knowledge. And how will we get the knowledge? By going to the cove.[154]

In one month, the student, a fisherman, and Michele courageously enter the cove and discover the Blue Grotto, remnants of an ancient sunken city that fill the world with the color blue in the cavern walls, arched dome, rocks, and water. The explorers become heroes, revealing truth that ends fear.

Courage, not fear, is dominant in Scott O'Dell's *Sing Down the Moon*,[155] for he says its theme is "human spirit when faced with injustice."[156] His story, which begins in Arizona in 1864, is told by Bright Morning, a fifteen-year-old Navaho shepherdess betrothed to Tall Boy. Spanish slavers kidnap her and force her to be a servant, but she escapes. When she returns home, Spanish soldiers compel her to join her people on The Long March, walking three-hundred miles to incarceration at Fort Sumner, New Mexico. Many die along the way, and most of the survivors lose initiative, but not Bright Morning. This nonstereotyped Native American prods her husband, Tall Boy, until they escape, and in freedom, she bears a child.

In an interview, Scott O'Dell relates that his title, *Sing Down the Moon,* is intended to convey the Navaho's doom. He attributes the title to Robinson Jeffers's version of Euripides' play, *Medea.* Here an enemy tyrant, Crion, repeats common belief in Medea's occult power, "Men say you can even sing down the moon."[157] O'Dell says his title implies that justice for the Navahos under their Spanish conquerors would never take place.

Betty Sue Cummings's *Hew Against the Grain* is another book with courage as its theme.[158] This account is seen from the eyes of Matilda, the youngest daughter in the Repass family of Virginia. With brothers fighting on both sides of the Civil War, she is opposed to slavery. The Repass home and crops are destroyed by soldiers, and her father succumbs to insanity as his family crumbles. A war wound for her is the loss of virginity at fifteen when she is raped by a man she later shoots. Helped by her friend, Docia, a slave she frees, Matilda fights what Grandpa Hume calls "dwindling," losing resources and courage to face life. She finds war is ugly, but she must be strong enough to avoid being winnowed out as she hews against the grain.

Courage is also the theme of Margot Benary-Isbert's *The Ark,*[159] a story of the Lechow family in post-World War II Germany. Since the death of her twin brother, Christian, fourteen-year-old Margret feels lost. With her father in a Russian prison camp, Margret and her older brother, Matthias, take farm jobs to support the family. Their home is a railroad car nicknamed The Ark. The prophecy, "It's going to be your ark to carry you over the rough seas of these times,"[160] is fulfilled when the family of five, including the father, begin life anew in The Ark.

*Patriotism*

**Middle and Upper Grades.** Patriotism is the theme of Marie McSwigan's World War II story, *Snow Treasure.*[161] Thirteen tons of Norwegian gold must be removed from German-occupied Norway. A group of children, led by twelve-year-old Peter Lundstrom, carry the gold secretly on sleds past German soldiers and bury it in snow, later to be loaded by men aboard ship. Heroic children risk their lives because of love for their homeland.

**Upper Grades.** A tale of medieval Poland, Eric P. Kelly's *The Trumpeter of Krakow*,[162] also has patriotism as its theme. With respect for country, Polish trumpeters play the Heynel hymn each hour of the day and night. The Heynal now ends with a broken musical phrase, for a trumpeter was shot while playing and couldn't finish the hymn. His martyrdom epitomizes sacrifice for Poland.

## Friendship

**Middle and Upper Grades.** Ruth Robbins's *The Emperor and the Drummer Boy* has the theme of loyal friendship.[163] After playing their drums in a French parade for Napoleon, Jean and Armand become true friends. They are separated at Boulogne when, despite storm warnings, Napoleon forces the ships to sail, including one with Armand aboard. His boat is wrecked, and Jean waits all night on shore for him.

> Napoleon asked, "Tambour, what keeps you here in this foul weather?"
>
> Jean replied, "I wait for my friend, Armand, Your Majesty."[164]

In the end, Armand floats ashore on his drum, and Jean rushes to help him.

## War's Effect

**Middle and Upper Grades.** The effects of war is the theme of a tale set in Paris after World War II, *Pancakes-Paris*.[165] A wartime widow and her two children, ten-year-old Charles and five-year-old Zézette Dumont, constantly compare their present life to days "BEFORE the war." Two American soldiers help by providing pancakes or crepes for Mardi Gras. Though the family is poor, they share their refreshments with equally poor playmates. For a short time, it's like "BEFORE the war."

**Upper Grades.** James Lincoln Collier and Christopher Collier wrote *My Brother Sam Is Dead* with the theme questioning justification of a war that divides families and punishes innocent victims.[166] In Connecticut during the Revolutionary War, a Tory father orders his sixteen-year-old son, Sam Meeker, an American patriot, to leave home, but another son, twelve-year-old Tim, is confused about loyalty. The antagonists never make up, for the father is captured and dies on a prison ship. Then Tim witnesses the execution of Sam, falsely accused of stealing his own cattle and killed as an example of General Putnam's discipline. Tim is left feeling the senselessness of the controversy.

The futility of war is the theme of William O. Steele's *The Perilous Road*,[167] which takes place in Tennessee during the Civil War. Eleven-year-old Chris Brabson wants to help the Confederacy, though his brother, Jethro, is a Union soldier. Later, Chris faces the reality of death and has difficulty justifying the war. He believes human values are sacrificed as the war becomes almost a sport and thinks, "Brother fighting brother, men that have gone to their duty starving and dying, turned into thieves and murderers by the pale horse of war."[168]

Harold Keith's *Rifles for Watie*,[169] set in Kansas from 1861 until 1865, has war's anguish as its theme. Sixteen-year-old Jeff Bussey is excited as he joins the Union army to preserve the nation and experience adventure. He no longer thinks of war as a lark after he witnesses cruelty, but concludes "that being alive was the biggest miracle in the world."[170] Jeff's anguish is heightened when he falls in love with a Rebel girl, Lucy Washbourne, is captured by Stand Watie's Cherokee Rebel forces, is treated kindly by them, and is nursed by a Rebel family when he is ill. In the end, Jeff is among the few soldiers who see both sides of the Civil War.

Another Civil War story, Irene Hunt's *Across Five Aprils*,[171] spans five years, 1861 until 1865, in southern Illinois. Its theme is war's destruction of a family. To nine-year-old Jethro Creighton, war means "shining horses ridden by men wearing uniforms finer than any suit in the stores of Newton."[172] His view changes after a teacher is seriously wounded, one brother dies in battle, another is a deserter, and yet another fights for the opposition, the South. Because of their rebel son, the family finds their barn burned. When the deserting brother returns home, the family fears prosecution for harboring him. To increase tension, the rebel brother is held captive in a camp where his union brother guards him. Jethro matures early as he experiences these war scars.

The remaining four books show the effect of World War II. Persecution is the theme of Hans Peter Richter's *Friedrich*,[173] set in Germany from 1925 until 1942. The story is about a fourteen-year-old Jewish boy, Friedrich Schneider, and his family—victims of anti-Semitism. Mr. Schneider loses his job because he is Jewish and later becomes a prisoner. More climactic are the deaths of Mrs. Schneider after the Germans beat her and of Friedrich, denied entrance into an air-raid shelter. The book's narrator and his family risk their lives to help the Schneiders, so friendship is a secondary theme.

In contrast with *Friedrich*'s persecution theme, humane treatment is the theme of Johanna Reiss's *The Upstairs Room*,[174] a story about the Netherlands in the 1940s. Two Jewish girls, twelve-year-old Annie de Leeuw and her older sister, Sini, spend two years hiding from Germans in an upstairs room of a kind Dutch farm family, the Oostervelds. Separated from an older sister, Rachel, a mother, now dead, and a father in another city, Annie and Sini are surprisingly positive, despite their fear. Credit goes to the Oostervelds who are anti-Nazi Protestants and willing to jeopardize their lives for Annie and Sini. They begin to feel like one family. This is evident when the war is over, and the two girls say farewell to Opoe, the Granny. She cries, "You're closer to me than my own family. What am I going to do now?"[175]

*The Upstairs Room* is less tragic than Myron Levoy's *Alan and Naomi*,[176] whose theme is trying to rehabilitate a war victim. Levoy tells about Jewish neighbors in New York City in 1944. Twelve-year-old Alan acts brotherly toward Naomi, a young war refugee from France. Ever since she saw her father beaten to death by Nazis, Naomi has been mentally impaired. She constantly tears paper, because her father told her to tear maps before the Nazis found them. Through a Charlie McCarthy doll, Alan helps Naomi. She begins to attend school, but when she witnesses bloodshed in a fight, she reverts back to her previous state, her hands tearing at empty air. Alan feels helpless as he sees the horrifying long-lasting effects of war.

A shameful World War II occurrence is placement of Japanese-Americans in detention camps as described in Florence Cranell Means's *The Moved-Outers*.[177] After the Japanese bomb Pearl Harbor on December 7, 1941, many U.S. citizens of Japanese descent suffer discrimination, the theme of this book. The author focuses on California's Ohara family consisting of Japanese-American parents born in Hawaii and four native-born children: Tad, who later dies serving in the U.S. Navy; Amy, enrolled at Wellesley, who stays East to avoid detention; and seventeen-year-old Kimio (Kim), a high school valedictorian who gets his diploma in the camp where he and his eighteen-year-old sister Sue are detained. In Cordova, California, Mr. Ohara must leave a fine home and sacrifice his nursery and florist business, for he is detained first. Then his wife and children, Sue and Kim, join him in the asphalt-floored Santa Anita, California camp. They wait in long lines to use the one bathhouse for fifteen thousand people. They continue to experience barbed-wire fences and night searchlights at a second camp in Granada, Colorado where people look upon them as "animals being herded into the zoo."[178] Kim particularly protests, "If it was the whole of America that was being evacuated! But this is class discrimination—."[179]

### Deception

**Upper Grades.** Katherine Paterson says in an interview that the theme of her *Master Puppeteer*[180] is "Nothing is as it appears to be."[181] Her suspenseful story is about lonely thirteen-year-old Jiro in eighteenth-century Osaka, Japan. During a famine, he apprentices at a puppet theater where he finds food, friends, and intrigue. Painfully, the curious boy detects the real master puppeteer, the secret Saburo or Robin Hood who robs the rich of rice and gives it to the poor. To serve Saburo, his father deserts his mother, and the hungry woman becomes a night rover until the theater shelters her. She then shows her first warmth to her son and gratitude to his kind puppeteer friend, Kinshi. The mother's true nature is unmasked along with the double identities of the father and Saburo.

### Greed

**Upper Grades.** Scott O'Dell states that greed is the theme of his book, *The King's Fifth*.[182] It consists of reminiscences by a fifteen-year-old mapmaker, Esteban de Sandoval, who served Coronado, the sixteenth-century explorer of the Southwest. One of six men who left Coronado to search for the legendary golden cities of Cíbola, he alone returns. He is imprisoned and tried for defrauding the Spanish king of one-fifth of discovered gold. He casts his treasure aside after seeing fellow conquistadores sacrifice their lives, consumed by lust for gold. At least in prison he is free from such madness.

The author, Scott O'Dell, confides, "If I were a young man, I would get a camera, and I would go out and film all my books, for instance, *The King's Fifth*."[183] He describes the locale in Veracruz, Mexico where Esteban was held, San Juan de Ulúa, as one of the greatest fortresses in the world. It is "a sixteenth-century dungeon with walls that are thirty-feet thick made of coral."[184]

### Assuming Responsibilities

**Middle and Upper Grades.** Beginning to assume responsibilities for others is the theme of Natalie Savage Carlson's *The Family under the*

*Bridge,*[185] set during the post-World War II housing shortage in France. A carefree Paris hobo, Armand Pouly, looks upon children as starling pests until he finds the poor Calcets, unable to pay rent, staying under the very bridge he always occupies in winter. Now that he feels needed, Armand becomes an apartment caretaker. Part of his pay is a dwelling for his three "grandchildren" and their mother.

**Upper Grades.** Vera and Bill Cleaver's *The Whys and Wherefores of Littabelle Lee,*[186] set in the early 1930s, has the theme of assuming responsibility. Orphaned sixteen-year-old Littabelle Lee lives with her grandparents, Paw Paw and Maw Maw, and Aunt Sorrow, an herb doctor, on a mountain farm. In late summer, lightning destroys their house and food supply so the family moves to the barn loft. Then Aunt Sorrow falls off her horse, becomes "not right in the head," and leaves to marry a hermit. It is winter and Littabelle has sole responsibility for her ailing grandparents. She thinks, "I am sick but I cannot be sick. I have got two old, helpless people depending on me . . . ."[187] She becomes a substitute teacher with a meager salary. Finally, she enlists a judge who forces her well-off, city-dwelling aunts and uncle to help support their parents. Feisty Littabelle begins to meet the whys and wherefores of obligations so she can be free to train herself as a teacher.

*Survival*

**Middle and Upper Grades.** Pearl S. Buck's *The Big Wave,*[188] which takes place in Japan, appeared in 1947, probably influenced by a major tidal wave that claimed 1,900 lives that year on the island of Honshu, Japan. The theme of this survival story is choosing life, not death. Kino, who lives on a mountainside farm, and Jiya, who stays in a seashore fishing village, are friends. Before a tidal wave sweeps away the fishing village, Jiya's family sends him to live with Kino so Jiya is the only survivor from the beach. While Jiya grieves for his decreased family, Kino's gentle father adopts him and declares, "He will be happy someday . . . for life is always stronger than death."[189] Sure enough, when Jiya matures, he happily marries Kino's sister and becomes a fisherman, building his home on the old beach. Unlike his father's house, Jiya's home faces the sea, so he can be ready to escape possible danger. Jiya puts family deaths behind him as he builds a new life.

The setting shifts from Japan to Sweden in the days of spinning wheels, part of life described in Nora Burglon's *Children of the Soil.*[190] As the title suggests, this book's theme is an industrious farm family's survival. The man of the household went to sea two years previously, and the woman, Olina, is left to her own devices, aided by a daughter, Nicolina, and a son, Guldklumpen, a second-grade pupil. The children are so poor they are barefoot in warm weather, but when it turns cold, Nicolina wears cast-off shoes, and Mother insists Guldklumpen wear his sister's old shoes to school. For Mother's birthday, the enterprising children earn enough to make her a rice-pudding treat, and on Saint Lucia Day, Nicolina serves Mother coffee in bed. Mother spins and weaves, Nicolina baby-sits, and Guldklumpen sells his wooden carvings—all pooling their money to pay the rent and buy two cows. The children credit a tomte or elf, not their own industry, for their progress.

**Upper Grades.** Scott O'Dell says reverence for life is the theme of his most famous book, *Island of the Blue Dolphins*.[191] It is based upon a newspaper clipping about a Native American who lived in isolation from 1835 until 1853. Karana is his name for the maiden who survives for eighteen years alone on Island of the Blue Dolphins (actually San Nicolás island), seventy-five miles southwest of California. Though a wild dog, Rontu, kills her brother, she befriends it and its pup. Her reverence for life extends to dolphins, sea otters, and birds, which she protects. She states:

> After that summer, . . . I never killed another otter. Nor did I ever kill another cormorant for its beautiful feathers. Nor did I kill seals for their sinews. Nor did I kill another wild dog, nor did I try to spear another sea elephant.[192]

Karana's words reflect the theme and O'Dell's purpose for writing his prizewinner. In an interview, he relates:

> I was damn mad at the hunters who came into our mountains and killed everything that walked or flew. I thought I might write a letter to the newspapers, and I realized right away that's ephemeral. Out of this anger, objectively I sat down right away to do a book that I thought would affect children, particularly girls. I thought that having read the book and someday having children, they would do something about this slaughter of innocent animals. This was why I wrote the book.[193]

Ironically, Karana, the gentle animal guardian, does not survive long after being rescued. Her story ends more tragically than Richard Wormser's *The Black Mustanger*,[194] whose theme is survival despite prejudice. In post-Civil War Texas, thirteen-year-old Dan Riker and his family are shunned, even refused help when the father breaks a leg, all because Mr. Riker is an ex-Union soldier. Dan risks further isolation by working for a cowboy or mustanger who is half Black and half Apache. The boy enhances his chances of survival by learning from the skilled mustanger.

In the South in the latter nineteenth century, prejudice and persecution prevail in William H. Armstrong's *Sounder*.[195] The primary theme is a loving Black family's struggle to survive, despite loss of the father. The father is a sharecropper who compassionately steals food for his hungry family. Before he is imprisoned, his dog, Sounder, is wounded by the sheriff. The father, crippled by a prison-quarry dynamite blast, comes home to die, and loyal Sounder dies soon after his master. The mother sacrifices so her family can survive. Hope stems only from the fact that the son is being educated.

*Sounder*'s author says the story was told to him fifty years ago by a gray-haired Black man, but critics argue it is unlikely a Black man would narrate a tale in which only the dog has a name. Regardless of source, Armstrong may use namelessness as a literary device to symbolize all oppressed Blacks made to feel like nonentities.

Harold Keith names his characters in *The Obstinate Land*,[196] a tale about Oklahoma in 1893 with a struggle-for-survival theme. After his father's death, thirteen-year-old Fritz tries to fulfill his father's dream of owning a farm. Homesteader friends help him endure when the land is hard to till, the weather is unpredictable, and there is hunger, sickness, and poverty.

The rest of the survival stories take place during World War II. In Esther Hautzig's largely autobiographical *The Endless Steppe: Growing Up in Siberia*,[197] the protagonist is eleven-year-old Esther Rudomin from Russian-occupied Vilna, Poland. The government forces her parents, grandmother, and her into exile in Siberia because they are a wealthy Jewish family. The theme, struggle for survival, is extracted from Esther's personal account of five years in a hut on the treeless Siberian plains. Even family togetherness is interrupted when Mr. Rudomin is ordered to front-line service. Ironically, their exile saved them from the German massacre of Polish Jews.

Italy during World War II is the setting for Erik Christian Haugaard's *The Little Fishes*.[198] The theme, fighting to survive, is evident as twelve-year-old Guido, an orphaned beggar, experiences hunger, loneliness, the destruction of Naples, and the deaths of many friends. This philosophy helps him endure poverty: ''It is understanding that makes the difference between us and the animals. And when you understand, you can feel a kind of happiness in the worst misery.''[199] Guido is more principled than many of the war orphans or ''little fishes,'' the inspiration for this commentary: ''These children are not bad. They are not good. They are little fishes—too poor to be either. But they have a right to live.''[200]

The final World War II story is Theodore Taylor's *The Cay*.[201] Its theme is a child, dependent on a Black man for survival, becoming less prejudiced. The narrator, eleven-year-old Phillip Enright, is traveling

from wartime Curaçao, an island near Venezuela, to the United States
on the freighter *Hato* when German submarines torpedo it. After the
shipwreck, Phillip finds himself on a raft steered by an illiterate, aged
Black man. His companion is Timothy, a man with no last name, who
comes from the Virgin Islands. At first, frightened Phillip finds Timothy
"black and ugly."[202] Then the boy becomes blind, the author's device
to cure his protagonist of color consciousness and increase his depen-
dency. Subservient Timothy calls Phillip "young bahss" and acts as if
he is inferior to the blind White child. Timothy dies while protecting the
boy with his own body against a hurricane, and Phillip acknowledges,
"Everyday, I learned of something new that Timothy had done so we
could survive."[203]

John J. O'Connor, a critic for *The New York Times,* says in a review
of *The Cay:* "Perhaps the time has come . . . to find material in which
the black becomes more than a disposable instrument for educating the
white."[204]

## Summary

Themes of historical fiction emerge after grouping 108 examples of prizewinners under twenty-eight headings. Survival, search for identity, determination, and the effect of war are among popular themes. More than
two-thirds of the titles are recommended only for those in upper-elementary grades, and the remainder are largely for those in middle through
upper grades. The majority of the books take place in this country, and
the early 1900s is a favorite time period. There are clusters of books set
in the seventeenth and eighteenth centuries, however, that deal with
colonists' relationships with Native Americans, and there are clusters of
books about the nineteenth century that concern Civil War issues.

Less than half of the books are set abroad, notably in the British
Isles, China, France, Germany, Japan, the Soviet Union, and Sweden.
Here clustering occurs around life in medieval Europe and around the
most popular of all topics, World War II or its aftermath.

Those who have written three prizewinners in the sample of historical
fiction include Meindert DeJong, Sid Fleischman, and Scott O'Dell. The
following have written two cited prizewinners in this category: Margot
Benary-Isbert, Claire Huchet Bishop, Robert Burch, Elizabeth Janet Gray,
Harold Keith, Lois Lenski, Eloise Jarvis McGraw, Katherine Paterson,
Kate Seredy, Mildred Taylor, and Alki Zei. They and others of their
caliber present themes in historical fiction with universal, timeless appeal.

**Notes**

1. "Elizabeth Gray Vining," *Profiles in Literature* (Philadelphia: Temple University, 1969).

2. Masha Kabakow Rudman, *Children's Literature, an Issues Approach* (Lexington, Mass.: Heath, 1976), pp. 256, 261–262.

3. In 1973, *Song of the Trees* won the Council on Interracial Books for Children Award in the African American category.

4. In 1977, *Roll of Thunder, Hear My Cry* won The John Newbery Medal and was a finalist for the National Book Award in the children's-book category. In 1979, it won the Pacific Northwest Library Association Young Reader's Choice Award.

5. Mildred D. Taylor, *Roll of Thunder, Hear My Cry* (New York: Dial, 1976), p. 152.

6. Ibid., p. 276.

7. In 1957, *Blue Mystery* won the Jane Addams Book Award.

8. Margot Benary-Isbert, *Blue Mystery* (New York: Harcourt, 1957), p. 65.

9. In 1962, *Winter Danger* won the Lewis Carroll Shelf Award.

10. William O. Steele, *Winter Danger* (New York: Harcourt, 1954), pp. 28–29.

11. Ibid., p. 29.

12. In 1947, *The Wonderful Year* was a Newbery Honor Book.

13. Nancy Barnes, *The Wonderful Year* (New York: Messner, 1946), p. 150.

14. In 1969, *Journey from Peppermint Street* was the first winner of the National Book Award in the children's-book category.

15. Meindert DeJong, *Journey from Peppermint Street* (New York: Harper, 1968), p. 198.

16. In 1968, *Down the Rivers, Westward Ho!* won the Western Heritage Award in the juvenile-book category.

17. Eric Scott, *Down the Rivers, Westward Ho!* (New York: Meredith, 1967), p. 168.

18. In 1980, *A Gathering of Days: A New England Girl's Journal, 1830–32* won The John Newbery Medal and The American Book Award in the children's-book category.

19. In 1947, *The Avion My Uncle Flew* was a Newbery Honor Book.

20. Cyrus Fisher, *The Avion My Uncle Flew* (New York: Appleton, 1946), pp. 18–19.

21. In 1953, *All-of-a-Kind Family* won the National Jewish Book Award.

22. In 1934, *The Apprentice of Florence* was a Newbery Honor Book.

23. In 1961, *Ten and a Kid* won the National Jewish Book Award.

24. In 1939, *Nino* was a Newbery Honor Book.

25. In 1976, *Dragonwings* was a Newbery Honor Book, won the Carter G. Woodson Book Award, and the International Reading Association Children's Book Award. In 1979, it won the Lewis Carroll Shelf Award.

26. Laurence Yep, *Dragonwings* (New York: Harper, 1975), p. 80.

27. In 1966, *Chancy and the Grand Rascal* won the Commonwealth Club of California Award.

28. In 1956, *The House of Sixty Fathers* won the Child Study Children's Book Committee at Bank Street College Award. In 1957, it was a Newbery Honor Book. In 1958, it won the Woodward Park School Annual Book Award and was put on the International Board on Books for Young People Honor List.

29. In 1977, *The Girl Who Had No Name* won the Golden Kite Award.

30. Berniece Rabe, *The Girl Who Had No Name* (New York: Dutton, 1977), p. 138.

31. In 1973, *North to Freedom* won the Lewis Carroll Shelf Award.

32. In 1973, *Summer of My German Soldier* won the Golden Kite Award and in 1974, was a finalist for the National Book Award in the children's-book category.

33. Bette Greene, *Summer of My German Soldier* (New York: Dial, 1973), p. 14.

34. Ibid., p. 31.

35. Ibid., pp. 113–114.

36. Ibid., p. 116.

37. Ibid., pp. 134–135.

38. Ibid., p. 198.

39. In 1928, *Downright Dencey* was a Newbery Honor Book.

40. Caroline Dale Snedeker, *Downright Dencey* (New York: Doubleday, 1927), p. 44.

41. Ibid., p. 234.

42. In 1944, *Bayou Suzette* won the Ohioana Book Award.

43. Lois Lenski, *Bayou Suzette* (Philadelphia: Lippincott, 1943), p. 10.

44. Ibid., p. 22.

45. Ibid., p. 116.

46. Ibid., p. 134.

47. Ibid., p. 208.

48. Ibid., p. 104.

49. In 1963, *A Boy of Old Prague* won the National Jewish Book Award.

50. Sulamith Ish-Kishor, *A Boy of Old Prague* (New York: Random House, 1963, p. 23.

51. In 1957, *Wolf Brother* won the Western Writers of America Spur Award.

52. In 1970, *Cayuse Courage* won the Western Writers of America Spur Award.

53. Evelyn Sibley Lampman, *Cayuse Courage* (New York: Harcourt, 1970), p. 82.

54. In 1969, *Edge of Two Worlds* won the Western Heritage Award.

55. Weyman Jones, *Edge of Two Worlds* (New York: Dial, 1968), p. 76.

56. In 1941, *Young Mac of Fort Vancouver* was a Newbery Honor Book.

57. Mary Jane Carr, *Young Mac of Fort Vancouver* (New York: Crowell, 1940), p. 237.

58. In 1953, *Moccasin Trail* was a Newbery Honor Book.

59. Eloise Jarvis McGraw, *Moccasin Trail* (New York: Coward, 1952), p. 241.

60. Ibid., p. 247.

61. In 1932, *Calico Bush* was a Newbery Honor Book.

62. Rachel Field, *Calico Bush* (New York: Macmillan, 1966), p. 128.

63. In 1931, *Meggy MacIntosh* was a Newbery Honor Book.

64. Elizabeth Janet Gray, *Meggy MacIntosh* (New York: Viking, 1969), p. 260.

65. In 1945, *The Silver Pencil* was a Newbery Honor Book.

66. Alice Dalgliesh, *The Silver Pencil* (New York: Scribner, 1954), p. 230.

67. In 1981, *Jacob Have I Loved* won The John Newbery Medal.

68. Katherine Paterson, *Jacob Have I Loved* (New York: Crowell, 1980), p. 156.

69. In 1936, *The Good Master* was a Newbery Honor Book.

70. Kate Seredy, *The Good Master* (New York: Viking, 1935), p. 188.

71. In 1940, *The Singing Tree* was a Newbery Honor Book.

72. Kate Seredy, *The Singing Tree* (New York: Viking, 1939), p. 244.

73. In 1969, *Skinny* won the Georgia Children's Book Award.

74. Robert Burch, *Skinny* (New York: Viking, 1964), p. 115.

75. Ibid., p. 115.

76. In 1969, *Constance* was a finalist for the National Book Award in the children's-book category and won the Lewis Carroll Shelf Award.

77. In 1968, *The Taste of Spruce Gum* won the Dorothy Canfield Fisher Children's Book Award.

78. In 1975, *An Old Tale Carved out of Stone,* (translated by Maria Polushkin) won the Mildred L. Batchelder Award.

79. A. Linevski, *An Old Tale Carved out of Stone,* (New York: Crown, 1973), p. 121.

80. In 1963, *By the Great Horn Spoon!* won the Western Writers of America Spur Award. In 1964, it was a notable book of the Southern California Council on Literature for Children and Young People Awards. In 1972, it won the George G. Stone Center for Children's Books Recognition of Merit Award.

81. In 1979, *Humbug Mountain* was a finalist for the National Book Award in the children's-book category.

82. In 1937, *Roller Skates* won The John Newbery Medal and in 1964, the Lewis Carroll Shelf Award.

83. In 1931, *Spice and the Devil's Cave* was a Newbery Honor Book.

84. Agnes Danforth Hewes, *Spice and the Devil's Cave* (New York: Knopf, 1930), p. 46.

85. Ibid., p. 9.

86. In 1975, *I Tell a Lie Every So Often* was a National Book Award in the children's-book category.

87. Bruce Clements. *I Tell a Lie Every So Often* (New York: Farrar, 1974), p. 116.

88. In 1975, *Wings* was a finalist for the National Book Award in the children's-book category.

89. In 1955, *The Wheel on the School* won The John Newbery Medal and in 1963, the Lewis Carroll Shelf Award.

90. Meindert DeJong, *The Wheel on the School* (New York: Harper, 1954), p. 6.

91. In 1955, *Banner in the Sky* was a Newbery Honor Book.

92. In 1962, *The Golden Goblet* was a Newbery Honor Book.

93. Eloise Jarvis McGraw, *The Golden Goblet* (New York: Coward, 1961), p. 247.

94. In 1933, *Young Fu of the Upper Yangtze* won The John Newbery Medal and in 1960, the Lewis Carroll Shelf Award.

95. In 1947, *The Hidden Treasure of Glaston* was a Newbery Honor Book.

96. In 1975, *Bert Breen's Barn* won the Christopher Award for ages twelve and up and in 1976, the National Book Award in the children's-book category.

97. In 1976, *Rifka Grows Up* won the National Jewish Book Award.

98. In 1963, *Annuzza, a Girl of Romania* won the Lewis Carroll Shelf Award.

99. In 1972, *The Tamarack Tree* won the Jane Addams Book Award.

100. Betty Underwood, *The Tamarack Tree* (Boston: Houghton, 1971), p. 179.

101. In 1969, *The Seeing Stick* won the Christopher Award in the children's-book category for ages six to nine.

102. In 1971, *The Witch's Brat* won the Lewis Carroll Shelf Award.

103. Rosemary Sutcliff, *The Witch's Brat* (New York: Walck, 1970), p. 142.

104. In 1977, *The Wheel of King Asoka* won the Christopher Award in the children's-book category.

105. Ashok Davar, *The Wheel of King Asoka* (Chicago: Follett, 1977), p. 39.

106. In 1946, *Strawberry Girl* won The John Newbery Medal.

107. In 1966, *Queenie Peavy* won the Child Study Children's Book Committee at Bank Street College Award. In 1967, it won the Jane Addams Book Award, in 1971, the Georgia Children's Book Award, and in 1974, the George G. Stone Center for Children's Book Recognition of Merit Award.

108. Robert Burch, *Queenie Peavy* (New York: Viking, 1966), p. 17.

109. Ibid., p. 143.

110. In 1962, *The Bronze Bow* won The John Newbery Medal and in 1964, it was put on the International Board of Books for Young People Honor List.

111. Elizabeth George Speare,'' *Profiles in Literature* (Philadelphia: Temple University, 1974).

112. In 1952, *The Defender* was a Newbery Honor Book.

113. In 1976, *The Great Brain Reforms* won the Pacific Northwest Library Association Young Reader's Choice Award.

114. In 1978, *What Are You Up To, William Thomas?* won the North Carolina Division American Association of University Women's Award in Juvenile Literature.

115. John D. Fitzgerald, *The Great Brain Reforms* (New York: Dell, 1973), p. 160.

116. In 1974, *The Treasure Is the Rose* was a finalist for the National Book Award in the children's-book category.

117. Julia Cunningham, *The Treasure Is the Rose* (New York: Pantheon, 1973), p. 93.

118. In 1970, *Otto of the Silver Hand* won the Lewis Carroll Shelf Award.

119. Howard Pyle, *Otto of the Silver Hand* (New York: Scribner, 1954), p. 136.

120. In 1942, *Paddle-to-the-Sea* was a Caldecott Honor Book.

121. Holling Clancy Holling, *Paddle-to-the-Sea* (Boston: Houghton, 1941), no page.

122. In 1972, *Samurai on Gold Hill* won the Commonwealth Club of California Award.

123. In 1976, *To the Green Mountains* was a finalist for the National Book Award in the children's-book category.

124. Eleanor Cameron, *To the Green Mountains* (New York: Dutton, 1975), p. 165.

125. "Eleanor Cameron," *Profiles in Literature* (Philadelphia: Temple University, 1972).

126. In 1935, *Dobry* won The John Newbery Medal.

127. Monica Shannon, *Dobry* (New York: Viking, 1967), p. 148.

128. In 1943, *Adam of the Road* won The John Newbery Medal.

129. "Elizabeth Janet Gray Vining," *Profiles in Literature* (Philadelphia: Temple University, 1969).

130. In 1958, *The Horsecatcher* was a Newbery Honor Book.

131. Mari Sandoz, *The Horsecatcher* (Eau Claire, Wisc.: Hall, 1957), pp. 127–128.

132. Ibid., p. 66.

133. In 1958, *The Great Wheel* was a Newbery Honor Book.

134. Robert Lawson, *The Great Wheel* (New York: Viking, 1957), p. 10.

135. Ibid., p. 10.

136. In 1922, *The Great Quest* was a Newbery Honor Book.

137. Charles Boardman Hawes, *The Great Quest* (Boston: Little, Brown, 1920), p. 59.

138. Ibid., p. 195.

139. Ibid., p. 248.

140. In 1974, *The Slave Dancer* won The John Newbery Medal.

141. In 1973, *Long Journey Home: Stories from Black History* was a finalist for the National Book Award in the children's-book category.

142. Julius Lester, *Long Journey Home: Stories from Black History* (New York: Dial, 1972), pp. 109–110.

143. In 1970 *Wildcat under Glass* (translated by Edward Fenton) won the Mildred L. Batchelder Award.

144. Alki Zei, *Wildcat under Glass* (New York: Holt, 1968), p. 12.

145. In 1974, *Petro's War* (translated by Edward Fenton) won the Mildred L. Batchelder Award.

146. In 1957, *Black Fox of Lorne* was a Newbery Honor Book.

147. In 1973, *Uncle Misha's Partisans* won the National Jewish Book Award.

148. Yuri Suhl, *Uncle Misha's Partisans* (New York: Four Winds, 1973), p. 41.

149. In 1942, *The Matchlock Gun* won The John Newbery Medal.

150. Walter D. Edmonds, *The Matchlock Gun* (New York: Dodd, 1941), p. 39.

151. Ibid., p. 17.

152. In 1952, *Twenty and Ten* won the Child Study Children's Book Committee at Bank Street College Award.

153. In 1953, *Red Sails to Capri* was a Newbery Honor Book.

154. Ann Weil, *Red Sails to Capri* (New York: Viking, 1952), p. 71.

155. In 1971, *Sing Down the Moon* won a Newbery Honor Book.

156. "Scott O'Dell," *Profiles in Literature* (Philadelphia: Temple University, 1976).

157. Robinson Jeffers, *Medea, Freely Adapted from the Medea of Euripides* (New York: Samuel French, 1948), p. 22.

158. In 1978, *Hew Against the Grain* was a finalist for the National Book Award in the children's-book category.

159. In 1976, *The Ark* won the Lewis Carroll Shelf Award.

160. Margot Benary-Isbert, *The Ark* (New York: Harcourt, 1953), p. 119.

161. In 1945, *Snow Treasure* won the Pacific Northwest Library Association Young Reader's Choice Award.

162. In 1929, *The Trumpeter of Krakow* won The John Newbery Medal.

163. In 1962, *The Emperor and the Drummer Boy,* illustrated by Nicholas Sidjakov, was a *New York Times* Choice of Best Illustrated Children's Book of the Year.

164. Ruth Robbins, *The Emperor and the Drummer Boy* (Berkeley: Parnassus, 1962), p. 30.

165. In 1948, *Pancakes-Paris* was a Newbery Honor Book.

166. In 1975, *My Brother Sam Is Dead* was a Newbery Honor Book and a finalist for the National Book Award in the children's-book category.

167. In 1958, *The Perilous Road* won the Jane Addams Book Award and in 1959 was a Newbery Honor Book.

168. William O. Steele, *The Perilous Road* (New York: Harcourt, 1958), p. 23.

169. In 1958, *Rifles for Watie* won The John Newbery Medal.

170. Harold Keith, *Rifles for Watie* (New York: Crowell, 1957), p. 139.

171. In 1965, *Across Five Aprils* was a Newbery Honor Book and in 1966, it won the Lewis Carroll Shelf Award.

172. Irene Hunt, *Across Five Aprils* (Chicago: Follett, 1964), p. 17.

173. In 1971, *Friedrich* won the Woodward Park School Annual Book Award and, in 1972, this book (translated by Edite Kroll) won the Mildred L. Batchelder Award.

174. In 1972, *The Upstairs Room* won the National Jewish Book Award and in 1973, was a Newbery Honor Book.

175. Johanna Reiss, *The Upstairs Room* (New York: Crowell, 1972), p. 195.

176. In 1978, *Alan and Naomi* won the Woodward Park School Annual Book Award.

177. In 1945, *The Moved-Outers* won the Child Study Children's Book Committee at Bank Street College Award, and in 1946, it was a Newbery Honor Book.

178. Florence Crannell Means, *The Moved-Outers* (Boston: Houghton, 1945), p. 89.

179. Ibid., p. 64.

180. In 1977, *The Master Puppeteer* won the National Book Award in the children's-book category.

181. "Katherine Paterson," *Profiles in Literature* (Philadelphia: Temple University, 1979).

182. In 1967, *The King's Fifth* was a Newbery Honor Book.

183. "Scott O'Dell," *Profiles in Literature* (Philadelphia: Temple University, 1976).

184. Ibid.

185. In 1959, *The Family under the Bridge* was a Newbery Honor Book.

186. In 1974, *The Whys and Wherefores of Littabelle Lee* was a finalist for the National Book Award in the children's-book category.

187. Vera and Bill Cleaver, *The Whys and Wherefores of Littabelle Lee* (New York: Atheneum, 1973), p. 113.

188. In 1948, *The Big Wave* won the Child Study Children's Book Committee at Bank Street College Award.

189. Pearl S. Buck, *The Big Wave* (New York: Day, 1947), p. 39.

190. In 1933, *Children of the Soil* was a Newbery Honor Book.

191. In 1961, *Island of the Blue Dolphins* won The John Newbery Medal and the Lewis Carroll Shelf Award. In 1961, it was also a notable book of the Southern California Council on Literature for Children and Young People Award. In 1962, it was put on the International Board on Books for Young People Honor List. In 1963, it won the William Allen White Children's Book Award and in 1964, the Nene Award.

192. Scott O'Dell, *Island of the Blue Dolphins* (Boston: Houghton, 1960), p. 156.

193. "Scott O'Dell," *Profiles in Literature* (Philadelphia: Temple University, 1976).

194. In 1971, *The Black Mustanger* won the Western Writers of America Spur Award and in 1972, the Western Heritage Award in the juvenile-book category.

195. In 1970, *Sounder* won The John Newbery Medal and the Lewis Carroll Shelf Award. In 1972, it won the Mark Twain Award and in 1973, the Nene Award.

196. In 1979, *The Obstinate Land* won the Western Heritage Award in the juvenile-book category.

197. In 1969, *The Endless Steppe: Growing Up in Siberia* was a finalist for the National Book Award in the children's-book category and won the Jane Addams Book Award. In 1971, it won the Lewis Carroll Shelf Award.

198. In 1967, *The Little Fishes* won the *Boston Globe-Horn Book* Award and in 1968, the Jane Addams Book Award.

199. Erik Christian Haugaard, *The Little Fishes* (Boston: Houghton, 1967), p. 213.

200. Ibid., p. 195.

201. In 1969, *The Cay* won the Commonwealth Club of California Award. In 1970, it won the Lewis Carroll Shelf Award, the Woodward Park School Annual Book Award, the Jane Addams Book Award, and it was a notable book of the Southern California Council on Literature for Children and Young People Award. In 1974, Bertha Jenkinson, chairperson of the Jane Addams selection committee, said, "I feel that the choice of *The Cay* . . . for our award in 1970 was a mistake." In 1975, Theodore Taylor returned his Jane Addams certificate.

202. Theodore Taylor, *The Cay* (New York: Doubleday, 1969), p. 33.

203. Ibid., p. 103.

204. *Interracial Books for Children* V, No. 6 (1974), p. 9.

## References of Prizewinning Historical Fiction in Time Sequence within Historical Periods

*(Estimated Reading Grade Level in Parentheses)*

*New World Setting*

**1500s:**

O'Dell, Scott. *The King's Fifth*. Illustrated by Samuel Bryant. Boston: Houghton, 1966 (6–9).

**1600s:**
Clapp, Patricia. *Constance*. New York: Lothrop, 1968 (6–9).

**1700s:**
Field, Rachel. *Calico Bush*. Illustrated by Allen Lewis. New York: Macmillan, 1966 (6–9).

Edmonds, Walter D. *The Matchlock Gun*. Illustrated by Paul Lantz. New York: Dodd, 1941 (3–5).

Gray, Elizabeth Janet. *Meggy MacIntosh*. Illustrated by Marguerite deAngeli. New York: Viking, 1969 (6–9).

Collier, James Lincoln and Christopher. *My Brother Sam Is Dead*. New York: Four Winds, 1974 (6–9).

Scott, Eric. *Down the Rivers, Westward Ho!* New York: Meredith, 1967 (5–7).

Steele, William O. *Winter Danger*. Illustrated by Paul Galdone. New York: Harcourt, 1954 (5–7).

**1800s:**
Snedeker, Caroline Dale. *Downright Dencey*. Illustrated by Maginel Wright Barney. New York: Doubleday, 1927 (4–6).

Carr, Mary Jane. *Young Mac of Fort Vancouver*. Illustrated by Richard Holberg. New York: Crowell, 1940 (5–9).

Jones, Weyman. *Edge of Two Worlds*. Illustrated by J.C. Kocsis. New York: Dial, 1968 (5–8).

Sandoz, Mari. *The Horsecatcher*. Eau Claire, Wisc.: Hall, 1957 (5–7).

Blos, Joan W. *A Gathering of Days: A New England Girl's Journal 1830–32*. New York: Scribner, 1979 (5–7).

Kjelgaard, Jim. *Wolf Brother*. Chippewa Falls, Wisc.: Hale, 1957 (4–8).

Underwood, Betty. *The Tamarack Tree*. Illustrated by Bea Holmes. Boston: Houghton, 1971 (6–9).

O'Dell, Scott. *Island of the Blue Dolphins*. Boston: Houghton, 1967 (6–9).

Cummings, Betty Sue. *Hew Against the Grain*. New York: Atheneum, 1977 (6–9).

Fox, Paula. *The Slave Dancer*. Illustrated by Eros Keith. Scarsdale, N.Y.: Bradbury, 1974 (6–9).

Clements, Bruce. *I Tell a Lie Every So Often*. New York: Farrar, 1974 (5–8).

Lampman, Evelyn Sibley. *Cayuse Courage*. New York: Harcourt, 1970 (5–8).

Fleischman, Sid. *By the Great Horn Spoon!* Illustrated by Eric Von Schmidt. Boston: Little, Brown, 1963 (4–6).

McGraw, Eloise Jarvis. *Moccasin Trail.* New York: Coward, 1952 (6–9).

Lester, Julius. *Long Journey Home: Stories from Black History.* New York: Dial, 1972 (6–8).

O'Dell, Scott. *Sing Down the Moon.* Boston: Houghton, 1970 (5–8).

Hunt, Irene. *Across Five Aprils.* Chicago: Follett, 1964 (6–8).

Keith, Harold. *Rifles for Watie.* New York: Crowell, 1957 (6–9).

Steele, William O. *The Perilous Road.* Illustrated by Paul Galdone. New York: Harcourt, 1958 (5–7).

Fleischman, Sid. *Chancy and the Grand Rascal.* Illustrated by Eric Von Schmidt. Boston: Little, Brown, 1966 (5–7).

Uchida, Yoshiko. *Samurai on Gold Hill.* Illustrated by Ati Forberg. New York: Scribner, 1972 (5–8).

Wormser, Richard. *The Black Mustanger.* Illustrated by Don Bolognese. New York: Morrow, 1971 (5–9).

Fleischman, Sid. *Humbug Mountain.* Illustrated by Eric Von Schmidt. Boston: Little, Brown, 1978 (4–6).

Armstrong, William H. *Sounder.* Illustrated by James Barkley. New York: Harper, 1969 (6–9).

Edmonds, Walter D. *Bert Breen's Barn.* Boston: Little, Brown, 1975 (6–9).

Lenski, Lois. *Bayou Suzette.* Philadelphia: Lippincott, 1943 (4–6).

Keith, Harold. *The Obstinate Land.* New York: Crowell, 1977 (6–8).

Lawson, Robert. *The Great Wheel.* New York: Viking, 1957 (5–7).

Sawyer, Ruth. *Roller Skates.* Illustrated by Valenti Angelo. New York: Viking, 1964 (4–6).

Fitzgerald, John D. *The Great Brain Reforms.* Illustrated by Mercer Mayer. New York: Dell, 1973 (5–8).

Jackson, Jacqueline. *The Taste of Spruce Gum.* Boston: Little, Brown, 1966 (5–7).

Yep, Laurence. *Dragonwings.* New York: Harper, 1975 (5–9).

Dalgliesh, Alice. *The Silver Pencil.* Illustrated by Katherine Milhous. New York: Scribner, 1944 (5–8).

Taylor, Sydney. *All-of-a-kind Family.* Illustrated by Helen John. Chicago: Follett, 1951 (3–6).

Lenski, Lois. *Strawberry Girl.* Philadelphia: Lippincott, 1973 (4–6).

Barnes, Nancy. *The Wonderful Year.* Illustrated by Kate Seredy. New York: Messner, 1968 (4–7).

Cameron, Eleanor. *To the Green Mountains*. New York: Dutton, 1975 (5–8).

Richard, Adrienne. *Wings*. Boston: Little, Brown, 1974 (5–6). Westminster, 1977 (6–9).

Newton, Suzanne. *What Are You Up To, William Thomas?* Philadelphia:

Taylor, Mildred D. *Song of the Trees*. New York: Dial, 1975 (3–5).

———. *Roll of Thunder, Hear My Cry*. New York: Dial, 1976 (6–8).

Rabe, Berniece. *The Girl Who Had No Name*. New York: Dutton, 1977 (6–8).

Cleaver, Vera and Bill. *The Whys and Wherefores of Littabelle Lee*. New York: Atheneum, 1973 (7 and up).

Burch, Robert. *Queenie Peavy*. New York: Viking, 1966 (4–7).

———. *Skinny*. New York: Viking, 1964 (4–7).

Holling, Clancy Holling. *Paddle-to-the-Sea*. Boston: Houghton, 1941 (3–6).

Paterson, Katherine. *Jacob Have I Loved*. New York: Crowell, 1980 (5–8).

Means, Florence Cranell. *The Moved-Outers*. Illustrated by Helen Blair. Boston: Houghton, 1945 (7 and up).

Greene, Bette. *Summer of My German Soldier*. New York: Dial, 1973 (6–9).

Taylor, Theodore. *The Cay*. New York: Doubleday, 1969 (6–9).

Levoy, Myron. *Alan and Naomi*. New York: Harper, 1977 (6–8).


*Old World Setting*


**Prehistoric Period:**

Livevski, A. *An Old Tale Carved Out of Stone*. New York: Crown, 1973 (6–9).


**Ancient Period:**

Davar, Ashod. *The Wheel of King Asoka*. Chicago: Follett, 1977 (2–4).

McGraw, Eloise Jarvis. *The Golden Goblet*. New York: Coward, 1961 (6–9).

Speare, Elizabeth George. *The Bronze Bow*. Boston: Houghton, 1961 (6–9).

Yolen, Jane. *The Seeing Stick*. Illustrated by Remy Charlip and Demetra Maraslis. New York: Crowell, 1977 (K–3).


**Medieval Period:**

deAngeli, Marguerite. *Black Fox of Lorne*. New York: Doubleday, 1956 (6–9).

the devil's property. He thinks, "They were Jews and accursed and the devil must have their black souls when they died."[50] Non-Jewish children, like Tomás, throw stones at ghetto Jews and place bets on their accuracy. Tomás changes after becoming bond servant to a Jewish master who helps the lad's starving family. He returns from a visit home to see the ghetto aflame and to mourn for the kind master and his daughter, victims of a pogrom or massacre. This book traces one boy's enlightenment.

*Search for Identity*

**Middle and Upper Grades.** The theme of the following five books is the protagonist's search for identity when torn between Native American and White cultures. In Jim Kjelgaard's *Wolf Brother,*[51] a sixteen-year-old Apache orphan, Jonathan, learns White culture in a nineteenth-century Arizona Jesuit school run by Father Harvey. He accepts the Jesuit's advice to return to the Apaches as a future leader, but finds them apathetic as a result of submission to Whites. He is confused by Whites who helped him learn, yet cause his people despair. After fighting with a cavalry sergeant, Jonathan flees and joins an ambushing band of Apaches under Cross Face who, like Father Harvey, sees the youth as a potential leader. He changes his name to Wolf Brother before Whites capture and exile him. He escapes and returns for a second time to his Apache brothers, helping them become ranchers, leaving the reservation designated by Whites. The primary theme is emphasized when he recognizes his bi-cultural background and finally changes his name to Jonathan Wolf.

**Upper Grades.** Like Jonathan Wolf, Samuel Little-Pony searches for identity, though confused by Cayuse and White influences, in Evelyn Sibley Lampman's *Cayuse Courage.*[52] In Oregon in 1848, he wants to be a great Cayuse hunter and warrior, but his dream is shattered when his arm is poisoned from a White man's abandoned trap. He goes to the mission of Boston Doctor, a White man, where he suffers amputation and learns English. He obeys Whites when there is a conflict with the Cayuse and, though torn, accepts the life of Whites until told to leave their mission. He is bitter because "They had taken everything from him, his arm, his people and now they were telling him to go."[53] He returns to the Cayuse, but when he overhears massacre plans, he warns mission residents, another example of ambivalence. The book ends with Samuel Little-Pony once more living among Whites as an interpreter.

Weyman Jones tells about life in Texas in 1827, and his theme is the same as his title, *Edge of Two Worlds.*[54] Fifteen-year-old Calvin

Sutcliff, Rosemary. *The Witch's Brat*. Illustrated by Richard Lebenson. New York: Walck, 1970 (6–9).

Gray, Elizabeth Janet. *Adam of the Road*. Illustrated by Robert Lawson. New York: Viking, 1964 (6–9).

Kelly, Eric P. *The Trumpeter of Krakow*. Illustrated by Janina Domanska. New York: Macmillan, 1966 (5–8).

Jewett, Eleanore M. *The Hidden Treasure of Glaston*. Illustrated by Frederick T. Chapman. New York: Viking, 1946 (6–9).

Pyle, Howard. *Otto of the Silver Hand*. New York: Scribner, 1954 (6–9).

Cunningham, Julia. *The Treasure Is the Rose*. Illustrated by Judy Graese. New York: Pantheon, 1973 (5–9).

Hewes, Agnes Danforth. *Spice and the Devil's Cave*. Illustrated by Lynd Ward. New York: Knopf, 1930 (8–12).

Kyle, Anne D. *The Apprentice of Florence*. Illustrated by Erick Berry. Boston: Houghton, 1933 (8–12).

## 1500s:

Ish-Kishor, Sulamith. *A Boy of Old Prague*. Illustrated by Ben Shahn. New York: Random House, 1963 (5–8).

## 1700s:

Paterson, Katherine. *The Master Puppeteer*. Illustrated by Haru Wells. New York: Crowell, 1976 (6–9).

## 1800s:

Robbins, Ruth. *The Emperor and the Drummer Boy*. Berkeley, Calif.: Parnassus, 1962 (3–6).

Hawes, Charles Boardman. *The Great Quest*. Illustrated by George Varian. Boston: Little, Brown, 1920 (8–12).

Weil, Ann. *Red Sails to Capri*. Illustrated by C.B. Falls. New York: Viking, 1952 (5–7).

Benary-Isbert, Margot. *Blue Mystery*. Translated by Clara and Richard Winston. Illustrated by Enrico Arno. New York: Harcourt, 1957 (4–6).

Kalashnikoff, Nicholas. *The Defender*. Illustrated by Claire and George Louden, Jr. New York: Scribner, 1951 (5–8).

Shannon, Monica. *Dobry*. Illustrated by Atanas Katchamakoff. New York: Viking, 1967 (5–8).

Burglon, Nora. *Children of the Soil*. Illustrated by E. Parin D'Aulaire. New York: Doubleday, 1931 (4–6).

Weilerstein, Sadie Rose. *Ten and a Kid*. New York: Doubleday, 1961 (5–7).

Ullman, James Ramsey. *Banner in the Sky*. Philadelphia: Lippincott, 1967 (6–9).

**1900s:**

Angelo, Valenti. *Nino*. New York: Viking, 1938 (5–9).

Burstein, Chaya. *Rifka Grows Up*. New York: Bonim, 1976 (5–7).

DeJong, Meindert. *Journey from Peppermint Street*. Illustrated by Emily McCully. New York: Harper, 1968 (4–7).

———. *The Wheel on the School*. Illustrated by Maurice Sendak. New York: Harper, 1954 (4–7).

Seuberlich, Hertha. *Annuzza, a Girl of Romania*. Illustrated by Gerhard Pallasch. Chicago: Rand McNally, 1960 (6–9).

Lewis, Elizabeth Foreman. *Young Fu of the Upper Yangtze*. Illustrated by Kurt Wiese. New York: Holt, 1965 (5–8).

Seredy, Kate. *The Good Master*. New York: Viking, 1963 (4–6).

———. *The Singing Tree*. New York: Viking, 1939 (4–6).

Zei, Alki. *Wildcat under Glass*. Translated by Edward Fenton. New York: Holt, 1968 (5–7).

Bishop, Claire Huchet. *Twenty and Ten*. Illustrated by William Pène du Bois. New York: Viking, 1952 (4–6).

DeJong, Meindert. *The House of Sixty Fathers*. Illustrated by Maurice Sendak. New York: Harper, 1956 (6–9).

Haugaard, Erik Christian. *The Little Fishes*. Illustrated by Milton Johnson. Boston: Houghton, 1967 (6–8).

Fisher, Cyrus. *The Avion My Uncle Flew*. Illustrated by Richard Floethe. New York: Appleton, 1946 (5–8).

Hautzig, Esther. *The Endless Steppe: Growing Up in Siberia*. New York: Crowell, 1968 (6–9).

Holm, Anne. *North to Freedom*. New York: Harcourt, 1963 (6–8).

McSwigan, Marie. *Snow Treasure*. Illustrated by Mary Reardon. New York: Dutton, 1942 (4–7).

Reiss, Johanna. *The Upstairs Room*. New York: Crowell, 1972 (5–8).

Richter, Hans Peter. *Friedrich*. Translated by Edite Kroll. New York: Holt, 1970 (6–8).

Suhl, Yuri. *Uncle Misha's Partisans*. New York: Four Winds, 1973 (5–8).

Zei, Alki. *Petro's War*. Translated by Edward Fenton. New York: Dutton, 1972 (5–7).

Benary-Isbert, Margot. *The Ark*. Translated by Clara and Richard Winston. New York: Harcourt, 1953 (5–9).

Bishop, Claire Huchet. *Pancakes-Paris*. Illustrated by Georges Schreiber. New York: Viking, 1963 (4–6).

Buck, Pearl S. *The Big Wave*. Illustrated by Hiroshige and Hokusai. New York: Day, 1947 (4–8).

Carlson, Natalie Savage. *The Family under the Bridge*. Illustrated by Garth Williams. New York: Harper, 1958 (3–5).

# 11 Realistic Animal Stories

*My brother Kevin's in sixth grade, and so is our neighbor Lucy. They're always arguing. She thinks* The Black Stallion *beats* Old Yeller, *but he won't listen. They're both wrong;* Shadrach's *best. That book's so great I named my rabbit Shadrach.*　　　　　　　　　—Kelly, aged seven

## Perspective and Standards

*Shadrach, The Black Stallion,* and *Old Yeller* are all realistic animal stories. Meindert DeJong's *Shadrach* is historical and set in the Netherlands while the other two are contemporary U.S. stories. Themes of these tales may revolve around maturing human as well as animal characters. The themes may depict animal loyalty, intelligence, and courage, either in a domestic or wild setting. Such stories are popular since children identify with a dependent pet, frequently considered a member of the family.

Walter Farley's *The Black Stallion* is a series book. Many realistic animal stories lend themselves to series presentation, like Beverly Cleary's books about Ribsy.

In Fred Gipson's *Old Yeller* and Marjorie Kinnan Rawlings's *The Yearling,* the protagonist is forced to kill a beloved pet for the good of the household. This painful act symbolizes the protagonist's assumption of responsibility and approaching manhood. However, readers may question if manhood requires being hardened.

In contrast with animal fantasy, which may feature animals as human beings, realistic tales show animals as animals and should always be accurate. Such serious literature may be useful in science classes. From Marguerite Henry's horse stories, for example, the characteristics of different breeds may be determined, facilitated by Wesley Dennis's illustrations. Each of her stories has a distinct, appropriate theme.

## Themes of Prizewinning Realistic Animal Stories Grouped under These Topics

### Life Revolving around Nature

**Middle Grades.** In Marguerite Henry's *Sea Star: Orphan of Chincoteague,*[1] the theme is life revolving around ponies. Paul and Maureen

Beebe, a brother and sister, care for orphaned Sea Star, whose mother's carcass is washed ashore from a neighboring island. They arrange for her to be nursed by a wounded mare.

**Middle and Upper Grades.** Preserving nature is the theme of Rutherford Montgomery's *Kildee House*.[2] Jerome Kildee's home has a hinged door, so raccoons and skunks, who live in a redwood tree next door, can enter and exit as part of his family without being domesticated. When a hunter, Donald Roger, threatens the animals, Kildee wins him over with the help of young Emmy Lou and almost creates a wildlife preserve on Kildee Mountain.

**Upper Grades.** Identification with animals is the main idea of Allan W. Eckert's *Incident at Hawk's Hill*,[3] which describes an incident in Canada in the 1870s. Six-year-old Ben is described as follows:

> He is shy and quiet around adults and even his family, rarely communicating with them, yet he feels a sense of belonging when he is with animals. Somehow these creatures sense his loneliness, his helplessness, his total lack of threat to them.[4]

Ben is lost for two months in the wilderness and is adopted by a female badger. He eats, plays, and fights like a badger. When he is reunited with his family at their Hawk's Hill farm, the badger follows him, and they sense that he has special gifts.

*Survival*

**Primary and Middle Grades.** Survival through seclusion is the theme of Glen Rounds's *Wild Horses of the Red Desert*.[5] In barren South Dakota Badlands, wild horses avoid hunters who ship horse meat to pet-food factories. "The first sight of distant riders brings a shrill alarm whinny from the mare on lookout, and the entire band quickly bunches for flight."[6] These horses consider men, mountain lions, and wolves to be enemies. They also learn to survive arid summers when waterholes are dry.

**Middle and Upper Grades.** Humanity that makes animal survival possible is the theme of Charlotte Baker's *Cockleburr Quarters*.[7] A low-rent district, Cockleburr Quarters, is the home of crippled, flea-infested Tory, a stray dog, and her eight puppies. She attaches herself to two kind Black males, Dolph Randall, a lad, and Jake Brown, a man, both of whom take odd jobs to support her and other homeless animals. Though poor themselves, the two raise money to spay cats and dogs, buy medicine to arrest mange, and provide food for animals. Jake confides, "I'd druther shoot them dogs than to let them be abused."[8]

## Helping the Disabled

**Middle and Upper Grades.** Glen Rounds creates stories about blind horses in the South Dakota Badlands. The theme of his first book, *The Blind Colt*,[9] is overcoming a disability. Compensating for being sightless, the colt develops keen smell and hearing which help him detect rattlesnakes and wolves. When snow chases him inside a ranch, a ten-year-old boy, Whitey, persuades his Uncle Torwal to accept the colt in the ranch herd.

The blind pony is less lonely in Rounds's second story, *Stolen Pony*,[10] than in his first tale, because his constant companion is a ranch dog. Trusting reliance, the primary theme, is reflected in the pony's dependence on the dog. Horse thieves steal the spotted pony and release him in the Badlands when they discover his disability, but the dog, who followed the thieves' van, guides his friend home. On the long journey, they face wild horses, a prairie fire, and the challenge of finding food.

## Adapting

**Middle and Upper Grades.** Animals need to adapt to new circumstances, as does the cat in Beverly Cleary's *Socks*.[11] Rivalry is the theme of this story about a pet cat who previously got a couple's total attention but now learns part of their love will go to their baby, Charles William Bricker. The cat's added discovery is that a baby can be fun.

## Maturing

**Middle and Upper Grades.** Maturing is the theme of Betsy Byars's *The Midnight Fox*,[12] which describes the development of nine-year-old Tom during a summer on his aunt's and uncle's farm. Though he previously was not interested in animals, he feels a sense of responsibility for a midnight fox and prevents his uncle from shooting it.

Similarly, in Elizabeth Yates's *Mountain Born* love of a lamb is a catalyst for early maturation,[13] the book's theme. When seven-year-old Peter lovingly cares for his tiny black lamb on the mountain farm, he becomes a responsible person, and at the same time, the lamb matures into a sheep called Biddy, leader of the flock. Peter announces his intention in a snowstorm to search for Biddy's own lost lamb, and his father now sees him "as a little boy no longer but as a young man whose ideas had to be reckoned with."[14] Aging Biddy dies, but Peter remembers her while touching his coat made of her wool and seeing her ewe offspring.

*Freedom*

**Middle and Upper Grades.** The theme of Helga Sandburg's *Joel and the Wild Goose* is memories of a freed bird replacing loneliness.[15] Young Joel is happy when he mends a goose's broken wing, but at first, he tries to prevent the bird's flight. Then he grants the goose freedom, realizing that memories of their friendship will keep him from feeling lonely again.

Another story about an assisted wild fowl is Selina Chonz's *Florina and the Wild Bird*.[16] Its theme is a freed bird's reward for human kindness. This anthropomorphic notion, giving the bird human traits, weakens the work. After Florina saves the life of a wild bird and cares for it, she reluctantly frees it. The bird leaves a crystal stone in his empty nest. "That was Florina's reward for her kindness. Florina prized her treasure."[17]

**Upper Grades.** Freedom quest is the theme of Mel Ellis's *Flight of the White Wolf,*[18] which shows how fifteen-year-old Russ tries to lead his white wolf, Gray, to freedom in the northern Wisconsin mountains. Gray instinctively killed a dog so a posse is after him. Challenged by starvation and chased by men with hounds, Russ and Gray find a mountain-wolf pack. Gray at last has freedom when he joins the pack.

*Wish Fulfillment*

**Primary and Middle Grades.** Alice Dalgliesh's *The Bears on Hemlock Mountain* has a wish-fulfillment theme.[19] It is about eight-year-old Jonathan, who travels across Hemlock Mountain to bring home an iron pot and wishes en route, "I would like to see a bear. I would rather see a bear than anything in the world."[20] Jonathan does see bears while completing his mission.

**Middle and Upper Grades.** Wish fulfillment is the theme of Byrd Baylor's *Hawk, I'm Your Brother,*[21] which features Rudy Soto, a young boy who wants to fly. He cages a hawk, hoping the bird's flying powers will be transferred to his own body. When Rudy realizes the hawk's frustration, he grants it freedom and, in his own mind, has the vicarious experience of flight.

Wish fulfillment sparked by love is the theme of Walt Morey's *Kavik the Wolf Dog*.[22] Kavik, which means wolverine to the Eskimos, is part malamute and part wolf. After he wins the Alaskan Sled Dog Derby, a new owner buys him, but he is sent aboard a plane that crashes in an Alaskan blizzard. The injured dog is trapped in freezing weather until fifteen-year-old Andy Evans rescues him, healing him with love. Once recovered, Kavik is taken to Washington by his owner. Separated by two thousand miles from Andy, Kavik breaks his bonds and travels over mountains and glaciers, finally returning to the Alaskan boy he loves.

**Upper Grades.** Friends fulfilling a wish, one similar to Kavik's, is the theme of Sheila Burnford's *The Incredible Journey*.[23] When the owner of three pets goes overseas, he leaves them with a trusted person, but the three animals travel over 250 miles to rejoin their master upon his return to Canada. Tested by starvation and wilderness, Tao, a Siamese cat, and Bodger, an old bull terrier, are led home by a young yellow Labrador retriever, Luath. The three, who form a lasting friendship, lament when the cat temporarily disappears. After her return, this is how they feel:

> It would have been impossible to find three more contented animals that night. The old dog had his beloved cat, warm and purring between his paws again, and he snored in deep contentment.[24]

It is an inseparable, worn-out trio that realizes its wish.

Wish fulfillment is also the theme of Marguerite Henry's *Black Gold*,[25] which takes place in Oklahoma in 1909. Two men have one desperate wish: to win the Kentucky Derby. Black Gold, the foal of thoroughbreds, answers their need. His owner, Al Hoot, dies before the Derby, but his wife keeps his dream alive. The other dreamer is young Jaydee, who rides Black Gold to Derby victory.

*Misunderstanding*

**Middle and Upper Grades.** An unresolved misunderstanding is the theme of Glen Rounds's *The Day the Circus Came to Lone Tree*.[26] When those in Lone Tree, a cow town, host their first circus, they misunderstand the lady-lion-tamer's act. A lion refuses to obey commands, part of the act, but the audience thinks the lady is in trouble and rushes into the ring with pistols and lariats. The frightened circus animals escape to the hills.

After finding them, the circus company promises never to return to Lone Tree.

### Determination

**Middle and Upper Grades.** Marguerite Henry's *Mustang: Wild Spirit of the West*[27] has the theme of determination to preserve the mustang. Wild Horse Annie initiates a protective campaign when she learns that mustangs on the Nevada range are slaughtered for pet food. After she speaks in Washington, D.C., congressmen pass a law to preserve the vanishing species.

**Upper Grades.** Persevering to change a workhorse into a thoroughbred is the theme of Marguerite Henry's *Justin Morgan Had a Horse*,[28] set in Vermont in the early 1800s. A schoolmaster, Justin Morgan, receives a weak colt. When the master dies, the colt is named for him. One of Morgan's students, Joel, gentles the horse, buys him at an auction, and with determination, transforms him into a racer. In the foreword, the author says this is the heritage of today's Morgan horses.

### Fixing Priorities

**Upper Grades.** Robert Burch's *Doodle and the Go-Cart* focuses on fixing priorities as its theme.[29] Twelve-year-old Danny (Doodle) Rounds is so anxious to own a two-hundred-dollar go-cart, he tries to earn the money by transporting passengers on his pet mule, Addie Flowers, making and selling scarecrows, trapping beavers and muskrats, and becoming a fishing guide. When he is fifty dollars short of his goal, a buyer wants to pay more than that amount for his pet mule, but he is too fond of Addie Flowers to sell her. His sentiments are as follows:

> He could see himself riding around it [the pasture] on a go-cart, his go-cart, till he came to the place Addie would be standing. When he tried to imagine himself in the go-cart without her there, the picture blurred and then disappeared altogether.[30]

Doodle keeps Addie but continues to raise money for a go-cart.

### Need for Acceptance

**Middle and Upper Grades.** A stray dog's need for acceptance is the theme of Meindert DeJong's *Along Came a Dog*.[31] The dog becomes the protector of a toeless red hen, farmhand Joe's pet, and wants to become part of Joe's household but is always chased away. When Joe finally does give him a home, the hen mothers the dog, for she has just begun to lay eggs, and that gives her an air of authority. "Now the little hen did not belong to him merely to guard and protect—she was his boss, he belonged to her. He belonged to someone!"[32]

**Upper Grades.** Acceptance of a stepfather is the theme of William Corbin's *Smoke*,[33] set in the Oregon Cascades. When his mother remarries, fourteen-year-old Chris Long is cold toward his stepfather, Cal Fitch. Then a stray German shepherd, Smoke, forces the two to relate. After Smoke attaches himself to Chris, the boy admits that Cal welcomes the dog. Smoke's former owner wants him back, so Chris and the dog run away. Cal feels time away will help the boy. Sure enough, Chris returns, prepared to relinquish Smoke, if necessary, but also willing to accept and respect Cal.

*Companionship*

**Middle and Upper Grades.** Companionship is the theme of Marguerite Henry's *Brighty of the Grand Canyon*,[34] a story of a free-spirited burro who enjoys company. An aged prospector, Old Timer, finds the donkey running wild along Bright Angel Creek and befriends him by sharing flapjacks. When Old Timer disappears, Brighty joins frontiersman Jim Owen (Uncle Jim). Theodore Roosevelt dedicates a new canyon bridge and honors the frontiersman by letting him cross first. Uncle Jim insists that Brighty, whose hoofs gouged out the trail, accompany him. Brighty expresses his feelings for Uncle Jim this way: "And the voice of Uncle Jim was something to hold to, like a rock in flood time."[35]

Meindert DeJong's *The Singing Hill* has friendship for a horse as its theme.[36] Six-year-old Raymond (Ray) Garroway is lonely when he moves to the countryside. While wandering on a singing hill, he finds and cares for an old horse that he names Thee-Rim. Ray's Grandpa happens to be the horse's owner and gives Thee-Rim to the boy. Joyous Ray sings, "Thee-Rim is my horse, and he is in our garage, and the rain can't rain on him any more . . ."[37]

A moose offers companionship in Phil Stong's *Honk, the Moose*,[38] set in northern Minnesota. Befriending a moose is the theme of this story about two ten-year-old boys, Ivar and Waino, who call the moose Honk and take him to the livery stable of Ivar's father during the winter. No one has the heart to shoot the moose so the boys become his owner.

Honk returns to the woods during the spring and summer, always visiting his human friends every winter, sharing warmth and hospitality.

The companionship of a boy and a more typical pet, his dog, is the theme of Beverly Cleary's *Henry and Ribsy*.[39] At the beginning, Henry's father tells him he can go salmon fishing if he can keep his dog Ribsy out of trouble for two months. Despite Ribsy's stealing a policeman's lunch and frightening the garbage man, the two do go fishing, and Henry catches the largest salmon.

**Upper Grades.** Will James's *Smoky the Cowhorse* is an adventure story about a spirited mouse-colored gelding who relates to only one man, Clint, a cowboy.[40] Companionship is its primary theme, though Smoky is forced to spend years away from Clint. The cow horse is stolen, sold to a rodeo, given to a livery stable, and forced to pull a vegetable wagon. During this time when he is abused, he learns to hate human beings, but in the end, he becomes a companion once more to Clint. Through love, Clint restores the horse's health and spirit.

*Love*

**Middle Grades.** Intense love for a pet is the theme of Meindert DeJong's *Shadrach*,[41] whose early twentieth-century setting is modeled after the author's childhood Netherlands village. Small Davie's grandfather and father try to strengthen him after he is ill by giving him responsibility for a black pet rabbit, Shadrach. Despite Mother's orders to stay in bed, Davie gathers clover for the pet he treasures. He exclaims:

> Every morning you woke up it was a miracle all over again, that there in a barn across the village sat a little rabbit, and he was yours. Something breathing, nibbling, hopping, and it was yours. In all the world it was yours.[42]

After finding lost Shadrach, Davie sings inside with happiness.

**Middle and Upper Grades.** Learning to love is the theme of Betsy Byars's *The House of Wings*.[43] Ten-year-old Sammie feels rejected when his parents leave him temporarily with his grandfather and go to Detroit to establish a new home. The boy runs away, chased by his grandfather, who calls him to help with an injured crane. After he feeds and cares for the crane, Sammy's attitude changes, and he begins to love both his grandfather and the crane. "He didn't know how it was possible to hate a person in the middle of one morning, and then to find in the middle of the next morning that you loved this same person."[44]

Eleanor Estes's *Ginger Pye*[45] and Beverly Cleary's *Ribsy*[46] have love for a dog as their theme. Estes is author-illustrator of her book about the Pye family. They grieve when they lose their cherished puppy, Ginger, and rejoice when they find him, thanks to a three-year-old boy called Uncle Benny.

Cleary's book also tells about a search for a lost mutt, Ribsy. His owner, Henry Huggins, finds him after the dog endures a bubble bath, an eccentric old lady, a football game, and high, rickety, fire-escape stairs.

Searching for the love and security that a home represents is the theme of Meindert DeJong's *Hurry Home, Candy,*[47] which is illustrated by Maurice Sendak. DeJong tells about a puppy who gets his name, Candy, from two loving children. When they go for a ride in the country, Candy gets lost. His lonely, hungry days end after he meets a kind sea captain and is reunited with him when lost again. Now "he would not merely have a pan of food, he'd have a home, he'd have a name, he'd have a love for a great, good man."[48]

**Upper Grades.** Love for a dog is the theme of Anthony Fon Eisen's *Bond of the Fire,*[49] set in the last glacial age 20,000 years ago. The first time Ash, a sixteen-year-old Cro-Magnon boy, camps alone, his fire attracts a dog, Arkla, and the two form a lifetime partnership. "By the light of the fire they stood together, and the hand of the boy controlled the dog and made them as one."[50] The two communicate, protect each other, and hunt together. The love Ash gives his dog is returned fourfold.

A girl's love for her dog is the theme of Louise Rankin's *Daughter of the Mountains,*[51] which takes place in Tibet during the last years of British rule. A young Tibetan girl, Moma, receives her heart's desire, a Lhasa terrier, Pempa, only to have him stolen and sold. Moma is so fond of her pet she leaves her family to search for him and travels alone through the mountains to the Indian coast. "Only one thought filled her mind and heart and put the strength of a giant into her legs: Pempa. I must get him back."[52] The story concludes when they are reunited.

Like Moma, fourteen-year-old Travis is attached to his dog, Old Yeller, and his love for his pet is the theme of Fred Gipson's *Old Yeller.*[53] The stray dog hunts for game, guards the crops from animal thieves, and protects the family when danger occurs. Unfortunately, after rescuing Travis's mother from an attack by a diseased wolf, Old Yeller gets hydrophobia. Travis says:

> It was going to kill something inside me to do it, but I knew then that I had to shoot my big yeller dog. I stuck the muzzle of the gun against his head and pulled the trigger.[54]

The ending of Marjorie Kinnan Rawlings's *The Yearling* is similar to that in *Old Yeller*, but her theme is love of a fawn.[55] Rawlings writes about lonely twelve-year-old Jody Baxter, a poor farmer's only child who grows up in the Florida wilderness with Flag, a fawn. When Flag becomes a mischievous yearling and destroys the family's scant crops, Jody's mother has to shoot him. The boy feels betrayed, for "he did not believe he should ever again love anything, man or woman or his own child, as he had loved the yearling."[56] After unsuccessfully trying to run away, Jody realizes his family's survival comes first.

In *Sasha, My Friend,*[57] Barbara Corcoran also shows the death of a pet, a wolf named Sasha, discovered as a pup in the Montana wilderness by a high school girl, Hallie. After her mother's death in an automobile accident, Hallie tries to revive her father's health by moving with him from California to his isolated boyhood ranch in Montana. Overcoming loneliness through love for her father and pet is the theme of this book. When Sasha is wounded in a trap, Hallie has to kill him, ending his misery. She gives undivided love to her ill father, forgetting previous feelings of solitude.

Love for a wolf is also the theme of John Donovan's *Wild in the World*.[58] John Gridley, a New Hampshire mountain youth, is the sole survivor of a thirteen-member family of homesteaders. In his loneliness, John develops a bond to a wolf who visits the farm, an animal he calls Son. That bond is strengthened when Son kills a rattlesnake to protect John. When John gets pneumonia, Son is his constant companion, as this quotation reflects: "John's coughing and shivering were back, and he held Son close to him on the couch."[59] After John dies, neighbors remove his body from the homestead, but Son returns to sit in the empty house and sleep on his master's bed.

In a lighter vein is Sterling North's *Rascal: A Memoir of a Better Era,*[60] whose theme is affection for a pet. This story takes place during World War I in a midwestern town. Raised by his father with animal friends, eleven-year-old Sterling remembers being with his raccoon, Rascal, "eating soft-shelled pecans, wishing we could stay side by side forever, sharing a meal and each other's company."[61] In the end, however, Sterling sets Rascal free to pursue a female raccoon.

Bears are other unusual pets, yet love between a boy and a bear is the theme of both René Guillot's *Grishka and the Bear*[62] and Walt Morey's *Gentle Ben*.[63] Guillot's book, set in primitive Siberia, tells how Grishka secretly accompanies men from his tribe who hunt and kill a mother bear. The lad adopts her cub, Djidi, remembering his banished father's advice to befriend mountain bears. A year later, the superstitious tribe wants to sacrifice Djidi, believing this will guarantee a bear-hunt's success, and Grishka runs away with his cub. The climax of their relationship occurs when tribal men searching for the missing lad injure Djidi. The wounded cub leads them to his unconscious master, then wanders away. Grishka's first words after he regains consciousness are "Djidi . . . Where's Djidi? Where is my little brother?"[64]

Like *Grishka and the Bear, Gentle Ben* is historical fiction since it takes place in Alaska before statehood. After his father refuses to buy Ben, a chained brown bear, Mark Andersen frees Ben and runs away with him. This is how Mr. Andersen finds them sleeping together:

> . . . just like a boy and his dog. How had Ellen [Mark's mother] put it last night? Something about a love that overcame fear and suspicion. A sort of Biblical "lion and lamb" kind of love.[65]

Ben and the Andersens feel such mutual affection, they save each other's lives.

More common than stories about bears are those whose theme is the love of a horse, such as Walter Farley's sequels, *The Black Stallion*[66] and *The Black Stallion Returns*.[67] In the first book, Alec Ramsay meets the Black when they alone survive a shipwreck, and the stallion leads the boy to safety on a deserted island. After their rescue and return to New York, Alec and the Black train to race against two famous horses and win. In the second book, the Black's original owner traces the stallion and returns with him to his native Arabia, leaving Alec in despair. A horse breeder who wants the Black to sire his thoroughbreds takes Alec to Arabia in search of the stallion. After many hardships, they find the horse, and Alec gets a last chance to ride him as victor in a race. Since the Black is not for sale, Alec's reward is the promise of his first foal. That will have to suffice, for those who know Alec and the stallion say, "Guess there's no love greater than yours for the Black, 'cept maybe his for you."[68]

Love for a horse versus money is the theme of Francis Kelnay's *Chucaro: Wild Pony of the Pampa*.[69] On the Argentine plains, twelve-year-old Pedro and Juan, a gaucho, lasso wild Chucaro and tame the horse. The rich rancher's spoiled son, Armando, offers Pedro thirty pesos for Chucaro. The boy says, "I know that thirty pesos is a lot of silver, but I wouldn't give up Chucaro if you gave me a million."[70] Juan offers a plan that allows Pedro's love to triumph over Armando's money. Armando can own Chucaro if he can lasso the horse. Since Armando is humiliated in his attempt, Pedro, his father, and Juan are forced to leave the ranch, but at least Chucaro goes with them.

Set in the United States, William Corbin's *Golden Mare* has the theme of love providing strength.[71] On a ranch, twelve-year-old Robin Daveen, a rheumatic-fever victim who cannot work or play like his brothers, draws strength atop his mare, Magic. The aged horse also draws strength from the boy. During a blizzard, the two prove their worth, getting help for Robin's mother after she breaks her leg. On their return, the boy, forced to kill an attacking cougar, collapses in the snow, protected by Magic. Robin revives, but the old mare dies, and others acknowledge, "It's only the boy's care and love that's kept her going this long."[72] Robin accepts the tragedy, strengthened by memories of Magic.

**Summary**

This chapter reviews forty-seven examples of realistic animal prizewinners for middle- and upper-elementary grades, including historical and contemporary fiction set in the United States or abroad. Most of these books are intended for those in or beyond fourth grade. Themes are discussed under thirteen headings with almost half the stories revolving around the theme of reciprocated love or companionship from an animal. A variety of animals are included. Half the accounts are about horses and dogs. Other animal subjects include the badger, bear, burro, cat, deer, fox, lamb, moose, mule, rabbit, raccoon, and wolf. Some stories have an ecological theme. Few of these prizewinners show animal or human stereotypes. Authors who have written several realistic animal prizewinners reviewed in this chapter are Marguerite Henry (five books), Meindert DeJong and Glen Rounds (four books each), Beverly Cleary (three books), and Betsy Byars and Walter Farley (two books each).

**Notes**

1. In 1952, *Sea Star: Orphan of Chincoteague* won the Pacific Northwest Library Association Young Reader's Choice Award.
2. In 1950, *Kildee House* was a Newbery Honor Book.
3. In 1972, *Incident at Hawk's Hill* was a Newbery Honor Book, and in 1975, it won the George G. Stone Center for Children's Books Recognition of Merit Award.
4. Allan W. Eckert, *Incident at Hawk's Hill* (Boston: Little, Brown, 1971), p. 17.
5. In 1969, *Wild Horses of the Red Desert* won the Lewis Carroll Shelf Award.
6. Glen Rounds, *Wild Horses of the Red Desert* (New York: Holiday House, 1969), pp. 14–15.
7. In 1973, *Cockleburr Quarters* won the Lewis Carroll Shelf Award.

8. Charlotte Baker, *Cockleburr Quarters* (Englewood Cliffs, New Jersey: Prentice Hall, 1972), p. 165.

9. In 1960, *The Blind Colt* won the Lewis Carroll Shelf Award.

10. In 1973, *Stolen Pony* won the Lewis Carroll Shelf Award.

11. In 1976, *Socks* won the William Allen White Children's Book Award.

12. In 1970, *The Midnight Fox* won the Lewis Carroll Shelf Award.

13. In 1944, *Mountain Born* was a Newbery Honor Book.

14. Elizabeth Yates, *Mountain Born* (New York: Coward, 1943), p. 113.

15. In 1965, *Joel and the Wild Goose* won the Lewis Carroll Shelf Award.

16. In 1954, *Florina and the Wild Bird,* illustrated by Alois Carigiet, was a *New York Times* Choice of Best Illustrated Children's Book of the Year.

17. Selina Chonz, *Florina and the Wild Bird* (New York: Walck, 1953), p. 22.

18. In 1972, *Flight of the White Wolf* won the Dorothy Canfield Fisher Children's Book Award and in 1974, the Sequoyah Children's Book Award.

19. In 1953, *The Bears on Hemlock Mountain* was a Newbery Honor Book.

20. Alice Dalgliesh, *The Bears on Hemlock Mountain* (New York: Scribner, 1952), no page.

21. In 1977, *Hawk, I'm Your Brother,* illustrated by Peter Parnall, won The Randolph Caldecott Medal.

22. In 1970, *Kavik the Wolf Dog* won the Dorothy Canfield Fisher Children's Book Award and in 1971, the William Allen White Children's Book Award.

23. In 1963, *The Incredible Journey* won the Dorothy Canfield Fisher Children's Book Award. In 1964, it won the Pacific Northwest Library Association Young Reader's Choice Award and the William Allen White Children's Book Award. In 1971, it received the Lewis Carroll Shelf Award.

24. Sheila Burnford, *The Incredible Journey* (Boston: Little, Brown, 1960), p. 101.

25. In 1960, *Black Gold* won the Sequoyah Children's Book Award.

26. In 1975, *The Day the Circus Came to Lone Tree* won the Lewis Carroll Shelf Award.

27. In 1967, *Mustang: Wild Spirit of the West* won the Western Heritage Award and in 1970, the Sequoyah Children's Book Award.

28. In 1946, *Justin Morgan Had a Horse* was a Newbery Honor Book.

29. In 1974, *Doodle and the Go-Cart* won the Georgia Children's Book Award.

30. Robert Burch, *Doodle and the Go-Cart* (New York: Viking, 1972), p. 121.

31. In 1959, *Along Came a Dog* was a Newbery Honor Book, and in 1960, it was put on the International Board on Books for Young People Honor List.

32. Meindert DeJong, *Along Came a Dog* (New York: Harper, 1958), pp. 112–113.

33. In 1970, *Smoke* won the Pacific Northwest Library Association Young Reader's Choice Award.

34. In 1956, *Brighty of the Grand Canyon* won the William Allen White Children's Book Award.

35. Marguerite Henry, *Brighty of the Grand Canyon* (Chicago: Rand McNally, 1965), p. 63.

36. In 1962, *The Singing Hill,* illustrated by Maurice Sendak, was a *New York Times* Choice of Best Illustrated Children's Book of the Year.

37. Meindert DeJong, *The Singing Hill* (New York: Harper, 1962), pp. 179–180.

38. In 1936, *Honk, the Moose* was a Newbery Honor Book and in 1970, it won the Lewis Carroll Shelf Award.

39. In 1957, *Henry and Ribsy* won the Pacific Northwest Library Association Young Reader's Choice Award.

40. In 1927, *Smoky the Cowhorse* won The John Newbery Medal.

41. In 1954, *Shadrach* was a Newbery Honor Book.

42. Meindert DeJong, *Shadrach* (New York: Harper, 1953), p. 100.

43. In 1973, *The House of Wings* was a finalist for the National Book Award in the children's-book category.

44. Betsy Byars, *The House of Wings* (New YorK: Viking, 1972), p. 141.

45. In 1952, *Ginger Pye* won The John Newbery Medal.

46. In 1966, *Ribsy* won the Dorothy Canfield Fisher Children's Book Award and, in 1968, the Nene Award.

47. In 1954, *Hurry Home, Candy* was a Newbery Honor Book.

48. Meindert DeJong, *Hurry Home, Candy* (New York: Harper, 1953), p. 244.

49. In 1965, *Bond of the Fire* won the Lewis Carroll Shelf Award.

50. Anthony Fon Eisen, *Bond of the Fire* (New York: World, 1965), p. 19.

51. In 1962, *Daughter of the Mountains* won the Lewis Carroll Shelf Award.

52. Louise Rankin, *Daughter of the Mountains* (New York: Viking, 1966), p. 44.

53. In 1957, *Old Yeller* was a Newbery Honor Book, and, in 1959, it won the Pacific Northwest Library Association Young Reader's Choice Award, the Sequoyah Children's Book Award, and the William Allen White Children's Book Award. In 1966, it received the Nene Award.

54. Fred Gipson, *Old Yeller* (New York: Harper, 1956), pp. 152–153.

55. In 1963, *The Yearling* won the Lewis Carroll Shelf Award.

56. Marjorie Kinnan Rawlings, *The Yearling* (New York: Scribner, 1938), pp. 427–428.

57. In 1972, *Sasha, My Friend* won the William Allen White Children's Book Award.

58. In 1972, *Wild in the World* was a finalist for the National Book Award in the children's-book category.

59. John Donovan, *Wild in the World* (New York: Harper, 1971), p. 82.

60. In 1964, *Rascal: A Memoir of a Better Era* was a Newbery Honor Book and won the Lewis Carroll Shelf Award. In 1965, it won the Dorothy Canfield Fisher Children's Book Award. In 1966, it won the Pacific Northwest Library Association Young Reader's Choice Award, the Sequoyah Children's Book Award, and the William Allan White Children's Book Award.

61. Sterling North, *Rascal: A Memoir of a Better Era* (New York: Dutton, 1963), p. 143.

62. In 1961, *Grishka and the Bear* won the Lewis Carroll Shelf Award.

63. In 1968, *Gentle Ben* won the Sequoyah Children's Book Award.

64. René Guillot, *Grishka and the Bear* (New York: Oxford University Press, 1959), p. 116.

65. Walt Morey, *Gentle Ben* (New York: Dutton, 1965), p. 44.

66. In 1944, *The Black Stallion* won the Pacific Northwest Library Association Young Reader's Choice Award.

67. In 1948, *The Black Stallion Returns* won the Pacific Northwest Library Association Young Reader's Choice Award.

68. Walter Farley, *The Black Stallion Returns* (New York: Random, 1945), p. 22.

69. In 1959, *Chucaro: Wild Pony of the Pampa* won The John Newbery Medal.

70. Francis Kalnay, *Chucaro: Wild Pony of the Pampa* (New York: Harcourt, 1958), p. 45.

71. In 1958, *Golden Mare* won the Pacific Northwest Library Association's Young Reader's Choice Award.

72. William Corbin, *Golden Mare* (Chippewa Falls, Wisc.: Hale, 1955), pp. 5–6.

## References of Prizewinners Arranged according to Type of Animal in Realistic Fiction

*(Estimated Reading Grade Level in Parentheses)*

*Assorted Animals*

Burnford, Sheila. *The Incredible Journey*. Illustrated by Carl Burger. Boston: Little, Brown, 1960 (6–9).
Montgomery, Rutherford. *Kildee House*. Illustrated by Barbara Cooney. New York: Doubleday, 1949 (4–6).
Rounds, Glen. *The Day the Circus Came to Lone Tree*. New York: Holiday House, 1973 (3–6).

*Badger*

Eckert, Allan W. *Incident at Hawk's Hill*. Illustrated by John Schoenherr. Boston: Little, Brown, 1971 (6–9).

*Bears*

Dalgliesh, Alice. *The Bears on Hemlock Mountain*. Illustrated by Helen Sewell. New York: Scribner, 1952 (1–4).
Guillot, René. *Grishka and the Bear*. Illustrated by Joan Kiddell-Monroe. New York: Oxford University Press, 1959 (5–7).
Morey, Walt. *Gentle Ben*. Illustrated by John Schoenherr. New York: Dutton, 1965 (5–7).

*Birds*

Baylor, Byrd. *Hawk, I'm Your Brother*. Illustrated by Peter Parnall. New York: Scribner, 1976 (3–5).
Byars, Betsy. *The House of Wings*. Illustrated by Daniel Schwartz. New York: Viking, 1972 (4–6).
Chonz, Selina. *Florina and the Wild Bird*. Illustrated by Alois Garigiet. New York: Walck, 1953 (3–6).
Sandburg, Helga. *Joel and the Wild Goose*. Illustrated by Thomas Daly. New York: Dial, 1963 (4–8).

*Burro*

Henry, Marguerite. *Brighty of the Grand Canyon*. Illustrated by Wesley Dennis. New York: Rand McNally, 1965 (4–6).

*Cat*

Cleary, Beverly. *Socks*. Illustrated by Beatrice Darwin. New York: Morrow, 1973 (4–6).

*Deer*

Rawlings, Marjorie Kinnan. *The Yearling*. Illustrated by Edward Shenton. New York: Scribner, 1938 (6–9).

*Dogs*

Baker, Charlotte. *Cockleburr Quarters*. Illustrated by Robert Owens. Englewood Cliffs, N.J.: Prentice-Hall, 1972 (3–7).
Cleary, Beverly. *Henry and Ribsy*. Illustrated by Louis Darling. New York: Morrow, 1954 (3–5).
————. *Ribsy*. Illustrated by Louis Darling. New York: Morrow, 1964 (3–5).
Corbin, William. *Smoke*. New York: Coward, 1967 (5–7).
DeJong, Meindert. *Along Came a Dog*. Illustrated by Maurice Sendak. New York: Harper, 1958 (4–7).
————. *Hurry Home, Candy*. Illustrated by Maurice Sendak. New York: Harper, 1953 (4–7).
Estes, Eleanor. *Ginger Pye*. New York: Harcourt, 1951 (4–6).
Fon Eisen, Anthony. *Bond of the Fire*. Illustrated by W.T. Mars. New York: World, 1965 (6–9).
Gipson, Fred. *Old Yeller*. Illustrated by Carl Burger. New York: Harper, 1956 (6–9).
Rankin, Louise. *Daughter of the Mountains*. Illustrated by Kurt Wiese. New York: Viking, 1966 (4–7).

*Fox*

Byars, Betsy. *The Midnight Fox*. Illustrated by Ann Grifalconi. New York: Viking, 1968 (4–6).

*Horses*

Corbin, William. *Golden Mare*. Illustrated by Pers Crowell. Chippewa Falls, Wisc.: Hale, 1955 (5–7).

DeJong, Meindert. *The Singing Hill*. Illustrated by Maurice Sendak. New York: Harper, 1962 (3–5).

Farley, Walter. *The Black Stallion*. Illustrated by Keith Ward. New York: Random House, 1941 (5–8).

———. *The Black Stallion Returns*. Illustrated by Harold Eldridge. New York: Random House, 1945 (5–8).

Henry, Marguerite. *Black Gold*. Chicago: Rand McNally, 1957 (5–8).

———. *Mustang: Wild Spirit of the West*. Illustrated by Robert Lougheed. Chicago: Rand McNally, 1966 (4–6).

———. *Sea Star: Orphan of Chincoteague*. Illustrated by Wesley Dennis. Chicago: Rand McNally, 1949 (2–4).

———. *Justin Morgan Had a Horse*. Illustrated by Wesley Dennis. Chicago: Rand McNally, 1954 (5–7).

James, Will. *Smoky the Cowhorse*. New York: Scribner, 1926 (6–8).

Kalnay, Francis. *Chucaro: Wild Pony of the Pampa*. Illustrated by Julian deMiskey. New York: Harcourt, 1958 (5–8).

Rounds, Glen. *The Blind Colt*. New York: Holiday House, 1941 (4–6).

———. *Stolen Pony*. Chippewa Falls, Wisc.: Hale, 1948 (4–6).

———. *Wild Horses of the Red Desert*. New York: Holiday House, 1969 (2–4).

*Lamb*

Yates, Elizabeth. *Mountain Born*. Illustrated by Nora S. Unwin. New York: McCann, 1943 (3–5).

*Moose*

Stong, Phil. *Honk, the Moose*. Illustrated by Kurt Wiese. New York: Dodd, 1955 (4–6).

*Mule*

Burch, Robert. *Doodle and the Go-Cart*. Illustrated by Alan Tiegreen. New York: Viking, 1972 (4–6).

*Rabbit*

DeJong, Meindert. *Shadrach*. Illustrated by Maurice Sendak. New York: Harper, 1953 (2–4).

*Raccoon*

North, Sterling. *Rascal: A Memoir of a Better Era*. Illustrated by John Schoenherr. New York: Dutton, 1963 (6–8).

*Wolves*

Corcoran, Barbara. *Sasha, My Friend*. Illustrated by Richard L. Shell. New York: Atheneum, 1969 (5–9).
Donovan, John. *Wild in the World*. New York: Harper, 1971 (5–8).
Ellis, Mel. *Flight of the White Wolf*. New York: Holt, 1970 (5–9).
Morey, Walt. *Kavik the Wolf Dog*. Illustrated by Peter Parnall. New York: Dutton, 1968 (4–8).

**Part IV
Contemporary Realistic
Fiction for Middle- and Upper-
Elementary Grades**

# 12 Contemporary Realistic Fiction about Families, Friends, and Problems

*For me, a good family story is* A Book for Jodan. *Jodan's mom and dad stop loving each other, but the main idea is they still love her. She still has a family. I know, because my parents are divorced, and that book helps me. I worry more about my dad than about my mom. I worry if my dad will die without me.*

*Maybe that's why the friendship story I picked tells about death. It's about a boy who dies in front of his pal. It's called* A Taste of Blackberries. *Both books are sad, but I feel better when I read them.*

—Michelle, aged eight

## Perspective

With almost half of U.S. marriages ending in divorce, some troubled children, like Michelle, turn to bibliotherapy, getting comfort and understanding from books. Even more carefree youngsters identify with characters in realistic fiction about families, friends, and personal problems. The early family stories cited only happy or adventurous experiences. Current accounts emphasize values and such problems as sibling rivalry, generation gap, poverty, divorce, remarriage, mental illness, and death. Family stories intertwine with friendship tales. The latter often dwell on loneliness, finding acceptance by peers, growing up, first romance, even death.

Family and friendship stories may discuss some of the same issues raised in personal-problem books, but not often as the central focus. Contemporary realistic-fictional prizewinners focus on such personal problems as drug sales and addiction; life in an orphanage, residential treatment center, foster home, and even in a subway niche; need for permanence, security, freedom, and love; identity crisis; being an outsider; and facing difficulties in school. This chapter examines themes of fifty-five sample prizewinners without differentiating stories about families, friends, and personal problems.

317

**Themes of Prizewinning Contemporary Realistic**
**Fiction about Families, Friends, and Problems**
**Grouped under These Topics**

*Adjusting*

**Middle Grades.** Adjusting to parents' separation is the theme of Marcia
Newfield's *A Book for Jodan*.[1] A nine-year-old only child, Jodan, copes
with the gradual breakup of her parents' marriage. She moves to California with her mother while her father stays in Massachusetts. The child
misses her father, visits him, and receives a book he made especially for
her. The book contains recorded memories, recipes, and advice, such as
"Learn to treasure what's gentle. When you love something that is alive,
try to help it grow and be itself."[2] The book helps Jodan realize how
important she is to her father.

**Middle and Upper Grades.** Adjusting to challenge is the theme of Katherine Paterson's *The Great Gilly Hopkins*.[3] Eleven-year-old Galadriel
(Gilly) Hopkins wants to live with her supposedly beautiful mother,
Courtney, instead of with fat, nearly illiterate Maime Trotter in a foster
home. The bright, unmanageable girl resents Trotter's other foster child,
seven-year-old William Ernest Teague, a slow learner, and the daily
dinner guest, Mr. Randolph, a blind Black lover of literature. Gilly writes
her mother that she wants to leave. After unsuccessfully trying to run
away, she begins to adjust, helping William Ernest learn to read and
even nursing flu-ridden family members. Though she now wants to remain with Trotter, her letter is forwarded to her maternal grandmother,
Nonnie, who claims her. Gilly lets Trotter know she loves her and tries
to adjust to Nonnie, thinking, "Trotter would be proud."[4]

   In an interview, Katherine Paterson says that the theme of *The Great
Gilly Hopkins* is: "Life is tough, but nothing's better than doing well at
a tough job."[5] She adds:

> The reason I wrote a book about a foster child is because I was a
> temporary foster mother. . . . We took two boys for what we thought
> was going to be two weeks. It turned out to be two months, and what
> I learned was that I'm a terrible foster mother. I would say to myself
> when something went wrong (and something went wrong many times
> every day), "I can't really deal with that, because he's only going to
> be here a short time. I was treating the child like a Kleenex, and there's
> nothing worse. . . . So I created the world's greatest foster mother
> (Maime Trotter) to make up for all my sins.[6]

   Flexibility is needed to live in different foster homes and to adjust
to changes in one's own family at times. Adjusting and learning to feel

accepted is Elizabeth Enright's theme in *Thimble Summer*.[7] A farmer's nine-year-old daughter, Garnet Linden, resents the fact that her older brother, Jay, gives all his attention to Eric, a thirteen-year-old orphan recently accepted by their family. She runs away, learning independence on her eighteen-mile trip to the town of New Conniston, but she returns with simple gifts for all family members, including Eric. Garnet attributes her adjustment and positive events to a lucky thimble, the story's symbol. She tells Eric:

> There was something wonderful about this thimble: everything began to happen as soon as I found it, why that very night the rain came and the drought was broken! And right after that we got money to build this barn, and you saw our kiln fire in the woods and came to be in our family. And then Citronella [her girl friend] and I got locked in the library, that was exciting, and I went to New Conniston by my-self. . . . And of course Timmy [her pet pig] won a prize at the fair. Everything has happened since I found it, and all nice things.[8]

Garnet is similar to ten-year-old Marly in Virginia Eggertsen Soren-sen's *Miracles on Maple Hill*,[9] a book with the theme of adjusting to changes or so-called miracles. Marly enjoys a winter vacation with her parents and older brother, Joe, at her grandmother's house. Upon enter-ing the house, she whispers to herself, "Please let there be miracles,"[10] and her wish comes true. Her first miracle occurs when sap rises in maple trees, is tapped, and becomes syrup. Miracles happen not only outdoors, but also inside people. Her nervous father, who has returned from a prisoner-of-war camp, adjusts so well to Maple Hill the family decides to remain there permanently.

In *Miracles on Maple Hill*, the author tends to stereotype Marly as a typical fearful female: "Marly couldn't pretend like Joe because she was always getting scared."[11] Marly, who's afraid of cows, feels safe when Joe invites her to walk with him.[12] Whether in the city or quiet countryside, the parents encourage their son to explore alone more than their daughter, as noted in these words:

> Even in the city Joe explored by himself. . . . It made her [Marly] feel cross that a girl couldn't explore by herself too, but Mother and Daddy would never let her.[13]

**Upper Grades.** Adjusting to parents' separation and divorce is Stella Pevsner's theme in *A Smart Kid Like You*.[14] The smart kid is Nina, a seventh-grader, who is forced to accept changes when her mother starts dating, her father remarries, and she has a mathematics class taught by her stepmother. She laments, "In our family we never saved anything.

We didn't even save the family.''[15] After she acknowledges her feelings, she begins to like her new stepmother and learns that pain can be replaced with love.

Adjusting to mother's remarriage is the primary theme of Eleanor Cameron's *A Room Made of Windows*.[16] In an interview, the author discusses the theme of her largely autobiographical story and memories of herself reflected in twelve-year-old possessive Julia:

> The central theme is the discovery by Julia that her mother is not her own private property. . . . I still wanted my mother to be mine, and I wanted to be hers. . . . Here came this man [Uncle Phil in the book], whom I had looked upon as a family friend, and all of a sudden, he loomed as someone who was going to take my mother away from me, so I put up a fight. Even after mother remarried, I continued to put up a fight. It was one of the most difficult periods that my precious mother had to face, and she faced many. . . . For the first time in my life, my eyes were opened to the fact that mother had her own life to live, that she had to think about her own future, and that she wanted the love of a man.[17]

Mrs. Cameron adds that she has no brother so Gregg in the book is based on her son, David. He gave her permission to state that his room is messy.

Like *A Room Made of Windows,* the theme of Kin Platt's *Chloris and the Creeps*[18] is adjusting to mother's remarriage. Eleven-year-old Chloris Carpenter is less flexible than her younger sister, Jenny, the book's narrator, who discusses adapting to life with their divorced mother. Their father is dead, having committed suicide after a second poor marriage. Chloris, loyal to the father she barely remembers, calls her mother's suitors creeps. She considers the biggest creep to be Fidel Mancha, the kind Mexican artist her mother marries. Disaster is narrowly averted after rebellious Chloris starts a fire in Fidel's workshop. Chloris begins to adjust when she says, ''Goodbye, almost-dear Daddy! . . . Now let's see what Fidel has to look at in his creepy old studio.''[19]

Coping with new members of a household may be traumatic. Adjusting to siblings is the theme of Marilyn Sachs's *Dorrie's Book*.[20] In her class, eleven-year-old Dorrie O'Brien writes a book about how happy she was previously, basking in attention as an only child. Now, with newly born triplets, her family moves from a fancy apartment to an old house. Neighbors Genevieve and Harold James, abandoned by their parents, help with the triplets and become foster children in the household. Dorrie resents sharing her room with Genevieve, who is neater than she is. Feeling rejected, Dorrie gets this guidance from Dad, ''Your problem is that you suffer from the 'Me-Mes.' It's common to only children and is seldom fatal, but it's very trying on friends and relations.''[21] In time, realizing her parents still love her, Dorrie feels more secure.

## Facing Death or Its Aftermath

**Middle and Upper Grades.** Doris Buchanan Smith's *A Taste of Blackberries* discusses the death of twelve-year-old Jamie, as witnessed by his best friend, John, the story's narrator.[22] This book's theme is acceptance of death. Jamie, a dramatic practical joker, pokes at a bee's nest, then falls to the ground. Peers think he is faking, but later learn his allergic reaction to bee stings causes his death. John cries hopelessly at his buddy's funeral. Afterward, he cannot eat, sleep, or play. One day, he brings blackberries to Jamie's grieving mother who asks him to substitute for her son in giving affection. He is relieved. Realizing he can cope with Jamie's death, he runs to play with other friends.

Coping with changes after his mother's suicide is the theme of Vera and Bill Cleaver's *Grover*.[23] Ten-year-old Grover Ezell is carefree in Thicket, Florida until his terminally ill mother takes her life. He remembers the two having long talks when she came home from the hospital. Now he needs to confide in someone, but his father is too grief-stricken. His father begins to adjust at the same time that Grover, assisted by friends, has the gumption to face change.

**Upper Grades.** Orin Woodward is three years older than Grover, but he has similar problems in Mary Stolz's *The Edge of Next Year*.[24] The book's theme is learning to accept a loved one's death. Orin's happy family is ripped apart when his mother, Rose, dies in an automobile accident. Orin's ten-year-old brother, Victor, reacts by giving all his time to keeping insects in a vivarium. His father, Elliot, seeks solace in alcohol. Orin resents their irresponsible response to grief, leaving him to do the cooking and housekeeping. The father, aware of Orin's attitude, joins Alcoholics Anonymous, and the adolescent feels some hope as spring approaches, the edge of next year. Orin concludes, ''You went on missing somebody, but after a while you sort of—relinquished them.''[25]

Finding the meaning of life and death is the theme of Carol Farley's *The Garden Is Doing Fine*.[26] Her twin brothers, Alan and Arthur, are too young, but Corrie Sheldon accompanies her mother on hospital visits to her father who has cancer. He asks about his garden, and Corrie feels she cannot lie about the frozen flower beds. Her mother explains:

> Some people, like me, why they're vegetables—useful, but solid and dull. Then other people, like Daddy, why they're flowers—frivolous,

but grand and beautiful. . . . If you want to have a full garden, why you need both kinds of things. You need both kinds of people to have a full life, too.[27]

Mrs. Sheldon feels Corrie is like her father and the twins, like herself. She concludes, "But what I'm trying to say, Corrie, is that if your dad should die, why we'd still have our flowers in the family."[28]

Corrie remembers her father telling her in the past, "It's a grand thing . . . to see the seeds that you plant grow into something good and useful. It's a fine thing to think they'll be living on even after you're dead and gone."[29] Now Corrie understands her father was talking as much about people as about seeds. She whispers, "I'm Daddy's garden! He planted the seeds of his thoughts in me, and he hoped something good would grow!"[30] She rushes to her father's bedside to report, "The garden is doing fine, Daddy."[31]

In Norma Fox Mazer's *A Figure of Speech*,[32] the rejection and eventual death of eighty-three-year-old Grandpa Pennoyer is seen through the eyes of his thirteen-year-old granddaughter, Jenny, the only member of the family who seems to love him. The theme is the need to treat older persons as sensitive individuals, not as senior citizens, a cliché or figure of speech. Jenny is incensed that Grandpa can't even talk about his boyhood without being reminded that everyone knows his tales. Jenny tells her mother, "You and Dad talk to Grandpa like he's dumb. Or a kid. You make him feel awful."[33] Jenny arises early every morning to visit Grandpa in his basement apartment attached to her parents' house, but at times, her mother won't let her go. When Jenny's older brother, Vince, returns from college with a wife, Valerie, the Pennoyers give Grandpa's apartment to the couple and move him into a shared bedroom. Grandpa isn't even consulted and begins to get sick often, so the Pennoyers plan to send him to a home for the aged. After Jenny warns Grandpa, the two go to a run-down farm he owns, but they can't survive there. He goes out one cold night, and Jenny finds him the next morning dead from exposure. Her parents think senility causes Grandpa to die, but Jenny knows he preferred death with dignity rather than placement in a home.

A relationship between a granddaughter and an ill grandfather also enters into Madeleine L'Engle's *A Ring of Endless Light*,[34] whose theme is coping with death. This is L'Engle's fourth book in the Austin family series which includes *Meet the Austins, The Moon by Night,* and *The Young Unicorns.* The narrator, Vicky Austin, almost sixteen years old, is joined by her parents and siblings John, Suzy, and Rob for what may be Grandfather's last summer in his Seven Bay Island home. He is dying of leukemia but officiates at a funeral for Coast Guard Commander Rodney. The Commander had a heart attack after preventing a suicide. Zachary Gray, the youth saved from suicide, and Leo Rodney, the Commander's son, turn to Vicky for help and romance. (Zachary's mother recently passed away, and his wealthy father has her body frozen rather than accept death's finality.) In addition, nineteen-year-old Adam Eddington, L'Engle's continuous character from *The Arm of the Starfish*, involves Vicky in research at the Marine Biology Center where she communicates with the wild dolphins he is studying. The title, *A Ring of Endless Light*, suggests existence in some form is infinite. Grandfather expresses:

> Simply the awareness that our mortal lives had a beginning and will have an end enhances the quality of our living. Perhaps it's even more intense when we know that the termination of the body is near, but it shouldn't be.[35]

## *Maturing*

**Middle and Upper Grades.** An aspect of maturing, admitting one's weaknesses, is the theme of Judy Blume's *Otherwise Known as Sheila the Great*.[36] While on summer vacation with her family in Tarrytown, New York, ten-year-old Sheila Tubman thinks she hides her fears of boys, dogs, and water, even from Mouse Ellis, a new friend who is the town's junior yo-yo champion. At Sheila's slumber party, the girls criticize each other in slam books. The hostess thinks:

> I know I don't have to worry about what they think of me, because I am careful to keep my bad points to myself. Sometimes I think I am really two people. I am the only one who knows Sheila Tubman. Everyone else knows SHEILA THE GREAT.[37]

However, the slam books reveal gaps in her armor, and Sheila herself gradually admits she doesn't know everything.

Growing up is the theme of another Judy Blume book, *Are You There, God? It's Me, Margaret*.[38] The author says this is her most autobiographical work, and there will be no sequels.[39] Margaret Simon celebrates her twelfth birthday in Farbrook, New Jersey after moving with her family from Manhattan. Margaret's father is Jewish and her mother, Christian, so she talks to God clandestinely to help her decide religious or nonreligious preference and to help her mature physically. She joins three other preadolescent girls in the Pre-Teen Sensations, a club that discusses boys and requires members both to wear bras and tell when they begin to menstruate. The book ends with Margaret thanking

God after she gets her first period. She says, "Now I am growing for sure. Now I am almost a woman!"[40]

**Upper Grades.** Growth is the theme of Vera and Bill Cleaver's *Queen of Hearts*,[41] but it is psychological rather than physical growth that is stressed in this view of twelve-year-old Wilma Omalie Lincoln. When Granny Lincoln has a stroke at age seventy-nine, Wilma is her summer housekeeper. At first, Wilma's six-year-old brother, Claybrook, joins them during the day, but he refuses to return after Granny makes false accusations. In time, Wilma begins to relate to Granny and notices how she is aging. She finds changes in herself, too, as the imaginary companions of her childhood disappear. She realizes, "It was over, really over, that other play-life of hers,"[42] and her parents, aware of her maturity, feel faint anxiety.

Maturing is also the theme of Irene Hunt's *Up a Road Slowly*.[43] Upon their mother's death, seven-year-old Julie Trelling and her nine-year-old brother, Christopher, move to the country home of maternal Aunt Cordelia and Uncle Haskell Bishop. Aunt Cordelia teaches them in a one-room schoolhouse where she has worked many years. When Julie enters high school, she is supposed to return to the home of her father, a professor. Instead, she chooses to stay with rather stern Aunt Cordelia whom she has learned to love. After Julie graduates as high school valedictorian, the aunt says, "Spinster Aunts serve a need, but they should know when the time comes to push young nieces out on their own. . . . You must have new experiences, be exposed to new ideas, Julie."[44] The book's title refers to the road of life which Julie gradually ascends.

When Julie discusses her future with Uncle Haskell, he offers this sexist advice: "Accept the fact that this is a man's world and learn to play the game gracefully, my sweet."[45] A liar and an alcoholic, the uncle is not a respected character, but neither Julie nor the author replies to his argument, and it may influence some readers.

Julie leaves her aunt when she is seventeen, the age of Angie Morrow in Maureen Daly's *Seventeenth Summer*.[46] The theme of this love story is a summer romance contributing to maturity. In the summer following high school graduation, Angie meets popular eighteen-year-old Jack Duluth. He becomes her first date, and she experiences new emotions with her first kiss and his declaration of love. As summer ends, the two part, for the Duluths are moving to Oklahoma and Angie will go to college in Chicago. Before she leaves, Jack gives her his class ring. Secure in his love, she realizes that each has to grow independently. Angie expresses the sadness she feels as she matures:

I could not help wishing that there wasn't so much sadness in growing up. . . . Growing up crowds your mind with new thoughts and new feelings so that you forget how you used to think and feel.[47]

The sadness in growing up is also apparent to sixteen-year-old Byron Douglas, narrator of S.E. Hinton's *That Was Then, This Is Now*.[48] Changing while maturing is the book's theme. Byron and Mark, who is a year younger, feel like brothers, because when his parents killed each other, Mark moved into Byron's house. The two prowl the streets, harass police, and fight street gangs. When the boys' lives are threatened outside Charlie's pool hall, Charlie tries to protect them and dies. Mark believes it's the hand of fate, but Byron questions being directionless and tough. Byron thinks, "It's kind of a good thing . . . when you know your own personality so you don't need the one the gang makes for you. . . . The difference is that was then, and this is now."[49] He adds, "I had learned something from everyone, and I didn't seem to be the same person I had been last year."[50] Byron falls in love with Cathy Carlson and begins to grow away from Mark. When Byron learns Mark is peddling drugs to adolescents, like Cathy's younger brother, M & M, he turns Mark over to authorities. It is a painful decision, and Byron laments, "I wish I was a kid again, when I had all the answers."[51]

*Adventure*

**Middle and Upper Grades.** The theme, adventurous discoveries, permeates another Elizabeth Enright book, *Gone-Away Lake*,[52] which describes how two cousins, eleven-year-old Portia and twelve-year-old Julian, enjoy exploring the area near their summer home. Their first discovery is a large Latin-inscribed stone that is dated July 15, 1891 and that seems to have belonged to an Italian poet and philosopher. Their second discovery is Gone-Away Lake, a swamp that previously was a lake, bordered by once-elegant abandoned summer houses, like Villa Caprice. Their discoveries are secret until Portia's younger brother, Foster, follows them and falls into quicksand. After the rescue, Portia's father sees Villa Caprice and thinks about buying it as a family retreat for future adventurous summers.

**Upper Grades.** Self-fulfilling adventure is the theme of E.L. Konigsburg's *From the Mixed-Up Files of Mrs. Basil E. Frankweiler*.[53] Eleven-year-old Claudia Kincaid, bored with her monotonous, straight-A life, decides to run away with her nine-year-old brother, Jamie, because he has more than twenty-four dollars to add to her five. She leaves home to experience her greatest adventure, living in the New York Metropol-

itan Museum. The two elude guards at the museum for a week, becoming
a team. "Becoming a team didn't mean the end of their arguments. But
it did mean that the arguments became part of the adventure, became
discussions, not threats."[54] Enchanted with an angel statue in the museum, they go to the home of its owner, Mrs. Basil E. Frankweiler, to
learn if Michelangelo was the sculptor. Mrs. Frankweiler answers them
on condition that they return home. Their adventure ends after Mrs.
Frankweiler includes a record of it in her mixed-up files and wills them
the statue, demanding that they keep its secret forever.

### Conservation

**Middle and Upper Grades.** A conservation problem, saving a historic
tree, is the theme of Mary and Conrad Buff's *Big Tree*,[55] which features
Conrad Buff's fine brown-and-white illustrations. The Buffs describe a
western U.S. tree as the biggest and oldest in the world, one that Native
Americans call Wawona. The authors telescope this redwood's five-thou-
sand-year history, telling how it may have sprouted when cave men
learned about fire. The tree survives because its bark is like asbestos so
no fire can burn it, and it is tannin-filled so no insect can gnaw it. The
book attributes human emotions to the tree, claiming, for example, "He
was in panic."[56] Men's saws cause the tree's panic until naturalists get
a declaration that Wawona's site is part of a park.

### Freedom

**Middle and Upper Grades.** Learning when to seek freedom is the theme
of Eve Bunting's *One More Flight*.[57] A constant runaway, eleven-year-
old Peter (Dobby) Dobson escapes from a Residential Treatment Center
after having previously run from five foster homes. On his latest excur-
sion, he spends several days in a barn with nineteen-year-old Timmer,
caretaker of injured birds of prey. Dobby complains about lack of freedom at the center, and Timmer helps by comparing him to birds. Timmer
releases his hawks and eagles when they can survive in the wilderness,
but one freed hawk, reluctant to leave, injures Timmer. While Timmer
is away being bandaged, Dobby tries to stop a man who sets the birds
loose. Dobby yells:

> "It's not time for them to go. They're not ready to be free.". . . .
> He was astonished by his own words. He wondered at the truth of
> them—that he saw the truth so clearly.[58]

Dobby is more appreciative when he returns to the center, promising not to run away again. He also promises himself that one day he will be free.

## Survival

**Upper Grades.** Survival is the theme of Felice Holman's *Slake's Limbo*,[59] the story of a thirteen-year-old nearsighted orphan, Aremis Slake, who flees into a subway when chased by gangs. He finds a dark, cold concrete room and uses it as a home for four months, sleeping on newspapers. He makes scant money reselling newspapers from subway trains and trash cans until he gets a job in a luncheonette. There he sweeps floors after the morning rush hour in exchange for a meal a day. When Slake realizes his hideaway will be destroyed by a subway repair crew, he becomes ill and collapses. A subway-train engineer, Willis Joe Whinny, rescues him, and the boy recuperates in a hospital where he gets needed eyeglasses. Preferring independent survival, he slips out of the hospital, not to the subway, but perhaps to a rooftop. As the story concludes, "Slake did not know exactly where he was going but the general direction was up."[60]

## Identity Crisis

**Upper Grades.** A boy's attempt to find himself is the theme of Julia Cunningham's *Come to the Edge*.[61] After four years at a foster farm, fourteen-year-old Gravel Winter overhears his father say:

"He'd be like a stone around my neck. The reason I left him here in the first place. Fact is—" and then it came "—I don't want him."[62]

Gravel runs away and finds a home in a small town with Mr. Paynter who begins to teach him sign painting. Before a gray feeling forces Gravel to leave, Mr. Paynter asks him what he might be if he could be transformed. Gravel's reply, "A rock,"[63] suggests a stone around his father's neck and prompts Mr. Paynter to say, "Then you've got to prod youself alive. . . . I trust you to come back, Mr. Winter."[64] He remembers this farewell when he moves to another town and gives himself piecemeal to three elderly persons. In return for shelter, he becomes Mr. Gant's eyes and in return for food, Mrs. Prior's legs. He also becomes the ears for Miss Ransome. After his three dependents urge him to learn a trade, he returns to Mr. Paynter and feels content for the first time.

A search for identity is also the theme of Robbie Branscum's *Toby, Granny and George*.[65] In the thirteen years since she was left on the elderly woman's doorstep, Toby has lived with her Granny in rural Arkansas. Toby's dog, George, is the third member of their household. When Granny's youngest daughter, Jolene, comes home after many years, Toby stares at her and knows instinctively she is Jolene's daughter. Afraid she will be taken from Granny, Toby runs away to hide at the home of Johnny Joe Treat, a fifteen-year-old mute boy. When Granny finds her, she assures the girl, "Leave, leave, not want you anymore? Why I told you, gal, I reckon I'd die without you and God, I swear I didn't know Jolene was your ma until she come here and told me."[66] Toby's mother leaves after she understands her daughter's preference to remain with Granny.

Older than Toby is seventeen-year-old Jacqueline Francis (J.F.) McAllister in Barbara Wersha's *Tunes for a Small Harmonica*.[67] Accepting oneself as unique is the theme of this book about an independent girl who is a misfit in the upper-class society of her birth. J.F.'s materialistic mother abhores her daughter's behavior and preference for masculine clothes. She gets no more love from her father, a Standard Oil executive who spends his time at work or at an exclusive businessman's club. J.F. is infatuated with the male poetry teacher in her girl's high school. She plays her harmonica on Manhattan streets, getting donations to help him go to Cambridge, England and complete his doctorate. The mid-sixties street experience teaches J.F. how unique she is, for she acknowledges:

> I didn't look like anybody else, or sound like anybody else, or act like anybody else. And I never had. I had spent my whole life worrying about being a peculiar person, when that was what I was meant to be in the first place.[68]

*Accepting Responsibility*

**Middle and Upper Grades.** Clyde Robert Bulla's *Shoeshine Girl* revolves around the theme of learning to accept responsibility.[69] Unmanageable ten-year-old Sarah Ida Becker visits Aunt Claudia in Palmville for the summer. Since her aunt won't give her spending money, Sarah gets a job shining shoes with Al Winkler. At first, Al is reluctant to employ a girl, but she works hard, and they become friends. When Al is hospitalized, Sarah continues the business and gives him the profits. After Al recuperates, she returns home to help her sick mother.

Less gutsy than Sarah is Benjie (Mouse) Frawley in Betsy Byars's

*The 18th Emergency.*[70] Here the theme is a boy's accepting responsibility for his actions after overcoming fear. Sixth grader Mouse imagines how to deal with seventeen of the world's greatest emergencies, but on the day he is confronted with his own eighteenth emergency, he has no answers. Under Neanderthal Man on the evolution chart in the school hallway, Mouse writes the name of the building's toughest fighter, Marv Hammerman, not knowing Marv is standing behind him. Mouse flees, but finally overcomes fear and takes his punishment. After accepting responsibility for his actions, standing up to a bully, and losing a fight honorably, his nickname seems inappropriate.

**Upper Grades.** A girl's learning to accept responsibility for her words is the theme of Louise Fitzhugh's humorous *Harriet the Spy.*[71] Harriet M. Welsch, an only child, relates best to her nursemaid, Ole Golly, and dislikes many of her sixth-grade classmates. Harriet, who wants to become a famous writer, has a daily routine spying through skylights and windows and hiding in dumbwaiters to observe and caustically record everything of interest in a secret notebook. She is candid and comical in her comments about her parents, classmates, and neighbors. After Ole Golly leaves to marry Mr. Waldenstein, pupils discover and read Harriet's notebook. They ostracize her, but Harriet retaliates. A letter from Ole Golly tells Harriet, "Remember that writing is to put love in the world, not to use against your friends. But to yourself you must always tell the truth."[72] After her parents secretly arrange with the principal for Harriet to be editor of a class paper, Harriet accepts responsibility for her journalistic misdeeds and in an editorial, apologizes to classmates.

Betsy Byars's *The Summer of the Swans* has the theme of accepting responsibility for a mentally retarded brother as part of growing up.[73] Following their mother's death and father's desertion, the three Godfrey children have lived with Aunt Willie. Sara is fourteen years old, her sister Wanda is nineteen, and her mentally disabled brother Charlie is ten. Sara feels the burden of caring for Charlie the night he gets lost looking for swans. When she finds him in a ravine, she begins to realize the meaning of responsibility. Initially envious of Wanda's appearance, Sara eventually senses that worth is not measured by external beauty, but by inner strength, which she tries to develop.

An older sister's accepting responsibility for her brother is the theme of another story, Eleanor Clymer's *My Brother Stevie.*[74] After their father's death, their mother deserts them, and twelve-year-old Annie Jenner and her eight-year-old brother, Stevie, move into their paternal grandmother's urban project apartment. Her mother's farewell request is for Annie to take care of her nearly delinquent brother. Impatient Grandma is ineffective when Stevie breaks into candy machines and throws rocks at trains. Annie, the narrator, gets her first help from Stevie's new teacher, Miss Stover, but when the teacher leaves, he reverts to attention-seeking behavior. Annie sacrifices to buy train tickets so she and Stevie can visit Miss Stover in the country. As a result of that visit, Stevie changes, grandmother stops hitting him, and Annie's responsibility diminishes.

A fourth story, Marilyn Sachs's poignant *The Bears' House*,[75] has the theme of accepting responsibility while yearning for a stable, loving home. Nine-year-old Fran Ellen Smith, ridiculed by fourth graders because she sucks her thumb and smells bad, skips school to care for her baby sister, Flora. Since their father left them, their mother has been so depressed, the children fend for themselves. Fletcher, her twelve-year-old brother, tells the others to keep their troubles a secret to avoid being sent to separate foster homes. He tries to shop and asks his eleven-year-old sister, Florence, to care for the baby and cook while Fran Ellen cleans. Florence is lazy so Fran Ellen does her sister's tasks and her own. She sneaks home during recess to give the baby a bottle of Kool-Aid, and even helps her five-year-old sister, Felice. Fran Ellen's only joy is fantasizing she is Goldilocks in a classroom dollhouse arranged for the three bears. Her teacher, Miss Thompson, delivers the dollhouse gift to the Smith apartment and promises help, a somewhat hopeful ending to this story of despair.

In order to stay under their own roof, the Luther family also conceals problems, as shown in Vera and Bill Cleaver's *Where the Lilies Bloom*.[76] Assuming responsibility and keeping promises is the theme of this book about a fourteen-year-old narrator, Mary Call, her five-year-old sister, Ima Dean, ten-year-old brother, Romey, and eighteen-year-old cloudy-headed sister, Devola. Their father, Roy Luther, a North Carolina mountain sharecropper, is dying of chest worms and makes Mary Call promise to bury him secretly, keep the family together, refuse charity, and prevent Devola from marrying landlord Kiser Pease. Mary Call assumes responsibility for the burial and for wildcrafting—collecting and selling medicinal herbs. She reneges on only one promise—Devola marries Kiser Pease after becoming more responsible. He, in turn, helps the family.

*Learning*

**Primary and Middle Grades.** Julia L. Sauer's *The Light at Tern Rock* has the theme of learning consideration.[77] Sauer tells about Byron Flagg, a lighthouse keeper, who asks Martha Morse to relieve him from several weeks of duty. The widow previously lived at Tern Rock Lighthouse when her husband was its keeper. Flagg promises to return by December 15, so her young nephew Ronnie, who lives with her, won't miss much school. By December 23, he still isn't back, so Aunt Martha cleans and cooks for Christmas. Ronnie finds a box with food, gifts, and a letter from Flagg, but they delay reading it. When Ronnie sulks, Aunt Martha says, ''Christmas, Ronnie, is something in your heart. It's a feeling that doesn't go with anger and hatred.''[78] After Christmas dinner, they share Flagg's letter, finding the sixty-year-old man had to trick them in order to spend the holiday with his niece's family, his first Christmas with young ones. Ronnie learns consideration and feels holiday satisfaction in lighting the beacon, feeling, ''We've lighted a candle tonight too—a big one.''[79]

**Upper Grades.** Learning from an experienced man is the theme of Jack Shaefer's *Old Ramón*.[80] A small boy's father tells him, ''You have had too much of printed books. You will watch Ramón and learn.''[81] The unnamed boy assures the shepherd, Ramón, ''You are my book about the sheep.''[82] From Ramón he learns about sheep, rattlesnakes, coyotes, sand storms, the difference between loneliness and being alone, and how to overcome fear. When a wolf kills Sancho, the boy's dog, Pedro is a comforting friend who teaches the lad how to face death.

Learning about oneself is the underlying theme in Norma Mazer's short-story collection, *Dear Bill, Remember Me? and Other Stories*.[83] In each story, a teenage girl learns about herself. In ''Up on Fong Mountain,'' Jessie finds she must change in order to relate to others. In ''Peter in the Park,'' Zoe tries to free herself from an overly protective family, and in ''Something Expensive,'' Maylee faces the reality that her mother is dating. ''Guess Whose Friendly Hands'' shows how Louise learns to live with cancer and tries to teach her family to face her impending death. ''Dear Bill, Remember Me?'' portrays Kathy, who realizes she is infatuated with her older sister's exboyfriend and painfully writes to congratulate him on his marriage.

*Outsiders*

**Middle and Upper Grades.** Seeking peer acceptance to avoid being an outsider is the theme of Judy Blume's *Blubber*.[84] After fat ten-year-old Linda Fischer makes an oral report on whales, her fifth-grade class nicknames her Blubber and treats her like an outsider. The cruelty is overdone, for leader Wendy develops *''HOW TO HAVE FUN WITH BLUBBER 1. Hold your nose when Blubber walks by. 2. Trip her. 3. Push her. 4. Shove her. 5. Pinch her. 6. Make her say, 'I am Blubber, the smelly whale of class 206' ''*[85] before she can use the toilet. The girls even compose a jump-rope rhyme, ''Oh what a riot, Blubber's on a diet, I wonder what's the matter, I think she's getting fatter and fatter and fatter and fatter, pop!''[86] The narrator, Jill Brenner, at first joins in ostracizing Linda, but later empathizes with her. Leader Wendy nicknames her new opponent Baby Brenner and makes Jill feel like an outsider. Jill says:

> A lot of people don't like me anymore. And for no good reason. I'm trying hard to pretend it does not matter, but the truth is it does. Sometimes I feel like crying but I hold it in.[87]

In the end, Jill challenges Wendy's authority and regains peer acceptance.
Upper Grades

Learning to feel less like outsiders and to accept common bonds between social classes is the theme of S.E. Hinton's *The Outsiders*.[88] Fourteen-year-old Ponyboy Curtis, the narrator, describes how he and his two older brothers, Sodapop and Darry, struggle to keep the family together after their parents' sudden deaths. Known as Greasers, the boys join other slum youths in protecting their turf from the Socs, upper-middle-class residents of Tulsa, Oklahoma. Ponyboy complains, "It wasn't fair for the Socs to have everything. We were as good as they were; it wasn't our fault we were Greasers.''[89] When a Soc accidently dies in a fight with Ponyboy and his friend, Johnny Cade, the two run away. They risk their lives in a fire to save several children, and Johnny ultimately dies. However, he and Ponyboy learn "Socs were just guys after all. Things were rough all over, but it was better that way. That way you could tell the other guy was human too.''[90]

*Impersonal or Tyrannical School Treatment*

**Upper Grades.** The individual versus technology is the theme of Sonia Levitan's *The Mark of Conte*,[91] a story about a high school freshman, Conte Mark. Confusion over his name results in the computer's printing two schedule cards, one for Conte Mark and another for Mark Conte. The lad assumes two identities and attends double the classes in order to graduate early. His friend, Greg, correctly assures him the caper is possible, because faculty members are not aware of his double existence. Though his work load is heavy, Conte is motivated to prove that the computer runs the school. Neglect of the individual is further shown when a lifeless dummy, Miss Valerie Valasquez, is registered as a substitute teacher and gets a high evaluation without administration realizing the hoax. Undetected, Conte leaves his mark at impersonal Vista Mar High.

A tyrannical secondary school is the setting for Robert Cormier's

*The Chocolate War,*[92] whose theme is misuse of power. At Trinity, a Catholic preparatory school, a teacher, Brother Leon, is in trouble because he has to repay school funds he misappropriated for his own use. He tries to raise money by selling chocolates at school and blackmails Archie Costello, leader of an intimidating school gang, the Vigils, to help in the sale. Archie proclaims, "I can con anybody. I am Archie."[93] However, even when Archie accuses freshman Jerry Renault of lacking school spirit, Jerry refuses to join in the sale. Jerry is inspired by a poster that questions, "Do I dare disturb the universe?"[94] The lone rebel suffers. He is falsely charged with being a homosexual and almost killed. The ending is pessimistic because the corrupt chocolate sale is a success, and Jerry believes his principled stand was futile.

*Permanence*

**Middle and Upper Grades.** A need for permanence is the theme of Lillie D. Chaffin's *John Henry McCoy,*[95] the story of an Appalachian boy. Since the big Kentucky coal mines closed, Mr. McCoy has had to travel to find work and constantly uproots his family. John Henry and Granny, who want to settle in one place, approach Mr. Thompson, a storekeeper, about his abandoned house. Granny says:

> I've come on business, house business. I don't have ten cents to my name, but you've got a house going to waste. Needs a fire in it to dry out the rot. Needs somebody to love it. Houses are like people, they fall apart when nobody cares. . . . Give you half on what I raise next year.[96]

Mr. Thompson agrees if John Henry agrees to help Granny. When Mr. McCoy gets a job in the city, but doesn't have a dwelling place for the family, John Henry convinces his mother to let them stay in their rural setting and ask his father to join them on weekends. Fulfilling his wish for permanence, John Henry thinks "about all the things he might have, . . . his school, his dog, his friends."[97]

*Need for Security or Love*

**Middle and Upper Grades.** A need for security is the theme of Eleanor Clymer's *Luke Was There.*[98] The narrator, twelve-year-old Julius, and his younger brother, Danny, abandoned by their father, stay in Children's House while their mother is in the hospital. At night Julius is frightened that his mother might die. His fears are assuaged by a new Black counselor, Luke Morehouse, who becomes the stable pillar in Julius's life. When Luke has to leave to do alternative service as a conscientious objector, Julius bitterly accuses him, "You're just like the rest. You make believe you like us, then you go away. My father, my uncle, José, you're all the same."[99] Lacking Luke's guidance, Julius gets into mischief and runs away. In Grand Central Station, he meets an abandoned seven-year-old boy, Ricky, whom he takes to Children's House though Julius knows he may face punishment. Best of all, Luke is waiting for him. His former counselor took time from work to search for him. The author shows no sex-role stereotyping when she states that hardened Julius cries upon seeing Luke. Several weeks later, Julius and Danny return home with their mother, but Julius remembers, "When I needed him [Luke] most, he was there."[100]

**Upper Grades.** A need for security and love is the theme of Julia Cunningham's *Dorp Dead*.[101] After his grandmother's death, eleven-year-old Gilly Ground resents living in an orphanage. He leaves to serve as an apprentice to Mr. Kobalt, a psychotic carpenter. Kobalt's padlocked stone house is orderly, and Gilly realizes, "Master Kobalt has not created this shiny, absolute precision out of love but because it creates safety for him."[102] Gilly's only friends are Kobalt's dog, Mash, and a mysterious hunter. Eccentric Kobalt beats his dog. When Gilly discovers a cage believed to be for him, he escapes. Kobalt chases him and tries to kill him. Mash returns Gilly's love by saving the boy's life. Gilly departs, presumably to find the hunter, after leaving Kobalt a message to Dorp Dead, a note he later discovers was misspelled.

    *Dorp Dead* is an allegory in which Kobalt represents evil, Gilly stands for all young people seeking security and love, and the hunter, whose gun has no bullets, symbolizes love. The hunter is nameless because he represents numerous rescuers. The author says, "I guess I did not give him a name because he has so many."[103]

*Family Relationships*

**Middle and Upper Grades.** A family's search for a name day is the theme of Jennie D. Lindquist's *The Golden Name Day*.[104] During her mother's illness, nine-year-old Nancy spends a year with her Swedish-American grandparents. As she begins to appreciate Swedish customs, she is disappointed to learn the Swedish Almanac lists no name day for Nancy. Grandpa Benson resolves the problem by finding one day, January first, with no listed name. He enters Nancy's name there, and other relatives follow his example.

The focus shifts from a granddaughter to a needed mother, the theme of Maia Wojciechowska's *"Hey, What's Wrong with This One?"*.[105] During the two years since their mother's death, three mischievous boys cause all their housekeepers to quit. For different reasons, the boys want a mother, not another housekeeper. Matt, the youngest, feels, "While she was alive . . . everything was right."[106] Davidson, the middle son, thinks, "When she was around, being good was not hard."[107] To Harley, the oldest, "She . . . understood how it was with the firstborn."[108] For these reasons, Matt goes with Dad to the supermarket to lead a search for a mother. When he sees a likely candidate, he asks Dad, "Hey, what's wrong with this one?"[109] Attracted by one woman, Matt knocks canned peaches her way, accidently injuring her. Dad visits her apologetically, and she calls on him. The boys prevail upon her to housekeep for them, a stereotyped role, while dating Dad.

In Emily Neville's account of life in New York City, *It's Like This, Cat,*[110] fourteen-year-old Dave Mitchell has a successful father who is a lawyer. The book's theme is a father/son relationship, which is antagonistic enough at times to cause his mother's asthma. Knowing his father is a dog lover, Dave deliberately chooses Cat as his pet. His father yells at him for playing his records, but Mr. Mitchell does help Dave's friend, Tom, and he is concerned about Dave getting his date, Mary, home safely. One evening when Dave and his father argue, Mr. Mitchell actually apologizes, a hopeful sign for improved communication.

In an interview, Emily Neville says that her book, *It's Like This, Cat* grew from a short story, "Cat and I," published in 1960 in the *New York Sunday Mirror*. She explains:

I started with this argument. . . . The father tells the boy how great it is to have a dog, so the kid will want to get a cat. I got that far. I had a boy, a cat, and a father. What happens to a cat? I thought what happened to our cats, only two things. It occasionally got lost, and it jumped out of a car on a parkway. What's the source of characters, like old Kate? I had a baby-sitter . . . who was a cat- and cottage cheese- and no-string-beans nut. She began bringing her sick cats to work, and we parted company. Writing the book from then on was a matter of adding another incident, another location, another person. I did not have the slightest idea of a real plot when I started. . . .

My editor said, "Your thread appears to be the boy and his father. Just be sure you strengthen that a tiny bit, and make sure that's where you end. That's where you began, so end with boy and father.''[111]

**Upper Grades.** A child assuming a mother's role is the theme of Betsy Byars's *The Night Swimmers*.[112] The night swimmers are three children of a deceased mother whose father, Shorty, an aspiring country-western singer, neglects them for his career. Shorty is away at night and busy by day, so young Retta (named for country singer, Loretta Lynn) tries to care for her still-younger brothers, Johnny (named for Johnny Cash) and Roy (inspired by Roy Acuff). Retta feeds them, making spaghetti with tomato soup and noodles, and entertains them by taking them for night swims in a pool of a colonel who retires early. When Roy almost drowns, Retta suffers guilt, for ''Retta had always been his daytime mother. Even when her real mother was alive, it had been Retta who looked after him.''[113] Retta's burden may be eased since there are hints that Shorty may remarry.

Learning family togetherness is the theme of Vera and Bill Cleaver's *Dust of the Earth*.[114] Fourteen-year-old Fern Drawn narrates the chronicles of her family after they inherit Grandfather Bacon's sheep ranch and try eking a living in the Badlands of South Dakota at Chokecherry. Grandfather looked upon the Drawns as ''the dust of the earth; we were below his salt.''[115] Fern has three siblings, sixteen-year-old Hobson, eight-year-old Madge, and three-year-old Georgie. Because they are poor as potato scrapings, Fern has to abandon school to tend the sheep. Normally family members are antagonistic or indifferent. Fern describes them as follows:

> We were not one. There were seldom any announcements of affection between us. We were like partridges in the wood, each scattered to his own interests except during meal and sleep times. We took pleasure in deviling one another. We were not friends. . . . The word love was not spoken in our house.[116]

However, the family members learn to communicate so they can tend their sheep. As a result, Fern finds them growing together, and the ''old feelings of desertion and aloneness have weakened between us.''[117]

The Drawns were previously isolated and learned to love each other, but the Devons, as shown in Jeanette Eyerly's *Escape from Nowhere*,[118] were formerly intimate and no longer are. Attempted escape from deteriorated family relations is Eyerly's theme. Teenager Carla Devon, the book's narrator, says that when her father is traveling on business, her mother drinks, but her father doesn't believe his wife has a problem. Carla's sister, Diane, away at college, is indifferent to her mother's alcoholism. One night, when her mother is in a drunken stupor, Carla leaves her house and accidently meets a popular school chum, Dexter Smith, who invites her to a party. Surprised to find guests smoking marijuana, she uses it. After trying more potent drugs, she becomes an addict and is jailed. On probation, she no longer needs drugs to hide from family problems and paves her own escape from nowhere. She says:

> For a while smoking pot had made me forget how lousy and unsatisfactory my life really was. But nothing had really changed. Now I knew that the only thing that would change it much was me.[119]

Several contemporary realistic prizewinners highlight relationships with fathers. The first, Annabel and Edgar Johnson's *The Grizzly*,[120] has the theme of relating to a separated father. David remembers painfully being hit by his father, Mark, before his parents separated. When his outdoorsman father takes the small-framed boy on a camping trip to the mountains, David is fearful. The strained father/son relationship improves after the two face a grizzly. David thinks, "And for a minute there, as they crouched together beside the truck, it had been almost as if the two of them were friends."[121] The grizzly attacks Mark, who is afraid for the first time. David proves courageous in a crisis, and the two learn from each other. David begins to realize his father is not cruel but is trying to make a man of him in too rugged a way.

A boy's reconciliation with his father is the theme of Paula Fox's *Blowfish Live in the Sea*.[122] Thirteen-year-old Carrie, a New York City apartment dweller, tells about her nineteen-year-old half-brother, Ben, a college dropout. He wears a leather hair thong and often writes or mumbles, "Blowfish live in the sea." When Carrie was born, Ben's father sent him a blowfish, claiming it came from the Amazon. Ben's knowledge of the true source of blowfish shows his disillusionment with his dishonest father. After six silent years, Ben's father, Mr. Felix, invites him to Boston, and Carrie accompanies her beloved Ben. Mr. Felix turns out to be a poor, unreliable alcoholic, but Ben decides to help him with his latest business, a motel. The boy lets Carrie have the one gift from his father, the ceramic blowfish. He doesn't require it now because he's found his father and feels needed.

*Independence*

**Upper Grades.** Jean Craighead George's *My Side of the Mountain* has a theme of learning to be independent through reverence for nature.[123]

Seventeen-year-old Sam Gribley runs away from his New York City
family to the Catskill Mountains. He dwells in a cave fashioned in a
giant hemlock tree, complete with clay fireplace and deerskin door. He
captures a falcon, Frightful, who helps secure his food, and is befriended
by a weasel, the Baron, and a raccoon, Jesse Coon James. Dressed in
animal skins, he cooks plants, such as tubers, surviving eight months
with reverence for nature until his parents intervene.

While discussing *My Side of the Mountain* in an interview, Jean
George says that her major themes are: (1) how the child "senses and
grows correctly among the plants and animals, the idealized way to live
as far as I'm concerned, and (2) finding himself."[124] She adds:

> That's the dream world—to be alone and independent of parents. What
> really influenced me were my parents' attitudes about this. They would
> take us to an island along the Potomac River and say, "Make a living
> off the place." My father taught me everything in that book. We ate
> everything I've described, all those delicious tubers and crayfish, so to
> me it was a way of life.
>
> I was rebellious. I resented authority. I was more or less a loner for an
> interesting reason. My brothers, who are ecologists too, are identical
> twins. They had this great thing going between them, and I was always,
> "Me too, let me come along."
>
> I also feel that this is like the development of the human child. They
> go through loving the father, the mother, the family group, and then
> that moment of independence comes when they've got to be alone with
> themselves before they can join the human society. This happened to
> Sam . . . [125]

*Loneliness or Friendship*

**Middle and Upper Grades.** Friendship is the theme of E.L. Konigsburg's
*Jennifer, Hecate, Macbeth, William McKinley, and Me, Elizabeth*.[126]
Ten-year-old Elizabeth is the loneliest only child in the whole United
States until she finds Jennifer, a witch, on Halloween. The two trick or
treat together and meet every Saturday. Though witches do not usually
make friends, Jennifer considers Elizabeth worthy if she follows instructions, first as apprentice and later as journeyman witch. Elizabeth has to
eat raw eggs, cast short spells, and help mix a potion that permits human
beings to fly. Jennifer becomes angry when Elizabeth refuses to throw
the toad, Hilary Ezra, into the bubbling potion, so the girls part. Later,
Jennifer visits Elizabeth, explaining that she is a neighbor, so they resume

their interracial friendship. The story concludes, "Neither of us pretends to be a witch anymore. Now we mostly enjoy being what we really are, just Jennifer, and just Me, just good friends!"[127]

Friends who are exceptional is the theme of Zilpha Keatly Snyder's *The Changeling*.[128] The story is told in retrospect by Martha Abbott, a slender, poised high school sophomore, who realizes how much she owes Ivy Carson, her playmate since they were both seven years old. Ivy claims to be in the large, troublesome Carson family as a changeling (an infant secretly exchanged without parents' awareness). In the early days, Ivy, a natural dancer, was light and fearless while Martha was fat and so easily scared her family called her Marty Mouse. Through friendship with imaginative Ivy, Martha develops acting talent and later stars in school productions. After the Carsons move away, Martha receives a letter from Ivy who is in New York studying to be a dancer. The letter says:

> I know I was right about being a changeling. I had to be. But lots of people are changelings, really. You might be one yourself, Martha Abbott, I wouldn't be surprised.[129]

**Upper Grades.** Another book by Zilpha Keatly Snyder, *The Witches of Worm*,[130] revolves around the theme of a lonely child's imagination. Deserted by her father, twelve-year-old Jessica is raised by attractive Joy who became the child's mother when she was eighteen years old. Joy works during the day and leaves Jessica alone at night to visit her boyfriend, Alan. While Alan may like Joy, the child realizes he does not welcome a ready-made daughter. In the Regency Apartment House, the only other child is Brandon, but he seems to have abandoned her, preferring his trumpet, bicycle, and male playmates. Jessica's loneliness is reflected in a recurring dream:

> There had been a time when she was afraid to go to sleep because of a dream that came back again and again. It was a terrifying dream about waking up all alone in an empty room that grew bigger and emptier until it filled the whole universe.[131]

Deprived of human companions, Jessica concentrates on an abandoned, newly born kitten, Worm. (The name derives from her mother's comment, "It reminds me of some kind of worm."[132]) After reading witchcraft tales, Jessica convinces herself Worm is bewitched. The child blames her own irresponsible behavior on Worm's magical control of her, claiming she has become a witch. In the end, Jessica tries to exorcize

Worm, and the cat almost dies. "Maybe you exorcized yourself, too,"[133] is the wise comment from Brandon who becomes a friend once more.

Overcoming loneliness is the theme of Ester Wier's *The Loner,*[134] the story of a young migratory worker with no family and no name. He looks after himself even when he is sick and left alone in a deserted camp. The first person to show an interest in him is Raidy, who tries to name him just before she catches her hair in a potato-digging machine. He witnesses her death. The dejected boy wanders until he is found by Boss, a large woman who manages a Montana sheep ranch. A loner herself, Boss nurtures the boy and gives him the name David. A third loner is the provisions tender, Tex. David reflects, "It had been Tex who had taught him how to stop being a loner, how to throw in his lot with others and work for everyone, not just for himself."[135] David learns his lesson well, for he saves Tex from a trap, nurses Boss, and slaughters the grizzly that killed Boss's son, Ben. David overcomes his loneliness as he gives and accepts warmth from those at the ranch.

A wealthier boy than David is oversized seventeen-year-old Franklin (Ox) Olmstead featured in John Ney's *Ox under Pressure.*[136] Ox is 6'8" tall, weighs 250 pounds, and is the only child of Palm Beach jet setters with a dubious family life. Preceded by *Ox: The Story of a Kid at the Top* and *Ox Goes North,* this third book in a series has the theme of friendship with a neurotic girl. The author tells how Ox accompanies his father and his father's female friend, Sally, staying on Long Island while his unconcerned mother visits Argentina. Ox befriends a troubled seventeen-year-old neighbor, tall, thin Arabella Marlborough who previously suffered from anorexia. She says, "I stopped eating because I was starved for affection."[137] When the wealthy woman with whom Arabella's family lives overhears the girl's criticism of the hostess, Ox takes Arabella to his home. She tells Ox, "I've been alone all my life, until I met you."[138] Then she moves to the Connecticut institution that cured her anorexia, hoping to learn independence in "hard places," and realizing "it's putting the pressure on you . . . to worry about me."[139] After the boy returns to Florida, he concludes, "Poor old Ox, under pressure he will always defend the weak, but when peace is restored, he wonders if it was worth it."[140]

The friendship and determination of misfits is the theme of Betsy Byars's *The Pinballs.*[141] Three children in a foster home band together to try to help each other. Adolescent Carlie is placed in the home because her stepfather beat and attacked her. Thirteen-year-old Harvey has lived there since his drunken father ran over him with a car and broke both of his legs. Eight-year-old Thomas J., abandoned at a farm run by two old women, worked for them until the women broke their hips. Authorities find he doesn't belong on the farm and put him in the foster home. Carlie looks upon the three in the following way:

> Harvey and me and Thomas J. are just like pinballs. Somebody put in a dime and punched a button and out we came, ready or not, and settled in the same groove.[142]

When Harvey goes to the hospital, Carlie tells Thomas J. she was wrong to compare the trio to pinballs. She explains:

> It's just that pinballs can't help what happens to them and you and me can. See, when I first came here, all I thought about was running away, only I never did it. . . . I know that doesn't sound like much, but it was me deciding something about my life. And now I have decided that when I go to this new school, I'm really going to try. . . . And as long as we are trying, Thomas J., we are not like pinballs.[143]

The friendship theme is also apparent in Katherine Paterson's *Bridge to Terabithia*,[144] an account of an imaginative ten-year-old boy and girl, Jesse Aarons and Leslie Burke. In the woods, the pair create a secret kingdom, Terabithia, which can be entered only by swinging across a creek on an enchanted rope. One rainy day, Leslie tries to visit Terabithia alone, falls off the rope, hits her head, and drowns. Jesse agonizes, then builds a bridge to Terabithia, crowning his young sister, May Belle, as the new queen in memory of Leslie, the real queen.

In an interview, Katherine Paterson says that the theme of her book, *Bridge to Terabithia,* is not death, but friendship. She explains:

> Most of the book is not about death, but friendship, and death of some kind is a part of every friendship. . . . The book grew out of a friendship that my twelve-year-old had with a girl, Lisa Hill, who was very dear to all of us, and she was killed. She was struck by lightning. This kid asked me yesterday why I didn't put that in the book, and I said, "Because nobody would believe it." . . .
>
> It was just after I had gone through a cancer operation. When I started writing the book, thinking I was going through the child's death, of course, what I was doing was facing my own death, which became a very difficult thing. When I came to the chapter where the child was supposed to die, it was many, many days before I could do it. Finally, a friend asked me, "How's your book coming?" I said, "I can't go through Lisa's death again." She replied, "It's not Lisa's death, Katherine." So I went home and faced my own death.[145]

## Summary

Themes of contemporary realistic fiction about families, friends, and problems are examined under seventeen headings. Most of the books have themes concerned with family relationships, adjusting, accepting responsibility, loneliness or friendship, maturing, and death. Overlapping occurs, but there are approximately thirty-two family stories, fourteen friendship tales, and fifteen books about problems. Over three-fifths of the sixty-one examples of prizewinners are intended for children in fifth grade or beyond, and the balance are mainly for those in or above fourth grade.

This chapter features multiple books by a number of authors. Four are by Betsy Byars and by Vera and Bill Cleaver, three are by Judy Blume, and there are two each by Eleanor Clymer, Julia Cunningham, Elizabeth Enright, S.E. Hinton, E.L. Konigsburg, Norma Mazer, Katherine Paterson, Marilyn Sachs, and Zilpha Keatly Snyder.

## Notes

1. In 1975, *A Book for Jodan* won the Woodward Park School Annual Book Award.

2. Marcia Newfield, *A Book for Jodan* (New York: Atheneum, 1975), pp. 28–32.

3. In 1978, *The Great Gilly Hopkins* won the Christopher Award in the children's-book category for ages nine to twelve. In 1979, it was the Newbery Honor Book and won the National Book Award in the children's-book category.

4. Katherine Paterson, *The Great Gilly Hopkins* (New York: Crowell, 1978), p. 148.

5. "Katherine Paterson," *Profiles in Literature* (Philadelphia: Temple University, 1979).

6. Ibid.

7. In 1939, *Thimble Summer* won The John Newbery Medal.

8. Elizabeth Enright, *Thimble Summer* (New York: Holt, 1966), p. 123.

9. In 1957, *Miracles on Maple Hill* won The John Newbery Medal.

10. Virginia Eggertsen Sorensen, *Miracles on Maple Hill* (New York: Harcourt, 1956), p. 23.

11. Ibid., p. 101.

12. Ibid., p. 70.

13. Ibid., p. 84.

14. In 1977, *A Smart Kid Like You* won the Dorothy Canfield Fisher Children's Book Award.

15. Stella Pevsner, *A Smart Kid Like You* (New York: Seabury, 1975), p. 189.

16. In 1971, *A Room Made of Windows* won the *Boston Globe-Horn Book* Award.

17. "Eleanor Cameron," *Profiles in Literature* (Philadelphia: Temple University, 1972).

18. In 1974, *Chloris and the Creeps* won the Southern California Council on Literature for Children and Young People Award.

19. Kin Platt, *Chloris and the Creeps* (Philadelphia: Chilton, 1973), p. 146.

20. In 1978, *Dorrie's Book* won the Garden State Children's Book Award.

21. Marilyn Sachs, *Dorrie's Book* (New York: Doubleday, 1975), p. 98.

22. In 1973, *A Taste of Blackberries* won the Child Study Children's Book Committee at Bank Street College Award and, in 1975, the Georgia Children's Book Award.

23. In 1971, *Grover* was a finalist for the National Book Award in the children's-book category.

24. In 1975, *The Edge of Next Year* was a finalist for the National Book Award in the children's-book category.

25. Mary Stolz, *The Edge of Next Year* (New York: Harper, 1974), p. 194.

26. In 1975, *The Garden Is Doing Fine* won the Golden Kite Award and the Child Study Children's Book Committee at Bank Street College Award.

27. Carol Farley, *The Garden Is Doing Fine* (New York: Atheneum, 1975), p. 110.

28. Ibid., p. 111.

29. Ibid., p. 181.

30. Ibid., p. 182.

31. Ibid., p. 185.

32. In 1974, *A Figure of Speech* was a finalist for the National Book Award in the children's-book category.

33. Norma Fox Mazer, *A Figure of Speech* (New York: Delacorte, 1973), p. 33.

34. In 1981, *A Ring of Endless Light* was a Newbery Honor Book.

35. Madeleine L'Engle, *A Ring of Endless Light* (New York: Farrar, 1980), p. 59.

36. In 1978, *Otherwise Known as Sheila the Great* won the South Carolina Children's Book Award.

37. Judy Blume, *Otherwise Known as Sheila the Great* (New York: Dell, 1972), p. 89.

38. In 1975, *Are You There, God? It's Me, Margaret* won the Nene Award and in 1976, the Young Hoosier Award.

39. "Judy Blume," *Profiles in Literature* (Philadelphia: Temple University, 1973).

40. Judy Blume, *Are You There, God? It's Me, Margaret* (New York: Dell, 1976), p. 148.

41. In 1979, *Queen of Hearts* was a finalist for the National Book Award in the children's-book category.

42. Vera and Bill Cleaver, *Queen of Hearts* (New York: Bantam, 1978), p. 98.

43. In 1966, *Up a Road Slowly* won The John Newbery Medal.

44. Irene Hunt, *Up a Road Slowly* (Chicago: Follett, 1966), p. 181.

45. Ibid., p. 31.

46. In 1969, *Seventeenth Summer* won the Lewis Carroll Shelf Award.

47. Maureen Daly, *Seventeenth Summer* (New York: Dodd, 1942), p. 179.

48. In 1978, *That Was Then, This Is Now* won the Massachusetts Children's Book Award.

49. S.E. Hinton, *That Was Then, This Is Now* (New York: Viking, 1971), p. 69.

50. Ibid., p. 155.

51. Ibid., p. 159.

52. In 1958, *Gone-Away Lake* was a Newbery Honor Book.

53. In 1968, *From the Mixed-Up Files of Mrs. Basil E. Frankweiler* won The John Newbery Medal and in 1970, the William Allen White Children's Book Award.

54. E.L. Konigsburg, *From the Mixed-Up Files of Mrs. Basil E. Frankweiler* (New York: Atheneum, 1972), p. 43.

55. In 1947, *Big Tree* was a Newbery Honor Book.

56. Mary and Conrad Buff, *Big Tree.* (New York: Viking, 1946), p. 30.

57. In 1976, *One More Flight* won the Golden Kite Award.

58. Eve Bunting, *One More Flight* (New York: Warne, 1976), pp. 69–71.

59. In 1977, *Slake's Limbo* won the Lewis Carroll Shelf Award.

60. Felice Holman, *Slake's Limbo* (New York: Scribner, 1974), p. 117.

61. In 1977, *Come to the Edge* won the Christopher Award in the children's-book category for ages twelve and up, and in 1978, it won the Lewis Carroll Shelf Award.

62. Julia Cunningham, *Come to the Edge* (New York: Pantheon, 1977), p. 6.

63. Ibid., p. 22.

64. Ibid., p. 22.

65. In 1977, *Toby, Granny and George* won the Friends of American Writers Award in the children's-book category.

66. Robbie Branscum, *Toby, Granny and George* (New York: Doubleday, 1976), p. 78.

67. In 1977, *Tunes for a Small Harmonica* was a finalist for the National Book Award in the children's-book category.

68. Barbara Wersha, *Tunes for a Small Harmonica* (New York: Harper, 1976), p. 173.

69. In 1976, *Shoeshine Girl* was a notable book of the Southern California Council on Literature for Children and Young People Award. In 1978, it won the Sequoyah Children's Book Award.

70. In 1975, *The 18th Emergency* won the Dorothy Canfield Fisher Children's Book Award.

71. In 1967, *Harriet the Spy* won the Sequoyah Children's Book Award.

72. Louise Fitzhugh, *Harriet the Spy* (New York: Harper, 1964), p. 276.

73. In 1971, *The Summer of the Swans* won The John Newbery Medal.

74. In 1968, *My Brother Stevie* won the Woodward Park School Annual Book Award.

75. In 1972, *The Bears' House* was a finalist for the National Book Award in the children's-book category.

76. In 1970, *Where the Lilies Bloomed* was a finalist for the National Book Award in the children's-book category.

77. In 1952, *The Light at Tern Rock* was a Newbery Honor Book.

78. Julia L. Sauer, *The Light at Tern Rock* (New York: Viking, 1951), p. 47.

79. Ibid., p. 62.

80. In 1961, *Old Ramón* was a Newbery Honor Book and winner of the Ohioana Book Award.

81. Jack Shaefer, *Old Ramón* (Boston: Houghton, 1960), p. 3.

82. Ibid., p. 3.

83. In 1976, *Dear Bill, Remember Me? and Other Stories* won the Christopher Award in the children's-book category for ages twelve and up. In 1978, it won the Lewis Carroll Shelf Award.

84. In 1977, *Blubber* won the Pacific Northwest Library Association Young Reader's Choice Award.

85. Judy Blume, *Blubber* (New York: Bradbury, 1974), pp. 71–72.

86. Ibid., pp. 79–80.

87. Ibid., p. 139.

88. In 1979, *The Outsiders* won the Massachusetts Children's Book Award for grades 7 to 9.

89. S.E. Hinton, *The Outsiders* (New York: Viking, 1967), p. 43.

90. Ibid., p. 104.

91. In 1977, *The Mark of Conte* was a notable book of the Southern California Council on Literature and Young People Award.

92. In 1979, *The Chocolate War* won the Lewis Carroll Shelf Award.

93. Robert Cormier, *The Chocolate War* (New York: Random House, 1974), p. 223.

94. Ibid., p. 123.

95. In 1971, *John Henry McCoy* won the Child Study Children's Book Committee at Bank Street College Award.

96. Lillie D. Chaffin, *John Henry McCoy* (New York: Macmillan, 1971), p. 72.

97. Ibid., p. 169.

98. In 1974, *Luke Was There* won the Child Study Children's Book Committee at Bank Street College Award.

99. Eleanor Clymer, *Luke Was There* (New York: Holt, 1973), p. 24.

100. Ibid., p. 74.

101. In 1966, *Dorp Dead* was a notable book of the Southern California Council on Literature for Children and Young People Award.

102. Julia Cunningham, *Dorp Dead* (New York: Pantheon, 1965), p. 29.

103. Julia Cunningham, "Dear Characters," *The Horn Book Magazine,* Vol. 43 (April 1967), p. 234.

104. In 1946, *The Golden Name Day* was a Newbery Honor Book.

105. In 1973, *"Hey, What's Wrong with This One?"* won the Georgia Children's Book Award.

106. Maia Wojciechowska, "Hey, What's Wrong with This One?" (New York: Harper, 1969), p. 3.

107. Ibid., p. 4.

108. Ibid., p. 4.

109. Ibid., p. 39.

110. In 1964, *It's Like This, Cat* won The John Newbery Medal.

111. "Emily Neville," *Profiles in Literature* (Philadelphia: Temple University, 1975).

112. In 1981, *The Night Swimmers* won The American Book Award for fiction.

113. Betsy Byars, *The Night Swimmers* (New York: Delacorte, 1980), p. 21.

114. In 1975, *Dust of the Earth* won the Western Writers of America Spur Award for fiction.

115. Vera and Bill Cleaver, *Dust of the Earth* (Philadelphia: Lippincott, 1975), p. 18.

116. Ibid., p. 20.

117. Ibid., p. 159.

118. In 1969, *Escape from Nowhere* won the Christopher Award in the children's-book teen-age category.

119. Jeanette Eyerly, *Escape from Nowhere* (Philadelphia: Lippincott, 1969), p. 182.

120. In 1967, *The Grizzly* won the William Allen White Children's Book Award.

121. Annabel and Edgar Johnson, *The Grizzly* (New York: Harper, 1964), p. 104.

122. In 1971, *Blowfish Live in the Sea* was a finalist for the National Book Award in the children's-book category.

123. In 1960, *My Side of the Mountain* was a Newbery Honor Book. In 1965, it won the Lewis Carroll Shelf Award and in 1969, the George G. Stone Center for Children's Books Recognition of Merit Award.

124. "Jean Craighead George," *Profiles in Literature* (Philadelphia: Temple University, 1974).

125. Ibid.

126. In 1968, *Jennifer, Hecate, Macbeth, William McKinley, and Me, Elizabeth* was a Newbery Honor Book.

127. E.L. Konigsburg, *Jennifer, Hecate, Macbeth, William McKinley and Me, Elizabeth* (New York: Atheneum, 1967), p. 117.

128. In 1970, *The Changeling* won the Christopher Award in the children's-book category for ages eight to twelve.

129. Zilpha Keatly Snyder, *The Changeling* (New York: Atheneum, 1970), p. 219.

130. In 1973, *The Witches of Worm* was a Newbery Honor Book and was a finalist for the National Book Award in the children's-book category.

131. Zilpha Keatly Snyder, *The Witches of Worm* (New York: Atheneum, 1974), p. 34.

132. Ibid., p. 39.

133. Ibid., p. 182.

134. In 1964, *The Loner* was a Newbery Honor Book.

135. Ester Wier, *The Loner* (New York: McKay, 1963), p. 152.

136. In 1977, *Ox under Pressure* won the National Book Award in the children's-book category.

137. John Ney, *Ox under Pressure* (Philadelphia: Lippincott, 1976), p. 45.

138. Ibid., p. 163.

139. Ibid., p. 227.

140. Ibid., p. 237.

141. In 1977, *The Pinballs* won the Woodward Park School Annual Book Award and, in 1979, the Georgia Children's Book Award.

142. Betsy Byars, *The Pinballs* (New York: Harper, 1977), p. 29.

143. Ibid., p. 136.

144. In 1978, *Bridge to Terabithia* won The John Newbery Medal and the Lewis Carroll Shelf Award.

145. "Katherine Paterson," *Profiles in Literature* (Philadelphia: Temple University, 1979).

## References of Contemporary Realistic Fictional Prizewinners about Families, Friends, and Problems

*(Estimated Reading Grade Level in Parentheses)*

*Family Stories*

Branscum, Robbie. *Toby, Granny and George*. Illustrated by Glen Rounds. New York: Doubleday, 1976 (6–8).

Byars, Betsy. *The Night Swimmers*. Illustrated by Troy Howell. New York: Delacorte, 1980 (5–8).

———. *The Summer of the Swans*. Illustrated by Ted Coconis. New York: Viking, 1970 (5–8).

Cameron, Eleanor. *A Room Made of Windows*. Illustrated by Trina Schart Hyman. Boston: Little, Brown, 1971 (6–8).

Chaffin, Lillie D. *John Henry McCoy*. Illustrated by Emanuel Schongut. New York: Macmillan, 1971 (4–6).

Cleaver, Vera and Bill. *Dust of the Earth*. Philadelphia: Lippincott, 1975 (5–8).

———. *Grover*. Illustrated by Frederic Marvin. Philadelphia: Lippincott, 1970 (4–7).

———. *Queen of Hearts*. New York: Lippincott, 1978 (6–10).

———. *Where the Lilies Bloom*. Illustrated by Jim Spanfeller. Philadelphia: Lippincott, 1969 (6–9).

Clymer, Eleanor. *My Brother Stevie*. New York: Holt, 1967 (5–8).

Enright, Elizabeth. *Thimble Summer*. New York: Holt, 1966 (4–6).

———. *Gone-Away Lake*. Illustrated by Beth and Joe Krush. New York: Harcourt, 1958 (4–6).

Farley, Carol. *The Garden Is Doing Fine*. Illustrated by Lynn Sweat. New York: Atheneum, 1975 (5–7).

Fox, Paula. *Blowfish Live in the Sea*. Scarsdale, N.Y.: Bradbury, 1970 (6–9).

George, Jean Craighead. *My Side of the Mountain*. New York: Dutton, 1959 (5–7).

Hunt, Irene. *Up a Road Slowly*. Chicago: Follett, 1966 (5–8).

Johnson, Annabel and Edgar. *The Grizzly*. Illustrated by Gilbert Riswold. New York: Harper, 1964 (6–9).

Konigsburg, E.L. *From the Mixed-Up Files of Mrs. Basil E. Frankweiler*. New York: Atheneum, 1972 (5–7).

L'Engle, Madeleine. *A Ring of Endless Light*. New York: Farrar, 1980 (6–8).

Lindquist, Jennie D. *The Golden Name Day*. Illustrated by Garth Williams. New York: Harper, 1955 (3–5).

Mazer, Norma Fox. *A Figure of Speech*. New York: Delacorte, 1973 (6–9).

Newfield, Marcia. *A Book for Jodan*. Illustrated by Diane de Groat. New York: Atheneum, 1975 (3–4).

Neville, Emily. *It's Like This, Cat*. Illustrated by Emil Weiss. New York: Harper, 1963 (4–6).

Pevsner, Stella. *A Smart Kid Like You*. New York: Seabury, 1975 (5–7).

Platt, Kin. *Chloris and the Creeps*. Philadelphia: Chilton, 1973 (5–8).

Sachs, Marilyn. *The Bears' House*. Illustrated by Louis Glanzman. New York: Doubleday, 1971 (5–7).

―――. *Dorrie's Book*. Illustrated by Anne Sachs. New York: Doubleday, 1975 (5–6).

Sauer, Julia L. *The Light at Tern Rock*. Illustrated by Georges Schreiber. New York: Viking, 1951 (2–4).

Snyder, Zilpha Keatly. *The Witches of Worm*. Illustrated by Alton Raible. New York: Atheneum, 1974 (5–8).

Sorensen, Virginia Eggertsen. *Miracles on Maple Hill*. Illustrated by Beth and Joe Krush. New York: Harcourt, 1956 (4–6).

Stolz, Mary. *The Edge of Next Year*. New York: Harper, 1974 (7–12).

Wojciechowska, Maia. *"Hey, What's Wrong with This One?"* Illustrated by Joan Sandin. New York: Harper, 1969 (3–6).

*Friendship Tales*

Blume, Judy. *Are You There, God? It's Me, Margaret*. New York: Dell, 1970 (4–6).

———. *Otherwise Known as Sheila the Great*. New York: Dell, 1972 (3–6).

Bulla, Clyde Robert. *Shoeshine Girl*. Illustrated by Leigh Grant. New York: Crowell, 1975 (3–5).

Byars, Betsy. *The Pinballs*. New York: Harper, 1977 (5–7).

Clymer, Eleanor. *Luke Was There*. Illustrated by Diane de Groat. New York: Holt, 1973 (4–7).

Daly, Maureen. *Seventeenth Summer*. New York: Dodd, 1942 (7–12).

Hinton, S.E. *That Was Then, This Is Now*. New York: Viking, 1971 (7–12).

Konigsburg, E.L. *Jennifer, Hecate, Macbeth, William McKinley, and Me, Elizabeth*. New York: Atheneum, 1967 (4–6).

Ney, John. *Ox under Pressure*. Philadelphia: Lippincott, 1976 (5 and up).

Paterson, Katherine. *Bridge to Terabithia*. Illustrated by Donna Diamond. New York: Crowell, 1977 (6–8).

Shaefer, Jack. *Old Ramón*. Illustrated by Harold West. Boston: Houghton, 1960 (6–8).

Smith, Doris Buchanan. *A Taste of Blackberries*. Illustrated by Charles Robinson. New York: Crowell, 1973 (4–6).

Snyder, Zilpha Keatly. *The Changeling*. Illustrated by Alton Raible. New York: Atheneum, 1970 (4–6).

Wier, Ester. *The Loner*. Illustrated by Christine Price. New York: McKay 1963 (5–8).

*Books about Problems*

Blume, Judy. *Blubber*. Scarsdale, N.Y.: Bradbury, 1974 (4–6).

Buff, Mary and Conrad. *Big Tree*. New York: Viking, 1946 (3–5).

Bunting, Eve. *One More Flight*. Illustrated by Diane de Groat. New York: Warne, 1976 (4–8).

Byars, Betsy. *The 18th Emergency*. Illustrated by Robert Grossman. New York: Viking, 1973 (4–6).

Cormier, Robert. *The Chocolate War*. New York: Random House, 1974 (9–12).

Cunningham, Julia. *Come to the Edge*. New York: Pantheon, 1977 (5–7).

———. *Dorp Dead*. Illustrated by James Spanfeller. New York: Pantheon, 1965 (5–8).

Eyerly, Jeanette. *Escape from Nowhere*. Philadelphia: Lippincott, 1969 (7–9).

Fitzhugh, Louise. *Harriet the Spy*. New York: Harper, 1964 (5–8).

Hinton, S.E. *The Outsiders*. New York: Viking, 1967 (7–12).

Holman, Felice. *Slake's Limbo*. New York: Scribner, 1974 (5–7).

Levitan, Sonia. *The Mark of Conte*. Illustrated by Bill Negron. New York: Atheneum, 1976 (6–9).

Mazer, Norma Fox. *Dear Bill, Remember Me? and Other Stories*. New York: Delacorte, 1976 (7–9).

Paterson, Katherine. *The Great Gilly Hopkins*. New York: Crowell, 1973 (4–7).

Wersha, Barbara. *Tunes for a Small Harmonica*. New York: Harper, 1976 (7 and up).

# 13 Contemporary Realistic Fiction about U.S. Minorities

*Though the theme of* Annie and the Old One *is sad, this book understands my people. TV shows us too often as warriors.*

—Running Dog, aged twelve

## Perspective and Standards

Like Running Dog, other minority-group members want to see themselves in print realistically. They ask to be represented in books as intelligent leaders who solve their own problems, not as token figures. They seek material written from their group's perspective, with an understanding of their history and value system. They want to be appreciated as individuals, not as a generalized mass, and when secure, will evaluate others in the same light. They expect accurate artwork and sensitive terminology.

The Council on Interracial Books for Children discourages loaded words, such as *savage,* and racial epithets. They prefer *Native American* to *Indian,* which can be confused with a resident of India, *rain forest* to *jungle,* and in North America, *nation* to *tribe.*

In this chapter, stereotypes in prizewinners are criticized. Generally, there is less paternalism in recent books than in earlier ones. The minority group of some authors and illustrators is specified in order to indicate that they create from the point of view of insiders.

## Themes of Realistic Fiction about U.S. Minorities Grouped under These Topics

*Accepting Death*

**Primary and Middle Grades.** The theme of Miska Miles's *Annie and the Old One* is young Annie's need to accept the impending death of her grandmother.[1] The Old One says she will be in Mother Earth when the new Navajo rug is done, so her granddaughter tries to delay the weaving. Then the Old One explains that no one can stop the inevitable.

353

*Fighting Loneliness*

**Middle and Upper Grades.** Fighting loneliness by accepting responsibilities is the theme of Jane Wagner's *J.T.*,[2] first presented as a CBS children's television production. Pictures taken by a Black photographer, Gordon Parks, Jr., convey the loneliness of a fatherless Harlem Black pupil, J.T. He assumes responsibility for a cat and helps his mother by getting a parttime job.

Harlem is also the setting for Mary Hays Weik's *The Jazz Man*,[3] whose poignant theme is loneliness and desertion. The author's daughter, illustrator Ann Grifalconi, projects in woodcuts the isolation of Zeke, a disabled nine-year-old Black boy. His quarreling parents desert him, returning only when he is starved and feverish. If the ending is not taken literally, it may be interpreted that the boy dies, and there is a rosy reunion in heaven. This is literature of despair that shows stereotyped, irresponsible Black parents.

*Acknowledging Growth*

**Middle and Upper Grades.** Acknowledging growth is the theme of Virginia Driving Hawk Sneve's *Jimmy Yellow Hawk*.[4] Ten-year-old Little Jim on a South Dakota Sioux reservation wants the diminutive dropped from his name. After an unusual accomplishment, the community recognizes his growth and calls him Jimmy Yellow Hawk.

**Upper Grades.** More complex is Joseph Krumgold's . . . *and Now Miguel*.[5] The twelve-year-old male narrator is patterned after a real boy living with his family on a sheep ranch near Taos, New Mexico. The book's theme is acknowledging the growth of a preadolescent. Author Joseph Krumgold states this more elaborately:

> The theme that came out of . . . *and Now Miguel* is a child growing up and being received into his family and community as an adult. It is the theme of confirmation. Two things are judged: the child (whether he is prepared to be an adult) and the society which is inducting him.[6]

In keeping with the theme, Miguel has a secret wish: to be considered mature enough to accompany family men on the summer trek with the sheep to the mountains. Older brother Gabriel gets drafted, and now Miguel, as the title declares, joins the mountaineers.

The book's illustrator, Jean Charlot, whose mother was Mexican, is a specialist in Mexican art. On the end papers, he portrays the Mexican-American lad pointing to the mountains, reinforcing the theme.

The history of . . . *and Now Miguel* exemplifies that the author's reason for writing and the theme are often linked. Joseph Krumgold, a documentary filmmaker, reveals that he wrote the book after producing a film by that same name for the U.S. Information Service, guided by anthropologist Margaret Mead. The film was to have been part of a series (that never materialized), showing the strength of U.S. families as economic and social units. However, Krumgold wrote a trilogy with the underlying purpose of the proposed film series in mind. The first volume in the trilogy, . . . *and Now Miguel*, has an agrarian setting. Companion books explore the implicit theme, acknowledging that a preadolescent is growing up, in different environments: *Onion John*,[7] in a small town and *Henry 3*, in suburbia.

### Need for Self-Determination

**Upper Grades.** In Krumgold's *Onion John*, acknowledging growth is a secondary theme. A dictatorial father concedes that his son, the twelve-year-old narrator, Andy Rusch, Jr., has matured enough to plan his own future. However, the apparent theme, self-determination, revolves around a tall childlike man, Onion John. Born in Europe, this devotee of Saint Stepan speaks an unidentified language with words ending in *ovitch* and *owsky* that only the narrator understands. Onion John finally hides in a cave, his expression of self-determination, rather than permit Rotarians to rebuild a home they think is proper for him.

The author says that Onion John is based on an actual person who ate onions with such appetite that, when he came on a bus, passengers moved to the back. In real life, Krumgold relates that the people of Belvedere, New Jersey "killed" Onion John "with utter love,"[8] for he died shortly after moving into a community-built house with appliances he could not safely operate. He did not have the strength to self-determine his residence, as the book character finally did.

### Career Choice

**Upper grades.** Pondering a jazz career is the theme of *Jazz Country* by Nat Hentoff, a jazz lecturer.[9] Tom Curtis, a White high school senior, chooses between the predictable world of college and the unknown challenge of becoming a jazz musician. Professional Black jazz performers are friendly after he becomes aware of their problems as Blacks and as musicians, but they steer him toward college.

A different career, that of medicine man, is the concern of *Younger*

Brother in Laura Adams Armer's *Waterless Mountain.*[10] The book's theme is the internal processes: the thoughts, feelings, and growth of an aspiring Navaho medicine man. The author studied Navaho culture in Arizona for eight years before writing her book which she illustrated with the help of her husband, Sidney.

The main weakness of *Waterless Mountain,* copyrighted in 1931, is that it does not feature minority members solving their own problems. The Big Man, a White or *Pelicano* trading-post owner, is the civil engineer who builds a needed reservoir. He cures Younger Brother's illness and lets the boy be the first Navaho to ride on an airplane. The flight convinces the boy's father "that white men are mightier than Navahos,"[11] damaging self-criticism in a book about a minority. Earlier, the Big Man's sister distributes Christmas presents, is repaid by the Navahos, and comments, "Didn't I always say the spirit of Christmas would win even a savage?"[12] Her terminology could not be less appropriate for humane, peaceful Navahos.

*Overcoming Fear*

**Middle and Upper Grades.** The same weakness in *Waterless Mountain,* though not as severe, is evident in Jonreed Lauritzen's *The Ordeal of the Young Hunter.*[13] Lauritzen's transcriptions are different than Armer's, his choice being *Navajo* and, for the White person, *Bellicano.* The theme of Lauritzen's book, overcoming fear, the young hunter's ordeal, is emphasized in several illustrations by Navajo artist, Hoke Denetsosie. Twelve-year-old Jadih has always lived in Arizona among The People, as the Navajos call themselves. A *Bellicano,* Mr. Jim of the trading post, leads Jadih to a hated cougar, which the boy kills with the adult's help. Then Mr. Jim drives the lad to a powwow where Jadih musters the courage to do a hunter's dance in a contest viewed by strange *Bellicanos.* The book suffers from Mr. Jim's paternalism instead of Navajos resolving their own problems.

*Integrated Education*

**Middle and Upper Grades.** The theme of Natalie Savage Carlson's *The Empty Schoolhouse* is seeking self-improvement and combating Black/White antagonism in integrated education.[14] In Louisiana, Black ten-year-old Lullah Royall, who wants a better education, leaves her segregated public school to enroll in an integrated Catholic school. (The book uses the dated terms *Colored* and *Negro.*) When violence keeps others away, only she and the nuns attend the empty schoolhouse. After an angry White wounds Lullah, many Whites change their attitudes toward her.

**Upper Grades.** A theme identical to that in *The Empty Schoolhouse* is at the core of Dorothy Sterling's somewhat-dated book, *Mary Jane,*[15] illustrated by Black artist Ernest Crichlow. The theme is seeking self-improvement and combating Black/White antagonism through integrated education. In the South, Mary Jane Douglas and Fred Jackson, twelve-year-old Black pupils (the book uses the term *Negro*), suffer abuse when they are first to integrate a junior high. Basketball skill helps Fred win friends, and Mary Jane is accepted when she shares a pet squirrel with Sally Wilson, a White classmate.

In *Sneakers* by Black author Ray Anthony Shepard, the theme is combating Black/White antagonism in integrated education.[16] In a newly integrated Massachusetts school, there is competition between Chuck, a Black eighth-grader on the football team, and Craig, his White peer. Fortunately, the boys put aside racial antagonism to plan strategy that brings their team victory. The two finally invite each other to their homes, ending their personal Black/White hostility.

### Trying to Improve Oneself

**Upper Grades.** Trying to improve oneself is the theme of *The Contender* by journalist Robert Lipsyte.[17] An orphaned Black high school dropout, Alfred Brooks, believes becoming a boxer may get him out of the ghetto. He begins to train, makes good friends, and plans to finish high school while continuing his job. After he loses an amateur bout, he realizes that trying to improve is what counts.

### Guidance Needed for Gang Members

**Upper Grades.** The theme of two prizewinners by Frank Bonham is guidance needed for gang members. In *Durango Street,*[18] the characters are Black, and in *Viva Chicano,*[19] they are Chicano. Both books show fatherless teenage parolees in urban California who return from detention to wary mothers in housing projects. In *Durango Street,* Black social worker Alex Robbins guides parolee Rufus Henry, a Moors gang member, to consider going back to school.

In *Viva Chicano,* parolee Keeny (Joaquín) Durán, aided by the Aztecs gang, hides from police. He gives himself up, subconsciously guided by his deceased Mexican father. In court, despite objections from his mother, parole officer Frank Baker convinces Judge Closson to place the youth in a parolees' boardinghouse where the resident advisor is landlady Peggy Sherwood. Unfortunately, the designers of a support system are all Anglos, a weakness in a book about Latinos.

### Poverty

**Upper Grades.** Memories of Puerto Ricans in South Bronx is the theme of *El Bronx Remembered* by Nicholasa Mohr, whose mother was Puerto Rican and whose father was Chinese-American.[20] Her collection of eleven short stories and one novella deal with problems, like poverty and unwed pregnancy, in New York City's *El Bronx,* an extension of Spanish Harlem.

Poverty is the theme of a humorous Mohr short story, "Shoes for Hector." A high school valedictorian, Hector López, has no money for new shoes. When he graduates, he wears a navy suit and his uncle's clashing pointed-toe orange shoes. He is afraid peers will call them:

> Roach killers. Man, the green horns wear them shoes to attack the cockroaches that hide in the corners. Man, they go right in there with them points and zap . . . zap . . . and snap . . . they're dead! *Matacucaracha* shoes.[21]

After he receives a graduation check, the valedictorian announces he'll "Buy me a pair of shoes! Any color except orange!"[22]

### Black in a White World

**Upper Grades.** Another collection of eleven short stories, *Guests in the Promised Land*[23] by Black author Kristin Hunter has the theme of being Black in a White world: "It ain't no Promised Land at all if some people are always guests and others are always members."[24] In one tale, "Bee Gee's Ghost," Frederick Douglass Jackson, a Black lad, is turned down by a White pet cemetery when he tries to bury his pure-white dog, Bee Gee, which stands for Brown Girl. (She has the name of a former pet, a brown police dog.) Confusion over color by the rejected child is thematic.

### Search for Identity

**Middle and Upper Grades.** A sheltered nine-year-old girl, Esther Lapp, is in Virginia Eggertsen Sorensen's *Plain Girl,*[25] whose theme is the search for identity in society as an Amish "plain girl." The girl's father has this narrow view of identity: "We are Plain People and so we wear plain clothes," but outsiders "don't know who they are. . . . They are nothing and nobody."[26] Forced by Pennsylvania school-attendance laws, the father lets his daughter go to school, though he is afraid she will forget Amish ties. She learns the benefit of farm machinery in the outside world and still appreciates good Amish customs, like helping harvest an injured farmer's crops. She decides to incorporate the best of the new world with her inherited values.

**Upper Grades.** A search for identity is the theme of Audrey Distad's *The Dream Runner*.[27] Fatherless twelve-year-old Sam "Many Troubles" McKee learns that the Sioux ancestors of his friend, old Clete, had traditional vision quests to seek a spirit to lead them into manhood. On his own vision quest, the boy imagines a Native American runner, who is none other than himself, a dream that convinces him to continue distance running.

The setting shifts to crowded Spanish Harlem, but the theme, searching for identity, prevails in the prose and representational art of *Nilda* by author-illustrator Nicholasa Mohr.[28] Ten-year-old Nilda Ramírez, who struggles for identity in a large Puerto Rican family, gets this advice from her dying mother:

> If I cannot see who I am beyond the eyes of the children I bore, then it was not worth the journey. . . . Hold on to yourself. . . . To give it all up, . . . you will lose what is real inside you.[29]

The mother encourages Nilda's identity as an artist. Her dream is fulfilled, for the novel is partially autobiographical, and Nicholasa Mohr is now a graphic artist.

Searching for identity, but as an Afro-American, is the theme of Kristin Hunter's *The Soul Brothers and Sister Lou*.[30] The author states: "It contains some of the milestones I have passed on my own continuing journey to discovering the meaning of my Afro-American identity and its worth."[31] In a northern ghetto, teen-aged Louretta Hawkins draws on the splendid legacy of Black music to form a highly successful vocal quartet, The Soul Brothers and Sister Lou.

Kristin Hunter hopes her story about a popular quartet will inspire Black readers, for she comments:

> The ghetto is a ferment of talent, and I want Black children themselves to see this. As to success in American terms, Blacks are a generation behind Whites in rejecting money. They don't want to go around barefoot and be poor; they've had enough of that.[32]

Lawrence Yep writes about his minority group in *Child of the Owl*,[33] whose theme is the search for identity as a Chinese-American. Previously raised by her widowed father, an addicted gambler, a twelve-year-old girl, Casey Young, says, "I knew more about race horses than I knew about myself—I mean myself as a Chinese."[34] While residing with her grandmother, Paw-Paw, in San Francisco's Chinatown, she discovers she is a child of the owl, because she feels alone inside. She thinks the owl story "tells me who I am."[35] It is her decision to stay permanently in Chinatown, "the first place I'd ever had roots in . . . Paw-Paw was spinning a lightweight, yet strong, silk cocoon about me."[36]

### Preserving a Historical Site

**Upper Grades.** Preserving a historical site, an underground-railroad museum, is the theme of *The House of Dies Drear* by Black author Virginia Hamilton.[37] Since abolitionist Dies Drear was murdered in his house (an underground-railroad station) the Black caretaker of the house, old Pluto, is fanatical about protecting it and its secret museum.

### Existence of Anti-Semitism

**Upper Grades.** The primary theme of Emily Cheney Neville's *Berries Goodman* is the existence of anti-Semitism.[38] The secondary themes reflect the positive values of loyal friendship, growing up in a big city, and a family's adjustment to a new environment. Nine-year-old Berries Goodman, a Mormon, experiences anti-Semitism in suburban New Jersey. First, a neighbor, Sandra Graham, taunts a Jewish lad, Sidney Fine, and then Berries's mother, a parttime realtor, confesses she sells houses to Jews only in restricted areas.

When asked what inspired *Berries Goodman,* the author emphasizes the primary theme:

> It grew out of my talking to my real estate friend who mentioned the problem of the restrictions understood by all the real estate brokers: don't sell north of Broad Street to anyone who's Jewish. . . . I was trying to get that situation into some book, and *Berries* was what it wound up in.[39]

### Revealing a Nazi Criminal

**Upper Grades.** The serious primary theme of M.E. Kerr's *Gentlehands* is an adolescent's decision to inform on his beloved grandfather, an evil

Nazi war criminal, and a lighter secondary theme is having a summer romance.[40] The only Jewish character, journalist Nick De Lucca, hunts Gentlehands, an ironically named SS officer who commanded Auschwitz dogs to kill Italian Jews. De Lucca's suspect is Frank Trenker, grandfather of protagonist Buddy Boyle. The boy laments that anti-Nazis killed Grandpa's dog, so his mother questions, "Do you expect me to feel sorry for his dog after what he let dogs do to human beings?"[41] When his girlfriend learns about Grandpa's past, the boy's summer romance is doomed. This is a skillful intertwining of primary and secondary themes.

Referring to *Gentlehands,* author M.E. Kerr says the romance of a policeman's son, "trying to get above his raisings,"[42] was based on fact, but the primary theme grew from reading Howard Blum's *Wanted! The Search for Nazis in America.* Some young people fail to note *Gentlehands*'s primary theme, so the author thinks she should have been more direct in warning that an animal or family lover may be evil.


*Friendship*

**Middle and Upper Grades.** Black characters are featured in *Sidewalk Story* by Black author Sharon Bell Mathis.[43] A loyal friend helping to stop injustice is the book's theme. When neighbors who cannot pay their rent are evicted, nine-year-old Lilly Etta Allen asks her mother, "Aren't you going to help? Mrs. Brown is your friend."[44] Despite her mother's intimidation, the girl publicly protests and involves a newspaper reporter whose sidewalk story brings assistance.

In another metropolitan tale, Mary Stolz's *The Noonday Friends,*[45] the primary theme concerns the friendship of two poor girls, and a secondary theme revolves around a father who is a scant provider. Two eleven-year-old schoolmates, Franny Davis, an Anglo, and Simone Orgella, a Puerto Rican, eat lunch together. Their families are friendly enough to help each other find employment.

Friendship between a Black and a White girl is the theme of Natalie Savage Carlson's *Ann Aurelia and Dorothy.*[46] In this nonstereotyped tale, a Black ten-year-old child, Dorothy Grant, is part of a loving, stable, middle-class family, and her White peer, Ann Aurelia Wilson, lives in a foster home until her mother returns.

Larger than Ann Aurelia Wilson's family is that of eleven-year-old Beth Lambert. Her life in rural Arkansas is discussed in Bette Greene's *Philip Hall Likes Me. I Reckon Maybe,*[47] which has the theme of a unique girl's friendship in a sexist society. Beth says, "I could see the chocolate brownness of my mama."[48] There are no other references to color in the text, but Black illustrator Charles Lilly effectively draws only Black characters except for a White storekeeper. Beth, the second-best pupil in her class, questions, "Is Philip Hall number one only 'cause I let him be? Afraid he wouldn't like me if I were best?"[49] Determined to go to college, bright Beth develops herself to the maximum, even if it means competing with her friend, Philip.

In an interview, Bette Greene says she prefers to write about unique girls. She knew the model for Beth Lambert who truly was unique.[50]

**Upper Grades.** Building interracial friendship is the theme of *South Town* by Black author Lorenz Graham, brother-in-law of the famous Black scholar, W.E.B. Du Bois.[51] In the South, two Whites help the Black Williams family protect themselves from night riders, because "It ain't every white man that's against colored folks."[52] When one of the Whites, Solomon Travis, dies, the Williams family moves North, and their experiences continue in sequels, *North Town, Whose Town?*, and *Return to South Town*.

Northern Black characters are featured in *Fast Sam, Cool Clyde, and Stuff*[53] by Black author Walter Dean Myers. The book's theme, neighborhood friendship, is developed when urban teenagers form the 116th Street Good People Club to care for each other in times of stress.

The primary theme of Zilpha Keatley Snyder's *The Egypt Game* is an individualistic child helped by friends.[54] Eleven-year-old neighbors, April Hall, an individualistic White child, and a Black peer, Melanie Ross, develop an imaginative Egypt game. They play it with a Chinese child, Elizabeth Chung, in old Professor's yard, motivating him to take new interest in life, a secondary theme of the book.

*Interracial Business Enterprise*

**Primary through Upper Grades.** The business enterprise of two friends is the theme of Jean Merrill's *The Toothpaste Millionaire*.[55] The author, an associate editor of Bank Street Readers, is interested in minorities, as is evident in this book prepared by Bank Street College. In Cleveland, Rufus Mayflower, an inventive twelve-year-old Black boy, and Kate Mackinstrey, a White girl with organizational skills, team to make and distribute inexpensive toothpaste. After banking a million dollars, Rufus plans a new business with his teammate.

*Need for Permanence*

**Middle and Upper Grades.** A need for permanence is the theme of Louisa R. Shotwell's *Roosevelt Grady*,[56] a story about a loving family of poor Black migratory workers. Roosevelt Grady dreams of staying in one school long enough to learn division. At Elliott's Bus Camp, his folks fulfill the dream when they choose a bus that can be a year-round home. Some readers criticize the mother's contentment with a dilapidated-bus home, but this is the first step toward full equality and establishing permanence.

## Homeland Preferred

**Upper Grades.** The theme of Hila Colman's *The Girl from Puerto Rico* is the homeland preferred after experiencing difficulties in New York.[57] Fifteen-year-old Felicidad Marquez and her family move from a Puerto Rican farm to New York City. After facing economic and social discrimination, they return to Puerto Rico to preserve their values.

## Family Relationships

**Middle and Upper Grades.** Love between a young boy and his great-great aunt, the theme of Sharon Bell Mathis's *The Hundred Penny Box*,[58] is emphasized in sepia drawings by Black illustrator Leo Dillon and his wife Diane. Michael Jefferson's mother wants to replace Aunt Dew's treasured old box that holds a penny for each of her hundred years. Michael shows his devotion by trying to save the box.

A different family relationship is depicted in Ruth White Miller's *The City Rose*.[59] When a timid Black girl, Dee Bristol, becomes an orphan, she moves from Detroit to a North Carolina farm. Struggling for acceptance is the book's theme. In her new home, she is sure Aunt Lulu wants her, but she is not sure of Uncle George. She also struggles for acceptance in her sixth-grade class with a biased White teacher who says, "So many Negroes have no respect for state property [textbooks]."[60] She earns teacher approval and realizes her uncle loves her when he files for adoption.

**Upper Grades.** A father is pivotal in *Our Eddie* by Jewish author Sulamith Ish-Kishor.[61] The book's theme is the effect of a fanatical, egotistical father, Mr. Raphel, on his family, especially on his older son, Eddie. The father chooses to teach Hebrew to the poor and relates only to his pupils. Mr. Raphel, an atypical Jewish father, neglects his family, and fifteen-year-old Eddie has to quit school to support them. Both Eddie and his mother are muscular dystrophy patients, but Eddie dies from attempted corrective surgery. Then Mr. Raphel is remorseful and more attentive to his other children.

The next two books concern Black characters. In *A Hero Ain't Nothin' but a Sandwich* by Black author Alice Childress, thirteen-year-old Benjie Johnson, deserted by his father, is almost hooked on heroin.[62] He desperately needs a father replacement. The book's apparent theme, overcoming addiction by adopting a father, is revealed through ten narrators. Benjie learns to love his stepfather, Butler Craig, after Craig saves his life. Bolstered by his mother and adopted father, Benjie feels he can live without heroin.

A more literary Black child is depicted in *Ludell* by Black author Brenda Wilkinson.[63] The book's theme is a preadolescent's relationship with her grandmother, neighbors, and teachers. In vernacular, the narrator relates the story, set in Waycross, Georgia, the author's hometown. It shows Ludell in her last three grades—fifth through seventh—of a segregated elementary school where one particular teacher inspires high-quality writing. Especially well described is the woman who raises Ludell, her loving grandmother, whom she calls Mama. Mama explains, "Sugar pie, you was my baby from the beginning."[64] Armed with a sense of humor, Ludell copes with pervasive poverty to establish warm relationships.

*Survival*

**Upper Grades.** The theme of Virginia Hamilton's highly original book, *M.C. Higgins the Great*,[65] is survival on an eroding mountain. The Black Higgins family lives in Ohio on inherited mountainous land that is endangered by mine stripping. The oldest son, M.C., instead of the father, begins construction of a wall to stop the erosion. He decides to stay, firmly planted on a safer mountain.

The theme of another Virginia Hamilton book, *The Planet of Junior Brown*,[66] is surviving while helping others. A Black eighth-grade student, Buddy Clark, abandoned by his mother, survived in an underground network of shelters. Now he supports others in his own shelter, living by his credo, "We are together because we have to learn to live for each other."[67]

After *The Planet of Junior Brown* was published, Virginia Hamilton discovered that similar self-help networks in large cities do exist. When asked about her book's theme in an interview, the author says she emphasizes survival.[68] Panelists agree that the main character is a survivor, but an unselfish, creative one who improves his surroundings.

Survival in a different environment, with wolves, is the primary theme of Jean Craighead George's *Julie of the Wolves*.[69] Miyax, called Julie in English, is a thirteen-year-old Eskimo girl who endures on the

North Slope of Alaska with a wolf pack. Some readers interpret the theme to be a girl pitted against nature for survival. However, ecologist Jean Craighead George does not think human beings and nature are in opposition. She says that her books often revolve around two themes: "(1) the child's relationship to the earth, and (2) the child becoming an independent person."[70]

Both themes are obvious in *Julie of the Wolves*. Survival with wolves is the primary theme, and becoming an independent person, a secondary theme. Most of the book tells about association with wolves, who have some human characteristics. When Julie is starving, wolves supply her with caribou, and she even drinks the milk of a nursing wolf mother. Her feeling of kinship to wolves, the primary theme, gives her the strength to develop independence, a secondary theme.

## Summary

This chapter reviews themes of forty-three examples of prizewinning works of realistic fiction about U.S. minorities. Featured in these books are American Black, Amish, Chicano, Chinese-American, Jewish, and Puerto Rican characters. Minority-group members give the insiders' perspective in that they authored almost half the award winners and illustrated more than one-third of those that are illustrated. Stereotypes are criticized where they are found in the books. About two-thirds of the listings are intended only for upper-elementary readers and most of the others, for those in a range of middle through upper grades. Themes are grouped under twenty-one headings.

Virginia Hamilton has written three prizewinners in the sample of realistic fiction about U.S. minorities. The following have written two: Natalie Savage Carlson, Kristin Hunter, Joseph Krumgold, Sharon Bell Mathis, and Nicholasa Mohr.

## Notes

1. In 1971, *Annie and the Old One* received the Christopher Award in the children's-book category for ages eight to twelve and the Commonwealth Club of California Award. In 1972, it was a Newbery Honor Book and won the Woodward Park School Annual Book Award.

2. In 1972, *J.T.* won the Georgia Children's Book Award.

3. In 1966, *The Jazz Man* was a *New York Times* Choice of Best Illustrated Children's Book of the Year, and in 1967, it was a Newbery Honor Book.

4. In 1970, *Jimmy Yellow Hawk* won the Council on Interracial Books for Children Award in the American Indian category.

5. In 1954, . . . *and Now Miguel* won The John Newbery Medal.

6. "Joseph Krumgold," *Profiles in Literature* (Philadelphia: Temple University, 1971).

7. In 1960, *Onion John* won The John Newbery Medal. Since Joseph Krumgold, its author, won the same medal for . . . *and Now Miguel* in 1954, he was the first to be honored twice with this coveted award.

8. "Joseph Krumgold," *Profiles in Literature* (Philadelphia: Temple University, 1971).

9. In 1966, *Jazz Country* won the Woodward Park School Annual Book Award.

10. In 1932, *Waterless Mountain* won The John Newbery Medal.

11. Laura Adams Armer, *Waterless Mountain* (New York: David McKay, 1931), p. 74.

12. Ibid., p. 66.

13. In 1954, *The Ordeal of the Young Hunter* won the Child Study Association of America Wel-Met Children's Book Award.

14. In 1965, *The Empty Schoolhouse* won the Child Study Children's Book Committee at Bank Street College Award.

15. In 1960, *Mary Jane* won the Woodward Park School Annual Book Award.

16. In 1970, *Sneakers* won the Council on Interracial Books for Children Award in the African-American category.

17. In 1967, *The Contender* won the Child Study Children's Book Committee at Bank Street College Award.

18. In 1967, *Durango Street* received the George G. Stone Center for Children's Books Recognition of Merit Award.

19. In 1971, *Viva Chicano* received the Woodward Park School Annual Book Award.

20. In 1976, *El Bronx Remembered* was a finalist for the National Book Award in the children's-book category.

21. Nicholasa Mohr, *El Bronx Remembered* (New York: Harper, 1975), p. 36.

22. Nicholasa Mohr, *El Bronx Remembered* (New York: Harper, 1975), p. 36.

23. In 1973, *Guests in the Promised Land* won the Christopher Award in the children's-book category for ages twelve and up. In 1974, it was a finalist for the National Book Award in the children's-book category.

24. Kristin Hunter, *Guests in the Promised Land* (New York: Scribner, 1973), p. 133.

25. In 1955, *Plain Girl* won the Child Study Children's Book Committee at Bank Street College Award.

26. Virginia Eggertsen Sorensen, *Plain Girl* (New York: Harcourt, 1955), pp. 76–77.

27. In 1978, *The Dream Runner* won the Friends of the American Writer Award for older children.

28. In 1973, *Nilda* was a *New York Times* Choice of Best Illustrated Children's Book of the Year, and in 1974, it won the Jane Addams Book Award.

29. Nicolasa Mohr, *Nilda* (New York: Harper, 1973), pp. 277–278.

30. In 1968, *The Soul Brothers and Sister Lou* won the Council on Interracial Books for Children Award for readers of ages twelve to sixteen. In 1971, it won the Lewis Carroll Shelf Award.

31. Kristin Hunter, *The Soul Brothers and Sister Lou* (New York: Scribner, 1968), dust jacket.

32. "Kristin Hunter," *Profiles in Literature* (Philadelphia: Temple University, 1969).

33. In 1977, *Child of the Owl* won the *Boston Globe-Horn Book* Award, and in 1979, it won the Jane Addams Book Award.

34. Lawrence Yep, *Child of the Owl* (New York: Harper, 1977), p. 3.

35. Ibid., p. 203.

36. Ibid., pp. 195–196.

37. In 1965, *The House of Dies Drear* won the Ohioana Book Award, and in 1969, it received the Edgar Allen Poe Award.

38. In 1966, *Berries Goodman* won the Jane Addams Book Award.

39. "Emily Cheney Neville," *Profiles in Literature* (Philadelphia: Temple University 1975).

40. In 1979, *Gentlehands* won the Louis Carroll Shelf Award.

41. M.E. Kerr, *Gentlehands* (New York: Harper, 1978), p. 158.

42. M.E. Kerr, "Changing Lifestyles in Children's Books," Drexel University and The Free Library of Philadelphia conference, March 25, 1981.

43. In 1969, *Sidewalk Story* won the Council on Interracial Books for Children Award for readers of ages seven to eleven.

44. Sharon Bell Mathis, *Sidewalk Story* (New York: Viking, 1971), p. 16.

45. In 1966, *The Noonday Friends* was a Newbery Honor Book.

46. In 1969, *Ann Aurelia and Dorothy* won the Woodward Park School Annual Book Award.

47. In 1975, *Philip Hall Likes Me. I Reckon Maybe* was a Newbery Honor Book.

48. Bette Greene, *Philip Hall Likes Me. I Reckon Maybe* (New York: Dial, 1974), p. 38.

49. Ibid., p. 5.

50. "Bette Greene," *Profiles in Literature* (Philadelphia: Temple University, 1981).

51. In 1958, *South Town* won the Child Study Children's Book Committee at Bank Street College Award.

52. Lorenz Graham, *South Town* (Chicago: Follett, 1958), p. 149.

53. In 1976, *Fast Sam, Cool Clyde, and Stuff* won the Woodward Park School Annual Book Award.

54. In 1968, *The Egypt Game* was a Newbery Honor Book. In 1970, it won the Lewis Carroll Shelf Award and in 1973, the George G. Stone Center for Children's Books Recognition of Merit Award.

55. In 1976, *The Toothpaste Millionaire* won the Dorothy Canfield Fisher Children's Book Award and in 1977, the Sequoyah Children's Book Award.

56. In 1964, *Roosevelt Grady* won the Lewis Carroll Shelf Award and the Woodward Park School Annual Book Award.

57. In 1961, *The Girl from Puerto Rico* won the Child Study Children's Book Committee at Bank Street College Award.

58. In 1976, *The Hundred Penny Box* was a Newbery Honor Book.

59. In 1977, *The City Rose* won the North Carolina Division of the American Association of University Women's Award in Juvenile Literature.

60. Ruth White Miller, *The City Rose* (New York: McGraw, 1977), p. 84.

61. In 1970, *Our Eddie* was a Newbery Honor Book.

62. In 1974, *A Hero Ain't Nothin' but a Sandwich* was a finalist for the National Book Award in the children's-book category, and it won the Woodward Park School Annual Book Award. In 1975, it won the Lewis Carroll Shelf Award.

63. In 1976, *Ludell* was a finalist for the National Book Award in the children's-book category and won the Woodward Park School Annual Book Award.

64. Brenda Wilkinson, *Ludell* (New York: Harper, 1975) p. 137.

65. In 1974, *M.C. Higgins, the Great* won the *Boston Globe-Horn Book* Award. In 1975, it won The John Newbery Medal, the National Book Award in the children's-book category, and the Lewis Carroll Shelf Award. In 1976, it was put on the International Board on Books for Young People Honor List.

66. In 1972, *The Planet of Junior Brown* was a Newbery Honor Book, a finalist for the National Book Award in the children's-book category, and a Lewis Carroll Shelf Award winner.

67. Virginia Hamilton, *The Planet of Junior Brown* (New York: Macmillan, 1971), p. 210.

68. ''Virginia Hamilton,'' *Profiles in Literature* (Philadelphia: Temple University, 1978).

69. In 1973, *Julie of the Wolves* won The John Newbery Medal and was a finalist for the National Book Award in the children's-book category.

70. ''Jean Craighead George,'' *Profiles in Literature* (Philadelphia: Temple University, 1974).


**References of Prizewinning Realistic Fiction Listed by U.S. Minorities**

*(Estimated Reading Grade Level in Parentheses)*

*American Blacks*

Bonham, Frank. *Durango Street*. New York: Dutton, 1965 (6–9).

Childress, Alice. *A Hero Ain't Nothin' but a Sandwich*. New York: Coward, 1973 (6–9).

Carlson, Natalie Savage. *Ann Aurelia and Dorothy*. Illustrated by Dale Payson. New York: Harper, 1968 (4–6).

———. *The Empty Schoolhouse*. Illustrated by John Kaufmann. New York: Harper, 1965 (3–5).

Graham, Lorenz. *South Town*. Chicago: Follett, 1958 (5–9).

Greene, Betty. *Philip Hall Likes Me. I Reckon Maybe*. Illustrated by Charles Lilly. New York: Dial, 1974 (4–6).

Hamilton, Virginia. *The House of Dies Drear*. Illustrated by Eros Keith. New York: Macmillan, 1968 (5–8).

———. *M.C. Higgins, the Great*. New York: Macmillan, 1974 (6–8).

———. *The Planet of Junior Brown*. New York: Macmillan, 1971 (6–9).

Hentoff, Nat. *Jazz Country*. New York: Harper, 1965 (6–9).

Hunter, Kristin. *Guests in the Promised Land*. New York: Scribner 1973 (6–9).

———. *The Soul Brothers and Sister Lou*. New York: Scribner, 1968 (6–9).

Lipsyte, Robert. *The Contender*. New York: Harper, 1967 (6–9).

Mathis, Sharon Bell. *The Hundred Penny Box*. Illustrated by Leo and Diane Dillon. New York: Viking, 1975 (3–5).

———. *Sidewalk Story*. Illustrated by Leo Carty. New York: Viking, 1971 (3–5).

Merrill, Jean. *The Toothpaste Millionaire*. Illustrated by Jan Palmer. Boston: Houghton, 1976 (2–5).

Miller, Ruth White. *The City Rose*. New York: McGraw, 1977 (4–7).

Myers, Walter Dean. *Fast Sam, Cool Clyde, and Stuff*. New York: Viking, 1975 (6–9).

Shepard, Ray Anthony. *Sneakers*. New York: Dutton, 1973 (5–6).

Sterling, Dorothy. *Mary Jane*. Illustrated by Ernest Crichlow. New York: Doubleday, 1959 (5–8).

Shotwell, Louisa R. *Roosevelt Grady*. Illustrated by Peter Burchard. Cleveland: Collins World, 1963 (4–6).

Snyder, Zilpha Keatley. *The Egypt Game*. Illustrated by Alton Raible. New York: Atheneum, 1968 (5–7).

Wagner, Jane. *J.T.* Photographs by Gordon Parks, Jr. New York: Van Nostrand Reinhold, 1969 (4–6).

Weik, Mary Hays. *The Jazz Man*. Illustrated by Ann Grifalconi. New York: Atheneum, 1966 (4–6).

Wilkinson, Brenda. *Ludell*. New York: Harper, 1975 (6–9).

*Amish*

Sorensen, Virginia Eggertsen. *Plain Girl*. Illustrated by Charles Geer. New York: Harcourt, 1955 (4–6).

*Chicanos*

Bonham, Frank. *Viva Chicano*. New York: Dutton, 1970 (6–9).

Krumgold, Joseph. *. . . and Now Miguel*. Illustrated by Jean Charlot. New York: Crowell, 1953 (6–9).

*Chinese-Americans*

Yep, Lawrence. *Child of the Owl*. New York: Harper, 1977 (6–9).

*Jews*

Ish-Kishor, Sulamith. *Our Eddie*. New York: Pantheon, 1969 (6–9).

Kerr, M.E. *Gentlehands*. New York: Harper, 1978 (6–9).

Neville, Emily Cheney. *Berries Goodman*. New York: Harper, 1965 (6–9).

*Native Americans*

Armer, Laura Adams. *Waterless Mountain*. Illustrated by Laura and Sidney Armer. New York: McKay, 1931 (5–7).

Distad, Audrey. *The Dream Runner*. New York: Harper, 1977 (5–8).

George, Jean Craighead. *Julie of the Wolves*. Illlustrated by John Schoenherr. New York: Harper, 1972 (5–8).

Lauritzen, Jonreed. *The Ordeal of the Young Hunter*. Illustrated by Hoke
Denetsosie. Boston: Little, Brown, 1954 (4–6).

Miles, Miska. *Annie and the Old One*. Illustrated by Peter Parnall. Boston: Little, Brown, 1971 (2–5).

Sneve, Virginia Driving Hawk. *Jimmy Yellow Hawk*. Illustrated by Oren
Lyons. New York: Holiday House, 1972 (3–5).

*Puerto Ricans*

Colman, Hila. *The Girl from Puerto Rico*. New York: Morrow, 1961
(6–10).

Mohr, Nicholasa. *El Bronx Remembered*. New York: Harper, 1975
(6–9).

———. *Nilda*. New York: Harper, 1973 (6–9).

Stolz, Mary. *The Noonday Friends*. New York: Harper, 1965 (4–6).

*Nonspecified*

Krumgold, Joseph. *Onion John*. Illustrated by Symeon Shimin. New
York: Crowell, 1959 (6–9).

# 14 Contemporary Realistic Fiction Set in Other Lands

*My teacher thinks I like to read only about Mexico, because my family comes from there, but that's not so. No one can get me to trade my copy of "What Then, Raman?. It tells about India. And I already let my Mom know what I want for my birthday—Pulga. That book is about Colombia. Good books are what I like, and they can be about anywhere.*

*—Emilio, aged ten*

## Perspective and Standards

For an elementary pupil, Emilio shows high standards and a precocious global perspective. His not-to-be-traded copy of *"What Then, Raman?"* is by Shirley L. Arora. Arora wrote her story after spending nearly four years in India, the country where both her husband and son were born. Emilio's requested birthday gift, *Pulga,* is by Siny Rose Van Iterson, who was born in the Netherland Antilles on the island of Curaçao. She writes in Dutch, and her books are translated into English. She has lived in Bogotá, Colombia, the setting of *Pulga.* In 1973, Van Iterson won the Hans Christian Andersen Award for all her children's books.

Since stories set in other lands must be as accurate as those that take place in this country, many authors, such as Arora and Van Iterson, have resided in the locale their books describe. When a book is not originally in English, translation should be in fluid style. A good example is Alexander and Alison Gode's version of *Pulga,* 1973 winner of the Mildred L. Batchelder Award for the best foreign book in translation.

When appropriate, authors should describe metropolitan life in other countries, not only quaint village customs. Nonstereotyped illustrations should be used, so all stories about Mexico, for instance, do not depict characters taking *siestas.* The literature should be so authentic it can enrich the social studies curriculum.

## Grouped under These Topics Are Themes of Prizewinning Contemporary Realistic Fiction Set in Other Lands

*Education*

**Middle and Upper Grades.** It is not surprising that the response to the question in Shirley L. Arora's title, *"What Then, Raman?"* is her book's

theme: learning, then teaching others.[1] The tale concerns Raman, a shy
boy in India who is first in his village to learn to read. When he reluctantly leaves school to help support his family, he is guided to teach
other villagers.

**Upper Grades.** A girl's struggle for an education is the theme of Minfong Ho's *Morning Song*,[2] a bilingual book with English and Chinese
on facing pages. The author writes in Chinese about her native Thailand.
In a Thai village, fourteen-year-old Dawan wins a scholarship to continue
her education in Bangkok, competing with her thirteen-year-old brother,
Kwai, who scored second highest on qualifying examinations. She has
to convince her father, who believes no girl needs further schooling. She
finally turns to Kwai for help. It was he who, after he started school
some years ago, got his father to allow Dawan to attend. Though the
decision is painful, Kwai gives this rationale for assisting his sister:

> "How can I say that I want to study more so I can help people later
> on, when the only way I can get this further schooling is by robbing
> my own sister of her chance to study?"[3]

When Kwai withdraws from competition, the father reluctantly permits
Dawan to accept the scholarship. As she departs, Kwai drops his last
remnant of bitterness, and the two sing their familiar morning song duet.


*Survival*

**Middle and Upper Grades.** Surviving by overcoming both a leopard and
a thief is the theme of Cecil Bødker's *The Leopard*,[4] which takes place
in Ethiopia and was originally written for Ethiopian children. Tibeso is
an Ethiopian boy who herds cattle for his widowed mother and others in
his mountain village. When a notorious leopard, The Big One, steals a
calf, Tibeso goes to The Great Man for advice. He is waylaid by The
Great Man's neighbor, a blacksmith, who has been robbing the countryside while claiming the leopard to be the thief. After Tibeso foolishly
tells the blacksmith at the crime scene there was a footprint with a scar
inside, the boy notices the blacksmith has such a footprint. It is too late!
The smith tries to kill Tibeso, and the lad struggles to survive. When
the leopard and smith slay each other, the boy returns home.

**Upper Grades.** Survival is the theme of *Pulga*,[5] a frightening story in
Bogotá, Colombia of malnourished, fourteen-year-old Francisco José or
Pulga, which means flea. In one squalid slum room, Pulga lives with his

grandmother and three younger siblings. Pulga feels especially responsible for Pedro, a brother with a twisted foot. Since his mother died and
his father abandoned them, Pedro is happy for the first time helping a
truck driver, Gilimón Naranjo, on a trip. When they visit the driver's
godmother, Mamá Maruja, she wants a boy like Pulga. He remembers
her words after returning to Bogotá. He finds his grandmother dead, his
sisters relocated, and Pedro homeless. The fast-paced book ends happily,
for Pulga's brother assists Mamá Maruja, and Pulga himself survives as
Gilimón's helper.

A suspenseful survival story is *The Black Pearl*,[6] which author Scott
O'Dell says has the theme, ''Safety cannot be bought.''[7] Sixteen-year-
old Ramón Salazar, son of the owner of Salazar pearl diving fleet, lives
in Lower California. While driving in the Vermilion Sea, Ramón seizes
the magnificent Pearl of Heaven, incurring the wrath of the fleet's finest
diver, Sevillano, and the dangerous octopus who guards the pearl, *Manta
Diablo*. When Ramón's father cannot sell the pearl at a high price, he
donates it to the church. Soon afterward, the father and all in his fleet
except Sevillano die in a storm. Ramón, feeling death is the Manta's
revenge, steals the pearl to fling it back into the sea. Sevillano prevents
this, explaining that his father died from taking chances, believing his
gift to the church put him under God's protection. Both Sevillano and
the sea creature die before Ramón gives the pearl back to the church.
He does so knowing that safety cannot be bought.

*Assuming Responsibilities*

**Middle Grades.** A boy's assuming a man's responsibilities is the theme
of Dorothy Rhoads's *The Corn Grows Ripe*.[8] The theme is emphasized
in Jean Charlot's drawings of a twelve-year-old boy, Tigre (Jaguar), who
helps the family after his father breaks his leg. Pictures show Tigre
getting a bonesetter, clearing the fields, and planting corn. Grandfather
echoes the theme as he hands Tigre a gun and says, ''He who does a
man's work should have a man's weapons as well.''[9] Fortunately, Tigre's
work is successful, for this modern Maya story in Yucatan ends: ''The
corn grew ripe.''[10]

**Upper Grades.** Responsibility for a retarded sibling is the theme of Babbis Friis-Baastad's *Don't Take Teddy*,[11] which takes place in Norway.
Thirteen-year-old Mikkel Grabseth takes care of his fifteen-year-old retarded brother, Teddy, who has the mind of a two-year-old. While playing baseball, Mikkel tries to baby-sit Teddy, who knocks out an opponent's
teeth. Mikkel, afraid Teddy will be arrested, runs away with his brother

to Uncle Bjarne's summer cottage. Both boys develop pneumonia from
the ordeal. When they recuperate, Teddy attends Lillebo, a special school.
After seeing Teddy's contentment as a day pupil, Mikkel begins to shed
his burden of responsibility.

*Courage*

**Primary and Middle Grades.** Anita Brenner's story set in a Mexican
village, *A Hero by Mistake,*[12] conveys the theme, accidental courage, in
its title. Little Dionisio, a cowardly Native American woodcutter, is so
frightened by loud noises he comforts himself by blowing a bugle, unaware he is driving away a robber band. In another circumstantial occurrence, he thinks he is capturing his escaped burro but lassos a dangerous
criminal. Jean Charlot helps convey the theme in illustrations that show
what actually happens and what Dionisio imagines. Villagers honor
Dionisio by calling him Don. The author summarizes:

> And did Don Dionisio get over being afraid? The truth is, he didn't.
> Only since people said he was brave, he acted brave, and somehow or
> other then he really *was* brave.
>
> How can you be brave when you are afraid? Well, if you do what you
> are afraid to do, that is brave.[13]

**Middle and Upper Grades.** More than one way to be courageous is the
theme of Carolyn Treffinger's *Li Lun, Lad of Courage.*[14] Ten-year-old
Li Lun, who lives on Blue Shark Island near China, is afraid of the sea.
He angers his father, Teng Lun, by refusing to go on a fishing trip. As
punishment, the father requires his son to plant seven rice grains atop
Lao Shan (Sorrow Mountain) and not return until he has grown seven
times the number of grains. A priest visits the boy on the mountain and
says, "You are brave, Li Lun. Braver than if you had gone fishing."[15]
The youth remembers those words during three and one-half moons on
the montain when gulls and rats destroy six plants. After his seventh is
ripe, he brings its ninety-nine grains to the temple where the priest asks
Li Lun to teach other boys to grow rice, and he earns the name Lad of
Courage.

Courage is also the theme of Armstrong Sperry's *Call It Courage,*[16]
the story of a fifteen-year-old South Sea Islander, Mafatu. He has been
afraid of the ocean since he saw his mother drowned when he was three
years old. Ridiculed as a coward, Mafatu conquers his fears by sailing
with an albatross and a mongrel dog, weathering a terrible storm. He
lands on another island before returning home, now socially accepted

due to his bravery. Unfortunately, there is a stereotyped reference to Black former occupants of the second island as *savages*.[17]

Courage and perseverance is the theme of Aimee Sommerfelt's *The Road to Agra*.[18] Set in India, the book is a result of the Norwegian author's visit to India with her husband, a UNESCO delegate. She tells about poor, thirteen-year-old Lalu who walks three hundred miles from Katwa down the road to Agra with his seven-year-old sister, Maya. She is the only one in a family of seven to attend school but will have to quit if her trachoma is not cured. After misadventures, the two reach Agra, where exhausted Maya is rejected at a hospital. As they courageously begin the long return walk, they are helped at a United Nations World Health Organization clinic. Maya begins treatment to restore her eyesight while Lalu lives in a doctor's house and earns money for their trip home.

*Wish Fulfillment*

**Middle Grades.** Wish fulfillment through effort is the theme of author-illustrator Nicola Simbari's *Gennarino*,[19] which takes place on the isle of Ischia, Italy. An orphan boy, Gennarino, whose leaky sailboat is destroyed in a storm, swims ashore at a gypsy camp. Gypsies promise a favor if Gennarino retrieves their Rainbow Bird, imprisoned by brigands inside Fire Mountain. When he fulfills the difficult task, gypsies loan him a sailboat with the decorative Rainbow Bird aboard. Gennarino sails in the *Grande Festa* on the Sea and achieves his goal by winning first prize, a new boat.

Not Italy but a Mexican forest is the setting for Laura Adams Armer's *The Forest Pool*.[20] Featured are Armer's full-color paintings of young Diego in a white homespun suit and straw hat with the iguana he unsuccessfully tries to keep. Diego's father goes to the pool of the Plumed Serpent to get the big iguana and finds it looking in a hole in a branch that Polly freshly scratched. Polly, a parrot, who only says, "I have been here before," came to Diego's family with a tobacco can tied to her leg and a note inside requesting, "Be kind to me. Pearls are in the pool."[21] Wanting to resolve Polly's mystery is the theme of this book, and that desire is realized. An iguana leads Father to a hole in a branch where he finds Polly's stringed pearls. Diego says, "I know that in some way the wise old one (iguana) would tell me what I wanted to know."[22]

**Primary through Upper Grades.** Finding cakes on Christmas Day is the wish-fulfillment theme of Ruth Sawyer's *The Christmas Anna Angel*,[23] set on a Hungarian farm. Anna dreams on Christmas Eve that her Christmas Anna angel makes the cakes. Actually, her mother hides enough white flour from inspecting soldiers to give Anna and younger brother Miklos this holiday treat.

A different kind of wish fulfillment is reflected in Maria Gripe's *Pappa Pellerin's Daughter*,[24] whose theme is an abandoned daughter craving her father. In a Swedish forest cottage, poverty-stricken twelve-year-old Loella cares for young twin brothers, Rudolph and Conrad, while their mother, a ship's cook, is traveling. Loella dresses a scarecrow in clothes belonging to the father she hasn't seen since she was two years old, the time her parents separated. (Her brothers have a different father.) Loella calls the scarecrow Pappa Pellerin and herself Loella Pellerin, though her father's name is Persson. When she learns her father wanted to be her custodian, she longs to meet him. At the end of the school year, her wish comes true, for standing where her scarecrow used to be is a tall, dark-haired man who says, "I have a daughter and I thought I might move in with her. . . . Her name is Loella."[25]

**Upper Grades.** Desire for a dog to share his solitude is the theme of Reginald Ottley's *Boy Alone*.[26] The story takes place at the edge of the Australian desert on a vast cattle station, Yamboorah homestead, similar to one where the author once worked. A nameless "wood-and-water joey" has no parents, relatives, or other children as companions. He is in contact with overseer Ross, old Kanga with his dog pack, and a kind cook, Mrs. Jones, who worries when the boy is caught in an Australian dust storm. The boy focuses on Kanga's dog, Brolga, and her puppy, Rags, but Brolga dies. When Kanga plans to train Rags as a ruthless dog pack leader, the boy flees with Rags to dangerous sandhills. Kanga saves him and lures him home by giving him Rags. The boy feels his risky flight worthwhile because Rags will share his solitude.

*Learning New Ways*

**Middle and Upper Grades.** Learning to trust a foreigner with new ways is the theme of Duane Bradley's *Meeting with a Stranger*,[27] which shows proud Ethiopians gradually accepting an American sheep expert. The author received help from an Ethiopian writer, Ato Tekle Ab Kassaye, and Dr. Edith Lord, former education advisor in the Ethiopian-United States Cooperative Education Program. The story focuses on a shepherd named Teffera. The lad is as skeptical as other villagers about the American, Sam Jones, who suggests new sheep-raising methods and tries to combat illiteracy. Jones is aware of the villagers' attitude, for he says, "If we trust each other and share what we know, both of our countries will be richer and better for it.''[28] Teffera is relieved to hear the American say he wants to share new ideas but not make Ethiopia like the rest of the world. When Jones leaves, the people trust him, and he has inspired Teffera to work toward environmental as well as personal improvement.

Mary and Conrad Buff's *Magic Maize* has a learning-new-ways theme and features Conrad Buff's fine illustrations of Guatamalan life.[29] The story concerns Fabian, a Guatemalan Native American boy. He follows his father's custom of offering hot corn mush to their Gods of Nature, hoping for a good harvest. At the same time, he defies old customs, accepts kernels of new corn, maize, from his brother, and secretly plants them with fine results. While planting, Fabian uncovers an ancient Maya jade earplug which interests archaeologists. Although Fabian's father was once skeptical, he learns that new and old ideas can work together, for he says:

> Even if you are strangers, and from afar, and not of my blood, *Señores,* you have saved us from the coffee plantation. And the boy may go to school if you and the President think he can really learn the new ways. I am too old to learn them.[30]

Changing from isolation to cooperation is the theme and new approach in Claire Huchet Bishop's *All Alone,*[31] a title that depicts the old ways in the French Alps. Feodor Rojankovsky's illustrations emphasize the setting. As the tale begins, two fathers preach, ''Each man for himself,'' so their sons feel guilty when they yodel to each other while tending three heifers apiece in the Alps. Ten-year-old Marcel Mabout is atop Little Giant, and his peer, Pierre Pascal, is on Big Giant. After Pierre oversleeps, his cows join the other boy's, and Marcel decides to move all cows to his friend's camp on Big Giant. The two boys huddle together in a storm that destroys Little Giant and blocks their exit. When rescued, they feel guilty for cooperating, but their two families start to share food and chores. Later, the mayor gives the two lads a tractor for joint use and says:

> We, the people of Monestier, have decided to tear down the age-old fences and hedges which enclose and separate our fields, and to work the whole land of the valley together—one common field under the sun.[32]

## Lovers of Africa

**Upper Grades.** Bonds between two who love Africa is the theme of *The Bushbabies* by William Stevenson, a Canadian who lived in Kenya.[33]

The true bushbaby or tarsier, Kamau, is the pet of thirteen-year-old Jackie Rhodes. The second bushbaby is Jackie herself, and the third is Tembo Murumbi, born in Kenya, Jackie's naive, devoted protector, the only one of the three to remain in Africa. As the story unfolds, an English game warden is leaving Kenya with his family, but his daughter, Jackie, cannot find her pet bushbaby's export license, so she slips off the ship to release the pet. The ship sails, Jackie is stranded, and she convinces Tembo, who formerly worked for her father, to take her to his home area, the tarsier's habitat, to free her pet there. News releases accuse innocent Tembo of kidnapping Jackie, so his life is in danger until the end. Tembo, the true hero, suffers from multiple forms of racism, even to the point of calling himself *savage*.[34] Tembo does not want to be uprooted, and Jackie shares his love of Africa. Her family considers it time for Africans to control their land, the one place where men, like Tembo, "still stand up tall, not hunchbacked under the burden of their own possessions."[35]

*Kindness*

**Primary and Middle Grades.** Eva-Lis Wuorio's *The Island of Fish in the Trees* has the theme of kindness.[36] This story takes place in Formentera on the Balearic Islands, a Spanish province off the coast of Spain. Without asking permission, Belinda and her younger sister, Lucy, travel to the island doctor, *Señor el Médico,* in a spirit of kindness. They want to help their mother, who has a toothache, and Belinda's headless doll, Maria-Carmen. On their journey, the island residents give them food and gifts, such as a goat and kitten. They find the doctor near some trees on which fish are drying, the source of the book's title. The doctor doesn't laugh about repairing a doll. He gives the girls a donkey before taking them to their mother and treating her toothache. Appreciative of the kindness, the mother reports, "Half the village has been here with a small present, to report on the children and inquire after my tooth."[37]

*Self-Choice*

**Middle and Upper Grades.** Choosing a family and occupation is the theme of Ann Nolan Clark's mystical *Secret of the Andes*.[38] High in the Peruvian Andes Mountains, young Cusi, who wears golden earplugs of Inca royalty, has always lived away from his family while tending llamas with old Chuto. Curious about his parents, Cusi meets his mother in the town of Ancient People that is later destroyed by a landslide. After he visits Cuzco searching for a family to join, Cusi decides Chuto is "Father of my choice,"[39] and "We are a family."[40] When Cusi voluntarily returns, Chuto shows him the secret cave where, for four hundred years, gold carried by sacred llamas has been hidden, though originally intended to ransom an Inca king. The Spaniards killed the king, so Incas hid the gold, kept royal llamas intact, and told only two herders the secret. As one who chooses to be a royal herder, Cusi now learns the secret.

**Upper Grades.** Independently choosing an occupation is the theme of Maia Wojciechowska's *Shadow of a Bull*.[41] Manolo Olivar feels cowardly in the shadow of his father, Spain's greatest bullfighter, who died in the bullring when only twenty-two. Townspeople expect Manolo to pursue his father's career despite his fears. When he is ten, reacting to community pressure, he begins to train. As his twelfth birthday approaches, he participates in his first bullfight. Afterward, with self-confidence, he tells his sponsors he will not be a bullfighter, but a doctor, a healer of men.

Wojciechowska, in writing about Manolo, was inspired by a boy she saw in Córdova, Spain who looked like the deceased Manolete, Andalucía's greatest bullfighter. He had Manolete's same eyes and long nose. The author was afraid men watching him might try to make him be a *torero,* though he spurned the thought and exercised self-choice.

**Summary**

Themes of examples of contemporary realistic prizewinners set abroad are discussed under nine headings in this chapter. Survival and wish-fulfillment stories are popular. Most of the tales are for readers in fourth grade and beyond. The twenty-three prizewinners take place in a surprisingly large number of locations: eighteen different countries and a group of Pacific South Sea Isles. The countries include Australia, China, Colombia, Ethiopia, France, Guatemala, Hungary, India, Italy, Kenya, Mexico, Norway, Peru, Spain, Sweden, and Thailand. There are four stories set in Mexico and two apiece in Ethiopia, India, and Spain.

**Notes**

1. In 1961, *"What Then, Raman?"* won the Jane Addams Book Award and the Woodward Park School Annual Book Award.
2. In 1971–1972, *Morning Song* won the Council on Interracial Books for Children Award in the Asian-American category.

3. Minfong Ho, *Morning Song* (New York: Lotus Book House), p. 90.

4. In 1977, *The Leopard* (translated by Gunnar Poulsen) won the Mildred L. Batchelder Award.

5. In 1973, *Pulga* (translated by Alexander and Alison Gode) won the Mildred L. Batchelder Award.

6. In 1968, *The Black Pearl* was a Newbery Honor Book.

7. "Scott O'Dell," *Profiles in Literature* (Philadelphia: Temple University, 1976).

8. In 1957, *The Corn Grows Ripe* was a Newbery Honor Book.

9. Dorothy Rhoads, *The Corn Grows Ripe* (New York: Viking, 1956), p. 54.

10. Ibid., p. 83.

11. In 1969, *Don't Take Teddy* (translated by L. McKinnon) won the Mildred L. Batchelder Award. In 1975, it won the Lewis Carroll Shelf Award.

12. In 1953, *A Hero by Mistake* was the *New York Times* Choice of Best Illustrated Children's Book of the Year.

13. Anita Brenner, *A Hero by Mistake* (Reading, Mass.: Addison-Wesley, 1953), p. 44.

14. In 1948, *Li Lun, Lad of Courage* was a Newbery Honor Book and a winner of the Ohioana Book Award. In 1959, it won the Lewis Carroll Shelf Award.

15. Carolyn Treffinger, *Li Lun, Lad of Courage* (Nashville: Abingdon, 1947), p. 60.

16. In 1941, *Call It Courage* won The John Newbery Medal.

17. Armstrong Sperry, *Call It Courage* (New York: Macmillan, 1940), p. 48.

18. In 1961, *The Road to Agra* won the Child Study Children's Book Committee at Bank Street College Award. In 1962, it won both the Jane Addams Book Award and the Woodward Park School Annual Book Award.

19. In 1962, *Gennarino* was a *New York Times* Choice of Best Illustrated Children's Book of the Year.

20. In 1939, *The Forest Pool* was a Caldecott Honor Book.

21. Laura Adams Armer, *The Forest Pool* (New York: Longmans, 1938), p. 16.

22. Ibid., p. 40.

23. In 1945, *The Christmas Anna Angel*, illustrated by Kate Seredy, won The Randolph Caldecott Medal.

24. In 1966, *Pappa Pellerin's Daughter* won the Lewis Carroll Shelf Award.

25. Maria Gripe, *Pappa Pellerin's Daughter* (New York: Day, 1966), pp. 155–156.

26. In 1971, *Boy Alone* won the Lewis Carroll Shelf Award.

27. In 1965, *Meeting with a Stranger* won the Jane Addams Book Award and the Woodward Park School Annual Book Award.

28. Duane Bradley, *Meeting with a Stranger* (Philadelphia: Lippincott, 1964), p. 79.

29. In 1954, *Magic Maize* was a Newbery Honor Book.

30. Mary and Conrad Buff, *Magic Maize* (Boston: Houghton, 1953), p. 76.

31. In 1954, *All Alone* was a Newbery Honor Book.

32. Claire Huchet Bishop, *All Alone* (New York: Viking, 1953), p. 88.

33. In 1967, *The Bushbabies* won the Woodward Park School Annual Book Award.

34. William Stevenson, *The Bushbabies* (Boston: Houghton, 1965), p. 233.

35. Ibid., p. 274.

36. In 1962, *The Island of Fish in the Trees*, illustrated by Edward Ardizzone, was a *New York Times* Choice of Best Illustrated Children's Book of the Year.

37. Eva-Lis Wuorio, *The Island of Fish in the Trees* (New York: World, 1962), p. 58.

38. In 1953, *Secret of the Andes* won The John Newbery Medal.

39. Ann Nolan Clark, *Secret of the Andes* (New York: Viking, 1952), p. 125.

40. Ibid., p. 119.

41. In 1965, *Shadow of a Bull* won The John Newbery Medal.


**References of Contemporary Realistic**
**Fictional Prizewinners Set Abroad,**
**Listed by Country of Setting**

*(Estimated Reading Grade Level in Parentheses)*

*Australia*

Ottley, Reginald. *Boy Alone*. New York: Harcourt, 1965 (6–8).

*China*

Treffinger, Carolyn. *Li Lun, Lad of Courage*. Illustrated by Kurt Wiese. Nashville: Abingdon, 1947 (4–6).

*Colombia*

Van Iterson, Siny Rose. *Pulga*. Translated by Alexander and Alison Gode. New York: Morrow, 1971 (5–7).

*Ethiopia*

Bødker, Cecil. *The Leopard*. Translated by Gunnar Poulsen. New York: Atheneum, 1975 (4–6).
Bradley, Duane. *Meeting with a Stranger*. Illustrated by E. Harper Johnson. Philadelphia: Lippincott, 1964 (4–6).

*France*

Bishop, Claire Huchet. *All Alone*. Illustrated by Feodor Rojankovsky. New York: Viking, 1953 (3–5).

*Guatemala*

Buff, Mary and Conrad. *Magic Maize*. Boston: Houghton, 1953 (3–5).

*Hungary*

Sawyer, Ruth. *The Christmas Anna Angel*. Illustrated by Kate Seredy. New York: Viking, 1944 (2–5).

*India*

Arora, Shirley L. *"What Then, Raman?"* Illustrated by Hans Guggenheim. Chicago: Follett, 1960 (4–6).
Sommerfelt, Aimée. *The Road to Agra*. Illustrated by Ulf Aas. New York: Criterion, 1961 (4–6).

*Italy*

Simbari, Nicola. *Gennarino*. Philadelphia: Lippincott, 1962 (3–4).

*Kenya*

Stevenson, William. *The Bushbabies*. Illustrated by Victor Ambrus. Boston: Houghton, 1965 (5–7).

*Mexico*

Armer, Laura Adams. *The Forest Pool*. New York: Longmans, 1938 (3–4).
Brenner, Anita. *A Hero by Mistake*. Illustrated by Jean Charlot. Reading, Mass.: Addison-Wesley, 1953 (2–4).

O'Dell, Scott. *The Black Pearl*. Illustrated by Milton Johnson. Boston: Houghton, 1967 (6–9). (Set in Southern California.)

Rhoads, Dorothy. *The Corn Grows Ripe*. Illustrated by Jean Charlot. New York: Viking, 1956 (3–4). (Set in Yucatan.)

*Norway*

Friis-Baastad, Babbis. *Don't Take Teddy*. Translated by L. McKinnon. New York: Scribner, 1967 (5–8).

*Peru*

Clark, Ann Nolan. *Secret of the Andes*. Illustrated by Jean Charlot. New York: Viking, 1952 (4–8).

*South Sea Isles* (nonspecific term for Pacific islands)

Sperry, Armstrong. *Call It Courage*. New York: Macmillan, 1940 (4–8).

*Spain*

Wojciechowska, Maia. *Shadow of a Bull*. Illustrated by Alvin Smith. New York: Atheneum, 1964 (5–7).

Wuorio, Eva-Lis. *The Island of Fish in the Trees*. Illustrated by Edward Ardizzone. New York: World, 1962 (2–4). (Set in Formentera, Balearic Islands.)

*Sweden*

Gripe, Maria. *Pappa Pellerin's Daughter*. Translated by Kersti French. New York: Day, 1966 (4–6).

*Thailand*

Ho, Minfong. *Morning Song*. Translated by Liu Ge. Illustrated by Kwoncjan Ho. New York: Lotus Book House (6–8).

# 15 Popular Contemporary Realistic Fiction: Mysteries and Humorous Stories

*I like different books for different moods. When I'm in the mood for mystery, I choose* Night Fall. *And when I'm in the mood to crack up, there's nothing funnier than* Henry Reed's Baby-Sitting Service. *I laugh so hard reading* Henry Reed, *I actually get the hiccups.*

—Kyoko, aged ten

## Perspective on Mysteries

Kyoko's initial choice, *Night Fall,* received the Edgar Allen Poe Award given by the Mystery Writers of America. It is a polished murder story without a detective.

The detective tale—one type of mystery—is said to have originated with Sir Arthur Conan Doyle, a physician born in 1859, who wrote about his Victorian years. He invented Sherlock Holmes, borrowing Oliver Wendell Holmes's surname. Holmes is patterned after the author's Edinburgh medical school teacher, hawk-faced Dr. Joseph Bell, who had the reputation for being able to deduce in five minutes a stranger's occupation and past history. Doyle's four novelettes and fifty-six short stories were so successful he became a full-time writer before his death in 1930.

Unlike Doyle, whose work was literary, Edward Stratemeyer's was not. Stratemeyer initiated the Nancy Drew mysteries under the pen name, Carolyn Keene, also used by his daughter and successor, Harriet Stratemeyer Adams. He wrote or directed others to write over eight hundred books. He employed hack writers, giving them three-page typewritten outlines in which he logically arranged characters' names and destinies. Hacks received $50 to $250 to enlarge the outline into a book quickly, and they released ownership claims. Stratemeyer used seventy pseudonyms, such as Arthur M. Winfield (Rover Boys), Laura Lee Hope (Bobbsey Twins), Victor Appleton (Tom Swift), and Franklin W. Dixon (Hardy Boys). His profits rose as he sold millions of factory formula tales.

Children who enjoy Nancy Drew may be enticed to more literary mysteries if adults orally share part of a recommended book, stop at an exciting point, and encourage those interested to read independently.

Mysteries help pupils increase their silent reading rates under suspenseful stimulus. Surprisingly, there are a variety of themes beyond whodunit.

## Themes of Prizewinning Contemporary Realistic Mysteries Grouped under These Topics

*Facing Challenge*

**Middle and Upper Grades.** Solving mysteries is the theme and challenge of Donald Sobol's *Encyclopedia Brown Keeps the Peace,*[1] *Encyclopedia Brown Lends a Hand,*[2] and other books in the series. Ten-year-old Leroy (Encyclopedia) Brown is the real brains behind his father, Chief of Police Brown, who conducts war on crime in the town of Idaville. For his twenty-five-cents-a-day detective agency and for his father, Encyclopedia solves ten entertaining mysteries per prizewinner. In *Encyclopedia Brown Lends a Hand,* Mr. Hunt claims he went to the bank on April Fool's Day to pay for an elephant left in his yard on Friday the thirteenth, but the young detective says Hunt is lying. ''As Encyclopedia knew, if in any month a Friday falls on the thirteenth, the first day of the month is Sunday. On Sunday banks are closed.''[3]

**Upper Grades.** Facing challenge is the primary theme of Phyllis A. Whitney's *Mystery of the Haunted Pool,*[4] set in the Hudson River community of Highland Crossing, New York. Twelve-year-old Susan Price is intrigued by a rumored secret haunting the fine old house her family rents from Captain Dan Teague. The captain is forced to rent his treasured home to pay medical expenses for his thirteen-year-old grandson, Gene Foster, whose left leg is in a brace. In a pool beside the Teague house, Susan discovers a face and is so bewildered she tells an antique lover, Altoona Heath, who removes the object of mystery. It is a ship's figurehead, a key to the resolution of Teague's financial problems.

Facing personal challenges is also the theme of Kin Platt's *Sinbad and Me,*[5] which is about twelve-year-old Steve Forrester and his bulldog detective, Sinbad, in Hampton, Long Island. Humorous dialogue lightens the tense story of an old Serbian storekeeper, Mrs. Teska, who is threatened with extortion by two thugs. Steve's curiosity is aroused when he sees Mrs. Teska's picture under another name in an old newspaper, and he tries to unravel the puzzle. To do so, he enters the cave of a deceased pirate, Captain Billy, when the tide is right, and he decodes a cave message. He also decodes messages at a mansion and on a tombstone. Steve's interest in codes and old houses makes it possible for him to help Mrs. Teska.

Older and more forlorn than Steve is sixteen-year-old Arnold Haithwaite. His challenge, the need to send a menacing stranger on his way, is the theme of John Rowe Townsend's *The Intruder,*[6] set in Skirlston on the treacherous English coast. Arnold helps his adopted dad, old Ernest Haithwaite, manage a guest house, but an unscrupulous intruder appears, pretends to be Ernest's relative, Arnold Haithwaite, and ousts the younger lad. The boy struggles to learn his own identity and to cope with the stranger who is poisoning Ernest. What happens to the intruder is part of the suspenseful climax.

The author of *The Intruder,* John Rowe Townsend, says in an interview, "It surprised me when *The Intruder* won the Edgar Award. I didn't realize I was a writer of mysteries until then."[7] When asked the age of his intended audience, Townsend quotes another English author, Joan Aiken, who jokes, "How do I know who it's for until I see who reads it?"

Joan Aiken is the creator of *Night Fall,*[8] another mystery set primarily in England. Nine-year-old Meg Frazer moves to London from the United States to be with her father (a physician) after the deaths of her mother (a movie star) and stepfather. The book's theme, solving a murder, is a challenge Meg faces when she is nineteen. To understand a recurring nightmare, she revisits Penleggen on the English coast where she had a brain concussion fourteen years ago. When she recalls a murder she witnessed there as a child, her life is in danger.

There is suspense in Aiken's tale and in Richard Peck's *Are You in the House Alone?*[9] The theme of this Connecticut story is facing rape and overcoming its effect. Sixteen-year-old Gail Osbourne is tormented by rape threats and receives a phone call asking if she is in the house alone. The mystery's climax occurs when Gail identifies her assailant. She soon learns the law punishes the innocent while criminals go free. The tense girl announces, "I'm never going to have anything to do with men for the rest of my life."[10]

*Survival*

**Upper Grades.** Survival is the theme of Robb White's *Deathwatch.*[11] Ben, a twenty-two-year-old college geology student, guides Mr. Madec, a cold, cunning executive, in a desert hunt for bighorn sheep. When trigger-happy Madec kills an old prospector instead of a bighorn, he feels it should be forgotten, but Ben wants to report the incident to the sheriff over forty miles away. Madec takes Ben's gun and forces him to remove his shoes and clothes. Ben struggles to stay alive without food or water, stalked by Madec. Ben's knowledge of the desert and his own ingenuity help him outwit Madec. With a bullet in his arm, his body blistered from

the sun and scratched from butte stones, he uses the prospector's slingshot to wound and capture Madec. Even then his troubles are not over.
The sheriff, believing Madec's lies that Ben murdered the prospector,
jails Ben. A physician, Dr. Saunders, is involved in the exciting
conclusion.

### Deception

**Upper Grades.** Deception is the theme of Scott Corbett's *Cutlass Island*.[12] Two junior-high lads, Skip Ellis and Harvey Harding, are hired
to investigate the peculiarities of John Hurd. He is caretaker of Cutlass
Island where there is a fortress with Civil War weapons. The secretive
caretaker contrasts with friendly Mal Sewell who brings the boys to the
island. When Skip injures his leg, John Hurd leaves to get help. Harvey
then freely explores the island, finds concealed dope, and learns that the
caretaker is an innocent victim of Mal's greed. Mal and his men are
routed as the others fight them with the fort's Civil War artillery. The
boys realize how deceived they have been, believing the wrong person
guilty.

Nothing is what it seems to be is the theme of Ellen Raskin's *The
Westing Game*.[13] The title comes from Samuel W. Westing's game in
which eight pairs of heirs try to discover his supposed killer. Each pair
gets unique clues and ten thousand dollars. When the players pool their
clues, they find the answer to the game but also learn that Westing, still
alive, is one of the players.

### Wish Fulfillment

**Middle and Upper Grades.** The primary theme of Phyllis A. Whitney's
*Mystery of the Hidden Hand* is fulfillment of a wish to discover one's
talents.[14] In Rhodes, Greece, vacationing twelve-year-old Gale Tyler and
her cousin, Anastasia Castelis, suffer by comparison with their gifted
older sisters. Anastasia practices ballet in imitation of her sister until she
realizes her talent is as a painter. The painter's grandfather, Thanos
Castelis, a sculptor, tries to force sculpting on his fifteen-year-old grandson, Nicos, but finally concedes Nicos's right to be a potter. The book's
title derives from the grandfather's secret possession of a marble hand
belonging to a museum statue. After the grandfather decides to return
the hand to his government, Gale helps him relate to his grandson. The
old man considers "a good mind and an understanding heart" to be
Gale's talents.[15]

Fulfillment of a different wish, that of belonging to a family, is the theme of Eleanor Cameron's *A Spell Is Cast*.[16] Orphaned, shy, ten-year-old Cory Winterslow believes Stephanie, an actress, adopted her years ago, but she did not. Cory learns the truth while at Tarnhelm, the California home of Stephanie's mother and handsome brother, Dirk. Cory unravels the mystery of Uncle Dirk's broken romance. She discovers his former fiancée is her friend, Laurel. She seems to cast a spell that reunites the couple, and they adopt her.

In an interview, Eleanor Cameron tells about the Pacific coast setting which contributes to an air of mystery in her book, *A Spell Is Cast*. The story takes place in Big Sur, part of Monterey Peninsula, 130 miles south of San Francisco. The author says, "It is a most beautiful place, I have loved it ever since I was twelve when we first started to go there." Then she discusses her unrestricted vocabulary in this and other books:

> I think all this restriction on words for children is absolutely absurd. Children can fight their way through most words. It's the difficult philosophical and sexual problems that children are shut off from, because they haven't really arrived at that state yet.[17]

Writers, like Eleanor Cameron, find children enjoy mysteries, a fact confirmed in interest surveys over the past fifty years. Humorous stories are equally popular with boys and girls.

### Perspective on Humorous Stories

Among prizewinners, contemporary realistic mysteries and humorous stories predominate, but mystery and humor may be found in any literary genre. There may be similar themes in mysteries and humorous stories, though they are treated differently. Humor may derive from plot, characterization, setting, illustration, and writing style. Certain books are episodic, giving a separate humorous incident per chapter. Some authors who specialize in humorous books often receive children's-choice awards. Such writers offer a panorama of themes as they provide welcome relief from somber stark realism and laugh at human foibles.

### Themes of Prizewinning Contemporary Realistic Humorous Stories Grouped under These Topics

*Being Trouble-Prone Entrepreneurs*

**Upper Grades.** Being trouble-prone entrepreneurs is the theme of Keith Robertson's *Henry Reed, Inc.*[18] and a sequel, *Henry Reed's Baby-Sitting*

*Service.*[19] In Grover's Corner near Princeton, New Jersey, adolescent Henry Harris Reed, accompanied by his beagle, Agony, spends frenzied, imaginative summers with his Uncle Al and Aunt Mabel Harris. In *Henry Reed, Inc.,* thirteen-year-old Henry and his twelve-year-old neighbor, Midge Glass, influenced by research at nearby Princeton University, start Reed and Glass, Inc., Pure and Applied Research. They think they discover oil only to find an old punctured fuel tank that nets them $39.75. Henry's projects succeed in spite of his antics, but one neighbor comments:

> These two children have created a public nuisance here on this lot. From the minute the sign [Henry Reed, Inc.] was painted on the barn we have not had a moment's privacy. . . . There is always some sort of chaos going on.[20]

In *Henry Reed's Baby-Sitting Service,* Henry is provoked when a neighbor robs him of a baby-sitting job. He and Midge begin a baby-sitting service and are challenged by a tot with a passion for hiding. Henry has so many unusual experiences, his Uncle Al tells him, ''You don't have to plan an accident. Something will happen naturally with you around.''[21]

In an interview, Keith Robertson speaks about Henry's prototype:

> Henry Reed is patterned after a fourth-grade school teacher. It seems rather ridiculous. We had a friend who taught school. It just seems that wherever she was, there was trouble. All sorts of activity and things went wrong, not her fault, of course, just a turmoil. Obviously, I could not have the central character be a fourth-grade schoolteacher and have children read it. I converted her into a boy, which was Henry.
>
> Some of the incidents are based on those my children got involved in. We live in a small town in New Jersey in an area similar to that described.[22]

The Henry Reed books are a perfect wedding of pictures and text that depict the theme of trouble-prone entrepreneurs. Robertson says, ''The illustrations were just as I had pictured Henry.''[23] Illustrator Robert McCloskey, who draws Henry in outlandish situations, confesses that he models Henry after himself.[24]

*Changing*

**Middle and Upper Grades.** Changing is the theme of Barbara Robinson's *The Best Christmas Pageant Ever.*[25] The six horrible Herdman children lie, steal, hit little kids, and set fire to an old, broken toolhouse. They talk dirty, curse their teachers, and take the Lord's name in vain. Even the girls smoke cigars. For three days, Leroy Herdman steals dessert from Charlie's lunch box. Then Charlie announces, "I don't care. I get all the dessert I want in Sunday school."[26] That's the wrong thing to say to keep the Herdmans away. Sure enough, the next Sunday school session, all Herdmans attend, eyeing refreshments. They alone volunteer for the Christmas play, threatening to put pussy willows in the ears of competing actors. They hear the Christmas story for the first time and interpret it in a novel way, wanting to fight Herod and give the Wise Men fine items. Leroy Herdman puts the church Christmas gift to his family, a ham, before the manger. The narrator, evaluating the changed Herdmans, concludes, "Well, it was the best Christmas pageant we ever had."[27]

## Persevering

**Middle and Upper Grades.** Persevering is the theme of Thomas Rockwell's *How to Eat Fried Worms*.[28] Billy Forrester accepts Alan Phelps's bet to eat fifteen worms in fifteen days for fifty dollars. Alan plots against Billy. He tries to keep Billy from eating a worm by stuffing him with hot dogs, and in an effort to scare him, writes a fake doctor's note saying worms are deadly. Billy persists, wins the bet, and develops such a taste for worms, he announces plans to continue eating them.

Persevering is also the theme of Beverly Cleary's *Henry and the Paper Route*.[29] Though he is rejected when he first requests to deliver newspapers, ten-year-old Henry Huggins becomes substitute paperboy after Scooter McCarthy gets chicken pox. When there is an opening, the job goes to Murph, genius inventor of a mechanical man, Thorvo. Murph stops working because a neighbor, four-year-old Ramona Quimby, who imagines she is a paperboy, removes his papers after he delivers them. Henry replaces Murph, coping with Ramona by making her a Thorvo outfit. To keep her from thinking she is a robot who delivers papers, he cautions, "Now remember, a mechanical man can't move very fast and he jerks along when he walks."[30]

In an interview, author Beverly Cleary says *Henry and the Paper Route* is part of a series that began with her first book, *Henry Huggins*. She says, "The theme of the series is the relationship of a boy to his dog, his family, and his neighbors. This is also the subject matter."[31] Each book has its own theme.

## Need for Loving Attention

**Middle and Upper Grades.** Judy Blume's *Tales of a Fourth Grade Nothing* has a need for loving attention as its theme.[32] A fourth-grade pupil, nine-year-old Peter Warren Hatcher, suffers because his parents and visitors seem to ignore him in favor of his two-year-old spoiled brother, Farley Drexel Hatcher (Fudge). On one occasion, Fudge unlatches Peter's bedroom door and eats his pet turtle, Dribble. After a weekend in the hospital, Fudge expels a dead turtle. When he returns home, he gets presents and kisses. Then Mr. Hatcher tells Peter, "Your mother and I think you've been a good sport about the whole situation. After all, Dribble *was* your pet."[33] Peter is surprised when they give him a pet Fudge can't swallow, a dog.

Readers feel Blume adds to humor with her choice of names, like Dribble and Fudge. In an interview, she talks about her naming process:

> I love to make up names. The first thing I do before I write a book is scribble names. I may know how many people are going to be in a family, and they all need names, of course. Before I know anything about them, before they're characters, I give them names. Then they grow, page by page, until I feel they're really my friends. I get very depressed when I finish a book, because it's like saying good-by to old friends, so the best therapy is to start another book right away.[34]

Beverly Cleary is another author who carefully names her characters, studying obituary columns and phone books for inspiration. One result of her efforts is Ramona Quimby, a recurring character already seen in *Henry and the Paper Route*. A need for loving attention is the theme of *Ramona the Pest,*[35] which shows Ramona at age five and her sister, Beezus, at age nine. Ramona is called a kindergarten pest when she "boings" another girl's curls. Ramona thinks, "People who called her a pest did not understand that a littler person sometimes had to be a little bit noisier and a little bit more stubborn in order to be noticed at all!"[36] The child is wounded when her teacher, Miss Binney, makes her leave. She returns only after Miss Binney sends her a welcoming note, a gesture showing she is still loved. *Ramona the Pest* and its sequel, *Ramona the Brave,* stress how important it is for a pupil to feel her teacher cares for her.

Author Beverly Cleary confides:

> I thought about *Ramona the Pest* for fifteen years before I wrote a word. . . . Ramona appeared almost by accident. When I was six years old, I did know a little girl and her big sister. The little girl called her big sister, "Beezus," but I have only one memory of the two girls. They were cutting through our yard on a trip home from the grocery store, and the little sister was licking a tube of butter as if it were an ice cream cone. Somehow, in my imagination, the character began to grow. . . .

Working as a children's librarian in Yakima, Washington confirmed my own childhood feelings that there weren't enough funny stories in the library, particularly not enough funny stories about real American children. I remember one boy wanted a funny story, so I gave him a book of folk tales I thought was humorous. He said, "I don't want to read about kings. I want to read about human beings."[37]

## Individuality

**Middle and Upper Grades.** Individuality is the primary theme of Beverly Cleary's *Ramona the Brave,*[38] a portrait of Ramona Quimby when she enters first grade. Her kindergarten teacher, Miss Binney, appreciates this unique, imaginative child.

> "Ramona Q! How nice to see you!" Miss Binney understood that Ramona used her last initial because she wanted to be different, and when Miss Binney printed Ramona's name, she always added ears and whiskers to the Q.[39]

Her first-grade teacher, Mrs. Griggs, is indifferent to Ramona. When a classmate copies Ramona's owl drawing and the teacher praises the copy, Ramona destroys it. Mrs. Griggs insists upon an apology, which Ramona makes. Her family helps the child regain her confidence without compromising her individuality.

## Maturing

Beverly Cleary's *Ramona Quimby, Age 8* emphasizes the theme of growing up.[40] Ramona writes atop her third-grade papers, "Ramona Quimby, Age 8," and "she liked being big enough to be counted on."[41] She even relishes the grown-up sound of the activity, Sustained Silent Reading. Her teacher, Mrs. Whaley, addresses the class as "you guys" and humiliates the child when she throws up in school. However, Ramona has the support of her family and tries to ignore shortcomings.

## Relationship with Father

**Middle and Upper Grades.** Father as a loving companion is the theme of Roald Dahl's *Danny: The Champion of the World.*[42] Nine-year-old Danny tells about his life in the English countryside. Since his mother died when he was four months old, he and his father, William, have lived alone in a gypsy caravan next to William's filling station. Though paupers, the two share a wealth of imagination. It is Danny's idea to poach pheasants with sleeping-powder-filled raisins. This escapade yields two hundred pheasants, making Danny champion of the world! The fun starts when the vicar's wife delivers the birds, and they come to life. Danny has such good times with William he doesn't invite friends home, "because I liked being alone with my father better."[43]

A more troubled father is in Beverly Cleary's *Ramona and Her Father,*[44] which depicts Ramona at seven years of age and her sister, Beatrice (Beezus), at eleven. The theme is family pressure as a result of unemployment. When Mr. Quimby loses his job and smokes heavily, his daughters start an antismoking campaign which angers him. Ramona reflects, "Nobody ever paid attention to second graders except to scold them. No matter how hard she tried to save his life, he was not going to let her save it."[45] In order to avoid depression, she becomes a sheep in a Sunday school play. Her father shows love for her when she is on stage, and he gives her a thumbs-up signal.

Beverly Cleary discusses the theme of *Ramona and Her Father* and the role of theme in her writing:

> The theme that unfolded in that book is the pressure on a family when a father loses his job. When I write a book, I don't intend any theme. I begin with a character and an incident and let the story unfold. I rarely begin at the beginning. The joy of writing is the surprise of what comes out of my imagination. I believe if I started with a theme, I might become a little didactic.[46]

**Summary**

Half of the twenty-three examples of contemporary realistic stories reviewed in this chapter are mysteries, most of which are intended for readers in fifth or sixth grade and beyond. Themes of mysteries are grouped under four headings. Half the mysteries have themes related to facing challenge.

While prizewinning mysteries include two books apiece by two authors, Donald Sobol and Phyllis A. Whitney, almost half of the humorous prizewinners are by Beverly Cleary. Four are sequels about Ramona Quimby, and one is about Henry Huggins. Among the humorous stories, Keith Robertson wrote two for pupils in upper-elementary grades, but most are for those in third grade and beyond. Themes of humorous contemporary fiction are grouped under seven headings.

The mysteries have earned single prizes, mainly the Edgar Allen Poe Award given by the Mystery Writers of America. Two humorous stories are Newbery Honor books, *Ramona and Her Father,* recipient of two other awards, and *Ramona Quimby, Age 8.*

Among humorous tales that have won multiple children's-choice awards are the following: *How to Eat Fried Worms,* six; *Ramona the Pest* and *Tales of a Fourth Grade Nothing,* four apiece; and *Henry Reed's Baby-Sitting Service,* three. It is no surprise that humorous, easy-to-read books are among those that are most frequently honored by children.

## Notes

1. In 1972, *Encyclopedia Brown Keeps the Peace* won the Pacific Northwest Library Association Young Reader's Choice Award.

2. In 1977, *Encyclopedia Brown Lends a Hand* won the Garden State's Children's Book Award.

3. Donald Sobol, *Encyclopedia Brown Lends a Hand* (New York: Nelson, 1974), p. 87.

4. In 1961, *Mystery of the Haunted Pool* won the Edgar Allen Poe Award.

5. In 1967, *Sinbad and Me* won the Edgar Allen Poe Award.

6. In 1970, *The Intruder* won the *Boston Globe-Horn Book* Award and in 1971, the Edgar Allen Poe Award.

7. "John Rowe Townsend," *Profiles in Literature* (Philadelphia: Temple University, 1975).

8. In 1972, *Night Fall* won the Edgar Allen Poe Award.

9. In 1977, *Are You in the House Alone?* won the Edgar Allen Poe Award.

10. Richard Peck, *Are You in the House Alone?* (New York: Viking, 1976), p. 124.

11. In 1973, *Deathwatch* won the Edgar Allen Poe Award.

12. In 1963, *Cutlass Island* won the Edgar Allen Poe Award.

13. In 1979, *The Westing Game* won The John Newbery Medal.

14. In 1964, *Mystery of the Hidden Hand* won the Edgar Allen Poe Award.

15. Phyllis A. Whitney, *Mystery of the Hidden Hand* (Philadelphia: Westminster, 1963), p. 166.

16. In 1964, *A Spell Is Cast* won the Commonwealth Club of California Award.

17. "Eleanor Cameron," *Profiles in Literature* (Philadelphia: Temple University, 1972).

18. In 1961, *Henry Reed, Inc.* won the William Allen White Children's Book Award.

19. In 1969, *Henry Reed's Baby-Sitting Service* won the Pacific

Northwest Library Association Young Reader's Choice Award and the William Allen White Children's Book Award. In 1970, it won the Nene Award.

20. Keith Robertson, *Henry Reed, Inc.* (New York: Viking, 1958), pp. 161–162.

21. Keith Robertson, *Henry Reed's Baby-Sitting Service* (New York: Viking, 1969), p. 62.

22. "Keith Robertson," *Profiles in Literature,* (Philadelphia: Temple University, 1972).

24. "Robert McCloskey," *Profiles in Literature* (Philadelphia: Temple University, 1977).

25. In 1976, *The Best Christmas Pageant Ever* won the Georgia Children's Book Award, and in 1978, the Young Hoosier Award.

26. Barbara Robinson, *The Best Christmas Pageant Ever* (New York: Harper, 1972), p. 21.

27. Barbara Robinson, *The Best Christmas Pageant Ever* (New York: Harper, 1972), p. 21.

28. In 1975, *How to Eat Fried Worms* won the Young Reader Medal for grades K–3 and the Mark Twain Award. In 1976, it won the Massachusetts Children's Book Award, the Nene Award, and the South Carolina Children's Book Award. In 1977, it received the Young Hoosier Award.

29. In 1960, *Henry and the Paper Route* won the Pacific Northwest Library Association Young Reader's Choice Award.

30. Beverly Cleary, *Henry and the Paper Route* (New York: Morrow, 1957), pp. 189–190.

31. "Beverly Cleary," *Profiles in Literature* (Philadelphia: Temple University, 1979).

32. In 1975, *Tales of a Fourth Grade Nothing* won the Pacific Northwest Library Association Young Reader's Choice Award. In 1977, it won the Georgia, Massachusetts, and South Carolina Children's Book Awards.

33. Judy Blume, *Tales of a Fourth Grade Nothing* (New York: Dutton, 1972), p. 120.

34. "Judy Blume," *Profiles in Literature* (Philadelphia: Temple University, 1973).

35. In 1970, *Ramona the Pest* won the Georgia Children's Book Award. In 1971, it won the Nene Award, the Pacific Northwest Library Association Young Reader's Choice Award, and the Sequoyah Children's Book Award.

36. Beverly Cleary, *Ramona the Pest* (New York: Morrow, 1968), p. 162.

37. "Beverly Cleary," *Profiles in Literature* (Philadelphia: Temple University, 1979).

38. In 1978, *Ramona the Brave* won the Mark Twain Award.

39. Beverly Cleary, *Ramona the Brave* (New York: Morrow, 1975), p. 61.

40. In 1982, *Ramona Quimby, Age 8* was a Newbery Honor Book.

41. Beverly Cleary, *Ramona Quimby, Age 8* (New York: Morrow, 1981), p. 19.

42. In 1979, *Danny: the Champion of the World* won the Young Reader Medal.

43. Roald Dahl, *Danny: the Champion of the World* (New York: Knopf, 1975), p. 106.

44. In 1978, *Ramona and Her Father* was a Newbery Honor Book. In 1979, it won the Nene Award, and in 1980 it was put on the International Board on Books for Young People Honor List.

45. Beverly Cleary, *Ramona and Her Father* (New York: Morrow, 1977), p. 101.

46. "Beverly Cleary," *Profiles in Literature,* (Philadelphia: Temple University, 1979).

## References of Popular Contemporary Realistic Fictional Prizewinners: Mysteries and Humorous Stories

*(Estimated Reading Grade Level in Parentheses)*

*Mysteries*

Aiken, Joan. *Night Fall*. New York: Holt, 1969 (6–9).

Cameron, Eleanor. *A Spell Is Cast*. Illustrated by Joe and Beth Krush. Boston: Little, Brown, 1964 (4–6).

Corbett, Scott. *Cutlass Island*. Illustrated by Leonard Shortall. Boston: Little, Brown, 1962 (5–8).

Peck, Richard. *Are You in the House Alone?* New York: Viking, 1976 (6–9).

Platt, Kin. *Sinbad and Me*. Philadelphia: Chilton, 1966 (6–9).

Raskin, Ellen. *The Westing Game*. New York: Dutton, 1978 (5–9).

Sobol, Donald. *Encyclopedia Brown Keeps the Peace*. Illustrated by Leonard Shortall. New York: Nelson, 1969 (3–5).

———. *Encyclopedia Brown Lends a Hand*. Illustrated by Leonard Shortall. New York: Nelson, 1974 (3–5).

Townsend, John Rowe. *The Intruder*. Philadelphia: Lippincott, 1970 (5–8).

White, Robb. *Deathwatch*. New York: Doubleday, 1972 (6–9).

Whitney, Phyllis A. *The Mystery of the Haunted Pool*. Illustrated by Tom Hall. Philadelphia: Westminster, 1960 (5–7).

————. *The Mystery of the Hidden Hand*. Philadelphia: Westminster, 1963 (5–7).

*Humorous Stories*

Blume, Judy. *Tales of a Fourth Grade Nothing*. Illustrated by Roy Doty. New York: Dutton, 1972 (3–5).

Cleary, Beverly. *Henry and the Paper Route*. Illustrated by Louis Darling. New York: Morrow, 1957 (3–5).

————. *Ramona and Her Father*. Illustrated by Alan Tiegreen. New York: Morrow, 1977 (3–5).

————. *Ramona Quimby, Age 8*. Illustrated by Alan Tiegreen. New York: Morrow, 1981 (3–5).

————. *Ramona the Brave*. Illustrated by Alan Tiegreen. New York: Morrow, 1975 (3–5).

————. *Ramona the Pest*. Illustrated by Louis Darling. New York: Morrow, 1968 (3–5).

Dahl, Roald. *Danny: The Champion of the World*. Illustrated by Jill Bennett. New York: Knopf, 1975 (3–5).

Robertson, Keith. *Henry Reed, Inc.* Illustrated by Robert McCloskey. New York: Viking, 1958 (5–7).

————. *Henry Reed's Baby-Sitting Service*. New York: Viking, 1969 (5–7).

Robinson, Barbara. *The Best Christmas Pageant Ever*. Illustrated by Judith Gwyn Brown. New York: Harper (4–6).

Rockwell, Thomas. *How to Eat Fried Worms*. Illustrated by Emily McCully. New York: Watts, 1973 (4–6).

# Appendix:
# Lists of Selected
# Prizes, Prizewinners,
# and Popular Themes

## The John Newbery Medal

Donated by the Frederic G. Melcher family, The Newbery Medal has been awarded annually since 1922 under the supervision of the Association for Library Services to Children of the American Library Association (50 E. Huron St., Chicago, IL 60611) to the author of the most distinguished contribution to literature for children published in the United States during the preceding year. Announced in January, the award is limited to residents or citizens of the United States. (Medal)

1922     *The Story of Mankind* by Hendrik Willem van Loon (Liveright)
Honor Books: *The Great Quest* by Charles Hawes (Little, Brown)
*Cedric the Forester* by Bernard Marshall (Appleton)
*The Old Tobacco Shop* by William Bowen (Macmillan)
*The Golden Fleece and the Heroes Who Lived Before Achilles*
      by Padraic Colum (Macmillan)
*Windy Hill* by Cornelia Meigs (Macmillan)

1923     *The Voyages of Doctor Doolittle* by Hugh Lofting (Lippincott)
Honor Book: No record

1924     *The Dark Frigate* by Charles Boardman Hawes (Atlantic-Little)
Honor Book: No record

1925     *Tales from Silver Lands* by Charles Finger (Doubleday)
Honor Books: *Nicholas* by Anne Carroll Moore (Putnam)
*Dream Coach* by Anne Parrish (Macmillan)

1926     *Shen of the Sea* by Arthur Bowie Chrisman (Dutton)
Honor Book: *Voyagers* by Padraic Colum (Macmillan)

1927     *Smoky, the Cowhorse* by Will James (Scribner)
Honor Book: No record

1928     *Gayneck, the Story of a Pigeon* by Dhan Gopal Mukerji (Dutton)
Honor Books: *The Wonder Smith and His Son* by Ella Young
      (Longman)
*Downright Dencey* by Caroline Snedeker (Doubleday)

1929     *The Trumpeter of Krakow* by Eric P. Kelly (Macmillan)

Honor Books: *The Forgotten Daughter* by Caroline Snedeker
    (Longmans)
*Millions of Cats* by Wanda Gág (Coward)
*The Boy Who Was* by Grace Hallock (Dutton)
*Clearing Weather* by Cornelia Meigs (Little)
*Runaway Papoose* by Grace Moon (Doubleday)
*Tod of the Fens* by Elinor Whitney (Macmillan)

1930    *Hitty, Her First Hundred Years* by Rachel Field (Macmillan)
        Honor Books: *Daughter of the Seine* by Jeanette Eaton (Harper)
        *Pran of Albania* by Elizabeth Miller (Doubleday)
        *Jumping-Off Place* by Marian Hurd McNeely (Longmans)
        *Tangle-Coated Horse and Other Tales* by Ella Young
            (Longmans)
        *Vaino* by Julia Davis Adams (Dutton)
        *Little Blacknose* by Hildegarde Swift (Harcourt)

1931    *The Cat Who Went to Heaven* by Elizabeth Coatsworth
            (Macmillan)
        Honor Books: *Floating Island* by Anne Parrish (Harper)
        *The Dark Star of Itza* by Alida Malkus (Harcourt)
        *Queer Person* by Ralph Hubbard (Doubleday)
        *Mountains Are Free* by Julia Davis Adams (Dutton)
        *Spice and the Devil's Cave* by Agnes Hewes (Knopf )
        *Meggy MacIntosh* by Elizabeth Janet Gray (Doubleday)
        *Carram the Hunter* by Herbert Best (Doubleday)
        *Odd-Le-Uk the Wanderer* by Alice Lide and Margaret Johansen
            (Little)

1932    *Waterless Mountain* by Laura Adams Armer (Longmans)
        Honor Books: *The Fairy Circus* by Dorothy P. Lathrop
            (Macmillan)
        *Calico Bush* by Rachel Field (Macmillan)
        *Boy of the South Seas* by Eunice Tietjens (Coward)
        *Out of the Flame* by Eloise Lownsbery (Longmans)
        *Jane's Island* by Marjorie Allee (Houghton)
        *Truce of the Wolf and Other Tales of Old Italy* by Mary Gould
            Davis (Harcourt)

1933    *Young Fu of the Upper Yangtze* by Elizabeth Lewis (Winston)
        Honor Books: *Swift Rivers* by Cornelia Meigs (Little)
        *The Railroad to Freedom* by Hildegarde Swift (Harcourt)
        *Children of the Soil* by Nora Burglon (Doubleday)

1934    *Invincible Louisa* by Cornelia Meigs (Little)

Honor Books: *The Forgotten Daughter* by Caroline Snedeker
  (Doubleday)
*Swords of Steel* by Elsie Singmaster (Houghton)
*ABC Bunny* by Wanda Gág (Coward)
*Winged Girl of Knossos* by Erik Berry (Appleton)
*New Land* by Sarah Schmidt (McBride)
*Big Tree of Bunlahy* by Padraic Colum (Macmillan)
*Glory of the Seas* by Agnes Hewes (Knopf )
*Apprentice of Florence* by Anne Kyle (Houghton)

1935    *Dobry* by Monica Shannon (Viking)
        Honor Books: *Pageant of Chinese History* by Elizabeth Seeger
          (Longmans)
        *Davy Crockett* by Constance Rourke (Harcourt)
        *Day on Skates* by Hilda Van Stockum (Harper)

1936    *Caddie Woodlawn* by Carol Ryrie Brink (Macmillan)
        Honor Books: *Honk, the Moose* by Phil Stong (Dodd)
        *The Good Master* by Kate Seredy (Viking)
        *Young Walter Scott* by Elizabeth Janet Gray (Viking)
        *All Sail Set* by Armstrong Sperry (Winston)

1937    *Roller Skates* by Ruth Sawyer (Viking)
        Honor Books: *Phebe Fairchild: Her Book* by Lois Lenski
          (Stokes)
        *Whistler's Van* by Idwal Jones (Viking)
        *Golden Basket* by Ludwig Bemelmans (Viking)
        *Winterbound* by Margery Bianco (Viking)
        *Audubon* by Constance Rourke (Harcourt)
        *The Codfish Musket* by Agnes Hewes (Doubleday)

1938    *The White Stag* by Kate Seredy (Viking)
        Honor Books: *Pecos Bill* by James Cloyd Bowman (Little)
        *Bright Island* by Mabel Robinson (Random)
        *On the Banks of Plum Creek* by Laura Ingalls Wilder (Harper)

1939    *Thimble Summer* by Elizabeth Enright (Rinehart)
        Honor Books: *Nino* by Valenti Angelo (Viking)
        *Mr. Popper's Penguins* by Richard and Florence Atwater (Little)
        *Hello the Boat!* by Phyllis Crawford (Holt)
        *Leader by Destiny: George Washington, Man and Patriot* by
          Jeanette Eaton (Harcourt)
        *Penn* by Elizabeth Janet Gray (Viking)

1940    *Daniel Boone* by James Daugherty (Viking)
        Honor Books: *The Singing Tree* by Kate Seredy (Viking)

*Runner of the Mountain Tops* by Mabel Robinson (Random)
*By the Shores of Silver Lake* by Laura Ingalls Wilder (Harper)
*Boy with a Pack* by Stephen W. Meader (Harcourt)

**1941**    *Call it Courage* by Armstrong Sperry (Macmillan)
Honor Books: *Blue Willow* by Doris Gates (Viking)
*Young Mac of Fort Vancouver* by Mary Jane Carr (Crowell)
*The Long Winter* by Laura Ingalls Wilder (Harper)
*Nansen* by Anna Gertrude Hall (Viking)

**1942**    *The Matchlock Gun* by Walter D. Edmonds (Dodd)
Honor Books: *Little Town on the Prairie* by Laura Ingalls Wilder (Harper)
*George Washington's World* by Genevieve Foster (Scribner)
*Indian Captive: The Story of Mary Jemison* by Lois Lenski (Lippincott)
*Down Ryton Water* by Eva Roe Gaggin (Viking)

**1943**    *Adam of the Road* by Elizabeth Janet Gray (Viking)
Honor Books: *The Middle Moffat* by Eleanor Estes (Harcourt)
*Have You Seen Tom Thumb?* by Mabel Leigh Hunt (Lippincott)

**1944**    *Johnny Tremain* by Esther Forbes (Houghton)
Honor Books: *These Happy Golden Years* by Laura Ingalls Wilder (Harper)
*Fog Magic* by Julia Sauer (Viking)
*Rufus M.* by Eleanor Estes (Harcourt)
*Mountain Born* by Elizabeth Yates (Coward)

**1945**    *Rabbit Hill* by Robert Lawson (Viking)
Honor Books: *The Hundred Dresses* by Eleanor Estes (Harcourt)
*The Silver Pencil* by Alice Dalgliesh (Scribner)
*Abraham Lincoln's World* by Genevieve Foster (Scribner)
*Lone Journey: The Life of Roger Williams* by Jeanette Eaton (Harcourt)

**1946**    *Strawberry Girl* by Lois Lenski (Lippincott)
Honor Books: *Justin Morgan Had a Horse* by Marguerite Henry (Rand)
*The Moved-Outers* by Florence Crannell Means (Houghton)
*Bhimsa, the Dancing Bear* by Christine Weston (Scribner)
*New Found World* by Katherine Shippen (Viking)

**1947**    *Miss Hickory* by Carolyn Sherwin Bailey (Viking)
Honor Books: *Wonderful Year* by Nancy Barnes (Messner)
*Big Tree* by Mary and Conrad Buff (Viking)

*The Heavenly Tenants* by William Maxwell (Harper)
*The Avion My Uncle Flew* by Cyrus Fisher (Appleton)
*The Hidden Treasure of Glaston* by Eleanore Jewett (Viking)

**1948**    *The Twenty-One Balloons* by William Pène du Bois (Viking)
Honor Books: *Pancakes-Paris* by Claire Huchet Bishop (Viking)
*Li Lun, Lad of Courage* by Carolyn Treffinger (Abingdon)
*The Quaint and Curious Quest of Johnny Longfoot* by Catherine
    Besterman (Bobbs)
*The Cow-Tail Switch, and Other West African Stories* by Harold
    Courlander (Holt)
*Misty of Chincoteague* by Marguerite Henry (Rand)

**1949**    *King of the Wind* by Marguerite Henry (Rand)
Honor Books: *Seabird* by Holling C. Holling (Houghton)
*My Father's Dragon* by Ruth S. Gannett (Random House)
*Story of the Negro* by Arna Bontemps (Knopf)

**1950**    *The Door in the Wall* by Marguerite deAngeli (Doubleday)
Honor Books: *Tree of Freedom* by Rebecca Caudill (Viking)
*The Blue Cat of Castle Town* by Catherine Coblentz (Longmans)
*Kildee House* by Rutherford Montgomery (Doubleday)
*George Washington* by Genevieve Foster (Scribner)
*Song of the Pines* by Walter and Marion Havighurst (Winston)

**1951**    *Amos Fortune, Free Man* by Elizabeth Yates (Aladdin)
Honor Books: *Better Known as Johnny Appleseed* by Mabel
    Leigh Hunt (Lippincott)
*Gandhi, Fighter Without a Sword* by Jeanette Eaton (Morrow)
*Abraham Lincoln, Friend of the People* by Clara Ingram Judson
    (Follett)
*The Story of Appleby Capple* by Anne Parrish (Harper)

**1952**    *Ginger Pye* by Eleanor Estes (Harcourt)
Honor Books: *Americans before Columbus* by Elizabeth Baity
    (Viking)
*Minn of the Mississippi* by Holling C. Holling (Houghton)
*The Defender* by Nicholas Kalashnikoff (Scribner)
*The Light at Tern Rock* by Julia Sauer (Viking)
*The Apple and the Arrow* by Mary and Conrad Buff (Houghton)

**1953**    *Secret of the Andes* by Ann Nolan Clark (Viking)
Honor Books: *Charlotte's Web* by E.B. White (Harper)
*Moccasin Trail* by Eloise McGraw (Coward)
*Red Sails to Capri* by Ann Weil (Viking)
*The Bears on Hemlock Mountain* by Alice Dalgliesh (Scribner)

*Birthdays of Freedom, Vol. 1* by Genevieve Foster (Scribner)

**1954**    *. . . And Now Miguel* by Joseph Krumgold (Crowell)
Honor Books: *All Alone* by Claire Huchet Bishop (Viking)
*Shadrach* by Meindert DeJong (Harper)
*Hurry Home, Candy* by Meindert DeJong (Harper)
*Theodore Roosevelt, Fighting Patriot* by Clara Ingram Judson
     (Follett)
*Magic Maize* by Mary and Conrad Buff (Houghton)

**1955**    *The Wheel on the School* by Meindert DeJong (Harper)
Honor Books: *Courage of Sarah Noble* by Alice Dalgliesh
     (Scribner)
*Banner in the Sky* by James Ullman (Lippincott)

**1956**    *Carry On, Mr. Bowditch* by Jean Lee Latham (Houghton)
Honor Books: *The Secret River* by Marjorie Kinnan Rawlings
     (Scribner)
*The Golden Name Day* by Jennie Lindquist (Harper)
*Men, Microscopes, and Living Things* by Katherine Shippen
     (Viking)

**1957**    *Miracles on Maple Hill* by Virginia Sorensen (Harcourt)
Honor Books: *Old Yeller* by Fred Gipson (Harper)
*The House of Sixty Fathers* by Meindert DeJong (Harper)
*Mr. Justice Holmes* by Clara Ingram Judson (Follett)
*The Corn Grows Ripe* by Dorothy Rhoads (Viking)
*Black Fox of Lorne* by Marguerite deAngeli (Doubleday)

**1958**    *Rifles for Watie* by Harold Keith (Crowell)
Honor Books: *The Horsecatcher* by Mari Sandoz (Westminster)
*Gone-Away Lake* by Elizabeth Enright (Harcourt)
*The Great Wheel* by Robert Lawson (Viking)
*Tom Paine, Freedom's Apostle* by Leo Gurko (Crowell)

**1959**    *The Witch of Blackbird Pond* by Elizabeth George Speare
     (Houghton)
Honor Books: *The Family under the Bridge* by Natalie Savage
     Carlson (Harper)
*Along Came a Dog* by Meindert DeJong (Harper)
*The Perilous Road* by William O. Steele (Harcourt)
*Chucaro: Wild Pony of the Pampa* by Francis Kalnay (Harcourt)

**1960**    *Onion John* by Joseph Krumgold (Crowell)
Honor Books: *My Side of the Mountain* by Jean Craighead
     George (Dutton)

*America Is Born* by Gerald W. Johnson (Morrow)
*The Gammage Cup* by Carol Kendall (Harcourt)

**1961**     *Island of the Blue Dolphins* by Scott O'Dell (Houghton)
Honor Books: *America Moves Forward* by Gerald W. Johnson
(Morrow)
*Old Ramón* by Jack Schaefer (Houghton)
*The Cricket in Times Square* by George Selden (Farrar)

**1962**     *The Bronze Bow* by Elizabeth George Speare (Houghton)
Honor Books: *Frontier Living* by Edwin Tunis (World)
*The Golden Goblet* by Eloise McGraw (Coward)
*Belling the Tiger* by Mary Stolz (Harper)

**1963**     *A Wrinkle In Time* by Madeleine L'Engle (Farrar)
Honor Books: *Thistle and Thyme* by Sorche Nic Leodhas (Holt)
*Men of Athens* by Olivia Coolidge (Houghton)

**1964**     *It's Like This, Cat* by Emily Cheney Neville (Harper)
*The Loner* by Ester Wier (McKay)

**1965**     *Shadow of a Bull* by Maia Wojciechowska (Atheneum)
Honor Book: *Across Five Aprils* by Irene Hunt (Follett)

**1966**     *I, Juan De Pareja* by Elizabeth Borten de Treviño (Farrar)
Honor Books: *The Black Cauldron* by Lloyd Alexander (Holt)
*The Animal Family* by Randall Jarrell (Pantheon)
*The Noonday Friends* by Mary Stolz (Harper)

**1967**     *Up a Road Slowly* by Irene Hunt (Follett)
Honor Books: *The King's Fifth* by Scott O'Dell (Houghton)
*Zlateh the Goat and Other Stories* by Isaac Bashevis Singer
(Harper)
*The Jazz Man* by Mary H. Weik (Atheneum)

**1968**     *From the Mixed-Up Files of Mrs. Basil E. Frankweiler* by E.L.
Konigsburg (Atheneum)
Honor Books: *Jennifer, Hecate, Macbeth, William McKinley,
and Me, Elizabeth* by E.L. Konigsburg (Atheneum)
*The Black Pearl* by Scott O'Dell (Houghton)
*The Fearsome Inn* by Isaac Bashevis Singer (Scribner)
*The Egypt Game* by Zilpha Keatley Snyder (Atheneum)

**1969**     *The High King* by Lloyd Alexander (Holt)
Honor Books: *To Be A Slave* by Julius Lester (Dial)
*When Shlemiel Went to Warsaw and Other Stories* by Isaac
Bashevis Singer (Farrar)

**1970** *Sounder* by William H. Armstrong (Harper)
Honor Books: *Our Eddie* by Sulamith Ish-Kishor (Pantheon)
*The Many Ways of Seeing, An Introduction to the Pleasures of Art* by Janet Gaylord Moore (World)
*Journey Outside* by Mary Q. Steele (Viking)

**1971** *Summer of the Swans* by Betsy Byars (Viking)
Honor Books: *Knee-Knock Rise* by Natalie Babbitt (Farrar)
*Enchantress from the Stars* by Sylvia Louise Engdahl (Atheneum)
*Sing Down the Moon* by Scott O'Dell (Houghton)

**1972** *Mrs. Frisby and the Rats of NIMH* by Robert C. O'Brien (Atheneum)
Honor Books: *Annie and the Old One* by Miska Miles (Atlantic-Little)
*The Headless Cupid* by Zilpha Keatley Snyder (Atheneum)
*Incident at Hawk's Hill* by Allan W. Eckert (Little)
*The Planet of Junior Brown* by Virginia Hamilton (Macmillan)
*The Tombs of Atuan* by Ursula K. Le Guin (Atheneum)

**1973** *Julie of the Wolves* by Jean Craighead George (Harper)
Honor Books: *Frog and Toad Together* by Arnold Lobel (Harper)
*The Upstairs Room* by Johanna Reiss (Crowell)
*The Witches of Worm* by Zilpha Keatley Snyder (Atheneum)

**1974** *The Slave Dancer* by Paula Fox (Bradbury)
Honor Book: *The Dark Is Rising* by Susan Cooper (McElderry/Atheneum)

**1975** *M.C. Higgins, the Great* by Virginia Hamilton (Macmillan)
Honor Books: *Figgs and Phantoms* by Ellen Raskin (Dutton)
*My Brother Sam Is Dead* by James Lincoln Collier and Christopher Collier (Four Winds)
*The Perilous Gard* by Elizabeth Marie Pope (Houghton)
*Phillip Hall Likes Me, I Reckon Maybe* by Bette Greene (Dial)

**1976** *The Grey King* by Susan Cooper (McElderry/Atheneum)
Honor Books: *Dragonwings* by Laurence Yep (Harper)
*The Hundred Penny Box* by Sharon Bell Mathis (Viking)

**1977** *Roll of Thunder, Hear My Cry* by Mildred D. Taylor (Dial)
Honor Books: *Abel's Island* by William Steig (Farrar)
*A String in the Harp* by Nancy Bond (McElderry/Atheneum)

**1978** *Bridge to Terabithia* by Katherine Paterson (Crowell)
Honor Books: *Anpao: An American Indian Odyssey* by Jamake Highwater (Lippincott)

*Ramona and Her Father* by Beverly Cleary (Morrow)

1979     *The Westing Game* by Ellen Raskin (Dutton)
         Honor Book: *The Great Gilly Hopkins* by Katherine Paterson
            (Crowell)

1980     *A Gathering of Days* by Joan W. Blos (Scribner)
         Honor Book: *The Road from Home: The Story of an Armenian
            Girl* by David Kheridian (Greenwillow)

1981     *Jacob Have I Loved* by Katherine Paterson (Crowell)
         Honor Books: *The Fledgling* by Jane Langton (Harper)
         *A Ring of Endless Light* by Madeleine L'Engle (Farrar)

1982     *A Visit to William Blake's Inn* by Nancy Willard (Harcourt)
         Honor Books: *Ramona Quimby, Age 8* by Beverly Cleary
            (Morrow)
         *Upon the Head of the Goat: A Childhood in Hungary, 1939–
            1944* by Aranka Siegal (Farrar)


## The Randolph Caldecott Medal

Donated by the Frederic G. Melcher family, The Caldecott Medal has
been awarded annually since 1938 under the supervision of the Association for Library Services to Children of the American Library Association (50 E. Huron St., Chicago, IL 60611) to the illustrator of the most
distinguished picture book for children published in the United States
during the preceding year. Announced in January, the award is limited
to residents or citizens of the United States. (Medal.)

1938     *Animals of the Bible* by Helen Dean Fish, illustrated by Dorothy
            P. Lathrop (Lippincott)
         Honor Books: *Seven Simeons* by Boris Artzybasheff (Viking)
         *Four and Twenty Blackbirds* by Helen Dean Fish, illustrated by
            Robert Lawson (Stokes)

1939     *Mei Li* by Thomas Handforth (Doubleday)
         Honor Books: *The Forest Pool* by Laura Adams Armer
            (Longmans)
         *Wee Gillis* by Munro Leaf, illustrated by Robert Lawson (Viking)
         *Snow White and the Seven Dwarfs* by Wanda Gág (Coward)
         *Barkis* by Clare Newberry (Harper)
         *Andy and the Lion* by James Daugherty (Viking)

1940     *Abraham Lincoln* by Ingri and Edgar Parin d'Aulaire
            (Doubleday)

Honor Books: *Cock-a-Doodle Doo, the Story of a Little Red Rooster* by Berta and Elmer Hader (Macmillan)
*Madeline* by Ludwig Bemelmans (Viking)
*The Ageless Story*, illustrated by Lauren Ford (Dodd)

**1941**  *They Were Strong and Good* by Robert Lawson (Viking)
Honor Book: *April's Kittens* by Clare Newberry (Harper)

**1942**  *Make Way for Ducklings* by Robert McCloskey (Viking)
Honor Books: *An American ABC* by Maud and Miska Petersham (Macmillan)
*In My Mother's House* by Ann Nolan Clark, illustrated by Velino Herrera (Viking)
*Paddle-to-the-Sea* by Holling C. Holling (Houghton)
*Nothing at All* by Wanda Gág (Coward)

**1943**  *The Little House* by Virginia Lee Burton (Houghton)
Honor Books: *Dash and Dart* by Mary and Conrad Buff (Viking)
*Marshmallow* by Clare Newberry (Harper)

**1944**  *Many Moons* by James Thurber, illustrated by Louis Slobodkin (Harcourt)
Honor Books: *Small Rain: Verses from the Bible* selected by Jessie Orton Jones, illustrated by Elizabeth Orton Jones (Viking)
*Pierre Pigeon* by Lee Kingman, illustrated by Arnold E. Bare (Houghton)
*The Mighty Hunter* by Berta and Elmer Hader (Macmillan)
*A Child's Good Night Book* by Margaret Wise Brown, illustrated by Jean Charlot (Scott)
*Good Luck Horse* by Chin-Yi-Chan, illustrated by Plao Chan (Whittlesey)

**1945**  *Prayer for a Child* by Rachel Field, illustrated by Elizabeth Orton Jones (Macmillan)
Honor Books: *Mother Goose*, illustrated by Tasha Tudor (Walck)
*In the Forest* by Marie Hall Ets (Viking)
*Yonie Wondernose* by Marguerite deAngeli (Doubleday)
*The Christmas Anna Angel* by Ruth Sawyer, illustrated by Kate Seredy (Viking)

**1946**  *The Rooster Crows* (traditional Mother Goose) illustrated by Maud and Miska Petersham (Macmillan)
Honor Books: *Little Lost Lamb* by Golden MacDonald, illustrated by Leonard Weisgard (Doubleday)

Sing Mother Goose by Opal Wheeler, illustrated by Marjorie Torrey (Dutton)

My Mother Is the Most Beautiful Woman in the World by Becky Reyher, illustrated by Ruth C. Gannett (Lothrop)

You Can Write Chinese by Kurt Wiese (Viking)

**1947**  The Little Island by Golden MacDonald, illustrated by Leonard Weisgard (Doubleday)

Honor Books: Rain Drop Splash by Alvin Tresselt, illustrated by Leonard Weisgard (Lothrop)

Boats on the River by Marjorie Flack, illustrated by Jay Hyde Barnum (Viking)

Timothy Turtle by Al Graham, illustrated by Tony Palazzo (Welch)

Pedro, the Angel of Olvera Street by Leo Politi (Scribner)

Sing in Praise: A Collection of the Best Loved Hymns by Opal Wheeler, illustrated by Marjorie Torrey (Dutton)

**1948**  White Snow, Bright Snow by Alvin Tresselt, illustrated by Roger Duvoisin (Lothrop)

Honor Books: Stone Soup by Marcia Brown (Scribner)

McElligot's Pool by Dr. Seuss (Random House)

Bambino the Clown by George Schreiber (Viking)

Roger and the Fox by Lavinia Davis, illustrated by Hildegard Woodward (Doubleday)

Song of Robin Hood ed. Anne Malcolmson, illustrated by Virginia Lee Burton (Houghton)

**1949**  The Big Snow by Berta and Elmer Hader (Macmillan)

Honor Books: Blueberries for Sal by Robert McCloskey (Viking)

All Around the Town by Phyllis McGinley, illustrated by Helen Stone (Lippincott)

Juanita by Leo Politi (Scribner)

Fish in the Air by Kurt Wiese (Viking)

**1950**  Song of the Swallows by Leo Politi (Scribner)

Honor Books: America's Ethan Allen by Stewart Holbrook, illustrated by Lynd Ward (Houghton)

The Wild Birthday Cake by Lavinia Davis, illustrated by Hildegard Woodward (Doubleday)

The Happy Day by Ruth Krauss, illustrated by Marc Simont (Harper)

Bartholomew and the Oobleck by Dr. Seuss (Random)

Henry Fisherman by Marcia Brown (Scribner)

**1951**  The Egg Tree by Katherine Milhous (Scribner)

Honor Books: *Dick Whittington and His Cat* by Marcia Brown
(Scribner)
*The Two Reds* by Will Lipkind, illustrated by Nicolas Mord-
vinoff (Harcourt)
*T-Bone, the Baby Sitter* by Clare Newberry (Harper)
*If I Ran the Zoo* by Dr. Seuss (Random)
*The Most Wonderful Doll in the World* by Phyllis McGinley,
illustrated by Helen Stone (Lippincott)

1952    *Finders Keepers* by Will Lipkind, illustrated by Nicolas Mord-
vinoff (Harcourt)
Honor Books: *Mr. T.W. Anthony Woo* by Marie Hall Ets (Viking)
*Skipper John's Cook* by Marcia Brown (Scribner)
*All Falling Down* by Gene Zion, illustrated by Margaret Bloy
Graham (Harper)
*Bear Party* by William Pène du Bois (Viking)
*Feather Mountain* by Elizabeth Olds (Houghton)

1953    *The Biggest Bear* by Lynd Ward (Houghton)
Honor Books: *Puss in Boots* by Charles Perrault, illustrated and
translated by Marcia Brown (Scribner)
*One Morning in Maine* by Robert McCloskey (Viking)
*Ape in a Cape* by Fritz Eichenberg (Harcourt)
*The Storm Book* by Charlotte Zolotow, illustrated by Margaret
Bloy Graham (Harper)
*Five Little Monkeys* by Juliet Kepes (Houghton)

1954    *Madeline's Rescue* by Ludwig Bemelmans (Viking)
Honor Books: *Journey Cake, Ho!* by Ruth Sawyer, illustrated
by Robert McCloskey (Viking)
*When Will the World Be Mine?* by Miriam Schlein, illustrated
by Jean Charlot (Scott)
*The Steadfast Tin Soldier* by Hans Christian Andersen, illus-
trated by Marcia Brown (Scribner)
*A Very Special House* by Ruth Krauss, illustrated by Maurice
Sendak (Harper)
*Green Eyes* by A. Birnbaum (Capitol)

1955    *Cinderella, or the Little Glass Slipper* by Charles Perrault, trans-
lated and illustrated by Marcia Brown (Scribner)
Honor Books: *Book of Nursery and Mother Goose Rhymes*,
illustrated by Marguerite deAngeli (Doubleday)
*Wheel on the Chimney* by Margaret Wise Brown, illustrated by
Tibor Gergely (Lippincott)
*The Thanksgiving Story* by Alice Dalgliesh, illustrated by Helen
Sewell (Scribner)

**1956**    *Frog Went a-Courting* ed. John Langstaff, illustrated by Feodor
            Rojankovsky (Harcourt)
            Honor Books: *Play with Me* by Marie Hall Ets (Viking)
            *Crow Boy* by Taro Yashima (Viking)

**1957**    *A Tree Is Nice* by Janice May Udry, illustrated by Marc Simont
            (Harper)
            Honor Books: *Mr. Penny's Race Horse* by Marie Hall Ets
            (Viking)
            *1 Is One* by Tasha Tudor (Walck)
            *Anatole* by Eve Titus, illustrated by Paul Galdone (McGraw)
            *Gillespie and the Guards* by Benjamin Elkin, illustrated by
            James Daugherty (Viking)
            *Lion* by William Pène du Bois (Viking)

**1958**    *Time of Wonder* by Robert McCloskey (Viking)
            Honor Books: *Fly High, Fly Low* by Don Freeman (Viking)
            *Anatole and the Cat* by Eve Titus, illustrated by Paul Galdone
            (McGraw)

**1959**    *Chanticleer and the Fox,* adapted from Chaucer and illustrated
            by Barbara Cooney (Crowell)
            Honor Books: *The House that Jack Built* by Antonio Frasconi
            (Harcourt)
            *What Do You Say, Dear?* by Sesyle Joslin, illustrated by Maur-
            ice Sendak (Scott)
            *Umbrella* by Taro Yashima (Viking)

**1960**    *Nine Days to Christmas* by Marie Hall Ets and Aurora Labas-
            tida, illustrated by Marie Hall Ets (Viking)
            Honor Books: *Houses from the Sea* by Alice E. Goudey, illus-
            trated by Adrienne Adams (Scribner)
            *The Moon Jumpers* by Janice May Udry, illustrated by Maurice
            Sendak (Harper)

**1961**    *Baboushka and the Three Kings* by Ruth Robbins, illustrated
            by Nicholas Sidjakov (Parnassus)
            Honor Book: *Inch by Inch* by Leo Lionni (Astor-Honor)

**1962**    *Once A Mouse . . .* by Marcia Brown (Scribner)
            Honor Books: *The Fox Went Out on a Chilly Night,* illustrated
            by Peter Spier (Doubleday)
            *Little Bear's Visit* by Else Holmelund Minarik, illustrated by
            Maurice Sendak (Harper)
            *The Day We Saw the Sun Come Up* by Alice E. Goudey, il-
            lustrated by Adrienne Adams (Scribner)

**1963**    *The Snowy Day* by Ezra Jack Keats (Viking)
Honor Books: *The Sun Is a Golden Earring* by Natalia M. Belting, illustrated by Bernarda Bryson (Holt)
*Mr. Rabbit and the Lovely Present* by Charlotte Zolotow, illustrated by Maurice Sendak (Harper)

**1964**    *Where the Wild Things Are* by Maurice Sendak (Harper)
Honor Books: *Swimmy* by Leo Lionni (Pantheon)
*All in the Morning Early* by Sorche Nic Leodhas, illustrated by Evaline Ness (Holt)
*Mother Goose and Nursery Rhymes,* illustrated by Philip Reed (Atheneum)

**1965**    *May I Bring a Friend?* by Beatrice Schenk de Regniers, illustrated by Beni Montresor (Atheneum)
Honor Books: *Rain Makes Applesauce* by Julian Scheer, illustrated by Marvin Bileck (Holiday)
*The Wave* by Margaret Hodges, illustrated by Blair Lent (Houghton)
*A Pocketful of Cricket* by Rebecca Caudill, illustrated by Evaline Ness (Holt)

**1966**    *Always Room for One More* by Sorche Nic Leodhas, illustrated by Nonny Hogrogian (Holt)
Honor Books: *Hide and Seek Fog* by Alvin Tresselt, illustrated by Roger Duvoisin (Lothrop)
*Just Me* by Marie Hall Ets (Viking)
*Tom Tit Tot* by Evaline Ness (Scribner)

**1967**    *Sam, Bangs and Moonshine* by Evaline Ness (Holt)
Honor Book: *One Wide River to Cross* by Barbara Emberley, illustrated by Ed Emberley (Prentice)

**1968**    *Drummer Hoff* by Barbara Emberley, illustrated by Ed Emberley (Prentice)
Honor Books: *Frederick* by Leo Lionni (Pantheon)
*Seashore Story* by Taro Yashima (Viking)
*The Emperor and the Kite* by Jane Yolen, illustrated by Ed Young (World)

**1969**    *The Fool of the World and the Flying Ship* by Arthur Ransome, illustrated by Uri Shulevitz (Farrar)
Honor Book: *Why the Sun and the Moon Live in the Sky* by Elphinstone Dayrell, illustrated by Blair Lent (Houghton)

**1970**    *Sylvester and the Magic Pebble* by William Steig (Windmill/Simon & Schuster)

Honor Books: *Goggles* by Ezra Jack Keats (Macmillan)
*Alexander and the Wind-Up Mouse* by Leo Lionni (Pantheon)
*Pop Corn and Ma Goodness* by Edna Mitchell Preston, illustrated by Robert Andrew Parker (Viking)
*Thy Friend, Obadiah* by Brinton Turkle (Viking)
*The Judge* by Harve Zemach, illustrated by Margot Zemach (Farrar)

1971    *A Story—A Story* by Gail E. Haley (Atheneum)
Honor Books: *The Angry Moon* by William Sleator, illustrated by Blair Lent (Atlantic-Little)
*Frog and Toad Are Friends* by Arnold Lobel (Harper)
*In the Night Kitchen* by Maurice Sendak (Harper)

1972    *One Fine Day* by Nonny Hogrogian (Macmillan)
Honor Books: *Hildilid's Night* by Cheli Durán Ryan, illustrated by Arnold Lobel (Macmillan)
*If All the Seas Were One Sea* by Janina Domanska (Macmillan)
*Moja Means One* by Muriel Feelings, illustrated by Tom Feelings (Dial)

1973    *The Funny Little Woman* retold by Arlene Mosel, illustrated by Blair Lent (Dutton)
Honor Books: *Anansi the Spider* adapted and illustrated by Gerald McDermott (Holt)
*Hosie's Alphabet* by Hosea, Tobias, and Lisa Baskin, illustrated by Leonard Baskin (Viking)
*Snow-White and the Seven Dwarfs* translated by Randall Jarrell, illustrated by Nancy Ekholm Burkert (Farrar)
*When Clay Sings* by Byrd Baylor, illustrated by Tom Bahti (Scribner)

1974    *Duffy and the Devil* by Harve Zemach, illustrated by Margot Zemach (Farrar)
Honor Books: *Three Jovial Huntsmen* by Susan Jeffers (Bradbury)
*Cathedral* by David Macaulay (Houghton)

1975    *Arrow to the Sun* by Gerald McDermott (Viking)
Honor Book: *Jambo Means Hello* by Muriel Feelings, illustrated by Tom Feelings (Dial)

1976    *Why Mosquitoes Buzz in People's Ears* by Verna Aardema, illustrated by Leo and Diane Dillon (Dial)
Honor Books: *The Desert Is Theirs* by Byrd Baylor, illustrated by Peter Parnall (Scribner)

*Strega Nona* retold and illustrated by Tomie de Paola (Prentice)

**1977**   *Ashanti to Zulu: African Traditions* by Margaret Musgrove,
           illustrated by Leo and Diane Dillon (Dial)
           Honor Books: *The Amazing Bone* by William Steig (Farrar)
           *The Contest* retold and illustrated by Nonny Hogrogian
           *Fish for Supper* by M.B. Goffstein (Dial)
           *The Golem* by Beverly Brodsky McDermott (Lippincott)
           *Hawk, I'm Your Brother* by Byrd Baylor, illustrated by Peter
           Parnall (Scribner)

**1978**   *Noah's Ark* illustrated by Peter Spier (Doubleday)
           Honor Books: *Castle* by David Macaulay (Houghton)
           *It Could Always Be Worse* retold and illustrated by Margot
           Zemach (Farrar)

**1979**   *The Girl Who Loved Wild Horses* by Paul Goble (Bradbury)
           Honor Books: *Freight Train* by Donald Crews (Greenwillow)
           *The Way to Start a Day* by Byrd Baylor, illustrated by Peter
           Parnall (Scribner)

**1980**   *Ox-Cart Man* by Donald Wall, illustrated by Barbara Cooney
           (Viking)
           Honor Books: *Ben's Trumpet* by Rachel Isadora (Greenwillow)
           *The Garden of Abdul Gasazi* by Chris Van Allsburg (Houghton)
           *The Treasure* by Uri Shulevitz (Farrar)

**1981**   *Fables* by Arnold Lobel (Harper)
           Honor Books: *The Bremen-Town Musicians* retold and illus-
           trated by Ilse Plume (Doubleday)
           *The Grey Lady and the Strawberry Snatcher* by Molly Bang
           (Four Winds)
           *Mice Twice* by Joseph Low (McElderry/Atheneum)
           *Truck* by Donald Crews (Greenwillow)

**1982**   *Jumanji* by Chris Van Allsberg (Houghton)
           Honor Books: *Where the Buffaloes Begin* by Olaf Baker, illus-
           trated by Stephen Gammell (Warne)
           *On Market Street* by Arnold Lobel, illustrated by Anita Lobel
           (Greenwillow)
           *Outside Over There* by Maurice Sendak (Harper)
           *A Visit to William Blake's Inn* by Nancy Willard, illustrated by
           Alice and Martin Provensen (Harcourt)

**National Book Award and Successor:**
**The American Book Award**

*National Book Award: Children's-Book Category*

In 1969, the National Book Award included for the first time a prize in the category of children's books. Since 1978, the award has been administered by the Association of American Publishers and its General Publishing Division (One Park Ave., New York, NY 10016). The award is presented to a children's book that a panel of judges considers the most distinguished by an American citizen published in the United States in the preceding year.

1969    *Journey from Peppermint Street* by Meindert DeJong (Harper)
        Other finalists: *Constance* by Patricia Clapp (Lothrop)
        *The Endless Steppe* by Esther Hautzig (Crowell)
        *The High King* by Lloyd Alexander (Holt)
        *Langston Hughes* by Milton Meltzer (Crowell)

1970    *A Day of Pleasure: Stories of a Boy Growing Up in Warsaw*
        by Isaac Bashevis Singer (Farrar)
        Other finalists: *Pop Corn and Ma Goodness* by Edna Mitchell
        Preston (Viking)
        *Sylvester and the Magic Pebble* by William Steig (Windmill/
        Simon & Schuster)
        *Where the Lilies Bloom* by Vera and Bill Cleaver (Lippincott)
        *The Young United States* by Edwin Tunis (World)

1971    *The Marvelous Misadventures of Sebastian* by Lloyd Alexander
        (Dutton)
        Other finalists: *Blowfish Live in the Sea* by Paula Fox (Bradbury)
        *Frog and Toad Are Friends* by Arnold Lobel (Harper)
        *Grover* by Vera and Bill Cleaver (Lippincott)
        *Trumpet of the Swan* by E.B. White (Harper)

1972    *The Slightly Irregular Fire Engine* by Donald Barthelme (Farrar)
        Other finalists: *Amos and Boris* by William Steig (Farrar)
        *The Art and Industry of Sandcastles* by Jan Adkins (Walker)
        *The Bears' House* by Marilyn Sachs (Doubleday)
        *Father Fox's Pennyrhymes* by Clyde Watson (Crowell)
        *Hildilid's Night* by Cheli Durán Ryan (Macmillan)
        *His Own Where* by June Jordan (Crowell)

*Mrs. Frisby and the Rats of NIMH* by Robert C. O'Brien
(Atheneum)
*The Planet of Junior Brown* by Virginia Hamilton (Macmillan)
*The Tombs of Atuan* by Ursula K. LeGuin (Atheneum)
*Wild in the World* by John Donovan (Harper)

1973    *The Farthest Shore* by Ursula K. LeGuin (Atheneum)
        Other finalists: *Children of Vietnam* by Betty Jean Lifton and
            Thomas C. Fox (Atheneum)
        *Dominic* by William Steig (Farrar)
        *The House of Wings* by Betsy Byars (Viking)
        *The Impossible People* by Georgess McHargue (Holt)
        *Julie of the Wolves* by Jean Craighead George (Harper)
        *Long Journey Home* by Julius Lester (Dial)
        *Trolls* by Ingri and Edgar Parin d'Aulaire (Doubleday)
        *The Witches of Worm* by Zilpha Keatley Snyder (Atheneum)

1974    *The Court of the Stone Children* by Eleanor Cameron (Dutton)
        Other finalists: *Duffy and the Devil* by Harve Zemach (Farrar)
        *A Figure of Speech* by Norma Fox Mazer (Delacorte)
        *Guests in the Promised Land* by Kristin Hunter (Scribner)
        *A Hero Ain't Nothin' but a Sandwich* by Alice Childress (Coward)
        *Poor Richard in France* by F.N. Monjo (Holt)
        *A Proud Taste for Scarlet and Miniver* by E.L. Konigsburg
            (Atheneum)
        *Summer of My German Soldier* by Bette Greene (Dial)
        *The Treasure Is the Rose* by Julia Cunningham (Pantheon)
        *The Whys and Wherefores of Littabelle Lee* by Vera and Bill
            Cleaver (Atheneum)

1975    *M.C. Higgins, the Great* by Virginia Hamilton (Macmillan)
        Other finalists: *The Devil's Storybook* by Natalie Babbitt (Farrar)
        *Doctor in the Zoo* by Bruce Buchenholz (Studio/Viking)
        *The Edge of Next Year* by Mary Stolz (Harper)
        *The Girl Who Cried Flowers* by Jane Yolen (Crowell)
        *I Tell a Lie Every So Often* by Bruce Clements (Farrar)
        *Joi Bangla* by Jason Laure with Ettagale Laure (Farrar)
        *My Brother Sam Is Dead* by James Lincoln Collier and Chris-
            topher Collier (Four Winds)
        *Remember the Days* by Milton Meltzer (Zenith/Doubleday)
        *Wings* by Adrienne Richard (Atlantic-Little)
        *World of Our Fathers* by Milton Meltzer (Farrar)

1976    *Bert Breen's Barn* by Walter D. Edmonds (Little)

Other finalists: *As I Was Crossing Boston Common* by Norma
  Farber (Dutton)
*El Bronx Remembered* by Nicholasa Mohr (Harper)
*Ludell* by Brenda Wilkinson (Harper)
*Of Love and Death and Other Journeys* by Isabelle Holland
  (Lippincott)
*The Star in the Pail* by David McCord (Little)
*To the Green Mountains* by Eleanor Cameron (Dutton)

**1977**   *The Master Puppeteer* by Katherine Paterson (Crowell)
  Other finalists: *Never to Forget: The Jews of the Holocaust* by
    Milton Meltzer (Harper)
  *Ox Under Pressure* by John Ney (Lippincott)
  *Roll of Thunder, Hear My Cry* by Mildred D. Taylor (Dial)
  *Tunes for a Small Harmonica* by Barbara Wersba (Harper)

**1978**   *The View from the Oak* by Judith and Herbert Kohl (Sierra Club/
    Scribner)
  Other finalists: *Caleb and Kate* by William Steig (Farrar)
  *Hew Against the Grain* by Betty Sue Cummings (Atheneum)
  *Mischling, Second Degree: My Childhood in Nazi Germany* by
    Ilse Koehn (Greenwillow)
  *One at a Time* by David McCord (Little)

**1979**   *The Great Gilly Hopkins* by Katherine Paterson (Crowell)
  Other finalists: *The First Two Lives of Lukas-Kasha* by Lloyd
    Alexander (Dutton)
  *Humbug Mountain* by Sid Fleischman (Atlantic-Little) ·
  *The Little Swineherd and Other Tales* by Paula Fox (Robbins/
    Dutton)
  *Queen of Hearts* by Vera and Bill Cleaver (Lippincott)

*The American Book Award: Children's-Book Category*

The National Book Award was last given in 1979; in 1980, it was su-
perceded by The American Book Award, which to date has not settled
on a particular format. (Sculpture by Louise Nevelson and $1,000.)

**1980**   Hardcover-Fiction Recipient: *A Gathering of Days* by Jean W.
    Blos (Scribner)
  Other finalists: *The Road from Home: The Story of an Armenian
    Girl* by David Kherdian (Greenwillow)
  *Throwing Shadows* by E.L. Kongisburg (Atheneum)

*Words by Heart* by Ouida Sebestyen (Atlantic-Little)

Paperback-Fiction Recipient:
*A Swiftly Tilting Planet* by Madeleine L'Engle (Dell)
Other finalists: *Alan and Naomi* by Myron Levoy (Dell)
*Frog and Toad Are Friends* by Arnold Lobel (Harper)
*The Great Gilly Hopkins* by Katherine Paterson (Avon)
*Higglety Pigglety Pop! or There Must Be More to Life* by Maurice Sendak (Harper)

**1981**   Hardcover-Fiction Recipient: *The Night Swimmers* by Betsy Byars (Delacorte)
Other finalists: *The Alfred Summer* by Jan Slepian (Macmillan)
*Far from Home* by Ouida Sebestyen (Atlantic-Little)
*Jacob Have I Loved* by Katherine Paterson (Crowell)
*A Place Apart* by Paula Fox (Farrar)

Paperback-Fiction Recipient:
*Ramona and Her Mother* by Beverly Cleary (Dell)
Other finalists: *All Together Now* by Sue Ellen Bridgers (Bantam)
*The High King* by Lloyd Alexander (Dell)
*Tex* by S.E. Hinton (Dell)
*The Westing Game* by Ellen Raskin (Avon)

Hardcover-Nonfiction Recipient:
*Oh, Boy! Babies* by Alison Cragin Herzig and Jane Lawrence Mali (Little)
Other finalists: *All Times, All Peoples: A World History of Slavery* by Milton Meltzer (Harper)
*The Ballpark* by William Jaspersohn (Little)
*People* by Peter Spier (Doubleday)
*Where Do You Think You're Going, Christopher Columbus?* by Jean Fritz (Putnam)

**1982**   Hardcover-Fiction Recipient: *Westmark* by Lloyd Alexander (Dutton)
Hardcover Picture Storybook:
*Outside Over There* by Maurice Sendak (Harper)

Paperback-Fiction Recipient:
*Words by Heart* by Ouida Sebestyen (Bantam)
Paperback Picture Storybook:
*Noah's Ark* by Peter Spier

Hardcover-Nonfiction Recipient:
*A Penguin Year* by Susan Bonners (Delacorte)

Book-Illustration Graphic Award:
*Jumanji* by Chris Van Allsburg (Houghton)

## Edgar Allen Poe Award

*Best-Juvenile-Mystery Category*

First awarded in 1961, an Edgar is given by the Mystery Writers of America (105 E. 19th St., New York, NY 10003) for the best juvenile mystery published in the previous year. (Ceramic bust of Poe.)

**1961**   *The Mystery of the Haunted Pool* by Phyllis A. Whitney (Westminster)

**1962**   *The Phantom of Walkaway Hill* by Edward Fenton (Doubleday)

**1963**   *Cutlass Island* by Scott Corbett (Atlantic-Little)

**1964**   *The Mystery of the Hidden Hand* by Phyllis A. Whitney (Westminster)

**1965**   *The Mystery at Crane's Landing* by Marcella Thum (Dodd)

**1966**   *The Mystery of 22 East* by Leon Ward (Westminster)

**1967**   *Sinbad and Me* by Kin Platt (Chilton)

**1968**   *Signpost to Terror* by Gretchen Sprague (Dodd)

**1969**   *The House of Dies Drear* by Virginia Hamilton (Macmillan)

**1970**   *Danger at Black Dyke* by Winifred Finlay (Philips)

**1971**   *The Intruder* by John Rowe Townsend (Lippincott)

**1972**   *Night Fall* by Joan Aiken (Holt)

**1973**   *Deathwatch* by Robb White (Doubleday)

**1974**   *The Long Black Coat* by Jay Bennett (Delacorte)

**1975**   *The Dangling Witness* by Jay Bennett (Delacorte)

**1976**   *Z For Zachariah* by Robert C. O'Brien (Atheneum)

**1977**   *Are You in the House Alone?* by Richard Peck (Viking)

**1978**   *Alone in Wolf Hollow* by Dana Brookins (Seabury)

**1979**   *The Kidnapping of Christina Lattimore* by Joan Lowery Nixon
             (Harcourt)

**1980**   *The Seance* by Joan Lowery Nixon (Harcourt)

**1981**   *Taking Terri Mueller* by Norma Mazer (Avon)


## Hans Christian Andersen Award

This is given biennially since 1956 by the International Board on Books
for Young People to one author and one illustrator (since 1966) in recognition of his or her entire body of work. (Medals.)

**1956**   Eleanor Farjeon (Great Britain)

**1958**   Astrid Lindgren (Sweden)

**1960**   Erich Kästner (Germany)

**1962**   Meindert DeJong (United States)

**1964**   René Guillot (France)

**1966**   Author: Tove Jansson (Finland) Illustrator: Alois Carigiet
             (Switzerland)

**1968**   Authors: James Krüss (Germany); José María Sanchez-Silva
             (Spain) Illustrator: Jiri Trnka (Czechoslovakia)

**1970**   Author: Gianni Rodari (Italy) Illustrator: Maurice Sendak (United
             States)

**1972**   Author: Scott O'Dell (United States) Illustrator: Ib Spang Olsen
             (Denmark)

**1974**   Author: Maria Gripe (Sweden) Illustrator: Farshid Mesghali
             (Iran)

**1976**   Author: Cecil Bødker (Denmark) Illustrator: Tatjana Mawrina
             (Soviet Union)

**1978**   Author: Paula Fox (United States) Illustrator: Svend Otto S.
             (Denmark)

**1980**   Author: Bohumil Říha (Czechoslovakia) Illustrator: Suekichi
             Akaba (Japan)

**Regina Medal**

Given annually since 1959 by the Catholic Library Association (461 W. Lancaster Ave., Haverford, PA 19041) for "continued distinguished contribution to children's literature." (Silver medal.)

| | |
|---|---|
| **1959** | Eleanor Farjeon |
| **1960** | Anne Carroll Moore |
| **1961** | Padraic Colum |
| **1962** | Frederic G. Melcher |
| **1963** | Ann Nolan Clark |
| **1964** | May Hill Arbuthnot |
| **1965** | Ruth Sawyer Durand |
| **1966** | Leo Politi |
| **1967** | Bertha Mahony Miller |
| **1968** | Marguerite deAngeli |
| **1969** | Lois Lenski |
| **1970** | Ingri and Edgar Parin d'Aulaire |
| **1971** | Tasha Tudor |
| **1972** | Meindert DeJong |
| **1973** | Frances Clarke Sayers |
| **1974** | Robert McCloskey |
| **1975** | Lynd Ward and May McNeer Ward |
| **1976** | Virginia Haviland |
| **1977** | Marcia Brown |
| **1978** | Scott O'Dell |
| **1979** | Morton Schindel |
| **1980** | Beverly Cleary |
| **1981** | Augusta Baker |

**Laura Ingalls Wilder Award**

First awarded in 1954, this medal has been given every five years, from 1960 to 1980, but now is offered every three years. The award is given in recognition of an author or illustrator whose books published in the United States have made a substantial and lasting contribution to literature for children. Administered by the Association for Library Services to Children, a division of the American Library Association (50 E. Huron St., Chicago, IL 60611). (Bronze medal.)

**1954**    Laura Ingalls Wilder

**1960**    Clara Ingram Judson

**1965**    Ruth Sawyer

**1970**    E.B. White

**1975**    Beverly Cleary

**1980**    Theodore S. Geisel (Dr. Seuss)

### Cited Children's-Book Awards

Children's-choice awards are asterisked in this list, compiled largely with information from *Children's Books: Awards & Prizes*.

1.  Jane Addams Book Award: The Women's International League for Peace and Freedom and the Jane Addams Peace Association (777 United Nations Plaza, New York, NY 10017) has been giving this award since 1953 to a children's book published the previous year that promotes peace, social justice, and world community. (Certificate.)
2.  American Institute of Graphic Arts Book Show: Their annual show of books selected for excellence in design and manufacture has been in existence since 1923 (1059 Third Ave., New York, NY 10021).
3.  Mildred L. Batchelder Award: Donated as of 1966 by the Association for Library Services to Children, this citation honors their former executive secretary. The association is part of the American Library Association (50 E. Huron St., Chicago, IL 60611). The award is given to an American publisher of a children's book (pre-nursery through eighth grade) originally published in a foreign language in a foreign country and later published in the United States. (Citation.)
4.  Irma Simonton Black Award: In memory of a children's-book author

and faculty member of The Bank Street College of Education (610 W. 112th St., New York, NY 10025), this award is given each spring to an outstanding book for young children. (Scrolls to author and illustrator.)

5. *Boston Globe-Horn Book* This is an annual award by *The Boston Globe* and *The Horn Book* (Park Square Building, 31 St. James Ave., Boston, MA 02116) to outstanding fiction, outstanding non-fiction, and outstanding illustration. ($200 to the winner in each category.)

6. The Randolph Caldecott Medal. (See separate list in appendix.)

7. Lewis Carroll Shelf Award: The University of Wisconsin (School of Education, Lewis Carroll Shelf Award Committee, Box 66, Education Bldg., Madison, WI 53706) gives annual awards to pub-lisher-nominated titles considered equal to *Alice in Wonderland*. Final selections are made by a committee of librarians, teachers, parents, and writers. (Gold Chesire-Cat seals.)

8. Child Study Children's Book Committee at Bank Street College Award: This is an annual award (Bank Street College of Education, 610 W. 112th St., New York, NY 10025) to a distinguished book from the previous year for children dealing with problems in their world.

9. Christopher Award: Given by the Christophers (12 E. 48th St., New York, NY 10017), this award honors the best current fiction or nonfiction. Candidates must be published in the calendar year the award is given, enjoy popular acceptance, and represent a high level of human and spiritual values. (Bronze medallion.)

10. Colorado Children's Book Award:* The fiction winner is chosen by Colorado schoolchildren from a master list compiled by a book-selection committee. On even-numbered years, the books are for preschool through grade 4; on odd-numbered years, for grade 5 and beyond. (Dr. William J. Curtis, Chairman, Colorado Chil-dren's Book Award, University of Colorado, Cragmor Rd., Col-orado Springs, CO 80907.)

11. Commonwealth Club of California Award: This is an annual award to the finest juvenile book on any subject by a Californian (Mon-adnock Arcade, 681 Market St., San Francisco, CA 94105).

12. Council on Interracial Books for Children Award: This award is now discontinued, but previously a $500 prize was given to new writers of children's books who are African-American, American Indian, Asian-American, Chicano, and Puerto Rican (Council on Interracial Books for Children, 1841 Broadway, New York, NY 10023).

13.  Ethical Culture School Book Award:* This is an annual award to
     the author of the best humorous book published in the preceding
     year. The award is determined by votes from children in grades
     4–6 from the Ethical Culture School (The Midtown School, 33
     Central Park West, New York, NY 10023). (Scroll.)

14.  Dorothy Canfield Fisher Children's Book Award:* This award is
     co-sponsored by Vermont State PTA and State Department of Li-
     braries. The winner is chosen by Vermont children from a list of
     thirty titles published the previous year (Vermont PTA, 138 Main
     St., Montpelier, VT 05602). (Scroll.)

15.  Friends of American Writers Award: This award recognizes an
     illustrator, an author of a book for four-to-eight-year-olds and an
     author of a book for ten-to-fourteen-year-olds published in the year
     preceding the award presentation. The winner must be a native or
     resident, of at least five-years' duration, of one of sixteen Mid-
     western states or one of those states must be the locale of the
     winning book. (Various stipends.)

16.  Garden State Children's Book Award: This award is for authors
     and illustrators ofbooks for early and middle grades (2–5) pub-
     lished three years prior to the award year. Winners are determined
     by the Children's Services Section of the New Jersey Library As-
     sociation (221 Boulevard, Passaic, NJ 07055). (Certificate.)

17.  Georgia Children's Book Award:* Begun in 1969, this award is
     sponsored by the College of Education of the University of Georgia
     (Athens, GA 30602). The winner is chosen annually by Georgia
     schoolchildren (grades 4–7) who vote for their favorite title from
     a selected list of twenty books written by authors in residence in
     the United States and published five years preceding the current
     award year.

18.  Golden Archer Award and Little Archer Award:* This award is
     given to an author for books published in the previous five years.
     The recipient is judged by votes of Wisconsin schoolchildren in
     grades 4–8. For the Little Archer Award, children in grades K–3
     vote on a picture book published in the previous five years to
     determine recipient. Sponsor of both awards is the Department of
     Library Science (University of Wisconsin, Oshkosh, WI 54901).
     (Medallion and certificate.)

19.  Golden Kite Award: This award is presented annually by the So-
     ciety of Children's Book Writers (P.O. Box 296, Los Angeles,
     CA 90066) to members whose award-year books of both fiction
     and nonfiction show excellence in writing and genuine appeal.
     (Pewter statuette.)

20. Coretta Scott King Award: The annual award honoring Dr. and
    Mrs. Martin Luther King, Jr. is for a book that promotes intercul-
    tural understanding. Sponsors are A & M Alabama University
    School of Library Media, Encyclopedia Brittanica, Johnson Pub-
    lishing Company, World Book Encyclopedia, and Xerox Corpo-
    ration (Awards Chairwoman: Ms. Glydon Flynt Greer, 2914 Moss
    Rd., N.W. Huntsville, AL 35810).

21. Massachusetts Children's Book Award:* The award is given an-
    nually to two or more books selected from two master lists by
    Massachusetts schoolchildren in grades 4–6 and 7–9. (Sponsored
    by Salem State College, Education Dept., Att: Dr. Helen Constant,
    Salem, MA 01970.)

22. National Book Award and Its Successor, The American Book
    Award, children's-book category. (See separate list in appendix.)

23. National Jewish Book Awards: This annual award is given by the
    Jewish Book Council of the National Jewish Welfare Board (15 E.
    26th St., New York, NY 10010) to the author of the best children's
    book on a Jewish theme published in the previous year. (Citation
    and $500.)

24. The John Newbery Medal. (See separate list in appendix.)

25. Nene Award:* The annual award is given to a book receiving the
    most votes from Hawaiian schoolchildren in grades 4–6. Spon-
    sored by the Children's Section of the Hawaii Library Association
    and Hawaii Association of School Librarians. (Plaque.)

26. *New York Times* Choice of Best Illustrated Children's Books of the
    Year: A panel of three judges selects the best-illustrated children's
    books of the year for *The New York Times* (229 W. 43rd St., New
    York, NY 10036).

27. North Carolina Division American Association of University
    Women's Award in Juvenile Literature: This award is given an-
    nually through the North Carolina Literary and Historical Associ-
    ation (109 E. Jones St., Raleigh, NC 27611). The author must
    have maintained state residency for three years. (Cup.)

28. Ohioana Book Award (Juvenile-Book Category): This award is
    given annually by the Ohioana Library Association (Room 1105,
    65 S. Front St., Columbus, OH 43215) to an Ohio author with a
    book published the previous year. The author must be born in Ohio
    or be a five-year resident of the state. (Medal.)

29. Pacific Northwest Library Association Young Reader's Choice
    Award:* The Pacific Northwest Library Associaton presents the
    award to an author of a book published three years earlier. Children
    in grades 4–8 from Alaska, British Columbia, Idaho, Montana,

Oregon, and Washington vote on twelve to fifteen titles prepared by children's librarians. (Scroll.)

30.  Edgar Allen Poe Award. (See separate list in appendix.)

31.  Sequoyah Children's Book Award:* The award is determined by Oklahoma school children in grades 3–6 based on a master list. The Sequoyah Children's Book Award Committee is a subcommittee of the Oklahoma Library Association (2500 N. Lincoln, Oklahoma City, OK 73105). (Plaque.)

32.  South Carolina Children's Book Award:* The South Carolina Association of School Librarians, the University of South Carolina College of Librarianship, and the State Department of Education sponsor the award. South Carolina pupils in grades 4–8 vote from a master list of books published in the previous five years. (Bronze medal.)

33.  Southern California Council on Literature for Children and Young People Award: The Southern California Council on Literature for Children and Young People gives awards to authors, illustrators, and others who contribute to children's literature (Fullerton Public Library, 353 W. Commonwealth Ave., Fullerton, CA 92632). (Bronze plaque.)

34.  George G. Stone Center for Children's Books Recognition of Merit Award: The Claremont Reading Conference gives a scroll to an author or artist of a children's book that has "power to please and to heighten awareness of children and teachers as they have shared the book in their classrooms" (Claremont Graduate School, Claremont, CA 91711). (Scroll.)

35.  Mark Twain Award:* Missouri schoolchildren, grades 3–8, choose one winner annually from a master list assembled by an awards committee with suggestions from Missouri organizations interested in children and reading. Co-sponsors are Missouri Library Association (403 South Sixth St., Columbia, MO 65201) and the Missouri Association of School Librarians. (Bronze bust of Twain.)

36.  Western Heritage Award: The National Cowboy Hall of Fame and Western Heritage Center give a trophy annually to a juvenile book that best portrays the authentic American West (1700 N.E. 63rd St., Oklahoma City, OK 73111). (Trophy.)

37.  Western Writers of America Spur Award: The Western Writers of America, Inc. give a plaque annually to the best western juvenile-category book published the previous year (1505 W. D St., North Platte, NE 69101). (Plaque.)

38.  William Allen White Children's Book Award:* The William Allen

White Library at Emporia State University (Emporia, KS 66801) presents a bronze medal annually to the creator of a book chosen by Kansas pupils in grades 4–8. The children vote on a list chosen by specialists. (Bronze medal.)

39. Carter G. Woodson Book Award: Named for a historian and educator, the annual award is for one social studies book for young readers that is sensitive to ethnic minorities and race relations. The sponsor is the National Council for the Social Studies (2030 M St., NW, Washington, DC 20036). (Plaque.)

40. Woodward Park School Annual Book Award: The award is given for the children's book that best demonstrates good human relations. Pupils raise money and give it to an organization benefiting children that is designated by the winning author.

41. Young Hoosier Award:* The Association for Indiana Media Educators awards a plaque annually to a fictional work published in the previous five years. Indiana pupils in grades 4–8 use a master list to vote on a winner (1120 E. 49th St., Marion, IN 46952). (Plaque.)

42. Young Reader Medal:* This award is given annually, sometimes in three categories, to works of fiction by a living author published within the previous five years. The award is decided by the votes of California schoolchildren in grades K–12 (California Reading Association, 3400 Irvine Ave., Suite #211, Newport Beach, CA 92660). (Medal.)

## Winners of Three or More Awards

Listed below are U.S. prose fictional books that have won three or more awards cited in *Children's Books: Awards and Prizes*. The total number of prizes includes children's-choice awards. The number of children's-choice awards is given in parentheses. Also stated are genre, author, and illustrator (if the author is not also the illustrator).

*Winners of Six Prizes: Fantasy*

1. O'Brien, Robert C. *Mrs. Frisby and the Rats of NIMH,* illustrated by Zena Bernstein (3).

*Winners of Six Prizes: Historical Fiction*

2.  North, Sterling. *Rascal: A Memoir of a Better Era,* illustrated by John Schoenherr (4).
3.  O'Dell, Scott. *Island of the Blue Dolphins* (3).

*Winners of Six Prizes: Contemporary Realistic Fiction*

4.  Rockwell, Thomas. *How to Eat Fried Worms,* illustrated by Emily McCully (6).
5.  White, E.B. *The Trumpet of the Swan,* illustrated by Edward Frascino (3).

*Winners of Five Prizes: Contemporary Realistic Fiction*

6.  Gipson, Fred. *Old Yeller,* illustrated by Carl Burger (4).
7.  Hamilton, Virginia. *M.C. Higgins, the Great.*

*Winners of Four Prizes: Historical Fiction*

8.  Armstrong, William H. *Sounder,* illustrated by James Barkley (2).
9.  Burch, Robert. *Queenie Peavy,* illustrated by Jerry Lazare (1).
10. DeJong, Meindert. *The House of Sixty Fathers,* illustrated by Maurice Sendak (1).
11. Taylor, Theodore. *The Cay* (1).
12. Yep, Laurence. *Dragonwings.*

*Winners of Four Prizes: Contemporary Realistic Fiction*

13. Blume, Judy. *Tales of a Fourth Grade Nothing,* illustrated by Roy Doty (4).
14. Burnford, Sheila. *The Incredible Journey,* illustrated by Carl Burger (3).
15. Cleary, Beverly. *Ramona the Pest,* illustrated by Louis Darling (4).
16. Miles, Miska. *Annie and the Old One,* illustrated by Peter Parnall (1).

*Winners of Four Prizes: Fantasy (Picture Storybooks)*

17.   Van Allsburg, Chris. *The Garden of Abdul Gasazi.*


*Winners of Three Prizes: Fantasy*

18.   Cleary, Beverly. *The Mouse and the Motorcycle,* illustrated by Louis Darling (3).
19.   Selden, George. *The Cricket in Times Square,* illustrated by Garth Williams (1).
20.   Steig, William. *Dominic.* (1).
21.   White, E.B. *Charlotte's Web,* illustrated by Garth Williams.
22.   Yolen, Jane. *The Girl Who Cried Flowers.* Illustrated by David Palladini.


*Winners of Three Prizes: Historical Fiction*

23.   Fleischman, Sid. *By the Great Horn Spoon!,* illustrated by Eric Von Schmidt.
24.   Hautzig. Esther. *The Endless Steppe: Growing Up in Siberia.*
25.   Taylor, Mildred D. *Roll of Thunder, Hear My Cry,* illustrated by Jerry Pinkney (1).


*Winners of Three Prizes: Contemporary Realistic
Fiction*

26.   Atwater, Richard and Florence. *Mr. Popper's Penguins,* illustrated by Robert Lawson (1).
27.   Childress, Alice. *A Hero Ain't Nothin' but a Sandwich* (1).
28.   Cleary, Beverly. *Ramona and Her Father,* illustrated by Alan Tiegreen (1).
29.   George, Jean Craighead. *My Side of the Mountain* (1).
30.   Hamilton, Virginia. *The Planet of Junior Brown.*
31.   Hunter, Kristin. *The Soul Brothers and Sister Lou.*
32.   Mohr, Nicholasa. *Nilda.*
33.   Paterson, Katherine. *The Great Gilly Hopkins.*
34.   Robertson, Keith. *Henry Reed's Baby-sitting Service,* illustrated by Robert McCloskey (3).
35.   Snyder, Zilpha Keatley. *The Egypt Game,* illustrated by Alton Raible (1).

36. Sommerfeit, Aimée. *The Road to Agra*, illustrated by Ulf Aas (1).
37. Treffinger, Carolyn. *Li Lun, Lad of Courage*, illustrated by Kurt Wiese.


*Winners of Three Prizes: Folk Literature*
*(Picture Storybook)*

38. Yashima, Taro. *Seashore Story* (1).


*Winners of Three Prizes: Fantasy (Picture Storybook)*

39. Lionni, Leo. *Alexander and the Wind-Up Mouse.*
40. Sendak, Maurice. *Where the Wild Things Are.*
41. Steig, William. *Amos & Boris.*
42. ———. *Sylvester and the Magic Pebble.*


*Winners of Three Prizes: Historical Fiction*
*(Picture Storybook)*

43. Shulevitz, Uri. *The Treasure.*


## Most Popular Themes or Topics under Which Themes Are Grouped

The most popular themes or topics under which themes are grouped are listed below in rank order. Tabulated beside each is the number of books in which that theme is primary, regardless of genre. The rank orders reflect several ties. Since there are 717 books in the sample, clustering is relatively slight.

| Rank | Theme or Topic under Which Theme Is Grouped | Number of Books |
|------|---------------------------------------------|-----------------|
| 1 | Friendship | 60 |
| 2 | Family Relationships | 42 |
| 3 | Love | 40 |
| 4 | Survival | 28 |

| 5 | Determination and Courage | 23 |
| 6 | Maturing/Maturity | 20 |
| 6 | Nature | 20 |
| 8 | Adventure | 18 |
| 9 | Search for Identity | 16 |
| 10 | Good Overcoming Evil | 14 |
| 10 | Virtue Rewarded | 14 |

**Chapters 2 to 15: Number of Books per Topic under
Which Themes Are Grouped**

*Chapter 2: Prose Classics (65 Books)*

Friendship (4); Loyalty (2); Adventure (2); Courage (2); Materialism (2); Finding a Home and Permanence (2); Give or Take with Animals (7); Animal Fantasy (1); Revenge (2); Love (5); Humor (2); Negative Emotions (4); Maturity (2); Positive Experiences (2); Negative Experiences (3); Self-Knowledge (2); Virtue Rewarded (4); Inner Spirit (1); Destiny (1); Family Relationships (11); Relationship to Society (4)

*Chapter 3: Traditional or Folk Literature in Picture
Storybooks (36 Books)*

*Pourquoi* Tales (4); Animal Importance in the Bible (1); Contentment (6); A Chase and a Search (2); Resourcefulness (4); Luck (1); Cooperation (4); Excessiveness (2); Frivolity (1); Greed (2); Deceit (2); Selfishness (1); Bravery (1); Determination (5)

*Chapter 4: Modern Fantasy in Picture Storybooks
(37 Books)*

Personification (2); Wind (2); Accomplishments Despite Small Size (2); Night (2); Nature (3); Mischief and Magic (2); Excessiveness (2); Etiquette (1); Indifference (1); Christmas (2); Virtue Rewarded (3); Good and Evil (2); Ingenuity (1); Friendship (3); Love (1); Dreams and Wishes (6); Imagination (2)

*Chapter 5: Animal Fantasy in Picture Storybooks*
*(73 Books)*

Nature (6); Maturing (3); Changing (2); Young and Old (2); Pretense and Imagination (2); Self-Awareness (4); Mischief Maker (2); Learning to Give (2); Ingenuity (4); Origin (1); Sharing (3); Cooperation (2); Virtue Rewarded (3); Heroism (3); Seeking Peace (3); Getting a Second Chance (2); Danger from Trusting Flattery (1); Learning (2); Family Relationships (3); Relationship with One Parent (4); Treachery Punished (1); Love (2); Friendship (15); Individualized Contribution (1)

*Chapter 6: Realistic Fiction in Picture Storybooks*
*(77 Books)*

**Historical Fiction.** Money and Treasure (2); Friendship (1); Value of Honesty (1); Virtue Rewarded (3); Self-Sufficiency (1); Change (1)

**Contemporary Fiction.** Concepts (6); Inviting Pleasant Dreams (1); Discovery (2); Nature (3); Winter Preparations and Survival (4); Birds (2); Patience Rewarded (2); Fish (4); Growth (2); Imagination (3); Impression (1); Resolving Problems (3); Deciding What Is Best (2); Establishing a Creative Tradition (1); Contentment (4); Responsibility (3); War (1); Bored or Challenged by Neighborhood (2); Family Relationships (3); Chinese Culture (2); Chicano Culture (2); Laughter (1); Friendship (14)

*Chapter 7: Traditional or Folk Literature (26 Books)*

Capabilities and Limitations (4); Cleverness (4); Outwitted (2); Cooperation (3); Good Overcoming Evil (2); Determination (3); Individualism (1); Inner Spirit (1); Keeping a Secret (1); Patience (1); Survival (1); Love (3)

*Chapter 8: Modern Fantasy (72 Books)*

Good Overcoming Evil (9); Maturing (1); Deviltry or Trickery (2); Revenge (2); War (1); Obedience (1); Destiny (1); Immortality (1); Fusion of Past, Present, or Future (10); Ingenuity (3); Determination (2); Wish

or Dream Fulfillment (2); Adventure (6); Kindness (1); Insight (1); Preferring Myth (1); Personification (5); Family Relationships (3); Individuality and Freedom (2); Learning and Wisdom (2); Love (2)

**Science Fiction.** Survival (1); Ingenuity (1); Adventure (3); Service (1);
Maturing (1); Self-Identity (1); Immortality (1); Insight (1); Destiny (1);
Truth (1); Freedom (1); Love (1)

*Chapter 9: Animal Fantasy (26 Books)*

Animals with Human Traits (2); Virtue Rewarded (3); Quest (4); Survival
(3); Courage and Determination (2); Excessive Size (1); Love (2); Running Away (1); Wish Fulfillment (1); Friendship (7)

*Chapter 10: Historical Fiction (108 Books)*

Resistance (2); Nature (2); Maturing (5); Family Relationships (7); Love
(3); Being Accepted (3); Search for Identity (9); Adjustment and Resistance to Change (6); Adventure (5); Mysticism (1); Determination (6);
Female Educational Goals (3); Overcoming a Disability (2); Positive
Replacing Negative (8); Good Overcoming Evil (2); One Dream Fulfilled
and Others Aborted (3); Occupational Choice (4); Slavery (3); Freedom
from Fascism (2); Revenge (2); Fear and Courage (6); Patriotism (2);
Friendship (1); War's Effect (9); Deception (1); Greed (5); Assuming
Responsibilities (1); Survival (9)

*Chapter 11: Realistic Animal Stories (47 Books)*

Life Revolving around Nature (3); Survival (2); Helping the Disabled
(2); Adapting (1); Maturing (2); Freedom (3); Wish Fulfillment (5); Misunderstanding (1); Determination (2); Fixing Priorities (1); Need for Acceptance (2); Companionship (5); Love (17)

*Chapter 12: Contemporary Realistic Fiction about
Families, Friends, and Problems (61 Books)*

Adjusting (8); Facing Death or Its Aftermath (6); Maturing (6); Adventure (2); Conservation (1); Freedom (1); Survival (1); Identity Crisis (3);
Accepting Responsibility (7); Learning (3); Outsiders (2); Impersonal or

Tyrannical School Treatment (2); Permanence (1); Need for Security or Love (2); Family Relationships (8); Independence (1); Loneliness or Friendship (7)

*Chapter 13: Contemporary Realistic Fiction about U.S. Minorities (43 Books)*

Accepting Death (1); Fighting Loneliness (2); Acknowledging Growth (2); Need for Self-Determination (1); Career Choice (2); Overcoming Fear (1); Integrated Education (3); Trying to Improve Oneself (1); Guidance Needed for Gang Members (2); Poverty (1); Black in a White World (1); Search for Identity (5); Preserving a Historical Site (1); Existence of Anti-Semitism (1); Revealing a Nazi Criminal (1); Friendship (7); Interracial Business Enterprise (1); Need for Permanence (1); Homeland Preferred (1); Family Relationships (5); Survival (3)

*Chapter 14: Contemporary Realistic Fiction Set in Other Lands (23 Books)*

Education (2); Survival (3); Assuming Responsibilities (2); Courage (4); Wish Fulfillment (5); Learning New Ways (3); Lovers of Africa (1); Kindness (1); Self-Choice (2)

*Chapter 15: Popular Contemporary Realistic Fiction (23 Books)*

**Mysteries.** Facing Challenge (7); Survival (1); Deception (2); Wish Fulfillment (2)

**Humorous Stories.** Being Trouble-Prone Entrepreneurs (2); Changing (1); Persevering (2); Need for Loving Attention (2); Individuality (1); Maturing (1); Relationship with Father (2)

# Glossary

**Alliteration**   repeated initial consonant sound

**Antagonist**   force, usually a character, opposing protagonist

**Character**   individual featured in literature

**Classic**   famous book that has stood the test of time

**Denouement**   final climactic action

**Didacticism**   moralistic instruction

**Explicit theme**   precisely stated theme

**Fable**   brief moralistic story, generally with animal characters

**Fantasy**   a story that often has a nonexistent setting and/or supernatural actions

**Fiction**   an imaginary story

**Foil**   a character who by way of contrast enhances the features of the main character

**Folktale**   a story handed down orally

**Hyperbole**   exaggeration used as a figure of speech

**Implicit theme**   inferred theme

**Legend**   an unverified story from the past, often based on history

**Metaphor**   comparison, as in ''He is foxy!''

**Myth**   nonscientific folktale explaining phenomena

**Nonfiction**   factual prose work

**Onomatopoeia**   word whose sound reflects its meaning, as ''buzz'' or ''bang''

**Parody**   satire on a literary work

***Pourquoi* tale**   imaginative explanation for origin, as ''Why the Elephant Has a Trunk''

**Primary theme**   a story's main underlying idea

**Protagonist**   a story's leading character

**Rebus**   a riddle consisting of pictures that suggest word sounds

**Science fiction**   a story based on an extension of the natural world, avoiding the supernatural

**Secondary theme**   a story's minor pervading idea

**Setting**   the time and place of a story

**Simile**   comparison using like or as, like ''as old as petrified wood''

**Stereotype**   a conventionalized character given more group than individualized traits

**Theme**   a story's underlying concept which often shows significance behind action

**Trade book**   literary work as opposed to textbook

# Index

Aardema, Verna, 11, 61, 64
*ABC Bunny, The,* 17
*Abel's Island,* 233
Abrashkin, Raymond, 210, 211, 218
Acceptance, theme of need for, 300–301
Accepted, theme of being, 252–253
Accomplishments despite small size,
  theme of, 81–82
*Across Five Aprils,* 272
*Adam of the Road,* 245, 265
Adams, Adrienne, 102
Adams, Harriet Stratemeyer, 387
Adams, Richard, 233
Adapting, theme of, 297
Adjusting, theme of, 318–321
Adjustment, and resistance to change,
  theme of, 256–257
Adventure, theme of, 29–30, 200–202,
  211–212, 257–258, 325–326
*Adventures of Huckleberry Finn, The,*
  28–29
*Adventures of Obadiah, The,* 133
*Adventures of Tom Sawyer, The,* 29
Aesop, 8, 40, 107
Africa, theme of bonds between lovers
  of, 379–380
Aiken, Joan, 186, 389
*Alan and Naomi,* 273
*Alberic the Wise and Other Journeys,*
  195
Alcott, Bronson, 45
Alcott, Louisa May, 45
Aleichem, Sholem (pseud., Solomon J.
  Rabinowitz), 131, 132
Alexander, Lloyd, 10, 59, 185, 187–188,
  189–190, 200–201, 218
*Alexander and the Wind-Up Mouse,* 114–
  115
*Alice's Adventures in Wonderland,* 26, 47
*All Alone,* 379
*All in the Morning Early,* 66–67
*All-of-a-kind Family,* 249
*Along Came a Dog,* 300–301
*Always Room for One More,* 62
*Amazing Bone, The,* 88
American Institute of Architects, 60
American Library Association, 17
*Amos & Boris,* 117
Analysis, generalization versus, 4
*Ananse the Spider,* 172
*Anansi the Spider,* 61
*Anatole,* 103

*Anatole and the Cat,* 103–104
Andersen, Hans Christian, 5, 14, 26, 34,
  35, 37, 40, 43
*. . . and Now Miguel,* 354–355
*Androcles and the Lion,* 107
*Andy and the Lion,* 107
*Andy Says Bonjour,* 11
*Angry Moon, The,* 70–71
Animal(s): with human traits, theme of,
  229–230; importance in Bible, 62;
  topic of give or take with, 32–33. *See
  also* Animal fantasy; Animal stories,
  realistic
*Animal Fair, The,* 98
*Animal Family, The,* 205–206
Animal fantasy, 33–34, 229; perspective
  on, 229; in picture storybooks, 97
  perspective on, 97
  summary of, 118–119
  themes of, 98–118
  summary of, 239; themes of, 229–239
*Animals of the Bible,* 62
Animal stories, realistic, 295; perspective
  and standards, 295; summary of, 306;
  themes of, 295–306
*Ann Aurelia and Dorothy,* 361
*Annie and the Old One,* 16, 353
*Annuzza, a Girl of Romania,* 260
*Anpao: An American Indian Odyssey,*
  174–175
Anti-Semitism, theme of existence of,
  360
Appiah, Peggy, 172
Applebee, Arthur N., 4
*Apprentice of Florence, The,* 249
*April's Kitten,* 144
*Arabian Nights, The,* 60
Ardizzone, Edward, 147
*Are You in the House Alone?,* 389
*Are You There, God? It's Me, Margaret,*
  14, 323–324
*Ark, The,* 270
Armer, Laura Adams, 356, 377
Armer, Sidney, 356
*Arm of the Starfish, The,* 323
Armstrong, William H., 16, 277
Arora, Shirley L., 373–374
*Arrow to the Sun: A Pueblo Indian Tale,*
  70
Artzybasheff, Boris, 173
Asch, Frank, 111
*As Right as Right Can Be,* 146